WORKING AMERICANS

1770–1869

Volume IX:
From the Revolutionary War
to the Civil War

WORKING AMERICANS

1770–1869

Volume IX:
From the Revolutionary War
to the Civil War

3 1336 08133 7892

by Scott Derks
and Tony Smith

A Universal Reference Book

Grey House
Publishing

PUBLISHER:	Leslie Mackenzie
EDITORIAL DIRECTOR:	Laura Mars-Proietti
MARKETING DIRECTOR:	Jessica Moody
AUTHORS:	Scott Derks and Tony Smith
CONTRIBUTORS:	Ellen Brown and Jimmy Copening
COPYEDITOR:	Elaine Alibrandi
COMPOSITION & DESIGN:	ATLIS Graphics

A Universal Reference Book
Grey House Publishing, Inc.
185 Millerton Road
Millerton, NY 12546
518.789.8700
FAX 518.789.0545
www.greyhouse.com
e-mail: books @greyhouse.com

While every effort has been made to ensure the reliability of the information presented in this publication, Grey House Publishing neither guarantees the accuracy of the data contained herein nor assumes any responsibility for errors, omissions or discrepancies. Grey House accepts no payment for listing; inclusion in the publication of any organization, agency, institution, publication, service or individual does not imply endorsement of the editors or publisher

Errors brought to the attention of the publisher and verified to the satisfaction of the publisher will be corrected in future editions.

Publisher's Cataloging-In-Publication Data
(Prepared by the Donohue Group, Inc.)

Derks, Scott.
   Working Americans . . . / by Scott Derks.

   v. : ill. ; cm.

Title varies.
"A universal reference book."
Additional author for Vol. 9: Tony Smith.
Includes bibliographical references and indexes.
Contents: v. 1. The working class—v. 2. The middle class—v. 3. The upper class.—v. 4. Their children.—v. 5. At war—v. 6. Women at work—v. 7. Social movements—v. 8. Immigrants—v. 9. From the Revolutionary War to the Civil War.
   ISBN: 1-891482-81-5 (v. 1)
   ISBN: 1-891482-72-6 (v. 2)
   ISBN: 1-930956-38-X (v.3)
   ISBN: 1-59327-024-1 (v. 5)
   ISBN: 978-1-59237-101-3 (v. 7)
   ISBN: 1-59327-101-9 (v. 7)
   ISBN: 978-1-59237-197-6 (v. 8)
   ISBN: 978-1-59237-371-0 (v. 9)

1. Working class—United States—History.   2. Labor—United States—History.   3. Occupations—United States—History.
4. Social classes—United States—History.   5. United States—Economic conditions.   I. Smith, Tony (Charles Anthony), 1969-   II. Title.

HD8066   .D47 2000
305.5/0973/0904

Printed in the USA

ISBN: 978-1-59237-371-0

PREFACE

This book is the ninth in a series examining the social and economic lives of working Americans. In this volume the focus shifts back in time to examine the lives of working Americans from the Revolutionary War to the Civil War. Along the way we meet a Dutch entrepreneur whose goal in 1793 was to corner the sugar maple tree market, a New Orleans slave trader known for the quality of his merchandise, and a woman who was simply told one morning that the family was leaving the farm she loved and moving west—discussion was not the custom of the day. In addition, doctors, lawyers, store clerks, soldiers, farmers, woodworkers, gunsmiths, whiskey merchants and preachers all make an appearance in this tableau of American history. Most found some form of success, but not all found satisfaction.

The first volume in this series, *Working Americans 1880 to 1999: The Working Class*, explores the struggles of the working class through the eyes and wallets of three dozen families. Employing pictures, stories, statistics and advertisements of the period, it studies their jobs, wages, family life, expenditures and hobbies throughout the decades. The second and third volumes, *The Middle Class* and *The Upper Class*, capture the struggles and joys of families possessing progressively greater wealth and their roles in transforming the economy of America from 1880 to 1999. The fourth volume, *Their Children*, builds upon the social and economic issues explored in previous volumes by examining the lives of children across the entire spectrum of economic status. Issues addressed include parenting, child labor, education, peer pressure, food and fun. *Volume V: Americans at War*, examines the life-changing elements of war and discusses how enlisted personnel, officers and civilians handle the stress, exhilaration, boredom and brutality of America's various wars, conflicts and incursions. *Volume VI: Women at Work* celebrates the contributions of women, chronicling both the progress and the roadblocks along the way. This volume highlights the critical role of women in the forefront of change.

Working Americans VII: Social Movements explores the various ways America's men and women felt called upon to challenge accepted convention, whether the issue was smoking cigarettes in 1901 or fighting construction of a massive hydroelectric dam in 1956. *Working Americans VIII: Immigrants* examines the lives of first- and second-generation immigrants, with a focus on their journey to America, their search for identity and the emotions they experienced in a new land.

This newest title, *Working Americans IX: From the Revolutionary War to the Civil War* jumps back in time to chronicle the lives of 30 families whose struggles shaped the economic and political concepts that eventually congealed into a place called the United States of America. In this volume, we meet a 63-year-old Boston merchant caught in the crosscurrents of the Revolutionary War in 1778; a Southern slave struggling to raise both her children and those of her master; a native New Englander practicing law in South Carolina; and a fur trader who daily risks his life in the wilderness of 1836. As part of this examination of early America we pan for gold in California, work in textile mills in Mass-achusetts and watch a young man grow cynical about the expanding role of the postal service.

As in previous books, each story is unique as each of us is unique. All the profiles are modeled on real people and events although, as for the earlier volumes, names have been changed and details added based on statistics, the then current popularity of an idea, or writings of the time. Otherwise, every effort has been made to profile accurately each in-dividual life in America, his or her work experience, and the struggle to find love or pros-perity. To ensure that each profile captures the emotions and thoughts of the subject, let-ters, biographies, magazine articles and doctoral theses were consulted, as were diaries and journals, many of which are quoted throughout the volume. In some cases the peo-ple profiled represent regional trends and feelings, but mostly, they represent themselves. Ultimately, it is people—their actions, investments, spending decisions, time commit-ments, jobs and passions—who shape society in our changing world.

INTRODUCTION

Working Americans 1770–1869 Volume IX: From the Revolutionary War to the Civil War is the ninth volume in the Working Americans series. Like its predecessors, this work profiles the lives of Americans—how they lived, how they worked, how they thought—decade by decade. Unlike previous volumes, which were organized by income or other criteria and covered from 1880 to the present, this work, for the first time in the series, focuses on an earlier era—1770–1869, from one major American war to another.

All nine volumes, regardless of economic status or time period, offer a unique, almost uncanny, look at those Americans whose talents, desires, motivations, struggles, and values shaped—and continue to shape—this nation. Without exception, the nearly 300 individuals profiled in the nine volumes of this Working Americans series are working toward their version of the American dream.

Volume IX: From the Revolutionary War to the Civil War takes you:

- To Boston, MA in 1772, where Anna Baffin was sent from Nova Scotia to live with relatives and attend school;
- Alongside Pennsylvania gunsmith Karl Zimmer in 1787, who works for 10 days on each of his sought-after rifles;
- To the Ohio farm of Banks Copening in 1813, where he left his four motherless children, when he was called upon to fight in the War of 1812;
- Into the classroom of Litchfield, CT headmistress Sarah Goodwin in 1826, as she incorporated her strong religious convictions into the lessons at the nationally acclaimed Female Academy;
- On the journey of young Gail Warlick in 1846, as she ran from a troubled childhood in Barnard, VT to work at a textile mill in Lowell, MA;
- Into the political campaign of Abraham Lincoln in 1864, for which 24-year old Alan Marsh worked tirelessly, to the dismay of his overburdened wife.

Arranged in 10 decade-long chapters, this newest *Working Americans* includes three **Profiles** per chapter for a total of 30. Each profile offers personal insight using *Life at Home*, *Life at Work* and *Life in the Community* categories, which are followed by historical and economic data of the time. **Historical Snapshots** chronicle major milestones. Various **Timelines**, on *Slavery* and *Maple Sugaring* for example, outline the progress of these issues. A variety of **News Features** puts the subject's life and work in context of the day. These common elements, as well as specialized data, such as **Selected Prices**, in currency of the time, punctuate each chapter and act as statistical comparisons between decades. The 30 men, women, and children profiled in this volume represent 17 American states, and a wide variety of ages and occupations. The Table of Contents following this Introduction provides a detailed list.

Like the other eight volumes in this series, *Working Americans 1770–1869 Volume IX: From the Revolutionary War to the Civil War* is a compilation of original research (personal diaries and family histories) plus printed material (government statistics, commercial advertisements, and news features). The text, in easy-to-read bulleted format, is supported with hundreds of graphics, such as photos, advertisements, pages from printed material, letters, and documents.

All nine *Working Americans* volumes are "point in time" books, designed to illustrate the reality of that particular time. Some Americans portrayed in this 9th volume realized the American dream and some did not. Many of their stories continue.

Praise for earlier volumes—

"The eighth volume takes a thematic approach . . . typifying the immigrant experience. . . . Accompanying the profiles are . . . items providing sense of the period."

". . . the Working Americans approach to social history is interesting and each volume is worth exploring . . ."

"these interesting, unique compilations of economic and social facts, figures, and graphs . . . support multiple research needs [and] will engage and enlighten patrons in high school, public, and academic library collections."

Booklist

"the volume succeeds at presenting various cultural, regional, economic and age-related points of view . . . [it is] visually appealing [and] certainly a worthwhile purchase . . ."

Feminist Collections

". . . easy reading that will help younger students come to an understanding of the lives and situations of American women."

"The volume 'promises to enhance our understanding of the growth and development of the working class over more than a century.' It capably fulfills this promise . . . recommended for all types of libraries."

Stories from Social Movements . . . *"succeed in capturing the spirit of the issue and the times . . ."*

ARBA

"[the author] adds to the genre of social history known as 'history from the bottom up,' which examines the lives of ordinary people . . . Recommended for all colleges and university library collections."

Choice

"this volume engages and informs, contributing significantly and meaningfully to the historiography of the working class in America . . . a compelling and well-organized contribution for those interested in social history and the complexities of working Americans."

Library Journal

TABLE OF CONTENTS

Dedicated to our families who lovingly support us in the pursuit of our creative endeavors and passion for history.

ACKNOWLEDGEMENTS

It is always an honor and a joy to be in the midst of energetic, intelligent people. Without their support and knowledge, climbing book-mountain would be impossible. In fact, librarians may be the greatest invention in the history of person-kind. The authors were particularly dependent upon the library staff of the University of South Carolina and the South Carolina State library, Blue Ridge Regional Library, Wake Forest University and the resources of Salem College. The authors also express their deep appreciation for the work of contributing writers Ellen Brown and Jimmy Copening, each of whom made major contributions. Thanks also go Ingrid Smith, Mathew Butler, Lindsey Myers, Jamie Martin, Jim and Lucy Andrews, Will Zimmer, Ellen Hanckel and Bill Gaillard. Finally, our appreciation for the support of Elaine Alibrandi and Laura Mars-Proietti. Surviving the process of writing a nine book series is not always easy.

1770–1779

The political turmoil and war that dominated the decade of the 1770s found its origins in Britain's triumph in the costly French and Indian War which ended in 1763. England's King George III, determined to prevent further territorial conflicts and to recoup the cost of fighting the hated French in America, first restricted Western expansion in the colonies, then championed the Sugar Act 1765, which increased duties on non-British goods. For the first time in the 150-year history of the British colonies, the Americans were told they must pay taxes directly to England. Boycotts, riots, and protests followed. As a result, the 13 separate, independent-minded colonies in America began to find unity in their opposition to British domination, particularly the power to tax.

When the Continental Congress boldly signed the Declaration of Independence, it was a dangerous challenge to the mother country and its outcome was far from certain. The colonial militias were outnumbered five to one by one of the most powerful nations in the world. The British Navy was fully capable of a complete blockade of the American coast. The British army was seasoned and feared. America's scattered, rural citizenry included thousands of loyalists still eager to do the bidding of the king. Of the 700,000 potential soldiers within the colonies, approximately a third sided with England or opposed the war and another third did little or nothing to help the cause. The entire money supply in the colonies was under $10 million. Nor did Congress have the power to tax a disparate, disunified people, so it turned to the printing press to finance its revolution against the England. In all, the revolutionary government printed and floated $450 million in paper money to purchase goods to support the military, an action that drove down the value of colonial money and inspired the phrase, "Not worth a continental." As a result, wages for labor doubled to a dollar a day, in specie, or coin, compared with $6.60 a month paid in colonial dollars to the revolutionary soldiers.

The American advantages were a few: an aroused leadership, a hatred of taxation, and a difficult location for England to reach and supply an army. America possessed few major cities to attack. Britain's large, highly organized army disliked doing battle in scattered communities reachable on poorly maintained roads that hampered the procurement of supplies and the deployment of troops. To make full use of its meager assets, the Americans adopted a defensive strategy that forced the British to spread their resources fighting over wide areas, resulting in an eight-year, very expensive and tiresome war.

In addition to battling the British, the American revolutionaries were attacked by both rapid inflation and blockade-imposed shortages. As early as 1775, the country faced acute shortages of such essential items as powder, flints, muskets, and knives. Even salt, shoes, and linens were in short supply. To fight back, wide swaths of the population decided the public good should come before private gain. This belief liberated crowds of people, frequently women, to physically set upon traders in tea or salt and demand that they charge no more than the "just price" which the buyers set for themselves.

The war economy also spoke with a distinctly French accent. Eighty thousand muskets and 60 percent of the gunpowder the colonials used came from France. In all, during the War for American Independence, the French contributed $8 million in loans plus thousands of military men. Their involvement arrived early, in 1777, when the British were still in an excellent position to quell the revolution. But when the British Army's attempt to cut off New England ended in a series of defeats including the Battle of Saratoga, New York, direct French military support began to flow, a critical turning point in the war. At the decisive battle of Yorktown, Virginia, all the military and half the army were French. In addition, Britain's other European enemies join the battle for their own purposes. Spain entered the war hoping to regain Gibraltar, which it had lost to the British in 1713, as did Holland, major commercial rival of England and a prominent financier of the American war effort. For decades the Navigation Act had locked the Netherlands out of the burgeoning American market; the revolution offered the perfect opportunity to reset the rules.

As the decade came to a close, John Adams was named to negotiate the Revolutionary War's peace terms with Britain, the Luddite riots began in Lancaster, England, in reaction to the introduction of machinery for spinning cotton, and Louis XVI of France freed the last remaining serfs on royal land.

1772 Profile

Anna Baffin left Nova Scotia for Boston for better educational opportunities for young girls, including learning the household arts of British society.

Life at Home

- Nova Scotia served as a delightful backdrop for Anna Baffin's childhood, despite a paucity of educational opportunities.
- Her father, Joshua Baffin, was a commissary (supplier of goods), to the British regiments stationed there.
- Concerned that Anna's education was too limited, he decided that the 12-year-old should complete her education in Boston, where he and his wife both grew up.
- They understood the necessity of education and that a young lady must be prepared for the domestic expectations of a housewife in British society—even in the Colonies.
- Anna's departure from her family home, known as Cumberland, was sad.
- It was especially hard leaving her mother whom she loved dearly.
- Her mother comforted her that she would be part of an extended family in Boston and that she would write often to her.
- She encouraged Anna to practice her writing through keeping a diary, which was also a way that they could share her activities in Boston.
- Anna would do anything for her mother.
- After a sad farewell to her mother and a challenging sea journey with her father, Anna was welcomed by her Aunt Sarah Deming, her father's oldest sister, in Boston.
- Her father only stayed in the city a few days before he was called away on business, which upset Anna.
- She was not yet familiar with her new home or her newly discovered family members.

Anna Baffin was sent as a young girl to live with relatives in Boston.

Boston offered a variety of opportunities for young Anna.

- Anna's fear and nervousness was not new to Aunt Deming, who had seen the nervous smiles of dozens of young women away from home for the first time.
- Aunt Deming eked out a small income by boarding young ladies who came to Massachusetts to attend the highly regarded Boston schools.
- Anna's room had a feather bed bolster, a dress closet, a black walnut desk and stool.
- Eager to please, Anna worked diligently on her studies which encompassed training in spinning linen thread and woolen yarn, stitch work, dancing and fine writing.
- Aunt Deming was taken aback that Anna had never worn a shift, a linen slip for under a dress, prior to arriving in Boston.
- Wearing linen from her waist to her knees seemed strange to Anna.
- It was not uncommon for Anna's aunt to correct her on improper school instruction.
- Anna learned the spelling of the fourth day of the week as "wednessday" but Mrs. Deming informed her that it should be "wednesday."
- In good weather Anna often visited her Aunt Elizabeth Storer on Sudbury Street as soon as writing school ended for the day.
- Often Aunt Storer sent a chaise, a two-wheeled carriage, to bring Anna for a visit to a large three-story home made of wood.
- Anna enjoyed those late afternoon teas in the drawing room decorated with a rich crimson and green Persian carpet.
- She and her aunt sat on the green damask window seat to enjoy the sun's warmth late in the day.
- On those late afternoons the two drank tea from delicate English china and discussed the sermons they had heard at Old South Church or Anna's daily school adventures.

Furnishings from Aunt Storer's sitting room, where Anna spent many afternoons.

- Between tea and dinner, Anna was permitted upstairs to marvel at her Uncle Ebenezer's (Ned) library on the second floor.
- It housed numerous books on religion, history, philosophy and astronomy and, also, her uncle's prized solar microscope.
- She also learned that her uncle was once attracted to her mother and even kissed her before her father even knew her.
- Anna found it amusing and odd to think of her mother liking any other person than her father.
- Recently, Uncle Ned broke his leg while driving a chaise in the snow.
- Returning from Watertown, the horse fell down while descending an icy hill and Uncle Ned fell out of the chaise.
- Anna was sure that it was God's grace that he was not run over by one of the wheels during the accident.
- Fortunately, he survived with only a broken right leg that didn't pierce the skin but the horse, too, broke his leg.
- Anna often visited her uncle after the accident to bring news, letters and books from other family members while he recovered.
- Structure was clearly part of Anna's life at home, reading from the Bible to her Aunt Deming every morning, and if time permitted, from other books as well.
- A cousin gave her some books, including *The Puzzling Cap, The Female Orators,* and *The History of Gaffer Too-shoes.*
- After school at Aunt Deming's involved Scripture readings, which Anna would discuss during her afternoon tea and record her thoughts about in her catechism book.
- During tea it was not uncommon for Lucinda, Aunt Deming's slave girl, to provide Sarah Deming with paper and scissors for her artwork.
- Anna was amazed at the skill and swiftness with which her aunt could create a decorative image from paper cuttings.
- Many gentlewomen were known to be of great skill in the art of papyrotamia, decorative paper cutting, in the Boston area.
- Anna thought Aunt Deming was most talented and generous in sharing the paper artworks with family in correspondences.
- She even provided a few to Uncle Ned while he recovered from his broken leg.

An example of Anna's Aunt Deming's decorative paper cutting.

Life at Work

- In Aunt Sarah Deming's Boston house, hard work was the rule
- Physical pain or sickness were no excuses for slothfulness.
- Early each morning, weather proving to be good, Anna Baffin departed home to attend both her sewing and writing schools.
- During the winter, her writing teacher Master Holbrook did not have class in the afternoon, so she had sewing half the morning and all afternoon.
- Sitting behind the spinning wheel for long periods created a number of pains and injuries, especially to Anna's sensitive little hands.
- But excuses were viewed as a character weakness.
- Even with painful sores on her fingers and a great boil on her right hip, Anna was expected to produce results in sewing class.
- Because she couldn't work the needle well with finger injuries, she spent more time spinning yarn.

- On a good day she could spin a "10 knot skane" of yarn, or roughly eight yards.
- To help cure the sores and boils, she took half an ounce of Globe Salt and stayed in her bedroom reading the Bible.
- The treatment was a disagreeable potion and upset her greatly.
- Her aunt placed plaster on her finger—"with the worse discomfort"—to help heal it properly.
- Typically, a good day's work for Anna embraced a variety of tasks and skills, including mending two pairs of gloves, sewing on the bosom for her uncle's shirt, mending for the wash two hand-kerchiefs and sewing on half a border for Aunt Deming's lawn apron.
- Reading and writing were also important aspects of Anna's learning, as was learning catechism.
- Every Wednesday evening at Old South Church, Aunt Deming and Anna attended the assembly's catechism lectures.
- On cold winter evenings, they would take a blanket and a foot-stove, a small metal box that held hot coals, to keep warm in the church.
- Sessions traditionally started with Reverend Beacon asking a question, such as, "What does it take to glorify God?" followed by a lecture to the assembly.
- Huddled in their blankets and with their fireboxes by their feet, members listened intently to the message.
- Once catechism ended, one assembly member would stay and inspect the church for stray foot stoves left behind that could accidentally burn the wooden building.
- Recently, Aunt Deming gave Mrs. Walters, an assembly member, a white satin pincushion for the birth of her newborn son.
- On one side was an embroidery of flowers, while the reverse had the words "Josiah Waters Welcome little Stranger."
- Pincushions were common gifts for mothers with a young child to receive in New England and Aunt Deming was known for giving a number of such gifts.

- Arriving home from church in the early evening, Aunt Deming required Anna to reflect and write what she learned from catechism lecture.
- Even under candlelight Anna made a point of writing well in her neat penmanship to explain the lecture.
- When Aunt Deming reviewed what she wrote, she not only corrected her spelling but noted mistakes about the lecture.
- Anna often worked as hard with her writing as with her sewing.
- She made certain not to be too sloppy in mixing her ink powder so the ink wouldn't run or be too thin when writing.
- A number of the students, especially the boys, tended to be sloppy with their writing.
- Students with ink stains on their hands betrayed how poorly they wrote.
- Proper writing required proper control of the pen to keep each letter neat, clean and at a proper size.
- Anna was proud of her writing skill
- In one communication to her mother Anna said, "Aunt says I can write pretily."
- Anna also wrote a fair amount outside of class in the evening, often in her diary or in letters to her parents in Nova Scotia, writing, for example, about the Christmas decorations on Boston's streets.

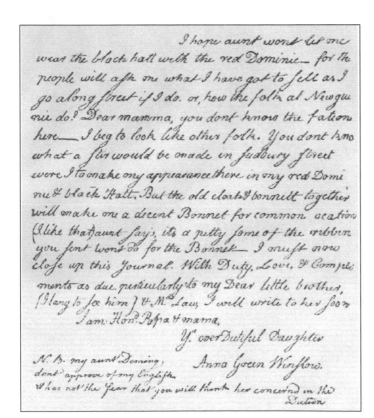

Example of praiseworthy penmanship.

- Anna and her family did not celebrate the holiday because Christmas was not part of the Puritan custom.
- This was because the holiday did not have a date within the Bible.
- Nonetheless, Anna enjoyed the decorations and merriment she encountered around the town during the season
- On Christmas she stayed at home and did a very good day's work.
- On New Year's Day, it was common tradition, especially among Puritans, to exchange gifts and good wishes.
- Though Anna did not bestow any gifts to family members, she did receive one from her Aunt Deming—a handsomely bound book entitled *The History of the Adventures of Joseph Andrews*.
- This was one of the few books Anna could truly call her own and she cherished the adventure stories found between the leather covers.

Life in the Community: Boston, Massachusetts

- Several days later in the mail Anna Baffin and her Aunt Sarah Deming received a New Year's greeting from Anna's Grandmamma.
- Enclosed for each of them was one-eighth of a dollar piece.
- With the money she had saved and this added money, Anna decided to go shopping.
- But buying goods in Boston was a challenge.
- Many Bostonians were self-proclaimed Sons and Daughters of Liberty and had pledged not to buy English-made goods or tea sold by the British.
- Anna also chose to call herself a Daughter of Liberty and wear as much Massachusetts-made goods as possible.
- She decided to purchase, with her aunt's permission, a beautiful white hat with a bit of white holland with the feathers sewn on it, as unsullied falling snow.
- While out shopping, Anna saw her dear friend Mary Scollay with her mother.
- While the two girls gave a quick hug hello, Mrs. Scollay thanked Anna for being so helpful in writing the invitation cards for Mary's birthday party.
- Mrs. Scollay praised Anna's writing to Aunt Deming while the two girls chatted about the upcoming party and what they were going to wear.
- She thought her penmanship was nicer than most adults who have written for years.
- On the day of Mary's birthday party, Anna was quite undecided about what to wear.
- She dearly wanted to wear her new hat but decided on an entirely different outfit.
- Her outfit consisted of a hair comb with pasted black feathers and garnet marcasite.
- The comb complemented her black and blue striped tucker (a piece of linen or frill of lace worn by women around the neck and shoulders), black bib and apron.
- Her yellow coat and silk shoes completed the outfit.
- Upon arrival at the Scollay home that evening at five o'clock, she first noticed the large company assembled in the spacious upper room of the house
- Music from two fiddlers provided merriment as the young girls scampered around.
- Many of the young girls were very genteel and gave pleasure to the evening's mistress, their friend Mary.
- Because Anna helped with the invitations, she was given the honor to open the evening's diversions in a slow and graceful minuet.
- A great variety of food and drink were on hand on dark maple tables including cakes, raisins and a diversity of nuts.
- The Scollays also had both hot and cold wine and rum punch.
- All the guests, including the young girls, had their fill of all items.
- Besides dancing, there were a number of games played by the girls that evening while the "elderly part of the company" was only observing.

- The first game was Woo'd the Widow, followed by Hunt the Whistle, Thread the Needle and Playing of Pawns.
- Anna's favorite game was Hunt the Whistle, in which all the girls sat on the floor forming a circle.
- One girl was blindfolded in the center while one in the circle was given a tin whistle.
- The blindfolded player had to find the whistle as it was passed around in various directions, while occasionally a player would blow the whistle.
- If caught with the whistle by the blindfolded person, you were then designated to be the blindfolded person.
- The night was so much fun, ending, to Anna's regret, at ten o'clock. Many of the girls could have danced and played for most of the evening.
- The last time Anna recalled having that much fun was the past summer watching the fireworks on Boston Common during the King's Coronation celebration.
- Regretfully, Anna now avoided certain areas of the Common.
- The king's 29th Regiment was encamped there and a number of problems had developed around the city.
- The biggest calamity occurred two years ago on March 5 with the massacre of five townspeople by the king's soldiers.
- Many of the town's citizens continued to treat the day as a solemn holiday with religious sources.
- Those active as a Son or Daughter of Liberty also attended services in memory of the cause of liberty.
- Anna knew of one young girl and family acquaintance, Betty Smith, who caused trouble among the soldiers.
- Betty started taking company with many of the men of the 29th Regiment on the Common and soon started stealing from them.
- The first time Betty was caught she was sent to jail and then punished at the public whipping post.
- The red whipping post was in a prominent location in Boston on State Street—right under the window of Anna's writing school!
- Betty was sent to jail a second time after she was caught pilfering the regiment's supplies.
- Anna had no idea what was to become of Betty until she was tried for her sinful crimes.
- As she learned from Reverend Beacon's sermons at Old South Church, when one person falls onto the slippery slope of sin, it's not easy to stop.
- Sin was not the only concern of the Puritans in Boston.
- The king, with the support of the colony's governor, was sending more Episcopal clergy to Massachusetts.
- The Puritans from Old South Church and other assemblies in Boston were upset at the arrival of this religious group and the potential poisoning of the city with their Romanist, Catholic-like, tendencies.
- Anna's Uncle Baffin commented that the Episcopal bishops "all have popes in their bellies."
- Regardless of the religious issues encountered, Anna noticed a great deal of energy in the city.
- Discussions of current events puzzled her.
- Talk regarding Tories and Whigs confused her.
- One of Aunt Deming's friends explained the details and differences, but that confused her even more.
- Issues regarding Britain, the governor and trade constantly became the subject of conversations at many adult gatherings—matters suitable, Anna was told, for adults, not young little girls.
- For Anna, the principles of God, family and hard work were what were required for a young girl.

HISTORICAL SNAPSHOT
1772

- The Boston Assembly demanded the rights of the colonies and threatened secession
- George Frederic Handel's Messiah was first performed in Germany
- World explorer Captain James Cook left England on his second voyage
- The total population of the American colonies was estimated to be 2,205,000
- In the art of tarring and feathering individuals, the community began following a standard protocol: First, strip a Person naked, then heat the Tar until it is thin, & pour it upon the naked Flesh, or rub it over with a Tar brush. . . . After which, sprinkle decently upon the Tar, whilst it is yet warm, as many Feathers as will stick to it. Then hold a lighted Candle to the Feathers, & try to set it all on Fire; if it will burn so much the better
- William Herschel and his sister Caroline discovered eight comets and 14 nebulae using telescopes they built together
- The London firm of Flight and Kelly produced the first barrel organ
- Of the 3,500 physicians practicing in the colonies, only 400 were medical doctors by formal training and degree
- Daniel Rutherford and Joseph Priestly independently discovered nitrogen
- Samuel Adams formed the Committee's Correspondence of Massachusetts to communicate its concerns to the other colonies and call for action against England
- The waltz was becoming fashionable in Vienna
- American poet Mercy Otis Warren published *The Adulateur,* a play designed to be read rather than performed
- Judge William Murray ruled in the Somerset case that a slave was free upon landing in England
- The first independent Anglo-American government was founded by the Watauga Association in East Tennessee; the written agreement allowed for a five-man court to act as the government
- New Jersey passed a bill requiring a license to practice medicine
- The Mission of San Luis Obispo de Tolosa formed in California
- The British customs cutter HMS *Gaspee,* charged with enforcing the Stamp Act of 1865, was attacked and burned off the coast of Warwick, Rhode Island; the English Crown offered a 500-pound reward for the capture of the terrorists
- The Inquisition was abolished in France
- A Moravian missionary constructed the first schoolhouse west of the Allegheny

Selected Prices

Ale, Bottle . . . . .8 Pence
Man's Hat . . . . .15 Shillings
Woman's Silk Handkerchief . . . . .3 Shillings
Molasses, Gallon . . . . .1 Shilling
Coffee, Pound . . . . .6 Pence
Coal, Bushel . . . . .2 Shillings
Tea, Pound . . . . .3 Shillings
Axe . . . . .1 Shilling
Hatchet . . . . .1 Pound
Gun and Bayonet . . . . .3 Pounds

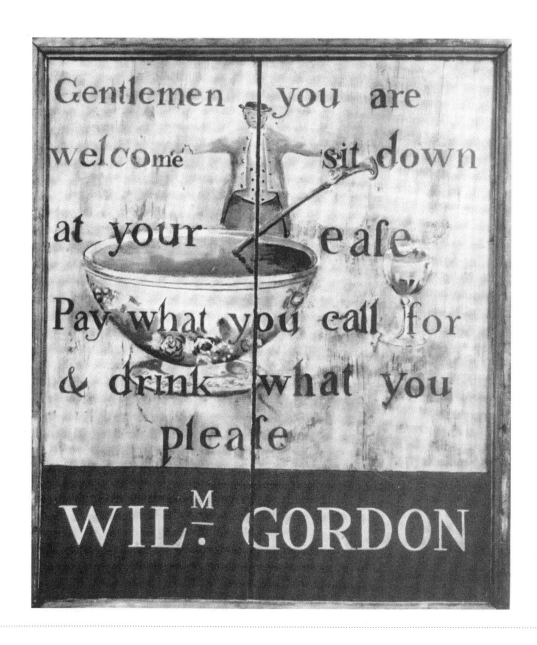

Flower-making Advertisements, *Boston Gazette,* October 19, 1767:

To the young Ladies of Boston. Elizabeth Courtney, as several Ladies have signified of having a desire to learn that most ingenious art of Painting on Gauze & Catgut, proposes to open a School, and that her business may be a public good, designs to teach the making of all sorts of French Trimmings, Flowers, and Feather Muffs and Tippets. And as these Arts above mentioned (the Flowers excepted) are entirely unknown on the Continent, she flatters herself to meet with all due encouragement; and more so, as every Lady may have a power of serving herself of what she is now obliged to send to England for, as the whole process is attended with little or no expense. The Conditions are Five Dollars at entrance; to be confin'd to no particular hours or time: And if they apply Constant may be Compleat in six weeks. And when she has fifty subscribers school will be opened, &c, &c.

"Boston Whipping Post," Writing of Samuel Breck, 1771:

The large whipping-post painted red stood conspicuously and prominently in the most public street in town. It was placed in State Street directly under the windows of a great writing school which I frequented, and from them the scholars were indulged in the spectacle of all kinds of punishment suited to harden their hearts and brutalize their feelings. Here women were taken in a huge cage, in which they were dragged on wheels from prison, and tied to the post with bare backs on which thirty or forty lashes were bestowed among the screams of the culprit and the uproar of the mob. A little further in the street was to be seen the pillory with three or four fellows fastened by the head and hands, and standing for an hour in that helpless posture, exposed to gross and cruel jeers from the multitude, who pelted them incessantly with rotten eggs and every repulsive kind of garbage that could be collected.

Foot-Stove Concerns, Records of Old South Church, Boston, January 16, 1771:

Whereas, danger is apprehended from the stoves that are frequently left in the meeting-house after the publick worship is over; Voted that the Saxton make diligent search on the Lords Day evening and in the evening after a Lecture, to see if any stoves are left in the house, and that if he find any there he take them to his house; and it is expected that the owners of such stoves make reasonable satisfaction to the Saxton for his trouble before they take them away.

Dancing School Advertisement, *Boston Gazette,* circa 1772:

Mr. Turner informs the Ladies and Gentlemen in Town and Country that he has reduced his price for teaching from Six Dollars Entrance to One Guinea, and from Four Dollars per month to Three. Those ladies and Gentlemen who propose sending their children to be taught will notice no books will be kept as Mr. T. has suffered much by Booking. The pupils must pay monthly if they are desirous the School should continue.

Sewing Instruction Advertisement

All kinds of Needleworks viz: point, Brussels, Dresden Gold, Silver and silk Embroidery of every kind. Tambour Feather, India & Darning, Spriggings with a Variety of Open-work to each. Tapestry plain, lined, and drawn. Catgut, black & white, with a number of beautiful Stitches. Diaper and Plain Darnings. French Quiltings, Knitting, Various Sorts of marking with the Embellishments of Royal cross, Plain cross, Queen, Irish, and Tent Stitches.

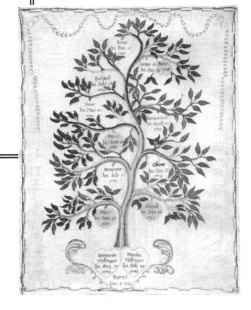

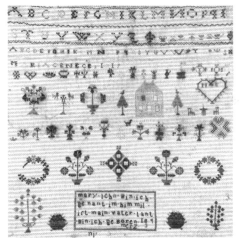

"Of the Rattle Snake," from Mark Catesby, *The Gentleman's Magazine*, London, England, 1753:

This snake is the largest and most terrible of all the viper kind: Some of them are eight feet long, and weigh about eight or nine pounds. Its bite is most deadly. If the fangs penetrate a vein our artery, inevitable death ensues in less than two minutes. When the bite is in a fleshy part, it must be immediately cut out to stop the current of the poison. They are very inactive and slow moving, and are never the aggressor; when provoked they give warning by shaking their tails. The charming or attractive power of this snake is generally believed in America. It is said that birds and squirrels no sooner spy this snake than with distracted gestures and outcries, regardless of everything else, they will gradually descend from the tops of the loftiest trees to the snake, who instantly devours them.

Mr. Catesby adds, but it is not uncommon for them to come into houses. In the month of February, 1723, when he was in the house of Colonel Blake in Carolina, the servant making the bed in a ground room, but a few minutes after he left it, on turning down the clothes, found a rattlesnake, lying coiled between the sheets. He thinks the deadliness of the snake is in proportion to the largeness of the snake, and the greater or lesser quality of poison injected. When the bite is slight the Indians sometimes suck the wound with good success, but the recovered person never fails of having annual pains at the time they were bit.

Of roots, that the Indians relied upon most for cure, and which those of Virginia and Carolina carry in their pallets, is a small tubers root which they chew, and apply the juice of, to the wound.

BENJAMIN FRANKLIN.
Ne à Boston, dans la nouvelle Angleterre le 17 Janvier 1706

1776 PROFILE

Father Francisco Mourelle, a Franciscan missionary following in St. Francis of Assisi's foot-steps, spread the Christian message among the Indians of the sun-battered Sonora Desert.

Life at Home

- Franciscan missionary Father Francisco Mourelle was appointed to spread Christianity to the Native American nations within New Spain's Sonora Desert region.
- Nowhere was the struggle for life harder.
- The natives scattered throughout this stretch of the dry, hot southwestern region were said to be some of the continent's most primitive.
- They lived a simple, difficult life.
- Ministry to these people required extensive travel and long leaves from his assigned community of San Xavier del Bac.
- He felt it important to become familiar with the each nation's tribe.
- That meant exploration of the region for extended periods, often with only a few companions.
- The recent outbreak of war pitting the English in Great Britain against the English in the American colonies was a world away.
- Of far greater concern was a place to live for several months, safe from the elements, following a long and arduous trip through the water-starved desert.
- In December 1776, his resting place was far from what Father Francisco Mourelle would call a home.
- The xacalli, or sand house, was a low structure dug out from the ground with three walls made of dirt that would permit the temporary storage of supplies and a place to rest his head.
- Staying in temporary dwellings was not uncommon for Father Mourelle during his constant travels throughout the desolate Sonora desert.
- The Franciscans represented a Catholic religious order founded by Francis of Assisi in Italy in the thirteenth century.
- The Church later recognized him as a saint because of the holy life he led.
- On Father Mourelle's most recent journey, he traveled approximately 40 days through a dry and treacherous Sonora.

Father Mourelle was a Christian missionary in the Sonora Desert.

St. Francis of Assisi was an inspiration to Father Mourelle.

- After so many trips out into the region, he was becoming familiar among the native tribes along the Gila and Colorado rivers, where Father Mourelle catechized and gave religious instruction with only the help of a single translator.
- His latest journey was the first time he had traveled with a large expedition.
- Acting on the orders of the viceroy of New Spain, he recently traveled across the Sonora to the Rio Colorado with Lieutenant-Colonel Don Juan Bautista de Anza's expedition from Tubac with two other priests.
- The expedition was quite large, comprising 240 individuals, 136 of them settlers of both sexes for the new mission at the Puerto de San Francisco.
- Over 690 mules and horses carried baggage while 355 head of cattle followed for sustenance during the journey.
- Some of the cattle was to be used for the new settlement and missions at Puerto de San Francisco.
- Roughly 28 soldiers protected the train of people and wagons against any possible attacks from the native population.
- Early on, attacks from the Apaches concerned one of the expedition's other priests, Father Pedro Carrasco.
- When the caravan did not encounter any attacks, he attributed it to the community's patronage of the Virgin of Guadalupe.
- Father Carrasco assured the expedition that the most holy Virgin of Guadalupe would be a tower of strength the whole way, attributing this miracle to faith and prayer to God.
- Even with God's protection, death still met the expedition early on when a soldier's wife died while giving birth to a healthy child.
- Several days outside of Tucson, a couple of muleteers attempted to hide from the expedition, intending to desert.
- This frustrated the commander.
- Lieutenant-Colonel Anza published a proclamation commanding all persons to behave in such a manner that the natives should have no bad examples set for them, in word or deed, from the Españoles, or the latter would face rigorous punishment for disobedience.
- A couple of days later, the runaways were discovered and placed back into the custody of the expedition.
- One was given 12 lashes while the second received 25 for desertion.
- Throughout the early portion of the trip, finding fresh water and grass was challenging.
- Sources of water, commonly in rain lagoons, had alkaline or other impurities, making it undrinkable.
- With water scarce early in the journey, Anza established the use of tardeada, two short marches between two watering holes.
- Overnight encampment was traditionally between the watering locations, so a tardeada meant a night without access to water.
- Later in the expedition they followed the desert's rivers where fresh water was commonly found, and stops at Indian rancherias allowed the expedition to rest.
- Along the way, the expedition commonly encountered Pima tribes near the Santa Cruz River outside of Tucson, and later Yuma tribes along the Gila River.
- Father Mourelle had visited a number of these rancherias during past journeys and knew some of the community members.

Father Mourelle and his expedition often encountered Pima and Yuma tribes.

- He had tried to increase a desire within them to be Christian.
- During the stops, the soldiers sometimes bartered with the Pima and Yuma tribes for items of interest.
- Poultry, goats or horses from the tribes were exchanged for red baize, a bright scarlet woolen cloth.
- Tobacco and glass beads were often given as gifts to the tribes by the expedition as a token of peace and goodwill.
- When the expedition arrived at the confluence of the Gila and Colorado Rivers, they noticed that the ford, the crossing point, was deeper than expected.
- The Yumas informed the expedition that the rivers rise deep this time of year, thus making the traditional fords difficult to cross.
- Discussions of crossing with rafts were dismissed by Lieutenant-Colonel Anza because it would be a long, tedious job to cross such a train of people and supplies.
- After a couple of days of searching for a crossing, they found a spot where the river divided into three branches.
- Based upon the Spanish measure of a vara, approximately 33 English inches, Father Mourelle estimated the river crossing was 400 varas in width.
- Mourelle arranged to have three Yumas take him across the river on their shoulders, his body stretched out stiffly between them like a corpse.
- He made it across safely and kept himself dry from the cold river.
- Father Carrasco, who was sick, went across on horseback with three servants leading his horse, making sure he didn't fall into the river.
- Once the expedition crossed, Father Mourelle departed from Anza's expedition, which was headed to the Puerto de San Francisco.
- Anza constructed Mourelle's xacalli structure near the home of Captain Salvador Palma, a native commander of all in the Yuma nation.
- The expedition left supplies for both him and Father Quimper so they could preach to the Indian nations along the Colorado until Anza passed through on his return.
- Anza ordered various supplies be left to help the two priests on their mission, which included tobacco, beads, assorted foods and cooking supplies.
- Five oxen were included among the horses and mules.
- Also remaining to aid Fathers Mourelle and Quimper were four Indians, including Sebastian Tarabel, who had accompanied Mourelle in past travels.

Yuma Indians.

Life at Work

- With the expedition safe, Father Francisco Mourelle said farewell and departed to do what the viceroy had ordered him to do—visit the nations of the Colorado River and investigate their willingness to learn about Christianity.
- Wearing the gray robe common to the Sonora Franciscans, Mourelle packed his mules with supplies and presents for the journey.
- It was impossible to keep his robe clean.
- Traveling south he first encountered Yumas at the Rancherias de San Pablo.
- To better communicate Christian salvation, he used images on a linen print to explain what they were hearing.
- On one side of the linen print was an image of the Virgin Mary, and on the other, a lost soul in hell.
- Sebastian often helped with the translation because he was familiar with the Yuma language.
- Many of the Yumas at San Pablo, and other rancherias, had heard of the Virgin Mary from the Pimas and informed Mourelle that she was a nice lady.
- They also knew that the lost soul was bad and that he would go down under the ground with the ugly wild beast.
- It was not the sacred theology Mourelle wanted to communicate on Christianity, but it was a start.
- He learned to adapt his expectations to the cultural and intellectual differences of New Spain.
- That required that he slowly introduce the ideas of the Christian faith to the various Indian nations.
- After discussing religion, Mourelle laid before them the proposition: would the Yumas wish to have the Españoles and priest come live in their land?
- They answered "Yes" in expectation of being well supplied with meat and clothing.
- Mourelle did not get this kind of welcome with all the tribes he visited along the Colorado.
- Some tribes of the Cajuenche nation reacted in horror at the image of the lost soul and did not want to look at it.
- On other occasions he sent Sebastian ahead to deliver greetings, especially where he had journeyed along the Colorado before.
- Often the natives in the area would gather for his arrival and wait to see Father Mourelle.
- To remind them that he had been with them in the past, Mourelle often showed them the crucifix, his prayer book and his compass—items that he traditionally carried on his person and shared with the tribes as visual reminders.
- After his discussion through a translator and use of visual aids, he would provide tobacco and glass beads to various tribe members.
- Whenever possible, Mourelle used his sextant to take a measurement of latitude to help indicate his location on the river.
- Such measurements were used to track the boundaries of tribes and the availability of fertile soils with grass and water conditions along the Colorado River.
- When he reached the mouth of the Colorado, he encountered beaches along the shoreline.
- The water moved like tides and tasted like salt.
- Near the mouth of the river, Mourelle encountered many mountain Indians he referred to as Serranos.
- Mezcal, a native plant, was a huge staple of the tribe's diet.
- They appeared poor and dirty but nonetheless, they welcomed the priest and were affable.

- Apparently they had never seen domesticated animals before, especially mules.
- Sebastian said they saluted the mules as if they were people.
- During the visit Mourelle had to act as peacekeeper when one of the Indians stole Sebastian's knife.
- The tribe was angry that their guest had been dishonored and wanted to destroy the home of the petty thief.
- Mourelle intervened and encouraged the tribe not to worry about the stolen knife.
- He believed the memory of such forgiveness would leave a lasting impression on the tribe longer than retribution for the knife.
- Similarly, a young Jalliquamay Indian had attacked a Cajuenche tribe member with a flint spear.
- The Jalliquamay spear penetrated through the shoulder and came near the heart.
- The incident upset the entire tribe, and many of the men wanted to kill the young Jalliquamay man.
- Father Mourelle told the tribe's captain that the fighting was senseless and would only cause further problems.
- The captain indicated that since the incident had happened, the killing could not be helped.
- Sebastian and the other Indian servants were terrified and, fearing injury, wanted to leave in haste.
- Understanding the possible threat, the Franciscan agreed, but not without first catechizing to the wounded man as well as he could.
- It appeared to him that the man joyfully received holy baptism.
- After a month of travel up and down the Colorado, Father Mourelle arrived at the Puerto de la Concepcion, where he visited with his dear friend, Father Quimper.
- Father Quimper was content serving as priest to the Yumas in the area and explained that the people had served him well.
- At Mass the Yumas reverently sang the psalms taught by the priest.
- A large number came to hear the Mass.
- During the service many imitated the most devout in making the sign of the cross, beating the breast and other signs of worship.
- This was a change in religious practices from some of the tribal beliefs.
- Father Mourelle and his Franciscan brethren often discussed the tribes' pre-Christian beliefs.
- Some of the tribes, especially the Pimas, believed that their origin was from near the sea where an old woman created their ancestors.
- When Pimas died, their ghosts would go toward the western sea, while others went and lived like owls.
- When the priests asked more about this Indian cosmogony, a theory of the origin of the universe, they were unable to say much more because they did not understand it themselves.
- Father Mourelle had the opportunity to share his recent observations to his Franciscan brethren about the Pimas near San Xavier del Bac.
- There, the Pimas raised large crops of wheat, cotton, maize and calabashes, which were a credit to the good construction of irrigation canals along the Santa Cruz River.
- The canal was common to all and divided to owners of different water circuits to care for their crop lands.
- Many of the Pimas dressed in Indian blankets of their own cotton or wool.

Father Quimper, longtime priest of the Yuma tribe and dear friend of Father Mourelle.

- Not all news was good during Mourelle visit.
- He learned that two or three tribal nations united on the seacoast near the Mission de San Diego.
- Word had it that they killed a priest and burned his house.
- Many in the Yuma nation were careful to communicate to the Españoles traveling through that they were not part of this incident at the Mission de San Diego.
- Even with this frightening news, Father Mourelle continued on his journey to catechize to the natives in the area.
- His next trip, he thought, was west toward the coast and, if possible, to visit the Franciscan Mission de San Gabriel.
- Father Quimper wished him a safe journey and prayed he would return prior to Lieutenant-Colonel Anza's return in the spring.

Life in the Community: San Xavier del Bac, Sonora Desert

- The rancheria of San Xavier del Bac was a small town diminishing in population in New Spain's Sonora Desert.
- For over 70 years, Spanish settlers worked and lived in this location with the native people, but changes in the area influenced the local population.
- Due to the remains of numerous ancient adobe pueblos in the vicinity, the first Spanish explorers called it Bac.
- The word *bac* means house or adobe.
- It was after the missionary Father Kino, a member of the Society of Jesus, or Jesuits, explored the area that the community's named changed to San Xavier del Bac.
- Father Kino's first priority in establishing a missionary in 1700 was to construct a church in San Xavier del Bac.
- The church was the first structure built in adobe fashion with light porous stone, with enough space for a large congregation to attend religious services.

The community of San Xavier del Bac in the Sonora Dessert.

- Other buildings were developed to help support the growing presence of Jesuit missionaries.
- Over time, the Jesuits instructed the native populations in the area and had a strong influence on the Pima nation.
- One of the influences was the construction of canals on nearby native lands for irrigation of local crops.
- This irrigation system, yielding a multitude of crops, helped develop the Pima population along the Santa Cruz Valley.
- Large quantities of beans, squash, maize and cotton were grown that enriched the population.
- The missions appeared to be having a positive influence on the native populations in accepting Christianity, but also Spanish rule.
- Under the orders of the Spanish crown, two goals of the Jesuits were to Christianize the native population and to gradually turn them into tax-paying citizens to the crown.
- With the efforts of both the Jesuits and the Spanish government, Spain anticipated this acceptance to occur over time from the native population.
- With the native people's conversion to Christianity, the Jesuit mission became a large operation that required a significant amount of oversight.
- The priest hired supervisory staff of both Spaniards and converted Indians to run the extensive operations within the mission.
- Activities included maintaining the mission property and grounds, cattle and horse ranching, drying and salting of food and construction of new buildings.
- Over the years much of the native population began to lose its autonomy, influenced by the increasing number of Spanish settlers moving into the region.
- Anger grew among those within the Pima nation with the encroachment of Spanish and other non-native Indians upon their tribal lands.
- The growth of the population brought heads of cattle to their rich grasslands as well as miners searching for precious metals.
- By 1751, the Pima population revolted against the Spanish for a two-year period.
- Hundreds of Spanish settlers in the Sonora region were killed.
- San Xavier del Bac was abandoned during that time and plundered by the Pimas.
- When peace was restored by the Spanish government, the New Spain government investigated the cause of the uprising.
- Leaders in Spain were upset about the revolt and angered that it was not suppressed immediately.
- Some of the blame was placed upon the Jesuit missions, but in general the Spaniards saw the Pima population as inferior and unable to operate in an orderly Spanish structure.
- Because of his distrust of the Jesuits, the Spanish King Charles III banned them from Spanish lands in the Americas.
- Much of this distrust was a result of the Church's political influence within Spain and suspicion of Jesuit involvement in riots caused in 1766.
- All religious properties in New Spain were placed under the care of the Spanish government and run by the Franciscans.

Spaniards were hired to run missions that were converted to Christianity.

- Due to neglect after the Pima revolt, the mission at San Xavier del Bac was in poor condition and the local population reduced in size.
- In 1764, the population was just under 400 individuals, and by 1772, it was 270.
- The mission encountered problems with other Indian attacks, especially from the Apache.
- With the development of a presidio, or fort, approximately 3.5 leagues (nine miles) north in Tucson in 1776, the population moved.

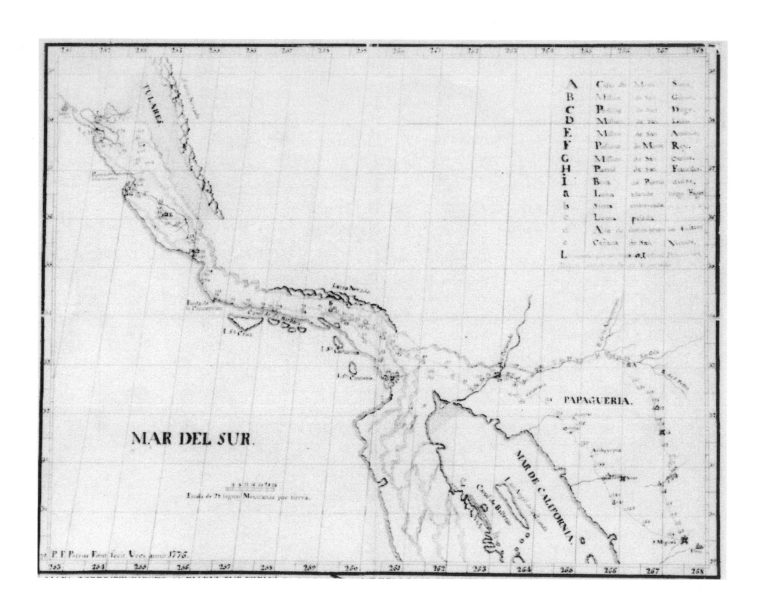

HISTORICAL SNAPSHOT
1776

- Thomas Paine published *Common Sense,* a scathing attack on King George III's reign over the colonies; it sold more than 500,000 copies in just a few months

- British forces evacuated Boston, Massachusetts, after George Washington placed artillery overlooking the city

- Virginia adopted a Bill of Rights that protected an individual's enjoyment of life and liberty and the acquisition of and possession of property

- The $2 bill was issued by the Continental Congress to pay for the "defense of America"

- Juan Bautista de Anza founded the site for the Presidio of San Francisco

- Rhode Island became the first American colony to renounce allegiance to King George III, two months before the Declaration of Independence was adopted

- The Virginia Convention instructed its delegates to propose a declaration of independence from Great Britain

- American invaders skirmished with British at Trois-Rivières, Quebec

- The Continental Congress adopted a resolution severing ties with Great Britain, though a formal Declaration of Independence was not adopted until July 4

- David Bushnell's *Turtle,* a submarine, attacked the British sailboat *Eagle* in the bay of New York

- Captain James Cook began his third voyage on *Resolution* to the Pacific Ocean

- Phi Beta Kappa was organized at William and Mary College in Williamsburg, Virginia

- Rhode Island established wage and price controls to curb inflation: limits included $0.70 a day for carpenters and $0.42 for tailors

Selected Prices

Candle . . . . .5 Shillings
Hayfork . . . . .1 Shilling
Indigo, Pound . . . . .8 Shillings
Jamaican Rum, Gallon . . . . .20 Shillings
Lace, Yard . . . . .7.5 Pence
Man's Cloak, Black Silk . . . . .2 Pounds
Mutton, Pound . . . . .3.5 Pence
Wheat, Bushel . . . . .4 Shillings

Typical Indian basket.

Account of Uprising at San Diego, Diary of Father Pedro Carrasco, Herbert E. Bolton's English translation *Anza's California Expeditions, Volume IV,* 1931:

Monday, January 1, 1776—I said Mass, and in it I said a few words to the people concerning the character of the holiday, exhorting them to renew their good resolutions, since we were now beginning a new year, etc. At daylight the ground was as white as if it had snowed, from the frost which fell early this morning. Because yesterday's journey was long and the cattle had arrived late, it was decided to do no more today than to cross the river, for although it is narrow it has a great deal of water, is very rapid, and has very high banks, as I said yesterday. Consequently the ford was repaired after Mass at the cost of considerable labor. About ten o'clock in the morning the courier who was sent on December 27 arrived with a reply from the mission of San Gabriel, a soldier from there, and seventeen saddle animals sent by the fathers to relieve those of ours which were badly worn. They also brought the distressing news that the Indians of the port and mission of San Diego rebelled in the month of November, killing a friar and wounding the soldiers. Of this event I shall speak more at length later on, in its proper place.

The ford being arranged, at two o'clock in the afternoon we began to cross the river; and in an hour it was successfully passed, halt being made on the other side near its banks. Most of the people crossed over on a bridge formed by a large cottonwood which had fallen and lay athwart the river. Near it was another cottonwood which the former expedition used as a bridge. This place is like all the rest, a fertile and beautiful country, with rose bushes, grapevines, blackberry bushes, and other plants which by their verdure are pleasing to the sight. In a word, all this country from the Puerto de San Carlos forward is a region which does not produce thorns or cactus. In fact I did not see in all the district which I traveled as far as the port of San Francisco any spinous trees or shrubs such as there are in the interior, except some prickly pears and some nettles which I saw near the port of San Diego; nor are any thorns encountered on the plants except on the blackberries and rose bushes. Finally, this country is entirely distinct from the rest of America which I have seen; and in the grasses and the flowers of the fields, and also in the fact that the rainy season is in winter, it is very similar to Spain.

Supplies Left for Fathers Mourelle and Quimper at the Colorado River, *On the Trail of a Spanish Pioneer: The Diary and Itinerary of Francisco Mourelle,* 1776:

One tercio of tobacco; two boxes of beads; one arroba of chocolate; one arroba of sugar; one arroba of lard; five oxen; three tercios of jerked beef; one carga of beans; one carga of coarse flour; a little fine flour; one almud of peas; a box of biscuit; three hams; six cheeses; one frying pan; one other pan; one ax; twelve cakes of soap; twelve wax candles; and one jug of wine.

Excerpt of Lieutenant Don Josef Joachín Moraga's Account of the Founding of San Francisco, 1775:

The Mission of San Francisco, which was founded at the Laguna and Arroyo de los Dolores, a site very beautiful and abundant in water, wood, and stone, is now also completed, and so handsomely built that I can do no less than marvel to see in so brief a time erected in the face of such a shortage of men a presidio and a mission such as in many years these northern California establishments will not have seen.

Now returning to the explorations which I have made of these lands, in which I was accompanied by the reverend fathers, toward the southeast I encountered timber sufficient to build commodious houses, and I saw the land to be well pastured and able to maintain a great number of cattle, and to support no small plantings of the necessary grains. Moreover, I saw that the heathen had burned many patches, which doubtless would produce an abundance of pasturage. In the rest of the explorations which I have made in the vicinity of the mission and the presidio I have found good lands, some large lagoons, little arroyos, and innumerable springs of fresh water which are permanent, although the year has been so short of rain. The Indians in the vicinity of the presidio and mission are of such good disposition that ever since the day when we arrived at this destination they have daily frequented one establishment and the other with such satisfaction on our part that we hope soon to see harvested the fruit which so Catholic a breast as that of your Excellency desires.

PIMO VILLAGE

Letter to Don Juan Bautista de Anza from Father Mourelle, 1776:

The Indians expect to be advised to go out to campaign. They are very wild, without doctrine even in their own language, because, although they pray together, no one by himself understands. Even the most advanced respond with any word, so I endeavor to get them to come to catechism. Yet it is not achieved unless it is in the greater number of youngsters who do it well. On the contrary are those who have already reached adulthood: these only attend on feast days. They say that they have always been reared so that adults go to the fields and the children to catechism. For the present I do not urge earnestly until I see how things are.

Selected Cost for the Anza Expedition to San Francisco
Wardrobe for a Man

3 shirts of good Silesian linen	18 reales each
3 pairs of underdrawers of Puebla cloth of 4 varas	2 reales each
2 cloth coats which with their lining and trimmings are worth	9 pesos, 3 reales
2 pairs of trousers, ditto	5 pesos, 3 reales
2 pairs of stockings	2 reales each
2 pairs of chamois-skin boots	10 reales each
3 pairs of gaiter shoes	5 reales each
1 cloth cape lined with thick flannel	11 reales each
1 hat	6 reales
2 Puebla powder-cloths	2 reales each
1 ribbon for the hat and hair	4 reales

Wardrobe for a Woman

3 shirts	4 pesos
3 pairs of white Puebla petticoats	12 reales
2 pairs of petticoats, some of silk serge, others of thick flannel, and an underskirt	Total cost of 16 pesos
2 varas of linen stuff for two linings	5 reales
2 pairs of Brussels stockings	4.5 reales
2 pairs of hose	2 reales
2 pairs of shoes	6 reales
2 women's shawls	12 reales
1 hat	6 pesos

8 reales equals 1 peso.

Clothing for Ninety Boys

5 pieces of cloth containing 180 varas	Total cost of 270 pesos
12 pieces of Puebla cloth for linings and white trousers	6 pesos, 4 reales each
270 varas of linen stuff for shirts of about 3 varas	Total cost of 168 pesos 3 reales
50 hats	4 reales each
8 dozen shoes for children of various sizes	4 pesos each

Clothing for an Equal Number of Girls

270 varas of linen stuff for shirts	Total cost of 168 pesos, 6 reales
4 pieces of Puebla cloth 6 for petticoats and linings	6 pesos, 4 reales each
90 cloths for women's shawls of all sizes	10 reales each
2 pieces of thick flannel for little petticoats	45 pesos each
4 pieces of cloth of about 34 varas for undershirts	12 reales each
12 pieces of ribbon for bands	Total cost 20 pesos
16 ditto of fine rope	Total cost 5 pesos
8 dozen shoes for girls of various sizes	4 pesos per dozen
120 blankets, single bed size for all	15 reales each
120 shepherd's blankets	5 reales each

8 reales equals 1 peso.

Source: Charles Edward Chapman, *The Founding of Spanish California; The Northwest Expansion of New Spain, 1687-1783,* 1916. The Macmillan Company, New York.

1778 Profile

Jonathan Forbes, a successful British merchant living in Boston, Massachusetts, considered himself a British subject torn between two worlds during the outbreak of the American Revolution.

Life at Home

- Jonathan Forbes had just turned 63 years old, and was confused, highly agitated and ailing financially.
- Even though the doctors had "made an apothecary shop of his stomach," his health was fine and Jonathan's greatest concern was about the future.
- Massachusetts was a mess, with the Boston economy in a shambles.
- An unnecessary war was underway throughout the Colonies.
- Trade was difficult, often risky.
- And no one knew who their friends were anymore.
- Merchants he had worked with for decades no longer spoke to him.
- Friends were dying and more would die.
- In the end, when the British crushed the Colonial army, some of the Colonies' best men would be hanged.
- Business would not return to normal for years.
- For decades Jonathan had joined—even led—his fellow merchants and civic leaders to oppose the repressive trade regulations that Britain was imposing.
- Through petitions and speeches he'd made it clear he was not in sympathy with England's aggressive taxation policies.
- Jonathan had served on grievance committees and been praised publicly for his service.
- He had even served as chairman of the committee designed to prevent "importations, particularly of foreign superfluities, and to encourage domestic produce manufacture."
- But while he considered the conduct of the British government toward the Colonies impolite and harsh, he was "indisposed" to forcible resistance and the cause of independence.

Jonathan Forbes was living in Boston during the outbreak of the American Revolution.

Jonathan imported many goods from London.

- He was born a British subject and would die a British subject, although for years he had been careful both to celebrate the king's birthday on June 4 and to attend the Sons of Liberty annual dinner.
- With the outbreak of armed conflict, he was expected to declare himself either a patriot or a loyalist.
- He was simply a successful merchant who was born in Britain and lived in America—both a patriot and a loyalist.
- Since he did not join the patriot exodus from Boston when the siege began, in order to protect his property, this was counted against him by the patriots.
- Subsequently, he was subjected to "rude treatment" by ruffians in the crowd when he attempted to attend the funeral of a fellow Mason.
- This humiliation was followed by the looting and pillaging of his warehouse by the British army during its occupation of Boston.
- War was good business for some, but not for Jonathan.
- Jonathan was born in Exeter, England, in 1715, where his grandfather held a number of prestigious government offices including sheriff and mayor.
- Jonathan and his brother Jacob immigrated to America when they were in their teens
- Jonathan went to Boston, while Jacob went to Québec.
- In 1736, when he was only 21 years old, Jonathan purchased a warehouse on Long Wharf that launched him into business.
- For several decades he used the highly efficient harbor of Boston to bring in salt, women's merchandise and steel farming tools not made in America.
- He had a knack for knowing how to cater to the needs of both Boston, with its growing wealth, and the agricultural countryside outside the city, which had dramatically expanded to meet the needs of city people.
- With this uniting of city and country came newly improved roads, better security for shipping goods, and small factories to meet everyday needs.
- Jonathan occasionally returned to England on buying trips and to visit London, but he considered Boston his home.
- Early on, Jonathan showed great interest in Trinity Church, where he was married in 1743
- That same year, he purchased pew number 82 to support the church and to establish his place in society.
- Throughout his life he was a generous giver and rarely absent from Sunday services.
- His diary religiously recorded his impressions of the sermons, both good and bad.
- On August 22, 1773, he wrote that clergyman Mr. Walter "is so good a man that my pen cannot describe his virtues."
- He also recorded his displeasure with very long sermons, including one lasting an hour and 40 minutes.
- But even the church experience was altered by the drumbeat of war.
- Tension was so pronounced in July 1776, the rebels interrupted church services during the prayers for the king, threatening bodily harm to preacher and building alike.

Jonathan's wife, whom he married in 1743.

- The vestry decided that the only alternative to shutting up the church in view of the temper and spirit of the people was to request the minister omit the part of the liturgy which referred to the king.
- One member of the Trinity Church clergy had already returned to England in light of the outlandish events and fear for his life; only God knew what was next.

Life at Work

- Since the insurrection against the British erupted five years earlier at the hands of his friends and neighbors, Jonathan Forbes had been praying for a solution.
- Clearly the Crown had unnecessarily riled the colonists with the Stamp Act of 1765, the Townsend Act of 1767, and the Boston Massacre in 1770.
- Jonathan found these events reprehensible and harmful to business.
- But it was the Crown's attempt to tax tea that catalyzed the colonists into action.
- In December 1773, Jonathan found himself uncomfortably in the middle of a major dispute concerning tea, a product he did not handle.
- Tea was a staple of colonial life, and the king assumed the colonists would pay a fair tax to enjoy the pleasure of a cup of it.
- Under the Tea Act, the East India Company was authorized to sell tea directly to the colonists without payment of any customs duties whatsoever—a fair deal.
- Jonathan understood this meant that tea was cheaper in the Colonies than in England, but it also meant that the English East India Company could undercut the prices of colonial merchants and smugglers, including John Hancock, who had profited considerably since he had helped initiate the boycott of English tea.
- During the boycott, tea sales by the British East India Company had fallen in the Colonies from 320,000 pounds to 520 pounds.
- By 1773 the East India Company had accumulated huge debts and huge stocks of tea in its warehouses with no prospect of settlement.
- Colonial smugglers were importing tea from Holland without paying import taxes.
- On November 29, a community meeting was called concerning the arrival of three East India ships carrying tea.
- Jonathan stepped in as mediator and agreed to talk to the ship's captain and "prevail upon him to act with reason in this affair."
- But to little avail.
- While Jonathan negotiated for the ship to leave, Samuel Adams whipped up the growing crowds protesting the importation of tea; each meeting was larger than the one before.
- An estimated 8,000 people were said to have attended the rally at Boston's Old South meeting hall on December 16.

Faneuil Hall, Boston

The tea tax mobilized the colonists into action.

A ship carrying tea into the Boston Harbor.

- On that same evening, "a number of people wearing Indian dresses then went onboard the three ships *Hall, Bruce,* and *Coffin.* They opened the hatches, hoisted out the tea, and flung it overboard; this might, I believe, have been prevented. I was sincerely so sorry for the event. 'Tis said near 2,000 people were present at this affair."
- By dawn 342 casks of tea, containing 90,000 pounds in total, had been consigned to the waters of Boston Harbor.
- The British Crown's response was disastrous.
- They punished the Sons of Liberty by closing Boston Harbor, shutting off business.
- At first Jonathan thought he was out of business.
- Despite the on-and-off boycott of British goods, business had been excellent.
- The export of Pennsylvania grain to Europe was keeping his ships busy.
- One recent shipment was marketed to Poland, Jonathan was amazed to learn.
- The cost of the destroyed tea had to be less than the economic impact of closing a port city.
- He agreed with printer-politician Ben Franklin, who said the cost of the destroyed tea should be repaid.

Benjamin Franklin. *The Pennsylvania Gazette,* May 9, 1754.

- In Britain, even those politicians considered friends of the Colonies were appalled.
- For a period, the highly fractious Parliament united all parties against the Colonies.
- What could the Colonies possibly want?
- The tax on the tea was a penny, while the average wage in New England was between one and two shillings per day.
- Now everyone was talking about abstaining from tea drinking, turning instead to balsamic hyperion made from raspberry leaves.
- Jonathan knew this would not last long.
- On June 1, 1774, Jonathan wrote in his diary, "This is the last day any vessel can enter this harbour until this fatal act of Parliament is repealed. Poor unhappy Boston. God knows only thy wretched fate. I see nothing but misery will attend thy inhabitants."
- On June 28, another town meeting was held, pitting John Adams and his committee against the merchants.
- "The debates very warm on both sides. . . . This affair will cause much evil, one against the other. I wish for peace in this town. I fear the consequences."
- In addition to closing the harbor, Parliament annulled the charter of the colony, and gave complete control of town meetings to the British governor, effectively giving the governor control over who was elected.
- Great Britain hoped that these acts would isolate radicals in Massachusetts from the rest of the Colonies and re-establish the authority of Parliament.
- The Administration of Justice Act granted British officials virtual immunity in all of the Colonies
- They could not be tried in local courts for capital offences, but were rather to be extradited to Britain and tried there.
- In 1775, the Quartering Act was expanded to include occupied buildings, which gave the British army the right to legally quarter itself in people's homes, eat up all their food, mess up their houses, threaten the men and leer at the women, and leave the farms in a physical and economic shambles.
- Repeatedly, Jonathan's warehouses were ransacked by the British army; officers openly told Jonathan that for the bribe of a case of wine, his property would be protected.
- Martial law was declared, all assemblies were banned, and a campaign was launched to confiscate weapons in the colony.

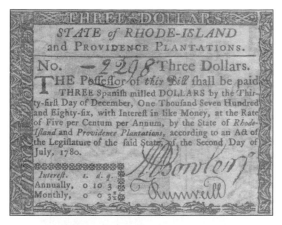

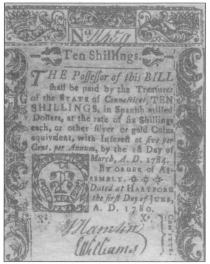

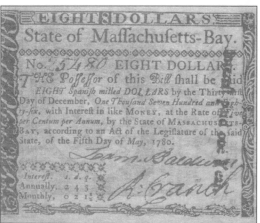

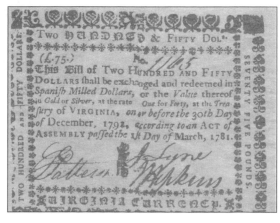

Colonies were issuing their own currency to help finance the war.

- After Boston Harbor was secured, the British imposed a naval blockade and captured the major American seaports of New York, Newport, and Philadelphia.
- Worst of all, the Colonies were issuing their own individual currencies to help finance expenditures.
- Not only did the value of the script change frequently, the British, in an effort to destroy the funding system of the Continental Congress, were counterfeiting the Continental dollar.
- Up and down the Colonies, merchants like Jonathan and his wife were leaving for British-held Nova Scotia, just to the north.
- Following the evacuation of Boston by the British forces in 1776, more than 1,400 of the inhabitants of Massachusetts went into a voluntary exile in Halifax with the British army.
- Among these were some of the most eminent in the Colony—lawyers, clergymen, representatives of some of the oldest European blood in New England—the Winslows, the Tilleys, and others, descendants of those who came over on the *Mayflower.*
- Jonathan had not yet declared himself a Tory for the king, but neither had he taken up arms as a patriot.
- Repeatedly, Jonathan had been warned that "a Tory is a thing whose head is in England, its body in America, and its neck liable to be stretched."
- Already 8,000 Loyalists from Boston had sought refuge in London.
- But many had found life disappointing in England, where they were isolated as a fringe group and found employment difficult.
- Jonathan's brother was urging him to join him in Québec.
- Jonathan kept telling his wife the war was only temporary, while his financial condition grew more perilous daily.
- In Rhode Island, thousands of Loyalists had been placed under house arrest or expelled from the community for refusing to sign a loyalty oath to the Colonies.
- By 1778, food shortages were persistent in Boston.
- Smuggler ships attempting to run the blockade were often sunk by the British.
- Jonathan was too old to start over, he kept telling himself.
- "Time to move on," his wife kept whispering.
- "What will become of my home?" he asked.
- "We will manage," she answered.

Jonathan's loyalties were divided between Britain and America.

Life in the Community: The New England Colonies

- The American Revolution forced more than 200,000 Loyalists into voluntary exile
- The majority were a mixture of affluent businessmen and craftsmen, shopkeepers and seamen.
- They were united in their distrust of the radical change underway, along with a deep respect for the traditions of Britain.
- The hurdles confronting the Americans in achieving independence were formidable.
- The British navy had virtual control of the Atlantic and could attack anywhere along the American coast at will.
- The British army boasted a large corps of seasoned officers experienced in the large-unit tactics of eighteenth-century European warfare.
- The new United Colonies were attempting to form a government and fight a war simultaneously.
- Congress still had to define the institutional relationship between it and the former Colonies.
- The Articles of Confederation gave Congress neither the power to tax nor the power to regulate commerce
- No tax system to generate revenue made it very difficult to borrow money.
- The war was to be financed through voluntary payments to Congress by the states, which were quick to pass loyalty statutes but slow to tax.
- In Rhode Island, death and confiscation of estate were the penalties provided for any person who communicated with the British ministry or its agents.
- To speak, write or act against doings of Congress or of the assembly of Connecticut was punishable by disqualification for office and imprisonment.
- In Massachusetts, a person suspected of enmity to the Whig cause could be arrested under warrant and banished, unless he would swear fealty to the Friends of Liberty.

King George.

HISTORICAL SNAPSHOT
1778

- British Captain James Cook explored the Sandwich Islands, now known as the Hawaiian Islands, and sighted the Oregon coast at Yaquina Bay, and Nootka Sound in Vancouver

- Puccini's opera *Roland* premiered in Paris

- The Colonies' Articles of Confederation were ratified by the first state, South Carolina

- England declared war on France, which then recognized the United Colonies and signed a treaty of aid

- Voltaire published *Irene*

- Oliver Pollock, a New Orleans businessman, created the "$" symbol

- Mary Ludwig Hayes, who became known as "Molly Pitcher," provided aid to the American patriots during battle

- The Liberty Bell was returned home to Philadelphia after the British Army left the city

- George Washington's troops engaged the British at the Battle of Monmouth, New Jersey

- Beethoven was first presented by his father as an eight-year-old prodigy

- American troops stationed at West Point nicknamed the place "Point Purgatory"

- Congress prohibited the importation of slaves in the United States

- Joseph Bramah from Yorkshire, England, constructed an improved water closet

- In England, the Catholic Relief Act ignited unrest in London

- German-Prussian army officer Baron von Steuben joined the Continental Army at Valley Forge and began drilling and training the troops

- English troops occupied Savannah, Georgia, the state's capital

- Loyalists and Iroquois Indians in New York killed 40 American settlers in the Cherry Valley Massacre

- David Rittenhouse observed a total solar eclipse in Philadelphia

- The Rhode Island General Assembly authorized the enlistment of slaves

Selected Prices

Barrel	.9 Pence
Bed, Sheets and Blankets	8 Pounds
Branding Iron	.4 Pence
Flask	.1 Pence
Gunpowder, Quart	.6 Shillings
Hay, Stack	.1 Pound
Man's Shoe and Knee Buckles, Silver	.1 Pound
Salt, Bushel	.3 Pence
Turpentine, Barrel	.15 Shillings
Woman's Cloak	.15 Shillings

Flier distributed throughout Boston, November 3, 1773

To the Freeman of this and the Neighboring towns, you are desired to meet at Liberty Tree this day at Twelve of Clock at noon, then and there to hear the Persons to whom the Tea shipped by the English East India Company is consigned to make a publick Resignation of their Offices as in Consignees upon Oath and also swear that they will re-ship any Tea that may be consigned to them by said Company by the first vessel sailing from London.

—O.C., Secretary, Boston

Flier distributed throughout Boston, November 30, 1773

Friends, Brethren and, Countrymen! That worst of Plagues, the Detestable Tea, ship'd for this Port by the East India Company, is now arrived in this harbour; the Hour of Destruction or manly opposition to the machinations of Tyranny stares you in the Face; every Friend of this Country, to himself and posterity is now called upon to meet at Faneuil Hall at nine o'clock, this Day, (at which time the bells will Ring) to make a united and successful Resistance to this last worst and most Destructive Measure of Administration.

Letter from Lord Percy to Adjutant General Edward Harvey in England, April 1775, concerning the outbreak of hostilities:

Whoever looks upon them as an irregular mob will find himself much mistaken. They have men amongst them those who know very well what they're about, having been employed as Rangers against the Indians and Canadians, and this country again much covered with wood and hills is very advantageous for their method of fighting.

Nor are several of their men void of a spirit of enthusiasm, as we experienced yesterday, for many of them concealed themselves in houses and advanced within ten yards to fire at me and other officers, though they were mortally certain of being put to death themselves in an instant.

You may depend upon it, that as the rebels have now had time to pre-prepare, they are determined to go through with it, nor will the insurrection here turn out so despicable as it is perhaps imagined at home. For my part, I never believed, I confess that they would have attacked the King's troops or have had the perseverance I found it in them yesterday.

The high cost of living during the war, from Mrs. Sarah Bache to her father, Philadelphia, 1778:

I had been obligated to pay 15 pounds and 15 shillings for a common calamanco petticoat without quilting, I once could have had for 15 shillings. I buy nothing but what I really want, and wore out my silk ones before I got this.

The Colony of Rhode Island Test Act, to be administered to those suspected of being unfriendly to the cause of the United American Colonies, 1776:

I, the subscriber, do solemnly and sincerely declare, that I believe the War, Resistance, and Opposition, in which the United American Colonies are now engaged against the Fleets and Armies of Great Britain, is on the part of said colonies just and necessary; and that I will not directly, nor indirectly, afford assistance of any sort or kind whatever to the said Fleets and Armies during the continuance of the present war; but I will hardily assist in the defence of the United Colonies.

* *

Thursday, June 12, 1776, pursuant to the order of the General Assembly:

WHEREAS, Messieurs Richard Beale, John Nicholl, Nicholas Lechmere, Thomas Vernon and Walter Chaloner having been examined before this Assembly, and refused to subscribe to the Test ordered by this Assembly to be tendered to suspected persons; and it appearing that while they continue in the principles by them avowed before this Assembly, or justly be deemed unfriendly to United Colonies; it is therefore

VOTED AND RESOLVED, that the Sheriff of the County of Newport forthwith remove said (dissent individuals) to the town of Gloucester in this Colony, where they shall be permitted to go at-large within the limits of the town, they giving of honor to continue there until further orders from this Assembly. That if either of them shall forfeit his parole, he shall, upon being apprehended, be committed to Gaol and closely confined until further orders from this Assembly.

* *

The diary of Thomas Vernon, loyalist and prisoner under house arrest by the Colonies:

Thursday, July 4, 1776. I rose at ten minutes after five o'clock. A very clear, cool morning. The wind still continuing at northwest. We tarried chiefly in the house this forenoon in shaving and cleaning ourselves. Our diversion was chiefly an innocent chat. We daily experience the good nature and civility of this family, which I cannot pass unnoticed. Our breakfast was coffee. We dined upon salt pork and greens, and a nap as usual; after we had drank a dish of tea, we walked out and assist our landlord and his sons in raking hay until evening. Having purchased a lamb of Mr. Keetch for our table, Mr. Beale saw it dressed. It is a tolerably good one. Our supper was a few eggs, boiled, and milk. Went to bed at half after nine.

Friday, July 5, 1776. Being more sleepy than usual I did not get up until 10 minutes before six. The wind was southwest, cloudy and almost calm, but as the sun grew higher the wind increased. We spent the day in and about the house. I amused myself in whittling a walking stick. At 12 o'clock we used the last lemon, and were not forgetful of our Newport friends. Dined half after 12 upon the forequarter of the lamb purchased yesterday, roasted, and the head pry'd with mint, and a sorrel salad. At two o'clock a small shower of rain. The wind still continuing very windy and cloudy. Half after five very considerable (to use the term of the country) showers of rain until almost sun setting, attended with thunder and sharp lightning and some hail. In the evening we all took a walk out, it being very pleasant, and soon after returned. Joseph, the boy of the house, by some accident cut his foot with the drawing knife, very badly; it bled much. . . .

Saturday, July 6, 1776. I rose at 10 minutes before five. A clear, calm morning. The wind about northwest. The weather, I think, very cool for the season; it continued so all the forenoon. Our time before breakfast employed in cleaning our shoes, shaving, etc. The whole forenoon has been spent chiefly in the house and chatting with the girls. We lament greatly the want of a book to amuse us, which we have neglected. Stephen, our landlords eldest

continued

The Colony of Rhode Island Test Act, to be administered to those suspected of being unfriendly to the cause of the United American Colonies, 1776 . . . *(continued)*

son, told us that he is a member of a company at Scituate, who some time past, have collected money which they have laid out in books, to be loaned out to the company. It is called as Scituate library. Our landlord attended the funeral of a young man who died suddenly. The procession passed by our house at one o'clock to the Baptist meeting-house, where is a sermon on the occasion. Esquire Wilmut called in to see us for the first time, with whom we had conversation respecting our suffering; he tarried with us about half an hour, and promised to see us again soon. I made a bowl of currant punch. Dined upon stewed veal and pork, with the sorrel salad. The weather growing very warm induced me to take a nap in the chair, which was very refreshing. We received a small keg of biscuit from Colonel Bowen. Took a walk in the fields at six to visit the haymakers. The wind all estate continued northerly; our supper, milk and bread, and as usual went to bed at half after nine.

A Retrospect of the Boston Tea-Party, a Memoir of George R. T. Hewes, 1834:

It was now evening (December 16, 1773), and I immediately dressed myself in the costume of an Indian, equipped with a small hatchet, which I and my associates denominated the tomahawk, with which, and a club, after having painted my face and hands with coal dust in the shop of a blacksmith, I repaired to Griffin's wharf, where the ships lay that contained the tea. When I first appeared in the street after being thus disguised, I fell in with many who were dressed, equipped and painted as I was, and who fell in with me and marched in order to the place of our destination.

When we arrived at the wharf, there were three of our number who assumed an authority to direct our operations, to which we readily submitted. They divided us into three parties, for the purpose of boarding the three ships which contained the tea at the same time. The name of him who commanded the division to which I was assigned was Leonard Pitt. The names of the other commanders I never knew. We were immediately ordered by the respective commanders to board all the ships at the same time, which we promptly obeyed. The commander of the division to which I belonged, as soon as we were on board the ship, appointed me boatswain, and ordered me to go to the captain and demand of him the keys to the hatches and a dozen candles. I made the demand accordingly, and the captain promptly replied, and delivered the articles; but requested me at the same time to do no damage to the ship or rigging. We then were ordered by our commander to open the hatches and take out all the chests of tea and throw them overboard, and we immediately proceeded to execute his orders, first cutting and splitting the chests with our tomahawks, so as thoroughly to expose them to the effects of the water.

In about three hours from the time we went on board, we had thus broken and thrown overboard every tea chest to be found in the ship, while those in the other ships were disposing of the tea in the same way, at the same time. We were surrounded by British armed ships, but no attempt was made to resist us. . . .

The next morning, after we had cleared the ships of the tea, it was discovered that very considerable quantities of it were floating upon the surface of the water; and to prevent the possibility of any of its being saved for use, a number of small boats were manned by sailors and citizens, who rowed them into those parts of the harbor wherever the tea was visible, and by beating it with oars and paddles so thoroughly drenched it as to render its entire destruction inevitable.

Memoirs, by Boston King, escaped South Carolina slave who joined the British Army serving in New York, 1783:

. . . About that time (1783), the horrors and devastation of war happily terminated, and peace was restored between America and Britain, which diffused universal joy among all parties, except us that escaped from slavery, and taken refuge in the English army; for a report prevailed in New-York, that all slaves, in number 2,000, were to be delivered up to their masters, although some of them had been three or four years among English. This dreadful rumour filled us all with inexpressible anguish and terror, especially when we saw our old Masters coming from Virginia, North-Carolina, and other parts, seizing upon their slaves in the streets of New-York, or even dragging them out of their beds. Many of the slaves had very cruel masters, so that the thoughts of returning home with them embittered life to us. For some days we lost our appetite for food, and sleep departed from our eyes. The English had compassion upon us in the days of our distress, and issued out a Proclamation, importing, "That all slaves should be free, who had taken refuge in the British lines, and claimed a sanction and privileges of the proclamations respecting the security and protection of Negroes." In consequence to this, each of us received a certificate from the commanding officer at New-York, which dispelled all our fears, and filled us with joy and gratitude. Soon after, ships were fitted out, and furnished with every necessity for conveying us to Nova Scotia.

The Americans have tarred and feathered your subjects, plundered your merchants, burnt your ships, denied all obedience to your laws and authority; yet so clement and so long forbearing has our conduct been that it is incumbent on us now to take a different course. Whatever may be the consequences, we must risk something; if we do not, all is over.

—British Prime Minister Lord North, promoting British retaliation for the Boston Tea Party, 1773

Well, boys, you have had a fine, pleasant evening for your Indian caper, haven't you? But mind, you have got to pay the fiddler yet.

—British Admiral Montague as the Sons of Liberty returned from the Boston Tea Party, 1773

1776 News Feature

Defending New York City from the British in July, 1776, A Narrative of Some of the Adventures, Dangers and Sufferings of a Revolutionary Soldier, **by Joseph Martin, published 1830:**

. . . At the lower end of the street were placed several casks of sea bread, made, I believe, of canel and peas-meal, nearly hard enough for musket flints; the casks were unheaded and each man was allowed to take as many as he could as he marched by. As my luck would have it, there was a momentary halt made; I improved the opportunity thus offered me, as every good soldier should upon all important occasions, to get as many of the biscuit as I possibly could; no one said anything to me and I filled my bosom and took as many as I could hold in my hand, a dozen or more in all, and when we arrived at the ferry stairs stowed them away in my knapsack. We quickly embarked on board the boats. As each boat started, three cheers were given for those on board, which was returned by the numerous spectators who thronged the wharves; they always wished us good luck, apparently; although it was with most of them perhaps nothing more than a ceremony.

We soon landed at Brooklyn, on the Island, marched up the ascent from the ferry to the plain. We now began to meet the wounded men, another sight I was unacquainted with, some with broken arms, some with broken legs, some with broken heads. The sight of these a little daunted me, and made me think of home, but the sight and thought vanished altogether. We marched a short distance, when we halted to refresh ourselves. Whether we had any other victuals inside the hard bread I do not remember, but I remember my gnawing at them; they were hard enough to break the teeth of a rat. . . .

While resting here, which was not more than twenty minutes or half an hour, the Americans and British were warmly engaged within sight of us. What were the feelings of most of the young soldiers at this time, I know not, but I know what were mine. But let mine or theirs be what they might, I saw a lieutenant who appeared to have feelings not very enviable; whether he was actuated by fear or the canteen I cannot determine now. I thought it fear at the time, for he ran around among the men of his company, sniveling and blubbering, praying each one if he had aught against him, or if he had injured anyone that they would forgive him, declaring at the same time that he, from his heart, forgave them if they had offended him, and I gave him full credit for assertion; for had he been at the gallows

with a halter about his neck, he could not have shown more fear or penitence. A fine soldier you are, I thought, a fine soldier's officer, an exemplary man for young soldiers! I would have then suffered anything short of death rather than have made such an exhibition of myself. . . .

We were soon called upon to fall in and proceed. We had not gone far, about half a mile, when we overtook a small party of the artillery here, driving a heavy twelve-pounder upon a field carriage, sinking halfway to the naves in the sandy soil. They pled hard for some of us to assist them to get on their piece; our officers, however, paid no attention to the entreaties, but pressed forward towards a creek, where a large party of Americans and British were engaged. By the time we arrived, the enemy had driven our men into the creek, or rather millpond, where such as could swim got across; those who could not swim, and could not procure anything to buoy them up, sunk. The British, having several field pieces stationed by a brick house, were pouring the canister and grape upon the Americans like a shower of hail. They would doubtless have done them much more damage than they did, but for the twelve-pounder mentioned above; the men, having gotten it within sufficient distance to reach them, and opening a fire upon them, soon obliged them to shift their quarters. There was in this action a regiment of Maryland troops (volunteers), all young gentleman. When they came out of the water and mud to us, looking like water rats, it was a truly pitiful sight. Many of them were killed in the pond, and more were drowned. Some of us went into the water after the fall of the tide, and took out a number of corpses and a great many arms that were sunk in the pond and creek. . . .

Just at dusk, I, with one or two others of our company, went off to a barn, about half a mile distance, with intent to get some straw to lodge upon, the ground and leaves being drenched in water, and we as wet as they. It was quite dark in the barn, and while I was fumbling about the floor someone called to me from the top of the mow, inquiring where I was from. I told him. He asked me if we had not had an engagement there, having heard us discharging our guns, I told him we had into severe one, too . . . I then heard several others, as it appeared, speaking on the mow. Poor fellows, they had better have been at their posts than skulking in a barn on account of a little wet, for I have not the least doubt that the British had possession of their mortal parts before the noon of the next day.

I could not find any straw, but I found some wheat in the sheaf standing by the side of the door; I took a sheaf or two and returned as fast as I could to the regiment. When I arrived the men were all paraded to march off the ground; I left my wheat, seized my musket and fell into the ranks. We were strictly enjoined not to speak, or even cough, while on the march. All orders were given from officer to officer, and communicated to the men in whispers. What such secrecy could mean we cannot divine. . . . We marched on, however, until we arrived at the ferry, where we immediately embarked on board the bateaux and were conveyed safely to New York, where we landed about three o'clock in the morning, nothing against our inclinations.

1780–1789

The decade of the 1780s opened with the continued conflict between those striving for and against American independence. The American forces had suffered numerous defeats, but ultimately America's vast size, Britain's attempts to control the southern colonies, and several key American military victories led to American independence at Yorktown by 1781. The 1783 Treaty of Paris formalized the war's end and the new nation embarked on the difficult process of forming a unified country, exposing a succession of internal conflicts and philosophies that dominated the political life of this decade.

Even with the war's end, prosperity for America was elusive. American merchants lost their favored position with Britain as a trading partner. Reduced wartime demand diminished agricultural prices. Cities experienced high unemployment. British merchants flooded the newly opened American market with luxuries. American merchants began limited trade with China in the 1780s, but Mediterranean trade was hampered by pirate attacks because American ships no longer had the protection of the British Navy.

As important, the losers in the battle for independence included many of the leading lights of America: wealthy merchants; professionals; prominent priests; and politicians who had stayed loyal to the crown during the war. In retaliation, the property of many was confiscated. Nearly 100,000 loyalists, or

Tories, were expelled to Canada, the Caribbean or South America. Large estates belonging to loyalist families were broken up into smaller plots, some of which were first set aside for educational purposes. The ancient British practice of passing on the family's entire estate to the eldest son, known as primogeniture, largely ended. Both these policies provided increased opportunities for small, independent farmers.

The weak government formed under the Articles of Confederation prevented the new nation from raising funds through taxation, thus hindering the government's ability to operate effectively and meet its debt obligations. Economic hardship crippled the country from 1784 through 1788, hurting businesses, especially the nation's fishermen and farmers. Nearly all activities that employed American-built ships from cod fishing to whaling to mercantile were depressed during the early years of independence. The financial hardships during this time influenced a New England revolt under Daniel Shays of 1,100 men who wanted economic reforms. These issues propelled the new nation's leaders to resolve the structural weaknesses of the Articles of Confederation by creating a new Constitution in Philadelphia in 1787.

Intellectual life continued, regardless of the War for American Independence. The American Academy of Arts and Sciences was founded in Boston in 1880. A serial publication, *The Federalist,* a work on political theory written by Alexander Hamilton, James Madison and John Jay, gained widespread popularity. Chemist Benjamin Rush emerged as the new American nation's foremost medical scientist, publishing *An Inquiry into the Effects of Spiritous Liquors on the Human Body and Mind* in 1884.

During the decade, theater life was becoming acceptable in the nation's larger cities. In New York, the first American comedy, *The Contrast,* was an immediate success in 1787. Pennsylvania repealed its prohibition on theater performances as other states accepted the art. Publishing started to grow as the first daily newspaper, the *Pennsylvania Evening Post,* entered circulation in Philadelphia in 1883. A few writers started to receive acclaim, as J. Hector St. John de Crèvecoeur's *Letters from an American Farmer* became a popular book. The work was translated into French and German editions which provided the Frenchman's impression of the New World, its farm life and geography. Philip's Freneaus's published work *Poems* marked him as one of America's major poets, with "The Wild Honey Suckle" considered his finest poem.

The pace of public transportation was slow within the new nation. By 1785, regular stage routes linking New York City, Boston, Albany and Philadelphia were established. The average travel time between New York and Boston was six days.

Near the decade's end, early signs of improvements in commerce were noticeable. American cabinetmakers and furniture designers were becoming equal artistically with other nations. The Commonwealth of Virginia authorized construction of the Little River Turnpike, the nation's first turnpike that would improve regional commerce. Manufacturing started to slowly emerge with the first cotton factory formed in Beverly, Massachusetts. Quickly manufacturing societies were being formed in Philadelphia, Boston and New York City to promote textile production. To support the nation's commodities, Congress passed its first tariff bill to protect the nation's key products from foreign competition.

1780 PROFILE

Rachel Findley was a slave in the western part of Virginia, where she and her "husband" Peter longed to be free to raise their family and own their own land.

Life at Home

- Rachel Findley was a mother and a slave; her day began before sunrise and stretched long past dark.
- Every morning she tended to her own children before hurrying to the main house to see about the fire and start breakfast for the missus.
- Rachel and her daughter, Judah, had been with John Draper for seven years; they were the first female slaves to arrive when he had only owned three field slaves.
- Since the new Mrs. Draper moved in, the household expanded to include her two children and more slaves.
- Now there were more mouths to feed and more work to be done.
- Rachel had been a slave in eastern Virginia, until 1773, when her master, Thomas Clay, sent her and Judah away, separating them from their kin.
- Mitchell Clay, Thomas's son, brought the woman and girl to the western Virginia backcountry.
- Not long afterwards, he traded them to Mr. Draper for 1,000 acres of land.
- In the process, Rachel lost contact with all of her loved ones including her grandmother Chance, her aunts and cousins, and her brother Samuel.
- Now Rachel lived in a small cabin with Peter, a field slave who had been with the Drapers for many years.
- Although not formally married, Rachel and Peter were happy to be together, and Rachel's family had grown to include several younger children.

Western Virginia homestead where slave Rachel Findley lived.

- The Drapers had a big family, with George, John, Alley, James, Silas, Mary and Elizabeth, all children of Bettie, the first Mrs. Draper.
- Rachel had been sorry when the first missus died.
- Bettie had been kind to her, and they had grown to respect and rely on each other during times of trial, such as childbirth or the terror of an Indian attack.
- In her youth Bettie was captured by Shawnee during the attack at Draper's Meadows in 1755 and held prisoner in Ohio for over six years.
- Rachel and Bettie talked several times about Bettie's ordeal, prompted by Rachel's persistent questions about life among the Indians.
- When Bettie asked Rachel why she took such an interest in the Shawnee customs, Rachel explained that her grandmother was a Catawba Indian, not a Negro, and she wanted to know more about her people.
- Bettie knew little about the Catawba Indians, but she remembered vividly the exotic customs of the Shawnee.
- She faced terrible grief and fear during the first months of her captivity, when she was separated from the other captives, including her sister-in-law Mary Ingles, and adopted into the family of an old chief.
- Gradually, her fears subsided and she settled into a dazed routine, learning how to make herself useful by sewing shirts for the warriors.
- She described how skillful the Shawnee women were in treating deer skins, making beautiful dresses and leggings.
- Bettie admired the respect Shawnee showed toward their elders, giving older men and women a voice in decision making.
- She admitted to Rachel that she sometimes missed the women who had become her friends but hastened to add that the settlers in their New River community of Virginia would not like to hear her say that she felt "friendly" toward the Shawnee.

The second Missus Draper was bossy and impatient.

- Rachel knew that Bettie was right, and figured that Bettie should not be calling her slave a "friend," either.
- Rachel told Bettie her story of how her grandmother was captured by Mitchell Clay's grandfather, and brought to Virginia, 50 or more years ago.
- Rachel described how the courts declared her grandmother an Indian and therefore free, but that her master had sent her away to avoid receiving the court order.
- Bettie had expressed sympathy, but was reluctant to tell her husband, afraid of what he might say or do; he would never agree to give up some of his slaves.
- Bettie wondered if Rachel's story was true, and looked for an opportunity to ask advice from someone familiar with the law.
- She died before she found that opportunity.
- The new Missus Draper was much less sympathetic; Rachel thought her bossy and impatient.
- She complained that the slaves had not been trained properly, had no discipline and showed little respect.
- The Draper children had trouble adjusting to their new stepmother, too.
- The older boys didn't spend much time around her, but the younger children had strict rules to obey and were always reminded to keep clean!
- The boys had to take lessons in music, reading and arithmetic, while the girls were taught to do fancy needlework.

- Change was all around Rachel.
- In the seven years that she lived on the Virginia frontier, more and more travelers were coming through in hopes of finding land farther to the west, often stopping by to visit along the way.
- They brought the latest news of the war against England and helped the Drapers feel connected to the rest of Virginia.
- Rachel never stopped hoping that someone from back East would bring news of her family and friends.

Life at Work

- Since the new missus arrived, Rachel Findley's workload increased with more washing, sewing, cooking, gardening and cleaning.
- All of Rachel's children had daily chores, too, in the barn, chicken coop, stables and the garden.
- Her daughter Judah, now 14, was being trained by the new missus to become a domestic slave and learned the finer points of cooking and sewing.
- These changes seemed strange and pretentious to Rachel, especially with the war threatening to disrupt everything.
- She heard the missus give a long list of items to Mr. Draper to buy, including Bohea tea, cake sugar, needles, buttons and muslin.
- She said that she couldn't entertain visitors without the proper provisions, and that she needed to provide the house slaves with proper clothing.
- Mr. Draper didn't seem too eager to make any of these purchases, but he didn't argue with her.
- He reminded her that, until normal trade could be resumed, wives in the New River settlements would not be serving any imported tea.
- She did not need to be reminded that salt was scarce, severely limiting the availability of salt pork.
- He explained other war-related problems, such as the high taxes and fear and mistrust spreading throughout the neighborhood with some families, especially German-speaking settlers, declaring loyalty to England, with others demanding loyalty to Virginia and the patriotic cause.
- He was afraid that he soon would be called into service to protect the prosperous lead mines near the New River or perhaps to break up a Tory rebellion.
- The military supply wagon had already passed through the community impressing needed supplies for the soldiers.
- When it left the Draper land, it carried bacon, several barrels of corn, six sheep and at least two smoothbore rifles.
- Rachel knew that threats had been made against William Preston, a county surveyor, and that many of the wealthy landowners were armed and ready to fight.
- Peter had told her that some of the smaller farmers blamed Preston for cheating them and preventing them from getting proper deeds to their land claims.

Samplers were used to practice sewing skills, and often depicted family life.

- Rachel could understand the anger that some families felt; they made claims, cleared fields and built houses, and had been waiting for years to get surveys or a fair hearing in the courts.
- She wondered if there would ever be any justice for slaves or the poor as long as wealthy men held so much power.
- In this time of civil war and unrest, people were forced to get by with home-grown substitutes, using molasses instead of sugar, sassafras instead of imported tea, and hard cider instead of brandy.
- For the women in the Draper household (slaves and free), war meant more hard work producing homespun fabrics, from preparing the flax, to weaving the fabric.
- For the Draper men, it meant more work too: growing hemp to make ropes for the shipping industry; corn for cattle fodder, corn meal and whiskey; and a full range of other agricultural products including cotton and tobacco.
- Cattle and horses were an essential part of the daily life and routine, and all the men and boys were expected to help with herding and branding.
- Rachel's children were assigned chores such as collecting eggs, weeding the vegetable garden, milking the cow and churning butter.
- Although Rachel and Peter appreciated the beauty of their surroundings and were glad they had food and a place to sleep, they longed to be free—to have their own little cabin and their own piece of land.
- They wanted their children to learn to read and develop skills, and be ready for independence, if it came.
- They wondered what independence would mean for slaves.
- Peter learned many useful skills, such as carpentry and blacksmithing, and was aware that his master could never have built his home or developed his land without the hard work and advanced skills of his slaves.

Life in the Community: New River, Virginia

- Rachel Findley and her children always looked forward to court day.
- It was exciting to load the wagons with produce and hand-made goods to take to the market at Fort Chiswell, the county seat.
- Many of the gentry and smaller landowners were there hoping to resolve disagreements or questions pertaining to runaway slaves or land disputes.
- Others came to enjoy the excitement of watching a trial or perhaps an execution.
- Situated at the junction of the Great Trading Path and the Richmond Road, near the New River, the community was named after a frontier fort built in 1758 as an outpost during the French and Indian War.
- For two decades, pioneers cultivated fields and built churches, recreating the middle class lifestyle most of them had known on the Eastern seaboard.
- Some of the earliest settlers were from Loudoun County, VA; Chester County, PA; and Burlington County, NJ, all predominantly Quaker areas.
- The bustling marketplace at Fort Chiswell lured hundreds into town, even though few people had cash.
- Bartering, however, allowed men, women and even children to trade their homemade items for whatever treasures they desired.
- Young girls traded eggs for thread or ribbons; men traded animal skins for salt or lead, and boys traded hand-carved toys for a new pen-knife or a set of marbles.
- Rachel's children brought a number of homespun items.
- Politicians were making speeches and handing out free cups of rum or brandy.
- Rachel avoided the lively scene, preferring to watch from the comfort of a shady tree and gossip with a slave named Jessie, who lived over at Ingles Ferry.

- They enjoyed seeing each other on court days, and they always had interesting news to share.
- Jessie was alarmed about the recent Indian attacks in the far western settlements of Virginia and Tennessee.
- She told Rachel that her missus, Mary Ingles' son, Thomas, was living in Burke's Garden with his wife and three children.
- Jessie's brothers, Moses and Ben, were living there too.
- Years ago, Mary, her two sons and several neighbors were captured along with Bettie Draper and taken to Ohio by the Shawnee.
- Mary stayed captive only a few months before escaping and starting the long journey home through the wilderness.
- Miraculously, she and a German captive walked hundreds of miles, arriving safely home in late November 1755.
- She was now living at Ingles Ferry with her four youngest children.
- William and Mary Ingles owned land on both sides of the New River where they operated a ferry, tavern and store.
- Jessie worked in the tavern, and was kept busier than usual in recent weeks, as scores of families journeyed along the Great Road, crossing the New River at Ingles Ferry and spending the night in the tavern.
- Life was austere, but the lure of land overcame any fear of Indian attacks or other hardships.
- Some women and slaves seemed less confident, however, as they listened to stories of scalpings, burned cabins, torture and other violence on the frontier.
- The war between the British and the Americans was forcing all to reconsider their identity.
- German families had no quarrel with the king of England, but they did have serious complaints about the local officials who, through greed and favoritism, had denied them opportunities to get deeds to the land.
- Negro slaves also wanted the chance to be free to own land, learn a trade, and learn to read, but no one could say for sure whether the Continental or the British army would be victorious.

Many families feared Indian attacks.

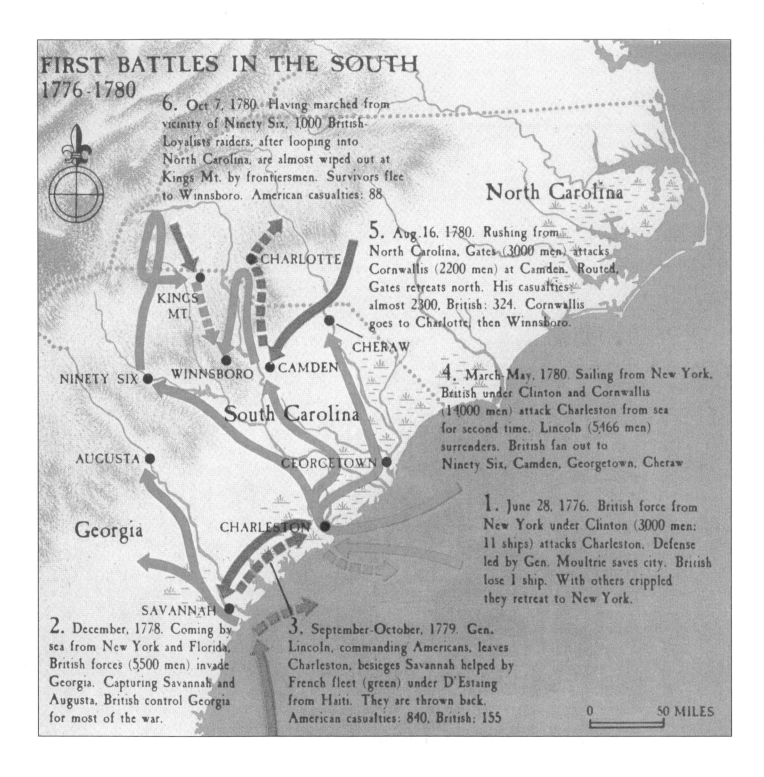

FIRST BATTLES IN THE SOUTH
1776-1780

6. Oct. 7, 1780. Having marched from vicinity of Ninety Six, 1,000 British-Loyalists raiders, after looping into North Carolina, are almost wiped out at Kings Mt. by frontiersmen. Survivors flee to Winnsboro. American casualties: 88

North Carolina

5. Aug. 16, 1780. Rushing from North Carolina, Gates (3000 men) attacks Cornwallis (2200 men) at Camden. Routed, Gates retreats north. His casualties almost 2300, British: 324. Cornwallis goes to Charlotte, then Winnsboro.

CHARLOTTE

KINGS MT.

CHERAW

NINETY SIX   WINNSBORO   CAMDEN

South Carolina

4. March-May, 1780. Sailing from New York, British under Clinton and Cornwallis (14000 men) attack Charleston from sea for second time. Lincoln (5,466 men) surrenders. British fan out to Ninety Six, Camden, Georgetown, Cheraw

AUGUSTA

GEORGETOWN

1. June 28, 1776. British force from New York under Clinton (3000 men; 11 ships) attacks Charleston. Defense led by Gen. Moultrie saves city. British lose 1 ship. With others crippled they retreat to New York.

Georgia

CHARLESTON

SAVANNAH

2. December, 1778. Coming by sea from New York and Florida, British forces (5,500 men) invade Georgia. Capturing Savannah and Augusta, British control Georgia for most of the war.

3. September-October, 1779. Gen. Lincoln, commanding Americans, leaves Charleston, besieges Savannah helped by French fleet (green) under D'Estaing from Haiti. They are thrown back. American casualties: 840, British: 155

0   50 MILES

HISTORICAL SNAPSHOT
1780

- Charleston, South Carolina, fell to the British, with losses of 5,400 men, four ships and a military arsenal, in the worst American defeat of the Revolutionary War

- The Americans were decisively defeated by the British at the Battle of Camden in South Carolina

- American militiamen defeated the British near Kings Mountain, North Carolina, forcing Cornwallis to abandon his invasion of the colony

- Esther de Berdt Reed assumed a leadership role in organizing, fundraising, purchasing materials, and working on the production of shirts in Philadelphia for the American Continental Army

- To consolidate revolutionary war debts, Alexander Hamilton proposed the creation of a central bank

- Pennsylvania began mandating the freeing of newborn children of slaves

- London exploded in riots in opposition to the Catholic Relief Act of 1778

- King Louis XVI abolished torture as a means of forcing the confessions of suspects in crimes

- A giant Mosasaurus dinosaur head was discovered in the Netherlands

- The Peruvian Indians revolted against Spanish rule

- James Baker and John Hannon started the first chocolate factory in the United States in Dorchester, Massachusetts

- Potter's apprentice Thomas Minton originated the pattern Blue Willow

- Steel pen points began to replace quill feathers for writing letters

- The second oldest scholarly society in the United States, the American Academy of Arts & Sciences, was formed in Boston

- American General Benedict Arnold secretly promised to surrender the fort at West Point to the British Army

- Britain declared war on Holland, igniting a four-year battle

- The first British Sunday newspaper appeared, the *British Gazette & Sunday Monitor*

- The circular saw was invented

- The Continental Congress established a court of appeals

- William Herschel discovered the first binary star, Xi Ursae Majoris

- Luigi Galvani conducted experiments with muscles and electricity

Slavery Timeline

1619
Twenty captive Africans were sold into slavery at Jamestown, Virginia, in the British American colonies.

1641
Massachusetts became the first colony to legalize slavery.

1654
Virginia courts granted blacks the right to hold slaves.

1657
Virginia passed a fugitive slave law.

1660
Charles II, king of England, ordered the Council of Foreign Plantations to devise strategies for converting slaves to Christianity.

1667
Virginia declared that Christian baptism would not alter a person's status as a slave.

1676
Black slaves and black and white indentured servants in Virginia banded together to participate in Bacon's Rebellion.

1682
Virginia declared that all imported black servants were slaves for life.

1691
Virginia forbade marriages between whites and blacks or whites and Native Americans.

1696
The Royal African Trade Company lost its monopoly and New England colonists entered the slave trade.

1705
The Virginia slave code codified slave status, defining all slaves as real estate, acquitting masters who killed slaves during punishment, forbidding slaves and free colored peoples from physically assaulting white persons, and denying slaves the right to bear arms or move abroad without written permission.

1723
Virginia abolished manumissions.

1733
Quaker Eli Coleman published *A Testimony against That Anti-Christian Practice of Making Slaves of Men.*

1758
Pennsylvania Quakers forbade their members from owning slaves or participating in the slave trade.

Timeline . . . *(continued)*

1767

The Virginia House of Burgesses boycotted the British slave trade in protest to the Townsend Acts.

1774

The First Continental Congress banned trade with Britain and vowed to discontinue the slave trade.

1775

The slave population in the colonies neared 500,000.

In Virginia, the ratio of free colonists to slaves was approximately 1:1.

The first abolitionist society was formed in Philadelphia, Pennsylvania.

General George Washington first announced a ban on enlistment of free blacks and slaves in the colonial army and then reversed the ban, ordering the army to accept the services of free blacks.

1777

Vermont became the first of the 13 colonies to abolish slavery.

1780

Delaware made it illegal to own slaves.

Pennsylvania began gradual emancipation.

Massachusetts enfranchised all men regardless of race.

Selected Prices

Coal, Bushel . . . . .4 Pence
Eggs, Dozen . . . . .7 Pence
Horse . . . . .25 Pounds
Indentured Servant, Boy . . . . .5 Pounds
Men's Breeches . . . . .2 Shillings
Milk Pan . . . . .6 Pence
Plow . . . . .7 Shillings
Rum, Gallon . . . . .1 Pound
Slave, Woman . . . . .77 Pounds
Tobacco, Hogshead . . . . .5 Pounds

Journal entry written in 1779 by Henry Hamilton, a British governor captured during the American Revolution, who spent the night at Ingles Ferry as he was on his way, under guard, to Williamsburg:

A beautiful girl, his [William Ingles's] daughter, sat at the head of the table and did the honors with such ease and graceful simplicity as quite charmed us. The scenery about his home was romantic to a degree. The river was beautiful, the hills well wooded, the low grounds well improved and well stocked. Mrs. Ingles in her early years had been carried off with another young woman by the savages and tho carried away into the Shawnee country had made her escape with the female friend & tho exposed to unspeakable hardships, and having nothing to subsist on but wild fruits, found her way back in safety from a distance of 200 miles. However, terror and distress had left so deep an impression on her mind that she appeared absorbed in a deep melancholy, and left the arrangement of household concerns & the reception of strangers to her lovely daughter.

Letter written by William Ingles to Col. William Preston in 1763:

I have the Plesher to inform you that I had the hapyness to falling in with a party of Indians in thire Return from Smiths River with sum prisoners and a great maney horses and after Exchanging about seventy shots we got possession of the Ground and all the plunder we Kild two on the Ground and I expect to find severl more to morrow as I am convinst that there is meney more Kild but as the Ground where they tuck Refuge in was so weddy and full of shrubs we did not search it we had two men wounded and one very mortal the men all behaved Like Good Soldiers and the Indians was as loath to give way the Battel lasted more than half an ower and the shouts of both parties could be hard I Dare say Neer two miles we are informed by one of the prisoners that there is a nother party of Indians Gon Down the meho River and the are to follow those and I think God willing to try my Corage wanst more with them If Providence would be so kind as to Direct our steps in so friendly a maner up to there Camp Mr. Robinson can give you the particulers as he Came up just as we had Drove them of I sent you a shot pouch that we tuck in the plunder wich I belive was the Captain's it is but a small present and I Beg you will Except it as a small trophie of our Victory we Got 30 horses and abundance of small Plunder We are in Great wont of Sum Powder and Lead for we are just out I hope sir you will Indever to porswed Colo Lewes to cintinew me at this Post as I find I can be of Great Sarves to the settlements Both of hallafax and that of yours for I find that the go within a little ways of this place when the go to Smiths River and thataway and we ly as handy to the Narrows as of aney other place Colo Phelps refused to Cumply with your ordors and would not Recave mr. Armstrong nor send anney of his men with mr. Cloyd But would go with his own men wheare he thought fit But at last I prevaild with him to Let a few of his men that Would Cum as Volenters with me and ten of them turned out wich I Left at the fort all but three and one of them was so unfortunate as to be shot Sir your instructions as often as you can conveniently send them will Give Sattesfaction to your obedient Sarvet

W Ingle   Sept ye 13th 1763

Symbol of America.

"Letter III, What Is an American?" *Letters from an American Farmer,* by Michel-Guillaume St. Jean de Crevecoeur, 1782:

I wish I could be acquainted with the feelings and thoughts which must agitate the heart and present themselves to the mind of an enlightened Englishman, when he first lands on this continent. He must greatly rejoice that he lived at the time to see this fair country discovered and settled. He must necessarily feel a share of national pride when he views the chain of settlements which embellish these extended shores. When he says to himself, this is the work of my countrymen, who, when convulsed by factions, afflicted by a variety of miseries and wants, restless and impatient, took refuge here. They brought along with them their national genius, to which they principally owe what liberty they enjoy what substance they possess. Here he sees the industry of his native country displayed in new manner, and traces, in their works, the embryos of all the arts, sciences, and ingenuity, which flourish in Europe. Here he beholds fair cities, substantial villages, extensive fields, an immense country filled with decent houses, good roads, orchards, meadows, and bridges, where, a hundred years ago, all was wild, woody, and uncultivated! What a train of pleasing ideas this fair spectacle must suggest! It is a prospect which must inspire a good citizen with most heartfelt pleasure! The difficulty consists in the manner of viewing so extensive a scene. He is arrived on a new continent: a modern society offers itself to his contemplation, different from what he has hitherto seen. It is not composed, as in Europe, of great lords who possess every thing, and a herd of people who have nothing. Here are no aristocratical families, no courts, no kings, no bishops, no ecclesiastical dominion, no invisible power giving to a few a very visible one, no great manufacturers employing thousands, no great refinements of luxury. The rich and the poor are not so far removed from each other as they are in Europe. Some few towns excepted, we are all tillers of the earth, from Nova Scotia to West Florida. We are a people of cultivators, scattered over an immense territory, communicating with each other by means of good roads, navigable rivers, united by the silken bands of mild government, all respecting the laws, without dread in their power, because they are equitable. We are all animated with the spirit of an industry which is unfettered and unrestrained, because each person works for himself.

Estate of first-generation frontiersman John Hashe, Montgomery County, Virginia, 1784:

A feather bed, large pot, frying pan, butter dish, beacon and six spoons, two spinning wheels, one riding saddle, and furniture.

"Choice of a HUSBAND," by a Gentlewoman of Prudence, *Wilmington Centinel,* and *General Advertiser,* North Carolina, June 25, 1788:

To meet a man perfectly agreeable (though the person is least to be regarded) may be a gift to some difficulty, to a nice and discerning woman. His qualifications must be great to recommend him: But I shall offer some particulars, which, if observed, may contribute to a good choice, and are worthy of election, though seldom to be met with in one person. First; it is necessary that he be a man of virtue and morality, having a large share of natural sense and acquired knowledge, proceeding from a liberal education; that he may indeed be well read, and a man of conversation, so as to have a general knowledge of men and things; to be pretty much, if not entirely, master of his passions, but not without courage, though with discretion to use; naturally good-humored and loving, but not jealous, nor meanly submissive; one not a perfect stranger to vice, but has seen enough of it to have a good notion of the folly and fatal tendency of it; he may be moderately addicted to all decent pleasures, and manly diversions; love his friend and bottle a little, but so as to not draw off his affection from his wife; to be a man of manners (though by no means foppish) enough to oblige and civilly treat persons of all temper; not to be too profuse, but have conduct enough not to live beyond his circumstances, and application enough to his own businesses, to keep the world from imposing upon him.

1781 PROFILE

Jacob Nevell led a busy life as an apprentice doctor to his uncle while working at odd jobs and pursuing a romantic interest.

Life at Home

- Twenty-two-year-old Jacob Nevell was an apprentice doctor in war-torn America.
- One of his earliest experiences was mending a soldier's arm four years earlier in Philadelphia under his uncle's supervision.
- Once certified, he planned to practice medicine in the West Indies or some exotic location.
- The youngest of four boys, Jacob was born the son of a merchant in New Haven, Connecticut.
- With education of great importance to his family, Jacob attended the prestigious Hatfield Academy under his father's instruction, who hoped he would become a lawyer like his older brother Thomas.
- Many Hatfield graduates attended Yale College.
- Jacob had no interest in law, but proved to have a strong command of Latin and fine penmanship.
- Jacob's life and destiny changed when his father's ship did not return to port in 1775; the entire crew was believed to have perished in a storm.
- A year later, when money was no longer available to finish his studies, Jacob wrote to his older brothers.
- His oldest brother Thomas agreed to help him in Philadelphia where he practiced law.
- After much discussion with their uncle, Doctor Robert Nevell, it was agreed that Jacob would apprentice with him in the medical arts.
- With the revolt in the colonies underway, rapidly rising prices and general uncertainty, Jacob graduated from Hatfield and accepted the opportunity in Philadelphia.
- Packing only necessities for his journey, Jacob rode a horse for several weeks to Philadelphia.

Jacob Nevell was an apprentice doctor to his uncle.

Jacob attended the prestigious Hatfield Academy in New Haven, Connecticut.

- Upon arrival he was greeted by his brother, who took him to mark the occasion with a drink of cherry rum at a local tavern.
- Thomas introduced Jacob to his uncle who he had never met, as Doctor Nevell left New Haven years earlier when he was a young man.
- His education and journeys in youth eventually brought him to Philadelphia.
- The doctor sized Jacob up quickly to see what sort of apprentice he would become.
- Doctor Nevell had other apprentices under him, especially since the medical college in Philadelphia was not operating; it ceased operating after his majesty's army had occupied the city in 1776.
- At the doctor's home, Jacob met Edward Loxley, also an apprentice.
- The two were to share the garret, an unfinished room under the roof, during their studies.
- The doctor's workspace and office had a unique atmosphere, with dozens of jars of powders and potions including mercury, sulfur, cinnamon, zedoary and asarum.
- Also on display was an extensive set of medical books that Doctor Nevell had acquired over the years, along with a collection of human bones.
- On one shelf was a human skull.
- Jacob learned that his apprenticeship would last several years, depending upon how well he conducted his studies.

Dr. Nevell's home was full of activity.

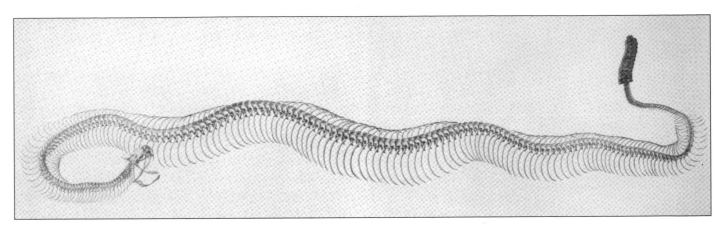

One of many skeletal specimens in Dr. Nevell's office.

- Hard work and memorization would be important for the apprenticeship to lead to a certificate.
- Initially, Jacob did not learn too much about being a doctor.
- He did a number of jobs around the house and doctor's office, including cutting wood, making fires, and running packages to patients.
- Gradually, he learned how to cut proper splints and make various bandages.
- Most of his work required memorization from a number of medical books, followed by intensive questioning by his uncle.
- Gerard van Swicten's *Commentaries upon Boerhaaves Aphorisms* demanded a significant amount of time studying and learning.
- Life was not just about studying, however.
- Philadelphia was a large town filled with local taverns, such as Tun Tavern.
- Jacob often dined with his brother Thomas, and met members of the local community.
- During one dinner with friends he met two women who would end up complicating his life.
- Abigail and Catherine Hawley were sisters with Abigail the older by just a year, and the same age as Jacob.
- Though both sisters were charming, he pursued Abigail for more than a year.
- Afternoons after his work and studies, he would have tea with Abigail and her friends.
- Other times she would join him in the evenings with his friends, often sharing conversation and debating current events in the colonies.
- He often entreated her, both in person and through letters, to grant him exclusive access to her company.
- Jacob confessed that his intentions were honorable.
- His brother and uncle objected, however, wanting him to marry more advantageously than the daughter of a tailor.
- After several months of courtship, Abigail departed to visit relatives in Nazareth, Pennsylvania.
- During the months of Abigail's departure, Jacob often spent time with friends at their houses or in a local tavern.

Tun Tavern, where Jabob often dined with his brother Thomas.

- One tavern they frequented was the Indian Queen near the Delaware River.
- There he would order a bowl of flip—a drink of heated rum or wine mixed with spices and sugar—for a few pence.
- It was not uncommon for him to stay out until 10 or 11 at night gambling with friends—playing backgammon, tumbling dice or playing cards.
- Other nights he would write letters to Abigail expressing his love for her, even though he had developed a wandering eye toward other women.
- He started spending time with Abigail's sister Catherine, who he discovered had a merry disposition and a superior intellect.
- The clandestine relationship between Jacob and Catherine lasted a few months.
- One event was so intimate he recorded it in Latin in case someone read his diary's personal accounts.
- "After C and I went into Clausum et in Cubito cecidisse et ubi agimus untill tres [a closed room and fell into bed and remained there until three] when Edward arrived were we obliged to part."
- He immediately appealed to his roommate Edward to swear him to secrecy.
- Jacob still cared deeply for Abigail and wanted no word of the incident to reach her.
- To end the relationship with Catherine and keep it a secret from Abigail, he helped Catherine draft letters to her sister describing her interest in another man.
- When Abigail returned, Jacob renewed the courtship he had pledged so ardently in his letters.

Life at Work

- After months of study and work, Doctor Nevell offered Jacob Nevell a chance to make some medicine.
- Under the observation of his roommate Edward, Jacob made Ehiopes Mineralis, a medicine for worms found in young children.
- The recipe required mixing flowers of sulfur with clean and crude mercury in equal quantities for five to six hours.
- The entire afternoon was required just to produce four ounces of the medicine.
- Jacob manufactured other medicines over time: Hier Picka, also known as holy bitters, was made of cinnamon, zedoary, asarum, saffron and cardamom seed and was often used as a purgative or a digestive stimulant.
- When typhoid or other contagious diseases were suspected in the city, work around contaminated patients caused concern.
- Doctor Nevell vividly described Philadelphia's smallpox outbreak in 1773 and how approximately 300 people had died.
- Nonetheless, the hours of work and studies afforded Jacob little money; the apprenticeship covered the cost of his education and board.
- Other sources of income were necessary.
- The British blockade and occupation had introduced tough financial times that continued after the British army's departure.
- Costs of goods were rising rapidly.
- A common razor, without a case, with bone in the setting cost 20 pounds and a small Dutch six-inch-by-four-inch worn looking-glass cost eight pounds.
- Jacob's diary detailed the high costs he paid to merchants, "I told them it was high time for a Bedlam to be built here in Philadelphia," reference to the Bethlehem Hospital and Bedlam, a hospital for lunatics in London.

- With his fine penmanship and command of Latin, Jacob often wrote "blanks" for his brother Thomas's legal practice.
- Most of the documents were form documents Thomas used to assist his clients.
- Jacob typically worked on these in his room early in the morning when the light came through his window.
- To save money on ink, he boiled crushed walnut shells with vinegar and salt.
- Once boiled down and set, the concoction produced a brown ink acceptable for writing.
- Even though the task of writing these blanks was tedious and boring, he consistently maintained a steady hand to keep from smudging the ink.
- Once done writing, he spread sand over the document to absorb the excess ink and blew it off the paper.
- Thomas was not fond of the walnut ink, preferring that Jacob use indigo instead for his documents, and eventually returned to a local printer to produce his blanks.
- Over time, Jacob gained more experience by visiting patients with his uncle, learning how to properly bleed a person, redress bandages or diagnose sicknesses.
- On one occasion they visited a woman with a fever, which they both diagnosed as Erisipilas (Erysipelas), or Saint Anthony's fire.
- Typically, the person is feverish for a few days with drowsiness.
- At times the patient experiences delirium followed by a superficial inflammation of the skin, tending to an apoplexy or abscess.
- Jacob's first patient without his uncle's help complained of a toothache, which Jacob treated by pulling the tooth for eight pence.
- Despite the long hours necessary to earn hard money, he managed to find time to spend with Abigail.
- He passed time by having tea with her in the afternoons and conversing.
- One topic was based upon a discovery within the novel, *The History of Sir Charles Grandison*, which discussed the conduct of the ideal gentleman and how to perform in society.
- It also addressed methods in acquiring the prefect wife, including a written covenant between the people seriously considering marriage.
- So Jacob drafted a covenant for him and Abigail, "the Purport of which was that we solemnly Engaged ourselves to one another, and never to have any Connections with any other Persons in a way of Courtship."
- The covenant was the subject of serious discussion over the course of several days.
- Abigail disliked the idea of marrying if Jacob fully intended to practice medicine in the West Indies.
- Also, she questioned if he could be truly faithful to her.
- After the discussion, the two signed the covenant, based upon support of both families, even though Jacob's family still had reservations.
- Because of Jacob's hard work and ability, he hoped his uncle would provide his certificate early, but that did not occur.

THE
HISTORY
OF
Sir CHARLES GRANDISON.
IN A
SERIES *of* LETTERS

Publiſhed from the ORIGINALS,

By the Editor of PAMELA and CLARISSA.

In SIX VOLUMES.

To the Laſt of which is added,

An Hiſtorical and Characteriſtical INDEX.

AS ALSO,

A Brief HISTORY, authenticated by Original Letters, of the Treatment which the EDITOR has met with from certain Bookſellers and Printers in Dublin.

Including OBSERVATIONS on Mr. Faulkner's Defence of Himſelf, publiſhed in his Iriſh News-paper of Nov. 3. 1753.

VOL. I.

The SECOND EDITION.

LONDON:

Printed for S. Richardſon;

And Sold by C. HITCH and L. HAWES, in *Pater-noſter Row*; By J. and J. RIVINGTON, in *St. Paul's Church-Yard*; By ANDREW MILLAR, in the *Strand*; By R. and J. DODSLEY, in *Pall-Mall*; By J. LEAKE, at *Bath*; And By R. MAIN, in *Dublin*.

M.DCC.LIV.

A topic of discussion for Jacob and Abigail.

Jacob traveled outside Philadelphia to see patients that his uncle was too busy for.

- Instead, he sent Jacob to meet with patients outside the town of Philadelphia.
- Uncle Nevell was fully occupied with the arrival of sick soldiers who had been prisoners in New York.
- On one visit to Haverford, Jacob passed a number of patriot soldiers, one of whom he recognized.
- He was the owner of the sawmill up the road.
- The two conversed briefly, and Jacob learned that his son cut his leg notching a log with an adze.
- Jacob visited the man's home and dressed his son's wound.
- The man's widowed mother was also present and inquired about a development on her breast.
- He was not familiar with what he saw but suspected it was cancer from his readings.
- He discussed the widow's ailment with his uncle upon arriving home, and they both returned to the widow's house the next day.
- Jacob redressed the boy's wound while his uncle talked with the widow for about an hour.
- Doctor Nevell diagnosed that she had cancer and provided her with a potion and a jalap, a laxative made from various roots.
- On the way home, his uncle explained that medicine was complex, and thus Jacob's apprenticeship was to take a number of years.

Life in the Community: Philadelphia, Pennsylvania

- Philadelphia, Pennsylvania, was a city of culture with an active port and commerce before the outbreak of war.
- The city derived its name from a city in Asia Minor important in early Christian history.
- Situated between the Delaware and Schuylkill Rivers, Philadelphia was the destination of the first colony of Swedes arriving in 1627, followed by the Dutch three years later.
- War occurred between the English and the Dutch in 1632, with the English seizing the city and the lands controlled by the Dutch.
- William Penn was granted the colonial lands, which included the area of Philadelphia, from King Charles II in 1681.
- The original city plan for William Penn was made by Thomas Holmein in 1683 and published in London to "the Society of Free Traders."
- The group was the largest purchaser of land in Britain.
- The intent was to create Philadelphia as a rural English town instead of a large city.
- The plan consisted of nine streets running east and west intersected by 20 streets running north and south, creating right angles.
- Two streets, High and Board Streets, were 100 feet wide and intersected at the the town square where public buildings were to be constructed.
- The city grew rapidly.
- In 1683, there were only 80 dwelling homes.
- By 1760, there were almost 3,000 homes with over 18,000 inhabitants, including Quakers and others seeking religious freedom.
- By 1780, the population was estimated to be close to 30,000.
- Philadelphia established institutions not commonly found during the colonial period, including the first hospital and a public library.

Example of one of Philadelphia's finest homes.

- The city had a central role during the period of colonial independence in the 1700s.
- The First and Second Continental Congresses occurred there.
- The Second Continental Congress adopted the Declaration of Independence in 1776.
- The city feared attack from the British and constructed defense works on the Delaware River and surrounding the city.
- In November of 1776, it was estimated that Philadelphia had 150 fire floats and two floating batteries.
- Due to its importance for trade and its influence on the patriot government, British troops seized the city in 1777.
- In 1781, as the war progressed into its fifth year and British troops were concentrated on the southern American colonies, new freedoms opened for the city's commerce.
- By the 1780s, over 700 sloops and schooners arrived annually.
- Many were trading goods, a large number of them manufactured in Philadelphia, for items from all over the world.
- The city housed shipyards, tanners, rope walks and multiple other trades.
- Philadelphia also supported a silk industry in which women would grow silk worms, feeding them common mulberries.

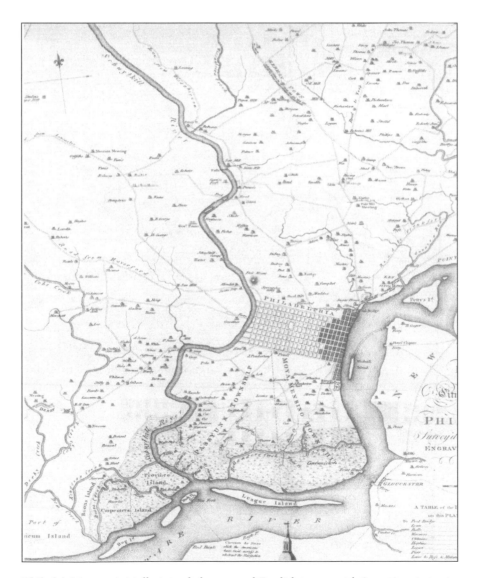

Philadelphia was initially intended as a rural English town, with 9 east/west streets and 20 north/south streets.

HISTORICAL SNAPSHOT
1781

- William Herschel saw what he first thought was a comet, which turned out to be the planet Uranus, during a telescopic survey of the northern sky

- British General Cornwallis's troops suffered heavy losses at the Battle of Guilford Court House, North Carolina

- Cornwallis surrendered to Washington at Yorktown, precipitating the end of the American Revolutionary War of Independence

- A British naval expedition led by Benedict Arnold looted and burned the port of New London, Connecticut

- The Peace Commission composed of John Adams, John Jay, Benjamin Franklin, Henry Laurens and Thomas Jefferson was instructed to seek independence and sovereignty

- The Bank of North America was incorporated in Philadelphia

- Carl Scheele discovered element number 42, molybdenum (Mo), in ore

- Charles Messier published his catalogue of nebulae

- Immanuel Kant published *Critique of Pure Reason*

- Joseph Priestly created water by igniting hydrogen and oxygen

- John Hanson was elected the first "President of the US in Congress assembled"

- Serfdom was abolished in parts of Austria

- Heinrich Olbers showed that Uranus was a planet, not a comet

- Los Angeles was founded in Bahia de las Fumas by 44 settlers

- Moses Mendelssohn published *On the Civil Amelioration of the Condition of the Jews*

Selected Prices

Bible . . . . .6 Shillings
Butter, Pound . . . . .9 Pence
Corn, Bushel . . . . .15 Shillings
Ironing Table . . . . .2 Shillings
Microscope . . . . .5 Pounds
Nutmeg, Pound . . . . .2 Shillings
Spinning Wheel . . . . .6 Shillings
Toothache Powder . . . . .5 Shillings
Trunk . . . . .15 Shillings

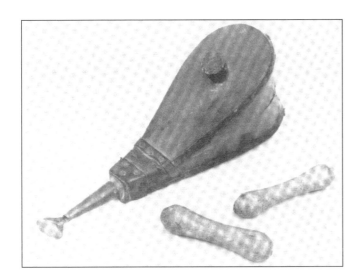

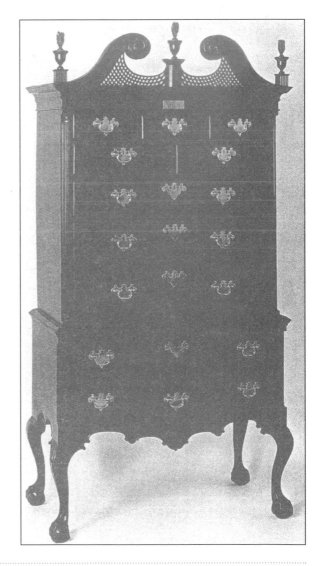

Excerpt from the Diary of Christopher Marshall, 1780:

July 4, 1780

Commencement began at [the] Philadelphia College this forenoon, at which many attended. . . . This being the anniversary of our freedom from English bondage, sundry vessels saluted the town. . . . The company of Artillery and Invalids' Regiment marched to the State House, where the Congress, President of the State and Council with a number of officers attended; bell ringing, guns firing till the evening and until numbers were so drunk as to reel home. As my sons had declined paying their quota for the raising [of] two men in their districts, and Capt. McLane calling, I snatched up some money of theirs and paid him, being Four hundred and eighty Pounds.

The History of Sir Charles Grandison, by Samuel Richardson, 1753–1754:

He attended the two ladies to their lodgings in his coach. He owned to Dr. Bartlett, that Lady Olivia was in tears all the way, lamenting her disgrace in coming to England, just as he was quitting it; and wishing she had stayed at Florence. She would have engaged him to correspond with her: he excused himself. It was a very afflicting thing to him, he told the doctor, to deny any request that was made to him, especially by a lady: but he thought he ought in conscience and honour to forbear giving the shadow of an expectation that might be improved into hope, where none was intended to be given. Heaven, he said, had, for laudable ends, implanted such a regard in the sexes towards each other, that both man and woman who hoped to be innocent, could not be too circumspect in relation to the friendships they were so ready to contract with each other. He thought he had gone a great way, in recommending an intimacy between her and his sisters, considering her views, her spirit, her perseverance, and the free avowal of her regard for him, and her menaces on his supposed neglect of her. And yet, as she had come over, and he was obliged to leave England so soon after her arrival; he thought he could not do less: and he hoped his sisters, from whose example she might be benefited, would, while she behaved prudently, cultivate her acquaintance.

Decoded Letter from Benedict Arnold to John André. 1890:

I wrote to Captn B[eckwith]-on the 7th of June, that a F[rench]-fleet and army / were expected to act in conjunction with the A[merican]-army. At the same time / I gave Mr. S[tansbury]-a manifesto intended to be published in C[anad]-a, and have / from time to time communicated to him such intelligence as I thought / interesting, which he assures me he has transmitted to you. I have / received no answer from my Letter, or any verbal Message - I expect soon / to command W[est] P[oin]t and most seriously wish an interview with some / intelligent officer in whom a mutual confidence could be placed. The / necessity is evident to arrange and to cooperate - An officer might / be taken Prisoner near that Post and permitted to return on parole, / or some officer on Parole sent out to effect an exchange.

General W[ashington]-expects on the arrival of the F[rench]-Troops to collect / 30,000 Troops to act in conjunction; if not disappointed, N[ew] York is fixed / on as the first Object, if his numbers are not sufficient for that Object, / Can-a- is the second; of which I can inform you in time, as well as of / every other design. I have accepted the command at W[est]. P[oint]. As a Post in which / I can render the most essential Services, and which will be in my disposal. / The mass of the People are heartily tired of the War, and wish to be on / their former footing - They are promised great events from this / year's exertion If - disappointed - you have only to persevere / and the contest will soon be at an end. The present Struggles are / like the pangs of a dying man, violent but of a short duration-

As Life and fortune are risked by serving His Majesty, it is / Necessary that the latter shall be secured as well as the emoluments / I give up, and a compensation for Services agreed on and a Sum / advanced for that purpose - which I have mentioned in a letter / which accompanies this, which Sir Henry will not, I believe, think / unreasonable. I am Sir, your humble Servant. / July 12, 1780 J. Moore / Mr. Jn Anderson / P.S. I have great confidence in the Bearer, but beg Sir Henry / will threaten him with his resentment in case he abuses the con- / fidence placed in him, which will bring ruin on me. / The Bearer will bring me 200 Guineas, and pay the remainder to / Captn A-who has requested to receive the deposit for Mr. Moore

It is happy for us that we have Boston in the front & Virginia in the rear to defend us. We are placed where Cowards out to be placed, in the middle.

—William Brandford, Jr concerning Philadelphia, Pennsylvania

Proclamation for a day of Thanksgiving, November 1780:

Whereas, The Hon'ble the Congress of the United States of America, by their resolve of the eighteenth of October last, did recommend in the following words, to wit:

"Whereas, It hath pleased Almighty God, the Father of all Mercies, amidst the vicissitudes of war, to bestow blessings on the people of these States, which call for their devout and thankfull acknowledgements, more especially in the late remarkable interposition of his watchfull Providence in rescuing the person of our Comander-in-Chief and the army from imminent dangers, at the moment when treason was ripened for execution; in prospering the labors of the husbandman, and causing the earth to yield its increase in plentifull harvests; and, above all, in continuing to us the enjoyment of the Gospel of peace.

"It is, therefore, recommended to the several States to set apart Thursday the seventh of December next, to be observed as a day of publick thanksgiving and prayer; that all the people may assemble on that day to celebrate the praises of our Divine Benefactor; to confess our unworthiness of the least of his favours, & to offer our fervent supplications to the God of all grace, that it may please him to pardon our heinous sins and transgressions, and incline our bears for the future to keep all his laws; to comfort and relieve our brethren who are in anywise afflicted or distressed; to smile upon our husbandry and trade; to direct our publick councils, and lead our fources by land and sea to victory; to take our illustrious ally under His special protection, and favour our joint councils and exertions for the establishment of speedy and permanent peace; to cherish all schools and seminaries of learning, and to cause the knowledge of Christianity to spread over all the earth."

Wherefore, as well in respect of the said recommendation of Congress, as the plain dictates of duty to acknowledge the favor and goodness of Providence, and implore its further protection, we do hereby earnestly recommend to the good people of Pennsylvania, to set apart Thursday the seventh day of December next, for the pious purposes expressed in the said resolve, and that they abstain from all labour on that day. Given,&ca., this 10th of November, 1780.

Excerpt of letter from Benjamin Franklin to his English friend Jonathan Shipley, 1786:

You seem desirous of knowing what Progress we make here in improving our Governments. We are, I think, in the right Road of Improvement, for we are making Experiments. I do not oppose all that seem wrong, but the Multitude are more effectually set right by Experience, than kept from going wrong by Reasoning with them.

Dr. Benjamin Rush on the value of bleeding to cure yellow fever patents, 1785:

By the proximate cause of fever I have attempted to prove that the inflammatory state of fever depends upon morbid and excessive action in the blood-vessels. It is connected, of course, with preternatural sensibility in their muscular fibers. The blood is one of the most powerful stimuli which act upon them. By abstracting a part of it, we lessen the principal cause of the fever. The effect of bloodletting is as immediate and natural in removing fever, as the abstraction of a particle of sand is to cure an inflammation of the eye, when it arises from that cause.

1787 Profile

Thirty-eight year old Karl Zimmer has been crafting guns for 20 years, and his work is now in high demand.

Life at Home

- Craftsman Karl Zimmer was widely recognized throughout southern Pennsylvania as the finest gunsmith in the region.
- His highly carved maple gun stocks were prized by any man privileged enough to own one.
- Now 38, married and father of seven, Karl was convinced that hard times were behind him.
- Since the end of the Revolutionary War, Karl had access to quality saltpeter, German-made steel, fine carving tools and polishing stones.
- The cost of materials stopped rising, more customers carried hard money, and the hard-working, tight-fisted Germans in and about Lancaster, Pennsylvania, were in a buying mood.
- Karl had the experience to provide the weapon they wanted: lock, stock and barrel.
- For decades the Pennsylvania flintlock, long rifle had been recognized as the colonies' most accurate long-range gun—a reputation Karl worked hard to maintain.
- Equipped with a .45 caliber ball, at 300 yards, a properly tuned Zimmer could bark a squirrel from the tallest tree.
- Karl constructed a rifle that weighed from seven to nine pounds with an overall length of about 55 inches from muzzle to butt plate.
- As a rule, mindful of needing to see the muzzle while loading, he built a rifle no longer than the height of a customer's chin.
- The longer barrel gave the black powder more time to burn, increasing the muzzle velocity and hence the accuracy.
- The longer barrel also allowed for finer sighting and thus greater accuracy.
- Each rifle took 10 days to build.

Karl Zimmer was recognized as the finest gunsmith in southern Pennsylvania.

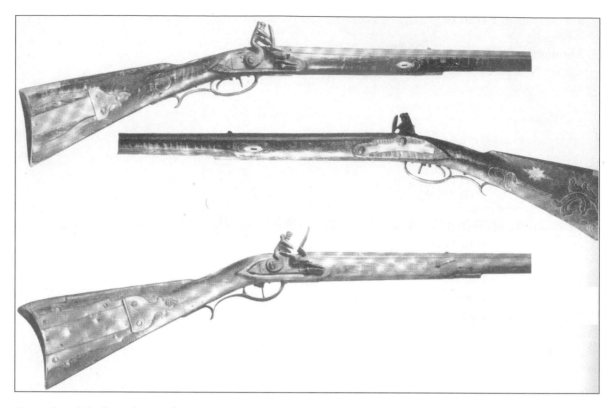

Examples of Karl's craftsmanship.

- Karl charged from $20 to $50 each, depending upon the ornamentation and engraving requested.
- The lock mechanism was entirely handmade, down to the smallest screws, springs and pins.
- The stocks were made of native curly maple, selected for the beauty of its grain and embellished with intricate carved designs.
- Patchboxes, thimbles, trigger guards and butt plates were fashioned from brass or silver and decorated with delicate hand engravings designed by Karl or his eldest son.
- Of the 40 to 50 parts that went into the gun's construction, the barrel was the most important and required the most skill.
- The last step was browning the barrel with cider vinegar to prevent rusting.
- When Karl's father emigrated to Pennsylvania from Germany, the weapon of choice on the frontier was the smooth bore musket or trade gun, built in France or England.
- This gun had an effective range of less than 100 yards.
- A good rifleman could hit a man-sized target up to 300 yards away with a long rifle, but the price for such accuracy was time.
- The long rifle required a full minute to load, longer than a musket.
- But for frontiersmen making their living harvesting deer hides for the British leather industry, accuracy was paramount.
- Originally rather plain, the long rifle eventually became a source of pride for its owner, who demanded intricate designs on every surface.
- As a result, gunsmiths like Karl, who loved to carve the stocks, were recognized as the preeminent craftsmen of their day.
- An accomplished gunsmith had to be a skilled blacksmith, whitesmith, wood carver, brass and silver founder, engraver and wood finisher.

- Karl learned the craft of gunmaking more than two decades earlier as a 15-year-old apprentice.
- Throughout Europe the standard apprenticeship was usually seven years, or until the subject became 21.
- In the colonies the time of indenturement was shrinking, driven by the critical need for crafts-labor and the general spirit of unbridled ambition that pervaded frontier America.
- In America a cooper could be trained in three years to make barrels, a leather britches maker was bound for only two years, and a blacksmith apprenticeship needed only one year and eight months.
- Karl served as an apprentice to a German gunsmith for three years and four months, ending his service in 1766.
- He was to be instructed in "the art and mystery" of the gunsmith with all its various branches by a qualified gunsmith who was obligated to provide "decent clothing both common and to go to church, board and wash and in every respect find said apprentice comfortable lodging."
- In addition, his agreement permitted him to leave his learning for nine days each fall to harvest grain beside his brothers and father.
- When the apprenticeship was complete, he was given, as was customary, a set of tools.
- Personal tools were critical, and a gunsmith was expected to carry his own hand tools from shop to shop.
- Many masters believed that the condition and care provided a man's tools were a direct reflection of future workmanship.

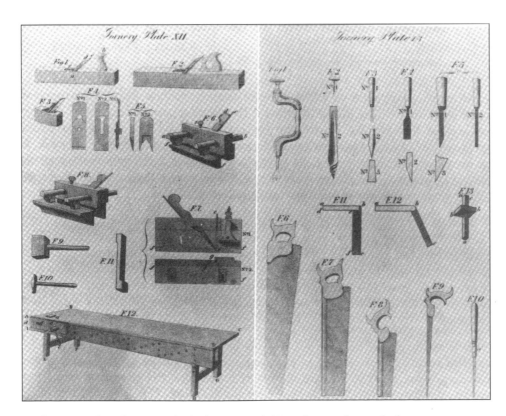

Karl's personal tools, most of which went with him wherever he worked.

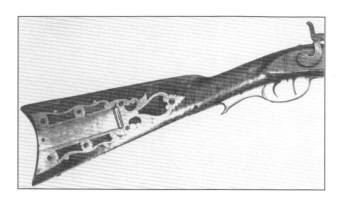

- Karl concluded his apprenticeship by constructing a meister-struck, or masterpiece, to demonstrate his skills.
- Karl worked so hard on the rifle's stock and carvings he dreamed about it every night.
- Most of the gunsmiths of Pennsylvania no longer required their apprentices to construct an meisterstruck, but Karl's mentor, Christian Hanckel, was from Germany and believed in maintaining the old country's standards.
- Years later knowledgeable hunters would debate Christian's influence on Karl's style, especially the origins of his distinctive stock carving with its highly festive loops that interlocked into a decorative pattern.

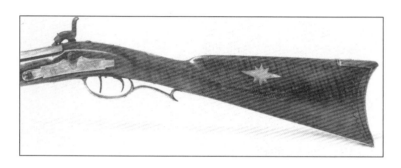

Life at Work

- By 1787 Karl Zimmer had been in business 20 years.
- The first few years were tough despite his gunsmithing skill.
- Learning to read people was perplexing, deciding who to trust, who to ignore, when to ask advice, when to trust your instincts, which suppliers would honor their word, and which hunters could be trusted with credit.
- Now with the children nearly raised, his wife Kate handled the orders, managed the books and talked with customers.
- Karl still controlled all the money and ordered all materials needed in the shop.
- Kate once accepted a load of maple without noticing the embryonic signs of checking (structural imperfections), within the drying wood.
- Now they inspected every load together.
- Thanks to Kate, Karl no longer had to change money from English pounds to the American dollar, decide if money was counterfeit, or calculate interest on debts.
- He didn't intend to marry a Moravian, but he met Kate at a Moravian church social where flirting was allowed (even encouraged!) and he chased her until she caught him.
- After their marriage, the seven children came regularly, some less than 18 months apart.
- The early years were lean for the novice gunsmith and his family.
- In addition to carving stocks or boring a barrel, he made extra money by sharpening coffee mills, making rope wheels, mending compasses, building dozens of rat traps and preparing written deeds.
- Several years in a row, Karl turned hundreds of weaver's shuttles for Christmas money and even taught English to a few of his fellow craftsmen in exchange for a pull of German refreshment.
- During his 20-year career he had watched Pennsylvania long rifles evolve.
- Stocks were much thinner, the carving more elaborate and the rifling inside the barrel far more sophisticated.
- Karl believed in every fiber of his six-foot frame that it was destiny that the rifle was invented in Germany in the fifteenth century and perfected in Lancaster, Pennsylvania.
- Who else but Germans could create such a thing of beauty?
- Surrounded by fellow, equally proud Germans, guaranteed that few argued.

- During the past 200 years, German-made firearms had been dramatically improved by German craftsmen.
- The progenitor to the Pennsylvania long rifle was the Jaeger, used for hunting big game in Central Europe.
- Relatively short at 36 inches, it boasted an octagonal barrel with a caliber of .60 to .75 and a stock made of walnut or fruit wood.
- The distinctive Pennsylvania rifle had been developing in Lancaster County around 1729, the year the county was founded.
- Early improvements included the use of a hinged brass patchbox cover, the use of long, shallow trigger guards attached with a screw instead of the stud and a pin, and a thin stock with improved angles to the barrel that increased accuracy.
- The secret to accuracy—the real purpose of a rifle—was the many steps required to make a barrel accurate enough to deliver a round ball every time.
- When Karl was an apprentice, barrels were made by welding strips of iron and short links around the core rod repeatedly until a tube of the desired length was formed.
- This rough, welded iron tube was reamed and smoothed inside, while the outside was smoothed with a hand file or grindstone, until the desired size and shape was achieved.
- The barrel was then straightened, and rifled, by cutting precision grooves inside the barrel with a hand-operated rifling machine.
- Twenty years later an equally labor-intensive process of drilling a barrel was coming into fashion using Whitworth steel and a twist drill that produced a more reliable barrel but remained the toughest part of constructing a quality rifle.
- Karl was proud that Pennsylvania rifles made by Germans (who were trained by Germans) in America, were described as the world's finest weapon.
- English buyers would humorously suggest his surname was too German and should be changed to something easier, more American, such as Lewis.
- Karl listened politely and then refused to sell them the rifles they desired, explaining that he always engraved his full, German name in his gun stocks.

Life in the Community: Pennsylvania

- Pennsylvania was largely an English colony until William Penn recruited a large number of Germans and the Swiss came to live in Penn's "Holy Experiment."
- Penn was a close friend of George Fox, the founder of the Quakers, at a time when the Society of Friends were called heretics because of their refusal to swear oaths of loyalty to Cromwell or the king.
- The Society's rejections of rituals and oaths, its opposition to war, and its simplicity of speech and dress soon attracted attention, usually hostile.
- In 1668, Penn was imprisoned for writing a tract, *The Sandy Foundation Shaken,* which attacked the doctrine of the trinity.
- Despite the unpopularity of his religion, Penn was socially acceptable in the king's court because he was trusted by the Duke of York, who became King James II.
- King Charles II owed William Penn £16,000, money which Penn's father had lent him.

William Penn was granted the land of Pennsylvania by King Charles in the late 1600s as a place where Penn's Quakers could live in religious freedom.

- Penn wanted a haven in the New World for persecuted Friends, and asked the king to grant him land in the territory between Lord Baltimore's province of Maryland and the Duke of York's province of New York.
  - The king wanted a place where religious and political outsiders like the Quakers could have their own colony, far away from England.
  - The freedom of religion in Pennsylvania brought not only English, Welsh, German and Dutch Quakers to the colony, but also Huguenots, Mennonites, Amish, Catholics, Lutherans from Catholic German states, and Jews.
    - Although William Penn was granted all the land in Pennsylvania by the king, he and his heirs chose not to grant or settle any part of it without first buying the claims of Indians who lived there.
    - In this manner, all of Pennsylvania except the northwestern third was purchased by 1768.
    - The Pennsylvania Germans belonged largely to the Lutheran and Reformed churches, but there were also several smaller sects: Mennonites, Amish, German Baptist Brethren or "Dunkers," Schwenkfelders and Moravians.
- The volume of German immigration increased after 1727, coming largely from the Rhineland.
- The Pennsylvania Germans settled most heavily in the interior counties of Northampton, Berks, Lancaster and Lehigh, and neighboring areas.
- Their skill and industry transformed this region into rich farming country.
- Wheat and corn were the leading crops, though rye, hemp and flax were also important.
- The English settled heavily in the southeastern counties, which soon became the center of a thriving agricultural and commercial society.
- Philadelphia became the metropolis of the British colonies and a center of intellectual and commercial life.

  - Thousands of Germans were also attracted to the colony and, by the time of the Revolution, comprised a third of the population.
  - By 1776, the Province of Pennsylvania had become the third largest English colony in America.
  - Although next to the last to be founded, Philadelphia had become the largest English-speaking city in the world, next to London.
  - The abundant natural resources of the colony made for early development of industries.
  - Sawmills and gristmills were usually the first to appear, using the power of the numerous streams.
  - Textile products were spun and woven mainly in the home, though factory production was not unknown.
  - The Pennsylvania long rifle was an adaptation of a German hunting rifle developed in Lancaster County.
  - Its superiority was so well recognized that by 1776, gunsmiths were duplicating it in Virginia, Georgia, North Carolina and Maryland.
  - The Conestoga wagon was also developed in Lancaster County.
  - Capable of carrying as much as four tons, it was the prototype for the principal vehicle for American westward migration, the prairie schooner.

HISTORICAL SNAPSHOT
1787

- George Washington was elected president of the Philadelphia Constitutional Convention
- The college of electors or Electoral College was established at the Constitutional Convention
- A majority of delegates completed and signed the Constitution of the United States at the Constitutional Convention, and submitted it to the states for ratification
- The first of the 77 essays comprising the Federalist Papers was published in newspapers
- Britain continued exporting its convicted criminals to the United States despite the Treaty of Paris
- The Abolition Society was formed by British Quakers to halt the importation of African slaves to the British colonies and America
- Alexander Hamilton became the first secretary of the United States Treasury
- A private mint struck the first penny made of copper, later called the Fugio cent
- The Northwest Ordinance established the rules for governing the Northwest Territory
- Inventor John Finch demonstrated his steamboat on the Delaware River
- Philadelphia's Free African Society was formed
- Mozart's Opera *Don Giovanni* opened in Prague with Mozart as its conductor
- Marie Jean Antoine Nicolas de Condorcet published *Letters from a Bourgeois of Newhaven to a Citizen of Virginia,* demanding political rights for women
- The first Unitarian minister in the United States was ordained in Boston
- Antoine Lavoisier developed a system for naming chemicals
- Publication of *Botanical Magazine* by William Curtis began, dedicated to introducing exotic plants
- A United States law passed, providing that a senator must be at least 30 years old
- The moons of Uranus—Titan and Oberon—were discovered by William Herschel
- Jacques-Alexander Charles postulated a law of gas expansion with temperature, which became known as "Charles's Law"

Selected Prices

Beehive $1.00
Blanket . . . . .1 pound
Eight-day Clock . . . . .12 pounds
Featherbed $12.00
Grindstone $4.00
Gun Lock . . . . .1 shilling, 11 pence
Gunpowder Flask . . . . .5 shillings
Musket $12.30
Pitchfork . . . . .1 shilling
Rifle . . . . .4 pounds, 6 pence

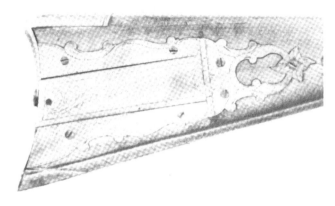

Proclamation by the citizens of Lancaster County, Pennsylvania, on the subject of American Independence and the effectiveness of their weapons, 1774:

Resolved from Hanover Township, Lancaster County, June 4, 1774; that in the event of Great Britain attempting to force unjust laws upon us by the strength of arms, our cause we leave to heaven and to our rifles.

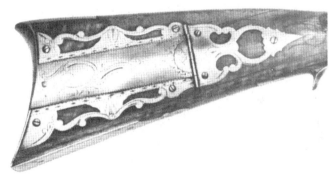

Karl was proud that Pennsylvania rifles, made by Germans, were described as the world's finest weapon.

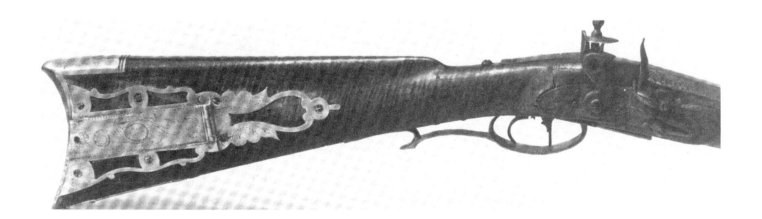

EIGHT DOLLARS REWARD, *Lancaster Journal,* September 16, 1795:

Ran away the 15th instant, from the subscriber living in Lancaster, indentured servant lad named John Mc-Can is about 19 years of age, 5 feet, 6 or 7 inches tall, of a dark complexion, and has a long nose. He speaks both English and German, but English best: and is by trade a gunsmith. He had on when he went away a good hat, a light-coloured cassimer coatie, and a nankin waistcoat and breeches.

Whoever apprehends the said runaway so that the Master might get him, shall receive the above reward and reasonable charges if brought home, from Christian Klein, gunsmith.

Inventory of Tools Found Within a Gunsmith Business, 1771:

Two bellows	One saw
Rifling engine	Stocking tools
Old stocks of wood	Drill stock
One anvil	Tumbler tool
One beck iron	Two pairs old shears
Five pairs of tongs	Boaring mill
A polishing leather	Boaring rods
Wheel bearing bits and floats	Two pairs nippers
Forging tools	One compass saw
Barrel anvil	One square
One vise	Three saw plates
Two small hacks	Six double tricksters
Two saw frames	20 cherrys
12 smooth files	One pair bullet molds
Two vise claps and three wedges	Two spring hooks
Two rasps	Two picks to cast tools and sand
Eight bench hammers	One grindstone
One ax and hatchet	One half-finished gun
12 large screw plates and britchen tools	One smooth rifle
One small screw plate	One new gun lock
Six pairs pliers	One powder proff
Seven pairs compasses	Needsfoot oil
One pair large stillyards	Two soddern irons
To draw knives	Six planes
Four ramer bits	Half-finished pistols and barrels
For old guns	

I have many times asked the American backwoodsman what was the most their best marksmen could do; they have constantly told me that an expert marksman, provided he can draw good & true sight, can hit the head of a man at 200 yards.

—British officer Col George Hanger, who witnessed his bugler's horse shot out from under him at a distance of a "full 400 yards"

Report of Reverend Mr. Roschen, *German Tracks,* 1789:

Marriages here are of two varieties. The one, according to the church discipline, calls for three successive announcements of the banns. In the other case, which occurs with equal frequency, the procedure is in general as follows: The groom secures a certificate from the Superior Officer at Salisbury (NC), comes riding along with his friends of both sexes, the bride riding by his side, to the pastor, or if none is available, to the Justice of the peace where the ceremony is performed. He enters holding in his right hand his flask of rum, greets with a "good morning," drinks to the health of the one officiating, produces his certificate and goes back to get his bride in the rest of the party.

The questions directed to the groom are: whether he has stolen (that is, kidnapped) his bride, which occurs frequently, and whether the parents have given their consent. If one steals his bride and has a license from Salisbury the objections of the parents are of no avail. As a rule in this country the son, as soon as he has reached his twenty-first year, and the daughter as soon as she is 18 years old, no longer stand under the control of their parents. In the case of marriages, which, by the way, are often contracted very early in life, provision for the future need not be any great cause for worry. Whoever is willing to work can easily obtain a plantation and poor people are generally not to be seen here at all.

Goldsmith's oil stones, letter from the Reverend Samuel Webster to Mr. Caleb Kennett, January 24, 1783, *Memoirs of the American Academy of Arts and Sciences,* Boston, 1785:

I have found what the goldsmith's use, and call an oil stone, equal, if not superior, to those imported from Turkey. But as it was so small as only to make two, one for each of my sons, who are goldsmiths, it is not in my power to send you a sample. It is extremely hard, and somewhat brittle; so that I easily broke it into two pieces. When it is ground it is exceedingly smooth, and serves to smooth engraving tools. I found it in my field by accident, and was excited, from its uncommon appearance, to take it up, not knowing, at the time, what it was. It is somewhat curdled with light and dark brown, or, when ground, it approaches to a light chocolate colour, somewhat clouded. Before it was ground some compared to Castile Soap. I have made considerable search for more, without success. I doubt not, however, that we have them in the country perhaps in plenty. I found this in moist ground. These stones are necessary for all who make use of engraving tools, and are now very scarce in dear.

"Raising the Meetinghouse, 1791," by Charles Kaufman, *The History of Boscawen and Webster, New Hampshire,* 1733 to 1878:

The raising of the meeting-house was a great event, and people came from the surrounding towns to aid in the work. They came early in the morning, with pike-poles and pitch-forks and iron bars—pike-poles and pitch-forks to lift with when the broadside should be well up in the air, and iron bars to hold against the foot of the post to slide them in the mortises of the sills. On such an occasion there was plenty of rum.

The first thing to be done was to take a drink, to give strength for the labor of the day. Then came the bringing together of the timbers. The sills were already laid and levelled. . . .

The broadside was then pinned together. Then came the drinking of more rum, and the marshalling of the crowd, the coolheaded men holding the iron bars, the strong and experienced men in places of responsibility. When all were ready, the master workman, standing in the rear where he could see all that was going on, commanded silence. We hear him say, "Are you ready all?". . ."Take hold all!" The men bend, and place their shoulders beneath the posts. A swarm take hold of the plate, another hold of the girts. The men at the iron bars spit on their hands. "Now, then." The frame rises. . . . It is up on their shoulders. "Now she rises!" Those by the plates seize their pike-poles and pitch-forks. At each corner and in the middle are "shores," with a crowd of men and boys lifting on each. . . . They lift with all their might, and grow red in the face. The pike-poles bend, handles for the pitch-forks are ready to snap. "Steady there!" Now comes a tug-of-war at the foot of the posts. The iron-bar men are bracing with all their might.

"Heave-ho," from the master.
"Now she goes!" from the men.

continued

"Raising the Meetinghouse, 1791," . . . *(continued)*

Higher, still higher, up to the perpendicular. The tendons slide into the mortises in the sills, the "shore" men hold back on the poles, the first broadside of the house of God stands in its appointed place. The men then wipe their brows, and take another drink of rum. There is a congratulatory dram all around, in preparation for the opposite broadside. That, too, rises. In come the connecting girts and plates, and then the lifting of the beams for the galleys, and the high beams, the putting up with sleepers, flanks and boards, rafters and purlins, and, last of all the ridge-pole. When the last is in place, a crowd of men sit astride it, take full drams from the bottles of rum passed up to them, and then dash the bottles to the ground. This is the last of the dedicatory dram.

Such was the scene on that day.

So complete were the arrangements, so excellent the workmanship of Samuel Jackson, so numerous the men, so early at work in the morning were they, that the first broadside was up before nine o'clock, the last dram drunk before noon, and the rising was over.

1786 News Feature

"Of the Mode of Education Proper in a Republic," from *A Plan for the Establishment of Public Schools and the Diffusion of Knowledge in Pennsylvania*, by Benjamin Rush, 1786:

The business of education has acquired a new complexion by the independence of our country. The form of government we have assumed, has created a new class of duties to every American. It becomes us, therefore, to examine our former habits upon this subject, and in laying the foundations for nurseries of wise and good men, to adapt our modes of teaching to the peculiar form of our government.

The first remark that I shall make upon this subject is, that an education in our own, is to be preferred to an education in a foreign country. The principle of patriotism stands in need of the reinforcement of prejudice. And it is well known that our strongest prejudices in favour of our country are formed in the first one and twenty years of our lives. The policy of the Lacedemonians is well worthy of our imitation. When Antipater demanded fifty of their children as hostages for the fulfillment of a distant engagement, those wise republicans refused to comply with his demand, but readily offered him double the number of their adult citizens, whose habits and prejudices could not be shaken by residing in a foreign country. Passing by, in this place, the advantages to the community from the early attachment of youth to the laws and constitution of their country, I shall only remark, that young men who have trodden the paths of science together, or have joined in the same sports, whether of swimming, skating, fishing, or hunting, generally feel, thro' life, such ties to each other, as add greatly to the obligations of mutual benevolence.

I conceive the education of our youth in this country to be peculiarly necessary in Pennsylvania, while our citizens are composed of the natives of so many different kingdoms in Europe. Our schools of learning, by producing one general, and uniform system of education, will render the mass of the people more homogeneous, and thereby fit them more easily for uniform and peaceable government.

I proceed in the next place, to enquire, what mode of education we shall adopt so as to secure to the state all the advantages that are to be derived from the proper instruction of youth; and here I beg leave to remark, that the only foundation for a useful education in a republic is to be laid in Religion. Without this there can be no virtue, and without virtue there can be no liberty, and liberty is the object and life of all republican governments.

Such is my veneration for every religion that reveals the attributes of the Deity, or a future state of rewards and punishments, that I had rather see the opinions of Confucius of Mahomed inculcated upon our youth, than see them grow up wholly devoid of a system of religious principles. But the religion I mean to recommend in this place, is that of the New Testament.

It is foreign to my purpose to hint at the arguments which establish the truth of the Christian revelation. My only business is to declare, that all its doctrines and precepts are calculated to promote the happiness of society, and the safety and well being of civil government. A Christian cannot fail of being a republican. The history of the creation of man, and of the relation our species to each other by birth, which is recorded in the Old Testament, is the best refutation that can be given to the divine right of kings, and the strongest argument that can be used in favor of the original and natural equality of all mankind. A Christian, I say again, cannot fail of being a republican, for every precept of the Gospel inculcates those degrees of humility, self-denial, and brotherly kindness, which are directly opposed to the pride of monarchy and the pageantry of a court. A Christian cannot fail of being useful to the republic, for his religion teacheth him, that no man "liveth to himself." And lastly, a Christian cannot fail of being wholly inoffensive, for his religion teacheth him, in all things to do to others what he would wish, in like circumstances, they should do to him.

I am aware that I dissent from one of those paradoxical opinions with which modern times abound; and that it is improper to fill the minds of youth with religious prejudices of any kind, and that they should be left to choose their own principles, after they have arrived at an age in which they are capable of judging for themselves. Could we preserve the mind in childhood and youth a perfect blank, this plan of education would have more to recommend it; but this we know to be impossible. The human mind runs as naturally into principles as it does after facts. It submits with difficulty to those restraints or partial discoveries which are imposed upon it in the infancy of reason. Hence the impatience of children to be informed upon all subjects that relate to the invisible world. But I beg leave to ask, why should we pursue a different plan of education with respect to religion, from that which we pursue in teaching the arts and sciences? Do we leave our youth to acquire systems of geography, philosophy, or politics, till they have arrived at an age in which they are capable of judging for themselves? We do not. I claim no more then for religion, than for the other sciences, and I add further, that if our youth are disposed after they are of age to think for themselves, a knowledge of one system, will be the best means of conducting them in a free enquiry into other systems of religion, just as an acquaintance with one system of philosophy is the best introduction to the study of all other systems in the world.

Next to the duty which young men owe to their Creator, I wish to see a regard to their country, inculcated upon them. When the Duke of Sully became prime minister to Henry the IVth of France, the first thing he did, he tells us, "Was to subdue and forget his own heart." The same duty is incumbent upon every citizen of a republic. Our country includes family, friends and property, and should be preferred to them all. Let our pupil be taught that he does not belong to himself, but that he is public property. Let him be taught to love his family, but let him be taught, at the same time, that he must forsake, and even forget them, when the welfare of his country requires it. He must watch for the state, as if its liberties depended upon his vigilance alone, but he must do this in such a manner as not to defraud his creditors, or neglect his family. He must love private life, but he must decline no station, however public or responsible it may be, when called to it by the suffrages of his fellow citizens. He must love popularity, but he must despise it when set in competition with the dictates of his judgement, or the real interest of his country. He must love character, and have a due sense of injuries, but he must be taught to appeal only to the laws of the state, to defend the one, and punish the other. He must love family honour, but must be taught that neither the rank nor antiquity of his ancestors, can command respect, without personal merit. He must avoid neutrality in all questions that divide the state, but he must shun the rage, and acrimony of party spirit. He must be taught to love his fellow creatures in every part of the world, but he must cherish with a more intense and peculiar affection, the citizens of Pennsylvania and of the United States. I do not wish to see our youth educated with a single prejudice against any nation or country; but we impose a task upon human nature, repugnant alike to reason, revelation and the ordinary dimensions of the human heart, when we require him to embrace, with equal affection, the whole family of mankind. He must be taught to amass wealth, but it must be only to encrease his power of contributing to the wants and demands of the state. He must be indulged occasionally in amusements, but he must be taught that study and business should be his principal pursuits in life. Above all he must love life, and endeavour to acquire as many of its conveniences as possible by industry and economy, but he must be taught that this life "is not his own," when the safety of his country requires it. These are practicable lessons, and the history of the commonwealths of Greece and Rome show, that human nature, without the aids of Christianity, has attained these degrees of perfection.

While we inculcate these republican duties upon our pupil, we must not neglect, at the same time, to inspire him with republican principles. He must be taught that there can be no durable liberty but in a republic, and that government, like all other sciences, is of a progressive nature. The chains which have bound this science in Europe are happily unloosed in America. Here it is open to investigation and improvement. While philosophy has protected us by its discoveries from a thousand natural evils, government has unhappily followed with an unequal pace. It would be to dishonour human genius, only to name the many defects which still exist in the best systems of legislation. We daily see matter of a perishable nature rendered durable by certain chemical operations. In like manner, I conceive, that it is possible to combine power in such a way as not only to encrease the happiness, but to promote the duration of republican forms of government far beyond the terms limited for them by history, or the common opinions of mankind.

To assist in rendering religious, moral and political instructions more effectual upon the minds of our youth, it will be necessary to subject their bodies to physical discipline. To obviate the inconveniences of their studious and sedentary mode of life, they should live upon a temperate diet, consisting chiefly of broths, milk and vegetables. The black broth of Sparta, and the barley broth of Scotland, have been alike celebrated for their beneficial effects upon the minds of young people. They should avoid tasting Spirituous liquors. They should also be accustomed occasionally to work with their hands, in the intervals of Study, and in the busy seasons of the year in the country. Moderate sleep, silence, occasional solitude and cleanliness, should be inculcated upon them, and the utmost advantage should be taken of a proper direction of those great principles in human conduct—sensibility, habit, imitations, and association.

The influence of these physical causes will be powerful upon the intellects, as well as upon the principles and morals of young people.

To those who have studied human nature, it will not appear paradoxical to recommend, in this essay, a particular attention to vocal music. Its mechanical effects in civilizing the mind, and thereby preparing it for the influence of religion and government, have been so often felt and recorded, that it will be unnecessary to mention facts in favour of its usefulness, in order to excite a proper attention to it.

I cannot help bearing a testimony, in this place, against the custom, which prevails in some parts of America, (but which is daily falling into disuse in Europe) of crowding boys together under one roof for the purpose of education. The practice is the gloomy remains of monkish ignorance, and is as unfavorable to the improvements of the mind in useful learning, as monasteries are to the spirit of religion. I grant this mode of secluding boys from the intercourse of private families, has a tendency to make them scholars, but our business is to make them men, citizens, and christians. The vices of young people are generally learned from each other. The vices of adults seldom infect them. By separating them from each other, therefore, in their hours of relaxation from study, we secure their morals from a principal source of corruption, while we improve their manners, by subjecting them to those restraints which the difference of age and sex, naturally produce in private families.

From the observations that have been made it is plain, that I consider it is possible to convert men into republican machines. This must be done, if we expect them to perform their parts properly, in the great machine of the government of the state. That republic is sophisticated with monarchy or aristocracy that does not revolve upon the wills of the people, and these must be fitted to each other by means of education before they can be made to produce regularity and unison in government.

1790–1799

The newly independent, but hardly unified young nation of the 1790s continued to wrestle with a wide range of political and economic philosophies, especially the proper role of the individual states versus the federal government, as well as the repugnant immorality of slavery versus its wealth-generating opportunities. Even though a centralized government ran counter to the fundamental beliefs of many who had fought to be free from British control, the creation of the Constitution was a major landmark in political and monetary development. The original Articles of Confederation simply provided for the establishment of a perpetual "league of friendship" for common defense and general welfare among the 13 states. Under it each state retained its sovereignty and its independence in all rights not given to the central government. But it quickly became clear that the country also needed a chief executive, the power to tax and the power to control commerce to be successful. Heavily in debt, the country was torn between differing state interests, and was vulnerable to another foreign invasion. The new Constitution was an economic and political document that gave the federal government a framework for balancing competing interests through an executive department distinct from the legislative and judicial departments, the right to issue money and the power to regulate interstate and foreign commerce. "The Federal Constitution was the work of the commercial people, the seaport towns, the slave holding states, of the officers of the Revolutionary Army, and the property holders everywhere," according to John Adams. Above all else, to clarify a system of property rights in America, including patent protection. With greater assurance of capitalizing on the gains of their ideas, inventors emerged in abundance.

The new nation, with its abundance of rich land and a long heritage of shipping, was aided by two events in 1793: the invention of the cotton gin and the outbreak of yet another war between England and France that lasted till 1815. America sent tobacco to France and the Netherlands as well as rice, wheat, flour and corn to Britain. While most of Europe was drawn into the conflict, America remained neutral and traded with both sides, becoming more self-sufficient. It was a time of full employment and sharply rising urbanization. Entrepreneurs amassed vast personal fortunes. In America laborers earned a higher wage than their British counterparts; at the end of the century American farm workers could earn a dollar a day, enough to buy a 15-pound turkey. In Philadelphia nearly 4,000 women were employed to spin materials in their homes for the newly established textile plants. There was a sharp increase in the number of artisan workshops and a dramatic increase in the production of beer, whiskey and other domestic alcoholic beverages in the colonies—which competed with foreign imports for the American market.

Peace also ignited a Western wanderlust. By 1790, the United States embarked on an era of expansion. After decades of abiding by the king's prohibition against Western movement, Americans rushed to lay claim to the land beyond the Appalachian Mountains. The Land Ordinance of 1784 had already provided for the formation of 10 states northwest of the Ohio River. This was followed by an ordinance that prescribed that the land should be systematically surveyed into townships of six miles square, each subdivided into 36 sections of 640 parcels each, costing one dollar per acre. These decisions placed the new government and its legions of settlers in direct conflict with the culture and tradition of the Native American peoples.

1793 Profile

Quriryn Kester was a Dutch-born entrepreneur who saw so much potential in the new America of the 1790s, that he applied for citizenship as soon as possible, and became a citizen two years after arrival—the minimal time required.

Life at Home

- Born the youngest of three children in Amsterdam, Quriryn Kester had been studying at the Academy of Geneva, Switzerland, since he turned 11.
- In 1782, when he was 14, he was summoned home.
- His father had died and with him, money for Quriryn's education.
- His mother died the following year and was buried in the old Lutheran church beside her husband.
- In desperation and despair, orphan Quriryn joined the Dutch navy and excelled, earning the title of Lieutenant ter zee shortly after turning 17 years old.
- By the time he reached 22, he had visited most of the important ports in Europe and Asia and spent time working in Smyrna and Ceylon.
- In 1790 he obtained permission for a two-year leave of absence from the ship *Guilderland* to travel to North America.
- He was sponsored by the Holland Land Company and was accompanied on his trip to America by a man who was an experienced Dutch sugar refiner.
- The Holland Land Company wanted to determine if making sugar with sugar cane and slave labor could be undercut by making sugar using hard sugar maple trees.
- Of immediate concern was the cost of acquiring up to 30,000 acres of sugar maple trees to launch the business.
- People on West Indian islands such as Jamaica, Barbados and San Domingo had grown wealthy because of sugar plantations, on which slaves were often worked literally to death.

At 22, Quriryn Kester traveled to North America from his home in Amsterdam.

- By cornering the American maple sugar market, the Holland Land Company planned to simultaneously control the domestic sugar market and cut the financial legs out of the Caribbean sugar cane business.
- Plus, large land holdings of quality property could be very profitable for investors willing to be patient, as the price of frontier lands could double within a decade.
- Quriryn, who had never seen a "mapple tree" before, was being asked to survey thousands of acres of the valuable trees for possible purchase.
- The Native Indians of New England had been making sugar from the sweet sap of the maple tree for centuries.
- Early explorers recorded the Indians' process for making maple sugar as early as 1606.
- Indian legend reported that maple sugar was discovered by Iroquois Chief Woksis after throwing his tomahawk into a maple tree one late winter evening.
- When he removed it the following sunny, warm morning, sap began to flow from the cut in the tree.
- According to legend, the sap was used to cover the meat for dinner and as the water in the sap boiled away, a sweet maple taste flavored the meat.
- Quriryn believed, however, that maple sugar was discovered by eating "sapsicles," the icicles of frozen maple sap that form at the end of broken twigs.
- Either way, sugar was influential enough that Indians moved entire families into the forest to establish sugar camps during early spring to capture the maple sap.
- Hardened, dry maple sugar was easily stored and was used as gifts, to trade with, and to mix with grains, berries and bear fat.
- Quriryn was under pressure to buy enough maple trees to compete with the Caribbean sugar cane plantations controlled by Denmark, England and France, the latter of which had just declared war on Holland.
- In early 1790 two Quaker delegations, one from New York and one from Philadelphia, presented petitions to the U.S. House of Representatives to put an immediate end to the African slave trade.
- This action had reinvigorated public discussion on the morality and economics of the slave trade, including the viability of producing America's sugar crop domestically using maple trees.

America's maple trees were seen as a way to produce sugar domestically.

- This economic war on slavery had captured the highly visible support of Benjamin Rush and Secretary of State Thomas Jefferson, who personally and publicly bought 50 pounds of refined maple sugar as a contribution to the cause.
- Benjamin Rush began promoting the cause in 1788 by publishing an essay on the "Advantages of the Culture of the Sugar Maple Tree" in a Philadelphia monthly.
- In 1789 he founded, with a group of Philadelphia Quakers, the Society for Promoting the Manufacture of Sugar from the Sugar Maple Tree.
- He even staged a scientific tea party to prove the potency of maple sugar.
- The guests—Alexander Hamilton, Quaker merchant Henry Drinker, and "several Ladies"—sipped cups of hyson tea, sweetened with equal amounts of cane and maple sugar.
- All agreed the sugar from the maple was as sweet as the cane sugar.

- Rush's aim was "to lessen or destroy the consumption of West Indian sugar, and thus indirectly to destroy negro slavery."
- Jefferson wanted to break his country's reliance on both Britain and its Caribbean-grown sugar at a time when Americans drank as many as 15 cups of tea every day and wanted every cup sweetened.
- Sugar was one of the nation's leading imports and subject to English tariffs.
- Jefferson believed there were enough maples to produce sugar "adequate to the consumption" of every American and some Europeans, too.
- Jefferson wrote to a friend in England that the maple tree, "yeilds a sugar equal to the best from cane, yeilds it in great quantity, with no other labor than what the women and girls can bestow. . . . What a blessing to substitute a sugar which requires only the labour of children, for that which it is said renders the slavery of the blacks unnecessary."
- Jefferson and Rush proclaimed that they could not, "put sugar in coffee without being saddened by the thought of all the toil, sweat, tears, suffering and crimes that have hitherto been necessary to procure this product."
- Promoters declared sugar maples to be the "diamonds of America" and Jefferson declared that America would soon be a net exporter of sugar, just as Quriryn was attempting to corner the market in trees.

Benjamin Rush founded the Society for Promoting the Manufacture of Sugar from the Sugar Maple Tree.

Life at Work

- Quriryn Kester encountered his first maple tree in the great swamps of Pennsylvania in August 1791.
- He and his partner, who were on horseback, dismounted and took considerable time to admire the sugar maple tree growing there, knowing they were about to buy thousands of acres as agents of the Holland Land Company.
- "Mr. Boon, at that instant, seemed to descry beneath its bark the treasures of Peru, while I, for my part, would have wished to carve on it the name of my sweetheart," he wrote in his journal.
- It was not the last maple he would see in that hardwood tree-rich land.
- On August 11, he recorded, "where we looked to find expensive works, buildings, and workmen, at least we had the satisfaction to find here a quantity of maple trees 15 to 20 inches in diameter, in some of which we still saw the holes where they were tapped, and the pipes with the reservoirs where the sap had run."
- That particular landowner owned 12,000 acres, 3,000 of which had large stands of maple trees, most boasting 30 trees per acre.

Quriryn was sent to America by the Holland Land Company to purchase land with maple sugar trees.

```
                    ITINERARY.

        Route from Bennington to Burlington Bay.


 Bennington                    Mr. Dewey.
 Shaftsbury         7 miles  "  Galusha.
 Arlington          7  —     "  Merwins.
 Sunderland         4  —     "  Seamon.
 Manchester         4  —     "  Allis.
 Dorset             5  —     "  McMarsters.
 Harwich            7  —     "  Gerrits.
 Danby              6  —     "  Antony.
 Wallingsford       7  —     Mrs. Hulls.
 Clarenden          3  —     Esqr Smith.
 Rutland            7  —     Mr. Williams.
 Pittsford          10 —     Mr.
 Middlebury         18 —     Col¹ Shapman.


 Middlebury Falls   4  —     Mr. Demon
 Vergennes          13 —     Col. Brosh.
 Charlotte          13 —     Mr. Riches.
 Burlington         13 —     Col¹ Keys.

 The whole          128 miles.
                       79
```

Quriryn's travel diary.

- Quriryn calculated that a tree 20 inches in diameter would produce 25 gallons of sap annually "& 5 gallons gives a pound of sugar."
- Usually 40 years are required to produce a maple tree large enough to tap, and the minimum diameter of a useable maple is at least 10 inches.
- That night, they turned out their horses to graze, built a fire at the foot of a superb maple tree, caught trout, which they boiled, and, after satisfying their appetite, spread slept near the fire, without wakening, until 7 o'clock the next morning.
- That day, Quriryn met a newcomer to the land who claimed to have produced 200 pounds of sugar—all of which he sold at a satisfactory price—from 150 trees on his property.
- The following day brought more acreage and pricing and descriptions of the roads they traversed based on whether they were "tolerable" or "mud to the horses' belly."
- Day after day Quriryn and his partner rode through forests, forded streams, dodged rattlesnakes, assisted fallen horses and looked for a safe place to sleep at night.
- As they transitioned from Pennsylvania into New York, Quriryn also learned a little something about Yankee bravado—namely, don't bet against it.
- While enjoying a beer one evening, he was introduced to a man who claimed his horse could move a heavy log 500 pounds or more mired in the road.
- None of the local draft horses, he claimed, had been able to budge it.
- Quriryn carefully inspected the skinny little horse but declined to wager whether he could "skid" the log out of the road.
- After a few more beers, the wager grew to pulling the log with three heavy men sitting atop, and Quriryn could not resist the bet.
- The entire bar emptied to witness the epic contest, in which Quriryn lost money, but gained friends.
- Quickly, Quriryn took a liking to wagering—especially on horse racing—and the thrill it produced.
- For nearly a week he hung around the area to participate in the afternoon racing.
- Typically, after a few drinks, one man would collect a bag of coins from everyone at the bar and place it on a tree branch a quarter mile down the road.
- The men would mount their horses, usually bareback, and race down the road.
- The first one to grab the purse won.
- Quriryn won enough to love the custom and write home about it.
- Then it was back to the road, 12 to 20 miles per day pricing land and talking to farmers about wheat prices, the weather, the predictions of the latest *Farmer's Almanac* and what price his neighbor paid for his land.
- By the time Quriryn reached Vermont, he had perfected the best way to get information from truculent farmers—farm gossip.
- Isolated in the backcountry with only their families to talk with, farmers were usually happy to exchange information they thought might earn them cash.
- Quriryn's journal quickly filled with the names of farmers, number of acres and prices available to the Holland Land Company once it started buying.
- "Passed through Clarendon to Rutledge, we stopped on the way at the house of Thomas Rice, whom we had seen in Genesee Country, where he had bought 400 acres at one dollar per acre with the intention of settling there. . . ."

- "It is astonishing to see a man 50 years old who has spent the best part of this life in clearing his land and enhancing its value, leaving it all just as he begins to enjoy the fruits of his labor, in order to bury himself anew in the forest, and expose himself to all the difficulties of forming a new settlement! But it is usually the case with Americans."
- In Vermont, the new American frontier was saturated by maple trees and sprinkled with a handful of people.
- The state of Vermont claimed 85,706 souls, located in seven counties with each county divided into townships of six miles square.
- By public policy, large landholders were discouraged because the legislature believed that granting a small number of acres to each person would prevent one person from having too much power.
- This made Quriryn's job of acquiring large, contiguous tracts more difficult and also tended to increase the price of land.
- In addition, although he found a considerable number of maple trees, few farmers could be persuaded to turn the forests into sugar factories for six weeks per year, or to work cooperatively with neighboring towns.
- In the southern part of the state the pioneers "cut down all the trees, keeping only a small quantity necessary for their consumption."

The Vermont landscape: many maple trees and few people.

- In the north, where there was more forest, the trees "were no more prized and too distant from all markets."
- The ultimate goal was not only to marshal together large tracts of trees but to organize the settlers into a sprawling cooperative, responsible for tapping, boiling and producing lucrative sugar blocks from maple sap.
- Quriryn, who was not sure these isolated people were interested in working together even for profit, and carefully avoided this sentiment when filing his periodic reports.
- By 1793 land buying by the Holland Land Company had begun in earnest and there was no turning back.

Life in the Community: Eastern United States

- The Holland Land Company was formed in 1789 by four Amsterdam investment firms, which employed several Dutch agents to keep them informed of financial developments in America and invest money for them.
- The Club of Four, as it was called, invested widely in American funds, including the South Carolina Funded Debt, the Massachusetts Deposit and the Pennsylvania Population Company.
- They also invested in American canal construction companies in the northeast.
- By the end of 1793, the Dutch consortium controlled four million acres in the bustling but fragile United States, including 700,000 acres east of the Allegheny River in Pennsylvania, 77,000 acres in central New York, and 23,000 acres in maple tree-rich Vermont.
- In the early 1790s plant science had gained an institutional respect throughout the United States; lectures on botany were offered widely and colleges regularly joined forces with agricultural societies to promote botanical research.

- The Massachusetts Society for Promoting Agriculture, established in Boston in 1792, offered cash premiums for "the cultivation of wheat and other grains; the improvement of land, including the reclamation of salt marshes; the raising of trees; the greatest stock maintained on the least land; the best vegetable food for wintering stock; the most and best wool from a given number of sheep; the best process for making cider, maple sugar, butter, cheese, flax, and salted provisions; and for the best farming journals, manures, tree plantations, advances in ploughs and ploughing techniques, and farms in general."

- The first two premiums the society awarded were $50 for the best account of natural history of the canker-worm, and $100 for the best way to eradicate the pest.

- Fully understanding the natural resources of America was an economic and political necessity.

- Following the Revolutionary War in 1783, the defeated British repeatedly increased tariffs and sugar to the coffee and tobacco coming to America.

- These higher costs, which the Americans could not control, spurred additional agricultural research.

- Secretary of the Treasury Alexander Hamilton wrote that the tariff increases by Britain gave domestic producers an incentive to enter the market.

- As the average duty on imports more than doubled from 29 percent in 1790 to 66 percent in 1794, learned societies began to offer premiums for research that targeted the specific commodities most impacted by high tariffs—such as sugar.

- At the same time, businessmen from the Netherlands were seeking economic opportunities in America now that it was no longer an English colony.

- Since the middle of the seventeenth century, when the Dutch controlled shipping throughout the world, Amsterdam had emerged as the economic capital of Western Europe.

- The scope of this economic empire started to falter in the eighteenth century because of wars, a lack of domestic raw materials and taxation.

- At the same time, France and England began to catch up economically.

- Holland remained Europe's financial center, and in the 1770s Dutch banks controlled 40 percent of British debt.

- In 1793 the majority of America's national debt—accumulated during the Revolutionary War—was on loan from Dutch banks.

American countryside in the late 1790s.

HISTORICAL SNAPSHOT
1793

- France declared war on England
- The "Reign of Terror," a purge of those suspected of treason against the French Republic, began in France
- Louis XVI was executed by guillotine
- Jean Pierre Blanchard made the first balloon flight in North America, in Philadelphia
- The German Reformed Church was established in the United States by Calvinist Puritans
- China's emperor turned away the British fleet and declared that China possessed all things in abundance and had no need of British goods
- Christian Sprengel published detailed descriptions of the manner in which different flowers are pollinated
- Claude Chappe established the first long-distance semaphore telegraph line
- Eli Whitney invented the cotton gin and applied for a patent
- French troops conquered Geertruidenberg in the Netherlands
- Noah Webster established New York's first daily newspaper, *American Minerva*
- Tennis was first mentioned in an English sporting magazine
- The Republican calendar replaced the Gregorian calendar in France
- The first American fugitive slave law passed which required the return of escaped slaves
- President George Washington's second inauguration speech required only 133 words
- The Humane Society of Philadelphia was organized
- Benjamin Rush successfully treated an epidemic of yellow fever
- The Louvre in Paris opened as a museum
- The first U.S. state road was authorized, running from Frankfort, Kentucky, to Cincinnati, Ohio

Maple Sugaring Timeline

1540
Jacques Cartier, the French explorer traveling up the St. Lawrence River, made the first written observation of North American maple trees.

1557
French scribe Andre Thevet wrote the first record of maples in North America yielding a sweet sap.

1606
Marc Lescarbot described the collection and "distillation" of maple sap by Micmac Indians of eastern Canada.

1788
Quakers promoted the manufacture and use of maple sugar as an alternative to West Indian cane sugar production with slave labor.

1790
The "Maple Sugar Bubble" grew, with national leaders promoting homegrown maple sugar as an alternative to slave-produced West Indian cane sugar; advocates included Thomas Jefferson, Dr. Benjamin Rush and Judge James Fenimore Cooper.

1791
A Dutch company bought 23,000 acres of Vermont land and attempted to hire local workers to make sugar to compete with cane from the West Indies.

Thomas Jefferson and George Washington discussed plans to start "maple orchards" on their Virginia plantations; most of the trees died or failed to thrive.

Maple sugaring.

Selected Prices

Boards, 100 Feet of Sap Pine $8.00
Cloth, Yard of Cotton $0.09
Cupboard . . . . .1 pound
Flatware, Dozen Knives and Forks .2 shillings
Hand Saw $0.50
Ox Chain . . . . .4 shillings, 6 pence
Men's Gloves, Silk . . . . .3 shillings
Hat Pin . . . . .2 pence
Potatoes, Bushel . . . . .11 shillings, 1 pence
Writing Desk . . . . .1 pound

"Spanish Moss, Travels through the United States of North America in the years 1795, 1796, 1797," Duc de la Rochefoucauld-Liancourt, London, England, 1800:

To several trees adheres a yellow grey moss, which hangs several feet down, like a beard, and is known by the name of Spanish beard. It retains the same color, both in winter and summer, and bears small blue flowers in spring. It clings especially to the oaks and elms; plantains, maples, cucumber trees, and pines are generally free from it. This moss injures only the beauty of the trees, but alters neither their growth nor leaves. In gardens which are well kept, it is taken off with iron rakes; the Negroes frequently pull it off the trees in the woods with their hands, and sell it to the upholsterers of Charleston, who stuff with it mattresses and chairs. For the same purpose, pretty large quantities of it are transmitted to Philadelphia, New York, and even to the northern states; for though it constantly preserves a certain unpleasant smell, yet is much used, from its being cheaper than wool or hair. In winter it affords good food for cattle.

Letter from A. Ridgely to her sons attending Dickinson College, September 25, 1796:

A young lady visited here just last week profess'd herself "astonished to find your sisters at work," and declared in a sweet simper, that she never had Sizars, thimble, needle or thread about her, for it was terrible in a lady to wear a pair of pockets French ladies never did such a thing. What can such a poor vain piece of affectation and folly be worth? Nothing if she possess'd the wealth of the Indies and I was a man I would scarcely even pay her the complement of a word.

Sugar made at home must possess a sweeter flavor to an independent American of the north, than that which is mingled with the groans and tears of slavery.

—A Vermont Almanac

Letter from Simon Taylor, Kingston, Jamaica sugar cane plantation manager, to Chaloner Arcedekne, England, May 29, 1788:

My Dear Sir

I have before me your letter of 28 March, and I find that you have received my letter of 26 January. We had no Storms nor Floods last year, and matters were going on very smoothly and prosperously untill the 22nd of this month, when we had the severest and heaviest flood, that we have had for these 23 years, indeed infintely higher than in any of the Hurricanes which has done every Estate in the River a very great deal of damage indeed, by carrying of the Trash intirely of some pieces, laying it on other, tearing up some Canes by the Roots, washing out the young Plants, and laying trash on some of them, indeed had it happened earlier in the Crop, it would have intirely destroyed it, but as it is it will do this one a great deal of Injury, and I am afraid hurt the next one. . . .

I bought for you 7 New Negroes and then 13. I on the 22 Inst bought 33 seasoned ones for Batchelors Hall, they are men, women and children, been seasoned near the place, and will I am hopefull by and by establish there a good gang of Negroes, we must have some more by and by, I am to pay for these £2205. One third down, 1/3 in July next year, & the Ballance the year after, by this you will have no Occasion to hire Negroes to clean your Pastures. I will this year putt in some Guinea Grass and make fences, next year will do the same, I think with about 20 New Negroes by and by, I will make the place profitable, both by fattening your old Cattle, as well as by selling Steers, but the first business they should go on will be making houses, and putting in more Cocos and Yams. As for Cruelty there is no such thing practised on Estates, I do not believe that the Mad Men at home wish to hurt themselves, but they should endeavour to regulate their own Police, and show Humanity to their own Poor, before they think of making regulations for our Slaves, who think themselves well of it as matters are at present situated, and do not wish for their Interference. God knows if they were treated as these Miscreants report, they would have cutt all our throats allready, from what they have allready heard from home. There is a man now at Golden Grove doing the Views, and I will get a Plan of the Estate made out to send you home by him, or another good one, who can do it, and mark all you want, but as for woodland you have none, but brush, but he shall mark out where the Guinea Grass Pastures are to be, which will be hilly land, and where your Provisions are. . . .

Excerpt from essay by Benjamin Rush:

There are in the states of New York and Pennsylvania alone at least ten millions of acres of land which produce the sugar maple tree, in the proportion of thirty trees to one acre. Now suppose all persons capable of labor in a family to consist of three, and each to attend 150 trees, and each tree to yield 50 pounds of sugar in a season, the product of the labor of 60,000 families would be 135,000,000 pounds of sugar, and allowing the inhabitants of the United States compose 600,000 families each of which consumed 200 pounds of sugar in a year, the whole consumption would be 120,000,000 pounds in a year, which would leave a balance of 15,000,000 pounds for export. Valuing the sugar at 6/90 of a dollar per pound, the sum saved the United States would be 8,000,000 dollars by home consumption, and the sum gained by exportation would be 1,000,000 dollars.

In contemplating the present opening prospects in human affairs, I am led to expect that a material part of the general happiness which heaven seems to have prepared for mankind will be derived from the manufacture and general use of maple sugar.

—Thomas Jefferson, 1791

Proper care of a watch, letter from Alexander Elmsley to Samuel Johnson, London, March 24, 1774:

Your watch cost 20 guineas and his good work. You must take care when she is not in your pocket and keep her lying horizontally. At present she is regulated and orderly and keeps very good time; if you hang her up at night, instead of laying down on the table she must be made to go about two minutes in the day slower which you can easily duped by altering the regulator. This is a secret in watch making I suppose you did not know before. You are also to take notice that in very hot weather all watches go slow, and in very cold weather fast, and must be regulated accordingly.

1798 PROFILE

Andrew Bartling, raised in Massachusetts by his aunt and uncle, was a young farmer who developed a farm and homestead in Vermont in preparation for his bride joining him.

Life at Home

- Twenty-one-year-old Andrew Bartling was a farmer fixated on nature's diverse rhythms that controlled his fate in Vermont.
- Awareness of the changes in the wind, temperature, sun or moon during the seasons was learned while growing up on his Uncle Robert's Massachusetts farm.
- For a farmer there is a proper time for everything.
- Andrew was often told that the earth has an appointed time to do work.
- In this way he understood the wisdom of cutting lumber in March to fuel a fire or build fences so the year ahead would help dry the green wood.
- Beginning in early childhood, Andrew spent considerable time caring for the livestock around the farm, cleaning manure from the stables, hauling firewood and clearing the fields of stones.
- One of his first activities—which he executed with pride—was helping his cousins paint the barn's interior.
- The finished product was a constant reminder of one of his first contributions to the family farm.
- His three older cousins showed him how to make white paint with a gallon of skimmed milk, a pound of lime and eight ounces of linseed oil.
- All the boys made a mess, but every corner inside the barn was properly christened with a coat of white paint that summer.
- Andrew's parents died when he was four years old, his father dying while in service with the Continental Army and his mother from a series of fevers.

Andrew Bartling left the family farm in Massachusetts to begin life as a Vermont farmer.

- Uncle Robert, his mother's brother, took him and his older sister in, in whose home faith in God, hard work and education were fundamental principles.
- Andrew often spent the evenings at the family table reading chapters and memorizing Scripture verses from the Bible by candlelight.
- Andrew appreciated the candlelight when the days shortened during the winter, which would not happen without the hard work of his aunt, who made candles each fall.
- She acquired the waste fat of oxen during November's "killing-time" and melted, pressed and sieved it several times to purify it into a fine wax tallow.
- By dipping and cooling homemade cotton wicks into a barrel of hot tallow, she gradually produced enough candles for the winter season.
- In addition to his Scripture readings at night, Andrew regularly attended Sunday church services with his relatives.
- At one church service during his seventeenth year in 1794, his focus turned to the blue ribbon in a young lady's shiny brown hair.
- After the service, Andrew learned from his aunt that the girl's name was Anna Boyer and she was visiting relatives in Westford during the summer months.
- During those few months Andrew courted Anna with the time he could spare from his work responsibilities.
- By Lammis Day, the first day of August, the Boyers joined Andrew and his family for the traditional celebration for a good harvest.
- Andrew and his cousins laid out a turf maze the previous day from sheaves of grain to keep the young children busy.
- Anna was impressed with the difficulty of the one-acre maze, while at the same time pleased that it was not so challenging as to discourage the children.
- At the afternoon meal, discussion grew around the new hard currency the American government was minting.
- It was a hot topic that rapidly escalated into angry talk.
  - American gold and silver dollars were being added to the other currencies already issued by the states, plus the British currency that was still in circulation.
  - Determining proper exchange rates was already cumbersome, especially when inflation was rampant, several men argued.
  - Hard metal currencies, such as the British and Spanish coins, were preferred over the paper currency issued by the states.
  - Already farmers and merchants suspected that the Bank of the United States was harming the very business interests it was supposed to protect by increasing interest rates.
  - Also, there was continued bitterness over the government's tax on distilled spirits in many western communities.
  - To halt the debate on the new currency and avoid the bitterness of stories about past monies lost to speculators, Andrew proposed a toast to the year's harvest and to the new saw mill being built in the community.
  - Later that day, he learned that Anna was returning home the following week.
  - They both agreed to write to each other.
  - A few weeks later, while mailing his first letter to Anna, word reached Westford regarding a rebellion in Pennsylvania.
  - Farmers were protesting the tax on distilled spirits, such as whiskey.
  - Talk within the town questioned what this event would mean locally, especially a few years after Shays' Rebellion in Massachusetts.

Andrew and future wife, Anna, at apple harvest.

- The news created concern in Andrew's home.
- Uncle Robert believed that a farmer was capable of taking care of himself.
- Governments come and go, he said, but people will always need grain for bread.
- It was November before the national government stepped in and discussion of the Pennsylvania rebellion died down.
- Over the next couple of years Anna wrote to Andrew from her family's home in Melrose and visited during the summer months.
- When Andrew turned 19, he realized he would not have the opportunities to continue farming in Westford, Massachusetts as the land was too costly.
- Nor would he likely acquire land from his uncle's inheritance because he stood behind his three cousins.
- Advertisements for farmland in Vermont attracted his attention with the offer of virgin timber and good land.
- His cousin John, the youngest and two years older than Andrew, was considering the possibility of moving west.
- After much discussion, they both agreed to purchase land in Vermont outside of Montpelier.
- Andrew discussed the move to Vermont with Anna in his letters during the early autumn months of 1796.
- She did not say much about it in return letters except that it was a matter for him to decide.
- By October, Andrew purchased 100 acres of wooded timberland with access to a small stream.
- John acquired 150 acres a half mile away along the same stream.
- Andrew then wrote a letter to Anna's father detailing his prospects and requesting his blessings to marry his daughter.
- The wait for a response letter took over a month.
- Mr. Boyer wrote that Andrew's meager prospects would cause a great deal of difficulty for his daughter, but gave his blessing.
- Andrew traveled to visit Anna and her family in early January, where they celebrated the end of the Christmas season.
- They agreed he would prepare his land in Vermont and build a house before the two would marry at his uncle's home.
- Uncle Robert, fully realizing that the undertaking would be difficult for both of the young men, provided each an ox as a parting gift.
- Andrew was equally pleased to learn that John had spent January at Uncle Robert's forge barn striking a small barrel full of nails from the nail rods he purchased from a slitting mill.
- Heating the nail rods over a fire, breaking them into individual nails and pounding each one with a nail head took considerable time.
- After purchasing a good wagon and loading it with the necessary tools and supplies, they departed in the beginning of March to get an early start clearing the lands.

Anna waited in Massachusetts while Andrew built their home in Vermont.

The trip from Massachusetts to Vermont was difficult for Andrew and his brother.

It took the pair three weeks to reach Montpelier from Westford, Massachusetts.

Life at Work

- The journey for Andrew Bartling and his cousin John on the cold, wet roads of New England was tough.
- The oxen proved most helpful in slowly moving the young men to Montpelier.
- The trip took them longer than planned—over three weeks—putting them behind schedule.
- Montpelier was growing quickly with several hundred people living in the area.
- A saw and grist mill was operating and good roads had been built.
- Andrew saw opportunity in the Montpelier community.
- After walking their land to see what they had purchased, they selected a spot near the stream and close to a road on Andrew's property to clear first.
- Between the two of them and their oxen, they managed to tame two acres of land over the next month.
- They used the oxen pair to help move the trees and remove stumps, which were then moved along the side of the road to construct a stump fence.
- The fence placed the top end of the stump facing the inside of the cleared land.
- Gaps between the stumps were filled with brush wood to create a simple structure capable of keeping the oxen secure during the evenings.
- Never had Andrew appreciated long woolen drawers so much, finding the thickness of the heavy underwear an enormous help during those cold nights.
- The cold weather reinforced the need to build a shelter promptly.
- Because they had so little land to plant, they had the time to construct a simple log cabin.
- After digging a square trench about two feet down by 10 feet by 20 feet, Andrew and John closely placed logs on top of one another to build up the wall.
- Once the logs were above the ground, they filled in the space in the trench to secure the wall's foundation.
- Building the house walls took only a few days.
- Then they constructed a temporary roof from birch bark, then a chimney.
- Their last task was filling in the wall's gaps with mud, stones and sticks.
- With a house built, crops planted and the season warming up, Andrew returned to Westford to marry Anna.

Word of Indian sightings made Anna fearful.

- John stayed to clear some of his land and finish making his harrow, a wooden block with teeth, to weed between the rows of corn.
- A month later, Andrew returned with his new wife and showed her their home.
- Anna was disappointed with the condition of the house, especially the unevenness of the dirt floor.
- The men had failed to make a wooden floor rake to rake the floor daily to keep it even.
- Soon, the floor was the least of Anna's worries.
- Word of Indian sightings swept through the community.
- Andrew kept his rifle loaded near the door for protection, whether it was man or beast that proved a threat to his farmstead.

- One time while out in the field, Andrew saw two Indians walking along the side of the road, traveling toward the mountains.
- He kept still until they were out of sight and did not say anything to Anna.
- The chiefs of the lower Canadian tribes had claimed areas of Vermont as part of their hunting grounds, and conflict was possible.
- The first year's harvest was small, just enough to get Andrew and Anna through the Vermont winter.
- Over the previous year, Andrew noticed the maple trees in the area and knew that they could produce a fair amount of maple sugar in the late winter.
- A local cooper agreed to provide credit on the buckets they needed for their first year's collection.
- During the slow winter months, they whittled dozens of spiles, or wood spouts, from sumac to draw the maple sap from the trees.
- It was discovered that inserting a spile into a maple tree was better for the tree than slashing the tree's trunk.
- During the month of March, Andrew collected two pails full of sap, roughly one pound a day from each maple tree.
- Anna boiled down the sap in a large kettle, it taking about two weeks.
- During the harvest, Andrew and Anna made roughly 50 pounds of maple sugar blocks from 25 trees.
- They sold the sugar to a Boston merchant, and earned enough income to pay down part of the cooper's credit and invest in the farm.
- A few days later, they were shocked when two Indians arrived at their home during the midday.
- Though they could not speak to them, it was evident they wanted to barter their maple sugar with Andrew.
- Andrew did not need any more sugar but decided to trade with the Indians as a gesture of goodwill.
- He offered two rabbit skins he had tanned in return for one pound of sugar.
- He watched the discussion the Indians had about the rabbit skins and noticed little to no expression on their faces.
- They accepted Andrew's offer, and left without a farewell.

Montpelier, Vermont experienced rapid growth in the early 1800s.

Life in the Community: Vermont

- Early explorers, such as Jacques Cartier and Samuel de Champlain, visited the Vermont region during the sixteenth and seventeenth centuries.
- By 1666, the first white settlement was established by the French with a small outpost called Fort St. Anne constructed on Isle La Motte along Lake Champlain.
- British troops started developing the region in 1690 and increased their presence over the next 40 years.
- The French and British wrestled for control of this region over much of the eighteenth century.
- After the French and Indian Wars, peace was established between the British and French, but arguments developed between the borders of the New York and New Hampshire colonies.
- By 1764, New Hampshire offered land grants to soldiers to settle the territory between New York and New Hampshire.
- The colony of New York protested that these lands belonged to New York.
- By 1770, the colony declared the New Hampshire land grants invalid.
- With the events of the American Revolution and the concerns over their property through the New Hampshire grants, the citizens of Vermont declared it a republic.
- They adopted a constitution that included universal male suffrage, public schools and a ban on slavery.
- By 1791 the Vermont voters ratified the United States Constitution, and the U.S. Congress admitted Vermont to become the fourteenth state, the first admitted to the Union after the original 13 colonies.
- To resolve boundary issues, Vermont paid the government of New York $30,000 in compensation for that state's diminished territorial reach.
- Soon afterwards, a Dutch company bought 23,000 acres of land in Vermont and attempted to hire local workers producing maple sugar to compete against sugar cane from the West Indies.
- The project failed because many from Vermont preferred to work their own land.
- Settlers from Massachusetts began arriving in the city of Montpelier in 1787.
- The city of Montpelier had a population of 113 in 1792.
- Over the next several years, the city experienced a rapid population growth.
- During that time it saw the construction of grist and saw mills, roads, schools, churches and inns.

HISTORICAL SNAPSHOT
1798

- Congress agreed to pay a yearly tribute to Tripoli to protect U.S. shipping
- Russia appointed the first Jewish censor to review Hebrew books
- Representative Matthew Lyon of Vermont spat in the face of Representative Roger Griswold of Connecticut in the U.S. House of Representatives after an argument
- The Federal Street Theater in Boston was destroyed by a fire
- The British boarded the U.S. frigate *Baltimore* and impressed into service a number of crewmen as alleged deserters
- The Republic of Switzerland was formed
- The United States Department of the Navy was established by an Act of Congress
- Judith Sargent Murray wrote *The Gleaner*, essays on women's education and alternatives to marriage
- The Mission San Luis Rey de Francia was founded in California
- U.S. passed the Alien Act which allowed the president to deport dangerous aliens
- The Sedition Act prohibited "false, scandalous and malicious" writing against the president and U.S. Government
- The U.S. Public Health Service was formed and the U.S. Marine Hospital was authorized
- Napoleon Bonaparte's army annexed Egypt, seized Malta and captured Naples
- The Eleventh Amendment regarding judicial powers was ratified
- Twenty-two sea captains founded the East India Marine Society, which later became the Peabody Essex Museum, in Salem, Massachusetts, to preserve the exotic treasures they brought back from their voyages
- The concept of manufacturing interchangeable parts was incorporated by Eli Whitney in the production of firearms for the U.S. Government
- A patent for a screw threading machine was awarded to David Wilkinson of Rhode Island
- Samuel Taylor Coleridge and William Wordsworth published *Lyrical Ballads*

Selected Prices

Beans, Bushel . . . . .4 shillings
Bucket, Leather . . . . .2 shillings, 6 pence
Chicken Coop . . . . .15 shillings
Flax Seed, Bushel . . . . .3 shillings, 9 pence
Hoe, Grubbing . . . . .1 pound, 5 shillings
Linseed Oil, Jug . . . . .1 shilling
Oats, Bushel . . . . .1 shilling, 6 pence
Plow and Irons . . . . .1 pound
Scythe . . . . .6 shillings, 6 pence

Communication to the Governor of Vermont from the Chiefs of Seven Nations, 1798:

To the Hon. Issaac Tichenor, Esq. Governor of the State of Vermont,

GREAT BROTHER, We the Chiefs and Councillors of the Seven Nations of lower Canada Indians, send our love and respect to you, and to treat about our hunting lands, that lie in your state. Beginning on the east side of Ticonderoga, from thence to the great falls on Otter Creek, and continues the same course to the height of land, that divides the streams between Lake Champlain, and the river Connecticut; from thence along the height of lands to opposite Missisque and then down to the Bay: That is the land belonging to the seven nations, which we have sent to settle for with you, as we have settled with York state. So we hope you will be pleased to receive our agents, and that it will be settled, so that both sides will be contented.

Cognahwaghat, the 29th of September, 1798

Signed by twenty Chiefs of the different nations.

"Descriptions of New England Harrows," *New England Farmer*, Samuel Deane, 1797:

The square harrow is armed with sixteen, or with twenty five tushes, or teeth. The sharper these teeth are, the more they will pulverize the soil. If they be steeled at the points, they will hold their sharpness the longer, and stir the ground more effectually. And the cost of doing it is so little, that it is surprising to see that it is so generally neglected by our farmers. . . .

Some use harrow with wooden teeth, but they are of so little advantage to the land, unless it be merely for covering seeds, that they may be considered as unfit to be used at all. The treading of the cattle that draw them, will harden the soil more, perhaps, than these harrow will soften it.

"U.S. Price of Postage in 1798, per Mile," *The Old Farmer and His Almanack,* George Lyman Kittredge, 1920:

Miles	Cents
30	6
60	8
100	10
150	12½
200	15
250	17
350	20
450	22
For more than 450	25

No allowance is to be made for intermediate miles. Every double letter is to pay double the said rates; every triple letter, triple; every packet weighing one ounce, at the rate of four single letters for each ounce.

Community gathering.

Alien Act of 1798

SECTION 1. *Be it enacted by the Senate and House of Representatives of the United States of America, in Congress assembled*, That it shall be lawful for the President of the United States, at any time during the continuance of this act, to *order* all such *aliens* as he shall judge dangerous to the peace and safety of the United States, or shall have reasonable grounds to suspect are concerned in any treasonable or secret machinations against the government thereof, to depart out of the territory of the United States within such time as shall be expressed in such order; which order shall be served on such alien, by delivering him a copy thereof, or leaving the same at his usual abode, and returned to the office of the Secretary of State, by the marshal, or other person, to whom the same shall be directed. And in case any alien, so ordered to depart, shall be found at large within the United States after the time limited in such order for his departure, and not having obtained a *license* from the President to reside therein, or having obtained such *license*, shall not have conformed thereto, every such alien shall, on conviction thereof, be imprisoned for a term not exceeding three years, and shall never after be admitted to become a citizen of the United States: *Provided always, and be it further enacted*, That if any alien so ordered to depart shall prove, to the satisfaction of the President, by evidence, to be taken before such person or persons as the President shall direct, who are for that purpose hereby authorized to administer oaths, that no injury or danger to the United States will arise from suffering such alien to reside therein, the President may grant a *license* to such alien to remain within the United States for such time as he shall judge proper, and at such place as he may designate. And the President may also require of such alien to enter into a bond to the United States, in such penal sum as he may direct, with one or more sufficient sureties, to the satisfaction of the person authorized by the President to take the same, conditioned for the good behaviour of such alien during his residence in the United States, and not violating his license, which license the President may revoke whenever he shall think proper.

SECT. 2. *And be it further enacted*, That it shall be lawful for the President of the United States, whenever he may deem it necessary for the public safety, to order to be removed out of the territory thereof any alien who may or shall be in prison in pursuance of this act; and to cause to be arrested and sent out of the United States such of those aliens as shall have been ordered to depart therefrom, and shall not have obtained a license as aforesaid, in all cases where, in the opinion of the President, the public safety requires a speedy removal. And if any alien so removed or sent out of the United States by the President shall voluntarily return thereto, unless by permission of the President of the United States, such alien, on conviction thereof, shall be imprisoned so long as, in the opinion of the President, the public safety may require.

SECT. 3. *And be it further enacted*, That every master or commander of any ship or vessel which shall come into any port of the United States after the first day of July next shall, immediately on his arrival, make report in writing to the collector or other chief officer of the customs of such port, of all aliens, if any on board his vessel, specifying their names, age, the place of nativity, the country from which they shall have come, the nation to which they belong and owe allegiance, their occupation, and a description of their persons, as far as he shall be informed thereof, and on failure, every such master and commander shall forfeit and pay three hundred dollars, for the payment whereof, on default of such master or commander, such vessel shall also be holden, and may by such collector or other officer of the customs be detained. And it shall be the duty of such collector or other officer of the customs, forthwith to transmit to the office of the Department of State true copies of all such returns.

SECT. 4. *And be it further enacted*, That the Circuit and District Courts of the United States shall respectively have cognizance of all crimes and offences against this act. And all marshals and other officers of the United States are required to execute all precepts and orders of the President of the United States, issued in pursuance or by virtue of this act.

continued

Alien Act of 1798 . . . *(continued)*

SECT. 5. *And be it further enacted*, That it shall be lawful for any alien who may be ordered to be removed from the United States, by virtue of this act, to take with him such part of his goods, chattels, or other property, as he may find convenient; and all property left in the United States, by any alien who may be removed as aforesaid, shall be and remain subject to his order and disposal, in the same manner as if this act had not been passed.

SECT. 6. *And be it further enacted*, That this act shall continue and be in force for and during the term of two years from the passing thereof.

1799 Profile

Brothers Benjamin and Joshua Morse were immensely proud of their reputation as the most skilled (and expensive) cabinetmakers in Annapolis, Maryland.

Life at Home

- Some in the Annapolis community thought the Morse brothers, especially Joshua, were arrogant and overbearing, but no one doubted their skills as furniture makers.
- After working together for 23 years, they had the talent to match Europe's finest furniture makers, and showed great ability for crafting one-of-a-kind designs of their own.
- Their collaborations began early in life during troubled times.
- Benjamin and Joshua were orphans three times over—a distinction they bore stoically.
- Their parents had died of scarlet fever—within days of each other—when the boys were small.
- Their uncle adopted the boys and provided a home and schooling—which emphasized cabinetmaking—until he succumbed to consumption four years later.
- Their older sister then took charge, only to disappear during a sea-going trip from Baltimore to New York, of which the ship was never found.
- That is when the two, at 14 and 16, vowed to stay together for life—no one else could be trusted.
- They also pledged to remain bachelors, even through the temptation of their years as apprentices.
- Their training period with a British-trained cabinetmaker lasted four years.
- As the older brother, Joshua set the artistic standard for the pair and allowed no room for compromise.
- Benjamin was the smiling face of the Morse Brothers who kept customers happy and Joshua calm.
- Between them they carved out a sound reputation for quality and earned enough money to buy a brick home together near the state capitol building.

Benjamin Morse was considered one of the most skilled cabinetmakers in Annapolis.

Benjamin's brother, Joshua.

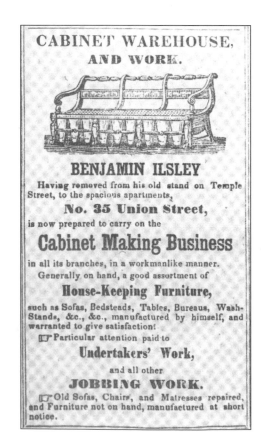

CABINET WAREHOUSE,
AND WORK.

BENJAMIN ILSLEY

Having removed from his old stand on Temple
Street, to the spacious apartments,

No. 35 Union Street,

is now prepared to carry on the

Cabinet Making Business

in all its branches, in a workmanlike manner.
Generally on hand, a good assortment of

House-Keeping Furniture,

such as Sofas, Bedsteads, Tables, Bureaus, Wash-
Stands, &c., &c., manufactured by himself, and
warranted to give satisfaction!

☞ Particular attention paid to

Undertakers' Work,

and all other

JOBBING WORK.

☞ Old Sofas, Chairs, and Matresses repaired,
and Furniture not on hand, manufactured at short
notice.

- The two-story home quickly became known for its sophisticated décor and lavish parties.
- No one ever went home from a Morse brothers' party hungry or entirely sober.
- As a result, Benjamin and Joshua knew all the city's key figures and most of the gossip that swirled around them.
- The parties were also a showcase for the extraordinary furniture crafted by the brothers and the exotic beauty of Benjamin's two Irish wolfhounds.
- The large, agile dogs were his constant companions and protectors.
- For many of the newly rich merchants and plantation owners, owning a piece of Morse Brothers furniture was a symbol of their newfound wealth and success.
- During the Revolutionary War Benjamin was a patriot who proudly served.
- Despite his love of precision, however, he detested the ritual of marching in line and keeping in step.
- Even more, he hated the quasi-war currently underway with the French.
- Ever since the French pirates had begun preying on merchant ships along the United States coastline, critical furniture making supplies were scarce.
- Mahogany from Cuba and rosewood from Brazil was stolen by French-affiliated sailors the prior month, delaying the building and delivery of two dining tables, 24 chairs and three chests.
- More embarrassing was the unavailability of British brass pulls, due to a shipment of pulls from England being plundered at sea by the French, leaving half a dozen chests sitting in the shop unfinished.
- With no pulls, the cabinetwork could not be completed and the brothers were unpaid for commissioned work.
- To fight back, Benjamin worked with the Annapolis city fathers to draft a resolution to President John Adams demanding American retaliation.
- The result was short of a declaration of war, but an authorization by Congress for U.S. warships to seize "armed vessels operating under authority or pretense of authority from the Republic of France."
- Benjamin believed that America had to show its teeth if France and other world powers were to respect its rights on the ocean and its right to free trade as a neutral and independent nation.
- Joshua said he didn't care if America declared war on the British Empire and the Republic of France simultaneously—if he could just get the materials he needed to do his work.

Life at Work
- Work for Benjamin and Joshua Morse started at sun-up, and they were kept on schedule by roosters living throughout downtown Annapolis.
- Benjamin started each day sharpening the chisels, saws and scrapers that were essential to their work.
- He planned the day's work schedule for himself, Joshua and the three craftsmen who were employed to haul lumber, rough-cut boards and endlessly sand furniture.

- Then he began crafting tapered legs, cutting ogee feet or book matching boards so they would display well on a chest top.
- Joshua carved the ball and claw feet, fluted the quarter columns and mixed the finishes.
- They often worked in partnership on their furniture: "Four hands with one mission," Benjamin liked to say.
- Benjamin was mindful of customers looking to buy, pay for, or check the progress of, an ordered piece.
- Despite the prices they charged, cash was a constant problem and the books were balanced weekly to track progress and keep workers paid.
- Payments to the Morse Brothers came in a variety of ways.
- Recently, a high chest sold to a plantation owner living 20 miles outside Annapolis for 90 pounds, was partially paid for with Indian corn and a delightful evening of drinking rum with the happy customer.
- Like many Annapolis merchants, Benjamin Morse offered discounts to customers who paid in hard currency, knowing from experience that the value of American paper money could vary widely from month to month and place to place.
- The secrets to earning a quality living, Benjamin preached, was a quality reputation and the ability to produce furniture on time.
- Joshua was obsessed with the first rule and lackadaisical about the second.
- After years of experimentation, Benjamin had calculated that, to be profitable, they needed to build a bedstead in two days, a chair in one day, a case of drawers in 17 to 22 days, and a desk in 14 to 19 days.
- One of their principal competitors was a Scottish-born cabinetmaker named Robert Travers whose shop produced a prodigious array of Chippendale and Federalist furniture based on English fashions.
- Robert was a businessman first, a craftsman second.
- Robert was so foppish, according to Joshua, he was willing to construct anything—even a "true Madame table," also known as a billiards table—if there was money to be made.
- Benjamin thought Robert's cabinet work showed sacrifices in detail.
- Their other competitor was the city of Baltimore, a center for social and mercantile activity, including furniture making.
- In recent years, some of their best customers had convinced themselves that the finest woodworking in America could only come from urban centers—especially seaports—influenced daily by European ideas and shipments.
- Annapolis' wealthy residents would often order a breakfront or high boy while on a shopping excursion to Baltimore, assuming it was the pinnacle of craftsmanship because it came from Baltimore.

Example of Morse Brothers' craftsmanship.

- "Trust your eyes," Joshua seethed, when word of the purchase reached Annapolis.
- To compete, Benjamin recruited a number of journeymen to work in the shop, including a musical instrument maker from Manchester, England, and a blacksmith capable of molding unique hinges
- Their employment lasted only as long as Joshua didn't comment on their work.
- A single shouting explosion would send the new recruit out the door, angry and determined to seek revenge.

Life in the Community: Annapolis, Maryland

- Annapolis, Maryland, was remarkably prosperous in the years immediately preceding the revolution.
- Extensive trade with England and Scotland bolstered the city's commerce.
- As the state capital, Annapolis was the center of Maryland's political and social pursuits as well.
- Wealthy planters and the rising merchant class flocked to the city, built substantial townhouses and purchased both imported and domestic luxuries.
- As a result, the city's residents developed a taste for elegant and refined living, including a desire for quality furniture made by expert craftsmen and lush, well-tended gardens with a formal, English look.
- Unlike many cities along the Eastern seaport, Annapolis nurtured an elite community with the "meaner sort" of dock-workers, sailors and prostitutes encouraged to settle in bustling Baltimore.
- Annapolis was settled in 1649 where the Severn River meets the Chesapeake Bay.
- In 1694, soon after the overthrow of the Catholic government of the lord proprietor, it was named capital of the royal colony and named Annapolis after Princess Anne, soon to be the queen of Great Britain.
- During the Revolution, Annapolis was at the center of Maryland's effort where vessels carrying soldiers and supplies regularly skirted the blockade of English ships.
- Always in the shadow of the phenomenal growth of nearby Baltimore, colonial Annapolis cultivated sophisticated tastes thanks to an international community.
- After 1780, when Baltimore was made a port of entry, oyster-packing, boatbuilding and sailmaking became the chief industries of Annapolis.
- Annapolis became the temporary capital of the United States after the signing of the Treaty of Paris in 1783, and Congress was in session there from November 1783 to June 1784.

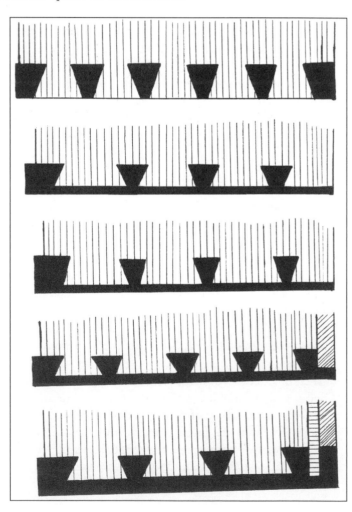

Diagram of various dovetails used by cabinetmakers.

HISTORICAL SNAPSHOT
1799

- George Washington died at age 67 at his Mount Vernon, Virginia home
- The *USS Constellation* captured the French frigate *Insurgente*
- Napoleon Bonaparte participated in a coup and declared himself first consul, or dictator, of France; five nations united against France
- Western agriculturalists first described the qualities of sweet corn, which was being grown by the Iroquois
- Pennsylvania pioneered the printed ballot
- The Rosetta Stone was discovered in Egypt by an officer in Napoleon's army
- Edward Jenner's smallpox vaccination was introduced
- The Bank of Manhattan opened in New York City
- The metric system was established in France
- An American patent for a seeding machine was granted to Eliakim Spooner of Vermont
- The last known blaauwboch or blue antelope was shot in Africa
- The Russian government granted the Russian-American Company a trade monopoly in Alaska
- Jacques-Louis David painted *The Rape of the Sabine Women*
- Eli Whitney received a government contract for 10,000 muskets
- The first American law regulating insurance was passed in Massachusetts
- The Dutch East India Company fell bankrupt

Selected Prices

Bedstead and Cord . . . . .7 shillings
Chair, Windsor . . . . .4 shillings
Chest of Drawers, Mahogany $20.00
Handkerchief, Woman's . . . . .5 shillings
Honey, Gallon . . . . .4 shillings, 8 pence
Sherry, Gallon . . . . .7 shillings, 6 pence
Shoe Buckles, Silver, Men's $1.50
Spade . . . . .2 shillings, 6 pence
Sweet Potatoes, Bushel . . . . .1 shilling
Wardrobe . . . . .13 pounds

"Matches," *The Gentleman's Magazine*, September 1803:

As the consequences of fire are of such serious and terrible nature, too much care cannot be taken to guard against them. I deem it therefore incumbent on me to make known the following circumstance, as it may surprise many of an immediate danger, where they have probably no more suspicion of it than I had.

Having occasion to be frequently sealing packets, that I might not give my servant the trouble of coming upstairs every time I wanted a lighted candle, I bought a phosphorous matchbox, for the purpose of furnishing myself readily with a light.

One day I dipped my match, rubbed it according to the directions on the cork at the bottom of the tin box, and it took fire; but the flame went out before I could light my taper. In consequence I applied the same match, which was perfectly extinguished in appearance, to the part containing phosphorus, pressing it hard as usual; when to my great surprise, the reservoir of phosphorus itself instantly caught fire. To extinguish it, I shut up the box; supposing in this state air being excluded, it must necessarily cease to burn. Still, however, I heard a hissing noise in the box as it stood on the table; and this noise, instead of diminishing, continued to increase. Alarmed at this, I took up the box, in order to extinguish the phosphorus by some other means, or to remove it to a place of less danger; but its heat was now so great that it presently burnt my fingers, and occasioned me to drop it on the floor. The green baize with which this was covered instantly caught; and the fire was spreading under it on all sides with rapidity, in spite of my endeavors to smother it by trampling on it; in doing which I burnt the soles of my shoes and scorched one of my feet; when one of my people came into the room, took up the box by the help of his doubled handkerchief, which it burnt, and threw it out the window into the yard. We now subdued the fire between us, by tearing up the baize and smothering it as well as we could; but not before it had communicated to the floor itself. Had such an accident happened in the night-time, when perhaps things of this kind are most frequently used, the event might have been deplorable indeed.

Though I hope this caution may serve to prevent similar accidents with a chemical composition that burns more ferociously than most, if not than any other substance, it may not be amiss to add, that nothing is said to extinguish phosphorus so speedily as urine.

Drums, and elegant prints, Advertisement of John Shaw, *Annapolis Maryland Gazette,* August 6, 1800:

A few elegant prints of Thomas Jefferson, Esq., vice-president of the United States, in handsome gilt frames, ditto the Washington family, dressing glasses, tea caddies, portable writing desks, gentlemens chest of tools, plate baskets lined with tin, house bells, chamber lamps with wick for burning in the night, gilt oval frames for pictures, boxes of paints for drawing, black lead and camel hair pencils, fifes, billiards sacks, wood-saws, wire fenders, maps of Maryland, a variety of household furniture.

Thomas Jefferson.

Commercial News, New-England Palladium, October 29, 1802:

Bermuda—Several English West Indies islands have shut their ports against the Americans, owing to their having such a number of their vessels and seamen unemployed. There are also here a great number of vessels unemployed, as well as seamen; and some measures must be taken to put a stop to the present trade between these islands and America or some new regulations take place, otherwise every dollar will vanish.

In whale fishery has been so productive this year that a greater number of ships and never was known are expected to be fitted out the next season both for the South-sea and Greenland, from England.

ADVERTISEMENTS, New-England Palladium, October 29, 1802:

JUST ARRIVED a supply of those highly celebrated GERMAN BITTERS invented by Abraham Van Vleeck, M.D.

Unlike many new and untried composition these valuable Bitters claim the test of more than sixty years' experience; approved and used by the citizens of New York during the Doctor's lifetime, who held them in high esteem. As a domestic medicine, a pleasant Bitter and cordial stomachie, no preparation now exant can be put in competition with them. During the war in America, when the bilious, autumnal, malignant and prison fevers prevailed in New York, their daily use as a preventative against taking the fevers from the sick; and as a cordial restorative after a fit of sickness and when a want of appetite and great debility retarded a recovery these Bitters were in great esteem.

They may be used freely as a Stomach Bitter, by all ages and sexes, in sickness and health; they're the best restorative and strengthener of any in use in Jaundice, Indigestion, Dropsy, Hysterics, Consumption, Hypochondriacal Complaints, all kinds of fevers after a crisis, particularly the putrid, flow, nervous and typhus fevers; and in all cases of weakness and debility; children with worms, and Diarrhea, Colic, Rickets and Convulsion etc.

* *

A WET NURSE

Married woman with a young breast milk wishes to go into a family to nurse a child. Inquire of the printers.

* *

WANTED

A YOUNG MAN, who hath experience in the mercantile business—and is acquainted with bookkeeping and accounts and has been on several voyages, withes for employment in some situation suitable to his capacity. He can produce sufficient testimonial of recommendation, and would engage on very favorable terms. Apply to the printers.

Letter from Rebecca Alexander Samuel to her parents from Petersburg, Virginia, in 1791:

You cannot know what a wonderful country this is for the common man. One can live here peacefully. Hyman made a clock that goes very accurately, just like the one in the Buchenstrasse in Hamburg. Now you can imagine what honors Hyman has been getting here. In all Virginia there is not a clock like this one, and Virginia is the greatest province in the whole of America, and America is the largest section of the world. Now you know what kind of country this is. It is not too long since Virginia was discovered. This is a young country. And it is amazing to see the business they do in this little Petersburg. At times as many as a thousand hogshead of tobacco arrive at one time, and each hogshead contains 1,000 and sometimes 1,200 pounds of tobacco. The tobacco is shipped from here to the whole world. When Judah comes here, he can become a watchmaker and a goldsmith, if he so desires. Here it is not like Germany where a watchmaker is not permitted to sell silverware. The contrary is true in this country. They do not know otherwise here. They expect a watchmaker to be a silversmith too. Hyman has more to do in making silverware than with watchmaking. He is a journeyman, a silversmith, a very good artisan, and he, Hyman, takes care of watches. This work is well paid here, but in Charleston, it pays even better.

Concerning Annapolis, by William Eddis, Letters from America, 1769:

At present, this city has more the appearance of an agreeable village than the metropolis of an opulent province, as it contains within its limits a number of small fields, which are intended future erections. But in a few years it will probably be one of the best built cities in America, as a spirit of improvement is predominant and the situation is allowed to be equally healthy and pleasant with any on this side of the Atlantic.

"Practical Information on Consumption of the Lungs,"
The Gentleman's Magazine, September 1803:

The title of the tract is, "On Consumption of the Lungs"; in which a new Mode of Treatment is laid down, and recommended to public attention; as having been found powerfully efficacious, particularly in the first stages of tuberculosis Consumption, before purulent Expectoration commences. . . .

Let ten grains of crude opium be well rubbed with thirty grains of mild volatile alkali, two drachms of syrup of white poppies, two drachms of volatile spirit of ammonia, and one ounce and a half water, or peppermint, or ani-feed-water. Of this, well shaken together, one tea-spoon should be taken in cold water two, three, or four times a day, increasing the dose to one and a half or two tea-spoonful, if necessary.

If the cough be slight, half the quantity of opium may be sufficient; if fevere, the opium may be increased to 12 or 15 grains. In short, any of the articles may be increased or diminished as circumstances may require; and in many cases other active additions will be found necessary.

"New York City," *New Travels in the United States of America,*
by J.P. Brissot de Warvillel, 1788:

If there is one city in the American continent which above all others displays English luxury that is New York, where you can find all the English fashions.

The women wear silk and gauze dresses, hats, and even elaborate hairdos. Carriages are rare, but the few that exist are elegant. The men dress more simply than the women, and they still distain to wear frills, but they compensate for this simplicity when they sit down at table, where the most expensive wines make their appearance. Luxury is already breeding in this city the most dangerous class of men—bachelors. They are afraid to marry because it is so expensive to keep a wife. . . .

Let those who doubt the prodigious effects of liberty on man and on his industry come to America! What miracles they will witness! While almost everywhere in Europe towns and villages were falling into ruin, here new buildings are rising on every hand. New York was partially destroyed by fire during the last war, but the traces of this terrible conflagration are disappearing. The activity which reigns on all sides announces the prosperity of the future. Everywhere streets are being widened and extended. Elegant buildings in the English style are replacing the gabled Dutch houses, which there are some still left. . . .

I take a walk along North River. What rapid changes in a few weeks! Two hundred feet of land have been reclaimed from the river by a very simple device. They construct a kind of box built up of very large logs laid one upon another at right angles with spaces between and fastened together at right angles by strong uprights. This floating dike is towed to the spot where it is to be located and where the water is often as much as forty feet deep. When it reaches its destination it is loaded with enormous rocks brought out on barges and is sunk. Then the space full of water behind the rocks is rapidly filled in.

On all sides houses are going up and streets are being laid out; everywhere I see workers filling land, excavating, building, laying pavements, erecting public pumps.

Address to John Adams, The President of the United States, from the citizens on Annapolis, Maryland, June 28, 1798:

That gratefully sensible of the blessings we enjoy under a government freely adopted, after mature deliberation, by the American people, and desirous of perpetuating these blessings to the latest posterity, we view with no less surprise than indignation, the treatment of our envoys by the French Directory. . . .

Threatened, as we are, with conditions harder than these, with a dismemberment similar to that of Venice, and with revolutionary systems, which the rulers of France, intoxicated with success, and insatiable of plunder, have produced among several European states within their grasp, we cannot doubt, that all true Americans will unite cordially in defence of their independence, and, by union, avert these calamities with which a timid and temporising policy has overwhelmed those countries, the victim of avarice, ambition, and intrigue.

Believing, as we do, that the executive of the united government has maintained an impartial neutrality, and that it has sedulously and faithfully endeavored to cultivate the friendship of France, to reconcile subsisting differences, and to remove every just cause of complaint against the United States (if any there be) we are determined to support, to the utmost of our abilities, the measures which the government may think proper to adopt protection of commerce, defence of the country, and in vindication of the insulted rights of an independent nation.

We should lament the necessity of engaging in a war, which the American people and government have anxiously sought to avoid; but war with all its horrors, would be preferable to base submission. On the removal of the present rulers of France, it may be expected that a milder policy will succeed that spirit of aggrandizement and conquest which has disorganized Europe; that the French nation whose sagacity equals its courage, will embrace a different conduct towards us; it must reprobate the measures which may force us to be its foe; a speedy reconciliation and reparation of injuries, we confidently hope would result from such a change. But as this event may be distant, it is prudent to be prepared against the worse; plans, therefore, now adopted, by congress, for putting this country in the best posture of defence, meet our entire approbation. We believe this to be a very general sentiment, and we wish its expression to be as general, that the directory may cease to project on the supposed disunion of our citizens, the dismemberment and ruin of our country.

We admire, sir, and applaud, the firmness of temper which, as the chief magistrate of a free people, you have displayed during your administration. Averse from war, and dreading its concomitant evils, you have evinced an earnest disposition to preserve the peace of our country, while it could be preserved without the sacrifice of its honor and its rights. Persevere, sir, in the same line of conduct; we trust you may rely on the hearty support of the American people, whose calm good sense discerns their true interests, and whose firm deliberate courage, under the protection of Providence will maintain them.

Signed by order of the citizens,
Nicholas Carroll, Chairman

1797 NEWS FEATURE

Inaugural Address of President John Adams, Philadelphia, March 4, 1797:

When it was first perceived, in early times, that no middle course for America remained between unlimited submission to a foreign legislature and a total independence of its claims, men of reflection were less apprehensive of danger from the formidable power of fleets and armies they must determine to resist than from those contests and dissensions which would certainly arise concerning the forms of government to be instituted over the whole and over the parts of this extensive country. Relying, however, on the purity of their intentions, the justice of their cause, and the integrity and intelligence of the people, under an overruling Providence which had so signally protected this country from the first, the representatives of this nation, then consisting of little more than half its present number, not only broke to pieces the chains which were forging and the rod of iron that was lifted up, but frankly cut asunder the ties which had bound them, and launched into an ocean of uncertainty.

The zeal and ardor of the people during the Revolutionary war, supplying the place of government, commanded a degree of order sufficient at least for the temporary preservation of society. The Confederation which was early felt to be necessary was prepared from the models of the Batavian and Helvetic confederacies, the only examples which remain with any detail and precision in history, and certainly the only ones which the people at large had ever considered. But reflecting on the striking difference in so many particulars between this country and those where a courier may go from the seat of government to the frontier in a single day, it was then certainly foreseen by some who assisted in Congress at the formation of it that it could not be durable.

Negligence of its regulations, inattention to its recommendations, if not disobedience to its authority, not only in individuals but in States, soon appeared with their melancholy consequences: universal languor, jealousies and rivalries of States, decline of navigation and commerce, discouragement of necessary manufactures, universal fall in the value of lands and their produce, contempt of public and private faith, loss of consideration and credit with foreign nations, and at length in discontents, animosities, combinations, partial conventions, and insurrection, threatening some great national calamity. In this dangerous crisis the people of America were not abandoned by their usual good sense, presence of mind, resolution, or integrity. Measures were pursued to concert a plan to form a more perfect union, establish justice, insure domestic tranquility, provide for the common defense, promote the general welfare, and secure the blessings of liberty. The public disquisitions, discussions, and deliberations issued in the present happy Constitution of Government.

Employed in the service of my country abroad during the whole course of these transactions, I first saw the Constitution of the United States in a foreign country. Irritated by no literary altercation, animated by no public debate, heated by no party animosity, I read it with great satisfaction, as the result of good heads prompted by good hearts, as an experiment better adapted to the genius, character, situation, and relations of this nation and country than any which had ever been proposed or suggested. In its general principles and great outlines it was conformable to such a system of government as I had ever most esteemed, and in some States, my own native State in particular, had contributed to establish. Claiming a right of suffrage, in common with my fellow-citizens, in the adoption or rejection of a constitution which was to rule me and my posterity, as well as them and theirs, I did not hesitate to express my approbation of it on all occasions, in public and in private. It was not then, nor has been since, any objection to it in my mind that the Executive and Senate were not more permanent. Nor have I ever entertained a thought of promoting any alteration in it but such as the people themselves, in the course of their experience, should see and feel to be necessary or expedient, and by their representatives in Congress and the State legislatures, according to the Constitution itself, adopt and ordain.

Returning to the bosom of my country after a painful separation from it for 10 years, I had the honor to be elected to a station under the new order of things, and I have repeatedly laid myself under the most serious obligations to support the Constitution. The operation of it has equaled the most sanguine expectations of its friends, and from an habitual attention to it, satisfaction in its administration, and delight in its effects upon the peace, order, prosperity, and happiness of the nation I have acquired an habitual attachment to it and veneration for it. What other form of government, indeed, can so well deserve our esteem and love?

There may be little solidity in an ancient idea that congregations of men into cities and nations are the most pleasing objects in the sight of superior intelligences, but this is very certain, that to a benevolent human mind there can be no spectacle presented by any nation more pleasing, more noble, majestic, or august, than an assembly like that which has so often been seen in this and the other Chamber of Congress, of a Government in which the Executive authority, as well as that of all the branches of the Legislature, are exercised by citizens selected at regular periods by their neighbors to make and execute laws for the general good. Can anything essential, anything more than mere ornament and decoration, be added to this by robes and diamonds? Can authority be more amiable and respectable when it descends from accidents or institutions established in remote antiquity than when it springs fresh from the hearts and judgments of an honest and enlightened people? For it is the people only that are represented. It is their power and majesty that is reflected, and only for their good, in every legitimate government, under whatever form it may appear. The existence of such a government as ours for any length of time is a full proof of a general dissemination of knowledge and virtue throughout the whole body of the people. And what object or consideration more pleasing than this can be presented to the human mind? If national pride is ever justifiable or excusable it is when it springs, not from power or riches, grandeur or glory, but from conviction of national innocence, information, and benevolence.

In the midst of these pleasing ideas we should be unfaithful to ourselves if we should ever lose sight of the danger to our liberties if anything partial or extraneous should infect the purity of our free, fair, virtuous, and independent elections. If an election is to be determined by a majority of a single vote, and that can be procured by a party through artifice or corruption, the Government may be the choice of a party for its own ends, not of the nation for the national good. If that solitary suffrage can be obtained by foreign nations by flattery or menaces, by fraud or violence, by terror, intrigue, or venality, the Government may not be the choice of the American people, but of foreign nations. It may be foreign nations who govern us, and not we, the people, who govern ourselves; and candid men will acknowledge that in such cases choice would have little advantage to boast of over lot or chance.

Such is the amiable and interesting system of government (and such are some of the abuses to which it may be exposed) which the people of America have exhibited to the admiration and anxiety of the wise and virtuous of all nations for eight years under the administration of a citizen who, by a long course of great actions, regulated by prudence, justice, temperance, and fortitude, conducting a people inspired with the same virtues and animated with the same ardent patriotism and love of liberty to independence and peace, to increasing wealth and unexampled prosperity, has merited the gratitude of his fellow-citizens, commanded the highest praises of foreign nations, and secured immortal glory with posterity.

In that retirement which is his voluntary choice may he long live to enjoy the delicious recollection of his services, the gratitude of mankind, the happy fruits of them to himself and the world, which are daily increasing, and that splendid prospect of the future fortunes of this country which is opening from year to year. His name may be still a rampart, and the knowledge that he lives a bulwark, against all open or secret enemies of his country's peace. This example has been recommended to the imitation of his successors by both Houses of Congress and by the voice of the legislatures and the people throughout the nation.

On this subject it might become me better to be silent or to speak with diffidence; but as something may be expected, the occasion, I hope, will be admitted as an apology if I venture to say that if a preference, upon principle, of a free republican government, formed upon long and serious reflection, after a diligent and impartial inquiry after truth; if an attachment to the Constitution of the United States, and a conscientious determination to support it until it shall be altered by the judgments and wishes of the people, expressed in the mode prescribed in it; if a respectful attention to the constitutions of the individual States and a constant caution and delicacy toward the State governments; if an equal and impartial regard to the rights, interest, honor, and happiness of all the States in the Union, without preference or regard to a northern or southern, an eastern or western, position, their various political opinions on unessential points or their personal attachments; if a love of virtuous men of all parties and denominations; if a love of science and letters and a wish to patronize every rational effort to encourage schools, colleges, universities, academies, and every institution for propagating knowledge, virtue, and religion among all classes of the people, not only for their benign influence on the happiness of life in all its stages and classes, and of society in all its forms, but as the only means of preserving our Constitution from its natural enemies, the spirit of sophistry, the spirit of party, the spirit of intrigue, the profligacy of corruption, and the pestilence of foreign influence, which is the angel of destruction to elective governments; if a love of equal laws, of justice, and humanity in the interior administration; if an inclination to improve agriculture, commerce, and manufacturers for necessity, convenience, and defense; if a spirit of equity and humanity toward the aboriginal nations of America, and a disposition to ameliorate their condition by inclining them to be more friendly to us, and our citizens to be more friendly to them; if an inflexible determination to maintain peace and inviolable faith with all nations, and that system of neutrality and impartiality among the belligerent powers of Europe which has been adopted by this Government and so solemnly sanctioned by both Houses of Congress and applauded by the legislatures of the States and the public opinion, until it shall be otherwise ordained by Congress; if a personal esteem for the French nation, formed in a residence of seven years chiefly among them, and a sincere desire to preserve the friendship which has been so much for the honor and interest of both nations; if, while the conscious honor and integrity of the people of America and the internal sentiment of their own power and energies must be preserved, an earnest endeavor to investigate every just cause and remove every colorable pretense of complaint; if an intention to pursue by amicable negotiation a reparation for the injuries that have been committed on the commerce of our fellow-citizens by whatever nation, and if success cannot be obtained, to lay the facts before the Legislature, that they may consider what further measures the honor and interest of the Government and its constituents demand; if a resolution to do justice as far as may depend upon me, at all times and to all nations, and maintain peace, friendship, and benevolence with all the world; if an unshaken confidence in the honor, spirit, and resources of the American people, on which I have so often hazarded my all and never been deceived; if elevated ideas of the high destinies of this country and of my own duties toward it, founded on a knowledge of the moral principles and intellectual improvements of the people deeply engraven on my mind in early life, and not obscured but exalted by experience and age; and, with humble reverence, I feel it to be my duty to add, if a veneration for the religion of a people who profess and call themselves Christians, and a fixed resolution to consider a decent respect for Christianity among the best recommendations for the public service, can enable me in any degree to comply with your wishes, it shall be my strenuous endeavor that this sagacious injunction of the two Houses shall not be without effect.

With this great example before me, with the sense and spirit, the faith and honor, the duty and interest, of the same American people pledged to support the Constitution of the United States, I entertain no doubt of its continuance in all its energy, and my mind is prepared without hesitation to lay myself under the most solemn obligations to support it to the utmost of my power.

And may that Being who is supreme over all, the Patron of Order, the Fountain of Justice, and the Protector in all ages of the world of virtuous liberty, continue His blessing upon this nation and its Government and give it all possible success and duration consistent with the ends of His providence.

1800–1809

At the turn of the century, change was the defining characteristic of the American nation at every level. The new city of Washington in the District of Columbia succeeded Philadelphia as the capital in 1800. That same year the nation voted to move away from the Federalist Party and support the Republican Party's presidential candidate, Thomas Jefferson. Political influence and real power spread to the untested U.S. Supreme Court, which established the doctrine of judicial review during the case of *Marbury v. Madison*.

America continued to show its potential strength on the international stage. America defended its self-interest during the Tripolitan War in North Africa to prevent Barbary pirates from preying upon the American merchant ships. Exports from the American states to both France and England continued to grow until 1808. As the two European nations battled during the Napoleonic War, each country prevented American merchants from visiting the other. In an attempt to flex the country's commercial strength, Jefferson signed the Embargo and Non-Intercourse Acts that prohibited trade with either nation. The action ultimately hurt American shipping and commercial interest, especially in New England, and caused a significant loss of customs revenue.

During this time of change, the nation began embracing various political opinions found in many newspapers and journals. The New York *Evening Post* and *The Port Folio* in Philadelphia became prominent publications. But other publications, such as John Marshall's *Life of George Washington,* Isaiah Thomas's *History of Printing in America* and Washington Irving's *History of New York* were popular works during the 1800s.

Growth of the young nation occurred in other areas, most noticeably with the purchase of the Louisiana territory from France in 1803. The nation's population witnessed the westward migration into the Northwest Territory and areas west of the Appalachian Mountains. Migration was further influenced by Lewis and Clark's exploration of the Louisiana territory and Zebulon Pike's exploration of the Southwest. As people settled in the Western areas, a religious revival began to spread, and it was common to hear evangelical sermons under grove trees or open fields. Also typical of this expansion was the opportunity to grow into areas of enterprise and transport goods along the Ohio and Mississippi Rivers to New Orleans.

The new opportunities foreshadowed the direction of the young nation's commercial future. Manufacturing continued to grow, mostly in New England, which could be seen in the production of textile products and metal works. In Waterbury, Connecticut, the establishment of the nation's first brass mill helped the city become the national center for brass manufacturing. Transportation improvements encouraged commercial opportunities. The completion of the Santee Canal system in South Carolina and the Western Inland Lock Navigation Company's project in New York started a boom in canal construction. Robert Fulton's steamboat *Clermont* allowed travel under a new mode of nautical transport. Businesses were also experiencing issues with labor costs from the 1806 shoemakers strike in New York City to the 1808 closing of African slave importation in the entire United States.

Still, the upstart nation showed considerable signs of being honorable to a world watching for a misstep. Few in Europe had really expected the young, restless country to survive for very long. Not only was there a danger of being drawn into the Napoleonic Wars raging in Europe, but as the century began, America was hardly a financially sound nation. The money supply was no more than $30 million, or less than six dollars per person. The nation's transportation network was so poorly developed that it cost $9.00 to both ship a ton of goods 3,000 miles from Europe to America's seacoast towns, as well as move the same goods 30 miles from the coast to the interior of the nation. Yet, America retained the same brash, ambitious nature that ignited the revolt against England a quarter century before. Even Thomas Jefferson's goal of reducing the size and power of the central government was shelved when Napoleon Bonaparte offered to sell 1.2 million acres in the Louisiana purchase, doubling the land size of the United States.

1800 Profile

John Ingles saw himself as a new breed of ambitious businessman, ready to reap the rewards of a new era of peace and prosperity after the turmoil of the prior two decades.

Life at Home

- John Ingles' community store was located on the west bank of the New River where the Great Wagon Road crossed at Ingles Ferry, Virginia.
- To weary travelers, the little community known as "Ferry Hill" offered food, shelter and hospitality as well as provisions; to locals, the store provided necessary tools, cloth, flour, medicine and even luxury items.
- John was also the owner of several parcels of land on both sides of the New River, which he had inherited from his father, William, who established a claim to this land prior to the French and Indian War and later launched several enterprises, including a ferry, a tavern, and a general store.
- Now, at the turn of a new century, the wars had ended, settlers were heading west in record numbers, and the Ferry Hill community was bustling with activity.
- That allowed the store to operate as a retail store for individual shoppers, a consignment venue for families throughout the neighborhood, and a regional depot handling large orders for other merchants.
- Success depended upon a steady flow of travelers, stocking the right quantity of merchandise, understanding the competition, and careful maintenance of financial records.
- Most resident customers lived off credit 10 to 12 months a year; individual accounts mostly were settled just once a year, following harvest time.
- Every transaction within the store was neatly recorded in a large day book, using a quill pen made at the store and dipped in ink created by the storeowner; manufactured writing pens made of fine steel in England were available at this time, but were rarely used in frontier Virginia.

John Ingles was an enterprising store owner in Ferry Hill, Virginia.

Margaret Crockett married John in 1794.

- Because some local farmers were afraid to keep money at home, John also served as a banker; the farmers simply deposited the harvest profit with John to withdraw when needed or to buy supplies throughout the year.
- John's best customer was also his cousin, John Draper, and owner of the Ferry Hill tavern.
- Another important partner, John Crockett, negotiated contracts with John for the purchase, shipping and hauling of supplies from Richmond and Baltimore.
- These three young men saw themselves as a new breed of ambitious and energetic businessmen, poised to enjoy the new era of peace and prosperity after the turbulence of the prior two decades.
- John Ingles married Margaret Crockett in 1794, and by 1800 they were living in a new frame house on the east side of the New River, a few hundred yards from the cabin where John's mother still lived.
- In the year 1800, John and Margaret had several young children, some slaves, and an extended family of siblings and cousins who lived along the New River.
- John's sister, Susannah, was married to Abram Trigg, a prosperous landowner and newly elected member of Congress.
- On the first day of January, 1800, the day book recorded that one of Trigg's sons, Daniel, came to the store to buy corduroy, tobacco, a hank silk, paper, three bushels of salt, and a sack bag.
- Another nephew, William Trigg, appeared later that week to buy a double-bladed knife.
- Susannah herself came in to buy sheep shears, two papers of pins, five pounds of coffee, one soup spoon, five skeins of thread, 12 pounds of sugar, and one five-pound loaf of sugar.
- John was the principal buyer for the store, which required him to make periodic trips to Richmond and Baltimore to select goods from other merchants.
- His wife and sisters helped prepare his shopping list, suggesting items popular in sophisticated homes back East as well as community needs like teapots, tureens, measuring tins, candlesticks, funnels, earthen plates, cups and saucers, decanters, pitchers, glasses and chamber pots.

John and his family lived happily in a newly built home on the east bank of the New River.

- Inventory for meal preparation was becoming more sophisticated, too; the store carried Hysom, Bohea, and green tea, beeswax, peppermint, nutmeg, molasses, allspice and rhubarb, as well as sugar, salt, coffee, hams, rice, brandy and cheese.
- To try to keep up with the latest fashions, the store carried 40 different styles of fabric, including chintz, scarlet cardinal, striped coating, Nankeen, gingham, India cotton and calico.
- Other items of clothing were available, ready-made, such as cloaks, shawls, fine hats, gloves, knee buckles, bonnets, garters, stockings and boots.
- To make life easier for the men, the store carried lead, powder, shot, fish hooks, gun flints, sickles, scythes, claw hammers, augers, awl blades, steel, pewter, compasses, door latches, files, rasps, pocket knives, drawing knives, shovels, tongs, whetstones, riding whips, men's and ladies' saddles, and bridles.

Life at Work

- John Ingles spent much of his 12-hour day serving the needs of his customers: filling orders, making entries in the day book, balancing accounts, and making trips to market.
- He also managed a farm with the help of several slaves, where he raised cattle and other livestock, and grew crops of corn, hemp and oats.
- Running a profitable store involved both bartering with customers, who exchanged potash and beeswax for pen knives and cloth, and negotiating with wholesalers.
- With a wholesaler of goods, cash was king—but whose cash?
- The currency might be in British or Spanish coins, state-issued paper money or federal currency.
- Failure to fully understand the highly volatile exchange rate of a large transaction could result in bankruptcy for a small store.

Forty varieties of the latest fabrics were sold in the Ingles' store.

- In addition to the complexity of the exchange rates for the various state and federal money, John handled goods from England, France and Spain and needed to intimately understand the packaging and weight measurements of each country.
- Even measuring off cloth required special skills and a separate table.
- Years earlier, Margaret Ingles had marked off a section of the counter with brass tacks in which a yard was divided into four squares with each square divided into 2¼-inch segments known as thumbs—an ancient measurement system that pronounced the length of a man's thumb to the second joint to be 2¼ inches, or a rule of thumb.
- The placement of the brass tacks on her counter allowed her to quickly measure cloth for a customer no matter the pattern she favored: four quarters represented one American yard, three quarters was one Ell Flemish, five quarters was one Ell English and six quarters one Ell French.
- In addition, she had to know that three barley-corns made one inch, 40 feet of round timber or 50 feet of hewn timber equaled one ton, or that a properly stacked cord of wood measured eight feet long by four feet wide and four feet high.
- Once that was mastered, John and Margaret had to set the price they wanted for the store goods, incorporating the costs of going to market, their ability to replace sold goods, the price they had been charged, and then, of course, profit.
- To assist their memories, code phrases were marked on the products such as Black horse, So friendly, Now be sharp or any other letter combinations in which no letter was repeated to serve as a reminder of the asking price.
- Not everyone was charged the same price.
- Once, when John got wind that the Brown family had bought an entire set of pots and pans from a Yankee traveling salesman, he kept their prices high for a year as payback.
- Buying from a stranger like that offended John.
- Cousin John Draper, as innkeeper, ordered great quantities of produce and supplies through the store; during the first half of the year, orders were filled for French brandy (15 gallons and two quarts), 50 pounds of sugar, 6.5 pounds of beeswax, 35 gallons of rum, and six pounds of coffee.

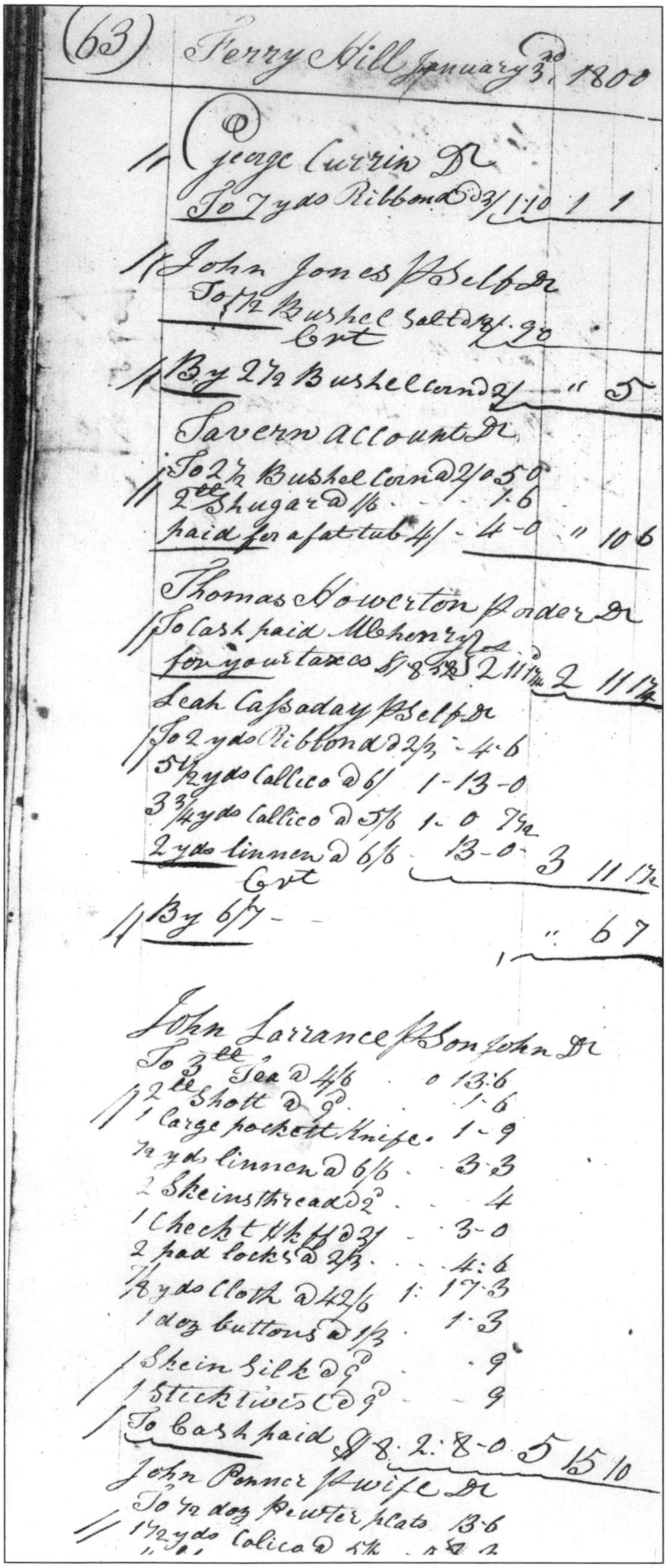

(63) Ferry Hill January 3rd 1800

George Currin Dr
To 7 yds Ribbon @ 3/ 1 1 0 1 1

John Jones pr Self Dr
To 1/2 Bushel Salt @ 8/ . 90
Crt
By 2 1/2 Bushel corn @ 2/ " 5

Tavern account Dr
To 2 1/2 Bushel Corn @ 2/ 0 5 0
2 lb Shugar @ 1/6 . 7.6
paid for a fat tub 4/ - 4-0 " 10 6

Thomas Howerton pr order Dr
To cash paid McHenry
for your taxes $/8 3/2 2 11 1/2 2 11 1/2

Leah Cassaday pr Self Dr
To 2 yds Ribbon @ 2/3 - 4-6
5 1/2 yds Callico @ 6/ 1-13-0
3 3/4 yds Callico @ 5/6 1-0 7 1/2
2 yds linnen @ 6/6 13-0 3 11 1/2
Crt
By 6/7 " 6 7

John Larrance pr Son John Dr
To 3 lb Tea @ 4/6 0 13:6
2 lb Shott @ 9d 1-6
1 Large pockett Knife 1-9
1/2 yds linnen @ 6/6 3-3
2 Skeins thread @ 2d 4
1 Checkt Hkff @ 3/ 3-0
2 pad locks @ 2/3 4:6
7/8 yds Cloth @ 42/6 1: 17:3
1 doz buttons @ 1/3 1-3
1 Skein Silk @ 9d 9
1 Stick twist @ 9d 9
To Cash paid $8 2:8-0 5 15 10

John Penner pr wife Dr
To 1/2 doz Pewter plate 13-6
1 1/2 yds Calico @ 5/6

Customer inventory for the Ferry Hill store.

- He, too, encountered ordering complexities in his business: four gills made one pint, 31.5 gallons made a barrel, 42 gallons a tierce, 63 gallons a hogshead and two hogsheads equaled one pipe.
- Only a few women's names appeared in the Ferry Hill day book in the year 1800, although several widows made purchases or received credit on their own individual accounts.
- Ruthey Beckett provided for herself by spinning and was credited with sundry spinning worth two pounds, five shillings.
- Other women came and went at the store to conduct business, but they were listed under their husbands' names.
- Some women received credit for weaving fabric or spinning thread, while others must have spent considerable time sewing, as evidenced by the high number of purchases of imported fabrics, ribbons, buttons, and sewing needles.
- Their husbands hauled in kegs of butter, bushels of corn and other produce, receiving credit that allowed them to purchase tools, pewter, gunpowder, nails, and other necessary and useful goods.
- In this way, the store took in many locally produced items such as corn, whiskey or skeins of thread, listing each transaction under the name of a certain customer with "cr," or credit, and then selling these items to account holders, making the notation "d" for debit.
- Both men and women also earned store credit by bringing in skins, whiskey, butter and other produce.
- Many of the goods handled at the store could be kept on the shelves indefinitely, but other "goods" could only be transported or hauled in certain seasons, requiring the coordinated efforts of a great number of people.
- For example, John Ingles had to make arrangements for cattle to be gathered, driven and kept in pastures over the course of about 35-40 days.
- About 40 men signed on to drive cattle to Richmond and received pay for their labor.

Life in the Community: Ferry Hill, Virginia

- In 1800 the Ferry Hill community had become a crossroads—and an oasis—for American pioneers seeking new lands to the west in the wilds of Tennessee and Kentucky.
- Families living in eastern Virginia who were desirous of moving to Kentucky with their household furnishings, livestock and slaves had two choices: either travel over land by way of the Great Wagon Road through southwestern Virginia, or go by wagon to Cleveland, where they were transferred onto a riverboat and floated down the Ohio River.
- Thousands of families chose to take the wagon road through southwest Virginia, crossing the New River at Ingles Ferry, before continuing westward over the Cumberland Gap into Kentucky.
- Early on, John's father William Ingles recognized the economic significance of this river crossing, and records show that he obtained a license to operate a ferry as early as 1762.
- He also purchased land on both shores of the river, building a fort, cabin and farm on the eastern side, and on the opposite shore, a ferry house, tavern and store.
- To distinguish the two communities that developed, the Ingleses came to refer to the farm on the eastern shore as Ingleside, and the settlement across the river as Ferry Hill.

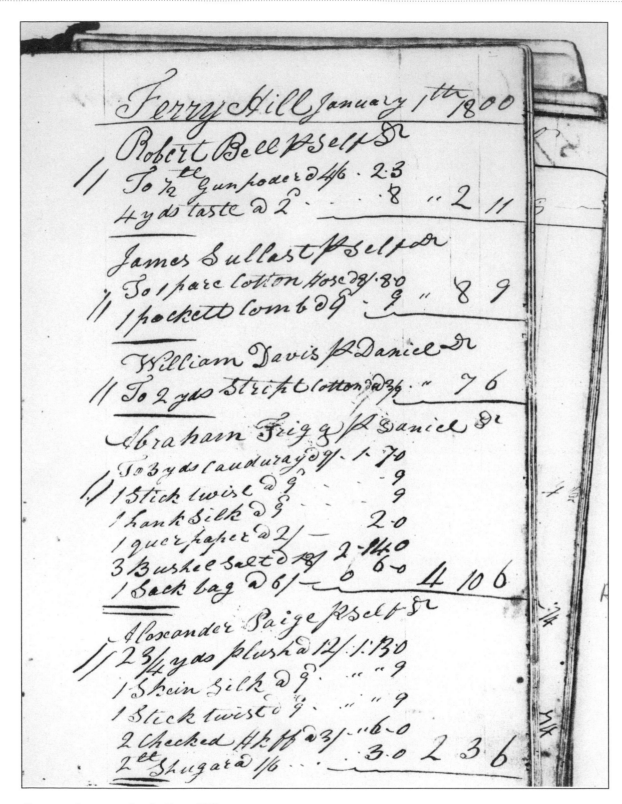

Customer inventory for the Ferry Hill store.

- Travelers probably referred to Ingles Ferry as their destination, but could have obtained a variety of services on either shore, including lodging, fodder and pasturage for livestock; food and drink; and supplies for the journey.
- The Ferry Hill community consisted of people with many skills, including farmers, cobblers, blacksmiths, tailors, spinners and weavers who lived near the ferry, many of whom offered services or produce to the families heading west or to the wagon drivers hauling freight back East.
- Breeding thoroughbred horses also was becoming popular in southwest Virginia.
- One breeder, who owned a stud horse named Federalist, carefully kept "a list of mares brought to my horse, Federalist, the season of 1801 at four dollars each and a quarter to the groom."
- Although most of the larger rivers in Virginia served as major conduits for trade and transportation, the New River, which originated in North Carolina and flowed in a northwesterly direction, represented more of an obstacle than an aid to transportation.
- Due to warfare and the threat of Indian attacks, Virginia's western frontier had been slow to develop roads, towns and commercial enterprises.
- By the late 1790s, however, local officials were planning the first towns in the region, such as Christiansburg and Blacksburg, and men were purchasing lots for homes and businesses.
- A community known as New Dublin, just a few miles farther west along the wagon road from Ferry Hill, had taverns and stores in operation during this same time period.
- John Allen, who had a license to operate a tavern in New Dublin, purchased 22¼ gallons of whiskey from the Ferry Hill store in June 1799; in March 1799, he had brought in 29 pounds of skins for credit.
- Another store in operation during these years was run by the Cloyd family.
- Located about 10 miles away from the Ferry Hill store, the Cloyd family store served a community along a new secondary road; based on the day book of both stores, they had 80 customers in common.
- Other business ventures were being created throughout the region, including John Crockett's involvement in ordering and transporting goods to his business on the Clinch River.
- Recordkeeping could be complex.
- Most families, especially the Scots-Irish, kept alive the tradition of naming children for their parents and grandparents, thus producing a bewildering jumble of similar names.
- Compounding this problem were difficult names and poor spelling; one German family had its name entered variously as Stobaugh, Stobough, Stobuck, Stoebuck, and Stobo.

Opposite banks of the New River.

Ferry Hill Entry for May 10, 1800
Account: John Crockett & Company (Virginia Money)

Debit:	Item:	Price (Pounds/Shillings/Pence)		
	To amount goods sent Clinch	695	5	8
	Expenses of Waggonage to New River from Baltimore	41	8	0
	To expenses paid to Clinch	2	2	7
	Total	738	16	37

Credit:	Item:			
	By cash per John Crockett	143	14	9
	By John Inglish put in goods	143	14	37

Entry for September 5, 1880
Account: John Crockett & Company (Virginia Money)

Debit:	Item:	Price (Pounds/Shillings/Pence)		
	To 92 lbs. nails	3	9	0
	75 lbs. steel	3	5	7½
	50 lbs. Copras	1	12	6
	31 lbs. alum	1	3	3
	100 lbs. lead	2	10	0

Entry for September 12, 1800:
Account: John Crockett & Co. (per Wilson)

Debit:	Item:	Price (Pounds/Shillings/Pence)		
	1¾ yards casimer	1	6	3
	1 dozen buttons	3		
	2 large buttons	6		
	1 stick twist&hand silk	6		
	¼ yd. Holland	1	10	4½

Ferry Hill store diary.

DRY GOODS. GROCERIES. NOTIONS.

HARDWARE,

And everything generally kept in a Country Store.

Goods sold Cheap for Cash or Good Produce.

HISTORICAL SNAPSHOT
1800

- The Library of Congress in Washington, DC, was created with a $5,000 allocation
- The French regained the territory of Louisiana from Spain by secret treaty
- John Adams became the first president to live in the White House
- William Herschel discovered infrared radiation from the sun
- The population of New York topped 60,000
- The world population was believed to be 800 million people, double the population in 1500
- Rev. Mason Locke Weems authored *A History of the Life and Death, Virtues and Exploits of General George Washington*
- Martha Washington set all her slaves free
- Robert Fulton tested a 20-foot model of his torpedo-armed submarine
- In the presidential voting, Thomas Jefferson and Aaron Burr tied, forcing the decision into the House of Representatives, which selected Jefferson on the thirty-sixth round
- A letter mailed from Savannah, Georgia, to Portland, Maine, required 20 days
- Congress convened for the first time in Washington, DC
- John Chapman, known as Johnny Appleseed, began planting tree orchards across western Pennsylvania, Ohio and Indiana
- Alessandro Volta demonstrated an early battery known as an electricity pile
- Belgium's textile industry dramatically expanded after a working spinning machine was smuggled from Britain and then widely copied
- The free black community of Philadelphia petitioned Congress to abolish slavery
- The first commercial Valentine greeting card appeared

John Adams.

Selected Prices

Backgammon Box $2.50
Chair, Mahogany $4.58
Harrow, Iron-Toothed $3.00
Hay, 1,000 Pounds $5.00
Hoe $0.80
Pistols, Pair $25.00
Pork, Pound $0.06
Spinning Wheel $2.00
Theater Ticket, Box Seat $1.00
Tobacco, 100 Pounds $5.00

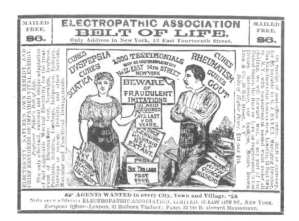

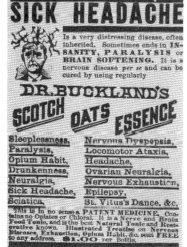

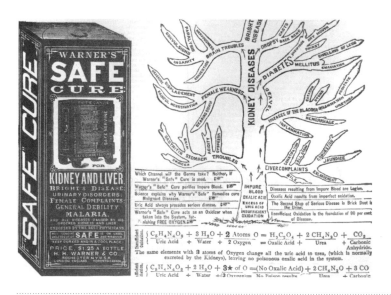

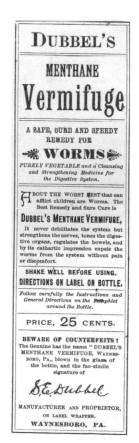

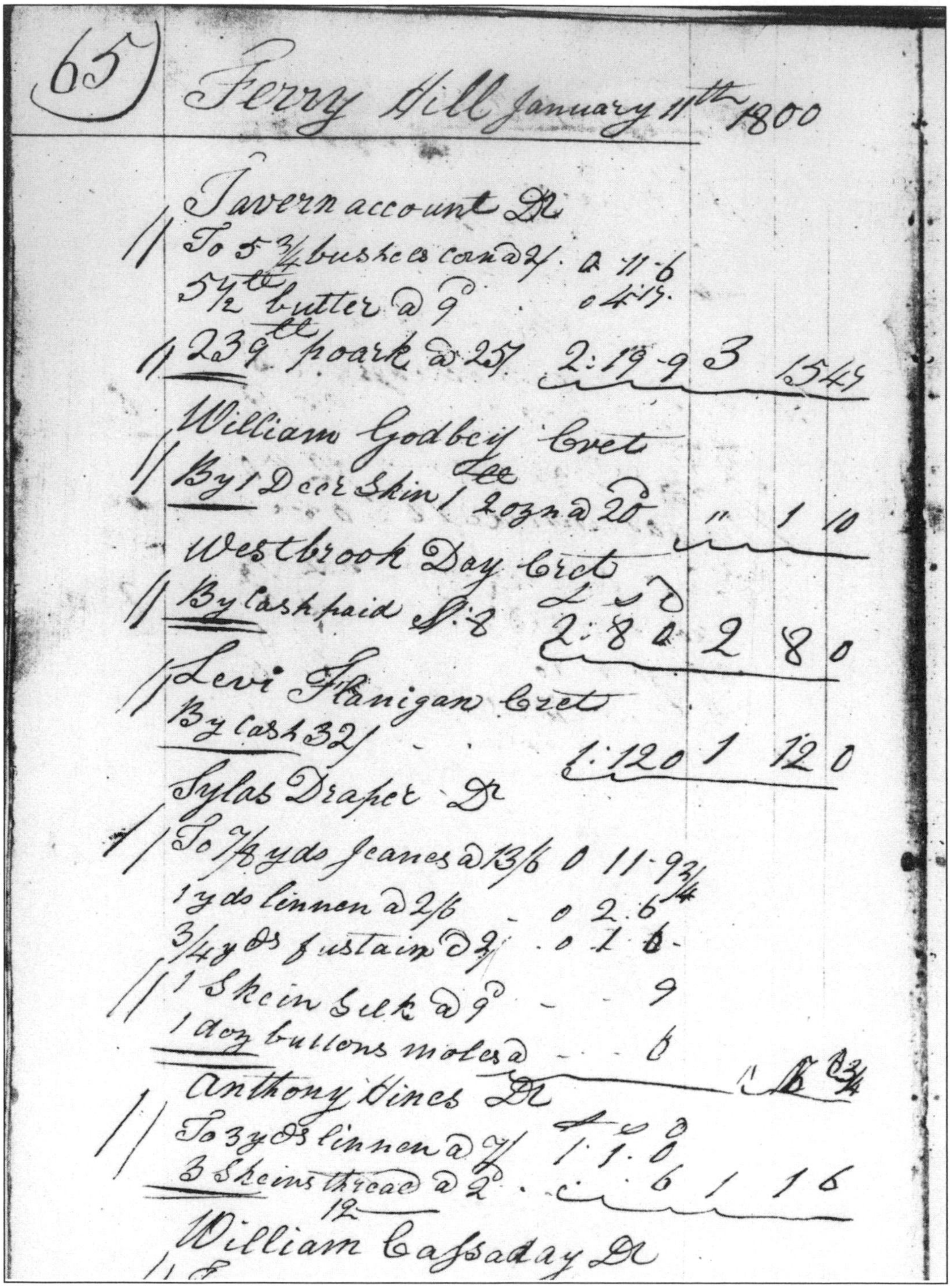

65 Ferry Hill January 11th 1800

Tavern account Dr
To 5 3/4 bushels corn @ 2/ . 0 11 6
5 1/2 lb butter @ 9 . 0 4 1½
239 lb poark @ 25/ 2:19:9 3 15 4½

William Godbey Cret
By 1 Deer Skin 1 2 oz @ 20 11 1 10

Westbrook Day Cret
By cash paid £:8 £ s d 2:8:0 2 8 0

Levi Flanigan Cret
By cash 32/ 1:12:0 1 12 0

Sylas Draper Dr
To 7/8 yds jeanes @ 13/6 0 11 9¾
1 yds linnen @ 2/6 0 2 6
3/4 yds fustain @ 2/ 0 1 6
1 Skein silk @ 9 9
1 doz buttons moles @ 6

Anthony Hines Dr
To 3 yds linnen @ 7/ 1 1 0
3 skeins thread @ 2 6 1 1 6

William Cassaday Dr

Customer inventory for the Ferry Hill store.

One day's shopping list for Abram Trigg and his wife Susannah:

Item	Price (in pounds/shillings/pence)
1 doz shallow earthen plates	12
½ doz soop plates	6
1 large jug	4/6
1 ditto blew	3
1 doz cups & sersers	9
1 mug	1/3
2 dishes	4
2 ditto	5
22 pounds shugar	1/9/4
2 chamber pots	6

Estate of Henry Helvey— inventory—Ferry Hill, September 17, 1792, recorded September 12, 1800:

Cows and calves; 10 sheep; 14 geese; mares, colts, horses; 24 hogs; wagon and gears; plow and harrow; kettle and hooks; hoes, mattock, saws, augers, files, gimblets, chisels, square, planes, hammer and anvil, loom, gears, saddlebags, saddle, chest, 2 casks and a cock, bed and furniture, tubs, churns, pails, kegs, barrels, large wheel, three gun barrels, lock and "bayonette," skillet, pots and hooks, dishes, 19 spoons, "basons," pewter, tea pot, watering can, iron spindle, crank, several pounds of old iron, 30 pounds of wool, three bee-hives, razors, bottles, bags, 330 pounds of new iron, and cash.

Ague Cure or Blood Purifier (1)

Take one pound of sassafras, one pound of sarsaparilla, one pound spikenard, one pound wild cherry bark, one-half pound bloodroot, one-fourth ounce of mandrake, put in four gallons of water and boil until reduced to one gallon. Strain and add one quart of rye whiskey and one-half ounce of oil of peppermint. Adult dose is one tablespoonful three times a day. (I)

Compound Ague Pills (2)

Take extract of Beef Gall and best Peruvion Bark; of each equal parts by weight; mix them well together; add sufficient water or book-binder's paste to make a stiff mass. Make the pills of common size. (C)

Antispasmodick Powders (3)

Take meadow cabbage, Indian turnip and pleurisy root, equal quantities, all made fine and well mixed together. Dose from a quarter to three quarters of a teaspoonful. If all the roots cannot be had, they may be used separately given in a tablespoonful of water. (C)

Apoplexy (4)

The head is to be shaved and cupped, a blister applied to the back of the neck and the head, and mustard poultices to the feet. (M)

Asthma (5)

A muskrat skin worn over the lungs with the fur side next to the body is certain relief for asthma. (I)

Asthma (6)

The fried roots of the thorn apple and skunk cabbage are smoked through a pipe. Take a quantity of Indian tobacco leaves, stem and pods, put them into a bottle and fill it with brandy or spirits, let it stand several days; this tincture should be taken at a teaspoonful at a time. (M)

Bleeding and Cuts (7)

To stop blood, bind on goose feathers, pressing them into the wound. Allow them to remain until they come off.

or

Tie up fresh cuts with warm ashes from the stove.

or

Stop bleeding by placing soot from a stove pipe on the cut. (This however may leave a black mark that cannot be removed.) (I)

Bowel Inflammation (8)

Take soft clay from the bottom of the creek where the water runs all the time and spread it about one inch thick on cheesecloth. Cover with another cloth to protect the clothing, and apply it as a poultice. (I)

Boils (9)

Peel the skin carefully from a boiled egg, wet it and apply it to the boil. It will draw the matter and relieve the soreness in a few hours. (I)

Gathering Breasts (10)

Melt together mutton tallow, beeswax and flaxseed oil, spread on a cloth and apply to the breast as hot as can be borne. When cool apply another. (I)

Cataarh (11)

Give twenty drops of hartshorn in half a pint of warm vinegar whey. Hoarhound and boneset tea taken in large quantities are very helpful also. (M)

or (12)

Make use of snuff several times a day, made of Indian physick and wild ginger in equal parts. (C)

Catarrhal Fever (13)

Grease the chest well and apply a hot pack made by filling a sack of suitable size with bran heated till brown. Have it as hot as the patient can bear and renew with another like it as fast as it cools off. Bruise fresh rue, put it on cloth and lay on the forehead, letting it come down over the temples, and on the wrists and the soles of the feet. (I)

Remedies for physical ailments.

"Venison, a Tour of America in 1798, 1799, 1800," by Richard Parkinson, London, 1805:

Venison is brought to market in waggons, and sold at the price of beef; it is shocking stuff. It is commonly salted, smoked, and served up raw at breakfast. When dressed in the fresh state, is usual to cut it into a saddle, by chopping the shanks off about the pope's eye, and just warming it at the fire: every gentleman has a chafing dish, and may be said to be his own cook; for, what with the wood-embers and the stew of the venison, the room is like the kitchen of Dolly's chop-house in London. About eight gentleman will eat all the flesh off the hind-quarters, and nearly pick the bones.

Letter by Elizabeth Southgate to her mother, Boston, Massachusetts, 1800:

Now Mama, what do you think I am going to ask for? A wig. Eleanor has got a new one just like my hair and only five dollars, Mrs. Mayo has one just like it. I must either cut my hair or have one, I cannot dress it at all stylish. Mrs. Coffin bought Eleanor's and says she will write to Mrs. Sumner to get me one just like it; how much time it will save in one year we could save that in pins and paper, besides the trouble. At the Assembly I was quite ashamed of my head, for nobody has long hair. If you consent to my having one do send me over a five dollar bill by the post immediately after you received this, for I am in hopes to have it for the next Assembly do send me word immediately if you can let me have one. Eliza

WANT ADS: New-England Palladium, Boston, Massachusetts, October 29, 1802:

Lamp Lighters Wanted

Wanted men to Light the Town lamps, the ensuing season, it is expected the applicants will bring a good recommendation those who lit the lamps last season, will have a preference, if they apply immediately to David Tilden, Battery-March-Street

* *

Wanted to hire

A smart girl that understands cooking and domestic housework. None need apply unless they can produce good recommendations.

* *

Ten Dollars Reward

Ran away from this subscriber, a Negro man named Prince 19 years of age, about six feet high, walks a little slopping, combs his hair, sometimes wears it tied; wore and carried away with him a gray striped outside jacket, one striped Nankeen under jacket, one silk ditto, striped Nankeen overalls, a pair of boots. Whoever will take up said runaway and returning to subscriber or secure him in any of our gaols so that his master may have him again, shall receive the above reward, also any necessary charges. All makers of vessels are forbid carrying said Negro off under the penalty of law, signed Oliver Arnold October 8, 1802

* *

AT SAMUEL CLAP'S OFFICE

Four packages just arrived, containing a variety of elegant and fashionable fox, luster wolf, bear, Russian hare, real sable, muffs and tippets, swansdown bosom friends and stocks, ell wide shawls, lined with fur; ladies black gypsy hats, men's and boys hats, ladies shoes, lined and trimmed with fur.

* *

FOR NORFOLK

The fast-sailing fch'r Greyhound, now lying at the Long Wharf, will positively sail in 10 days, having part of her cargo engage. For freight or passage, apply to Cornelius Coolidge No 32, Long Wharf

"Bedsteads for the Sick," *The Domestic Encyclopedia; or, A Dictionary of Facts and Useful Information,* by A.F.M. Willich, 1802:

BEDSTEAD, a frame for supporting him a bed. Among the various materials used for bedsteads, iron is not only the most durable, but the most beneficial with respect to health. Oak is excellent for this purpose, being almost impervious to worms, if felled in the proper season, and allowed to become dry; but cedar, were it not for its strong odour, would be still more efficacious in preventing the inroads of bugs, or other vermin. Hence, the beams and posts of a bedstead, made of any hardwood, might be inlaid with cedar.

On this occasion, we cannot, in justice to Mr. Lambert of Berwick-street, Soho, omit to give a concise description of his newly invented Bedstead of the Sick and Wounded, which he terms the Royal Patent Fracture Bed, which is ably calculated to alleviate the painful situation of the aged, the infirm or diseased. This ingenious contrivance, therefore, affords a comfortable accommodation to persons confined by fractures, gout, palsy, &c. It is particularly adapted to lying-in women. The bed may be made, and the linens changed, without in the slightest manner disturbing the patient, which renders it highly serviceable in camps and hospitals. . . . The whole apparatus may be attached to any four post bedstead by a common carpenter.

BEDSTEAD for the SICK & WOUNDED, Invented by Mr Lambert.

"Definitions," *Schoolmaster's Assistant,* **by Nathan Daboll, 1802:**

Gross weight, which is the whole weight of any sort of goods, together with the box, cask, or bag, etc., which contains them.

Tare, which is an allowance, made by the buyer, for the weight of the box, cask, or bag, etc. which contains the goods bought, and is either at so much per box, etc. or at so much per cwt, or at so much in the whole gross weight.

Trett, which is an allowance of 4 pounds in every 104 pounds for waste, dust, etc.

Suttle, is what remains after one or two allowances have been deducted.

1805 Profile

New England-bred Edward Jenkins had anticipated that practicing law in the Southern United States would be unique; he never imagined how unique.

Life at Home

- A native of Farmington, Connecticut, Edward Jenkins was the youngest child of a Revolutionary officer and a direct descendent of a minister who shared in the founding of the colony of Connecticut.
- Finding his place in the world was important, as was a sense of adventure.
- His opportunity came in the form of a letter while attending Yale College in 1804.
- The communication was from his older brother John who invited him to join his successful law firm in Columbia, South Carolina, upon graduation.
- A few months later, with his newly acquired degree in hand, Edward began the long journey to South Carolina via a clipper ship.
- Upon arrival in Charleston, South Carolina, he bought a horse and rode for four days to reach the state's new capital in Columbia.
- As he crossed the Congaree River, he could see the State House two miles away through the trees.
- The sight of the building pleased him; although his journey was coming to an end, Edward was not in high spirits.
- According to his journal, he had been reflecting—glumly—during his bug-swatting travels about his future in this foreign-looking place.
- Arriving at his brother's office a few days earlier than expected, Edward caught John by surprise.

Edward Jenkins graduated from Yale College and joined his brother's law firm in Columbia, South Carolina.

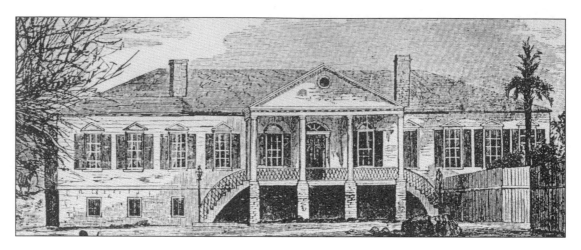

Edward's second job was at the College of South Carolina.

- The long anticipated welcome was pleasant but brief; John had to leave for the circuit court straight away but directed Edward to a boarding house across the street.
- It was an excellent choice.
- In addition to working with his brother, Edward had arranged a second job as a tutor at the newly developed College of South Carolina.
- The college had about 30 students, many of whom were staying at the same boarding house, along with a number of tutors.
- Even though the college buildings were still under construction only a quarter of a mile from the State House, near to the town center, they gave the appearance of being in a reclusive location, Edward observed in his journal.
- There were no houses around the property and the surrounding land was dominated by lofty pines and wild shrubs.
- Two long buildings had been completed to house the chapel, a library, a Philosophical Chamber and Recitation Rooms.
- Plans to build a President's house, dining hall and Professor's house were awaiting money provided by the state's legislature; $50,000 from the public treasury had been allocated to build the first two buildings.
- When not practicing law, Edward often met his students at the boarding house, which was situated perfectly between the school and his brother's office.
- Time was spent helping them improve upon their Latin and Greek memorization; to his disappointment, his students were often distracted or preoccupied with other activities in the boarding house.
- At Yale, students rarely spent much time with a tutor until it was close to the examination period, but the needs were greater here.
- Fortunately for Edward, he was paid for assistance during the prescribed times and not on the success of the academic performance.
- Legal work was Edward's primary obligation.
- His brother John's practice required a lot of support.
- Mornings were spent writing briefs and affidavits for the courts, always preparing numerous copies—each the length of half a sheet.
- A copy was required for the judge prior to trial.
- If it was a case for the Court of Appeals, one copy was required for each of the six justices.
- As Edward recorded in his journal, it was "a common saying that the Carolinians are industrious in nothing but law business."

- Whatever the truth of that remark, Edward was pleased with the efficiencies within the South Carolina courtroom.
- A judge rarely adjourned the court for dinner and tolerated no delays.
- If a juryman or officer of the court was not at his post, the judge often reprimanded or fined the offender.
- It was also the practice to have two sets of jurymen available so that as soon as one case retired to make a verdict, the other was available to begin a new trial.
- Often Edward had to travel for work, and it bothered him to do so on a Sunday, a day for him to attend church and respect God.
- Many of the Carolinians did not seem to focus too much on this subject, although the laws did not expressly encourage the violation of the Sabbath.
- But those violations did occur, especially within the law profession.
- It was not uncommon for lawyers to be detained at court until Saturday night and then be obliged to attend another court hearing 20-40 miles away the next Monday morning, which resulted in travel on the Sabbath.
- It was also common for the legislature to begin its sessions on Monday, thus requiring people to travel on Sundays.
- Regardless, Edward tried to attend a church service even when traveling.
- On one such journey in the western part of South Carolina near Table Mountain, he and his traveling companion heard the shrill-sounding voice of a mountain preacher along the Woolenoy River.
- The gloom of the forest only served to heighten the sacred silence of the scene with the preacher surrounded by oak trees.
- The lawyers' entrance caused a bit of a disruption to the sermon, but they were welcomed to sit and listen.
- Edward heard the whispers of the congregation, made up entirely of mountain people.
- "I had heard of the simple manners of the mountain people, but I had not expected to find simplicity itself out-simplified," he recorded.
- Many of the women were without stockings or shoes.
- Their attire only comprised a shirt and petticoat.
- The men, including the preacher, were mostly barefooted and, using a common phrase, in their shirtsleeves.
- After the service, the preacher was kind enough to invite Edward and his companion for dinner at his one-story frame house.
- The meal consisted of fresh pork and sweet potatoes cut up and set on a large tin without any bread or sauce; salt was the only accompaniment for the meal.
- A chest not higher than Edward's knees served as a table; he and his companion sat in the only chairs in the house.
- The preacher employed the end of another chest for his seat.
- On another occasion, when traveling to Camden with another lawyer, Edward caused a bit of consternation on the topic of law and natural liberty.
- The topic was struck when Edward was complimenting the merits of Connecticut's laws over South Carolina's.
- Edward expressed the view—favored by many in New England—that some regulations were needed for the greater good of all, especially to prevent harm toward others or property.
- His companion was outraged over the suggestion and informed Edward that such regulations would be despised by Carolinians, who have a high sense of liberty.
- For many in South Carolina, the opinion prevailed that every man had a right to do what he pleased; the public has no right to interfere in his affairs.
- Eventually the two men agreed to disagree on the subject.

Invention of the cotton gin allowed the work of 2,000 slaves to be replaced by two horses, a man and two boys.

- A short time later, Edward returned one forenoon to Columbia by the way of Charles Pickney's home and watched a group of negroes collecting cotton.
- The negroes were busily cleaning the cotton from its seed using a cotton gin; Edward had no conception of Mr. Eli Whitney's device until he saw it in operation.
- A first-rate gin, he was told, when put in motion by two horses and well attended by a man and two boys, could clean as much cotton in one day as 2,000 slaves could by hand.
- Based on Edward's observation, if one quarter of it was true, then the labor savings must be prodigious.

Life at Work
- Legal work dominated Edward Jenkins's time.
- He often spent considerable time at what Carolinians called the Court of Common Pleas.
- For him, it would be better understood as Court of Common Law.
- Typically, it involved criminal cases, both great and small, as well as civil cases that were beyond the jurisdiction of the justice of the peace.
- Edward usually handled cases of debt, agreements made orally or in writing, which did not exceed $12.00.
- The justice court could handle cases up to $75.00, but Edward's brother John traditionally handled these larger cases.
- The business of the court was preceded by a sermon; traditionally a minister was paid $10.00 or $12.00 for each session.

- Most of the forenoon was taken up in the forming of juries and calling the cases.
- The oddness of names around the Columbia region amused Edward, particularly the German inhabitants, whose names were rather awkward and harsh to hear.
- He wondered why many had not changed the pronunciation to soften the sound or adapt them to an English idiom.
- Outside of the Germans, Edward was unsettled by the appearance and manners of the South Carolina country people.
- Edward saw them as rude and unpolished.
- Both men and women dressed in coarse homespun cotton of a mixed color with no consideration of fashion, taste or refinement about them.
- Women wore short loose-gowns, petticoats and sun-bonnets of the same cloth; many filled the courtroom without any sense of common decency.
- The Carolinians often crowded the bar and peered over the shoulders of the lawyers sitting at their benches.
- Edward also came into contact with many of the state's politicians working at the State House.
- As efficient as the legal system may be, he questioned the industriousness of the politicians at the State House.
- The members took more satisfaction in walking about the streets looking important than addressing the public's business.
- When the two houses of the legislature were called into session, three or four days were required to form a quorum because so many legislators were otherwise occupied elsewhere in Columbia.
- Observing the legislative process was a welcome diversion for Edward, and when time permitted he often watched the proceedings.
- One piece of legislation pertaining to the slave trade caught his attention.
- One of the members of the House of Representatives had introduced a bill for shutting the ports for importation of slaves into the state.

Importing slaves into the region was hotly debated by the South Carolina legislature.

- The commercial activity of importing slaves into the state was prohibited by law from 1787 to 1803, but the slave trade resumed in late 1803 and would remain legal until January 1, 1808.
- Heatedly, the South Carolina legislature debated the issue.
- One side warned against the danger of increasing the number of blacks in the country and the injustice of human trafficking.
- It was said that increasing the number of slaves would destroy the equality of republican institutions and injure the real interest of South Carolina.
- Opposition to the bill did not directly argue the religious morality of the issue, but reminded the legislative body of its responsibility to uphold the interest of the state's constituents.
- The coastal plantations had grown prosperous and wealthy through the use of slave labor—especially now that the cotton gin had made cotton farming so profitable.
- The issue of supporting slavery would be unthinkable for most of Edward's New England.
- He was amazed that some of those strongly advocating the slave trade were steady Baptists.
- When the bill reached the South Carolina Senate, those who were against closing the ports to slave importation had the vote of 16 members, while the opposition had a vote of 15 members.
- The plan to prohibit further importation of slaves died by one vote.
- Edward observed the joy of the senators as some rose to congratulate each other with handshakes across tables and chairs.
- "Horrid exhibition of Horrid Republicanism!" he wrote in his journal that night.
- A week later Columbia was alarmed over a rumor of an insurrection of the negroes on the other side of the river a few miles away.
- Edward was told the negroes planned to first take possession of the munitions depot at the State House.
- Edward remained in his boarding house for most of the night and waited for news of the insurrection.
- He watched as the militia prepared to defend the town around sunset.
- No news of serious danger arrived.
- Prior to supper the owner wanted bread from the bakery for the evening's meal.
- No one in his boarding house wanted to leave out of fear.
- So Edward agreed to go with the owner, who crowded him closely out of fear being out on the streets.
- By nine o'clock that evening, the town was bustling; the militia was patrolling on both foot and horseback.
- An artillery piece was placed in a prominent location in front of the State House.
- One negro, who was suspected in being part of the rumored uprising, was committed to jail.
- The General Assembly stayed in the State House conducting business through the evening with the purpose of adjourning the session.
- The following morning no insurrection had occurred.
- One negro man was shot dead by the evening patrols on the north end of Columbia.
- It was later discovered he was following his master at no great distance.
- Both had been out of town, had not heard of the alarm and paid no regard to the patrol.

The Congaree River, South Carolina.

- By the afternoon the town was calm and the legislature quickly departed to return for the Christmas season.
- "It is indeed a calm after a storm; and it is really pleasurable to have once more such a season of tranquility," Edward wrote.

Life in the Community: Columbia, South Carolina

- A small town, only two miles square in the center of South Carolina, Columbia was the second planned capital in the United States.
- The state's capital was designated by the South Carolina General Assembly in 1787 based on its location at the state's geographic center near a traditional Indian gathering spot along the Congaree River.
- In 1792 the city and the surrounding area had a population of 3,921, 37 percent of whom were negroes.
- By 1799, Col. Wade Hampton erected a cotton gin near town that increased commercial activity; the following year, boats departed with 70 tons of cargo full of cotton, tobacco, corn, beeswax and other commercial articles.
- With the growth of commerce, businessmen started other industries; in 1802 an oil mill was built.
- The oil was extracted from agriculture products found in the area, especially cottonseed; one bushel of cottonseed could produce half a gallon of oil.
- Stephen Brown developed a rope walk in 1802 which promoted the cultivation of hemp by many of the local farmers.
- Within a year of operation, 80 tons of cordage, rope and cable were produced.
- Within a few years, Columbia saw the development of paper manufacturing and a brick kiln to support the city's rapid growth.
- Even with commerce growing, the city appeared small in size because much of the population worked on farms.
- During 1805, many of the streets were not yet opened, with only two or three buildings constructed upon them.

- It was common to discover several proposed streets in Columbia still unopened with bushes growing in the roads.
- Approximately a hundred buildings had been built by 1805, generally constructed of wood, and narrow to aid in ventilation.
- Because of the sandy soil in the area, the buildings were without cellars and sat upon a foundation of blocks or stones, which, too, were scarce.
- The dry and sandy soil produced little grass for ground cover.
- Only a few of the town's citizens were natives of South Carolina; some were from Virginia and the New England states.
- A fair number were foreigners from England, Scotland, Ireland, France and the various countries of the German Empire.

Stately South Carolina architecture.

HISTORICAL SNAPSHOT
1805

- The Michigan Territory was created and separated from the Indiana Territory; the city of Detroit was designated as its capital
- U.S. Marines attacked pirates on the Barbary Coast of North Africa on the shores of Tripoli
- Charles Wilson Peale founded the Pennsylvania Academy of Fine Arts
- Napoleon Bonaparte was crowned king of Italy
- The Lewis and Clark expedition crossed the Rocky Mountains and reached the Pacific Ocean
- American boxer Bill Richmond knocked out Jack Holmes in Kilburn Wells, England
- The Treaty of Pressburg ended hostilities between France and Austria
- Admiral Nelson defeated the French and Spanish fleet at the Battle of Trafalgar
- The *Times* of London published its first illustration January 10, showing the funeral of Lord Nelson
- The first American covered bridge spanned the Schuylkill River
- The Female Charitable Society, the first women's club, was organized in America
- William H. Wollaston discovered rhodium
- Tangerines reached Europe for the first time, coming directly from China
- Chief Justice Samuel Chase was acquitted by the Senate impeachment trial, ending the Republican campaign against the Federalist bench
- The first California orange grove was planted at San Gabriel Mission near Los Angeles
- Virginia required all freed slaves to leave the state or risk imprisonment or deportation
- The French Revolutionary calendar law was abolished

Selected Prices

Cider, Barrel	$1.50
Corn, Barrel	$3.33
Gunpowder, Pound	$0.40
Jars, Dozen	$1.60
Shoes, Women's	$1.00
Tomahawk	$0.25
Waistcoat	$2.00
Wardrobe, Mahogany	$6.00
Whip Saw	$5.00
Wool, Pound	.37½ cents

President Thomas Jefferson's defense of freedom of the press during his second inaugural address, 1805:

The artillery of the press has been leveled against us, charged with whatsoever its licentiousness could devise or dare. These abuses of an institution so important to freedom and science are deeply to be regretted, inasmuch as they tend to lessen its usefulness and to sap its safety. . . . Since truth and reason have maintained their ground against false opinions in league with false facts, the press, confined to truth, needs no other legal restraint; the public judgment will correct false reasoning and opinions on a full hearing of all parties, and no other definite line can be drawn between the inestimable liberty of the press and its demoralizing licentiousness.

Thomas Jefferson.

China's potential, statement of a South Carolina legislator, 1805:

In stating the inducements which exist for the exportation of specie thither, he observed that the population is so great in China, it cannot be increased—and public officers are appointed to go about the streets every morning, and bury or throw into the rivers the bodies of infants that have been cast out. This immense population makes the price of labor so very small that we in America and [Great Britain] who are accustom'd to such high wages and prices, can't have any conception of it. I have seen . . . a black silk vest that any beau in the States would be proud to wear, sold in Canton for seven pence (12½ cents) and a complete suit of nankeen from head to shoulders sold for half a dollar.

South Carolina College, excerpt from *A View of South Carolina, as Respects Her Natural and Civil Concerns*, by John Drayton, 1802:

And soon, we hope, the *South-Carolina College* will rise an ornament to the town; respectable from its establishment; but still more from the learning and friendship, which a national institution, like this, cannot fail to promote among the youth from all parts of this state; an object, particularly desirable to all true lovers of their country.

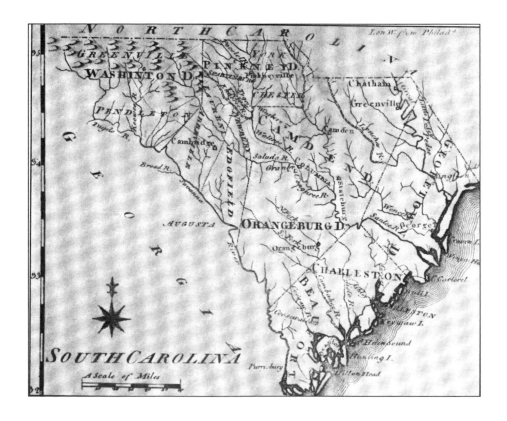

Slang found in South Carolina, Diary of Edward Jenkins, 1806:

The low country abounding with swamps, which often prove embarrassing to travelers, it has become common to say of one who has got into difficulty of any kind, He has got *swamp'd.* . . . *Cabin* is used for a long house or any poor mansion. *Raly* for *really. So help me* is an expression put by those who are not quite profane enough to annex the name of Deity, at the end of an affirmation which they wish to strengthen. . . . Instead of saying, I rode a little farther, the Carolinian says, I rode a *piece* farther. . . . *Good man* is often used for a man of property, even without limiting the meaning to characteristic punctuality. *"All but"* is a favourite expression for almost Eg. We *all but* turned over. . . . The common introductory address to a Stranger is *Stranger.* Eg. Stranger, will you tell me which of these roads leads to Abbeville?. . . . When one calls loudly to another, the interjection O, is often inserted. Eg. Edmund! Edmund! O, Edmund!. . . . Guess is a word, when used for believe, so confessedly Yankee.fied (as the Carolinians pretend) as to be made on principal criterion for determining who is a New Englander.

"Gilbert Stuart's English Portraits," *The Monthly Magazine,* London, England, 1805:

When we speak of him as the most accurate painter we mean to say, that having a very correct eye he gave the human figure exactly as he saw it, without any attempt to dignify or elevate the character; and was so exact in depicting its lineages that one may almost say of him what Hogarth said of another artist, "that he never deviates into Grace," and from all which we may fairly infer that he was never a favorite portrait painter with the ladies. He was, however, so well grounded in his profession that had not his eccentricities led him to quit this country it would have corrected his errors and figured very high in his art.

"An ingenious clock," *Travels in Some Parts of North America in the Years 1804, 1805 and 1806,* Robert Sutcliffe, York, England, 1811:

12 month, fourth day, 1805: At night I went to Batavia, New York and took up my quarters in the house of Joseph Ellicott and his brother, where I was kindly and generously entertained. . . . In the centre of a good room, in which I slept, was fixed one of the most beautiful and curious clocks I have ever seen. It was in the form of an elegant mahogany pillar, on the capital of which were four faces. On one of them was an orrery, shewing the motions of the earth and planets round the sun. On another face were marked the hours and minutes; and on the third face were marked the names of 24 musical tunes, with a pointer in the center, which being placed against any name, repeated that tune every quarter, until the pointer was moved to another. On the fourth face was seen, through the glass, the curious machinery of the clock. The value set upon this ingenious piece of mechanism was 1000 dollars. The cabinet work of the case, as well as the engravings and paintings about it, and also the movements, although done in a beautiful workmanlike manner, had been executed by men, none of whom served an apprenticeship to their respective lines of business. The mechanism was executed by the grandfather of the kind friend in those house it stands. This family are remarkable for ingenuity, and have rendered essential services to this country, by the improvements they have made in the machinery of flour mills. One of their progenitors had been clock-maker to a King of England, and was considered a first-rate mechanic in his day. Those propensities and talent sometimes run in families from one generation to another.

"Moravian handwork, 1803," *A Girl's Life 80 Years Ago: Selections from the Letters the Eliza Southgate Browne,* by Clarence Cook, 1887:

Bethlehem, August 9, 1803. We went to the Schools, first was merely a sewing school, little children, and a pretty single sister about 30, with her white skirt, white, short, tight waistcoat, nice handkerchief pinned outside, a muslin apron and a close cambric cap of the most singular form you can imagine. I can't describe it; the hair is all put out of sight, turned back before, and no border of the cap, very unbecoming but very singular, tied under the chin with a pink ribbon, blue for the married, white for the widows. Here was a Piano-forte, and another sister teaching a little girl music. We went thro' all the different schoolrooms, some misses of 16, their teachers were very agreeable and easy, and every room has a piano. I never saw any embroidery so beautiful; muslin they don't work. . . .

We went to a room where they keep their work for sale, pocket- books, pin balls, Toilette cushions, baskets, artificial flowers, etc. . ., etc. We bought a box full of things, and left them much pleased with the neatness and order which appeared thro'out.

"Eggnog on the Frontier, 1806," *Sketch of Western Settlements in 1806,* by George Sample:

There were 15 to 20 cabins at Manchester, one of which was called a tavern. It was at least a grog shop. There were about a dozen visitors at the tavern, and as the landlord was a heyday, wellmet tibbler with the rest, they appointed me to assist the landlady in making eggnog. I was inexperienced in the art, but I made out to suit them very well. I put about a dozen eggs in a large bowl, and after beating or rather stirring the eggs up a little, I added about a pound of sugar and a little milk to this mess; then I filled the bowl with whiskey, and set it on the table; and they sat around the table and supped it with spoons! Tumblers or glasses of any sort had not then come in fashion. They all began to cut up, and especially a professor of religion. I thought he ought to have set a better example. When I found out how the game was going, I resigned my commission and went to bed.

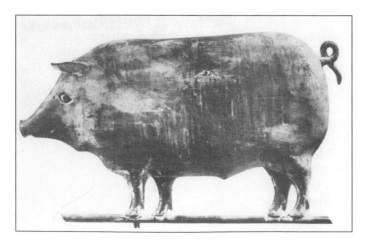

Decorative weathervanes were becoming popular.

1808 PROFILE

Even though John Eliot had been a Congregationalist minister for over 20 years in Salem, Massachusetts, he was continually envisioning ways to proselytize members within his community.

Life at Home

- Now comfortable behind the pulpit in his forty-ninth year, John Eliot didn't have to think hard to remember the turbulent days following his graduation from Harvard with high honors in 1777.
- Initially, based upon his mastery of foreign languages, he accepted an appointment in Boston as a teacher in a Latin grammar school.
- As his oratory skills and confidence slowly improved, he started preaching as a candidate in a Congregational church in Salem.
- But John's manner of reading the Scripture lesson during church services was peculiar to those familiar with tradition.
- Typically, he named the Scripture chapter and then paraphrased the reading.
- For him, the goal was to present God's message instead of the exact language in the Bible.
- Because it was not a method welcomed by the senior pastor, it hurt John's ability to become a full minister.
- After a few years, members of the church's committee argued on his behalf for him to become a minister.
- Only then was John Eliot given consent by the senior pastor.
- Over the years his church welcomed the messages he delivered and how he led by Christian example.
- He believed that a true Christian must deny himself and do all the good he can for others.
- In this spirit, he donated nearly half of his minister's salary to the poor and encouraged the wealthier members of his flock to contribute additional support.

John Eliot became a minister soon after his graduation from Harvard.

- Often he would receive large contributions from affluent merchants in his church to be distributed to the poor at his discretion.
- Once he received a $50.00 bill from a ship's captain who confided in one of his overseers about the distribution.
- The money was delivered to 10 widows, each receiving $5.00.
- When the senior pastor died, John was asked to fill his role.
- After becoming a full minister, he moved into a modest home on Essex Street.
- Typically, he spent his Mondays drafting two Scripture lessons for the upcoming Sunday lectures in his library.
- John's library was a collection of hundreds of religious books he had acquired over the years, but it also housed his hobbies—items acquired from his church members, mostly from the ship captains who sailed the world.
- He received a printing of *The Divine Comedy* by Dante Alighieri in Italian from Capitan Norton upon his return from Italy.
- Captain Norton also provided Tom, the squirrel-colored cat, from the same voyage as a pet.
- John was grateful for these gifts, as well as the coins from some Italian states to include in his extensive coin collection, which contained rare antique coins he was given.
- When Mr. Samuel Fowler was clearing some land he recently purchased, he discovered eight pieces of silver buried six inches under the soil beside a flat rock.
- Three were coins from Queen Elizabeth's reign dated 1563, 1569 and 1574.

John preached Christian values of faith, hope and love.

- A fourth was a James I coin that was larger than the Elizabethan coins and dated 1615.
- John spent considerable time reading about other Christian faiths and included these works within his library.
- He acquired a book for $0.18 titled *Free Communion & upon the conduct of the Baptists in withdrawing from the Other Churches.*
- Reading the book was an effort on his part to understand the newly arriving Baptist ministers.
- Many were coming to Salem to convert members of the local community.
- To him these Baptist ministers preached against his understanding of Christianity.
- He commented in his journal, "It is a painful reflection that this sect, from which we might promise something benevolent, assists to weaken everything but superstition."
- The other Christian clergy in Salem were also frustrated at the free plunder of their members from the various Baptist faiths recently formed in the area.
- Capturing particular notice was their practice of immersion baptisms, the washing away of Original Sin in the Christian faith and Biblical teachings, that aroused fear.
- When an earthquake occurred that lasted for several seconds one evening in May, a few Baptist ministers sparked deep concerns that Salem would be soon sunk by an earthquake, based upon the dreams of one local Baptist minister.
- Many of the Salem ministers discussed writing a refutation in the *Salem Gazette*, especially on the efforts of Baptists to re-baptize those who had received a sprinkle instead of total immersion in water.

Pride and selfishness were thought to be a path to Hell.

- John believed that errors of opinion may be tolerated only if reason was free to address them.
- Thus he spent most of his energies on improving the community, such as his involvement in the area's School Committee that was charged with education of the youth.
- Often he visited the schools to discern issues on the quality of education and matters regarding instructor pay.
- On one occasion, John Eliot learned about the pay of one Salem schoolmistress who received four pounds and two shillings for 16 weeks of instruction.
- She wished for a raise of an additional 16 pence per week, which the committee discouraged.
- John also met schoolmasters of a town school who printed their own books of class instruction.
- Therefore, he saw many titles he had never encountered in school, such as *Kneeland's Definition, Staniford's Art of Reading* and *Hubbard's Geography*.
- A local minister in Northfields, who spent time with the School Committee, observed how few negroes could read and write and discussed the usefulness of establishing a school to instruct them separately.
- A vote was taken by ballot by the committee with six out of seven votes in favor; within a month the school successfully opened with 40 young negroes enrolled.
- Outside of his work in education, John heard financial pleas from a number of missionary services.
- He received news from the missionaries admitted into China that thousands of Chinese had embraced Christianity in Peking.
- He commented in his journal, "We know not what degree of expectation to indulge from such reports."
- His church also was asked to fund the propagation of the faith among the Indians in America.
- Some parishioners claimed to John that they learned true morality from the naked hearts of Indians during their time out west.
- John supported causes to reach the Indians but questioned if they were effective.
- He had seen the worst characteristics of man develop when dealing with the natives of the country.
- One person who approached Salem's religious ministers on educating the Indians was Gideon Blackburn.
- Blackburn expressed the hope of teaching the Cherokee children to write in English and introduce them to agricultural pursuits.
- His goal was to encourage them not to speak in their own language because it was too guttural.
- Ultimately, he claimed to foster their hopes to become part of the Union and have their representatives in the Legislature.
- With the support of many of Salem's ministers, Blackburn preached one Sunday evening to a crowded house and ranted on the resurrection, heaven and anything that came his way.
- He also shared his vision for the Cherokee and indicated that he was helping 40 Indian children pray, write and read.
- By evening's end he collected about $300.00.

Life at Work
- Death was a common occurrence in John Eliot's life, and so were funeral services over which he presided.
- No one was safe from the tyranny of fatal fevers.

Shipwrecks and disease took the lives of many in the Salem, Massachusetts community.

- In addition, there occurred shipwrecks that resulted in the loss of men who were part of the life of his church in Salem.
- In one case Captain Rhuee and his ship struck the rocks along the French coast, dooming the entire ship and crew.
- The captain's wife was distraught at the loss; she was also suddenly without income to care for her two children.
- Death was brought by sinful habits acquired by some in Salem.
- During a period of a month, three young men were victims of intemperance, with one taken with convulsions and comatose about three days before expiring.
- John was also alarmed about his personal health when he caught influenza while riding toward Cambridge.
- He was seized with shivers and took to bed immediately with a blanket at an inn.
- He felt debility for a number of days with the most violent sweat he ever had experienced.
- He ate and drank sparingly during his days of sickness.
- Still weak, John returned to Salem, where the town's physicians said 500 had the influenza.
- Many believed the best way to fight the influenza was to know how it arrived.
- The most prevalent belief was that it came in with the long rains that made the atmosphere full of vapor for a long time.
- How to measure such vapor was unknown, but if it could be measured, then it could possibly be prevented, it was believed.
- Since the influenza had killed so many, John conducted a number of funeral services for those who succumbed to the same sickness from which he had so recently recovered.
- He even had to bury Benjamin Foye, a good friend and benefactor to his church.
- Besides losing an eighth of his income, John lost a confidant who provided prudent foresight on matters of daily life.

- After the succession of deaths, John Eliot made sure to spend time with his church members in non-church-related activities.
- His favorite place of amusement was the Nahant peninsula, 10 miles away.
- Recently, he invited the wives of two prominent ship captains out for an excursion one April Friday in a chaise, a four-wheel travel carriage.
- John carried with him lemons, apples, nuts, coffee and sugar for the day.
- Expenses that day included $2.00 for a hired horse, $0.54 for beef, $0.16 for bread, $0.25 for the toll and $0.12 for the gate into Nahant; the total expense for the day totaled over $6.00.
- In addition to visiting Nahant, John took the Custom House boat to Naugus for a day of fishing with church members.
- Afterward he stopped for dinner at Aunt Morse's ale house and took coffee on the shoreline's rocks.
- When he took a group of young pupils to the shore, they attempted to study the marine life as the tides changed.
- Studying the natural world was one of John's most pleasurable occupations, a passion that commonly brought him into discussions with many church members in Salem.
- The previous year, Mr. Hood had brought potatoes each filled with 12 to 20 one-inch-size worms.
- Upon inspection, it appeared that the crop active with the worms was planted at the foot of a hill in land that was low, clayey and very wet—a place to be avoided.
- He also loved talking with ship captains concerning the appearance of a comet he had spotted in the night sky.
- John first observed it in the southwest sky over his Essex Street home; to the naked eye it appeared as a common star.
- Disappointment fell upon John when he wanted a closer examination of the object with his Dolland telescope and there were none available in town with larger magnifying powers.
- His time outside in the evenings with others helped him pause and notice the new buildings that added to the town's growth.
- In 1798, there were a total of 1,577 buildings in the town that had expanded to 2,000 now.
- The increase of the town's size also increased the likelihood of fire.
- A few years prior, the town passed laws restricting the smoking of cigars after a careless smoker burned the town's ropewalk, also referred to as the Twine factory.
- Often the ropewalks were inhabited by the most lawless men, who on Sundays would crawl into such places to spend a day in concealment to smoke.
- Currently, the town officers assembled to discuss the use of stoves in shops and offices, especially the need to prevent careless fires.
- Recently a fire developed at Cushing & Co., a printing and bookbinding company.
- At two o'clock in the morning the alarm rang and woke many to fight the fire.
- Fortunately for Salem, the air was calm and the fire did not spread to other buildings.
- Regretfully, the entire building and its contents, including three printing presses, paper stock and printed books, were lost.
- The estimated value of the damage exceeded $10,000.
- John condemned those who claimed the fires were a judgment by God.
- Instead it was the consequence of leaving their homes unprotected.
- Once this occurred when parents left their children alone while attending a Scripture lecture.
- The home was still under construction and housed wood shavings in an unfinished room which the children used to feed a fire on a cold evening.

- This created a destructive fire that burned several homes and left a number of people homeless.
- John was thankful for the efforts of those who contributed from neighboring towns to help fight the fire.
- In his journal he commented, "The neighboring Towns gave generous & immediate assistance, for which they merit the public gratitude. They brought their engines with them."
- Fires were not the only items that caught the excitement of the town; political and judicial news traditionally sparked interest as well.
- One trial caught John's attention as it pertained to the divorce of West & West; the husband was the son from a prominent Salem family and master of his own vessel.
- The woman fell in love with the man and the two quickly eloped.
- Shortly thereafter she quickly sued for a divorce; many did not know whether to feel pity or contempt.
- Each spouse hired experienced lawyers from Salem or Boston to make their cases in court.
- The trial exposed their personal lives and insinuated a number of character flaws, mostly infidelity.

The divorce trial of a prominent Salem couple sparked the townspeople's interest.

- In his journal, John wrote while observing the trial, "Never has my mind felt such tumult, never did it experience such horror."
- The trial lasted five days and the court determined the divorce outcome with consent by both parties.
- The wife was to have the farm in Danvers and the real estate.
- She would also receive $3,000 a year.
- For many the trial was a welcome distraction from the weak economy, caused by the American embargo with Britain.
- In 1807 the British *HMS Leopold* attacked the *USS Chesapeake,* an American frigate that had just sailed from Chesapeake Bay.
- After several broadsides of cannon fire, the British boarded the ship, seized the men and abandoned the heavily damaged *USS Chesapeake.*
- Salem was outraged over the British maritime presence along the American coasts, especially when it interfered with commerce.
- Uncertain if war would occur over the matter, many of the town's merchants were afraid to trust valuable cargo at sea until they knew the state of negotiations with Britain.
- The fear in town created the impression of an embargo, a government order prohibiting the departure of commercial ships from its ports.
- By January 1808, President Jefferson actually issued an embargo in an attempt to oppress Britain, while avoiding war.
- By spring, John heard the concern and discussions of the merchants and captains regarding the embargo.
- British ships continued to seize returning American ships that had departed prior to the embargo and the American government was doing nothing.
- Jefferson's embargo was also hurting their trade, and many debated the need and potential longevity of the national measures.
- The concept of sacrifice for the common good meant financial hardship for merchants who supported the embargo.
- Instead a number of merchants ignored the embargo.
- John pondered if they could submit to a temporary sacrifice of their mercantile interest to help the country through this crisis with Britain.

Life in the Community: Salem, Massachusetts

- Salem, Massachusetts, was a bustling seaport, particularly because of its trade with China, and the residents often referred to themselves as "citizens of the world."
- Prior to the start of the nineteenth century, Salem was known for its role in the Salem witch trials that occurred in 1692.
- It was more importantly known as an active seaport.
- For most of the seventeenth and eighteenth centuries, ships left from its ports and entered into the North Atlantic in search of cod.
- Large quantities of the fish were harvested from the sea and dried for transport.
- It was a valuable commodity in European ports.
- During the War of Independence, Salem was an active location for privateers—private warships authorized by the American government to attack British shipping during the war.
- During the American Revolution, Salem was the most successful privateering port in America; Salem's 158 privateering vessels captured 445 English vessels.
- Once the war was over, many merchants and privateer captains converted their efforts to trade now that they were no longer held bound by the British mercantilist regulations.

- Salem ships began exploring the globe for opportunities with many nations.
- The ships returned with exotic cargoes such as Bohea tea and exotic woods such as teak and sandalwood.
- By 1790, Salem was the sixth largest city in the country, propelled by its involvement in trade and shipbuilding.
- The influence of the new goods from foreign destinations began to influence Salem and its wealth; Salem's Elias Hasket Derby became one of America's first millionaires.
- The growth of wealth influenced the town's architecture and changed the look and style of the city.
- Many of the city's wealthy merchants built grand homes with distinct Chinese influences.
- Some homes were even retrofitted with Chinese balustrades and displayed Chinese ornamental images.
- One common design element was the China coin symbol—often a sign of good fortune and wealth and a common image on much of the art and porcelain that arrived in the city.
- With an influx of capital into Salem, two banks were developed.
- The first was the Essex Bank which started with $300,000 in 1792; by 1803, the Salem Bank was formed with $200,000 in capital.
- Other businesses developed to support the increase of trade activity: marine insurance, baggage wagons and the expansion of shipbuilding.
- With the added wealth, Salem made investments into education for the city's population; private schools developed for young men and ladies.
- The city also invested in three public coeducational primary schools in 1801, which were thought to outperform the Boston schools.

HISTORICAL SNAPSHOT
1808

- The importation of slaves into the United States was banned as of January 1 by an act of Congress
- Napoleon invaded Spain with an army of 150,000, routing the Spanish
- Henry Crabb Robinson became the world's first war correspondent when the *Times* of London sent him to report on the Peninsular War in Spain
- Thomas Jefferson rejected petitions that he run for a third term, citing the example set by George Washington
- Anthracite coal was first burned as an experimental fuel by Wilkes-Barre in Pennsylvania
- Bavaria produced a written constitution that abolished serfdom and proclaimed the principle of equality of citizens before the law
- John Jacob Astor incorporated the American Fur Company with himself as sole stockholder
- The *S.S. Phoenix* was launched by New Jersey engineer John Stevens, the first steamboat with an American-built engine
- Inventor Richard Trevithick demonstrated his steam locomotive Catch-me-who-can on a circular track near London's Euston Road
- Parliament repealed an Elizabethan statute declaring theft from a person a capital offense

- French confectioner Nicolas Appert developed a method of vacuum-packing food in jars
- The first Parisian restaurant with fixed prices opened in the Palais Royal
- The first college orchestra in the United States was founded at Harvard
- Ludwig van Beethoven's Symphony No. 5 in C minor and Symphony No. 6 in F major were performed in Vienna
- The first U.S. land-grant university was founded at Ohio University in Athens, Ohio
- The Medical Society of the State of New York was founded
- Alexis Bouvard accurately predicted the orbital locations of Jupiter and Saturn
- The first volume of *American Ornithology* by Alexander Wilson was published

Selected Prices

Boots, Gentleman's $4.00
Cake, Sold by Confectioner $0.75
Cotton Gin $85.00
Cotton, Pound $0.25
Liquor Case $1.00
Shovel $0.25
Sugar, Pound . . . . .12½ cents
Thread, Pound $0.21
Tuition, Boys' School for Latin $16.00
Wagon, Four Horse $40.00

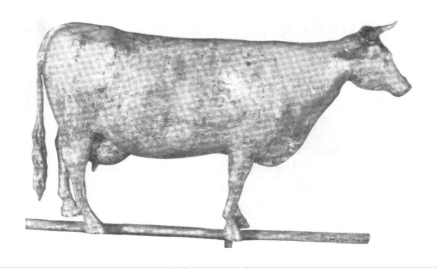

"The Chesapeake Affair," *Washington Federalist,* 1808:

We have never, on any occasion, witnessed the spirit of the people excited to so great a degree of indignation, or such a thirst for revenge, as on hearing of the late unexampled outrages on the Chesapeake. All parties, ranks, and professions were unanimous in their detestation of the dastardly deed, and all cried aloud for vengeance.

"An Address to Youth," *Staniford's Art of Reading,* Tenth Edition, 1814:

Youth is the season proper to cultivate the benevolent and humane affections. As a great part of your happiness is to depend on the connexions which you form with others, it is of high importance, that you acquire betimes the temper and the manners which will render such connexions comfortable. Let a sense of justice be the foundation of all your social qualities.

"Cherokees Visit Washington," *John Ross and the Cherokee Indians,* By Rachel Caroline Eaton, 1914:

A considerable difference existed at this time between the Upper and Lower Cherokees; the former were chiefly farmers while the latter, still hunters, were beginning to feel themselves hedged in by the narrowing boundaries of their hunting grounds. Differences of opinion growing out of these differences in occupations led to discontent. In May, 1808, a delegation of Upper Cherokees arrived in Washington, requesting that a line be drawn between their lands and those of the Lower Cherokees, that their lands be allotted them in severalty, and that they be admitted as citizens of the United States, while their brethren in the South might hunt as long as the game lasted. In his talk with them Jefferson encouraged removal, but informed them that citizenship could not be conferred upon them except by Congress.

Letter by William Gray in the *Salem Gazette*, August 12, 1808:

When the Embargo law passed, I thought it a Constitutional measure, and I did not think proper to oppose it. The policy of the measure has been much questioned; yet I think then existing circumstances rendered it prudent and necessary; as Great Britain had threatened and had at that time passed (though not officially known to us) the orders of council of the 11th November, 1807, authorizing the capture and condemnation of all vessels, bound from the United States, that should sail for France, or the countries of her allies. . . . It is insinuated that I am growing rich, while others are suffering by the Embargo: I have not reaped any advantages from it, that I know of, in any form whatever; those who best know me can say, whether I have benefited others, or taken advantage of their necessity. So far from reaping profit from the embargo, my estate has declined more than ten per cent in value since its operation, which I am ready to demonstrate to any person desirous of investigating the subject.

Jefferson's Authority to Suspend the Embargo, Letter to William Lyman from Thomas Jefferson, April 1808:

The decrees and orders of the belligerent nations having amounted nearly to declarations that they would take our vessels wherever found, Congress thought it best, in the first instance, to break off all intercourse with [Great Britain]. They passed an act authorizing me to suspend the Embargo whenever the belligerents should revoke their decrees or orders as to us. The Embargo must continue, therefore, till they meet again in November, unless the measures of the belligerents should change. When they meet again, if these decrees and orders still continue, the question which they will have to decide will be, whether a continuance of the Embargo or war will be preferable.

Punishment for Importation of Slaves, Statutes of the United States Concerning Slavery approved March 2, 1807:

SEC. 5 That if any citizen or citizens of the United States, or any other person resident within the jurisdiction of the same, shall, from and after the first day of January, one thousand eight hundred and eight, contrary to the true intent and meaning of this act, take on board any ship or vessel from any of the coasts or kingdoms of Africa, or from any other foreign kingdom, place, or country, any negro, mulatto, or person of colour, with intent to sell him, her, or them, for a slave, or slaves, or to be held to service or labour, and shall transport the same to any port or place within the jurisdiction of the United States, and there sell such negro, mulatto, or person of colour, so transported as aforesaid, for a slave, or to be held to service or labour, every such offender shall be deemed guilty of a high misdemeanor, and being thereof convicted before any court having competent jurisdiction, shall suffer imprisonment for not more than ten years nor less than five years, and be fined not exceeding ten thousand dollars, nor less than one thousand dollars.

Ballad

Why with sighs my heart is swelling
Why with tears my eyes o'er flow. . .

Ask me not, 'tis past the telling
Mute involuntary woe. . .

Why with sighs my heart is swelling,
Why with tears my eyes o'er flow, . . .

Who to winds & waves a stranger,
vent'rous tempt the raging seas. . .

In each billow fancies
Danger shrinks at ev'ry rising breeze. . .

Why with sighs my heart is swelling
Why with tears my eyes o'er flow

—Composed by Guglielmi, 1808

1802 NEWS FEATURE

An Oration on the Anniversary of the Declaration of Independence, Noah Webster, New Haven, Connecticut, 1802:

The history of the first English settlements in America, and of the measures which prepared the way for a revolution in the colonies, is too interesting not to be well understood by men of common curiosity and reading in this State. That history unfolds a series of great events, evidently suited to accomplish important purposes in the economy of Divine Providence . . . events which every American of expanded views must contemplate with admiration; and every Christian, with delight. . . .

In the lapse of twenty six years, since the date of our sovereignty, a large proportion of the inhabitants of the United States have been changed. Most of the civil and military characters, conspicuous in the revolution, are now in their graves; and a new generation has arisen to guide the public councils, and to guard the blessings which their fathers have purchased. The experience of the same period of time, has drawn in question some opinions respecting the superior excellence of a republican government; and clouded the brilliant prospect which animated the hopes of the revolutionary patriots. Numerous unexpected difficulties in the management of this species of government, and multifarious disappointments, under the best administrations have arisen in thick succession, to confound the wisdom, and blast the hopes, of the most discerning friends of their country. To trace the causes of these disappointments, is to prevent a repetition of them, or prepare ourselves to meet them with advantage.

It is worthy of observation, that nations sometimes begin their political existence, as young men begin the world, with more courage than foresight, and more enthusiasm than correct judgment. Unacquainted with the perils that await their progress, or disdaining the maxims of experience, and confident of their own powers, they expect to attain to supereminent greatness and prosperity, by means which other nations have found ineffectual, and bid defiance to calamities by which others have been overwhelmed. . . . Nations, like individuals, may be misled by an ardent enthusiasm, which allures them from the standard of practical wisdom, and commits them to the guidance of visionary projectors. By fondly cherishing the opinion that they enjoy some superior advantages of knowledge, or local situation, the rulers of a state may lose the benefit of history and observation, the surest guides in political affairs; and delude themselves with the belief, that they have wisdom to elude or power to surmount the obstacles which have baffled the exertions of their predecessors.

Such are the mistakes of reformers; and such have been the illusions of the enthusiastic friends of the revolution. Their imagination has been warmed with the belief, that the sequestered position of America, would exempt her citizens from the troubles which harrass Europe; that a general diffusion of knowledge, and superior attainments in policy, would enable them to form constitutions of government, less defective than any which have preceded them; and that their public virtue would secure a faithful, uncorrupt, and impartial administration. Whenever a doubt has been suggested, respecting the duration of a free republic, it has been repelled by one general answer, that the system of representation, supposed to be a modern improvement in free constitutions, is calculated effectually to obviate the evils which other states have experienced, from legislatures consisting of popular assemblies.

But does the wide ocean that rolls between the two continents, detach our citizens from a deep interest in the affairs of Europe? Will our commerce, a productive source of our wealth, permit a separation of interests? And will not our prejudices and our wants, in spite of reason and patriotism, continue, for a long period, to link us to the policy, the opinions, and the interest of European nations?

But if we had the power to insulate our country, our interest, and our hearts, can we assure ourselves that our citizens' supereminent wisdom, to frame systems of government, which shall be proof against the insidious advances of corruption, and the bold assaults of faction? What has prevented the enlightened sages of antiquity, from viewing man in all his attitudes; and learning all the possible modes, by which the human passions operate on society and government? After the experience of four or five thousand years, and numberless forms of government, how should it happen to be reserved for the Americans to discover the great secret, which has eluded all former inquiry, of infusing into a political constitution, the quality of imperishable durability? Is not the pretension to such superior light and wisdom in our citizens, rather an evidence of pride, self-sufficiency, and *want of wisdom?* If Moses, with an uncommon portion of talents, seconded by divine aid, could not secure his institutions from neglect and corruption, what right have we to expect, that the labors of our lawgivers will be more successful?

But great expectations are formed from *representation* in government, which is supposed to be a modern discovery, destined to give permanency to republics. If representation were a modern invention, every good citizen would wait impatiently for the result of a fair experiment; solicitous that the inventors might not be ultimately numbered among a multitude of dreaming projectors, who commence their schemes, "acribus initiis, incurioso fine," ["eager at the start, careless at the end"] with ardent zeal and splendid promises, which end in nothing. But representation is not a modern discovery. It was for ages practiced, not only in France, Spain, Denmark, and Sweden, as it has been in Switzerland and Great-Britain, but in many of the small states of antiquity; not, perhaps, in the same form prescribed by our constitutions, but in a variety of modes, in which the principles of it were fully and fairly tested.

Representation, by enabling a state to govern, without assembling all its citizens, lessens the chance of sudden and violent convulsions; but it neither humbles pride, subdues ambition, nor controls revenge and rivalry. It still leaves a state subject to the operation of all the turbulent, restless passions of man; changing only their direction. It is a popular opinion, but probably a great mistake, that corruption in a state is introduced by men in power; whereas, in fact, it usually originates with the candidates for preferment. Men in office, if respected and rewarded, have few temptations to abuse their trust; but strong and irresistible motives for fidelity and diligence. Their subsistence and their reputation are the most ample guaranty for a faithful discharge of their duties. Men, therefore, who *seek,* not those who *possess,* the honors and emoluments of government, are the first to introduce corruption. It is extremely important that this truth should be duly weighed; for popular jealousy is usually directed exclusively against the officers of government, when in fact, it ought to be employed to guard against the arts and address of *office-seekers.*

By corruption is here intended, not only the influence of money or favors, but an undue bias given to the minds of the electors, from violent passions and strong prejudices, which impel them to abandon *principle* to follow *men.* No man will deny that men in power sometimes abuse their trust; nor is it the intention of the writer to discountenance a proper watchfulness over public officers. This vigilance, however, is much better exercised by the legislature, than by candidates for office, printers, clerks and spies. The latter are incessantly exciting *groundless* alarms and popular suspicions, about officers whose conduct, on a regular inquiry, is found to be unimpeachable. Fraud and delinquency in public officers occasionally occur, and when detected, are universally reprobated and the guilty persons punished. About *real* crimes, there is rarely any difference of opinion . . . parties and factions arise on doubtful questions and imaginary evils. But the natural growth of corruption in a state, from the mismanagement of men in power, is extremely slow, compared with the vast increase under the impulse of the violent passions raised among electors by the candidates for office. When the electors enlist under *men,* they desert the true principles of elective governments . . . they follow *their leaders* and *their party,* without examining *measures* or *principles.* This has been the ruin of many states. It is an evil that seems to be *innate* in a republican government, that the electors never *remain free* and *unbiased.* This is a *perversion* of the true principles of an elective government, which is here called *corruption.* and it arises from factions originating mostly with office-seekers. For this evil, no remedy has ever been devised. One general effort of a party to change the administration in a government like ours, does more to introduce and confirm this species of corruption, than all that can be done by men in power, for half a century.

This truth being admitted, for it is authorized by history and observation, we have a clear rule by which to estimate the hazard to which a state is exposed, by a corruption of its true principles. The passions of men being every where the same, and nearly the same proportion of men in every society, directing their views to preferment, we observe that, in all governments, the object and efforts are the same, but the direction of those efforts is varied, according to the form of government, and *always applied to those who have the disposal of honors and offices.* In a monarchy, office-seekers are courtiers, fawning about the ministers or heads of departments . . . in a pure democracy, they are orators, who mount the rostrum, and harangue the populace, flattering their pride, and inflaming their passions . . . in a representative republic, they are the *friends of the people,* who address themselves to the electors, with great pretensions to patriotism, with falsehoods, fair promises, and insidious arts. In a monarchy, the minister may be corrupted, and the nation not be materially affected. In a democratic state, the populace may be corrupted by the arts or seduced by the eloquence of a popular orator. In a single hour, an Athenian assembly might be converted from the adorers, into the persecutors of their best magistrates and ablest generals. . . . In the morning, a Themistocles and a Phocion might be idolized by the people; and at evening, sentenced to exile, or condemned to swallow poison. But does a representative government effectually guard the magistrates from similar abuses of popular power? If the electors cannot assemble, to listen to the seductions of an artful orator, has modern invention supplied no means, by which their minds may be perverted, and their passions inflamed? What are gazettes, handbills and pamphlets, but substitutes for orators? A species of silent messengers, walking by night and by day, stealing into farm houses and taverns, whispering tales of fraud about public officers, exciting suspicion, spreading discontent, weakening confidence in government! What is the difference between the misguided zeal of an Athenian assembly, and of the citizens of America, except in the means and the time employed to effect the object? The one resembles a tornado, suddenly collecting and exhausting its force in undistinguishing, but momentary ravages; the other is like the slowly gathering tempest, whose lingering approach is announced by chilling blasts, and a lowering sky.

Whatever may be the form of government, therefore, corruption and misrepresentation find access to those who have the disposal of offices; by various means and different channels indeed, but proceeding primarily from demagogues and office-seekers, of bold designs and profligate principles.

It is said, however, that we have constitutions of government, or fundamental compacts, which proscribe abuses of power, by defining the exact limits of right and duty, and controlling both rulers and people. But how long will a constitutional barrier resist the assaults of faction? From the nature of things, the words of a fundamental code must be general, to comprehend cases which cannot possibly be specified; and of course, liable to be extended, or frittered away by construction. The danger from this quarter is imminent, and hardly admitting of a remedy, when popular jealousy is excited against the constitution, and the rights or the prejudices of the people are to be favored, by enlarging or abridging its powers. When a magistrate becomes more popular than the constitution, he may "draw sin as it were with a cart-rope" in the work of extending his power over the instrument which was intended to restrain usurpation. Whatever vanity and self-confidence may suggest, in favor of the restraints of a paper compact, all history and uniform experience evince, that against men who command the current of popular confidence, the best constitution has not the strength of a cobweb. The undisguised encroachments of power give the alarm and excite resistance . . . but the approaches of despotism, under cover of popular favor, are insidious and often deceive the most discerning friends of a free government. . . .

The eminent characters who have conducted the revolutions in England and America, have laid it down as a fundamental principle in government, that by nature all men are *free, independent,* and *equal,* and this principle, without definition or limitation, forms a main pillar of our constitutions.

If there were but a single man on earth, he certainly could have no masters, but the elements and the inflexible laws of nature. But political axioms, if not mere empty sounds, must have reference to a social state. How then, can men, exposed to each other's power, and wanting each other's aid, be *free* and *independent?* If one member of a society is free and independent, all the members must be equally so. In such a community, no restraint could exist, for this would destroy freedom and independence. But in such a state of things, the will of each individual would be his only rule of action, and his *will* would be supported by his *strength.* Force then would be the ultimate arbiter of right and wrong, and the wills of the weaker must bend to the power of the stronger. A society, therefore, existing in a state of nature, if such a state can be supposed in which there should be no law but individual wills, must necessarily be in perpetual anarchy or despotism. But no such state of society can exist. The very act of associating destroys the natural freedom and independence of each member of the society, anterior to any compact limiting their respective powers and rights; for it is a principle, resulting from the very nature of society, independent of any mutual agreement for the purpose, that one individual shall not exercise his own power to another's prejudice. Of course, by the very constitution of society, the will of each member is restrained by the laws of general utility, or common good, the details of which are to be regulated by the supreme power. Whatever may be the abstract reasoning of men on this subject, the practice has been, and by the nature of man, must continue to be, that the members of a state or body politic, hold their rights subject to the direction and control of the sovereignty of the state. It is needless to discuss questions of natural right as distinct from a social state, for all rights are social, and subordinate to the supreme will of the whole society. Nor, without such a supreme controlling power over all the members of a state, can an individual possess and enjoy liberty.

1810–1819

The most tenuous phase of the political experiment known as the United States of America began in 1812 with the Second War of Independence with England. For several years America had avoided another costly war through a self-imposed trade embargo that forbade land and seaborne commerce with foreign nations, virtually eliminating American exports, largely shutting down the East Coast seaports, and resulting in falling farm prices, failed industries and widespread unemployment. At the same time, traders and settlers in the West were convinced that England was both arming and inciting the Native Americans against them. War hawks, largely elected from the Western and Southern states, declared that America's rights must be asserted, despite the risks. President James Madison's war message cited British interference with American trade, a blockade of the Eastern seaboard, impressment of American sailors and British-inspired Indian attacks. The two-year battle resulted in several major battles over ownership of parts of Canada, the British invasion and burning of Washington, DC, and little territorial change. But the intensity of the War of 1812 had a psychological impact on the economy of the nation. Political conversations that insisted that secession was the right of every state virtually vanished as unity took precedence. Even the Federalists' attempts in 1814 to brand the conflict as "Mr. Madison's War" backfired. The Federalists were considered traitors and the party never recovered.

One lasting impact of the War of 1812 was the name Uncle Sam, a nickname for the United States. Workers at Samuel Wilson's meat packing plant in Troy, New York, which supplied provisions to the U.S. Army, joked that the U.S. stamped on the barrels bound for the troops actually stood for their boss Uncle Sam Wilson. The story spread and as time went on government property in general became referred to as Uncle Sam's.

Between 1790 and 1820 the population of the United States increased from nearly four million to 10 million people, resulting almost entirely from American births and not immigration. Only 250,000 new settlers came from abroad during these 30 years, and half of those after the War of 1812. During this time the Temperance Movement, the formation of labor union societies and the expansion of voting rights to non-property holders all got their start.

After the war, American industry grew, driven by new concepts in industrialization and energy supplied by steam engines, which measured their efficiency in horsepower, or how many horses the machine replaced. Expenditures for new and improved roads, bridges and canals also increased, including the publicly financed Erie Canal in New York State, which dramatically reduced freight charges on internal commerce. Economically, however, the United States was still tethered to Europe. With the shipping lanes liberated, the South could once again send most of its annual 125 million-pound cotton crop to England, whose industries continued to dominate manufacturing. Many American industries failed during this period because they were unable to produce the same quality textiles at a competitive price in this global atmosphere. America then suffered another economic blow in the Panic of 1819 with the collapse of European markets for American export products. This three-year depression revealed deep political and sectional divisions in the United States, marked by bank failure, the plummeting of farm prices, widespread joblessness and the collapse of the Western land prices.

The impact of the war also revealed that the nation lacked the financial resources to adequately support itself during times of war and peace. In 1811 Congress had decided that the Bank of the United States was undemocratic and declined to review its charter. Without a federal institution into which to deposit revenue, the federal government turned to local banks. Many of the local banks were organized with little or no restrictions and state legislatures lacked the experience to develop adequate guidelines for these private institutions. When war was declared in 1812 against Britain, the need for a national bank became obvious, leading to the incorporation of the Second Bank of the United States.

1810 Profile

Fifty-seven-year-old Lucy Childress, left with nothing but debts in Virginia, decided to travel with her family to western Kentucky to start a new life.

Life at Home

- Lucy Childress was grateful to have a house to live in, and proud to have helped build it herself.
- But she missed the comforts of her former life and the home she left behind in Virginia.
- Once the unchallenged matron of a Southern estate, Lucy, along with her husband and younger daughter, had been reduced to living in a rustic log dwelling in the wilderness of western Kentucky, on a small parcel of land belonging to her son, Randolph.
- She missed her eldest daughter, Elizabeth, and her son-in-law, Mr. Peyton, who had always been so generous and helpful; they stayed in Virginia when she moved west to escape years of accumulated debt.
- Without Mr. Peyton to lean on, Lucy could only turn to her husband and sons, who were preoccupied with problems of their own.
- Her husband, Col. Charles L. Childress, of Albemarle County, Virginia, had lost everything, and had nothing but debts to pass along to his sons.
- Formerly a wealthy landowner, slave holder and militia officer during the Revolutionary War, Col. Childress had accumulated so many debts in Virginia that he was forced to sell his land, slaves and most of his other property.
- The Colonel's reversal of fortune affected every member of the household and extended family; instead of having wealth and prestige to pass along to his sons and daughters, he had become a burden and an embarrassment.
- He was not alone.

Lucy Childress traveled to Kentucky with her family to start over.

Colonel Childress had always counted on others to manage his property and business.

- Decades of bad farming practices in Virginia had led to depletion of the soil and poor crop yields; years of war and political turmoil had disrupted the traditional European markets, leaving thousands of planters' finances in a shambles.
- In the fall of 1807, two of the Childress boys, Randolph and Lilburne, decided to make a new start and move their families to western Kentucky.
- They persuaded their parents to join them in making the arduous journey that started with a long, overland trip by wagon to Pittsburgh and culminated in a frightening sail aboard a flat boat down the Ohio River to western Kentucky.
- It was customary and cost effective for families to make long-distance moves in one big caravan; in all, the Childress party consisted of 21 family members and about 20 slaves.
- The two brothers purchased parcels of undeveloped land in Livingston County, Kentucky, and now were responsible not only for their wives and children, but for their parents and younger sisters, who came to Kentucky to keep the family together.
- But starting over was difficult.
- Col. Childress and Lucy were so destitute they were only able to bring four elderly slaves and a few meager possessions.
- The Colonel had never expected to be in this situation, and was ill-equipped to take responsibility for clearing land, planting crops, and building a new homestead in the wilderness.
- He had always depended on overseers to run his large holdings, and had never taken much interest in agriculture or the practical skills necessary for farming, such as plowing, animal husbandry, seed planting and carpentry.
- A year after the move, Randolph, Lucy's oldest son, was struggling with debts and the consequences of poor financial planning.
- He had virtually no cash to spare for any of their household needs.
- He charged $18.25 at a store in Salem, Kentucky in 1809; in 1810 he was summoned to court to pay up his overdue account.
- Lilburne, too, was short of cash, and had limited means of earning a living.
- He rented out some of his slaves on an extended basis for some income, but that left him with fewer workers in his own fields.
- When malaria and other serious illnesses struck his family, Lilburne ran up a large bill with the local doctor for house calls and medicine.
- Eventually, the doctor took him to court to force him to pay his debt.
- The youngest son, Isham, had stayed behind in Virginia; he didn't write letters very often, and Lucy wasn't sure when and if he might ever show up for a visit.
- Lucy worried about her three young daughters, wondering how they would attract eligible suitors without money for fine fabrics, shoes, handkerchiefs, books, dance lessons, or piano—all important for acquiring social skills and refinements.
- Since Lucy and her daughters no longer had servants, it was necessary for them to handle chores formerly beneath their station, such as cooking, laundry, gardening and weaving.
- Lucy could not expect much physical help from the old, frail slaves who accompanied them to Kentucky.
- Fortunately, though, the older slaves did know how the chores should be done, and they adapted well to the Spartan conditions, so they were a calming and steady influence for Lucy and her daughters.
- Among the seven slaves who came with Randolph, two were grown men, two were rented out, two were elderly, and one, Matilda, was 10 years old.
- Matilda, often called "yellow Matilda," was fathered by Col. Childress' son, Charles, and her mother was a slave in the Childress' family.

Lucy's daughters were now forced to help the servants with daily chores.

- Matilda's mother and other relatives were sold off in 1806, but Matilda stayed with the family—her master and uncle, Randolph Childress, and Lucy, her grandmother.
- Lucy often wondered how things would turn out for her grandchildren, who were forced to grow up with so little money for education and the finer things in life.
- She worried about Lilburne, too, who began associating with the wrong crowd and spending too much time in taverns, drinking too much whiskey.
- As for the Colonel, he seemed rather lost and angry.
- He wanted good meals served at his table, he wanted the neighbors to show him respect, and he often mumbled about the way things used to be.
- Each day he would walk out to the field and find fault with one thing or another, and then come back to sit idly on the porch and stare out toward the Ohio River.
- Lucy tried to soothe him and keep him cheerful, but it wasn't easy.

Life at Work

- Lucy Childress could barely remember how to perform the chores she had learned when a child, but now she had to perform those chores and many others.
- She remembered as a little girl watching one of her family's slaves warp the old loom, a process that would take many hours, and how another slave would start weaving.
- Lucy never did learn how to weave any of the complicated patterns, but she enjoyed watching the shuttle fly back and forth as sheets of cloth magically appeared.
- One of her neighbors in Kentucky offered to help Lucy and her daughters build a loom, since they had not brought one from Virginia, to make plain fabric.
- Lucy remembered how to spin, but she wasn't sure about all the steps involved in preparing flax, hemp or cotton.
- Unless something changed, Lucy realized that if the family was to have clothes and other household furnishings, she would have to relearn many of these domestic arts.
- She knew how to knit stockings, crochet coverlets, piece a quilt, and sew a dress or shirt, but weaving and flax hackling, were unfamiliar to her.
- Lucy was distraught to look down at her hands.
- They were once soft and white, with perfectly manicured nails—a sure sign of her privileged status.
- Now her fingers were puffy and red, with hard and calloused pads on her thumbs.
- Her rings had become so tight she often had to force them off.
- Lucy tried to keep her head and arms covered when she was in the fields to help with planting or harvesting, but she noticed freckles on her arms and ankles, and, alas, horrible welts caused by insect bites.
- She never imagined having hundreds of mosquitoes swarming through the air, eager to bite in every place imaginable.
- The unending drudgery of repetitive household chores, too, was more overwhelming than she had ever considered.
- The Colonel kept commenting on the fertility of the soil and the abundance of game and fish, but was oblivious to the work required to support the family's daily needs.
- He was brought up to expect a life of gentlemanly leisure, and always kept a safe distance from "women's work."

Relearning domestic arts, such as stitching and weaving, were necessary for Lucy and her daughters.

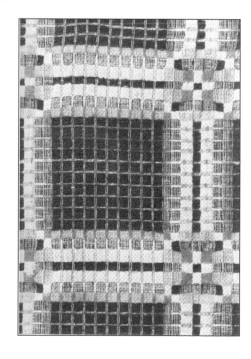

The Childress cabin in Kentucky was a far cry from their fine home in Virginia.

- And what a chore it was to prepare meals in that cramped little log house!
- Instead of a broad stone hearth equipped with cast iron trivets, gratings, and hinged hangars, the cabin had a modest fireplace with room for a few skillets and pans—not much better than the cooking arrangement in slave quarters back home.
- Lucy longed for the varieties of herbs and vegetables grown in the garden back home, too, and wondered how they would survive much longer in this place without a better food supply.
- Since there was no money to purchase sugar, tea and spices—"luxury" items that were now nearly unattainable—Lucy had to produce things they could barter with.
- In addition to teaching her daughters to spin and weave, they developed other skills with market value, such as raising chickens, hogs or sheep.
- Lilburne and Randolph always enjoyed hunting, but now, didn't have time for it.

Lucy's sons enjoyed hunting, but now had little time to for it.

- Lucy wished they could find time to hunt for fresh game—it would have been a welcome relief from the steady diet of chicken and ham.
- Lucy had never felt so tired, and at 57, the constant work load and worry began to sap her strength, leaving her vulnerable to illness that often surrounded her.
- And the Colonel did not have money to pay the local doctor for house calls.

Life in the Community: Western Kentucky

- Despite the relative isolation of their farm, Lucy Childress and her daughters had frequent opportunities to meet neighbors, make friends and participate in community-wide activities.
- There was a large gathering of families who helped Randolph and Lilburne construct their houses and barns.
- The population of Kentucky was growing dramatically, and many of the newcomers were old friends the family had known in Virginia.
- Since the Childress family had been prominent landowners in Virginia, they were initially greeted with respect by the local Kentucky families.
- Lucy was embarrassed to be living in a dwelling so much less spacious and elegant than her Virginia home, and avoided entertaining.
- She was alarmed to learn about the violence and lawlessness in Kentucky.
- She heard from her sons about cases of drunkenness, robbery and murder that were brought before the justices.
- Four towns had been erected in Livingston County: Eddyville, Centreville, Kirksville and Smithland.
- Eddyville was the largest town in the county and boasted a grist mill, paper mill, distillery and saw mill and, in 1805, an impressive shipyard, building ships up to 150 tons.
- Centreville became the new county seat of government in 1804 and by 1808 its population was about 40 whites and six slaves, with a log courthouse, a jail, two taverns, and a Presbyterian church.

Lucy was alarmed to learn of the violence and lawlessness in Kentucky.

- Kirksville was smaller, with fewer than 25 people, but located only about five miles from Cave-in-Rock, a cave made famous by visits from riverboat pirates.
- The men who lived in Cave-in-Rock preyed on unsuspecting boatloads of settlers coming down the Ohio.
- These men would pretend to be trained guides but then steer the boats into the worst and most dangerous section of the shoals, causing them to capsize.
- The pirates would let the folks drown, while accomplices waited to collect their property.
- Lucy also heard tales of taverns that allowed so much drinking that unruly customers sometimes bit off ears and gouged out their opponents' eyeballs.
- Smithland, the little town located about four miles from Lilburne's farm, at the mouth of the Cumberland, had a population of about 100 people, with two ferries and no churches.
- James McCawley, who became a good friend to Lilburne, operated a tavern in Smithland with the county's first billiard table.
- The shops in Smithland were designed to attract the business of rivermen, and business was good along a river that averaged about 15 craft a day.
- McCawley had a reputation for violence and was frequently brought before the court on charges of brutality, often in connection with his participation in a four-man gang that terrorized slaves and Indians.
- Court records revealed that John Gray was indicted for saying "God damn your fool soul," to his bay horse at Harkins stable.
- Joseph Woods, who ran a warehouse and inspection station, was charged with the failure to deliver 2,000 pounds of lead for a customer in Ohio, and in another case, found guilty of replacing tobacco with cotton in a large shipment of hogsheads.

HISTORICAL SNAPSHOT
1810

- The U.S. Census recorded the United States population of 7,239,881, 19 percent of whom were black
- The Maryland legislature authorized a lottery to build a memorial to George Washington
- The first United States fire insurance joint-stock company was organized in Philadelphia
- Spanish artist Francisco Goya began his series of etchings *The Disasters of War* depicting the Peninsular War
- Illinois passed the first state vaccination legislation in the U.S.
- Goats were introduced to St. Helena Island and began the devastation that eventually caused extinction of 22 of the 33 endemic plants
- An electrochemical telegraph was constructed in Germany
- The French Catholic Church annulled the marriage of Napoleon I and Josephine
- The first Irish magazine in America, *The Shamrock*, was published
- The British Bullion Committee condemned the practice of governments printing too much money and causing inflation
- King Kamehameha conquered and united all the Hawaiian Islands
- The first billiard rooms were established in London, England
- The sale of tobacco in France was made a government monopoly
- The Cumberland Presbyterian Church of Kentucky was excluded from the Presbyterian Church
- Napoleon ordered the sale of seized U.S. ships
- Tom Cribb of Great Britain defeated American negro boxer Tom Molineaus in 40 rounds in the first interracial boxing championship
- Simon Bolivar joined the group of patriots that seized Caracas in Venezuela and proclaimed independence from Spain
- Australian Frederick Hasselborough discovered Macquarie Island while searching for new sealing grounds

Selected Prices

Chamber Pot $0.37
Coffee Roaster $0.50
Men's Knee Buckles $2.00
Mule $80.00
Pitchfork $0.50
Scissors . . . . .12½ cents
Surgical Instruments $8.00
Toll, Horse Crossing Dan River $0.08
Wagon Whip $2.50
Watch, Gold $50.00

Letters from the South, New York, 1817:

In almost every part of the United States where I have chanced to be, except among the Dutch, the Germans, and the Quakers, people seem to build everything ex tempore and pro tempore, as if they looked forward to a speedy removal, or did not expect to want it long. Nowhere else, it seems to me, do people work more for the present, less for the future, or live so commonly up to the extent of their means. If we build houses, they are generally of wood, and hardly calculated to outlast the builder. If we plant trees, they are generally Lombardy poplars that spring up of a sudden, give no more shade than a broomstick stuck on end, and grow old with their planters. Still, however, I believe all this has a salutary and quickening influence on the character of the people, because it offers another spur to activity, stimulating it not only by the hope of gain, but the necessity to exertion to remedy past inconveniences.

Rural taste in silver, letter from William Pelham in Zanesville, Ohio, to Sidney Gardiner, Philadelphia silversmith, April 23, 1815:

In his letter to me Mr. Fletcher mentions that you will probably have many articles which I might find it advantageous to deal in. I should think you would not have many such, as your assortments will be calculated for the refined taste of an opulent city, whereas my trade must be necessarily limited to articles and necessity suitable to the first stages of civilized life.

**Letter from Lucy Childress to her brother upon leaving
Virginia for West Kentucky, 1807:**

Dear Brothar,

I now take up my pen to bid you a dieu supposing I never shall have the pleasure of again seeing you tomorrow we shall be on our way to the Mouth of the Cumberland River, you may think it strange that Ould people take so great a Journey. Nearly all my children remove to that place and their desire for their parents to go appears very great. . . . I feal much hurt at leaving two Brothers, for evar, and not seeing eather. I wish you all the happiness that can possibly be expressed by an affectionate Sister.

Letter, former President John Adams, 1813:

Science had liberated the ideas of those who read and reflect, and the American example kindled feelings of right in the people. An insurrection has consequently begun, of science, talents and courage against ranking birth, which have fallen into contempt. . . . Science is progressive, and talents and enterprise on the alert.

Cooking fish, *The Old Farmer's Almanac,* 1800:

Take the fish while still alive and scour and run him clean with water and salt, but do not scale him. Open him and put him with his blood and liver in a small kettle. Add a handful each of Sweet Marjoram, Thyme, and Parsley, and a sprig each of Rosemary and Savory. Bind the herbs in two or three small bundles and put them into the fish with four or five whole onions, twenty pickled oysters, and three anchovies. Pour on your fish as much Claret Wine as will cover him and season well with salt, cloves, mace, and orange and lemon rind. Cover the pot and put on a quick fire till it be sufficiently boiled. Then take out the fish and lay it with the broth in a dish. Pour upon him a quarter of a pound of fresh melted butter beaten with six spoonfuls of the broth, the yolks of two or three eggs, and some of the herbs, shredded. Garnish with lemons and serve it up.

1813 PROFILE

Banks Copening, an Ohio farmer whose wife had died in childbirth, had to leave his children alone when he was called to fight in the War of 1812.

Life at Home

- Banks Copening was plowing the southside of his property near the creek when his neighbor rode up on horseback with the news.
- For months Banks had been dreading this moment, when he would be called, as part of the Ohio militia, to fight the British in the Second War of Independence.
- News normally arrived slowly to Ohio—but not news of war.
- The fight with the British had begun a year earlier over shipping rights and the kidnapping of American sailors.
- Eager to invade Canada and take more territory from the British, war hawks in Congress had been rattling their sabers since 1805.
- Canada appeared ready for plucking, with 500,000 people, compared to 7.5 million people in the U.S., and a slice of those were of French origin and uncertain loyalty.
- And Banks was not convinced that the British were entirely to blame for all the Indian attacks in white settlements.
- He thought Indians were crazy enough on their own, and had to be stopped before they harmed the growth of the West.
- Banks stared at his neighbor silently for several moments, who responded to the silence sympathetically with "I know, I know. I feel the same way."
- He was to report in two weeks, not enough time to get a good crop planted.
- His only son, now 13, would have to support the three younger girls until—and if—he returned.

Banks Copening left his motherless children alone when he was called to fight in the War of 1812.

Pioneers greatly feared the Indians, who were being supplied with weapons by the British.

- When the war started, militia enlistments lasted for three months but now they were six months—just long enough to ruin an entire year's crop.
- Banks's wife Rebecca had died two years ago in childbirth after 16 hours of labor.
- Times had been hard ever since.
- Banks and Rebecca had moved to central Ohio, newly married, 21 years ago when he was 16 and she was 14.
- Their first crop and their first child failed to flourish.
- They quickly realized that they had a lot to learn if they were to survive.
- The crops for the next two years were both big harvests.
- With this hard-won prosperity came three children who all died of fever in a single week.
- They were buried next to their older brother on a small hill beneath a maple tree that turned into a blaze of fiery-colored leaves each fall.
- Rebecca visited the graves faithfully but Banks went only when Rebecca insisted, mostly on holidays.
- After she died, he visited them all each morning before the workday began while the girls dressed and fixed breakfast.
- It was during these treks that he first began to see more Indian activities—nothing threatening, but any sighting was cause for alerting neighbors to possible danger or theft.
- Now that the British were supplying the Indians with weapons and paying for pioneer scalps, only trouble could result.
- He thought about sending the children away while he was gone, but no place was safe and the neighbors were burdened enough.
- Numerous Indian nations were participating in the War of 1812—Shawnee, Miami, Delaware, Iroquois, Ottawa, Ojibwe, Dakota, Menomonie, Winnebago, Sauk and Fox.

Life at Work
- The day Banks Copening reported for duty was cloudless after three days of rain—a perfect time to plant.
- His children stood bravely as he rode away, only to collapse in a heap of tears the moment his horse passed the crest of the bend, just beyond the windbreak grove.
- He carried his own rifle, bedroll and canteen, hearing from others that essential supplies were scarce.
- Some felt the promised free musket for six months' service was not worthy of defending a man's life in battle.
- The standard issue weapon was the .70-caliber smooth-bore musket—a muzzle-loaded flintlock that fired a soft lead ball weighing an ounce and misfiring every sixth or seventh shot.
- The Ohio militia was formed in 1803; every state within the United States was mandated to recruit and maintain its own militia.
- The militia existed to protect a state's residents from attack, whether from Indians, other countries, or internal revolts.
- During the first call-up, 1,500 Ohio volunteer militiamen marched with the Fourth Regiment of the U.S. infantry.

- At the staging area at Urbana, Ohio, the enthusiastic, but unfocused, volunteers had little discipline, mostly because they didn't elect their officers themselves.
- Morale did not improve during the 200-mile march across unbroken wilderness so treacherous the supply wagon could not keep up.
- Entire regiments of several state militias left the army en masse in disputes over pay, food and the propriety of crossing the Canadian border.
- The stories Banks heard about the early days of the campaign came mostly from men who had deserted the army before William Hull surrendered at the battle of Detroit.
- Official and unofficial reports added up to the same thing — disaster.
- Early battles were victories for Britain, and hundreds of Ohio militiamen were captured.
- All able-bodied white men between the ages of 18 and 45 were required to participate in the militia, which supplemented the army.
- Most regular army officers had only disdain for state militias, saying it was impossible to plan a battle if you have no confidence your soldiers would fight.
- Soldiers who enlisted in the regular army at the start of the war accepted a five-year commitment in exchange for a bounty of $31 and 160 acres of land; when recruitment lagged the incentive was increased to $124 and 320 acres of land.

Early battles were victories for the British.

- Privates were paid $5 a month; non-commissioned officers $7 to $9 a month and officers $20 to $200, although rarely on time.
- The militia were paid $6 for three months in advance in addition to their anticipated United States pay of $5 per month.
- Once Banks arrived at Urbana, he learned that his company was to defend the American Northwest from British invasion—no small feat for these untrained farmers who were counting up the days until they could return home again.
- One aspect that united all the soldiers was their contempt for army food.
- "The flour," Banks wrote, "was mouldy and the beef and pork unfit to be eaten."
- To save money, the soldiers were fed via civilian contracts, whose profits were driven by their ability to buy low-cost foods.
- Well-fed or not, the army was expected to endure long bouts of boredom for the opportunity to fight the enemy and possibly die.
- Within the first month Banks was sent into battle—the siege of Fort Meigs—attacking a British and Indian force of 2,400 that surrounded the American fort.
- A fellow soldier described the two days of fighting, saying, "Everyone fired and struck at the enemy in wild madness."
- After a volley of firing and fear and retreat, Banks realized, "I had 20 rounds of cartridge in my box when I went to the battle ground, and when the firing ceased on examining my box I found the last was in my musket."
- A half dozen of his militia returned home that night, unnerved by the spectacle of battle, including part of a farmer's plowing arm left on the battlefield.
- Banks helped bury three soldiers, including the neighbor who had first brought news of the call-up.

- A dozen soldiers from his home county were down with the fever; another suffered from a severe nosebleed that rendered him delirious.
- Desperate to return home but fearful of the coward's brand, Banks wrote, "I lay down in despair, not caring what became of me."
- The next day his commander made a speech.
- "He began by saying he was surprised at us for not standing our ground at the bush fence."
- "This was too much," Banks recorded. "We believed that we had done all that men could do, and this was our thanks."
- The Indians continued to besiege the post at night and no one dared sleep.
- Two runners sent by the commander were turned back.
- Orderly Sergeant William Blundle and one other man went by land several days later and were successful in reaching safety, where they found reinforcements.
- Militiamen were being blamed for the break in the line.
- Once again the citizen-soldiers were the fall guys for bad military decisions.
- Banks thought seriously about leaving the military and returning home to his farm and children.

Life in the Community: Ohio

- The war that was officially declared on June 18, 1812, was the culmination of a series of events dating back to 1783.
- Like most wars, it was not fought for one reason alone.
- The end of the Revolutionary War had brought victory but left many issues unresolved, including the border between the new nation and the British colony of Canada.
- As a result, both sides claimed some of the same land, especially in Maine, giving rise to numerous border skirmishes.
    - War would allow American forces to take over Canada by gaining control of the Great Lakes and to free the West of the Indian menace fomented by the British.
    - And British fur traders refused to evacuate their lucrative Indian trading forts in Detroit, Niagara and Sandusky despite terms of the Treaty of Paris.
    - On the high seas the British routinely interfered with American shipping or captured sailors they accused of being deserters from the British navy.
    - The British navy, while on a war footing with the French, impressed approximately 6,000 American citizens by claiming they were British subjects.
    - Repeatedly, America seemed on the edge of war when shots were fired and sailors killed.
    - The Embargo Act of 1807 stopped armed conflict, but it also devastated the American economy.
    - Under the Embargo Act, American ships were forbidden to sail from a United States port to a foreign port, prohibiting American exports.
    - As a result, the nation's foreign trade came to a halt, while the British merchants scrambled to take over the foreign markets once controlled by America.
    - To the north, the Canadians did a healthy business in smuggled goods.

President James Madison.

- Throughout the Northeast, which was dependent on trade, shipping, and fishing, unemployment soared as thousands of seamen lost their livelihoods.
- In the South and West, farmers who were unable to sell their crops to Europe experienced surpluses, followed by declining prices and bankruptcy.
- The price of cotton plunged from $0.51 a pound in 1805 to $0.24 a pound three years later.
- President James Madison declared, in his war message to Congress, that free trade and sailors' rights were the leading causes of the conflict, but Western territorial expansion and the British army of Native Americans also played a part.
- Western settlers believed that the United States was destined to keep expanding to control the entire continent of North America.
- "We shall draw the British," remarked Tennessee pioneer Felix Grundy. "They will no longer have an opportunity of trade with the Indian neighbors."

America in 1812

- The United States declared war against Great Britain in 1812.
- America had almost doubled in size, thanks to the Louisiana purchase in 1803.
- Since 1783 the country had nearly doubled its population from four million inhabitants to 7.2 million.
- The ethnic makeup was 50 percent of English descent, 15 percent African, most of them slaves; 15 percent Celtic Americans, including the Scotch-Irish, Scotch and Welsh; and 15 to 20 percent German, Dutch and French.
- Approximately 100,000 American Indians lived on tribal territories in the Northeast and southeastern parts of the country.
- Four out of five Americans farmed for a living.
- The nation's city dwellers were concentrated along the East Coast in the seaport cities of New York (96,400), Philadelphia (53,700), Baltimore (45,500), Boston (33,000), Charleston (24,700), and New Orleans (17,200).
- Northern farmers worked the land with oxen, while farmers in the West preferred horses and Southerners tended to use mules.
- The most common farming tools were the hoe, the axe, the plow and the scythe.
- Many farmers could make what they needed to survive: barrels, bricks, furniture and horseshoes.
- The average household contained six persons; 40 percent of all households had eight to 12 members.
- The average white couple expected to have seven or eight children, one of whom would die before reaching the age of one; one of whom would die before reaching 21.
- Houses in the West consisted of one-room cabins about 12 feet long, and in the North the average farmhouse measured 20 to 24 feet and could contain two or three rooms; the well-to-do lived in two-story houses of brick, some with 10 or 12 rooms.

- People who lived alone were considered eccentric or mad.
- Before 1800, most American men dressed in homespun linen or wool cloth produced at home; by 1812, factory-made cloth of cotton and wool was used widely, even in rural areas.
- Most families owned a table, at least three chairs and several beds.
- Typically, families slept three or more to a single bed.
- Most homes were heated using wood-burning fireplaces.
- Whale oil lamps were beginning to replace candles; some housewives were cooking on stoves instead of kitchen fireplaces.
- The development of mass-produced clocks in 1806 dramatically expanded the number of households with a timepiece.
- Corn and pork were staples of the family table; hard cider was widely drunk in the North, whiskey in the South.
- Coffee drinking was increasing along with the level of sugar consumed annually.
- Horse racing, dog fighting, dice, cards, cock-fights and wrestling were all popular pastimes.
- The rate of exchange between the United States and Great Britain was one pound equaling $4.44.
- Other coinage in use included Mexican silver dollars; coins from England, France and the Netherlands; and even kopecks from Russia.

HISTORICAL SNAPSHOT
1813

- American forces captured Fort George, Canada
- Congress chartered the Second Bank of the United States
- American forces under General Zebulon Pike captured York, now Toronto
- The first pineapples were planted in Hawaii
- The *Demologos*, the first steam-powered warship, was launched in New York City
- The U.S. Congress authorized steamboats to carry mail
- The British announced a blockade of Long Island Sound, leaving only the New England coast to shipping
- The first mass production factory began making pistols
- A Swiss traveler discovered the Great and Small temples of Ramses II in Egypt
- David Melville of Newport, Rhode Island, patented an apparatus for making coal gas
- Jane Austen published *Pride and Prejudice*
- Simon Bolivar returned to Venezuela and took command of a patriot army, recapturing Caracas from the Spaniards
- Rubber was patented
- The first raw cotton-to-cloth mill was founded in Waltham, Massachusetts
- The U.S. invasion of Canada was halted at Stoney Creek
- Commander Oliver Perry defeated the British in the Battle of Lake Erie
- The Society for Preventing Accidents in Coal Mines in Sunderland was founded under the auspices of the Duke of Northumberland

Commander Oliver Perry.

Selected Prices

Axe $2.00
Coffee, One Pound $0.10
Loom $4.50
Musket, 1812 Model $15.00
Oats, 3 acres $18.00
Plough $15.00
Scythe, Grass $0.66
Table, Oval Breakfast $8.00
Trough $0.50
Wagon, Gear & Tent $130.00

The old officers [who had previously fought in the Revolutionary War] had very generally slunk into either sloth, ignorance, or habits of intemperate drinking.

—General Winfield Scott, concerning his fellow officers, 1814

Speech to the Delawares, 1812:

The Commissioners appointed to meet in Council the Indian tribes of the western frontier of the united states: To the Chiefs head men & Warriors of the Delaware tribe Children

Your Father the President when he heard that some of the Indian tribes had listened to the Messages of the british exciting to War, against his people had broken the bond of Friendship & violated the Treaty of Greenville, their conduct would have Justified him in Stretching out the Strong Arm of the United States for their distruction: But having regard for their welfare of all his Children, not willing to punish the Innocent with the guilty, & desirous that those who have been seduced by bad advice should have an opportunity to save themselves, from that destruction that inevitably awaits them, in case of hostility, has sent us to his Red Children with good advice Children listen, we speak the words of your Father the president, live at peace with your white and red Bretheren pursue your usual employments Provide for your Women and Children The Americans love peace, but do not fear war, they are able to fight their own Battles Your father does not ask your assistance, in the War in which he is now engaged with the british The red people have no concern in the dispute between the Americans and the British. They do not understand the causes of the war, and why should they take part in it? Consider well who are your best friends, the Americans, upon great chief, has sent you the good advice, to live in peace; or the British, who advise you to take war against your white brethern & excite the red people to war among themselves. Your old men can remember the conduct of the[m] in a former War, after engaging the red people on their side, when they were defeated they left them to the mercy of the conquerors, without their names, being mentioned in the Treaty of Peace. Children your Father has authorised his Commissioners to assure you, that if you follow his advice to live in peace with his people, & act the part of true friends, to the Americans, he will take you by the hand, will brighten the chain of friendship, & protect you against the enemies of the United States when you desire it that your Annuities shall be paid according to treaty. Your lands held sacred, & shall not be taken from you, or purchased without your express desire, & consent Children To preserve the chain of Friendship and entitle yourselves to the advantages of a lasting peace, you must watch over and be responsible for the peaceable conduct of your young men, and in case they Join the enemies of your white bretheren, you must deliver them up for Punishment You are to give notice, when the enemy are coming to attack our settlement, and by no means, to harbor in your towns the hostile Indians, in their approach or retreat from War Children It made our hearts glad to hear your determination to live in peace We will communicate your speeches to your father the president Every thing he has promised by us will be performed, we have smoaked the pipe of Peace, you have promised a lasting peace & friendship, we call the great spirit to witness the sincerity of your professions.

Anonymous Diary, War of 1812 "Second Detachment of Pennsylvania melisha (militia) commanded by jenaral Crooks."

Friday, January 1st, 1813

This day we lay in camp. The day was wet and disagreeable.

Saturday, 2nd

This day we lay at camp. This was a very snoey day and night.

Sunday, 3rd

This day we lay in camp. I went out to [rest missing].

Wednesday, 6th

This day arived at Lebanon. Major Ball rented a room for our company it not being large enough [for] our mess. Rented a room for our selves. The distance 10 miles.

Thursday, 7th

This day was taken up in making some arrangement for housekeeping.

Friday, 8th

Nothing to doo but take care of our horses and in the evening Joseph Waddle heard that Robert Henderson had reported that he had acted cawardly in the action which adgitated him very much.

Saturday, 9th

This morning Joseph Waddle and John Willson went down to Henderson's room to have [rest missing]

Monday, 11th

Nothing to doo but take care of our horses.

Tuesday, 12th

Was taken up examining the bills of lost property.

Wednesday, 13th

Was taken up in same business.

Thursday, 14th

The last of the Kentucky Caverly went home on furlough.

Friday, 15th

Pay roles was made out and sent to Cincinata.

Saturday, 16th

This day we lay in our srrom having nothing but feeding our horses.

Tuesday, 19th

This day the landlord moved from the sine (sign) of the swan to the Crasskees and we moved with him. His name was Samuel Hetan.

Wednesday, 20th

This day Captain Scott and Perce came in town and loged with us and informed us J. Weddel that his father was ded and that me pepel was all well. The [day] is cold.

Thursday, 21st

This day I road out to Company of Captain Scott and Perce. I went 4 [miles] and returned home.

continued

Anonymous Diary, War of 1812 . . . *(continued)*

Sunday, 24th

This day was very wet and the water was very hy.

Monday, 25th

Nothing happened worth riting.

Wednesday, 27th

This day I road out of town a few miles took linen and then returned back.

Wednesday, 27th (second entry)

Nothing for this day.

Thursday, 28th

Lay at Lebanon.

Saturday, 30th

Lay at the same place.

Sunday, 31st

This day the news came into Lebanon that General Winchester defeated and orders for Major Balls Squadron to March to the Rapids tho solders was unesy about then.

The Journal of Lt. John Le Couteur, 1814:

The old Christmas custom of the "First Footing" determined the fortunes of the family in the coming year by the first visitor on Christmas day: A good year was expected if a handsome man visited bearing coal or salt; whilst a poor old woman arriving at your door was considered a bad omen.

Lieutenant John LeCouteur, while stationed in Kingston, Upper Canada, gave them both:

After tea well over and arrangements were making for forfeits or some amusement to be fixed upon, I slipped out with Miss Ph—s, an ally who lent me one of Her Mother's dresses. In a short time I was fully equipped, slipped out of the back door, knocked at the front door, and requested to speak to the kind Old lady as a decayed Gentlewoman requiring aid. Miss Ph. was of course sent out to hear my story and thought it would be better the poor Lady should tell her own story to the whole party who might become interested in her welfare. This was reported and the decayed Lady told her piteous tale, loss of Husband, children, fortune. The old Lady herself was completely won and a large sum was preparing for her relief but a certain occasional twinkling in the unfortunate Lady's eye led one or two of the fair sparklers [to] suspect the truth—a whisper went about and screams of laughter following, the poor Lady had to cut and run.

**Letter from Thomas Jefferson
to John Adams,
October 28, 1813:**

Science had liberated the ideas
of those who read and reflect,
and the American example
kindled feelings of right in the
people. An insurrection has
consequently begun, of science, talents and courage
against ranking birth, which
have fallen into contempt. . . .
Science is progressive, and talents and enterprise on the
alert.

**Total number of deaths,
*Morning Chronicle and
Baltimore Advertiser,*
September 8, 1819:**

Total number of deaths in the last week, ending
Monday at sunrise:

Adults, 40
Children, 51
Total, 91

29 deaths of malignant fever east of the falls.
One death of malignant fever west of the falls.
61 from other diseases.

1815 Profile

For all intents and purposes, John Lewis was a logger. He was also known as the best whiskey maker in the mountains of Patrick County, Virginia.

Life at Home

- Logger and whiskey maker John Lewis, and his family, lived in the Bent, a mountain community near the rugged pinnacles of Buffalo Mountain, Virginia.
- The prosperity of John, his wife Colleen, and their children was fueled by hard work and several generations of well-earned mountain know-how.
- Alvin Lewis, John's grandfather, had moved west into Patrick County, Virginia, from Newcastle, Pennsylvania, in 1745, traveling southwest along the Great Valley Path.
- Originally an Indian trail known as the Warriors Path, the Great Valley Path was the route by which the Scotch-Irish made their way into Virginia and points south.
- For three generations their homes had been built of logs with two cribs, or rooms, covered by one roof which extended over both.
- Fireplaces with outside chimneys were located at each end.
- Their barns consisted of a covered central building with shed roofs on all sides.
- At the back of the Lewis house stood the smokehouse, which was used to cure, smoke and store meats.
- The wash kettle and the "battling" bench, where the laundry was scrubbed, was located near the edge of the river branch which flowed by the house.
- The Lewis boys, Charles, 16, and Micah, 15, demonstrated their loyalty to family two years earlier while their father was away for nine months fighting the British during the Second War of Independence, the War of 1812.

John Lewis was a logger, and the best whiskey maker in the mountains of Virginia.

- The Lewis girls, Mary, 13, and Alva, 11, also responded favorably to the increased workload during the war.
- Their father missed one entire harvest while away, but the winter was mild, the neighbors helpful and only one hog died and no more than a handful of chickens had disappeared into the talons of hawks or the jaws of foxes.
- The biggest loss was the cash money they traditionally earned from the whiskey still, so that year the children's shoes were not replaced (though they were split by mountain ice) and the girls did not get new ribbons at Christmas.
- Since no school was available for the four children, their parents, who were both able to sign their names, taught their children to read from the Bible.
- Both the Bible and John Lewis preached the same sermon—hard work was the secret of a good life.
- The only other reading material in the house was a *Farmer's Almanac* that Colleen loved to consult, and occasionally argue with, about its weather predictions.
- Her mother had taught Colleen how to predict the weather based on the goose bone method, which did not always agree with the almanac.
- At Thanksgiving, Colleen would serve a freshly killed goose that had been roasted and then carved so as not to cut the breast bone from the carcass.
- After the meal, she would carefully remove the breastbone and cut away all the meat and fat so the bone could be put on a shelf to dry.
- If the bone turned blue, black or purple, a cold winter lay ahead; white indicated a mild winter; purple tips were the sure sign of a cold spring; and a blue color toward the edge of the bone meant open weather until New Year's Day.
- Colleen also used the almanac to record planting dates and harvest yields, as well as for notes concerning which bug killers worked best.
- Everyone worked every day except Sunday, ensuring that the family had a good crop.
- The two boys plowed the fields while the whole family helped with seed sowing and cultivation.
- With three cows, 34 beehives, a sheep flock, an apple orchard and a herd of free ranging pigs, there was always something to do.
- But blessed with a cold spring in the yard, a vein of coal near the kitchen door, and a large deer population to harvest, the family was able to remain comfortable and, just as important, independent.
- During the summer months when the list of chores seemed endless, the fireplace occupied an important role in family life.
- Equipped with a built-in horizontal bar running from side to side about three feet off the fireplace floor, the hearth allowed for pots and kettles to be hung from hooks above the fire and used for cooking stews, vegetables and meats.
- With everyone busy with various tasks all day long, this type of cooking could be done with only periodic minding.
- Leather breeches beans, which were dried by sewing the bean pods on a string, served as a quick and convenient meal for this busy family.
- Colleen made ash cakes by mixing a thick cornbread dough, shaping small cakes, covering them with a cloth and putting them in a cleaned out corner of the fireplace.
- Hot ashes covered the cloth and hot coals covered the ashes, cooking the cakes in half an hour using its own moisture to prevent the cloth and cakes from burning.
- As the fall approached, activity shifted toward the harvest.
- The Lewises—like most of their Scotch-Irish neighbors—grew corn, beans and squash for their use.
- Food bartering among neighbors was rare since everyone grew similar crops.
- But the harvesting of the corn crop signaled the beginning of John Lewis's real source of income—distilling fine whiskey for the entire community.

Life at Work

- For all practical purposes, John Lewis was a logger.
- He was also known as the distiller of the best moonshine on the mountain.
- Logging was one of the ways a moonshiner could mask his activities and gain access to the ash, hickory and oak wood which was used to stoke still fires.
- Logging was hard work with meager rewards.
- Often it took an entire day to fell a large oak using an axe that needed to be repeatedly sharpened.
- Once the tree was felled, the task of laboriously pulling wood logs down the mountain was accomplished using a wagon and a working steer team.
- John preferred driving oxen for logging work because the steers were easier to handle than horses.
- Oxen were less expensive to feed on cottonseed meal and hulls, and if a steer was injured during work it could be butchered and eaten with minimal loss.
- John preferred to work Red Devon oxen, an old stock cattle breed the Scotch-Irish had raised for generations.
- The winter, after the ground had frozen, was the best time for logging because the logs were easier to skid on the icy ground.
- Mountain loggers got most of their work done during inclement weather, which kept farmers cabin-bound.
- John felt lucky to have two healthy boys to help him with the heavy work and also a father to dispense wisdom when the work got especially dangerous.

Felled trees were pulled down the mountain by steers.

- Loggers were better known in the mountains for their courage than their longevity.
- Working in the wintertime woods also placed John Lewis conveniently close to his whiskey-making still operation, located high in the northern facing slope with a quality stream running westward.
- The homemade still was hidden in a dense laurel thicket with a "room" for the whiskey production cut out in the center with easy access to cold running water.
- A pipe for running water from the stream was made by stripping wild chestnut bark intact from a slender pole.
- Making liquor was as natural as butchering a hog, and John had learned how from his father and was proud to teach his children.
- Before the run was started, corn was moistened and kept warm until it sprouted, then dried, and then was ground to make a cornmeal malt.
- The mash, made up of regular cornmeal, was then put into barrels, mixed with yeast and hot water and allowed to ferment until the base was ready for the addition of the malt.
- Good fresh white corn was preferred for the mash, requiring three gallons of water per bushel.
- For more than a week the mixture was kept just warm enough to ferment and batches that were allowed to chill down spoiled and were thrown away.
- After fermentation, the liquid was poured into the still, the fire lit and the vapors started through the copper spiral pipe.

Working in the woods put John close to his whiskey-making operation.

- The fuel of choice was ash, oak or hickory, which were found in abundance in the mountains of Patrick County.
- Ten- to 12-foot logs were fed slowly into the furnaces as they burned.
- Cooled by the running water surrounding the worm-like pipe, the vapors condensed into a liquid called singlings, which ran into a bucket.
- After a run, the still was emptied and the singlings poured back in to be distilled a second time into doublings, which emerged free of oils and impurities.
- While still warm the whiskey was put into jugs and carried away, often by John's two boys and two lifelong friends who could be trusted.
- Half of every batch was sent over the mountain for cash money; half was distributed to neighbors who paid John back when they could.
- Where whiskey was involved, a runner had numerous temptations, from drinking from the jug before delivery, to stealing the payment, to telling the law.
- Trust was always a delicate issue, especially after a shooting.
- Women always blamed liquor for a son's death.
- When John had extra liquor to sell he used the twig communication system; knowledgeable men recognized that a series of sticks cut in a particular fashion and thrown into the path was an advertisement for moonshine.
- John loved spending his winters in the woods—away from people—tending mash, even after a tree fell on his shoulder and produced a persistent throbbing when cold weather was about.
- There was something special about the mountains in wintertime that made John breathe better.

A logging community in the Blue Ridge Mountains.

Life in the Community: Patrick County, Virginia

- The Scotch-Irish began to arrive in the ports of Philadelphia and Newcastle shortly after the beginning of the 1700s.
- In 1737 Scotch Irishman Morgan Brian cleared an Indian trail known as Warriors Path, creating a new wagon trail from the Pontiac Potomac River to the Yadkin River in North Carolina.
- After 1740 the Scotch-Irish began moving into the Patrick County mountains in increasing numbers.
- The Buffalo Mountain settlement called the Bent was isolated by design, with neighbors living miles apart.
- This remoteness was conducive to mountain-style peace of mind, but not to the support of schools, which were nonexistent.
- If children were educated, it was at home, if their parents were literate themselves.
- Within this isolated community the church became the center of social life for the Scotch-Irish mountaineers.
- Most Scotch-Irish were Presbyterians.
- Presbyterian ministers were usually well-educated men of a type not eager to venture into the more remote areas.
- Few Presbyterian ministers were attracted to the opportunities of the untamed Blue Ridge Mountains.
- The spiritual void was filled by the Primitive Baptist faith, led by local men called to preach from the laity.

- Although unschooled, these preachers delivered rousing, sometimes eloquent sermons inspired by the spirit—not book learning.
- Too much education could get between a man and his Lord, they believed.
- Baptisms were performed in nearby rivers, creeks and streams, along with ritual foot washing practiced by the older members.
- Though not large in numbers, the Primitive Baptist religion set the social customs and patterns that dominated the Blue Ridge.
- The climax of the Primitive Baptist year, the August meeting, was the social event of the southern mountains.
- Preaching began early on Saturday mornings followed by baptisms in the river.
- A 100-foot table could barely hold all the picnic baskets brought by each family.
- Crowds would number as large as 800 or 900.
- Outside the church, large crowds would promenade in their best clothing, often purchased especially for the occasion.
- By late afternoon arguments and disagreements fueled by moonshine consumption grew in pitch and fury.
- Sometimes these altercations resulted in death.
- The Primitive Baptists allowed liquor on church grounds, even though most agreed liquor was a vice.
- The prevailing attitude was that drinking was an inalienable right for those who chose to partake.
- In 1791 when the federal Congress placed an excise tax on distilled liquors, a committee of citizens from Patrick and Henry counties sent a petition to the Congress in which they stated in part, "We are being deprived of one of the greatest God-given pleasures of life by a tax we cannot pay."
- They strongly urged that the tax be repealed.
- These mountaineers had been Washington's favored troops and took pride in their reputation.
- Whiskey was one of the few sources of cash income for most.
- Despite the tax, the Scotch-Irish continued to support the federal government and even fought in the War of 1812, the second war between the United States and Great Britain.
- Patrick County responded to the war with a regiment of soldiers under the command of Colonel Samuel Staples, who went to Norfolk, Virginia, and helped fight the British.
- John Lewis and many of his friends served in this regiment.

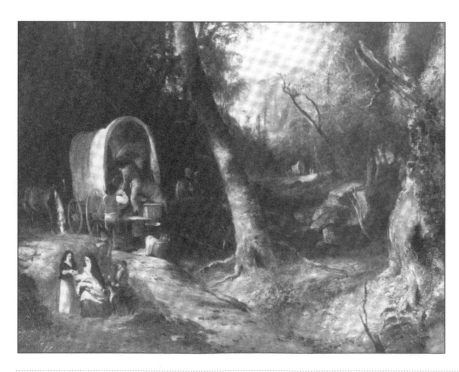

Baptisms were performed in rivers and creeks.

HISTORICAL SNAPSHOT
1815

- Andrew Jackson defeated the British at the Battle of New Orleans after the War of 1812 was officially over
- Napoleon and 1,200 men left Elba to start the 100-day reconquest of France but were defeated by British forces under Wellington at the Battle of Waterloo
- Humphry Davy invented the miner's safety lamp for use in coal mines, which allowed deep coal seams to be mined despite the presence of methane
- The world's first commercial cheese factory was established in Switzerland
- Congress appropriated funds for the restoration of the White House and hired James Hoban, the original designer and builder, to do the work
- John Roulstone of Massachusetts penned the first three lines of "Mary Had a Little Lamb" after a classmate named Mary was followed to school by her pet lamb
- The first New England missionaries arrived in Hawaii
- William Prout postulated that atomic weights of elements were multiples of that for hydrogen
- Three thousand post offices had been opened in the United States
- Austrian composer Franz Schubert produced two symphonies, two masses, 20 waltzes and 145 songs
- The Library of Congress, which was burned during the War of 1812, was re-established with Thomas Jefferson's personal library of 6,500 volumes
- Sunday observance in the Netherlands was regulated by law
- A United States flotilla ended the decades-old piracy of Algiers, Tunis and Tripoli when the U.S. declared war on Algiers for taking U.S. prisoners and demanding tribute

Selected Prices

Bible with Maps $2.00
Cigars, 10 Spanish $0.08
Colander $0.12
Corn, Barrel $3.33
Jars, per Dozen $1.60
Jelly, Pot of Strawberry $0.50
Spectacles and Case $1.75
Toothbrushes, Lot $0.50
Umbrella $1.00
Whiskey, Gallon $0.39

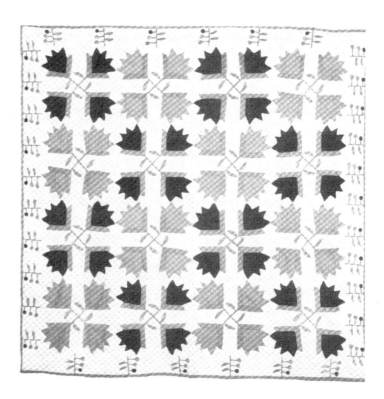

"Taste in America," *Baron Klinkowstrom's America,* 1818-1820:

In the states where I have been, English tastes are prevalent in the interior of the houses, the furnishings and furniture. However, in the country district where German colonists have settled, German architecture prevails. Long stretches of Pennsylvania have kept the Rhineland building and furnishing methods, but in the cities the English dimensions and custom of placing the narrow side of the house toward the streets are accepted.

Usually only two rooms are used, one as a dining room and the other as a living room. In the dining room there is always a very elegant Mahogany sideboard decorated with silver and metal vessels of the household as well as with beautiful cut glass and crystal. Carpets are in common use in this country even in the homes where, because of financial conditions, one would not expect to find them. In the parlor the sofa is placed at one end of the fireplace during the wintertime, and here the lady of the house always takes her place. Everyone gathers around the fire and when the group is small the evening is spent between the fireplace and a table always in the middle of the floor, whereon tea is served or water and cognac which is a popular drink here, without which one is seldom permitted to leave.

In intimate and family groups tobacco is smoked in the presence of women; cigars are used, not pipes; and the kind, unassuming American women allow it.

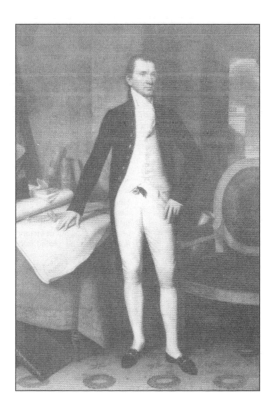

"Mahogany Furniture," *Sketches of America*, Henry Bradshaw Fearon, 1818:

Honduras mahogany is five-pence halfpenny to seven pence farthing the superficial foot; in St. Domingo, nine pence three farthing to 17 pence half-penny. Mahogany is used for cupboards, doors, and banisters, and all kinds of cabinet work. Curl maple, a native and most beautiful wood, is also much approved. Veneer is in great demand, and is cut by machinery. Chest of drawers are chiefly made of St. Domingo mahogany; the inside is faced with boxwood: shaded veneer and curl maple are also used for this purpose. I would remark, that the cabinet work executed in this city (New York) is light and elegant. Indeed, I am inclined to believe that it is superior to English workmanship. I have seen some with cut glass instead of brass ornaments, which had a beautiful appearance. . . . Cabinetmakers shops, of which there are several in Greenwich street, contain a variety, but not a large stock. They are generally small concerns, apparently owned by journeymen who had just commenced on their own account. These shops are perfectly open, and there is seldom any person in attendance. In the centre, the board is suspended with the notice, "Ring the bell." I have conversed with several proprietors: they state their business to have been at one time good, but there is now too much competition.

"George Washington's Last Will and Testament," *The life of George Washington*, David Ramsey, 1807:

To my brother, Charles Washington, I give and bequeath the gold-headed cane left me by Dr. Franklin, in his will. I add nothing to it, because of the ample provision I have made for his issue. To the acquaintances and friends of my juvenile years, Lawrence Washington and Robert Washington, of Chotanct, I give my two other gold-headed canes, having my arms engraved on them; and to each, (as they will be useful where they live) I leave one of the spy-glasses, which constituted part of my equipage during the late war. To my compatriot in arms, and old and intimate friend, Dr. Craik, I give my bureau, or, as the cabinetmakers call it, tambour-secretary, and the circular chair, an appendage of my study. To Dr. David Stewart, I give my large shaving and dressing table, and my telescope. To the reverend now Bryan Lord Fairfax, I give a Bible, in three large folio volumes, with notes, presented to me by the Rt. Reverend Thomas Wilson, a bishop of Sodor and Man. To Gen. De la Fayette, I give a pair of finely wrought steel pistols, taken from the enemy in the Revolutionary war. To my sisters-in-law, Hannah Washington and Mildred Washington—to my friends, Eleanor Stuart, Hannah Washington, of Fairfield and Elizabeth Washington, of Hayfield, I give each a mourning ring of the value of 100 dollars. These bequests are not made for the intrinsic value of them, but as mementos of my esteem and regard.

"Maryland Penitentiary, $160 Reward," *Morning Chronicle and Baltimore Advertiser,* September 8, 1819:

160 dollars will be paid for the apprehension and delivery at this institution, of the following convicts, who escaped at half past one o'clock yesterday morning. Their names and descriptions are as follows, viz:

ALEXANDER BEATTY, born in Connecticut, 34 years of age, 5'10" high, brown complexion, brown hair, a stout well-made man, has a vicious down look when spoken to.

JOHN CASEY, born in Frederick county, Maryland 30 years of age, fair complexion, brown hair, no visible mark.

JOHN LACY, born in Frederick county, Maryland, 30 years of age, fair complexion, brown hair, no visible marks, shows his teeth much when speaking.

EDWARD MARTIN, born in Philadelphia, brown complexion, 6 feet half an inch high, dark hair, no visible mark, 21 years of age.

WILLIAM KELLINGER, alias LEWIS SMITH, born in New-York, 23 years of age, fair hair, 5 feet 5 inches high, no visible mark.

JOSEPH BISHOP, born in Connecticut, 31 years of age, fair complexion, 5 feet 6 inches high, the thumb and three fingers of the left hand lost.

"A Curious Fact," *Farmer's Almanac,* 1795:

During several weeks of last summer, one of my milch-cows very frequently gave clotted blood from one of her tits, which, whenever this was the case appeared scratched and inflamed. The milkmaid insisted she was sucked by a snake, but I paid little attention at first. Observing the animal so affected, I had her put into a separate pasture, and then nothing happened for several days. Thinking she might now be suffered to graze with the other cattle, she was put into her former pasture, and immediately her milk and tit were affected as above. She seemed very uneasy toward evening; always repaired to the same spot on the field at that time and lowed violently as if she had lost her calf. One evening as I was walking toward her, I saw a large black snake very near her, measuring nearly four feet. . . . I think we may reasonably assume that the uncommon bloody appearance of her milk and tit must have arisen from being sucked by this huge reptile.

"Farmer's Calendar," *Farmer's Almanac,* 1812:

January: Feed your doves and spread ashes among their dung

February: Sled out your winter dung as you can carry much more on a sled than you can on a cart in April

April: Set trees; be sure to set that side south that was south before

July: Now all hands be haying; begin by mowing the ripest and thinnest first

September: Turn your pigs into the woods to gather acorns

November: Bleed your horses and fat cattle of all kinds

December: Now come on the long and social winter evenings when the farmer may enjoy himself and instruct and entertain his family by reading some useful books

---

In the event of a thunderstorm the safest place is within a few feet of your horse, which being then a more elevated animal, will receive the shock in preference.

—*Farmer's Almanac,* 1800

"Our Southern Highlanders," Horace Kephart, 1911:

The North of Ireland was settled by the Scotsman who had been imported by James I. They learned how to make poteen in little stills after the Irish fashion. By-and-by the Scotch-Irish fell out with the British government, and large bodies of them emigrated to America. They were a fighting race. They brought with them, too, an undying hatred of excise taxes, and a spirit of unhesitative resistance to any authority that sought to enforce such laws.

Morning Chronicle & Baltimore Advertiser.

I.] WEDNESDAY MORNING, SEPTEMBER 8, 1819. [No. 132.

AMSTERDAM,
...fast sailing Ship PHILIP,
...ROBERT LESLIE, will begin to
...articles of small bulk only
...freight, if immediate applica-
...For freight, or passage, having
...modations, apply to the cap-
...Cordery's wharf, or to
...AS. W. KARTHAUS & CO.
No. 50, South Gay-street.

AGE FOR DOVER,
...will land Passengers at Dover.

d2w

...on of Co-partnership
...ship heretofore existing between
..., under the firm of SEYLER &
...this day dissolved by mutual
...persons having claims against
...present them to Wm. Metzger
...; and all indebted to them, are
...red to make payment without
...as he is duly authorized to re-
...due to them.
FREDERICK SEYLER,
WM. METZGER.

TO LET,

Marine Bank of Baltimore,
September 4th, 1819.
THE BUSINESS of this BANK will be trans-
acted at No. 165½, BALTIMORE-STREET,
until further notice.
By order,
JB. BIER, Cashier.
sept 6   d6t

CARRE & SANDERSON'S
SEMINARY,
NO. 380, MARKET-STREET,
PHILADELPHIA.
MESSRS. CARRE & SANDERSON,
inform their friends respectfully, that the exercises of their school will recommence on
the first day of September. To merit a con-
tinuation of the public patronage, they shall
endeavor to maintain that organization of the
studies of their seminary, which, according to
their judgment and experience, may best promote the interests of their pupils, and to pursue that conduct in the duties of their profession, which ought to ensure them the esteem
of the worthy, and the approbation of those
who rightly appreciate the benefits of a liberal
education. And, at the same time, they have
to solicit the co-operation of the parents and
guardians of their pupils in supporting the
discipline and regulations which are indispensable to the progress of the scholar, as well as

THE NEW & ELEGANT
Steam-Boat MARYLAND,
CLEMENT VICKERS, Master,
Has commenced her regular route between
Easton, Annapolis and Baltimore—Leaving
Easton every Monday & Thursday at 8 o'clock,
A. M. for Annapolis and Baltimore, via Todd's
Point, in Dorchester county, and arrive at Annapolis at half past 1 o'clock, P. M. and
from thence at half past 2 o'clock, P. M. for
Baltimore.
Passengers bound to Philadelphia, will meet
the Union Line of Steam Boats, and arrive
there the next morning, making by this route
only 24 hours from Easton to that place—Returning leaves Baltimore for Annapolis and
Easton, every Wednesday and Saturday, at 8
o'clock, A. M. arrives at Annapolis at half past
11 o'clock, A. M. and starts from thence at
12 o'clock, P. M. arrives at Easton at
6 o'clock same evening, via Todd's Point, Ox-
ford, and a place known by the name of the
Double Mills. The Maryland will also take on
board Horses, Carriages, &c. All baggage at
the risk of the owners.
sept 4   1y
UNION LINE

SHERIFF'S SALES.
Great Bargains may be expected.
By virtue of a writ of fieri facias to me directed, will be exposed to Public Sale on the
premises, on THURSDAY, the sixteenth day
of September next, at 10 o'clock, A. M. at the
house lately occupied by Peter Hardt, in the
borough of York, that well known and valuable
Establishment, viz.

YORK RECORDER,
Together with the entire PRINTING and JOB
OFFICE attached thereto, consisting in part of
3 Printing Presses
12 Pair of Stands
60 do   Cases
1 Fount 14 line Pica Type
1 do   7 do   do   do
1 do   5 do   do   do
1 do   Cannon   do
1 do   Double Great Primer
5 do   Double Pica, English, and
       German
2 do   German Text
2 do   Pica, English and German
3 do   Small Pica do and do
1 do   Long Primer
2 do   Brevier
1 do   Nonpareil
With every other Article requisite for carrying
on the Printing Business on an extensive scale.
If the above are not sold at private...

City Bank of Baltimore,
August 15th, 1819.
The Stockholders in this institution are
hereby respectfully notified, that a GENERAL
MEETING will be held at their Banking
House, in the City of Baltimore, on TUESDAY
the 20th day of October next, at 11 o'clock, A.
M. when a statement of the affairs of the bank
will be laid before them for their consideration.
By order of the Board.
J. PINKNEY, Jr. Cashier.
august 14   d:200
The Annapolis Maryland Republican,
Easton Star, Hagerstown Gazette, and Frede-
ricktown Examiner, will publish the above
four times.

MARYLAND
PENITENTIARY STORE
220½
MARKET-STREET.
RICHARD B. SPALDING,
Sole Agent for vending the Manufactures of the
Maryland Penitentiary,
OFFERS FOR SALE,
Hats, fur and wool, well assorted
Shoes and Boots, leather and morocco, do.

GARDEN SEEDS, &c.
The Subscriber has for Sale a variety of
Cabbage,   Turnip,   Lettuce
Radish & other Seeds,
FIT FOR THIS SEASON:
Those Seeds have been warranted good, and
of a superior quality.
Country made up with care and despatch.
No. 2, Hanover-street, next door
sept 6   eo4t

WILLIAM MILES,
No. 3, Share-street, near Market-street,
HAS FOR SALE,
4to Post, gilt and plain   Super Royal do do
in cases   Royal   do do do
Folio Post do do   Medium do do
Foolscap assorted do   Demi   do do
Pot assorted   do   Tea Papers assorted
Bank Bill do do   Stainers' Printing Pa-
Wrapping Paper   pers
Kentish Cap do   Large & small, & blue
Ironmongers do   and white Band-box
Cotton Yarn do do   Boards
Double Wrapping do   Binders' do
Sheathing Paper   Saddlers' Trunk do
Cases uncut Pot & Cap   Sugar Loaf Paper

1819 NEWS FEATURE

"Benevolence," *Morning Chronicle and Baltimore Advertiser,*
September 8, 1819:

Times of severe affliction, when Divine Providence, to answer his own inscrutable purposes visits us with sickness and sorrows, these seasons are surely calls for the display
of every Christian grace. When we remember, that we are all but moving masses of dust
and ashes, liable every moment to crumble into nothing at the touch of death; that
however distinguished these phantoms of existence may be by opulence, by prosperity,
by character, or by talents above their fellows, yet that a few more fleeting suns will reduce us all to a mournful and silently equality; that the period approaches, when beauty
will no longer fascinate, opulence entice, power overawe, or splendor of intellect delight; these are surely reasons why these animated forms of dust and ashes, should be
kind and merciful to each other; but when in addition to all these ordinary evils with
which human life is waylaid and ensnared at every turn and angle, the Deity empties
upon us his vials of wrath; when death seems to walk amidst the blaze of noon, then
surely does it become us more specially, to exercise humanity and benevolence. Creditors should remember that honest, patient, persevering industry is now incapable of
finding employment—that he eats his daily bread in the sweat of his brow, and does
not mean to be dishonest—that by pressing their claims at a period like the present,
they drive their victims into the list of the insolvent debtors—that they compel them to
resort to bankruptcy, by the very means that they take to enforce the claim of debt—
that no alternative remains but bankruptcy, when a legal claim is so rigidly enforced at
such a season.

But it is not the only duty of Christians to remain satisfied, by such a display of benevolence; they are called on for the exercise of duties more active; duties more decidedly
benevolent; they are bound to administer comfort to the sick, and to lighten the load of
poverty—the evils inflicted by Divine Providence, we must all bear, as well as the opulent
as the poor; but it surely becomes us in a season like the present, not to add to such awful afflictions; not to render the malady with which the city is visited more insupportable;
not in fine to make ministry more wretched, and dejection more hopeless.

We are drawn to these reflections by a noble display of benevolence, that has lately
been manifested by some of the philanthropic citizens of Baltimore—two ropewalks

near the city have, we understand, been furnished for the accommodation of the suffering poor, who are now able to fly from the part which is the abode of the malignant disease, and to find a refuge, furnished by the humanity of their fellow citizens—1,000 of these unhappy fugitives have been accommodated already. But this is not enough, every man whose heart aches for the sorrows and suffering for a fellow being, whose nerves involuntarily shake, and whose eyes overflow with the tale, or the spectacle of distress; who remembers that while an animated compound of dust and ashes, implores charity from his hands that he is himself nothing more than dust and ashes, subject to the same infirmities, beset of the same temptations, prone to the same painful vicissitudes of misery, is bound to contribute all in his power for his suffering race.

We may if he is not able personally to contribute, suggest plans for ameliorating the distress of his fellow citizens—these may be examined, canvassed and discussed in our public journals, and those that are practical and abounding with benevolence, adopted. We should delight in the present afflicting season to enrich our columns with speculations of this character, and we hope this invitation will not be passed by without notice. A large expanded, systematic and comprehensive charity is demanded at this awful crisis. In the same degree as Heaven afflicts, should mankind be merciful to each other. To borrow an image from physical nature, it ought to be remembered, that in proportion to the darkness, turbulence and grandeur of the tempest, shines in the bow of the cloud, as if the angel of mercy had been contending with the demon of destruction, and had erected this triumphal arch in the heavens to commemorate his victory.

1820–1829

During the 1820s, explosive conflicts emerged between the Northern and Southern states around the issues of slavery. The formation of the Missouri Compromise provided a brief balance of power in Washington but forever prohibited slavery in the rest of the Louisiana Territory north of the parallel 36°30′ north line. Economic dependence on imports further upset Southern Americans as the Tariff of 1828 was signed into federal law protecting Northern American industry. The economic hardships encouraged some Southern Americans to cast their eyes toward Spanish-controlled Texas for future agricultural expansion.

The nation progressively moved west with its population center moving farther away from the East Coast. Many Americans began migrating west of the Mississippi River, while others entered areas not entirely controlled by the United States. To grow its North American territory, Spain welcomed Americans into Texas to settle the region and pursue agriculture development. Along the Pacific Coast, both Britain and the United States jointly occupied the Oregon Country that supported the fur trade which was lucrative for both countries.

During the 1820s, many trappers and explorers were discovering the secrets of the American West. Jedediah Smith's expedition crossed and mapped the Sierra Nevada and the Great Salt

Lake regions for future growth. Americans exploring the Oregon Territory for fur formed organizations for the region's settlement, eventually creating conflict between the American states and Britain. Border conflicts also arose with Native Americans as settlers entered their lands. In 1825, a treaty was signed by the Creek Indians in which they promised to turn over their lands in Georgia and migrate west.

Even as Native Americans were losing territory to U.S. expansion, many literary works were printed, such as *Yamoyden*; *Logan, an Indian Tale*; and *Ontwa, Son of the Forest*, that provided American citizens a romantic perception of Native American life. James Fenimore Cooper's *The Last of the Mohicans* was a phenomenal publishing success selling over two million copies.

Culturally, the American nation was finding distractions in other endeavors. Horse-racing was growing as a common spectator sport. The first major race with 100,000 spectators occurred at the Union Course on Long Island between two horses in 1823. The theater experienced competition when the historically dominant British performers were rivaled by American talent such as between American Edwin Forrest and British William Chare Macready in New York City. The new theater of white entertainers in blackface likely developed in 1828 with Thomas Dartmouth Rice's solo performance of dancing and singing "Jim Crow."

As the American industrial economy grew, so did the growth of canal construction to transport goods at lower costs. The completion of the 350-mile Erie Canal in 1825 proved commercially successful and encouraged many states to construct their own canal systems. By the decade's end, canal construction was common along the East Coast, including the $2.25 million Chesapeake and Delaware Canal. When completed in 1829, its cost was shared by the U.S. Government, Delaware, Maryland and Pennsylvania. Even as the growth of canals took place, a new technology was emerging using steam power, allowing a travel speed of 12 to 15 mph without exhaustion of an animal—more than double the 6 mph of the stagecoach. The development of the Baltimore and Ohio Railroad foreshadowed a shift in transport that would later influence the nation's development.

1823 Profile

Caleb Hope had already been to exotic China three times aboard merchant ships by the time he celebrated his twenty-second birthday; his first voyage across the ocean took place when he was only 13 years old.

Life at Home

- Caleb Hope, a seasoned sailor, dreamed of being the first mate of a merchant sailing ship.
- His every thought revolved around the ocean.
- The fifth of eight children, Caleb was born in Salem, Massachusetts; his father was a lawyer who took the last name of Hope to inherit a female relative's modest legacy.
- After his mother died when he was seven, Caleb was farmed out to his paternal grandmother in Newburyport, Massachusetts; she died a year later.
- Caleb and three of his brothers were then sent to separate boarding schools in Boston where as an 11-year-old he joined fellow Bostonians in repelling British soldiers raiding the harbor in the opening days of the War of 1812.
- After his father remarried, Caleb and his brothers were allowed to come home only twice a year: once in the fall to get their winter clothes, and once in the spring to get their spring clothes.
- "We were not allowed to be at home at the same time, so the years passed without our seeing one another," Caleb remembered.
- His only pleasure at school, under the strict rule of a Congregationalist minister, was attending church where he could fantasize about a pretty little girl in a straw hat who sat nearby; over the course of a year, he never spoke to her and never learned her name.
- Unlike his four brothers, who eventually attended college, Caleb was a lackluster, rebellious student; his father's solution was to send him to sea as a cabin boy.

Caleb Hope sailed to China three times by the time he was 22.

Caleb enjoyed the international flavor of sailing.

- According to the ship's manifest, Caleb's age was given as 13 years and two months, his height as 4'10" and all his various scars were listed to protect him from being impressed on board an English man-of-war, whose captain might claim he was an English subject.
- The merchant sailing ship was headed to Canton, China, to purchase a cargo of tea.
- "I felt as if I was doing something dreadful, and near as I remember, that feeling never left me until I got back from that voyage 18 months later."
- The crew consisted of 25 men, including the captain, first mate, a second mate, eight old sailors, six green hands, a cook, a steward, a supercargo and two other "ship boys" like Caleb.

As a young sailor, Caleb was often seasick.

- Caleb's specialty was climbing; on land no tree could meet his challenge, and at sea he was a human monkey.
- With his diminutive size and impressive arm strength, Caleb could scramble up the tallest mast to repair rigging in a raging storm.
- Yet, the inexperienced sailor was often seasick, which not only embarrassed the young boy, but did not prevent him from being assigned to a watch.
- The ship's watches lasted four hours, except the dog watches, which were from four in the afternoon until six and from six until eight, two hours each.
- The bell was struck every half hour, commencing at eight in the evening, which was called first watch, until 12 o'clock, which was eight bells, and from midnight to four which was called the middle watch; the time from four until eight was called the morning watch.

Public punishment was meant to set an example.

- All hands were awakened at seven bells, or half past seven, when they had half an hour to eat their breakfast and be prepared to work at 8 a.m.
- When the time arrived for one of Caleb's late night watches, he was too seasick to get up, so the first mate beat him repeatedly with a rope and poured a bucket of water over him to teach him how to stay awake.
- When that did not motivate the seasick lad, the first mate covered the cabin boy with tar and grease mixed together and rubbed it around his face and neck.
- The black concoction would not wash off with salt water, and Caleb wore the sticky concoction for weeks; the use of fresh water had been restricted since the first day out of port to three quarts a day per person, which had to be used for coffee, tea, and soup, as well as drinking.
- Some of the sailors said it was a shame to treat a little boy that way; others simply ignored him.
- A few used foul language to graphically describe how he looked.
- After that the old sailors used the midnight watch to tell Caleb long tales of adventures and share some superstitions of the sea: for example, black bears walking in the ship's yards were a sure sign that a heavy gale was going to blow.
- When the ship cut down to the equator and crossed the equatorial line, the captain celebrated the traditional superstition by giving the entire crew extra grog—New England rum—on that day.
- Anyone, including Caleb, who was crossing the line for the first time was then formally christened by an old seaman elaborately dressed as Neptune, complemented by a long beard and hair made from rope yarns.
- After five months the ship arrived in the cold winter climate of Chile, where the ship was to take aboard a cargo of copper destined for the market in Canton, China.
- Caleb was fascinated by the swarms of penguins marching along the shore and swimming around the ship.

- "On the beach they looked like men, as they were perfectly upright when they were on the land . . . there were several kinds, some three feet and over in height, with red and yellow feathers about the back of the head, with black bodies and white breasts," he wrote in letters home.
- From there the ship sailed through the Pacific Ocean to the distant Sandwich Islands (Hawaii) to take aboard a cargo of sandalwood; these were the same islands where British Captain James Cook was killed and said to be eaten by the natives in 1779.
- There the captain purchased yams, bread fruit and other edibles; the crew had eaten no vegetables for months and scurvy had began to show up among the ship's crew.
- Next stop: China.
- Ships intent on trading in Canton sailed up the Yellow River where they were met by a harpoon boat, headed by a comprador whose task it was to handle the transaction, and who, in this location, used broken English mixed with Portuguese, some Dutch and a little French.
- Caleb enjoyed fresh omelettes prepared by the Chinese and had his clothes washed and his hair cut for the first time in months.
- The ship lay at anchor for three months before being loaded with hundreds of barrels of tea for sale in New England, along with barrels of hard currency as payment for the copper and the sandalwood.
- Before the new cargo could be loaded, the crew discharged overboard much of the ship's ballast, made up of large paving stones, keeping only enough to hold the keel of the ship upright until the cargo had been loaded.
- Loading tea in China was an arduous, detailed task; the Chinese had a reputation for cheating, weighing down tea barrels with stones or filling the tea boxes with hulls of rice when no one was looking.
  - Every barrel had to be inspected twice.
  - Before leaving China, Caleb used his remaining money to purchase silks, china sets, carved ivory and tortoise shell work and a variety of oriental boxes for resale in America.
  - When he returned to Massachusetts, Caleb was determined never to see the sea again, but personal necessity and the new American practical navigator changed that resolve.
  - The total trip had consumed 19 months; Caleb was paid $90, minus $0.20 a month for hospital money, or $86.20 after the ship landed.
  - Some of his money was used to purchase Nathaniel Bowditch's book on navigation that was revolutionizing the business of long-distance sailing.
  - Thanks to the precise calculations and practical advice contained in the book, sailors could more precisely traverse the oceans.
  - Among the navigational aids used in Bowditch's book was the clip log and line, which was heaved over the stern on a line calibrated with knots.
  - With the ship steady on a given compass course, the number of knots run out in a minute, calculated using a sand-filled minute glass, indicated the ship's speed through the water.

Advertisement for Chinese tea.

It took five months to sail from Boston to Canton, China.

Life at Work

- Within six months, Caleb Hope was aboard another merchant ship returning to China.
- This was a finer ship than his last, staffed primarily with a crew from Cape Cod which included several men eager to take the altitude of the sun at meridian each day with the quadrants they had brought aboard so they could keep journals and practice their navigation skills.
- As for diet, it, too, was superior to that of the previous trip; the men had stipulated and the captain agreed that they should have flour puddings twice a week, beans in pork twice a week and vegetables every day, along with plenty of vinegar daily, plus, as much bread as they could eat.

- Unlike the previous voyage, provisions were also made for sufficient water so that the sailors could have good coffee each morning and tea each evening along with molasses and sugar.
- The crew did no work on Sundays except what was necessary for navigation; time was used for singing psalms and reading.
- Most of the sailors had brought their own songbooks aboard.
- The run to Canton, China, took five months; once there, Caleb was proud to lead the crew on a tour of the China he already knew well.
- That first night everyone stuffed themselves with fried fish, stewed meat and baked duck; after five months of dining on the ship's provisions, eating fresh food was a joy indeed.

Caleb purchased fine gifts to resell back home.

- The ship was in China for six weeks before returning; this time Caleb acquired ivory carvings and silks for resale plus a tattoo.
- One of his fellow sailors had bought a bottle of India ink in China and used his idle time aboard ship to ink tattoos using three common needles spaced evenly around a pointed stick.
- Caleb got sailing pictures on his arms, a heart for his mother on his back and his initials on his hands during the return voyage; he later regretted his decision.
- Also during the return voyage, the crew caught a large number of porpoises, dolphins and barracudas; the porpoise was called the sea pig because its internal organ arrangements were similar to a pig's; in addition, even though the meat was darker, it tasted like pork.
- Caleb also witnessed from a distance a mysterious sight during the return trip: a vessel on fire with smoke pouring out of her.
- He had a good view of the tragedy and watched for hours, sure the ship would sink into the sea at any moment.
- Only after arriving in Boston did he and the rest of the crew learn it was a steamship called the *Savannah* which was sailing for Russia to become the first ship ever to cross the Atlantic Ocean under steam power.
- Caleb's next voyage was to the West Indies, carrying lumber, mostly pine boards, enough to fill the hold and the deck from the bulkhead of the quarterdeck forward to near the foremast.
- It was an old ship that leaked the whole passage to Cuba; two men were required to be at the pump at all times.
- "To man the pumps we had to get down in this hold, the water washing under us, and the sea frequently breaking over, so that sometimes it was half of water, and we like drowned rats pumping for our lives."
- Caleb took turns pumping with another sailor, 10 minutes at a time, after which he would be so exhausted he had to sleep between shifts.

Caleb once swam shark-infested waters to escape from a dangerously unsafe ship.

- The trip aboard the slow, leaky ship took 40 days.
- Once in Cuba the cargo of lumber was discharged by tossing the boards into the bay until a large raft was created, so the rest of the lumber could be stacked and towed to the lumber yard of the purchaser, who was half a mile away from the vessel.
- Soon after unloading, the crew began to desert the ship, claiming the vessel was haunted and would never again arrive in the United States in one piece, the latter of which proved to be true.
- For the return trip the hull of the ship was filled with hogsheads of molasses, loaded by the few remaining sailors.
- Using family contacts, Caleb inquired about employment aboard a ship that lay half a mile away; the request was granted but the only way for him to get there was to swim— a dangerous undertaking considering the large, often aggressive sharks in the harbor.
- But driven by superstition and the number of men who had previously deserted the ship, Caleb was determined to leave the vessel.
- At midnight he tied a few of his possessions on his back, jumped overboard into the inky water and swam hard.
- He safely reached the new ship, but before he could sail, his previous captain had him arrested and placed in a Spanish prison, occupied by every kind of criminal, including the insane.
- There he stayed for three days and three nights before he was released and returned to his original ship, where he was assigned the worst possible duties, including blackening the yards with coal tar.
- Determined not to return to sea in that vessel, Caleb made the most trouble possible until he was assigned to a schooner in need of crew; both vessels were owned by the same man.
- It, too, was hauling molasses, but was manned by a clueless captain and a first mate without a timepiece to call watch.
- When Caleb arrived in Boston, his father and stepmother were amazed to see him.
- They believed he had drowned at sea.
- Recently, the newspapers had reported that his original ship was lost at sea and then sunk with all aboard drowned.

- Good luck and determination kept him alive once again.
- Caleb remained in port for six weeks before heading to China for the third time—this time as first mate.

Life in the Community: Boston, Massachusetts

- Boston, Massachusetts, was an exciting, newly chartered city in 1823, a transportation hub and the center of commerce in New England, where "no man would consent to be poor or expect to remain that way for long," according to local legend.
- Boston first became an international cargo port in 1630, after having served as a settlement and trading area for Native American tribes for at least 4,000 years.
- For most of the eighteenth century, Boston served the rapidly expanding colonies with imports of English finished goods in exchange for exports of lumber, fully constructed vessels, rum and salted fish.
- Boston, nicknamed "Athens of America," also gained wealth based on the "triangle route" in which sugar was brought to Boston to be made into rum which was then traded for slaves in Africa, who were then transported to West Indies sugar plantations to produce sugar for Boston's distilleries.
- But success brought conflicts.
- The great increase in Massachusetts wealth caused England's large population of merchant trading companies to demand that the colonies exclusively trade with the "mother" country.

Boston Harbor.

- To reduce their dependence on British trading ships, Bostonians sought greater independence by starting a vigorous shipbuilding industry of their own, and began to establish independent trading links with other colonies and countries to the north and south.
- Subsequent attempts to prevent Boston's merchants from engaging in world trade then stirred Boston's middle class to join the more radical elements in calling for revolution.
- In 1775 this power struggle culminated in an armed confrontation in the nearby town of Lexington, which formally began the American Revolution.
- After the revolution, Boston was one of the world's wealthiest international trading ports due to the city's consolidated seafaring tradition—exports included rum, fish, salt and tobacco.
- During this era, descendants of old Boston families became regarded as the nation's social and cultural elite.
- In 1822, Boston was chartered as a city and chose a mayor-council form of government.
- The original hilly Shawmut Peninsula upon which the city was built covered 800 acres surrounded by salt marshes, mudflats, and inlets of water.
- As Boston outgrew its site in the 1800s, most of the hills were leveled and used as fill to create the Back Bay district.
- Boston's tax base expanded when the city annexed neighboring towns such as Noddle's Island, which was renamed East Boston.
- In 1821, Boston opened Boston English High School, one of the nation's first high schools.
- Boston Harbor's success stimulated inland transportation by merchants eager to move goods to and from the port.
- In England the construction and maintenance of roads was a public responsibility; in America a private company built the roads and took the economic risk in hopes of profits.
- To cover the cost of building and maintaining turnpikes, users were charged fees at fixed points based on the number of wheels in the vehicle and by the number of head of cattle being hauled.
- A trip from Boston to Baltimore could take up to 26 days; these turnpikes permitted interstate commerce as far north as Boston and as far south as Augusta, Georgia.
- Viewed as competition for merchant sailing ships, the wagoneers amused themselves by painting the words "Mud Clipper" or "Sailor's Misery" on the sides of their vehicles.
- As the roads improved, through the use of wood planks or crushed stone, four and six teams of horses harnessed to shiny coaches could travel the 40 miles from Providence, Rhode Island, to Boston in fewer than five hours, and the drivers would be heard to brag, "Only lightning could have done it quicker."

HISTORICAL SNAPSHOT
1823

- Georgia passed the first state birth registration law
- The streets of Boston were lit by gas
- President Monroe proclaimed the Monroe Doctrine, stating "that the American continents . . . are henceforth not to be considered as subjects for future colonization by European powers"
- James Fenimore Cooper published *The Pioneers*
- The Reverend Hiram Bingham, leader of a group of New England Calvinist missionaries, began translating the Bible into Hawaiian
- The poem "A Visit from St. Nicholas" by Clement C. Moore, often called "'Twas the Night Before Christmas," was published in the *Troy Sentinel* (New York)
- The death penalty for more than 100 crimes was abolished in England
- The growing popularity of sending Christmas cards drew complaints from the Superintendent of Mail who said the high volume of the cards was becoming a burden on the United States Postal System
- The Mission San Francisco de Solano de Sonoma was established to convert the native Indians and develop local resources
- Charles Macintosh of Scotland invented a waterproof fabric useful in the creation of raincoats
- Franz Schubert composed his song cycle *Die Schone Mullerin*
- Former slave Thomas James helped found the African Methodist Episcopal Zion Society, the forerunner of the Underground Railroad
- Rugby football originated in Rugby School, England
- The British medical journal *The Lancet* began publication

Selected Prices

Beans, Bushel $18.00
Coffee Mill $18.00
Fiddle $140.00
Ink Powder $8.08
Molasses, Gallon $6.30
Plank, 100 Feet $18.00
Rum, Gallon $7.20
Silk, Ounce $162.00
Tea, Pound $10.80
Toll, Four-Wheel Carriage $3.60

Sailors enjoyed the local entertainment at various ports.

Two Years Before the Mast, Richard Henry Dana, 1840:

There is a witchery in the sea, its songs and stories, and in the mere sight of the ship, and the sailor's dress, especially to a young mind, which has done more to man navies, and fill merchantmen, than all the press gangs of Europe . . . many are the boys, in every seaport, who are drawn away, as by an almost irresistible attraction, from their work and schools, and hang about the decks and yards of vessels, with a fondness which, it is plain, will have its way. . . .

Yet a sailor's life is at best a mixture of a little good with much evil, and a little pleasure with much pain. The beautiful is linked with the revolting, the sublime with the commonplace, and the solemn with the ludicrous.

"The Physician, Diseases of the Dog-Days,"
New Monthly Magazine, London, 1824:

I cannot approve the practice of plunging liquids into ice in hot weather to render them cold. In all that we eat and drink, a certain proportion should be observed in the temperature, that we may not occasion too rapid and violent a change in the body. But let us only compare the degree of heat of the blood and stomach in the hottest of the Dog-days, with the icy coldness communicated to the liquids which we swallow, and is not this correcting one extreme by another? How liable are the overheated juices to become congealed by the great degree of cold! How easily may the minutest vessels in which they circulate be thereby contracted! And how soon may not these combined causes produce obstructions of the juices in the minute vessels! Hence arise the fatal inflammatory fevers which are so common in hot weather, and which we denominate inflammations of the stomach, and pleurisy. Seven days, and even shorter, are frequently sufficient to terminate in this manner the life of the person who was previously in robust health; and it is not the Dog-star, but the luxuriant gratification which we seek in cooling ourselves by refrigerants, that occasions this catastrophe.

"White Oak Logs or Plank," *The American*, New-York, July 19, 1820:

The Commissioners of the Navy will receive the first day of September next, proposals are furnishing 240,000 superficial feet of white oak plank, of various thickness from 4 to 7½ inches; and 80 to 100 white oak logs.

The planks must average 45 feet in length, none of it to be less than 35 feet, and must be 12 to 15 inches in width. The logs must be 16 to 24 inches square, and 30 to 60 feet long they may be either square or around.

The proposals may be for plank, or for logs suitable to make the plank. Persons proposing to furnish plank will be pleased to state their terms per 100 superficial feet; or proposing logs, their price per cubic foot.

The whole to be delivered at Portsmouth, N.H. at the expense and risk of the contractor, on or before the 1st May, 1821.

Advertisement: Newburgh and Buffalo Post Coach and Steam-Boat Line, *The American*, New-York, July 19, 1820:

The above line runs from Newburgh in Buffalo, and from Buffalo and Newburgh, three times a week, performing the route each way in four days.

The horses and carriages are good and convenient: the drivers sober and careful: the houses of accommodation are not surpassed by any in the state.

This Line is connected with a new and elegant Steam-boat on Cayuga Lake, which on the arrival of the coaches takes the passengers on board, and affords them a pleasing relief from the fatigues of traveling by land.

The passage of the Lake is the most delightful that can be imagined. The beauty and the variety of the scenery, the flourishing and handsome villages, and the large and well cultivated farms, which adorn its borders, at once delight and astonish the beholder. The boat is furnished in the first style; the accommodations on board are excellent; refreshments and provisions of the best quality, and every attendant is paid by the master to render the passage agreeable. The coaches from Cayuga bridge to Buffalo, for elegance and convenience, are not excelled by any in the United States.

Before the Wind: The Memoir of an American Sea Captain, 1808-1833, Memoir of Charles Tyng:

After we had been out two months or so, one very pleasant Sunday afternoon, I made a bet with William Hickling that I could go out to the trunk of the main mast, which is the tip top of the mast. The sky sail pole, as it was called, had no shroud, so it was a bare pole of 8 to 10 feet long, with a trunk in the end, as the ship was rolling, the end the pole was making something of a sweep in the skies. It was a rather dangerous exploit, but I did it and gained the bet, which was a dollar, which William paid me.

An hour afterwards, Maggie (the First Mate), having heard of it, called me aft, and took the dollar from me, and gave me a severe whipping with the end of a rope. That is what I got for trying to be smart. But it did not dampen my ardour for climbing, as by constant practice, I became an expert before the voyage was over. I could go up a rope hand over hand, higher than anyone on board. I could hold on with one hand longer, and in fact I had more confidence in my hands and arms, than in my feet when going about the ship, for I always felt safe long as I had hold of a rope. The practice was great benefit to me. It gave me great strength to the muscles of the arms, and many a time saved me pitching into the sea.

Before the Wind: The Memoir of an American Sea Captain, 1808-1833, Memoir of Charles Tyng:

[In China] the river was covered with boats, always sculled by women, who lived on board with their children, and they of all sizes until they were big enough to work on shore or to catch fish. Until they could crawl about, they were carried on the mothers' backs in a sort of band, which did not interfere with her work. When they got so they could crawl, they had fastened to their back a life preserver, which was made from a peculiar wood more like the pith of a reed than wood and was lighter than a cork. They frequently fell overboard. The mother, or anyone, would reach out and pick them up. Men were seldom seen in these boats, without they were very old and could not work. These boats seemed to be all alike, and very near of a size besides, about 12 feet long and 5 feet wide, each covered about half way over with a bamboo cover, under which they lived, and raised their families. They were sculled by an oar of a different shape from ours, being in two pieces spliced together, and resting on an iron pivot in the stern of the boat, and it was astonishing with what ease they could propel their boats along.

We lay at anchor at Whampo between two and three months, so that I got pretty well acquainted with the habits of the people and the appearances of things on the water. . . .

"Indiana," *The American*, New-York, July 19, 1820:

At the last session of the legislature, a law was passed, directing that any person (travelers excluded) wearing any dirk, pistol, sword in cane, or any other unlawful weapon, concealed, shall be deemed guilty of a misdemeanor, and, on conviction thereof by punishment or indictment, shall be fined any sum, not exceeding $100, for the use of country seminaries.

"A bold and atrocious attempt!" *The American*, New-York, July 19, 1820:

We understand an attempt was made on Saturday night last to murder and rob Mr. John C. F. Rommel, toll-gatherer on the Hackensack Bridge. About 11 o'clock three men, supposed to be Irishmen, applied to pass the bridge, stating they had nothing smaller than a two dollar bill to pay the toll. One of them stepped into the toll-house, but instead of his money drew a large knife from his coat pocket, and attempted to thrust it into the left breast of Mr. Rommel. Most fortunately he passed off the stroke with one hand, and with the other seized the villain and by the throat. A dog lying under the bed flew to the assistance of his master, and after a short struggle the desperados retreated, without seriously injuring the person of Mr. Rommel, and effected their escape. The dog, however, was very badly wounded. As the villains left the house, Mr. Rommel seized a loaded pistol, and one at least would have paid for his temerity had not the pistol flashed.

"Review of the Markets in Baltimore for the Past Week, July 9 to July 15, Inclusive," *The American,* New-York, July 19, 1820:

Cotton New Orleans, of middling quality, has been sold at $.20, and some very inferior at $.18.

Coffee Prices continue steady; St. Domingo 24 ? to .25 cents and prime green Havana 26.

Flour There continues a steady demand for fresh made flour, the price of which is $475.

Tobacco In Kentucky, nothing has been done; some small sales of Virginia have been made to the trade.

Molasses Considerable sales have been made at prices, varying from 24 and 30 cents per gallon.

Salt We notice the arrival of 3923 fanegas from Gibraltar, in 2500 bushels from Turks Island.

"Rotunda: Garden of Versailles," *The American,* New-York, July 19, 1820:

The palace and garden of Versailles are equaled by nothing of a similar description in the world. In adorning his favourite spot Louis XIV tasked the genius of the age, and dissipated the wealth of provinces. The apartments of the palace are literally composed of marble, gold, and paintings; and the garden, besides its magnificent fountains, grottoes, colonnades, and etc. is crowded with statues by celebrated masters; many of which are said to have cost 1000 sterling. The lake and the fountains are supplied from distant reservoirs; and to exhibit these superb waterworks in motion now done only on great occasions, is an expense of 30,000 francs. From this palace, the scene of their bright festive days, Louis XVI and Marie Antoinette watched the portentous cloud darken round them, which finally burst with such disastrous violence. The panorama of the Château and Garden of Versailles, now in the Rotunda, covers three thousand square feet of canvas. It was painted by Mr. John Vanderlyn, from sketches made on the spot in 1815; and, in point of execution, is not inferior to the best European exhibitions of the kind. To the fidelity of its details and general effect the writer of this paragraph can testify. So happily are the lights and shades disposed amid the vases, statues, and pyramids of foliage, that the objects stand out with the boldness of sculpture; and the eye seems actually to catch the motions of the gay groups that glide among them. It will remain in exhibition a few weeks longer at the Rotunda, in Chambers-Street, near City-Hall.

The doors are open every day (Sundays excluded) from 9 a.m. until 6 p.m. Admittance $.25, children half-price.

Before the Wind: The Memoir of an American Sea Captain, 1808-1833, Memoir of Charles Tyng:

One night went off the Cape, the wind blowing a gale, and the sea running high, which caused the ship to labour badly, Mr. Nash asked me if I could not send down the fore top gallant yard, as it was straining the mast when the ship pitched and rolled heavy. I jumped up the rigging, followed by Nat Carnes, who was one of the smartest. We soon had the tie stopped out on the yard and the yard was posted hoisted up a cock bill, the parrel was cut, and the lifts and braces taken off, and I followed the yard down the rigging, which with the sail soaking wet was very heavy, and every time the ship rolled to the leeward, the yard had to be held to the rigging by taking a turn round the shroud with the end of the gasket to keep it from swinging off.

I got down with it very well until I got down to the top, when the end of the gasket slipped from my hand, and the yard swung out some 50 feet with me clinging to it. I held on tight, looking at the heavy seas below me, until it swung back again, which fortunately for me, came in against the rigging with me outside. Had I been inside I should have been crushed between the yard and rigging. They lowered away on deck as quick as they could, and when within a few feet of the deck the rope broke and the yard came down on the deck with full force, it was a marvel to all that the rope did not break when it swung off with my weight on it. Had it broke then, that would have been the last of me.

1826 PROFILE

Sarah Goodwin was an active schoolteacher in Litchfield, Connecticut, and a driven educator who challenged numerous young ladies attending her academy from across the United States; her strong religious convictions shaped her expectations of her students.

Life at Home

- Sarah Goodwin had been active as a schoolteacher for over 30 years in Litchfield, Connecticut.
- She focused her energies on improving the minds of the young ladies attending her school.
- Sarah started her quest in 1792 with only one pupil under her instruction in her dining room.
- Over time her reputation spread and the number of students grew; parents sent their daughters to be molded with a rounded education focused on history, English and the arts.
- As her instruction and number of pupils grew, teaching in her home proved troublesome; by 1798 Sarah managed to convince Litchfield's prominent men to construct a school building.
- A number of subscribers agreed to contribute funding for the building; in all a total of $385 was raised.
- The one-room schoolhouse was roughly 30 feet by 70 feet with most of the space used to hold plain pine desks for the students, who sat on long plank benches.
- Sarah kept her materials on a small desk beside her elevated teacher's chair.
- These items represented all the building's furniture, excluding a small movable piano in one of the building's two closets.
- The second closet was used to house bonnets and other garments the students brought to class.
- With a permanent building for instruction, the school was called the Female Academy, attracting national recognition.

Sarah Goodwin was a schoolteacher in Litchfield, Connecticut.

- Over time, girls began to arrive from as far as Boston, New York and Savannah, Georgia, to receive instruction.
- When the summer term started in late May, most of the young ladies arrived in Litchfield by stagecoach.
- For some it was the first time away from home, and Sarah often assisted in placing them in respectable homes for boarding near the academy.
- The boarding expense was $1.75 to $2 per week, exclusive of washings, collected by the school, which reimbursed the families with whom the students resided.
- A number of girls were forced to share a room and expressed frustration over sleeping arrangements and sharing a bed.
- Sarah disliked the petty arguments the girls voiced and developed an extensive set of rules of conduct.
- Each young lady was expected to memorize the rules, most of which focused upon daily prayer, conduct within a family's home, personal behavior and academic excellence.
- One of the rules required that two hours must be "faithfully devoted" to close study each day while out of school.
- The ladies with whom the girls boarded were expected to report any student who failed to study the two hours required.
- Over the years Sarah heard a number of complaints; for new students it usually pertained to homesickness and not receiving letters from home.
- One young lady visited the post office too often, even on Fridays, knowing fully well that the mail from New York City did not arrive on that day.
- Sarah removed 30 credit marks from her grades for the homesickness.
- With over 30 years of instructing students, Sarah spent her time teaching her students history and geography.
- Sitting at their desks, students would write their lessons from her lectures within their books.
- One of the books each student was required to use was Sarah's *Universal History*.
- After years of trying to locate an adequate history book for the ladies to study, she gathered sufficient historical information from several texts into one book.
- After a week's instruction, she tested the ladies on their knowledge and memorization of materials.
- Each was called in turn to answer questions when addressed; a correct answer would earn the student credits.
- Sarah was disappointed with one student who grew up along the Delaware River but could not recall the source of the river.
- It was a simple answer for the child, who rapidly lost any appearance of thought.
- One student made a great error when called to parse, or break down a sentence into parts of speech.
- In her haste she placed a verb in the infinitive mode in the imperfect tense.
- She failed to catch the error in time and only earned five credits that day.
- With so many ladies to teach, Sarah was grateful for the assistance of those she hired.
- She was especially pleased with her nephew John Brace, who provided instruction in the areas of botany and natural history.
- Sarah thought it important to have a broad knowledge of the world, including the world of science.
- John would collect plant and insect specimens and present them in class.
- He had an extensive collection of bugs, including two from China that were in excellent condition.
- The remainder of the bugs were of Litchfield descent and John was capable of tracing the pedigree back to when Noah first entered the ark.

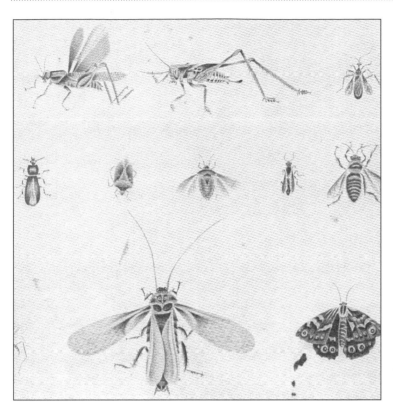

Sarah's nephew, John Brace, taught the students botany and natural history.

- Aside from insects, many of the girls enjoyed the botany lessons Sarah's nephew provided.
- Inspired by his lectures, the ladies acquired numerous wild plants, such as white braneberry, carrion flower, violets and Solomon's seal, to transplant them around the school.
- Most were placed in the beds by the school's door-yard.
- The sight pleased Sarah and reinforced the students' interest to apply their learning to the real world.
- Aside from learning about the world, its language and history, Sarah made Christian study an imperative for each student.
- Saving the student's immortal soul was of more importance than all the education she could provide.
- Each student was expected to read a portion of Scripture both morning and evening with meditation and prayer.
- Aside from the prayer and reflection, she expected her students to keep holy the Sabbath by attending church.
- Sarah even incorporated Scripture studies on Saturday after the ladies recited the school's rules.
- Often they read various passages from the Bible and Sarah would explain what they had read.
- During the weekly testing, she would provide credit marks for those who memorized the assigned Scripture verses and answered religious questions.
- One of Sarah's students, Eliza Sheldon, answered correctly to the question, "What is sin?"
- Eliza responded that "Sin is any want of conformity unto or transgression of the law of God."
- Sarah clearly understood that not all her students were responsive to learning about Christianity.
- When one student openly laughed during morning prayer, Sarah exclaimed that the student would possibly be cast into darkness where there is gnashing of teeth.

- The laughing young lady replied, "Then I suppose those who have no teeth will have to gum it!" which was followed by a chorus of giggles.
- Sarah Goodwin removed five of her credit marks for her poor behavior.
- With all the credits accrued by the students in all topics taught at school, Sarah recognized their accomplishments halfway in the term.
- Sarah permitted the girls to select their seats based upon the number of credit marks earned.
- Those with the most credit marks had the right to select their seat of choice, often a location near the window to get as much of the summer breeze as possible.
- Students with the lowest number of marks often had fewer options: those away from the window or next to girls they disliked.
- Girls who applied their talents also received invitations for tea with Sarah on Wednesday afternoons.
- During these periods, a circle of girls would gather around her tea table and engage in conversations that challenged their reasoning of what they had learned.
- On one occasion, while the girls ate shaved, smoked beef and some cakes with preserves, they discussed the opening of the Erie Canal, recited poetry they had written and sang songs they had memorized from their music lessons.
- Only years later would the young ladies realize that such gatherings were another lesson Sarah was providing: the ability to entertain and conduct oneself as a lady in a social setting was important, especially in acquiring a future spouse.
- A real treat occurred at one tea party when Edward Clarke, an older English gentleman visiting the area, brought his perspective glass for the girls to view.
- The device, also known as a zograscope, enabled them to look at hand-colored lithographic scenes through a reflecting glass and magnifying lens.

How to conduct oneself as a lady in social settings was an important lesson at the Female Academy.

Students learned to care for small animals and took music lessons.

- The scenes viewed through the perspective glass provided depth to the flat images and fascinated the young ladies greatly.
- Sarah was disappointed that Mr. Clarke had no images of American scenery.
- Nonetheless, she was pleased to allow the Englishman to show his country in a favorable light.

Life at Work

- Sarah Goodwin's life as headmistress of the Female Academy included the receipt of distressing news regarding the death of one of her students.
- It was common through the year to receive four such letters, which always upset her.
- She also hated to see a young lady leave the school upset over trivial differences and encouraged the parties to forgive one another before parting.
- It was also a part of preservation of one's soul to reconcile so that they all could meet in heaven.
- Recently, the school received a heartrending account of the *Albion*, a packet-ship that left New York for Liverpool.
- The ship was lost just off the coast and all on board were assumed lost as well.
- The entire academy was horrified because the news devastated one of the teachers, Miss Beecher.
- Her fiancé was on board the ship.
- After a week of waiting for any possible news of hope for survivors, a memorial service was held at the Congregational church next to the school.
- Most of the students conducted themselves well in church, knowing fully well it was offensive to God if they failed to do so, but they would receive deductions in their credit marks also.
- Bad behavior was rarely a problem, but issues did occur within the community.
- One problem arose outside of the Congregational church itself between the academy students and the girls of the Litchfield community.
- The battlefield was a set of two benches fenced in with conventional high lattice work and away from the adult church members.
- Each week one group of girls would arrive and monopolize both benches, preventing the other group from using the space.
- It was not uncommon for one of the groups to arrive early to "pack the seats" before church and prevent the other group from using the space; pin pricking, pinching and punches through the lattice also occurred.
- Within the town was an ale house by an animal pound, and it was frequently visited by the students from the Litchfield Law School.
- It was a common occurrence for students to write over the door "Ale by the pound."
- The act infuriated the ale keeper, who constantly complained to both Sarah and the proctor of the law school.

- Sarah would have nothing to do with the ale keeper because she viewed him as an impudent villain.
- She asked the law school's vice chancellor to handle the matter because it was not the place for a lady to converse with this character, especially a lady who has strong opinions on intemperance.
- Sarah viewed this as a community issue; years before, she helped form Litchfield's Temperance Society and wrote numerous articles in the local paper on the subject.
- In one article she wrote that married women should "make the house of your husband the most interesting place on earth."
- Sarah informed her readers that men typically are led into the habit of intemperance by the poor behavior of their wives at home.
- A home that is welcoming to the husband would not lead him to the evil habit.
- Watching the behavior of men was common in Sarah's world, especially boys studying at the law school who sought every opportunity to pass part of the day with the ladies from her school.
- During her afternoon walks she would encounter small groups of students walking together on Prospect Hill towards Echo Rock.
- Other times she heard of ladies taking boat rides on Lake Bantan during the summer days.
- These acts did not bother Sarah in the slightest, and it pleased her to know her ladies were behaving well.
- What infuriated her was when young men failed to heed her rules when visiting the young ladies boarding in her home on prescribed days and times.
- One method she employed to control the conduct of young men was providing access to the monthly balls for the young students.
- Only young men in good graces with Miss Goodwin received invitations.
- She often heard, to her pleasure, that the invitations were prized at the law school.
- This was primarily due to the fact that the number of ladies attending was traditionally double that of the men present.
- Many would arrive in their best party attire to enjoy an evening of dancing and conversation.
- Three or four musicians came to the school on a Saturday evening around 6 o'clock after all the invitees had arrived and played until 9 o'clock.
- Besides the traditional dances, the academy hosted a two-day public exhibition at the end of each term for the Litchfield community.

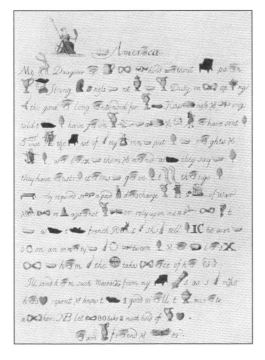

Creative penmanship was practiced.

- At this venue the ladies could display their talents, which included theater, art, poetry and music.
- In addition, Sarah expected each girl to bring home to her parents evidence of her studies.
- Those talented in watercolor drawings or embroidering could proudly display their work on the walls in family parlors.
- The less gifted were advised to paint their family coat of arms, which they could acquire with the assistance of the local Looking Glass & Picture Store.
- In exchange for the research assistance, there was a promise that the store would be employed to frame the students' works.
- Every year prominent members of the Litchfield community were asked to judge the students' best work.
- Their role was to evaluate each piece of artwork in the various categories and award the winners the Prize of Merit.
- The opinion of community leaders kept the judging without bias from those involved in the school, thus strengthening the significance of the award.
- Even with numerous works on display during the exhibition, the highlight was often the theater performance.
- The school's ladies invited young men to see them perform acts they had practiced diligently during their free time.
- Some of the plays were classics, but it was not uncommon to see performances written by Miss Sarah Goodwin herself.
- Those productions commonly involved events in history.
- At the end of the exhibition, Sarah presented her address to the students, thus concluding the summer term in late October.
- Afterwards, the students departed to visit family members for the month or travel with one of their classmates home.
- After several decades of teaching, Sarah appreciated the month-long respite the young ladies' absences offered.
- Nonetheless, she had to prepare for the start of the winter term and did not believe in being idle.

Life in the Community: Litchfield, Connecticut

- Litchfield, Connecticut, was a primary city in the western part of the state where significant commerce passed.

- Its location on a high road made it part of a great inland route from Boston to New York City as well as from West Point to Connecticut's capital, Hartford.
- The initial travel that occurred was postage coaches that rode daily through the town delivering mail along the way.
- Because of the strength of the roads into and out of Litchfield, daily mail routes were established between the city and Hartford, New Haven, Norwalk, Poughkeepsie and Albany.
- It was not uncommon to see the large, red, four-horse coaches roll through town making great noise with the drivers cracking their whips and blowing horns at a great pace.

- One could acquire fare at Deming's Tavern and leave Litchfield on a stage at 5 o'clock in the afternoon for New York or Albany and arrive by 1 o'clock the next day.
- Being a large city along a major roadway and with a population of over 4,600 people in 1810, Litchfield witnessed a great deal of commercial and industrial activity develop.
- Iron was the primary manufacturing activity in Litchfield, which boasted four iron forges, a slitting mill and one nail factory.
- It also had 18 saw mills, five grain mills, a paper mill, an oil mill and a cotton factory, to name only a few other industries.
- Other smaller tradesmen were located in the area to take advantage of the city's opportunities.
- One example of an entrepreneurial endeavor concerned the numerous carriages rolling into town.
- The city's central location between primary travel destinations encouraged two carriage makers to locate operations within the community.
- By 1820 Litchfield ranked fourth in the state's population, following only New Haven, Hartford and Middletown.
- The city boasted numerous natural resources, most prominently the mineral spring containing chalybeate and sulfurous waters only a half mile from the court house.
- Many visitors made a point to spend time there to enjoy the water's effectiveness in curing disease.
- One popular location was Prospect Hill where many walked for exercise and pleasure.
- Also present in this location was Echo Rock, where visitors would cast their voices and hear them call back to them.
- By 1827, the growth of the city's population and number of visitors encouraged an inventor to propose locating a machine that would raise individuals in one of four two-person carriages to a height of 50 feet into the air.
- He indicated that: "recommended by the most eminent physicians in the United States, the recreational device planned to help take an airing."

Litchfield residents enjoyed the countryside.

HISTORICAL SNAPSHOT
1826

- The American Temperance Society was formed in Boston

- Beethoven's String Quartet #13 in B flat major (Opus 130) premiered in Vienna

- Samuel Mory patented the internal combustion engine

- Weber's opera *Oberon* premiered in London

- The USS *Vincennes* left New York to become the first warship to circumnavigate the globe

- Russia and Norway established a border that superseded the arrangement made 500 years earlier in the Treaty of Novgorod

- Simón Bolívar helped the new South American republic of Bolivia gain independence and recognition from Peru

- Former U.S. presidents Thomas Jefferson and John Adams both died on July 4, the fiftieth anniversary of the signing of the Declaration of Independence

- A Pennsylvania law made kidnapping a felony, effectively nullifying the Fugitive Slave Act of 1793

- Explorer Gordon Laing became the first European to reach Timbuktu

- Lord & Taylor opened in New York at 47 Catherine Street

- Connecticut's six-mile Windsor Locks Canal opened to provide safe passage around the Enfield Falls and rapids in the Connecticut River 12 miles upstream from Hartford

- The first horse-powered railroad in America opened in Quincy, Massachusetts, at a granite quarry with three miles of track

- Gideon B. Smith planted the first of the new quick-growing Chinese mulberry trees in the United States and spurred development of the silk industry

- French chemist Antoine-Jérôme Balard discovered the element bromine

- After Pope Leo XII ordered that Rome's Jews be confined to the city's ghetto, thousands of Jews fled Rome and the Papal States

- Sing Sing Prison opened its first cell block some 30 miles north of New York City on the Hudson River

- The Zoological Gardens in Regent's Park were founded by the Zoological Society of London

Selected Prices

Bonnet, Silk $15.00
Candlesticks, Plated $11.00
Dictionary $3.50
Fabric, Velvet, Yard $5.50
Mirror $22.00
Pencil $0.22
Piano $2,000.00
Tea Kettle $18.00
Tea, Pound $15.50
Thimbles, Box $11.00

Terms of Tuition at Female Academy

1826
Litchfield Female Academy
Conducted by Miss Goodwin and Mr. Brace

Terms of Tuition

Writing, History, Geography, Grammar, Arithmetic, Rhetoric, and Composition, with plain Needlework, per quarter $5

The above, with Natural and Moral Philosophy, Logic, Chemistry, Mathematics, the Principals of Taste and Criticism, with the Latin and Greek Languages, per quarter $6

French Language $5

Drawing $3

Music 12

Board in respectable families near the Academy, from $1.75 to $2 per week, exclusive of washing.

The Summer Term, commences May 16.

The Winter, November 29.

Wood etchings.

Recipe for a toothache, Diary of George Youngglove Cutter, 1820:

1 Tablespoonful of spirits
1 Tablespoonful of vinegar
1 Teaspoonful of common salt

"An Address to the Moon," Ann M. Richards, New York:

Sweet Moon if like Cretona's sage
By any spell my hand should dare
To make thy disk my ample page
And write my thoughts my wishes there

How many a friend whose careless eye
Now wanders o'er that starry sky
Would smile upon that orb to meet
The recollection fond and sweet

The reveries of fond regret
The promise never to forget
And all my heart and soul would send
To many a dear lov'd distant friend

Stage Coach Advertisement, *Litchfield Monitor,* November 10, 1829:

Litchfield, New Milford, Danbury and Norwalk Mail Stage.

This stage leaves Josiah Park's Hotel, Litchfield, on Tuesdays, Thursdays and Saturdays at 3 in the morning, passing thro' New Preston, New Milford and Brookfield and arrives at Danbury to lodge: leaves Danbury next morning for Norwalk and arrives in time for passengers to take the steam boat for New York. No Night Travelling.

Fare through to New York 3.25

Returning Takes the Norwalk passengers at Danbury on Monday, Wednesday and Friday morning, and arrives in Litchfield the same day.

For seats apply at the Bar at Parks Hotel, Litchfield, H. Barnes, Proprietor

Boat Excursion Advertisement, *Litchfield Monitor*, June 27, 1826:

The new and elegant Horse boat, *Bantam*, having been recently built for the express purpose of accommodating pleasure parties on the Bantam Lake, is now completely prepared to accommodate ladies and gentlemen who may wish to take advantage of this safe and neat mode of taking a trip upon our pleasant waters. Parties wishing to engage the boat for a trip must give two days' notice to the subscriber residing at the north end of the Lake.

—Harmon Stone

"Partial list of Rules at Litchfield Ladies Academy,"
Chronicles of a Pioneer School,
Emily Vanderpool:

1st—You are expected to rise early, be dressed neatly and to exercise before breakfast. . . . You must consider it a breach of politeness to be requested a second time to rise in the morning or retire of the evening. . . .

8th—Every hour during the week must be fully occupied either in useful employments, or necessary recreation. Two hours must be faithfully devoted to close study each day, while out of school: and every hour in school must be fully occupied. . . .

12th—The truth must be spoken at all times though it might seem more advantageous to tell a falsehood. . . .

14th—Tale bearing and scandal are odious vices and must be avoided: neither must you flatter your companion by any remarks on their beauty, dress or any accomplishment, in order to increase their vanity, and let everyone thus flattered remember that such compliments are an insult offered to the understanding. . . .

17th—No young lady is allowed to attend any public ball, or sleigh party till they are more than 16 years old. . . .

19th—You must write a letter to be corrected and sent home to your friends once in four weeks—excepted excused. You must not write a careless note or any careless writing. . . .

23rd—You must not walk for pleasure after 9 o'clock in the evening. . . .

1829 PROFILE

Ian Llewellyn was working as a horse driver on the Erie Canal in New York and telling tall tales of his past to the tourists and cabin girls riding on the boats.

Life at Home

- For the last six years, 19-year-old Welchman Ian Llewellyn had been telling curious tourists on the Erie Canal in New York that he was an orphan left to find his own way at the age of six.
- The tale kept the meddling city women from trying to send him home and earned him considerable sympathy from the cabin girls who worked along the canal.
- But after a night of drinking and thinking, Ian had decided to be a convict.
- A sordid past would make for better stories in the course of a long day pushing horses up and down the canal, often 10 hours at a time; a past that included prison could start fights or prevent them—Ian wasn't sure which and didn't care.
- Now all he had to do was decide what he'd been in prison for: murder was too much, but robbery sounded like too little.
- In truth he had grown up, largely homeless, amidst the construction of the Erie Canal; his immigrant father began as a ditch digger in 1817 when Ian was seven years old.
- His mother left soon after the family arrived in America.
- "The land of opportunity," his father would say sarcastically; "I could have starved like this at home."
- Then came the Erie Canal's promise to pay workers a dollar a day.
- According to the newspapers, New York Governor DeWitt Clinton intended to spend $7 million for the canal's construction, and Ian's father figured some of that money would rub off on him.

Ian Llewellyn was a horse driver in the Erie Canal.

Governor Clinton of New York approved the plan to connect the Great Lakes with the Atlantic Ocean.

- First proposed in 1699, the Erie Canal was designed to link the eastern seaboard, especially New York City, with the interior of the United States as far west as Buffalo.
- Plans called for the canal to connect the Great Lakes with the Atlantic Ocean by running from Albany, New York, on the Hudson to Buffalo, New York, on Lake Erie, a distance of 363 miles.
- Even though the Dutch-owned Holland Land Company had invested in roads and turnpikes in upstate New York, better transportation was needed to link the farmers and their products to the New York ports.
- Although former President Thomas Jefferson called initial plans for the Erie Canal "a little short of madness," Governor Clinton envisioned the transportation link as essential to the continued expansion of western New York and cutting transportation costs by 95 percent.
- When construction began on July 4, 1817, in Rome, New York, Ian and his father were there.
- His father had been hired as one of a legion of ditch diggers, an occupation previously handled by slaves or convicts; Ian was a waterboy, a job that paid poorly but allowed him to ignore schooling.
- It was quite a celebration; the *Utica Gazette* even made special mention of how the ceremony unified employer and labor in the joy it brought them all.
- After the cheering stopped, the men went to work—blacksmiths, stonemasons and carpenters, along with laborers who shoveled and cut their way through New York's landscape, from rock-infested soil to water-soaked swampland.
- Many Americans believed that the four-foot-deep and 40-foot-wide, 363-mile-long canal was part of God's plan for Americans to reshape the human and physical world.
- Using gunpowder, ox carts and ingenuity, America was challenging the best intentions of nature to make life better for its people.
- Some scorned the entire plan, branding it Clinton's Folly, and predicted failure.
- Ian and his father worked 10- to 12-hour shifts and slept together in the nearest barn; Ian also learned to keep his food satchel under his body while he slept to protect it from the field mice.
- He also learned before the age of 10 that a visit to the grog shop with his father would take away the pain of a day's work.
- The first 15 miles, from Rome to Utica, took two years.
- The problem was not the digging of the ditch but the felling of trees to clear a path through the virgin forest.
- That's when Ian's father switched jobs and learned to pull tree stumps out of the ground with a huge, tripod-mounted winch.
- A three-man team with mules could then build a mile of canal a year.
- Ian's father worked the trees for four years before one of the massive chains broke unexpectedly and dropped the tree on him and two other men.
- In all, seven men died that week in accidents, explosions and cave-ins; newly arrived Irish immigrants eager for work took their place.
- Ian's father had hated the Irish immigrants and blamed them for keeping wages down; they were an ever-present plague on this opportunity to be prosperous.
- The promised dollar a day had turned out to be far less once housing, clothes washing and company-supplied liquor were deducted.

- Before he was crushed by the tree, Ian's father was making $14 a month.
- Ian made a dollar a week as a waterboy.
- At his father's funeral, the canal foreman expressed his regrets and offered Ian a job as a driver, as a favor to his father.
- Ian had just turned 13.

Life at Work

- Success came quickly to the Erie Canal, providing Ian Llewellyn with considerable job security.
- Day after day he guided the horse-drawn boats stacked high with wheat, barrels of oats or piles of logs up and down the Erie Canal.
- A shift could last 10 hours or more, depending on the distance to be traveled, which left plenty of time to chat with the steady flow of tourists, businessmen and settlers who flocked to the canal.
- Even though the boats only traveled at a rate of two miles per hour, the travel time between Albany and Buffalo was cut from six days to three.
- Luxurious packet boats carried tourists from the northern tour, a travel circuit that ultimately led to Niagara Falls; locals used the canal to visit relatives or conduct business.
- Anyone in upstate New York who had not voyaged on the tranquil waters at least once was considered a homebody.
- Riding the canal was an adventure—something to record in one's journal.
- Often passengers would step out of the canal boat and walk along with Ian asking questions about the horses he drove, the canal and sometimes about Ian himself.
- He was careful to cut back on his cussing during these times, having chased away more than one pretty girl prematurely.
- He loved the attention and especially the chance to talk to people from far away and hear their accents and smell their clothes.
- Canal packet boats were approximately 78 feet in length and 14.5 feet across and were designed to accommodate up to 40 passengers at night and more than a hundred in the daytime.
- During waking hours, the packet's central cabin served as a sitting room and could be transformed into a dining room for meals.
- Dinners were sometimes elegant with delicacies like roast beef, ham, plum pudding, and liqueurs to add enjoyment to the sightseeing.
- In addition to the waterway's locks, aqueducts, deep cuts and massive embankments, the canal carried passengers through deep forest and seemingly endless swamps.
- The canal also encouraged families to move farther west, comforted in the knowledge that they could still get supplies, mail, and visits from relatives.
- The bane of a canal traveler's existence was low bridges, constructed for farmers after their land was cut in two by the canal.
- Virtually every tourist carried home tales of fellow passengers forced to fling themselves against the deck or scramble into the cabin whenever a bridge was seen.
- The bane of Ian's existence as a driver was malfunctioning locks that lengthened his workday and frustrated previously pleasant passengers.
- Some businessmen, pressed for time, would transfer from canal boats to stagecoaches to avoid sections of the canal particularly laden with locks.
- Ian's biggest problem was working year-round; the frigid temperatures of upstate New York often shut down the Erie Canal for up to five months each year.

- This meant that the U.S. mail was often not delivered promptly to upstate New Yorkers, accustomed to speedy communications; crops did not get to market; and Ian went unpaid.
- At other times of the year, Ian was never able to get dry; it was the driver's job to keep the horses moving, pulling the freight-laden boat up the canal in the middle of the summer heat or during torrential rains: captains, merchants and passengers had schedules to keep.
- Rarely did Ian get a full night's sleep; bugles would sound in the middle of the night to alert him to the arrival of a boat needing a change of horses.
- Depending on the news of the canal, one shift could end at midnight and start again at 5:30 a.m.
- Then, after a 12-mile pull requiring seven hours' work, Ian might sleep on the floor of another barn for three hours before starting another 10-hour trip.
- He knew from experience that falling asleep while driving the horses would enrage the captain or tease death at one of the locks.
- Both were to be avoided.
- Approximately 3,000 boats used the canal, carrying four times that many cabin girls—all interested, he told himself, in getting to know him better, so, making the captain mad was not a good thing.

Life in the Community: Upstate New York

- In 1817 freight required several weeks to move from the ports of New York City to the interior of the state.
- By 1827 the Erie Canal had dramatically influenced the lifestyle of people within the canal corridor—the distance a wagon could travel in one day, about 20 miles, on either side of the man-made ditch.
- Ready access to markets in New York City gave farmers a greater sense of independence, whether they were selling wheat, apples, or cloth woven from their own sheeps' wool.
- Improved transportation also encouraged city merchants to sell their wares in the hinterlands—dramatically expanding the availability of farm tools, clothing and luxuries such as oysters.
- At the same time, the canal gave rise to towns composed of the very rich and the very poor.
- Swamps drained of water destroyed once vibrant forests, while changes to canal technology challenged the laws of nature, serving as a threat to America's special geographic and moral destiny by encouraging too much civilization.
- State funding for the Erie Canal was approved following President James Madison's veto of a federal funding bill, symbolizing the national debate concerning economic development.
- The Federalists supported a strong central government that was capable of sponsoring and funding commercial expansion, including roads and international trade.
- The Democratic-Republicans placed most of the power in the hands of the various states and promoted a limited role for the federal government.
- To finance the canal, New York planned to use toll revenue, the proceeds of land sales near the canal, lotteries, taxes on the improved land near the ditch and the payment of levies on products that moved through the canal, such as salt, or steamboat travel.

HISTORICAL SNAPSHOT
1829

- French mathematician Evarise Galois introduced the theory of groups
- The New England Asylum for the Blind, the first in the U.S., was incorporated in Boston
- Scottish explorer John Ross discovered the magnetic North Pole
- Jons Berzelius discovered element 90, thorium
- Andrew Jackson was inaugurated as the United States president
- The original Siamese twins, Chang and Eng Bunker, arrived in Boston for an exhibition to the Western world
- Giachinno Rossini's opera William Tell was produced in Paris
- Mormon Joseph Smith was ordained by John the Baptist—according to Joseph Smith
- Niépce and Louis Jacques Mandé Daguerre formed a partnership to develop photography
- William Austin Burt of Michigan received a patent for the typographer, a forerunner of the typewriter
- Stiff collars became part of a man's dress
- Slavery was abolished in Mexico
- The American Bible Society published Scripture in the Seneca Indian language
- Forty million buffalo inhabited the American West
- The Chesapeake Bay Canal was formally opened
- The length of a yard was standardized at 36 inches
- The British Parliament passed the Catholic Emancipation Act, which granted freedom of religion to Catholics and permitted Catholics to hold almost any public office
- The Indian custom of immolating a widow along with her dead husband was abolished in British India
- David Walker published *Walker's Appeal*, an American pamphlet that opposed slavery
- American annual per-capita alcohol consumption reached 7.1 gallons
- The cornerstone was laid for the United States Mint

Andrew Jackson.

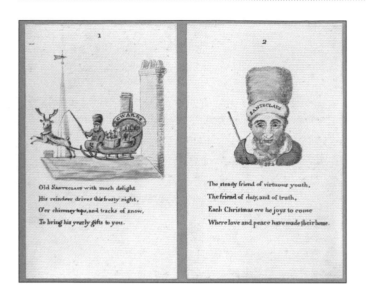

1

Old Santeclaus with much delight
His reindeer drives this frosty night,
O'er chimney tops, and tracks of snow,
To bring his yearly gifts to you.

2

The steady friend of virtuous youth,
The friend of duty, and of truth,
Each Christmas eve he joys to come
Where love and peace have made their home.

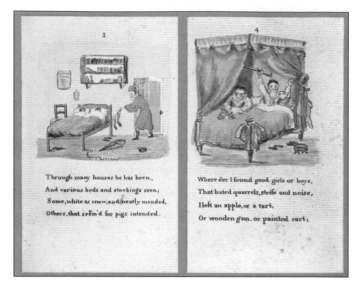

3

Through many houses he has been,
And various beds and stockings seen;
Some, white as snow, and neatly mended,
Others, that seem'd for pigs intended.

4

Where e'er I found good girls or boys,
That hated quarrels, strife and noise,
I left an apple, or a tart,
Or wooden gun, or painted cart;

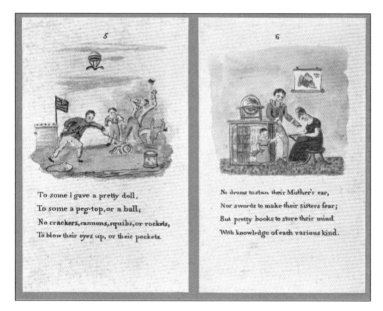

5

To some I gave a pretty doll,
To some a peg-top, or a ball;
No crackers, cannons, squibs, or rockets,
To blow their eyes up, or their pockets.

6

No drums to stun their Mother's ear,
Nor swords to make their sisters fear;
But pretty books to store their mind
With knowledge of each various kind.

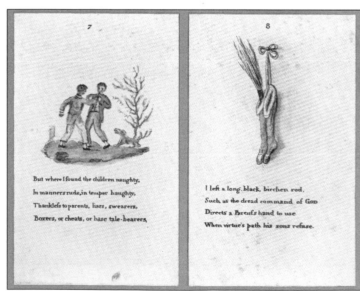

7

But where I found the children naughty,
In manners rude, in temper haughty,
Thankless to parents, liars, swearers,
Boxers, or cheats, or base tale-bearers,

8

I left a long, black, birchen rod,
Such as the dread command of God
Directs a Parent's hand to use
When virtue's path his sons refuse.

Pages from a children's book.

Erie Canal Timeline

1792
The Western Inland Lock Navigation Company incorporated to link the Hudson River to the Ontario and Seneca lakes.

1808
The New York State legislature authorized to survey of possible canal routes.

1811
The New York State canal commissioners asked for aid from the federal government and neighboring states.

1817
Erie Canal construction began with New York State funding when President James Madison vetoed federal funding of the canal.

1820
Navigation traffic began on the Erie Canal's eight-mile middle section, while work began on the eastern section.

1823
Boats first passed from the Erie Canal and the Champlain Canal into the Hudson River.

1825
A grand celebration marked the completion of the Erie Canal between Buffalo and Albany, New York.

Boats on the newly completed Erie Canal.

Selected Prices

Brandy, French, Ten-Gallon Cask $8.00
Collar, Man's $0.25
Crib $1.50
Glasses, Jelly, Dozen $1.00
Lard, Pound $0.05
Plough $2.00
Pocketbook, Woman's $0.25
Quilting Frame $0.50
Tea Set, Canton Chinaware $18.00
Wood, Cord $0.75

One year old, My New Birth Day, Letter from Joseph Hollingsworth to William and Nancy Rawcliff, South Leicester, New York, 1828:

Respected Aunt & Uncle,

Don't be astonished at my writing No. 4 before I have received No. 3 from you. One reason is this, viz. that this day being the first anniversary of my landing in America I wanted to celebrate it by writing a letter. . . .

I have lived in America exactly one year. I have seen all the Seasons and must confess that I prefer the American weather far before the English. I've never seen in this country a beggar such as I used daily to see in England, nor a tax gatherer with his Red Book as impudent as the D-v-L, taking the last penny out of a poor man's pocket. In this country there no Lords, nor Dukes, nor Counts, nor Marquises, nor Earls, no Royal family to support nor King.

The "President of the United States" is the highest titled fellow in this country. He is chosen by the people, of the people; holds his station for four years, if not re-chosen is no more than the rest of the people. The president when he makes his speech does not begin with "My Lords and Gentlemen" but with "Fellow Citizens." When we came from Poughkeepsie to this place we stopped at first at Amenia, New York. I was astonished to see the driver loose the horses off and leave the waggon by the road side. I spoke to Bro. John and told him I thout our goods would be stolen. He answered 'No danger." If I had not been well tired I believe I should not have slept that night for fear, but I had no occasion to fear, for our goods was as safe as when locked up in the yard at Manchester, and all the journey so thro' we never put our waggon under cover, always left it in the road or street (or where ever it happened to be) all night to the mercy of the Theives, if any there were. We have no lock on our doors, we never make them fast at night. This helps to confirm the truth of some of my old English poetry

A land where tyrany is no more
Where we can all be free
And men without a lock to th' door
Sleeps and tranquility

There is a factory sistem which breeds a kind of petty tyranny but ere long will be leveled as low as its the supporters I Hope.

Give my regards to Old Haigh and tell him if you please that my father has no occasion to hawk nuts in America as every body can have them for gathering in this country. Neither is he bound to carry Mes. Haighs wet pieces up Mirylane on his back nor to go roast himself in their stove every Sunday morning for nothing. I have got a new hat which cost five dollars and three quarters. I have a pair of boots making which will be four dollars and an half. I am still working in the Gig room for $17 per month. Father has been writing a letter for six months together to William Lockwood. He is not yet finished. It is to be so large, and so compleat with information, but I guess it will be like the mountain in labour, it may bring forth a mouse. The more I live in this country the better I like it.

You must excuse my brothers James and Jabez for not writing as they are both deeply engaged in Sparking. Jabez Sparks a Yankee girl James Sparks a Saddleworth girl, and on the 25th of November Joseph Kenyon took two English girls to a ball.

We are all in good health at present hoping you are the same. Jabez and James are little tickled at what I have just written so I will conclude.

Soloman Henkel Recipes and Cures: Henkel's Vermifuge, Compound Oil of Worm-seed, Newmarket, Virginia, 1832:

This medicine is a powerful anathematic and a mild cathartic, expelling every species of worms infesting intestinal canal. It is a medicine which has been compounded through an experience in the practice of medicine since 1796, and brought to its present improved state in 1832, and since used with great astounding success as a vermifuge.

Worms may be readily distinguished by the following symptoms, viz: variable appetite, fetid breath, acid eructations, and pains in the stomach, grinding of teeth during sleep, picking of the nose, paleness of the countenance, hardness and fullness of the belly, slimy stools, with occasional griping pains, more particularly about the navel, heat and itching about the mood seat, short dry cough, emaciation of the body, slow fever with the evening exacerbations, and irregular pulse, and sometimes compulsive fits.

As this medicine cleanses the stomach and bowels of whatever is foul or offensive, without causing griping or pain, experience has proved it to be equally valuable in many diseases besides those induced by worms, to which children are exposed. Adults have also used it with advantage.

"Dyeing Cabinet Woods Various Colors," *A New Family Encyclopedia; or Compendium of Universal Knowledge*, Charles A. Goodrich, Philadelphia, 1832:

Wood, for inlaying, veneering, &c etc., is dyed red by boiling it in water and alum; then taking it out, adding brazil to the liquor, and giving the wood another boil in it. Black, by applying a solution of logwood, boiled in vinegar, hot with a brush, and afterwards washing the wood over with a decoction of galls and sulfide of iron till it be of the hue required. Any other color may be given by squeezing out moisture of horse-dung through a sieve, mixing it with roche alum and gum arabic, and to the whole adding green, blue, or any other color desired. After standing two or three days, the wood, cut to the thickness of half a crown, is put into the liquor boiling hot, and suffered to remain till it is sufficiently colored. New mahogany may be made of a dark color, by smearing it over with a paste made of quick lime and water.

"A Ballet in New York City 1832," *America and the Americans*, Achille Murat, 1849:

It is only a few years since, that waltzing was proscribed in society, and only Scotch reels and quadrilles were danced. From the moment of its introduction the waltz was looked upon as almost indelicate, and, in fact, an outrage on female delicacy. Even preachers denounced in public the circumstance of a man who was neither love or nor husband, encircling the waist, and twirling a lady about in his arms, as a heinous sin and abomination. Nobody can forget the excitement caused by the arrival of the ballet corps in New York from Paris! I happened to be at the first representation. The very appearance of dancers in short petticoats caused an indescribable astonishment; but at the first "pirouette," when these appendages, charged with lead at the extremities, whirled round, taking a horizontal position, such a noise was created in the theater, that I question whether even the uproar at one of the Musard's carnival "bal infernal" at Paris, could equal it. The ladies screamed out for very shame, and left the theater, and the gentlemen, for the most part, remained crying and laughing at the very fun of the thing! while they only remarked its ridiculousness.

"Manufacturing Straight Pins," *The Edinburgh Encyclopedia*, Philadelphia, 1832:

The brass wire of which pins are made is first drawn to the proper thickness, and after being straightened it is cut into different lengths, each of which is sufficient for making several pins. The ends of these lengths are then well pointed on small grinding stones, and the length of the pin is cut off from each end, and the process repeated until the length of wire is exhausted. In order to make a head, a piece of metallic wire is spun on another, so as to form a hollow spiral when taken on. This spiral is then cut by shears into small parts of two coils each, which is sufficient for making the head. In putting on the head, the workman thrusts the blunt end of the pin among the heads, and when immediately placed under a heavy weight or pressure, the head is made secure by a blow and the pin can be completed in its form. It is then whited, by putting it in a copper colouring tin and the lees of wine. Twenty workmen are said to be employed on each pin, from the drawing of the wire to the arrangement of the pins on the paper.

The mechanican, not the magician, is now the master of life.

—Massachusetts Governor Edward Everett, 1832

Speech, by Reverend F. H. Cuming marking the completion of the Lockport locks along the Erie Canal in 1825:

The mountains have been levelled; the vallies have been filled; rivers and gulfs have been formed over them, by the exertions of art, a channel in which the waters of the distant Hudson, the waters of the still more distant Atlantic, will reunite with water to the remote west, and constitute a river.

Letter from Padraig Cundun, Irish farmer who had worked in the Erie Canal, 1834:

I have a fine farm of land now, which I own outright. No one can demand rent from me. My family and I eat our fill of bread and meat, butter and milk any day we like throughout the year, so I think being here is better than staying in Ireland, landless and powerless, without food or clothing.

"The Erie Canal," *The Connecticut Herald,* 1821:

When it is considered with how much ease families can remove to the land which they own in the West, and with what facility and delight emigrants thither can occasionally revisit their friends and the spot of their nativity, the mind is at once impressed with the magnitude and importance of this great inland communication.

1824 NEWS FEATURE

"Indian Anecdotes," *The New Monthly Magazine*, **London, England, 1824:**

Several attempts have been recently made to attract attention to the state of the North American Indians, both in our own possessions and those of the United States, with a view to ameliorate the condition and prevent their utter extinction. All that relates to the development of the character of man and his savage as well as civilized state, is calculated to accelerate the progress of knowledge and must be generally beneficial to mankind. Mr. Hunter, it is well known, lately published a work of a very singular character upon the subject, calculated to throw light upon the habits and manners of this singular race, who has scantily peopled the northern regions of America, prior to its discovery by Europeans, many tribes which have altogether disappeared. Numberless peculiar customs and singularities of language distinguish this people from the Aborigines of every other known territory, and it is doubtful whether any offer a more interesting subject of research. In the North American Indians stands in the highest rank of uncivilized man. His religious creed, at least that of many of the tribes west of the Mississippi, resembles that of the Jews, in being pure theism. He is a lover of freedom, and nothing can bend him to slavery, being indissolubly attached to roaming the vast forest and beautiful savannahs of his native land. He exhibits great nobleness of character, singular magnanimity, strong parental and filial attachments, a love of truth and sincerity in his intercourse with his friends, and a degree of bravery and sagacity in war, almost incredible. He is a cruel and revengeful enemy, but he rarely becomes an enemy without adequate cause. Persecuted, belied, and cheated by the whites, he has been represented as being destitute of virtues, worthless, and ferocious; when in reality he frequently exhibits great generosity, elevation of spirit, and energy of address, which are not surpassed among the inhabitants of civilized communities. The Indian attacks upon the whites have rarely or ever been made without ample provocation; among themselves they have been encouraged by the colonists in their internecine wars, have been paid by them per scalp, for the destruction of their brethren. The robberies and murders of Indians often perpetuated by backwoods-men and the knavery of white traders, the continual encroachments of the colonists upon them, the sufferings they have undergone from the introduction of ardent spirits, and the feuds that have been carefully promoted between the different tribes, have rapidly diminished the population; and the time approaches very fast when in all the vast tract east of the Mississippi not a single aboriginal American will remain. The traditions of the Iroquois abound with touching relations with the injustice they have sustained from the whites, from their first settling in the country. "We and our tribes," say they, "lived in peace and harmony with each other before white people came to this country; our council-house extended far to the north and to the south. In the middle of it we could meet from all parts to smoke the pipe of peace together; when the white man arrived in the south we received them as friends, we did the same when they arrived in the east. It was we, it was our forefathers, who made them welcome and let them sit down by our side. The land they settled on was ours. We knew not but the Great Spirit had sent them to us for some good purpose, and therefore we thought they must be good people. We were mistaken; for no sooner had they obtained a footing in our lands, than they began to pull our council-house down, first at one end and then at the other, and at last meeting in the center where the council-fire was yet burning bright, they put it out and extinguished it with our own blood sin! with the blood of those who with us had received them soon! who had welcomed them in our land! the blood ran in streams into our fire, and extinguished it so entirely, but not one spark was left us whereby to kindle a new fire; we were compelled to withdraw ourselves beyond the great swamp, and fly to our good uncle the Delamattenos, who kindly gave us a tract to live on. On we shall be permitted to remain in this asylum the great Spirit only knows. The whites will not rest contented until they shall have destroyed the last of us, and made us disappear entirely from the face of the earth."

The introduction of civilization into America and the establishment of a mighty empire there, has not been effected without the committal of many wanton crimes. The murders, robberies, injustice, and oppression of the native Indians, the kidnapping and carrying them out for slaves, the assembling them under peaceful pretences and betraying them, men, women, and children, to destruction, together with the occupation of their hunting grounds and native soil, form another singular example of the inscrutable government of mundane events; and how much national and individual injustice and crime are permitted to take place, to work out a remote and expensive good. The outrages committed upon the Indians never wanted an excuse, though nine times out of ten a provocation fully sufficient to justify them was given on the part of the whites. . . .

The Indian traditions have preserved with great accuracy the appearance of the whites among them, and the unprincipled conduct of the first settlers. The Dutch demanded from them as much land as a hide would cover, to raise greens for their soup; this being granted they cut the hide into strips and encircled a large piece of ground with it on the New York Island, "upon which they built strong houses" and "planted great guns" against them. The conduct of the English to their disgrace, is even less ceremonious than this. They asked no leave of the Indians, but took possession of what land they wanted, encroached upon the hunting and fishing-grounds, and very quickly got into disputes with them and spilled their blood. The tribe of Indians to whom the land belonged, which was thus occupied by the British, after having welcomed the destroyers of their shores and even hunted for them, fled into Pennsylvania and remained there until Miquon, the Englishman, (William Penn), whose name they even now regard with great reverence, came and procured an interval of peace for them. At his death they were again persecuted and driven afar from their new home. . . .

The attempts made to convert the Indians to Christianity have been generally unsuccessful, kept among the Moravians. This is to be accounted for in two ways: first because the whites have exhibited a bad moral character to the Indians, far inferior to that of the Indians themselves in many respects. They ask what treaty had Christians kept with them? "What promises had they not violated? Had they not been despoiled of their hunting grounds, of their lakes, and of their mountains? Had they not slain their old men and warriors? Had they not taught them to act as beasts, yea, worst than the beasts of the forest, by the use of spirituous liquors? Did they not give rum to them to deceive and cheat them; to take from them their fields and skins? Had they not derived loathsome diseases and other evils from these professing Christianity? Can the God of the Christians approve such acts?" The simple reasoning being overcome by whites and exemplary conduct and character residing among them, there is a second objection to the mode communicating instruction, which helps to account for that little progress hitherto made. To teach a savage to read and write, it is ignorantly supposed will be the same efficacy as endowing an illiterate member of a civilized community with the same acquirements. This is a serious mistake. The Indian is first to be made to approximate to the white in the habits and comforts of life. To have a success worthy of the attempt, a missionary should be a man of practical knowledge in the arts necessary to improve existence. He should begin by attending the sick and administering them medicine; he should teach his flock the arts of husbandry, direct them to innocent amusements, and instruct them how to make articles necessary to procure them additional comforts. He should remove their prejudices by degrees; and as their condition becomes better, instruct them, step by step, in their religious duties, and finally communicate to them the more central branches of education. Very little good is done by teaching the Indians to read and write in the first instance. The Moravians, by pursuing this wiser plan to a certain extent, have succeeded better than others in imparting moral instruction to them.

The number of Indians in all parts of the continent of North America, is calculated at two millions; but this is a very rough estimate, and the truth can never be exactly known. A treaty was concluded by the United States in 1794, which comprehended fifty-seven thousand Indian warriors. This would give a population of about half a million comprehended in that treaty, including the aged, the women, and the children. . . .

That a race which often exhibits traits of character worthy of being imitated in civilized countries, should be suffered to dwindle away, a prey to the vices and rapacity of the dregs of the white people, is deeply to be deplored. It is a good subject for that philanthropy to work upon, which is now extending itself upon nations much more rude and barbarous. We have also to repay these unfortunate Indians for the calamities we have been the means of inflicting upon them; and it is to be hoped that the laudable attempts of such men as Mr. Hunter . . . will kindle a candle of feeling the disinterested benevolence toward the aboriginal inhabitants of America, and induce the Canadian and American governments to punish any oppressions and insults they may receive from the colonies of these nations respectively.

A diligent examination of the subject must convince the most prejudiced, that the Indian detained in North America has fewer vices and more noble points of character, than can be found elsewhere on the globe among an unenlightened people, though none have been more wronged, belied, and persecuted.

1830–1839

During the 1830s, America was growing in size and character, showing no reluctance to test new ideas. During this critical time of peaceful expansion, both agriculture and industry underwent fundamental changes that resulted in improved productivity and more self-sufficiency. As a result, less labor was needed on the farms, freeing up workers for the burgeoning industries of New England eager to supply the national market. Lowell, Massachusetts, in particular, pioneered the industrial system, characterized by innovative technology, professional management and extensive use of female labor, as envisioned by Francis Cabot Lowell. Western migration accelerated in the 1830s as settlers from the northern free states followed the shores of the Great Lakes, bringing commerce to Michigan and Wisconsin. Land seekers from the coastal slave states found Mississippi, Alabama and points west to their liking. The population of some old-line eastern towns actually decreased, breathing life into Ohio, Kentucky, Tennessee and locations beyond. By the end of the decade more than 6.3 million people lived in the Western states, 4.1 million of whom had moved to the region since 1820.

This economic expansion was driven by the era of the canals that dramatically opened the interior of the country to Eastern manufactured goods. This grand innovation in travel then melted into the railroad age—a technology revolution that opened up a huge swath of the country to development, settlement and exploitation. Both canals and railroads suffered through periods of overbuilding and bankruptcy, but improved transportation changed the way Americans thought about their boundaries. Railroads in particular allowed people to reorient the West, opening up vast new territory to farming. At the same time, improved transportation and reduced freight rates played a critical role in ending the concept of self-sufficiency held so dear by many rural farmers.

The new economy was also creating an America less tied to agriculture and European manufactured imports and more toward homegrown factories and internal expansion. Factories with 10, 50, or 100 wage earners were common, producing gunpowder, wool blankets or cast-iron plates. These facilities provided real wages to farmers frustrated by intermittent crop failures and isolation. In exchange, workers in this new industrial age were expected to work 12-hour days, six days a week. At the same time, more work was sent to private homes, where it was often women who earned a weekly wage doing piecework. By 1831, in just the four largest cities, approximately 13,000 women worked at home making items such as paper boxes, hoop skirts, shirts and collars, artificial flowers and ladies' cloaks. When outworkers were calculated into the working rolls, women in 1839 made up almost half of all manufacturing workers in America and about two thirds of workers in New England. The wages were low and profits high. By the late 1830s ready-made clothing was sold for five times what it cost to produce. Women, on average, made $1.50 to $2.00 a week for sewing and many, based on high employer-set production levels, made less than $1.00 per week.

At the same time, Britain began repealing laws restricting immigration of its skilled artisans as a display of its commitment to an international economy. And emigrate they did. Thousands of skilled English, representing a broad segment of British society, flooded into America bringing specialized craft skills to a market both ripe and eager for innovation. More than 100,000 Europeans a year flowed to the land of the free, remaking the map of America: more than half the German immigrants found land west of the mountains, the Scandinavians found homes in Illinois, Wisconsin and Minnesota, while approximately 85 percent of the Irish, retreating from failed crops and starvation, stayed in the East. America's reputation as the land of opportunity was already well established and documented in the lives of millions of immigrant families.

The populist movement, whose roots went back decades, got its champion in 1829 with the inauguration of President Andrew Jackson, who invigorated the hopes of the common man and struck fear into the nation's most prosperous. When as president, for example, he vetoed the re-charter of the Second Bank of the United States in 1832, he pitted the common man against the Eastern money interests. That same year, Jackson tangled with Vice President John C. Calhoun over high tariffs. South Carolina opposed the cost of the taxes on imported goods, fearing that economic instability would damage its hold on slavery, already weakened by falling cotton prices and soil exhaustion. Calhoun and others began to reassert that the United States was actually a compact of states, each of which retained the right to declare certain laws null and void. This argument set the stage for Southern secession and the resulting Civil War three decades later.

1834 Profile

Joseph Lyons, having ventured away from his conservative Jewish background, was a shy, well-educated college graduate still uncertain about his place in the world.

Life at Home

- Although employed as a clerk working in a law office in Savannah, Georgia, 20 year old Joseph Lyons was troubled by his future.
- To find answers, he wrote in a journal each day, recording his opinions about politics and religion, writing poetry, as well as articulating his ambivalence about his future plans.
- A graduate of South Carolina College in Columbia, Joseph was the son of a prominent Jewish businessman.
- Joseph's parents lived in Columbia, South Carolina, where his father, Isaac Lyons, ran a grocery store and was active in the local synagogue.
- Joseph's father had been born in Bavaria in 1774; his mother, Rachel Cohen, was born in London in 1775.
- Her parents, Joseph's grandparents, Rebecca and Jacob Raphael Cohen, emigrated from London to Montreal, Canada.
- After the American Revolution, the family moved to Philadelphia, where Jacob became the hazan, the official of a synagogue who conducts the liturgical part of the service and serves as cantor, of Philadelphia's largest synagogue, Mikveh Israel.
- Isaac and Rachel were married in Philadelphia, and they soon had one daughter and five sons.
- Isaac began as a carpenter but soon became a merchant, heavily involved in civic affairs.

Upon graduating from South Carolina College, Joseph Lyons was uncertain about his future.

- The family moved south to Charleston in 1811, and Isaac became a member of the Hebrew Orphan Society, purchased three slaves, and opened a mineral warehouse business.
- By 1820, Isaac had been named to the governing council of Beth Elohim, a sign that the Lyonses had become accepted into Jewish elite society.
- During a period of economic decline and unrest due to a scare about slave rebellions, Isaac moved with his family to Columbia, a frontier market town.
- Isaac's business was described in the local paper, the *Telescope*, in 1827, as a "new Grocery Store" offering a variety of wines and liquors, sugars, coffee, tea, rice, flour, crackers, spices, soap, candles, powder, and shot.
- The store became widely known for its oysters, considered a very popular treat, especially among the young men of the town.
- By 1834, young Joseph had ventured away from his family and was living in Savannah, Georgia, working as a clerk in the law practice of Levi Sheftall D'Lyon, and learning "what it is to be a stranger."
- Although shy and unpopular among his classmates at South Carolina College, Joseph missed the intellectual exchanges he experienced there with a few close friends.
- He found some relief from his loneliness by writing in his journal on the big issues of life: ". . . what can a man make of himself unless he is in the region of Intelligence i.e. in a city, a fellow must starve where food is not to be had."

Main Street in Columbia, South Carolina.

- Joseph often corresponded with several friends from college and several cousins who were close to him in age and interests.
- He considered several different career paths, including medicine, surveying, mining, farming, mineralogy, and, of course, law.
- One other career path was as a hazan in a Jewish congregation.
- That would require study in Germany, and he thought longingly about how it might provide him with a steady income.
- However, since he was not certain about his own religious beliefs, he rejected that path as dishonorable.
- He was also unsure how to combine his Jewish heritage with the modern, progressive influences.
- At South Carolina College, the president of the college, Thomas Cooper, who believed in religious tolerance, refused to teach theology, and claimed that students "needed to be cured from religion."
- Ultimately, Joseph was more comfortable reading—Voltaire and Blackstone—and writing poetry.

Joseph ventured from the prescribed road to success.

- In his journal he wrote, ". . . I can write trash rhymes very readily and can play Hail Columbia on the fiddle and can do a heap of things, which are useful for all purposes but that of earning bread, for making me independent."
- Joseph's family was able to afford many things which other families might consider luxuries, such as college educations for their children and expensive trips out of town, by boat, to distant ports such as Philadelphia.
- He felt guilty for spending so much of his father's money, with nothing to show for it.
- Soon after his graduation, in December of 1833, Joseph celebrated by going to Charleston to visit friends.
- He described Charleston as a place "where bananas, Books and Oysters do abound."
- A major seaport, Charleston showcased markets and restaurants serving fruits and seafood that would be much harder to find in an inland town like Columbia.
- Charleston had a much more vibrant social life than Columbia, and Joseph was invited to several parties.
- At the first party, he felt "horrid, silent as a post and awkwardly dawdling . . . face burning, shrinking and enraged. . . ."
- At the next party he attended he played card games—first "lotto" (losing 25 coppers), and then "loo" (losing 500 coppers).
- His cousin, Raphael, celebrated his twenty-first birthday with a gentlemen's party, costing Joseph 600 coppers.
- He also attended a special Jewish ceremony—a circumcision of twins—a novel experience to him.
- Before coming home to start working in Savannah in a law firm, he decided to make an unexpected trip to Philadelphia with his cousin Raphael.
- He wrote to his parents asking permission, and debated whether he should go.
- His sister, Isabel, who lived in Charleston, advised him not to make the trip, but he decided to board the boat, with or without the blessings of his family.
- His parents had lived in Philadelphia many years before, and they still had family there.

Charleston, South Carolina offered Joseph more social opportunities than Columbia.

Joseph's cousin, Raphael.

Joseph and Raphael sailed unexpectedly to Philadelphia and enjoyed the city immensely.

- Joseph and Raphael were planning to stay with one of their cousins.
- Soon after stepping on board, they experienced seasickness for the first time.
- He and Raphael both wondered why they ever decided to go through such misery, and wished they had stayed on "terra firma" back in Charleston.
- Joseph eventually found his sea legs, and discovered the glorious beauty of the Gulf Stream, with its colorful fish, porpoises, and deep blue water.
- The discomforts of travel faded into a faint memory once the young men arrived in the beautiful old city of Philadelphia, with its wonderful architecture and lively mercantile business.
- They investigated Chestnut Street, with its banks, stores and theaters.
- They made reservations to attend the theater that evening, where they had the good fortune to see one of the best actresses of the day—Miss Fanny Kemble—performing in *The Stranger in Venice*.

Life at Work

- At the law office in Savannah, Georgia, Joseph Lyons's responsibilities were light, as he was also preparing for an oral examination in the law.
- Previously, he was present for such an examination of two young men and was alarmed at the detailed questions they were ready to answer.

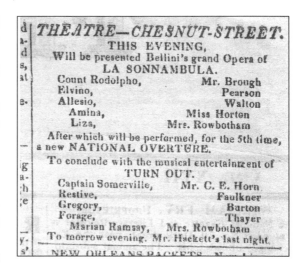

Joseph and his friends "sturgeon dragging" on a lake.

- He worried that his exams would prove to be an embarrassment.
- One day's plan of study: Starting at 10 a.m. until 1 p.m.—historical reading (or at times miscellaneous law); 1-2—music (violin); 3-5 Law, followed by miscellaneous reading; evening—noting and examinations on Law, then Spanish; go to bed.
- Even though Joseph had studied Spanish, French and Latin, and often interjected phrases in these languages into his writing, he was dissatisfied with his educational attainments, and felt "deep in the slough of despond."
- He asked: "What are my acquirements at 20; as to language a superficial notion of Latin, Greek, French and Spanish, a similar proficiency on flute and violin, a similar acquaintance with politics, metaphysics, and general literature. . . ?"
- He sometimes took time off from his work and studying, going out to see what was happening, or perhaps writing letters to friends.
- One Friday night, he and several friends went "sturgeon dragging" on a lake.
- This consisted of paddling slowly around in the lake, with two fellows at the bow with sturgeon hooks in their hands, which they let down in the water to rake up the fish that live in the muddy bottom.
- The next day they had better luck when they went out to hunt for catfish.
- They caught a "Rock," which Joseph later ate for his supper.
- But his ambivalence about his career path continued to resurface, and he regretted not having studied harder in college.
- "Now it is I feel the fruits of having gone through College as superficially as I did. Did I but understand mathematics now I could obtain a place in a school here which would yield me about 800 or 1,000 dollars a year, but it is impossible. I do not know a cubic equation from a simple, and co-signs and Co-tangents are almost Cabala to me."
- In Savannah, Joseph witnessed a cholera outbreak.
- He worried that his landlord, who had some of the symptoms, may have been in the early stages of the disease.

- To ward off the disease himself, Joseph was careful to eat grapes and persimmons.
- "I do not want to die of such a troublesome disease. . . . I hardly expect to escape fever, my exposure is perhaps too much for one unaccustomed to it."

Life in the Community: Charleston, South Carolina

- The Colony of South Carolina began welcoming Jews in 1669.
- "Jews, Heathens and other Dissenters" were allowed to settle there, but not Catholics.
- Jews and Huguenots were encouraged to come, in part because of their commercial talents, but also because they were considered European, in a colony that was becoming increasingly black.
- By 1800, Charleston had the largest Jewish population in North America, and this widely accepted, successful Jewish community was noted for both its high degree of integration into the mainstream and for its wealth and prominence.
- Joseph's father was on the governing council of Beth Elohim, which had been a largely conservative congregation, but in the early 1800s a reform movement emerged.
- The principal reform leader, Isaac Hardy, had opened an academy, attended by children from Charleston's elite families, both Jews and Gentiles, which encouraged an atmosphere of religious tolerance.
- One contentious issue centered on the proposal to purchase an organ for their new building.
- This issue split the congregation in two, pitting the conservative and reform-minded Jews in the Beth Elohim congregation against each other.
- The reform movement also divided the Lyons family along generational lines, with Isaac remaining a member of the conservative faction, and Joseph and his siblings leaning to the reformers' side.
- Also under debate was the issue of states' rights, or nullification.
- The debate in South Carolina was particularly fierce, saying that the American government had no right to impose tariffs, and wished these tariffs "nullified," or removed.
- Joseph was an enthusiastic "nullifier" and enjoyed wearing a special "palmetto" pin signifying his support for nullification.
- When he visited Philadelphia, he showed off his pin and happily identified himself as a proud believer in nullification, even to strangers.

Joseph ate grapes and persimmons to protect himself during a cholera outbreak.

HISTORICAL SNAPSHOT
1834

- Poker emerged as a Mississippi riverboat game
- Thirty-five thousand slaves were freed in South Africa as slavery was abolished throughout the British Empire
- New York and New Jersey made a compact over ownership of Ellis Island
- "Turkey in the Straw" became a popular American tune
- Sardines were canned in Europe for the first time
- One of New York City's finest restaurants, Delmonico's, sold a meal of soup, steak, coffee and half a pie for $0.12
- Louis Braille invented a system of raised dot writing to enable the blind to read
- Carl Jacobi discovered "uniformly rotating self-gravitating ellipsoids"
- Cyrus Hall McCormick patented a reaping machine
- Sandpaper was patented by Isaac Fischer Jr. of Springfield, Vermont
- The first railroad tunnel in the United States was completed in Pennsylvania
- The U.S. Senate censured President Andrew Jackson for taking federal deposits from the Bank of the United States
- The Spanish Inquisition was abolished
- Federal troops were used to control a labor dispute near Williamsport, Maryland, among Irish laborers constructing the Chesapeake and Ohio Canal

Selected Prices

Andirons, Brass $40.00
Cheese Press $10.00
Currant Wine, Barrel $228.00
Freezer, Tin $5.00
Man's Pants $100.80
Mutton, Pound $2.50
Rifle $332.50
Turkey, Whole $35.00
Wheelbarrow $5.00
Woman's Hose, Irish cotton $4.00

"Patent Shower Bath," *National Gazette*, Philadelphia, Pennsylvania, July 1, 1833:

This newly invented Shower Bath, combining usefulness with elegance, and the utmost cleanliness, but a very beneficial influence on the human body, being constructed in such a manner as to be conveniently put up in any private chamber, where the whole machine, when closed, forms a handsome piece of furniture, is respectfully offered to the public for inspection. . . . This Bath answering the purposes of the utmost privacy and convenience, may be put up in any bed chamber or nursery room, without the least trouble; it can be used in a standing, sitting or lying posture, and is formed by means of shower pipes, the water spouting through them like a gentle dew, whereby the temperature of the human body is not so suddenly affected; but the person bathing, if ever so delicate, agreeably refreshed; by these means preserved, and gradually hardened against the influence of the air; whereby colds and rheumatism are prevented, the nerves and the skin being greatly strengthened; whereas the common shower baths are rather indicated to produce a sudden shock not at all agreeable to delicate frames, or wanted for common bathing purposes.

"Fashion," *The New-York Mirror:* a Weekly Journal, Devoted to Literature and the Fine Arts, October 31, 1835:

Sleeves, a leading article of female attire, furnish us with a complete illustration of fickleness. In the olden time, sleeves were fashioned tight at the shoulder, descending whence, they gradually assumed width, until, near in the waist, they terminated in capricious ruffles.

Point-blank reverse is the present mode. "Bishops sleeves," as they are called, are now in the ascent; an inconvenient fashion in the first place; but what has fashion to do with convenience? In its wildest flight there might be some determinate object in view; but here all purpose defies inquiry. 'Tis a mode as much to be condemned for its distraction from any native beauty in the wearer, as for its intrinsick ugliness. The width of shoulder lent to the female figure by two overgrown balloons is unnatural and masculine. Is it attempted by artificial aid of contrast, to give a seeming miniature to the waist? if so, there is no true elegance at last obtained, for little satisfaction can there be in seeing a human body cut into like a wasp.

"Wallpaper," *United States Gazette*, Philadelphia, November 24, 1836:

The subscriber offers for sale at his Paper Hanging Warehouse, number 275 S. 2nd St, this splendid view of North America, the most spectacular article ever brought to this country. The whole of these views, collectively form a panorama of 48 feet in circumference, and may be divided into five principal parts from No. 1 to 6; exhibits a general view of New York, taken from Weehawk Hill, from which it is separated by the Hudson River. On the right of New York is seen Governor's Island with the fort which commands the bay. This part also contains several country views, fashionable promenades, &c. The 2d from 7 to 13 is a view of the military Academy at West Point, situated at a delightful spot on the banks of the Hudson, in the vicinity of stupendous rocks and highlands. . . . This series also represents a view which has attracted numerous spectators from the different parts of the country, and the monument erected in memory of General E. Wood is also seen in perspective. The 3rd from no. 14 to 21, a general view of Boston with its numerous splendid buildings, its port with steamboats and vessels of all nations flying to and fro, the unloading of cargoes and the general aspect of activity on its wharves, give an idea of the maritime importance of this city. . . . The other parts contain a calumet dance by the Winnebago Indians, Natural Bridge in Virginia, steamboats, railroads, falls of Niagara, and many other beautiful scenes too numerous to describe.

"Advice to Brides and Grooms on Brooms," *The Housekeepers Book*, Philadelphia, 1837:

The brooms of the domicile are various sorts; and, like every other article of domestic utility, but various qualities; nor are the best kinds to be ascertained by young housekeepers by intuition, neither should servants be entrusted with commission to purchase them. Shopkeepers are not always honest if servants are; and the less collusion that is allowed, or even hazarded between them on all occasions, the more advantageous it will be to a mistress. Experience alone, in a matter of brooms, can determine the good qualities and comparative merits of these essentials to household comfort.

We will begin with the carpet broom, that darling vehicle of the housemaid in her daily work of destruction to the beautiful woofs that grace our floors. With regret we have listened to the tearing sound of one of these vile bundles of harsh rushes scratching up the nap, under the strong arms and ruthless vigour of the servant! These gay brooms, begirt with gilded crimson leather, are one of the most expensive articles in the house; for they not only destroy the carpets, even when quite new, but quickly wear down; and, in that state of stubborn jagged twigs, a stable broom could commit less havoc. The best brush for our carpeted floors is a long-handled one, with rounded ends, the hairs very stiff, and about as long as those in a clothes brush. This, at all events, will suffice for the purpose of six days out of seven; so that only once a week, instead of every day, the genuine carpet broom may be permitted. Two house brooms should be always provided, one for the sleeping apartments (which should be kept upstairs) and one for the kitchen: and these, indeed all brooms, should have round ends; we deprecate those which are usually seen with ends sharp and square, and seem to have been invented expressly to chip the paint from the skirting boards.

"The Malagasy," *The Youth's Friend*, by the American Sunday School Union, July 1839:

The Malagasy: This is the name by which the inhabitants of the island of Madagascar are known. The above picture has been copied into the *Youth's Friend*, for the sake of bringing before the minds of its young readers a representation of the mode of living among these people. It would, probably, do much to increase our interest in heathen nations, if we had pictures of them in their various dwellings and employments. This would make us feel more the reality the degradation of the people who live with little or no civilization, and who have not the light of divine truth to guide them. Look at this view of the inside of a house in Madagascar, and think that millions are living this way; one room serving for all the family, and for the cow beside; no floor to cover the ground; no chimney to carry off the smoke; no windows to admit a cheerful light, and the only opening for this purpose being the door, and a hole in the roof. How few of the comforts of the humblest cottage are to be found in this hovel! What a wretched home for children! See that man and woman. In dress and appearance they seem to us being not much above the animal that is tied to the post. And the machine in which the woman is making cloth, how rude in its construction compared with the loom used in civilized countries!

Remember that this is not a picture of a dwelling remarkable in Madagascar for its want of comfort; or that these people would be curiosities there. It is but a sample of the thousands of homes and men and women in that island; and when compared with conditions from other nations, this dwelling would be considered fit for a king, so much better is it than the holes which millions of our race live.

Now suppose these people should be visited by a missionary. He talks with them about the mind and the soul, and makes them understand that they're capable of being instructed and enlightened. He tells them of God, of his word, of Christ, of eternity. He teaches them to read, and gives them a Bible in their own language. They assemble with him to pray and sing, and hear the Scriptures explained. They learn what their duty is to God, to their fellow-man. They feel as if a new world is open to them in the knowledge they have acquired. They are shown what advances other countries have made through their greater advantages of education in arts, and they see their own inferiority and that they have been living without the knowledge of the greatest blessings of life. Can you suppose that as they were instructed from week to week, no change would take place in this picture? No; you'll say at once, there would be a gradual improvement of their condition. They would desire proper clothing; they would learn the comforts of cleanliness; they would find another stable for the cow; they would build a chimney and find some covering for the floor of earth. Soon the whole appearance of things would be altered, until at last this miserable abode would be changed into a neat house with trees for shade, and vines to cover it, and a little garden surrounding it. And it is only for want of faith, if we cannot also expect to find a still more important change, and to see this family morning and evening reading the Bible and uniting in Christian worship.

Think of such a change in this one hut; and then extend your thought to a similar change in all the huts of Madagascar, of Africa, Asia, and the whole pagan world; and you will then perceive how blessed is the work of sending the Gospel to every creature.

The Panorama of Professions and Trades, or Every Man's Book, by Edward Hazen, Philadelphia, Pennsylvania, 1839:

To give the work a complete finish, four coats of varnish are successively applied; in addition to these, a particular kind of treatment is used after the laying on trying each coat. After the application of the first coat, the surface is rubbed with a piece of wood of convenient form; after the second, with sandpaper and pulverized pumice-stone; after the third, with pumice-stone again; after the fourth, with very finely powdered pumice-stone and rotten stone. A little linseed oil is next applied, and the whole process is finished by the application of flour, and by friction with the hand.

1836 PROFILE

Osborne Gibson was a mountain man roaming the Missouri and Oregon territories seeking to make a living in the fur trade; he had to learn to survive in the unsettled region and protect himself from the natural elements and the various Indian tribes.

Life at Home

- For the prior four years, Osborne Gibson had been trapping beaver and other wild game throughout the Rocky Mountains.
- Staying alive was a job in itself.
- The rugged life he found in the unsettled wilderness was not what he expected when he left his father and seven older siblings at age 17, searching for opportunity.
- After a seven-day walk to the New England coast, Osborne signed on first as a crew member of a clipper ship.
- He expected adventure as a member of the ship's crew but quickly learned the nautical definition of hard work.
- His non-stop duties on board the clipper, along with the seasickness, held little appeal, so when the ship arrived in New Orleans, he deserted his service.
- Still in search of adventure, he traveled along the Mississippi to St. Louis to join a trading company planning to trap beaver in the Rocky Mountains along the Snake River.
- Osborne was hired as an inexperienced hand for $250 for 18 months' service.
- Since he lacked the necessary gear to survive in the mountains, the company had to pay for his supplies, thus putting him in debt before he even left town.
- Osborne departed with 58 other men, and traveled hunter-like— wearing a flannel shirt, leather breeches, leggings, a coat made of blanket, a wool hat and moccasins made of dressed deerskin.
- He also carried his rifle with a powder horn and a bullet pouch attached to his belt.

Osborne Gibson lived as a mountain man, trapping animals for their fur.

St. Louis, Missouri.

Osborne's inexperience as a trapper put his life in danger.

- The trappers in the company wore similar garb but also rode with a sack containing six beaver traps, their butcher knives and a small wooden box containing bait for beaver.
- Aside from what he personally carried, each trapper traveled with an animal that carried his personal supplies such as extra powder horns, cooking utensils, salt and hatchets.
- The more experienced trappers carried supplies to trade with the Indians for furs.
- In addition to beads, some of the more popular supplies included woolen blankets and iron products, such as pots and pans.
- Half the company consisted of experienced trappers; Osborne was hired as a camp keeper, and was called a "Green horn" because he was inexperienced in the wilderness.
- His lack of experience was noticeable early on when he and a mulatto hire discovered a grizzly bear rummaging for roots near a grove of willow trees.
- Osborne and the man approached the creature and fired upon the bear, but only wounded it in the shoulder.
- Wanting to finish the bear with a shot, Osborne approached too closely and the angry bear charged and chased him though the marsh.
- The bear moved across the damp ground faster than Osborne could run.
- When he turned to face the bear with his rifle in hand, the grizzly stood erect and roared.
- Osborne froze with fear and thought it was his end.
- That was when the mulatto pierced the bear's heart with a rifle ball and saved Osborne's life.
- Osborne wrote in his journal, "I secretly determined in my own mind never to molest another wounded Grizzly Bear in a marsh or thicket."
- He was not the only inexperienced trapper.

- As the party stopped along a mountain slope to rest for part of an April day, it was discovered that the young English shoemaker from Bristol was missing.
- The expedition's leader ordered Osborne to go back and search for him—an impossible task since the rocky ground left no trail that may have led to his whereabouts.
- After firing his gun several times during the day's search, Osborne gave up after sunset without hopes of finding him.
- The following day he rode back downstream and returned to the party waiting at a fork in the river.
- When Osborne shared the news, the men were not surprised; the trappers assumed the Englishman was dead, and some had even wondered if Osborne would find his way back.
- Death was a common occurrence in the wilderness; rushing into a decision could get the group lost, cause them to stumble upon unfriendly Indians or get oneself killed.
- Osborne saw unsound emotions control a company member, like Abram Peterson, on a number of occasions.
- Abram was eager to cross the flood waters of the Salt River, move down the mountain and hunt some game for dinner.
- Melting mountain snow had flooded the river and the team commenced to make a number of bull boats to ferry their equipment over to the other side.
- Abram wanted nothing to do with the party's activity but waited with the group.
- Over the next couple of days, the men constructed boat frames of green willow branches and covered them with two raw buffalo hides sewn together and placed over the frame.
- A slow fire gradually dried the skins that created a buoyant vessel for the men and supplies.

Flood waters made crossing the Salt River difficult.

- Impatiently waiting for the boats to dry and irritable with some of the party members, Abram decided to cross the freezing Salt River on his horse.
- Halfway across the flood waters he fell from his horse and sank into the river.
- Osborne made a point of learning from the experienced mountain men about surviving in the woods.
- One thing he learned to do was make pemmican, a food item made from animal fat and meat.
- Osborne made batches of pemmican when a party member brought back bear or buffalo to the camp.
- He cut thin slices of meat and dried them slowly over the fire.
- Once dried, the meat was pounded into small pieces, mixed with melted animal fat and packaged into rawhide pouches.
- One time when he and a couple of trappers were lost, Osborne dreamed he had some pemmican—or any other food.
- Returning back to camp after several days of poor hunting, he and two other men realized they were trapped at a river crossing.
- Because rains had caused flooding that left the area destitute of game, the men lived chiefly upon roots for 10 days.
- After they managed to find a crossing point and return to camp, they discovered that the meat of two fat grizzly bears was being cooked into a stew.
- Inside his journal Osborne wrote, "The meal took a longer time to cook than any meal I ever saw prepared. It was also the best meal I had ever eaten. Of course that was the opinion of many of us starving."
- Starvation was only one of the dangers.
- While attempting to cross a river aboard a log raft, the raft, men and company's provisions were tossed into the heart of the rapids.
- The men swam to shore but the raft and the provisions continued downstream.

Osborne and fellow trapping company employees often found themselves off course and in unfamiliar territory.

- That was when Osborne questioned why he was in the wilderness and not back in St. Louis in a gay saloon swapping tales and drinking.
- The following day he was relieved to discover that the raft had drifted upon a gravel bar downstream with everything still safely secured.
- He saw it as a good omen, but most of the older trappers said it was just luck.
- Arguments started a few days later.
- The near loss of supplies did not settle well with the independent trappers working for the company who knew the territory better than did Joseph Sage, the leader.
- It was common to hear the trappers correct Sage on a river's name or a direction they should travel.
- Instead of listening, Sage would consult his handwritten directions and insist his sources were correct.
- When the party was seeking a proper course for Jackson's Hole, Osborne was sent ahead to find its location based upon Sage's directions.
- Instead of being gone for two days, he searched for a week without any success.
- When he returned, Osborne discovered that six trappers and a camp keeper had deserted to form their own camping company.

Life at Work

- When Osborne Gibson completed his 18-month service with the company, he decided to try his hand at independent trapping.
- At the start of the spring, he could make good money trapping and selling beaver skins at three or four dollars per pound.
- Working with experienced trappers, Osborne carried six used Newhouse traps, each weighing five pounds, into locations along the Yellowstone River.
- When the men discovered river streams active with beaver, they established a camp and spent seven to 10 days working the location.

When a stream was found active with beaver, trappers camped and worked 7-10 days in one spot.

- Osborne placed each trap in roughly 10 inches of water, allowing the river silt to cover the metal jaws; the chain was secured to a willow stake.
- On the willow leaves, trappers placed castoreum mixtures to attract the beavers; once snared, the animal would become drowned in the trap.
- As a former camp keeper, Osborne was familiar with processing the beaver into pelts: after skinning and cleaning the animal, the pelts were dried on willow branches in the sun.
- Inspecting and cleaning the traps throughout the day consumed his time.
- If one location was not too productive, Osborne had to locate another spot upstream where beaver were more active.
- While trapping, it was not uncommon to encounter other trapping companies.
- On one occasion Osborne met an American employed with the American Fur Company and who traded actively with the Crow Indians.
- Eager for news, he approached the American to inquire what was happening back East.
- Osborne learned that since the cholera epidemic that had struck St. Louis a couple of years earlier, the city was becoming more religious, with Protestant churches growing everywhere within the area.
- Religion was not something Osborne thought about, but he loved the natural beauty he saw all around him.
- By the middle branch of Henry's Fork, the beautiful cascading waterfalls of "Falling Fork" made him pause, as it did thousands of buffalo feeding upon valley grass along the Snake River.
- Osborne's journal recorded, "Buffaloe carelessly feeding in the green vales contribut to the wild and romantic Splendor of the Surrounding Scenery."

Osborne noted the "splendor" of buffalo feeding in the wild.

Osborne enjoyed trapping in the wilderness.

- Within that beauty were also numerous tribes of Indians, not all of whom were friendly to trappers.
- At one encounter, Osborne and his fellow trappers accidentally walked into a small tribe of Snake Indians in a small valley secluded among cottonwood trees.
- Osborne quickly communicated with the chief through his limited knowledge of the Snake language and some hand gestures, and an agreement was reached for the tribe to swap available skins for needed materials.
- In exchange for a couple of axes, kettles and a few small sacks of tobacco and ammunition, the tribe provided a large quantity of fine deer and elk skins.
- Because leather could not keep one warm in wet weather, the chief also wanted some woolen blankets.
- In exchange for a number of blankets, Osborne bartered for three neatly dressed panther skins.
- Not all encounters ended as well, especially with the Blackfeet Indians.
- At times they would ambush a lone trapper walking the rivers, scalp him and take his horses and traps.
- During one episode with a Blackfeet tribe, Osborne and his companions engaged in a gunfight with the Indians that lasted over three hours.
- During that attack three horses were killed by rifle balls shot by the Blackfeet; one of the trappers was hit in the knee by a rifle ball which remained lodged under the kneecap.

Indians often ambushed animal trappers.

- The injury poisoned him with fever and he died three days later.
- Once while traveling through the forest, Osborne's company encountered a small village with 15 lodges; initially they thought of attacking the camp to smite all the Blackfeet present.
- Within two miles of the village, the trappers were surprised to be greeted by unarmed Blackfeet humbly polite and willing to trade.
- Cautiously, they agreed and entered the tribe's camp.
- Once inside they saw the Indians weak and dreadfully sick.
- Writing in his journal that evening, Osborne commented, "We were ashamed to think of fighting a few poor Indians nearly dwindled to skeletons by the small Pox and approaching us without arms."
- Such thoughts of mercy were rare with the mountain men, who commonly agreed that a rifle was the best way to negotiate and settle disputes with hostile tribes—especially Indians who would steal their horses and furs during the middle of the night.
- Once when Osborne turned the horses loose to eat grass overnight, he lost two of his best animals.
- Upon investigation of the area, he found a grass trail made in the dew toward the horses' location from crawling Indians.
- If it had been a couple of days earlier, they might have taken the cache of furs he planned to unbury.
- Like the other trappers, he buried his extra supplies and beaver skin bundles in a pit lined with sticks and leaves.
- The cache was covered and well concealed from other trappers or Indians, only to be removed from the ground prior to the summer rendezvous with suppliers from St. Louis.
- Osborne arrived in St. Louis with a large party of 55 men and 20 mule-driven carts.
- Trappers responded with joy in receiving letters from family and friends; others focused upon conducting business and acquiring personal supplies.
- Because of the remote location and the demand for materials, Osborne was surprised at the inflationary increase in the materials he needed for the next year.
- Woolen blankets cost $20; common cotton shirts $5; sugar and coffee $2 per pint, tobacco $2 per pound and alcohol $4 per pint.
- The prices of these items were excessive, especially when Osborne received only $4 per pound for beaver skins.
- Market demand for beaver skins had started diminishing as they had slowly gone out of fashion and were being replaced by silk.

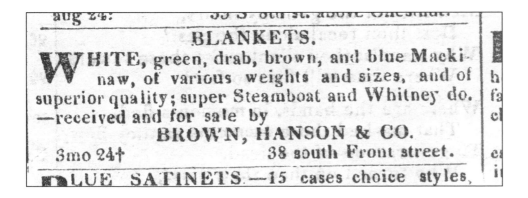

- One bundle of 60 beaver skins, which weighed approximately 80 pounds, yielded Osborne only $320 due to the mixed quality of skins.
- A few years earlier, prices were at $6 per pound for beaver skins.

Life in the Community: St. Louis, Missouri

- St. Louis, Missouri, was an active community rapidly growing from commerce due to its location along the Mississippi and Missouri rivers.
- Initially a small trading center operated by the French and Spanish, St. Louis became part of the United States under the Louisiana Purchase signed by President Thomas Jefferson in 1803.
- Since the Lewis and Clark expedition departed in 1805 to explore the Louisiana Territory, St. Louis had been viewed as a launching point into the western territory.
- Most of the activity in the west was initially led by mountain men and trapping companies exploring the western lands for beaver furs and sending them through St. Louis.
- The fashionable raw material was often used in the manufacture of coats and hats.
- The city's commercial activity increased with the arrival of *Zebulon M. Pike,* the first steamboat to port at the city's docks in 1817.
- Commercial activity rapidly grew with the industrial development of steam-powered engines which made it easier to deliver goods upstream against the Mississippi current.
- Between $200,000 and $300,000 worth of furs annually were being channeled through St. Louis to eastern American cities and Western Europe.
- The economic stimulus of the fur trade rapidly grew the city to support the trade and the city's development.
- Businesses started by individuals from various trades began to thrive within St. Louis.
- By the early 1820s, St. Louis had numerous industries, including a tannery, three soap and candle factories, two brickyards, a nail factory and two potteries.

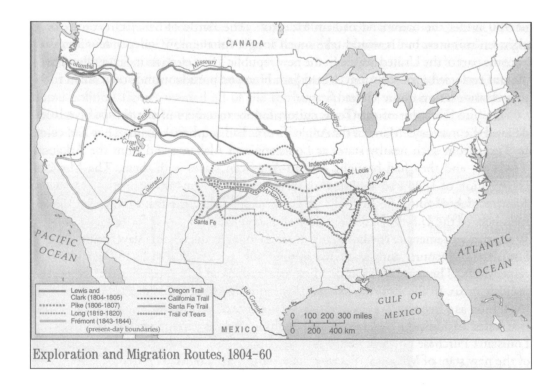

Exploration and Migration Routes, 1804–60

As steamboats became a regular sight in the port of St. Louis, the city worked hard to improve its wharf and levee.

- The basic needs of the rapidly growing west influenced the development of other businesses within the city.
- Manufacturers of wagons, guns, plows and stoves were commonly found.
- With the growth of economic activity and wealth, numerous churches and schools were developed in the city.
- By 1829, St. Louis College became the first college established west of the Mississippi; by 1835, the college created a medical department under the influence of the city's prominent physicians.
- As steamboats became more numerous along the riverfront, improvements of the city's wharfs and levee grew in importance.
- During the 1830s, it was common to see over 150 steamboats in and around the city delivering goods up the Mississippi River from destinations around the world.
- To contend with the its rapid growth, St. Louis established a chamber of commerce to meet the city's business and community needs such as a suitable theater, hotel, park, bank and library.
- Growth was not only an issue with local business, but with residents as well.
- As St. Louis' population settled and built outside the city limits, problems arose due to the lack of planning.
- Streets were constructed at inconsistent widths without concern of direction or size of street blocks.
- At times many of the new roads created dead ends, thus limiting the number of available roads into and out of town.
- The population of St. Louis was almost 15,000 by 1830, with over 11,000 counting themselves as white and approximately 2,800 slaves—a population that nearly doubled by 1836.

HISTORICAL SNAPSHOT
1836

- The Whig Party held its first national convention in Albany, New York
- The Alamo, defended by 182 Texans for 13 days, was besieged by 3,000 Mexicans lead by Santa Anna
- Samuel Colt patented the first revolving barrel multishot firearm
- Charles Darwin returned to England after five years aboard the HMS *Beagle*
- The Republic of Texas declared its independence from Mexico and elected Samuel Houston as its president
- Martin Van Buren was elected to the U.S. presidency
- Reconstruction began on Synagogue of Rabbi Judah Hasid in Jerusalem
- Arkansas entered the Union as the twenty-fifth state
- California gained virtual freedom from Mexico following a revolt led by Juan Bautista Alvarado
- Spain relinquished its territorial claims in Central America after years of fighting with the British
- Chile's dictator Diego Portales initiated a war with a Peruvian-Bolivian coalition over trade issues
- Abolitionist Angelina E. Grimké issued a pamphlet titled, "Appeal to Christian Women of the Southern States"
- Twenty-three of New York's 26 fire insurance companies declared bankruptcy as claims mounted for losses sustained in the 1835 Manhattan fire
- The Long Island Rail Road ran its first train between New York and Boston
- The S.S. *Beaver*, tested under steam at Vancouver, became the first steamboat to be seen on the Pacific Coast
- The hot-air balloon *Royal Vauxhall* lifted from London's Vauxhall Gardens and landed 18 hours later in the German duchy of Nassau.
- The first English-language newspaper, *Sandwich Island Gazette and Journal of Commerce*, was published in Hawaii
- The University of Wisconsin was founded at Madison
- Philadelphia's first penny daily, The *Philadelphia Public Ledger*, began publication
- The Prix du Jockey Club horse race had its first running outside Paris
- A phosphorus match was patented by Alonzo D. Phillips
- New York City's Park Hotel opened on the northwest corner of Broadway and Vesey Streets

Selected Prices

Blinds, Venetian, Pair $80.00
Chandelier $100.00
Churn, Stone $8.40
Cravat $3.75
Hair Tonic $20.00
Lantern, Glass $1.20
Razor, Strap and Box $40.00
Shotgun $80.00
Side Board, Mahogany $600.00
Theater, Opera Box $20.00

"Estimated Cost of Sending a Supply Train to the Central Rockies," *The Correspondence and Journals of Captain Nathaniel J. Wyeth,* **1833:**

Ins and Sundays	$160.00
Baling of the above and Sundrys bought at St. Louis	$100.00
50 pack saddles and 50 Riding saddles	$250.00
Hobbles and Halters for 100 animals	$150.00
Shoeing for 100 animals	$ 50.00
Corn and sundry for Horses	$ 50.00
Saddle Blankets	$100.00
50 men for 5 months at 15 per month	$3,750.00
Provisions to Buffaloe	$100.00
Pack Covers	$ 50.00
Ammunition	$100.00
100 animals	$3,000.00
Guns	$300.00
First cost of Goods	$3,000.00
Six months interest on all charges except wages	$222.00
	$11,382.00

Estimates of Beaver Production in the Rocky Mountains, 1832:

Number Packs (each containing 100 Pounds)	Company
90 Packs	from Santa Fe
30 Packs	American Fur Company party under Dripps and Fontennelle
140 Packs	Rocky Mountain Fur Company, brought home by Wm. Sublette
120 Packs	Traded by the American Fur Company at post on the Missouri
380 Packs	Total

Advertisement: *Missouri Gazette & Public Advertiser* Feb. 13, 1822:

TO: Enterprising Young Men,

The subscriber wishes to engage ONE HUNDRED MEN, to ascend the river Missouri to its source, there to be employed for one, two, or three years. For particulars enquire of Major Andrew Henry, near the Lead Mines, in the County of Washington, (who will ascend with, and command party) or to the subscriber at St. Louis.

Common Cooking Techniques, *The American Frugal Housewife*, Mrs. Child, 1833:

Calf's Head
Calf's head should be cleansed with very great care; particularly the lights. . . . It is better to leave the wind-pipe on, for if it hangs out of the pot while the head is cooking, all the froth will escape through it.

Roast Pig
Stew fine salt over it an hour before it is put down. It should not be cut entirely open; fill it up plump with thick slices of buttered bread, salt, sweet-marjoram and sage. Spit it with the head next to the point of the spit; take off the joints of the leg, and boil them with the liver, with a little whole pepper, allspice, and salt, for gravy sauce. The upper part of the legs must be braced down with skewers. Shake on flour. Put a little water in the dripping-pan, and stir it often. When the eyes drop out, the pig is half done. When it is nearly done, baste it with butter.

Election Cake
Old-fashioned election cake is made of four pounds of flour; three quarters of a pound of butter; four eggs; one pound of sugar; one pound of currants, or raisins if you choose; half a pint of good yeast; wet it with milk as soft as it can be and be molded on a board. Set to rise over night in winter; in warm weather, three hours is usually enough for it to rise. A loaf, the size of common flour bread, should bake three quarters of an hour.

Rocky Mountain Trapper.

"The Rocky Mountain Trapper," Louis Lacroix, *The New York Times*, December 12, 1856:

St. Paul, Saturday, Nov 1, 1856

Have lately met with a veteran Rocky Mountain hunter—a veritable specimen of the genius trapper—a man who has spent his whole life in threading the mazes of our western wildernesses; who for twenty-six years never visited a white settlement, and for eleven years was constantly trapping on the Rocky Mountains, in the employ of the American Fur Company; who stood upon the site of San Francisco long before the golden riches of California were discovered and passed five years about the great Salt Lake before it was desecrated by the Mormons; who has seen the names carved by LEWIS and CLARK upon the trees on the tributaries of the Columbia; and, in a word, who is also familiar with the mountains, rivers, and prairies of the vast extent of country as an old resident is with the streets, parks and public buildings of his native city.

The old forest-ranger, now verging on to 60 years, LOUIS LACROIX by name, resides with his Indian wife about 40 miles from St. Paul, which he thinks quite near enough to the abode of civilization; but he occasionally calls in to see us, and tells marvelous stories of his hair-breadth scrapes, daring exploits and encounters with the terrible Blackfeet; his warfare with hunger and the elements; his frequent campaigns with the renowned KIT CARSON and other famous hunters; and last, but not least, his excursions and explorations under the leadership of the Pathfinder of the Rocky Mountains. . . .

The hale old hunter says he is getting tired of civilized life; his honest soul recoils from contact with the scheming pale faces, and he is soon to retire again in to the country of the buffalo, to follow his old congenial calling; he is one of the few relics of that class of men soon to pass away forever, whose everyday realities were fraught with incidents both tragic and comic, more interesting than the wildest creations of fancy. But their mission has been fulfilled, the country around the Rocky Mountains is no longer *terra Incognita*, and they have been the guides to him who held the torch of science that illuminated its hidden mysteries. Nor will they wholly die, for the pen of IRVING has embalmed them in the memories of us all, and their own names, imperishable attached to their various mountain passes and peaks and the rivers where they trapped, will yet hand them down to future generations.

"Historical View of Trappers," Frederick Dellenbaugh, *Breaking the Wilderness*, 1905:

SIt so happened that this particular quality of fur was in great commercial demand in Europe for the making of hats. For some time it had constituted an article of profitable export from the eastern part of the continent, as the similar animal in Europe had been exterminated. Finally, the supply from America also diminished as the trappers pursued their merciless task. Then followed the discovery that the great wild region west of the Mississippi contained beaver in the immense numbers, and beaver trapping became the principal quest of many bold natures eager to stake their lives with Fortune, just as others later played a different game with the golden gravels of California. . . .

Stimulated by the prospect of riches and the excitement of new scenes, the trappers sought the innermost recesses of the mountain wilderness, slaying what opposed their way, taking beaver by the thousands and ten of thousands, and sending pack upon pack by way of St. Louis to the waiting markets of the Old World. The early returns may be estimated from the success of one enterprising man who, having employed a band of enterprising trappers, came out of the far regions on one occasion with nearly 200 packs, each worth in St. Louis about $100,000. Thus it was that the beaver became responsible for the first opening of the great Western Unknown.

1838 PROFILE

Colonel Edmund Gordon Lang, as he was known, had become rich selling slaves at weekly auctions in New Orleans, the main slave trading market in the United States.

Life at Home

- Colonel Edmund Gordon Lang was successful, rich and universally despised.
- As an experienced New Orleans slave trader, Colonel Lang—as everyone called him—had grown wealthy auctioning stout field hands and quality breeding stock in the coastal city, the epicenter of the slave trade market in America.
- Men from throughout the South courted Colonel Lang's attention when it was time to buy or sell slaves, but never considered him a potential dinner guest, someone a gentleman would invite to actually sit next to his wife.
- His auctions, held every Saturday, drew large crowds of onlookers; Lang specialized in high-quality Negroes and creative financing.
- This could involve the swapping of land, horses and other slaves to make a deal work; Lang was a creative man.
- Every auction was an event—spirited affairs in which the buyers were entertained with food and drink and the merchandise was well oiled, combed and groomed to impress the crowd and solicit the best bids.
- The elaborate home Lang owned in New Orleans was acquired after a plantation owner, who desired too many slaves, held too little cash in a year that cotton prices dropped dramatically.
- Colonel Lang loved that house and relished telling the story of how indignant the plantation owner became when he was forced to move out of his city house to pay his bills to a slave trader, a Southern shyster.

Colonel Lang became rich selling slaves at auction.

New Orleans, Louisiana was a center for the slave trade.

- Lang grew up without distinction or military experience.
- His mother worked the docks of northern Florida as a cook and part-time prostitute.
- Lang left home after his mother died of cholera when he was 12, intrigued by the chance to become a bounty hunter (a profession that paid good money to chase down runaway slaves throughout the swamps of Florida).
- The year he turned 16, he was asked to accompany a string of captured slaves to New Orleans; he never returned to Florida or spoke of it again.
- Everything about New Orleans was fascinating: the buildings, the languages, the chance to make real money selling slaves and the number of willing women available to a man of importance.
- After living in New Orleans a year he dropped his original name and picked up Lang from a sign he saw on the street.
- Privately, he joked to himself that he was truly a self-made man.
- The next few years were consumed with learning the business: how to grade, trade, auction, groom, fatten up and sell black people to white people.
- He also spent considerable time learning math; he had seen his illiterate mother cheated dozens of times and he had no interest in following that family tradition.
- He also learned how to entertain an audience while auctioning slaves; everyone had a good time at a Lang auction, except the slaves.
- Within a decade he had bought a building, established a network of runners and built a solid reputation as a clever man.
- The walls of the city were filled with posters advertising many of his competitors: Wilson, Kendig, White, Botts and Beard.
- But it was the interstate traders who were the best known: Franklin and Armfield of Virginia, the Woolfolk and Slatter families of Maryland and the Hagans of South Carolina.
- Each of the large firms transported and sold hundreds of people annually; their accounts in New Orleans were calculated in the hundreds of thousands of dollars.

- Often they would purchase or repurchase slaves no longer needed in the upper South for resale in Mississippi and Alabama, where the soil had not been depleted by the many years of cotton crops.
- The lifeblood of Lang's business was the small trader who handled a dozen or two dozen slaves each year.
- Most spent their fall purchasing slaves in the upper South for resale and quick profit in the New Orleans markets.
- To avoid trouble at the slave market itself, Lang preferred that his suppliers split families at the time of purchase.
- The last thing he needed on sales day was a hysterical female slave screaming when her son or husband was sold away at a good price.
- He had seen it all before, and it was bad for business.

Life at Work

- Every year Colonel Edmund Lang opened his books on the day before Christmas and then bought and sold men, women and children until mid-June.
- Most slaves from the upper South were sold in the months following the cotton harvest, when the slaves were no longer needed, and the cotton planters had more cash.
- The selling season for slaves was approximately six months long.
- Soon thereafter Colonel Lang fled the sweltering heat of New Orleans and the lingering threat of malaria.
- Most of the summer was spent visiting the homes of New Englanders who believed him to be a wealthy plantation owner; Colonel Lang was an energetic, entertaining guest to have around.
- For 16 years he had been calculating in his head the potential value of the men or women standing before him and whether food, clothing or grooming would improve their price.
- Taking a break from the pressures of slave trading was essential, particularly now that smuggling new slaves into the United States had become more difficult and he was forced to compete for the finest homegrown merchandise to sell.
- Slaves were a necessity for many plantation owners if crops were to be planted, hoed, cut and packed; the price of slaves paid year in and year out directly paralleled the price of cotton.
- When cotton prices jumped, so did the cost of field hands.
- This had led some planters to focus on buying better breeding stock—male and female—so they could glean profits from both a slave's labor in the field and nighttime pleasure too.
- Since the children could be sold at 12 or 13 years old and still get a quality price.
- Since 1829 Louisiana law had forbidden the separation by sale of children under the age of 10 from their mothers, so now buyers preferred older children of 13 who showed potential.
- Colonel Lang believed in having good-looking merchandise, even if it cost him a little more.
- His regular business purchases included dresses, shoes, stockings and head coverings for the women; suits with undershirts, socks, boots and hats for the men.

Slaves were essential to maintaining the South's cotton economy.

Lang's slaves were often noted for their style and neatness.

- Northern writers visiting the market often commented on the stylish neatness of the slaves he offered for sale.
- Throughout the South, the slave trading pens of New Orleans were much feared.
- Slaves in Kentucky and Virginia pledged to behave better in exchange for not being sold through the New Orleans slave market.
- To reduce the chances of unrest or rebellion when transporting slaves to market, slave traders made sure that the groups of people they were preparing to sell were unknown to one another.
- On the way to the market, even though the slaves were chained together, manacled into a single string of humanity, they were not permitted to speak.
- Traders routinely packed the slaves and price categories according to gender, age, height, weight, and skin color, the same way farmers prepared apples for market.
- Categories might include "extra women, number one women, second rate and ordinary women."
- Descriptions included skin color notations such as Negro, Griffe, Mulatto, or Quadroon.
- A good trader began to package his slaves for market weeks before they reached the slave pens of New Orleans.
- The heavy chains and galling cuff were removed so the skin would heal; beards were shaved, hair cut and grey hairs were plucked out and "blacking" dye applied.
- Old slaves, like old horses, brought poor prices.
- The women were thoroughly washed; tallow was added to their hair and they were provided fresh clothing.

Lang promised his slaves cash if they acted lively.

- Once they reached the slave pens prior to sale, the slaves were fed bacon, milk and butter to fatten them up; dancing was encouraged to improve muscle tone and make their skin shine.
- A local doctor visited the slave pens regularly to cull the sick and treat minor wounds; by custom, a buyer had a year to return sick slaves and Colonel Lang was willing to pull teeth or purchase medicine to make sure that his slaves stayed sold.
- His close friends still laughed about the time a clever Negro pretended to be deaf to void a sale—not once, but twice.
- As a final step before auction, Lang had his merchandise greased with sweet oil.
- Slaves entered the trade area alone and anonymous, separated from their families and communities; strangers in a strange place.
- Men were placed on one side of the room, women on the other; each line was arranged by height, tallest to shortest.
- The physical inspections of their nearly nude bodies had occurred earlier in the day as buyers searched for defects: whip marks, broken bones or signs of aging.
- Once the auction began, auctioneers like Lang humanized his merchandise by telling stories about where they were from and what skills they possessed.
- Sometimes the stories were even true.
- To solicit the best price, Lang promised each slave cash or clothing if they smiled and acted lively during the auction; many were told to lower their age, if asked, or hide the fact that they had been runaways in the past.
- For many slaves, their final auction price was a badge of distinction to be worn the rest of their days; aging field hands were known to brag, "I cost the master $1,200."

Life in the Community: New Orleans, Louisiana

- The American annexation of New Orleans following the Louisiana Purchase of 1803 brought population growth and economic development to the port city.
- The Louisiana Purchase removed most of the political barriers to development.

A lively social scene was evident in New Orleans.

- The 1810 Census revealed a population of 10,000, making New Orleans the largest city west of the Appalachians and America's fifth largest city; by 1830, New Orleans was America's third largest city, behind New York and Baltimore.
- From 1810 until 1838, New Orleans grew at a faster rate than any other large American city and represented 18 percent of all United States exports.
- Located at the mouth of the country's only major transportation network, the Ohio-Missouri-Mississippi river system, New Orleans boomed as the Northeastern and British demand for western foodstuffs and southern cotton exploded.
- At the same time, New Orleans benefited from the technological advances the cotton gin, spinning jenny, and steamboat that made the plantations of the lower Mississippi Valley highly efficient and profitable sources of cheap cotton for clothing the world.
- The increased output of cotton was borne by a new, more efficient means of water transportation—the steamboat—starting in 1812.
- In 1821, 287 steamboats arrived in New Orleans; by 1826, there were 700 steamboat arrivals.
- After 1830, steamboats were in general use on the Mississippi, allowing two-way packet lines to operate, carrying both cargo and passengers on regular schedules.
- Ninety percent of the city's trade consisted of downriver shipments of Midwestern foodstuffs; by the late 1830s, cotton became king.
- The growing world demand for cotton led to the development of vast, efficient slave plantations in the lower Mississippi Valley that produced more cotton at lower prices.
- Sugar and tobacco were distant runners-up to cotton, and foodstuffs made up the bulk of the rest of the exports.

British demand for southern cotton exploded . . .

. . . leading to vast slave plantations in the lower Mississippi Valley.

- Most of the cotton was shipped from New Orleans to Liverpool and other British ports, either directly, or via New York.
- Spurring this change in New Orleans, too, was the completion of the Erie and other canals in the 1820s and 1830s which drained away much of the upper Midwest grain trade to New York.
- Cotton was picked and baled from September through December.
- Shipments into the city ran from a low in October to a high in January, tapering off in the spring, with most of the year's crop exported by May.
- In summer, the port was virtually deserted as a result of the heat, humidity and falling water levels.
- Many merchants and their families left the city to avoid the heat, yellow fever, cholera and hurricanes.
- However, between January and March, plantation owners and their families would visit the city to partake of the social whirl of Mardi Gras, shopping and meeting with their cotton manufacturers, who acted as agents, bankers and financial advisors.
- As a major point of entry for the country, New Orleans also had a transient population of seamen, immigrants and tourists, drawn by the city's restaurants, theatres, operas, bars, gambling houses and red light establishments.
- The streets near the docks in, above, and below the French Quarter were lined by bars, flophouses and clip joints.

Historical Snapshot
1838

- The first telegraph message was sent using dots and dashes
- J. M. W. Turner painted *The Fighting Temeraire*
- The steamship the *Great Western*, built by British engineer Isambard Kingdom Brunel, sailed from Bristol to New York in a record 15 days
- New York passed the Free Banking Act, which popularized the idea of state-chartered banks
- The First Afghan War began; the British garrison at Kabul was wiped out
- Procter & Gamble Company was formed
- Charles M. Hovey introduced a strawberry grown from seed produced by hybridization, the first fruit variety that originated through breeding on the North American continent
- John Wright Boott received the first recorded shipment of tropical orchids to the United States
- Matthias Schleiden discovered that all living plant tissue was composed of cells
- The U.S. Mint in New Orleans began operation, producing dimes
- Thomas Henderson, Friedrich Struve and Friedrich Bessel made the first measurements of the distance to stars using the parallax method
- Samuel F. B. Morse made first public demonstration of the telegraph
- Mammoth Cave in Kentucky was purchased by Franklin Gorin as a tourist attraction
- Mexico declared war on France
- Frederick Douglass, American abolitionist, escaped slavery disguised as a sailor
- Tennessee became the first state to prohibit alcohol
- The Territory of Iowa was organized
- The first Braille Bible was published by the American Bible Society

Frederick Douglass.

New World Slavery Timeline

1501
Spanish settlers brought slaves from Africa to Santo Domingo on Hispaniola.

1522
The slaves rebelled on the Caribbean island of Hispaniola, which now comprises Haiti and the Dominican Republic.

1562
John Hawkins, the first Briton to take part in the slave trade, made a huge profit hauling human cargo from Africa to Hispaniola.

1581
Spanish residents in St. Augustine, the first permanent settlement in Florida, imported African slaves.

1619
Africans brought to Jamestown, Virginia, were the first slaves imported into Britain's North American colonies.

1662
Virginia law decreed that children of black mothers "shall be bond or free according to the condition of the mother."

1705
Virginia lawmakers allowed owners to bequeath their slaves and permitted masters to "kill and destroy" runaways.

1712
Slaves in New York City killed whites during an uprising, later squelched by the militia.

continued

Africans being prepared for slavery in America.

New World Slavery Timeline . . . *(continued)*

1739
Seventy-five slaves in South Carolina revolted, stole weapons and fled toward freedom in Florida.

1775
Anthony Benezet of Philadelphia founded the world's first abolitionist society.

1784
Congress narrowly defeated Thomas Jefferson's proposal to ban slavery in new territories after 1800.

1790
Nearly 700,000 slaves lived in a nation of 3.9 million people.

1793
The Fugitive Slave Act outlawed any efforts to impede the capture of runaway slaves.

1794
Eli Whitney patented his cotton gin for pulling seeds from cotton, turning cotton into the cash crop of the American South and creating a huge demand for slave labor.

1808
The United States banned the importation African slaves, but smuggling continued.

18020
Missouri was admitted to the Union as a slave state, and Maine as a free state.

1822
Freed slave Denmark Vesey led a rebellion in Charleston, South Carolina.

1831
Virginia slave preacher Nat Turner led a two-day uprising against whites, killing about 60.

1835
Southern states expelled abolitionists and forbade the mailing of antislavery propaganda.

Selected Prices

Bellows $3.40
Cloak, Woman's $125.00
Dressing Table $200.00
Hayfork $7.13
Slave, Boy $7,750.00
Slave, Girl $2,500.00
Slave, Man $10,000.00
Slave, Woman $8,500.00
Veal, per Pound $3.80
Whiskey, Pint $80.00

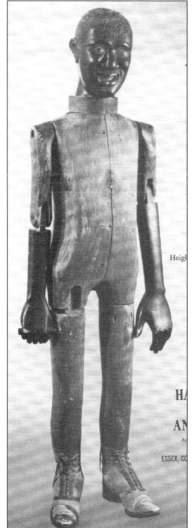

Letter from slave trader Tyra Glen to his business partner concerning slave sales, 1837:

I saw some fellows sold in Salisbury for 350 dollars, all others in proportion. Likely tall field fellows young and lively is bringing Heare from $1020 to $1050, likely tall field girls no one has been selling Heare from $800 & I think from what traders tell me women & Children, Boys and Girls & middle-aged men sell fully in proportion.

Memories of slave Moses Grandy at the sale of his wife:

I asked leave to shake hands with her which he refused, but said I might stand at a distance and talk with her. My heart was so full that I could say very little. . . . I gave her the little money I had in my pocket, and bade her farewell. I have never seen or heard of her from that day to this. I loved her as I loved my life.

"The Apple and the Chestnut, The Slave's Friend," American Anti-slavery Society, 1836:

A white man, whose name was Lorenzo, once teased a poor colored man, whose name was Mungo.

Lorenzo. Here, Mungo, said he, look at this apple, and then look at that chestnut.

Mungo. I do Massa; I see them.

Lorenzo. Well, this apple is the white man, and that chestnut is the negro.

Mungo. O, Massa, what you say is true. The chestnut has a dark skin, just like poor black man. But its *kernel* is all white, and sweet. The apple, though it looks so pretty, has many little black grains at the heart.

Now little boys and girls can't be abolitionists until they get rid of all those black grains in their hearts.

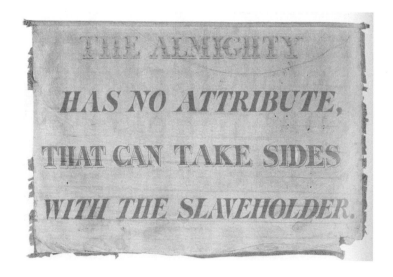
THE ALMIGHTY HAS NO ATTRIBUTE, THAT CAN TAKE SIDES WITH THE SLAVEHOLDER.

"Artificial Fire Works," *Parley's Magazine*, September, 1836:

New York, July 18, 1836.

Mr. Editor,

I was lately reading a book entitled "The Week Day Book," in which I observed a description of a boy making artificial fire-works. It referred to the Boy's Own Book. I have looked the Boy's Own Book all over, and I cannot find any thing about it. I think it must be in the English edition.

If you would be so kind as to insert the above, and give a description how to make the "artificial fire works," you would oblige me and many of your readers very much.

Yours, &c.

P. S.

Reply. We have looked over several books, in order to find out the method of making fire works, in the hope of gratifying P. S. and other readers; but have found nothing to the purpose, except the following, from the Encyclopedia Americana. Even this is in a style which we fear some of our readers will not be able fully to comprehend; but we have not thought it best to alter it.

"The ingredients (of artificial fire works) are, 1st, Saltpetre, purified for the purpose. 2d, Sulphur. 3d, Charcoal. gunpowder is likewise used in the composition of fire works; being first ground, or as it is technically called *mealed*. Camphor and gum-benzoin are employed as ingredients in odoriferous fire works.

"The proportions of the materials differ very much in different fire works, and the utmost care and precaution are necessary in working them to a state fit for use, and then in the mixing.

"When stars are wanted, camphor, alcohol, antimony and other ingredients are required, according as the stars are to be blue, white, &c. In some cases gold and silver rain is required; then brass dust, steel dust, saw dust, &c. enter into the composition. Hence the varieties may be almost indefinite.

"With respect to color, sulphur gives a blue, camphor a white or pale color, saltpetre a clear white yellow, salammoniac a green, antimony a reddish, rosin a copper color."

A laboratory, at the Castle Garden, in New York, was blown up a few weeks ago; and in it about $2,000 worth of artificial fire works. We suppose they are made in the laboratory, in large quantities, to sell.

On the whole we are hardly sorry that we can find nothing more definite on this subject, for we believe there are a thousand better ways of amusing ourselves, and others, than by means of artificial fire works.

Journal, Reverend Robert Walsh's account as he boards a slave ship, 1828:

When we mounted her decks we found her full of slaves. She was called the *Feloz*, commanded by Captain José Barbosa, bound to Bahia. She was a very broad-decked ship, with a mainmast, schooner rigged, and behind her foremast was that large, formidable gun, which turned on a broad circle of iron, on deck, and which enabled her to act as a pirate if her slaving speculation failed. She had taken in, on the coast of Africa, 336 males and 226 females, making in all 562, and had been out seventeen days, during which she had thrown overboard 55. The slaves were all inclosed under grated hatchways between decks. The space was so low that they sat between each other's legs and [were] stowed so close together that there was no possibility of their lying down or at all changing their position by night or day. As they belonged to and were shipped on account of different individuals, they were all branded like sheep with the owner's marks of different forms. These were impressed under their breasts or on their arms, and, as the mate informed me with perfect indifference "burnt with the red-hot iron." Over the hatchway stood a ferocious-looking fellow with a scourge of many twisted thongs in his hand, who was the slave driver of the ship, and whenever he heard the slightest noise below, he shook it over them and seemed eager to exercise it. I was quite pleased to take this hateful badge out of his hand, and I have kept it ever since as a horrid memorial of reality, should I ever be disposed to forget the scene I witnessed.

As soon as the poor creatures saw us looking down at them, their dark and melancholy visages brightened up. They perceived something of sympathy and kindness in our looks which they had not been accustomed to, and, feeling instinctively that we were friends, they immediately began to shout and clap their hands. One or two had picked up a few Portuguese words, and cried out, "*Viva! Viva!*" The women were particularly excited. They all held up their arms, and when we bent down and shook hands with them, they could not contain their delight; they endeavored to scramble up on their knees, stretching up to kiss our hands, and we understood that they knew we were come to liberate them. Some, however, hung down their heads in apparently hopeless dejection; some were greatly emaciated, and some, particularly children, seemed dying. . . .

The heat of these horrid places was so great and the odor so offensive that it was quite impossible to enter them, even had there been room. They were measured as above when the slaves had left them. The officers insisted that the poor suffering creatures should be admitted on deck to get air and water. This was opposed by the mate of the slaver, who, from a feeling that they deserved it, declared they would murder them all. The officers, however, persisted, and the poor beings were all turned up together. It is impossible to conceive the effect of this eruption—517 fellow creatures of all ages and sexes, some children, some adults, some old men and women, all in a state of total nudity, scrambling out together to taste the luxury of a little fresh air and water. They came swarming up like bees from the aperture of a hive till the whole deck was crowded to suffocation front stem to stern, so that it was impossible to imagine where they could all have come from or how they could have been stowed away. On looking into the places where they had been crammed, there were found some children next the sides of the ship, in the places most remote from light and air; they were lying nearly in a torpid state after the rest had turned out. The little creatures seemed indifferent as to life or death, and when they were carried on deck, many of them could not stand.

After enjoying for a short time the unusual luxury of air, some water was brought; it was then that the extent of their sufferings was exposed in a fearful manner. They all rushed like maniacs towards it. No entreaties or threats or blows could restrain them; they shrieked and struggled and fought with one another for a drop of this precious liquid, as if they grew rabid at the sight of it.

"Whitewashing," Memoirs of Benjamin Franklin, written by himself, Continued by his Grandson and Others, Philadelphia, Pennsylvania, 1837:

When a young couple are about to enter into the matrimonial state, a never failing article in the marriage treaty is, the lady shall have been enjoying the free and unmolested exercise of the rights of whitewashing, with all its ceremonies, privileges, and appurtenances. . . .

When the lady is unusually fretful, finds fault with the servants, is discontented with the children, complains much of the filthiness of every thing about her—these are signs that ought not be neglected; yet they're not decisive as they sometimes come and go off again, without producing any further effect. But if, when the husband rises in the morning, he should observe in the yard a wheelbarrow with a quantity of lime in it, or should see certain buckets with lime dissolved in water, there is then no time to be lost; he immediately locks up the apartment or closet where his papers or private property is kept, putting the key in his pocket, betakes himself to flight: for a husband, however beloved, becomes a perfect nuisance during the season of female rage; his authority is superseded, his commission is suspended, and the very scullion who cleans the brasses in the kitchen becomes of more consideration and importance than him. He has nothing for it, but to abdicate, and run from an evil which he can neither prevent nor mollify.

The husband gone, a ceremony begins. The walls are in a few minutes stripped of their furniture, paintings, prints and looking glasses lie in a huddled heap about the floor; the curtains are torn from the testers, the beds crammed into the windows; chairs and tables, bedsteads and cradles, crowd the yard; and the garden fence bends under the weight of carpets, blankets, cloth cloaks, old coats, and ragged breeches. . . .

This ceremony completed, and the house thoroughly evacuated, next operation is cleaning walls and ceilings, every room and closet with brushes dipped in a solution of lime, called white-washing; to pour buckets of water over every floor, and scratch all the partitions and wainscots with rough brushes wet with soap-suds, and dipped in stone-cutters sand. The windows by no means escape the general deluge. A servant scrambles out upon the pent-house, at the risk of her neck, and with a mug in her hand, and a bucket within reach, she dashes away innumerable gallons of water against the glass pane; to the great annoyance of the passengers in the street. . . .

Go ahead! is the order of the day. The whole continent presents a scene of scrabbing and roars with greedy hurry.

—Sculptor Horatio Greenough, 1836

Notice of Two Rocking-Chairs, James Freewin, *Gardener's Magazine*, London, England, December 1838:

In America it is considered a compliment to give the stranger a rocking chair as a seat; and when there is more than one kind in the house, the stranger is always presented with the best.

1837 NEWS FEATURE

"Balloon Ascension," *National Gazette and Literary Register,* **Philadelphia, Pennsylvania, September 1, 1837:**

Vauxhall Gardens was crowded during the whole of Monday afternoon by an immense assemblage of persons, drawn together to witness the hazardous and, we regret to add, fatal experiment of Mr. Cocking to descend from an altitude of upwards of a mile in a parachute of his own invention. No attempt to a similar description has been made since the experiment of Monsieur Garnerin, upwards of 30 years ago; and the greatest curiosity was naturally excited as to the result. Thousands of persons filled all the streets and avenues in the neighborhood of Vauxhall, and a joyous crowd swarmed on every eminence and open spot that commanded a fair view of the horizon. The time fixed for the ascent to the aeronaut was five o'clock, but on entering the gardens at that hour the process of inflation of Mr. Green's Nassau balloon was not yet completed. This afforded an opportunity of inspecting the parachute in which Mr. Cocking contemplated this awful descent.

Mr. Cocking explained that his parachute was constructed on a totally different plan from that of M. Garnerin. The latter he described as a form of umbrella, closed at the moment of dissent, but expanded by the atmosphere as it approached the earth, and forming a sort of canopy over the aeronaut. His parachute, on the contrary, was in the form of an umbrella reversed, the cavity containing the air being turned uppermost, with the view, he said, of preventing the oscillation which proved so disastrous for M. Garnerin.

The parachute was surrounded by a hoop, to which a basket or car was attached by several cords. Mr. Cocking expressed the utmost confidence in the result of his experiment, but it appeared that it was a confidence which he did not feel. His restless looks and nervousness of manner seemed to belie the bravery of his speech, and more than once it appeared that his mind was ill at ease, and that he would willingly have postponed the attempt until a less hazardous trial had assured him of its safety.

At six o'clock, Messrs. Green and Spencer entered their balloon, which was allowed to ascend to an altitude of about forty feet, that the parachute might be brought directly under it, and securely fixed. It was seven o'clock before all the preparations were completed, at which time the whole apparatus was distinctly visible to everyone in the gardens. The band of the Surry Yeomanry suddenly struck up the National Anthem, which being considered to be the signal for the cords to be loosened, a loud buzz proceeded from the gardens, and was re-echoed by the impatient mob outside. At this moment a tube or pipe linen was lowered by the Messrs. Green and Spencer from the car of their balloon through the orifice in the parachute, past the basket in which Mr. Cocking was to sit. This was for the conveyance of the ballast necessary to discharge on the ascent of the balloon, and which, if it had been thrown out in the usual manner, would have been lodged in the parachute. All the preparations having been completed, Mr. Cocking stepped into the car amid the acclamations of the company, and the cords were loosened, the balloon and its attendant parachute mounting into the heavens amid the renewed cheering of the crowd.

We regret to have to state that the experiment of the descent of the parachute was terminally fatal for Mr. Cocking, the gentlemen who projected it, and who ascended in it with the balloon. . . .The parachute was in the shape of an inverted cone, not very unlike an umbrella turned upside down. It was in circumference 107 feet 4 inches. From the bottom of the machine, which was constructed of fine Irish linen, a basket of wicker was suspended, in which Mr. Cocking placed himself. The distance between this basket and the car in which were Mr. Green and Mr. Spencer, was between 40 and 50 feet. The ascent of the balloon took place about twenty minutes before eight o'clock on Monday. When Mr. Cocking entered the basket of the parachute he was perfectly collected, and exhibited no appearance of want of nerve or indecision.

Mr. F. Gye, who was particularly anxious in his attention to the arrangements of the experiment, and who is entitled to every praise for the manner in which he exerted himself to prevent the possibility of an accident, continually in the course of the day, and up to the very moment of the ascent of the balloon, advised Mr. Cocking, if he felt the least timidity, to relinquish his attempt, and undertook to allay any ill feelings that might arise among the public at the disappointment. Mr. Cocking, however, professed himself most anxious to carry his announcement into execution; and after thanking Mr. F. Gye for his kindness and solicitude, professed himself most eager to ascend. At twenty minutes to eight o'clock, everything being in readiness and the parachute attached to the car of the balloon, the ascent took place. Nothing could be more majestic. The weight and great extent of the parachute apparently rendered the motion of the balloon more steady than on any former ascent, and the almost total absence of wind assisted in keeping the balloon in a perfectly perpendicular position. There was not the slightest oscillation; the balloon and parachutes sailed through the air with a grandeur which exceeded anything of the kind ever before witnessed, and continued in sight about 10 minutes. A great deal of ballast was discharged almost immediately over the enclosure after which the huge machine rose rapidly, but not so suddenly as to break the even current of its course. It was expected by those in the gardens that Mr. Cocking would have descended so near Vauxhall as to afford them a view of his descent. This was not the case. He was lost in the clouds, and the company were some time left in conjecture, but certainly not in anticipation of the result of the experiment. A son of Mr. Gye was the first person who announced the fatal catastrophe. This gentleman followed on horseback and arrived in the field, near Lee, in Kent, just in time to learn the parachute had descended with such violence that Mr. Cocking had lost his life in his experiment. The intelligence was not suffered to transpire for some time in the hopes that the account might be incorrect, and that Mr. Cocking might have only been stunned, or have fainted it being remembered that something of this sort occurred on the descent of Mr. Garnerin many years ago. It was, however, very shortly ascertained that the intelligence was too true. He moved his hand once after his fall, but exhibited no other signs of life. Several country people, who were close by, procured a waddled hurdle, placed him upon it, and conveyed him without delay to the Tiger's Head

Inn in Lee. He was immediately attended by Dr. Chowne, who was on the spot; but all medical assistance was unavailable. The arteries of his arms were opened, but it was to no purpose, life had fled. . . .

We have since been favored by an eyewitness with the following particulars of the fatal result:

Mr. R. Underwood, of Regent Street, followed on horseback in the direction taken by the balloon, to witness if possible, the descent of the parachute, and from that **gentleman** we have learned the melancholy details which follow. Mr. Underwood was in the neighborhood of Blackheath when he saw Mr. Green sever the cord which attached the parachute to the car. The parachute, thus left to itself, descended with the utmost rapidity, and swayed from side to side in the most fearful manner. Mr. Underwood immediately anticipated the worst. In a few seconds, the dreadful oscillations still continuing, the **basket** which contained the unfortunate aeronaut broke away from the parachute and Mr. Cocking was precipitated to the earth from a height of several hundred feet. Mr. Underwood immediately spurred his horse, and arrived in the field near Lee, where several laborers had picked up the parachute. They would not believe a man had fallen with it, but on Mr. Underwood's explanation, and an offer of five guineas to whoever should find the body of Mr. Cocking, they commenced a diligent search. After traversing four fields they heard groans proceeding from the field called Burnt Ash, near Lee, and on going in that direction they found the unfortunate Mr. Cocking literally dashed to pieces, and just as they were loosening his cravat he breathed his last in their arms. He was speedily conveyed to the Tiger's Head Inn, where four medical gentlemen attended. Their services were, however, needless. The unfortunate man was quite dead, and his body now lies to await the coroner's inquest.

1840–1849

Hostilities between the Northern and Southern states continued during the decade of the 1840s, even as the nation confronted international issues along its borders. America not only favored westward expansion, it displayed a willingness to fight for that right. Acceptance of the Republic of Texas as a state divided the nation, drawing it into war with Mexico. By 1848 under the Treaty of Guadalupe Hidalgo, America acquired over half a million square miles of territory, including California.

The growth of the nation across the continent increased the disputes, not only between slavery and antislavery forces, but also on the issues of religion. Hundreds of thousands of immigrants from Europe were arriving in the United States, many with Catholic or non-Protestant backgrounds, who motivated a strong anti-immigration effort during this period. The religious hostilities towards the immigrants commonly occurred in New York, Philadelphia and other urban centers through the decade. Religious hostilities also fell upon a new religious group, the Mormons, who fled west to the Great Salt Lake region to escape persecution.

Culturally, the decade saw a proliferation of publications of magazines, such as *The Dial, The Living Age* and *Brownson's Quarterly Review.* The publications provided readers a diverse collection of fiction, poetry and commentary. *The Dial,* a short-lived publication that ended in 1844, espoused a transcendental view that influenced New England writers. A number of contributing writers supported the magazine, including Ralph Waldo Emerson and Henry David Thoreau.

Temperance societies, started in the 1830s, grew rapidly during this period to confront America's burgeoning poor health and declining moral values. The Washington Temperance Society, formed in 1840, claimed membership of 500,000 intemperate drinkers and 100,000 confirmed alcoholics by 1843. Many employers supported the Temperance Movement under the premise that non-drinking workers **would be more** productive. Many Protestant ministers also supported the effort as a moral crusade for total abstinence.

Though the national debate on slavery was to predominate human rights topics, other key causes saw their early seeds planted during this period. In the 1842 case *Commonwealth v. Hunt,* the Massachusetts Supreme Court recognized the legality of labor unions and their right to strike. Also within Massachusetts, child labor legislation passed limiting the workday to 10 hours for those under the age of 12 years. Women's issues were becoming part of the national discussion and included in women's publications and journals. The 1848 women's convention at Seneca Falls, New York addressed a woman's right to vote, own property and divorce.

As the multiple debates took their prospective political stages, so did other discoveries take center stage. The telegraph, created by Samuel Morse, saw its first message sent from Washington, DC, to Baltimore in 1845, leading the nation to improve communications. Modern sewing machines improved textile production, and the use of anesthesia helped with the medical treatments of patients during operations. By the end of the period, news of gold at Sutter's Mill, California, greatly influenced the westward migration. The thought of quick wealth motivated many men to travel west to seek their fortune. By the end of 1849, 80,000 people had made their way to California and $10 million worth of gold was mined.

1846 Profile

Gail Warlick, who possessed a restless spirit that drove her from one job to another without apparent reason, decided to go to work at the textile mills in Lowell, Massachusetts.

Life at Home

- The daughter of a dispirited, lame farmer and an alcoholic mother, Gail Warlick decided to run away from the farm at age 15; the destination was not important.
- Her first job was as a domestic with a farming family in Bridgewater, Vermont, just a few miles from her family home in Barnard.
- But difficulties ensued and by her sixteenth birthday, she was employed in the textile mills of Lowell, Massachusetts, alongside nearly 8,000 young women seeking opportunity in the new emerging textile business.
- Before going to Lowell, Gail wrote her father asking his consent; "I can earn more to begin with than I can anywhere about here. I am in need of clothes which I cannot get if I stay about here and for that reason I want to go to Lowell or some other place."
- A month later she wrote her father from a boarding house in Lowell to announce that she had found work in the spinning room, earning $1.80 per week.
- Her trip by stagecoach had cost $3.00 and lodging during the trip $0.25; before beginning work she bought herself a bonnet to celebrate her arrival.
- Her aunt Nancy supplied her with a new alpaca dress for the trip.
- In the newly created town of Lowell, factory owners and their friends had built hundreds of boarding houses near the mills where textile workers could live year-round.
- Twenty-five women lived in Gail's boarding house; as was customary there were six mill girls assigned to a room and two to a bed.

At 16 years old, Gail Warlick was working in the textile mills in Lowell, Massachusetts.

- Her small, partially ventilated bedroom offered little privacy, but was an improvement over the bed she shared at home with three other sisters.
- As the newest person to the room, Gail was charged with emptying the chamber pots each morning; she hated the smell.
- Within days of arriving, Gail was mentored by several of the more experienced girls in the house on how to dress, how to talk to overseers and the general rules of the community— and how to get around them.
- She deeply resented needing the help, but quickly realized its value.
- Her first monthly paycheck was for $6.60; she had to pay $4.68 for her room and board and used the extra to purchase a pair of rubbers as well as a pair of shoes that cost $0.50.
- In her letters home, Gail occasionally described her pay in shillings, the British system, even though she was paid in dollars.
- Invariably she announced her pay not as the gross amount paid but the net of room and board.
- As standard practice, the wages of all the mill girls were posted on a blackboard showing the production and earnings of each worker several days before the monthly payday, so disputes could be addressed.
- As the Christmas season loomed that first year, Gail was thankful for her health.
- That week a female mill worker had slipped on the ice and broken her neck; the same day a man was struck and killed by the one of the cars of the Boston and Lowell Railroad; a third worker had died when he fell down and a bale of cotton landed on top of him.
- Even though the company rules stated that mill girls should contain their hair in a net, vanity prevailed and several girls Gail knew personally had been injured or killed when long hair was caught in heavy machinery.
- One of her roommates suffered from near total deafness—the price paid for hearing the overwhelming noise of the power looms for the past three years.
- One of the girls told Gail that after working in the mill for several years, she heard crickets chirping in her ears all the time.
- But poor air quality was by far the greatest risk of all.
- Throughout the mill, the windows were nailed shut and steam was regularly sprayed into the air to maintain humidity.
- This kept cotton threads from drying out and snapping in the looms.
- Fewer breaks meant less work for the mill girls, but with no outside breeze the air grew stale and loaded with free-floating cotton lint.

The textile mill was built next to the river.

Social gatherings were encouraged.

- The mills were illuminated by whale oil lamps which hung from a post at each loom, leaving many dark spots, especially on cloudy winter days.
- Gail longed for letters from home and often wrote her relatives to simply ask for mail.
- She cared little for the concerts and lectures regularly sponsored by the mill—except when the boys from town were included.
- But restlessness haunted her search for happiness.
- By the time Gail turned seventeen, she had quit Lowell, held two textile jobs and returned to the spinning room in Lowell.
- Her letters to her father often mentioned her desire to return home.

Life at Work
- The days at the factory began early for Gail Warlick and normally lasted more than 12 hours.
- At 5 o'clock in the morning the bell rang for everyone in the boarding house to get up for breakfast and go to work.
- At half past 12, she took a 30-minute lunch break, and then worked until 7:30 pm.
- During her 12- to 14-hour workday, Gail tended four sides of the warp spinning frames, each with 128 spindles.
- Saturdays normally were short days—just eight hours.
- Gail was proud of the fact she could "doff as fast as any girl in our room" and wrote her father "I think that the factory is the best place for me and if any girl wants employment I advise them to come to Lowell."
- Doffers worked intensively for about 15 minutes every hour and the rest of the time was their own.
- Often Gail was allowed to read, knit, or go outside the millyard to play, but had to remain on duty 12 hours or more per day.

- Books were banned from being brought into the mill itself, so Gail taped newspaper clippings or torn out pages from books to a space near her work area to cope with the repetitive work, especially after she moved to the carding room, where the pay was better, the girls more experienced and few breaks were allowed.
- But Gail hated to be told what to do.
- Mill girls were required to sign an agreement to abide by certain regulations including a minimum one-year commitment.
- Overseers had to approve any absences, and anyone not reporting to her station without good reason would be fired.
- Mill girls could also be discharged for immoral behavior or imbibing alcohol.
- If leaving on her own accord, a two-week termination notice was necessary in order to receive an "honorable discharge."
- Another requirement was mandatory church attendance on Sundays, although this rule was not strictly enforced.
- Some of the girls felt that they could not afford to pay pew rent, or did not choose to spend their money on the fine clothes that they deemed necessary to participate at services.

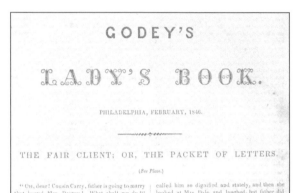

- Besides talking, Gail's favorite leisure activity was fashion.
- Her favorite fashion magazine was *Godey's Lady's Book,* even though the periodical criticized mill girls who donned expensive watches and dressed beyond their social class rank.
- In the fall of 1848, as Gail was making up her mind to leave for another position—possibly in Vermont—she was asked to help weave "negro cloth," a coarse composite cloth containing wool.
- This cloth was sent south for use in making slaves' clothing.
- But Gail knew the push for profits was back when all the girls were told the number of machines they had to work had doubled.
- And when several mill girls quit, immediately Irish immigrants, fresh off the boat and willing to do anything, took their places.
- They were soon followed by new hires from Greece, Poland, Russia, Portugal, and Colombia.
- Gail told everyone she was quitting so she could see her little brother Frank before he mustered out to fight in the war against Mexico.
- In her heart she just knew she was restless.

Life in the Community: Lowell, Massachusetts

- In 1814, businessman Frances Cabot Lowell built a textile mill next to the Charles River in Waltham, Massachusetts, the first integrated mill in the United States capable of transforming raw cotton into cotton cloth in one building.
- In 1821, Boston Manufacturing Company investors purchased land near Pawtucket Falls in East Chelmsford to expand the company's textile manufacturing operations.
- In less than 20 years, a sparse collection of family farms was transformed into the industrial city of Lowell, Massachusetts.
- By the mid-1830s, 10 textile corporations had opened 32 mills in the city of Lowell.
- Women throughout New England were recruited by agents telling tales of high wages available to "all classes of people."
- In 1840, the factories employed almost 8,000 workers, mostly women between the ages of 16 and 35, though some were as young as 10.
- Unlike the Rhode Island textile mills which preferred to employ entire families—including small girls—Lowell recruited rural teenaged girls ready to make their own money before settling down in marriage.

Lowell, Massachusetts.

- Worldwide, the industrial revolution was changing the face of commerce, and Lowell was central to this transformation in the United States.
- For decades, cotton mills were among the lowest forms of employment of women.
- In England the factory system had developed a well-earned reputation for brutal overseers who abused the mill girls and even "destroyed her purity."
- According to popular newspaper accounts, mill girls were slaves, to be beaten, pinched and pushed about at will.
- To overcome this prejudice, the mills at Lowell offered high wages to women that they might be "induced to become millgirls, in spite of the opprobrium that still clung to this degrading occupation," according to one writer of the time.
- Young girls were employed to take off, or doff, the full bobbins from the spinning frames and replace them with empty ones.
- Mill girls who had homes generally worked from eight to 10 months in the year; the rest of the time was spent with parents or friends; a few taught school during the summer months.

Lowell was a collection of family farms before being transformed into a mill town with 10 textile corporations and 32 mills.

- The most prevailing incentive to labor was to secure the means of education for some *male* member of the family.
- To make a *gentleman* of a brother or a son, to give him a college education, was the dominant thought in the minds of a great many of the better class of mill girls.
- Traditionally, women of the farm had always been pressed into a money saving role rather than a money earning member of the community.
- Besides, few respectable jobs were open to girls and women.
- As a servant, or "help," her wages were from $0.50 to $1.00 a week; or, if she went from house to house by the day to spin and weave, she could earn but $0.75 a week and her meals.
- The mills offered far more—including precious independence.
- A woman was not supposed to be capable of spending her own, or of using other people's money.
- In Massachusetts, before 1840, a woman could not legally be treasurer of her own sewing society, unless a man was responsible for her.
- As former mill worker Harriet Hanson Robinson explained, "The law took no cognizance of woman as a money spender. She was a ward, an appendage, a relict. Thus it happened that if a woman did not choose to marry, or, when left a widow, to remarry, she had no choice but to enter one of the few employments open to her, or to become a burden on the charity of some relative."

HISTORICAL SNAPSHOT
1846

- The Mexican-American War started with a battle between the Mexican and U.S. armies at Palo Alto in Texas

- The Oregon Treaty settled the boundary line between the U.S. and British possessions in Canada at the forty-ninth parallel

- By using the temperature of the Earth, Irish physicist William Thomson estimated that the planet was 100 million years old

- German chemist Christian Schonbein discovered that a mixture of sulfuric acid and saltpeter was explosive when it dried

- The double cylinder rotary press was introduced, capable of producing 8,000 sheets an hour

- Congress chartered the Smithsonian Institution

- Ether anesthesia was used for the first time by dentist William Thomas Green Morton in surgery at Massachusetts General Hospital in Boston

- The movement of the Mormons to settle in the west began

- Robert Thomson obtained an English patent on a rubber tire

- Iowa became the twenty-ninth state

- Elias Howe patented the sewing machine

- The saxophone was patented by Antoine Joseph Sax

- Michigan ended the death penalty within its borders

- The *Oregon Spectator* became the first newspaper to be published on the West Coast

Selected Prices

Buttons, Gross of Pearl Shirt Buttons $5.00
Corn, Barrel $32.20
Fabric, Hollins, Yard $7.40
Hog $129.26
Loom $123.50
Matting, Yard $2.30
Obstetric Instruments $46.00
Saddle, Leather $969.00
Suspenders $6.90
Thread, Linen, Pound $27.40

Factory Rules from the Handbook to Lowell, 1848:

All persons in the employ of the Hamilton Manufacturing Company, are to observe the regulations of the room where they are employed. They are not to be absent from their work without the consent of the over-seer, except in cases of sickness, and then they are to send him word of the cause of their absence. They are to board in one of the houses of the company and give information at the counting room, where they board, when they begin, or, whenever they change their boarding place; and are to observe the regulations of their boarding-house.

Those intending to leave the employment of the company, are to give at least two weeks' notice thereof to their overseer.

All persons entering into the employment of the company, are considered as engaged for twelve months, and those who leave sooner, or do not comply with all these regulations, will not be entitled to a regular discharge.

The company will not employ any one who is habitually absent from public worship on the Sabbath, or known to be guilty of immorality.

A physician will attend once in every month at the counting-room, to vaccinate all who may need it, free of expense.

Any one who shall take from the mills or the yard, any yarn, cloth or other article belonging to the company, will be considered guilty of stealing and be liable to prosecution.

Payment will be made monthly, including board and wages. The accounts will be made up to the last Saturday but one in every month, and paid in the course of the following week.

These regulations are considered part of the contract, with which all persons entering into the employment of the Hamilton Manufacturing Company, engage to comply.

TIME TABLE OF THE LOWELL MILLS,

To take effect on and after Oct. 21st, 1851.

The Standard time being that of the meridian of Lowell, as shown by the regulator clock of JOSEPH RAYNES, 43 Central Street.

	From 1st to 10th inclusive.				From 11th to 20th inclusive.				From 21st to last day of month.			
	1st Bell	2d Bell	3d Bell	Eve. Bell	1st Bell	2d Bell	3d Bell	Eve. Bell	1st Bell	2d Bell	3d Bell	Eve. Bell
January,	5.00	6.00	6.50	*7.30	5.00	6 00	6.50	*7.30	5.00	6.00	6.50	*7.30
February,	4.30	5.30	6.40	*7.30	4.30	5.30	6.25	*7.30	4.30	5.30	6.15	*7.30
March,	5.40	6.00		*7.30	5.20	5.40		*7.30	5.05	5.25		6.35
April,	4.45	5.05		6.45	4.30	4.50		6.55	4.30	4.50		7.00
May,	4 30	4.50		7·00	4.30	4.50		7.00	4.30	4.50		7 00
June,	"	"		"	"	"		"	"	"		"
July,	"	"		"	"	"		"	"	"		"
August,	"	"		"	"	"		"	"	"		"
September,	4.40	5.00		6.45	4.50	5.10		6.30	5.00	5.20		*7.30
October,	5.10	5.30		*7.30	5.20	5.40		*7.30	5.35	5.55		*7.30
November,	4.30	5.30	6.10	*7.30	4.30	5.30	6.20	*7.30	5.00	6.00	6.35	*7.30
December,	5.00	6.00	6.45	*7.30	5.00	6.00	6.50	*7.30	5.00	6·00	6.50	*7.30

* Excepting on Saturdays from Sept. 21st to March 20th inclusive, when it is rung at 20 minutes after sunset.

YARD GATES,

Will be opened at ringing of last morning bell, of meal bells, and of evening bells; and kept open Ten minutes.

MILL GATES.

Commence hoisting Mill Gates, Two minutes before commencing work.

WORK COMMENCES,

At Ten minutes after last morning bell, and at Ten minutes after bell which "rings in" from Meals.

BREAKFAST BELLS.

During March "Ring out"........at....7.30 a. m..........."Ring in" at 8:05 a. m.
April 1st to Sept. 20th inclusive.....at....7 00 " " .... " " at 7.35 " "
Sept. 21st to Oct. 31st inclusive.....at....7.30 " " .... " " at 8.05 " "
Remainder of year work commences after Breakfast.

DINNER BELLS.

"Ring out"............................∴.12.30 p. m..........."Ring in".... 1.05 p. m.

In all cases, the *first* stroke of the bell is considered as marking the time.

Massachusetts House Document, no. 50, March of 1845:

. . . Miss Sarah G. Bagely said she had worked in the Lowell Mills eight years and a half, six years and a half on the Hamilton Corporation, and two years on the Middlesex. She is a weaver, and works by the piece. She worked in the mills three years before her health began to fail. She is a native of New Hampshire, and went home six weeks during the summer. Last year she was out of the mill a third of the time. She thinks the health of the operatives is not so good as the health of females who do house-work or millinery business. The chief evil, so far as health is concerned, is the shortness of time allowed for meals. The next evil is the length of time employed—not giving them time to cultivate their minds. She spoke of the high moral and intellectual character of the girls. That many were engaged as teach-ers in the Sunday schools. That many attended the lectures of the Lowell Institute; and she thought, if more time was allowed, that more lectures would be given and more girls attend. She thought that the girls generally were favorable to the ten hour system. She had presented a petition, same as the one be-fore the Committee, to 132 girls, most of whom said that they would prefer to work but ten hours. In a pecuniary point of view, it would be better, as their health would be improved. They would have more time for sewing. Their intellectual, moral and religious habits would also be benefited by the change. Miss Bagely said, in addition to her labor in the mills, she had kept evening school during the winter months, for four years, and thought that this extra labor must have injured her health.

A Description of Factory Life by an Associationist, 1846:

In Lowell live between seven and eight thousand young women, who are generally daughters of farmers of the different States of New England; some of them are members of families that were rich the generation before.

The operatives work thirteen hours a day in the summer time, and from daylight to dark in the winter. At half past four in the morning the factory bell rings, and at five the girls must be in the mills. A clerk, placed as a watch, observes those who are a few minutes behind the time, and effectual means are taken to stimulate to punctuality. This is the morning commencement of the industrial discipline (should we not rather say industrial tyranny?) which is established in these Associations of this moral and Christian community. At seven the girls are allowed thirty minutes for breakfast, and at noon thirty minutes more for dinner, except during the first quarter of the year, when the time is extended to forty-five minutes. But within this time they must hurry to their boarding-houses and return to the factory, and that through the hot sun, or the rain and cold. A meal eaten under such circumstances must be quite unfavorable to digestion and health, as any medical man will inform us. At seven o'clock in the evening the factory bell sounds the close of the days work.

Thus thirteen hours per day of close attention and monotonous labor are exacted from the young women in these manufactories. . . . So fatigued, we should say, exhausted and worn out but we wish to speak of the system in the simplest language, are numbers of the girls, that they go to bed soon after their evening meal? and endeavor by a comparatively long sleep to resuscitate their weakened frames for the toils of the coming day. When Capital has got thirteen hours of labor daily out of a being, it can get nothing more. It could be a poor speculation in an industrial point of view to own the operative; for the trouble and expense of providing for times of sickness and old age could more than counterbalance the difference between the price of wages and the expense of board and clothing. The far greater number of fortunes, accumulated by the North in comparison with the South, shows that hireling labor is more profitable for Capital than slave labor.

Now let us examine the nature of the labor itself, and the conditions under which it is performed. Enter with us into the large rooms, when the looms are at work. The largest that we saw is in the Amoskeag Mills at Manchester. It is four hundred feet long, and about seventy broad; there are five hundred looms, and twenty-one thousand spindles in it. The din and clatter of these five hundred looms under full operation, struck us on first entering as something frightful and infernal, for it seemed such an atrocious violation of one of the faculties of the human soul, the sense of hearing. After a while we became somewhat inured to it, and by speaking quite close to the ear of an operative and quite loud, we could hold a conversation, and make the inquiries we wished.

The girls attend upon an average three looms; many attend four, but this requires a very active person, and the most unremitting care. However, a great many do it. Attention to two is as much as should be demanded of an operative. This gives us some idea of the application required during the thirteen hours of daily labor. The atmosphere of such a room cannot of course be pure; on the contrary it is charged with cotton filaments and dust, which, we were told, are very injurious to the lungs. On entering the room, although the day was warm, we remarked that the windows were down; we asked the reason, and a young woman answered very naively, and without seeming to be in the least aware that this privation of fresh air was anything else than perfectly natural, that "when the wind blew, the threads did not work so well." After we had been in the room for fifteen or twenty minutes, we found ourselves, as did the persons who accompanied us, in quite a perspiration, produced by a certain moisture which we observed in the air, as well as by the heat.

The young women sleep upon an average six in a room; three beds to a room. There is no privacy, no retirement here; it is almost impossible to read or write alone, as the parlor is full and so many sleep in the same chamber. A young woman remarked to us, that if she had a letter to write, she did it on the head of a band-box, sitting on a trunk, as there was not space for a table. So live and toil the young women of our country in the boarding-houses and manufactories, which the rich and influential of our land have built for them.

The Editor of the *Courier* and *Enquirer* has often accused the Associationists of wishing to reduce men "to herd together like beasts of the field." We would ask him whether he does not find as much of what may be called "herding together in these modern industrial Associations, established by men of his own kind as he thinks would exist in one of the Industrial Phalanxes, which we propose.

Boarding House Rules from the Handbook to Lowell, 1848:

REGULATIONS FOR THE BOARDING-HOUSES of the Hamilton Manufacturing Company. The tenants of the boarding-houses are not to board, or permit any part of their houses to be occupied by any person, except those in the employ of the company, without special permission.

They will be considered answerable for any improper conduct in their houses, and are not to permit their boarders to have company at unseasonable hours.

The doors must be closed at ten o'clock in the evening, and no person admitted after that time, without some reasonable excuse.

The keepers of the boarding-houses must give an account of the number, names and employment of their boarders, when required, and report the names of such as are guilty of any improper conduct, or are not in the regular habit of attending public worship.

The buildings, and yards about them, must be kept clean and in good order; and if they are injured, other-wise than from ordinary use, all necessary repairs will be made, and charged to the occupant.

The sidewalks, also, in front of the houses, must be kept clean, and free from snow, which must be removed from them immediately after it has ceased falling; if neglected, it will be removed by the company at the expense of the tenant.

It is desirable that the families of those who live in the houses, as well as the boarders, who have not had the kine pox, should be vaccinated, which will be done at the expense of the company, for such as wish it.

Some suitable chamber in the house must be reserved, and appropriated for the use of the sick, so that others may not be under the necessity of sleeping in the same room.

REGULATIONS
FOR THE
BOARDING HOUSES
OF THE
MIDDLESEX COMPANY.

THE tenants of the Boarding Houses are not to board, or permit any part of their houses to be occupied by any person except those in the employ of the Company.

They will be considered answerable for any improper conduct in their houses, and are not to permit their boarders to have company at unseasonable hours.

The doors must be closed at ten o'clock in the evening, and no one admitted after that time without some reasonable excuse.

The keepers of the Boarding Houses must give an account of the number, names, and employment of their boarders, when required; and report the names of such as are guilty of any improper conduct, or are not in the regular habit of attending public worship.

The buildings and yards about them must be kept clean and in good order, and if they are injured otherwise than from ordinary use, all necessary repairs will be made, and charged to the occupant.

It is indispensable that all persons in the employ of the Middlesex Company should be vaccinated who have not been, as also the families with whom they board; which will be done at the expense of the Company.

SAMUEL LAWRENCE, Agent.

JOEL TAYLOR, PRINTER, Daily Courier Office.

Cabinet Furniture, The American Labor Devoted to the Cause of Protection of Home Industry, July 1842:

This subject has received from the friends of Home Industry less attention, compared with its importance in the aggregate of American labor sought to be protected from foreign competition, than most other branches of business. The reason has then, that no representation of the evils under which American Cabinetmakers suffer has as yet been made, although few now need the fostering a protection more than they. Individual complaints of the depreciation of their business have often been made, and yet no statistical facts have been collected with the view to memorialize Congress on the subject.

That the interest of this class of our manufacturers should receive prompt and efficient attention there can be no doubt, when it is known that the wages of men employed in the business are now reduced from $12 and $14 per week to from $6 to $8. As an example washstands of mahogany which formerly sold for $2.50 and which cannot now be manufactured for less $1.75, are imported by the Agents of French manufacturers and sold at auction in this city for seventy-five cents. About the same comparative price prevails in numerous other articles of cabinet furniture imported and sold under like circumstances. The parts of these articles are made complete, with tenons and mortices, and in that state packed and shipped in the American market, where, being put together, they sell at a profit, though vastly below the prices at which an American laborer can live. The result is, that great quantities of French cabinet are sold at our auctions at prices corresponding with the difference between French and American labor, and hence with profit to the foreign manufacturers, but with notable destruction to our own. It may be fairly asked, under those circumstances if our legislators will look with indifference on the prostration of the labor of our country at the shrine of foreign cupidity.

Observations of Travelers on South Carolina, 1820-1860, by J. Ryan McKissick with reference to J. S. Buckingham's *The Slave States of America*, 1842:

A Georgia woman, who raised silkworms and wove silk cloth, told Buckingham she could sell to South Carolinians as much as she could weave at double the price of French and English silks. Her explanation was: "The people of South Carolina are all for living on their own resources, and having no dependence on other countries; they, therefore, readily paid double prices for silks grown and manufactured at home, because it shut up the foreign trader, and kept all the money in the country."

Travels in the United States in 1847, by Domingo Sarmiento, 1847:

Since, as they say, "As the nest, so the bird," I will say a word or two about the villager. If he is a tavern keeper, a storekeeper, or belongs to some other sedentary profession, his daily costume will consist of the following articles: patent-leather boots, pants and coat of black cloth, a black satin waistcoat, a tie of twilled silk, a small cloth cap, and, hanging from a black cord, a gold charm in the shape of a pencil or a key. At the end of this cord, and deep in his pocket, is the most curious item of a Yankee's dress. If you want to study the transformations the watch has gone through from its invention down to our time, ask a Yankee you meet what time it is. You will see fossil watches, mastodon watches, haunted watches, watches which are the home of vermin, and inflated watches three stories high with drawbridges and the secret stairways which you descend with a lantern in order to wind up.

I know no more about New York as it is now than the hermit of Saba. Such a mass of busy population, such noises of "armorers closing rivets up," such creaking of blocks, such pulling of ropes, such caulking of seams!

—Celebrated New Yorker Philip Hone, 1849

"Emancipation," *Newark Daily Advertiser*, March 14, 1849:

The subject of emancipation is just now exciting much feeling all over the State (of Kentucky), and the election for the approaching convention to revive the Constitution is absorbing all of the questions. The result of course cannot be foreseen. There are 99 counties in the state, and the whole number of delegates to the convention will be 100. The whole number of voters in the state is 141,620, and the number of slaves is 192,470. It appears that about one-fifth of the whole number of counties contain one-fourth only of the voting population, while they have one half of all the slaves in the State. And on the other hand, five-eights of the whole number of counties with more than one half of the voting population contains less than one fourth of the slaves in the state. . . . Woodford County has more slaves in proportion to her voting population than any other county—nearly five slaves to every voter. Johnson County has fewer slaves than any other—the proportion being 27 voters to one slave.

"Insanity," *Newark Daily Advertiser*, March 14, 1849:

Dr. Bingham, Superintendent of the Insane Asylum at Utica, says in his valuable report that he has found hereditary forms of insanity as curable as any other. . . . In Dr. Bingham's opinion the most frequent immediate cause of insanity, and one of the most important to guard against, is the want of sleep. "So rarely," he said, "do we see a recent case of insanity, that is not preceded by want of sleep, that we regard it as almost a precursor to mental derangement." He continues: "Some believe sleep was of little consequence. Though it may be well to rise with the sun, or when it is light, (not before, however) yet this is of minor importance, in comparison to retiring early to bed.

Dr. Bingham gives the following hints for the procuring of sound sleep: "It is important in the first place, that the mind should not be disturbed for several hours before retiring to rest. Retire early, neither when very warm or cold; sleep on a hair mattress, or on a bed not very soft. The bed-room should be large and well ventilated, and the bed should not be placed near a wall or near a window, as such an arrangement often exposes the person to currents of cold air. There should be nothing tight about the neck, and the Chinese rule of brushing the teeth before retiring, is a good one. Tea or coffee taken late in the evening is apt to disturb sleep. Strive to banish thoughts, as much as possible, on retiring to rest, or take up the most dull subject. Study during the evening is improper."

"Appointing Power," *Newark Daily Advertiser,* March 14, 1849:

The appointing power is a weakening feature of the president, according to the Union, which, in the course of an article on appointments yesterday, throws the following light upon the subject:

We repeat over and over, that this patronage is "not the thing which it has been cracked up to be." It weakens the Executive more than it strengthens him. Who is it that said, that for the one man you appoint, you offend ninety-nine others; and this 100th man is apt to be ungrateful? Certain it is, that for one who was appointed, there are many who are disappointed. We hear of many complaints and murmurs already from the Whigs, who have been soured by the unavailing applications for themselves or their friends. The present President might take some consolation from the history of his predecessor. We are satisfied that Mr. Polk suffered more by the loss of friends in consequence of disappointed office seekers than from any other cause. It is our firm impression that he would've been more popular at this moment if you've never had a fish or a loaf to give to the hungry expectant."

"Deaths," *Newark Daily Advertiser,* March 14, 1849:

Deaths in New York last week 300, of which 164 were children. Of apoplexy 6, bronchitis 5; consumption 52; croup 5; congestion of the lungs 7; debility 10; diarrhea 5; dropsy in the head 18; dysentery 5; fevers 32; inflammation of lungs 22; inflamed bowels 8; measles 7; old-age 5; smallpox 11

1848 PROFILE

Cooped up in his father's and uncle's general stores in Maine, Benjamin Reed dreamed of a better life for himself out west in New York or Ohio.

Life at Home

- Benjamin Reed had been active as a clerk for the past two years in Bangor, Maine, daily assisting the customers in his father's general store, Reed's Wholesale & Retail Grocery.
- Already seventeen, Benjamin knew this was not the life he had envisioned.
- The routine of the early morning hours bored him greatly.
- Almost every morning, he woke around five o'clock to open the store, remove its shutters, and hang the pasteboard tin-letter stamped signs outside indicating the availability of "Rye Meal," "Oats," "Eggs," and "Butter."
- Then he had to hang outside the available merchandise, such as tin buckets and grass mats, and sweep and mop the floors.
- With much of the store's walls used for shelving, few windows were present for light, so before his seven o'clock breakfast, he had to fill the oil lamps to create additional illumination within the store.
- Without the added light, customers complained that they were unable to see the merchandise in the store's shadows.
- Benjamin rarely completed his assigned duties before the numerous customers began arriving.
- One of the store's biggest customers, Mr. Macomber, often arrived at the start of the day to make purchases for his lumber operations.
- One morning, Mr. Macomber spent over $40 on groceries, including 10 bushels of salt and 500 pounds of fish.
- His purchases, including putting all of the goods into his wagons, consumed the entire morning.

Benjamin Reed dreamed of a life away from his family's general store.

- If Benjamin failed to wake up early to open the store, he could expect the wrath of his father, especially if a customer was left waiting.
- Once he woke up at 20 minutes to six upon hearing the passing of the baker's cart and the sound of his bells.
- Quickly changing from his night clothes into his work attire, Benjamin rushed down the street to open the store and saw the baker's assistant waiting for him to open the store.
- Pleased to learn the assistant had only just arrived, Benjamin could avoid a potential conflict with his father.
- Benjamin's father also tasked him with searching through shipped produce that was speculatively purchased.
- Once he purchased three boxes of lemons at $2.50 per box.
- Each box was supposed to have 300 lemons, but none of the boxes came close to half that count and all the lemons were decayed.
- Upset with the lemon speculation, Mr. Reed spent a solid 10 minutes yelling at Benjamin to search through the stack to find some that could potentially be sold.
- Later in the week he was yelled at again when his father caught him using the butcher's knife—designated to cut pork—to cut slices of soap and butter for customers.
- Too often he had heard his father's lecture that everything should be kept in its place and be "bright as a dollar."
- Upon opening the store at half past five one morning, Benjamin had to tend to a number of customers by himself as business began in earnest.
- Before breakfast he discovered he had made an error when a customer gave him a $2 bill for a $1.20 purchase.
- Instead of giving back 80 cents in change, he handed him back $1.80.
- In great distress, Benjamin left work early before dinner to resolve the error.
- He had to pay the ferryman one penny to cross the Penobscot River and found the customer at his home.
- With the event fresh in the customer's memory, Benjamin managed to collect the difference before his father could discover the error.
- Though he avoided conflicts with his father whenever possible, Benjamin enjoyed arguing and debating larger matters in the newspaper, the *Bangor Mercury*, under a pseudonym.
- Examples of his earlier letters included a commentary on Thoreau's protest of the Mexican War, local lumber businesses on the Penobscot River, and various scientific advances.
- After a lecture by a visiting speaker on slavery's harm to the nation, a local citizen argued in the local press that it was not the concern of New Englanders.
- The comments angered Benjamin, causing him to reply under an assumed name in the following edition.
- He wrote a lengthy argument and concluded his letter, "Every intelligent man in the State of Maine knows that Slavery is a violation of the first principles of humanity utterly, totally and fully wrong. All then remaining for us to do is convince the people in what manner our party proposes to abolish it."
- Benjamin was proud of this piece and several others over his months of writing.
- But signing each letter "A. Yeoman" proved to be a poor choice of a pseudonym; it was later discovered by the paper's editor that Yeoman's address was Benjamin's father's store.

- His clandestine methods upset both his parents, but his mother was a bit more understanding.
- She was pleased to see her son engaged in intellectual endeavors, a trait she valued, unlike her husband.
- Mrs. Reed enjoyed sharing her interests in science, politics and current events with her children; her husband tended to be focused solely on business.
- Benjamin viewed his mother as his strongest teacher, especially on subjects he did not learn at school.
- Through her instruction, he not only learned the importance of temperance from alcohol and the abolition of slavery, but also about clairvoyance and phrenology.
- Benjamin viewed phrenology as an important scientific breakthrough.
- The concept of studying a person's skull bumps to reveal personality traits fascinated him.
- One evening, he attended a series of lectures on phrenology and was shocked at the audience's lack of scientific knowledge.
- Only he and his brother Charles knew there were 240 bones and 400 muscles within the human body.
- Later in the lecture a head examination was made on one attendee during which it was discovered that his *Devotional Organs* were small.
- A few days later Benjamin paid six shillings to have his skull measured and examined to determine his personality strengths and deficiencies by the phrenologist.
- It came as no surprise that his *Amativeness*, the faculty for romantic love, was underdeveloped.
- The want of a sweetheart had been evident to Benjamin for some time, and reading Byron's *Don Juan* in the evenings only reinforced his interest in the girls in town.
- One summer afternoon while sweeping the front steps of the store, he noticed the way two girls walked by.
- A few weeks later, he made a point of stopping behind the Dye House to see the immersion of the same two young ladies by a Baptist minister in the Penobscot River.
- Benjamin wrote in his journal, "During the baptism, they had on loose gowns of black."
- Then came the party invitation.
- The receipt of an invitation for Susan Jane's "bring out" party on her sixteenth birthday thrilled Benjamin.
- He and his friend Nathan arrived that evening promptly at seven o'clock with the other guests.
- Many young men and women engaged in conversation for the first couple of hours, but by nine o'clock, Benjamin was wretched because much of the talking was interspersed with kissing.
- Upon the party's end around eleven o'clock, Nathan commented to Benjamin that he had behaved "martyr like" for not kissing any girls that evening, especially the girls he fancied.
- Benjamin focused most of his free time on attending performances at Bangor's new theater house, Market Hall.
- To guarantee a full house, performance managers at times provided low-price tickets to attract laborers.

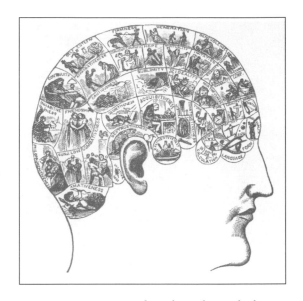

Benjamin was interested in phrenology which was determining intelligence by the shape of the human skull.

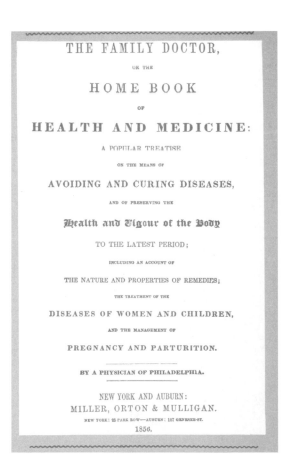

Benjamin and his friend Nathan were invited to Sarah Jane's "bring out" party.

- One show's cost was as low as 12½ cents and the hall's seats were filled a full 30 minutes before the seven o'clock performance.
- Although many in attendance appeared to be of genteel persuasion, the show's manager still reminded the audience of proper theater etiquette.
- For example, songs of merit should not be "manifested by whistling or shouting."
- But total excitement overwhelmed Bangor when Tom Thumb arrived to perform at Market Hall.
- At 15 years of age, Tom was only 27 inches high and weighed 15 pounds.
- The entire Reed family attended one of his three performances in Bangor.
- Benjamin's mother was thrilled to acquire Tom Thumb's visiting card upon entering the door.
- She also bought for 9 pence a gilt medal with his likeness on one side; the medal was also inscribed with the words "Victoria Regina" with Queen Victoria's head on the reverse side.
- During the performance, Tom Thumb performed a number of songs and dances.
- Benjamin especially enjoyed Thumb's miniature representations of Napoleon Bonaparte and Frederick the Great in full military dress.

Life at Work

- The unexpected death of Benjamin Reed's four-year-old little sister Emma was a shock to both him and his brother.
- Initially his mother thought the little girl had a slight ague, a fever, but it grew worse.
- The doctor confirmed that she had scarlet fever and stressed that it was no way preferable to yellow fever or smallpox.
- Two days later, Emma died.
- In his journal Benjamin wrote, "Half past 5, Emma is dead! As she died the face of heaven, which had before, it seemed, shed sympathetic tears, was lit up by a smile of sunshine. . . . The blow seemed excruciating to Mother."

Benjamin's mother insisted on family portraits.

- Benjamin tried to philosophize on the loss of Emma and how she was in the perfect bliss of heaven with two other siblings his mother lost prior to his birth.
- A few weeks later, his mother's fortieth birthday was a somber affair without Emma's presence.
- To mark the occasion, Benjamin gave her a present of an old American dollar dated 1795 with the injunction not to spend it.
- His mother was appreciative of the gift but wanted everyone's daguerreotype taken by the end of the month.
- Benjamin and Charles went to Mr. Woodbury's daguerreotype room to have their portraits taken in their best attire.
- Their mother had intended to have hers taken as well but did not have the time.
- In the early summer, with their limited cash tied to pending crops or business prospects, regular customers increased their personal accounts at the Reeds' store.
- At times it was a challenge to record accounts.
- Benjamin was taken aback when a 10-year-old girl entered the store to acquire a bar of soap.
- When asked what her parents' names were, she responded with "marm" and "par."
- It took Benjamin a full five minutes questioning the girl to determine who her father was and where to charge the soap.
- One customer with outstanding obligations passed away without leaving any assets or money for his wife or children.
- Benjamin's father had to turn the widow away when she asked to acquire clothes for her little daughter.
- During the hot summer days and added free time, reading was a common activity for Benjamin because customers were few.
- Tired of reading "light literature," he spent time reading new works, such as Currer Bell's *Jane Eyre* and a tract on Fourierism.
- The conflict Charles Fourier discussed between the rich and the poor interested Benjamin, but he could not see it as conceivable.

- Society working together with the same long-term plan to help one another was not what Benjamin saw in reality in Bangor or the national press.
- The amount of wealth acquired by John Jacob Astor, who died a few months prior, appalled Benjamin.
- Astor's millions were used for his own personal amusement and not for the greater good of society.
- Though concerns for society were lofty, daily business was the priority, especially when the general store's finances were decidedly poor.
- Every dollar was used to help pay the mortgage on the Reed home.
- Business declined rapidly in the fall when father's liquor license expired, which also influenced the amount of trade within the store.
- By late October, without discussion, Benjamin learned that he was going north to Weston, Maine, to work in his Uncle Samuel's general store.
- Uncle Samuel was in dire need of help in the booming lumbering community.
- Benjamin was not pleased with this responsibility but accepted it to help earn money for the family.
- His father also indicated that Benjamin needed to start acquiring letters of reference for future job prospects.
- Upon saying farewell to his family, Benjamin mounted Whitney's Express Stage for Weston with five other passengers.
- For the rugged two-day journey, he contended with the nausea from cigar smoke produced by two men.
- Uncle Samuel greeted Benjamin when the stagecoach arrived in front of his business, B.F. Brown & Company, a story and half structure, 20 by 50 feet in size.
- The store's primary space was large with a sizable cylinder stove to warm the space in the cold months.

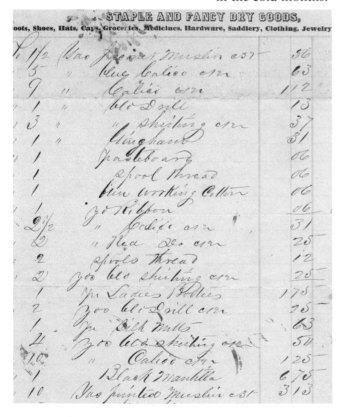

Benjamin kept the accounts for his Uncle Samuel's store.

- Two counters were painted blue, with one on the south side, 18 feet long, being used to serve customers with groceries and medicines.
- The northwest corner was used for barrels of molasses and oil and dry goods, while buttons and hardware were kept on the north side of the room.
- Benjamin immediately realized that Weston was not like Bangor when he first encountered a customer's four-year-old boy smoking a cigar.
- The fact that he was doing so with the ease and nonchalance of an experienced smoker shocked him as well.
- Boasting a diversity of customers, Uncle Samuel's store was busy and Benjamin was put to clerking immediately upon arrival.
- Regretfully, he was not familiar with the store and had difficulty helping the customers.
- After a few days of poor service, Benjamin was assigned to keeping the account books.
- This, too, was a challenging task, primarily because of all the exchange of credit with the lumbermen.
- In between opening the store early and assisting customers, the task of writing account books neatly in ink burdened Benjamin.
- During these monotonous tasks he contemplated a more prosperous life elsewhere in the United States.

- Often he thought of leaving Maine and going west to make his fortune in trade.
- Dreams of buying great bargains from western farmers and selling them for a profit attracted Benjamin.
- He discussed the concept with his uncle of buying crops in the fall for two or three dollars a barrel.
- One then could transport them by one's own vessel to large cities and sell them for four or five dollars—possibly more.
- Uncle Samuel tossed aside Benjamin's thoughts and encouraged him to work hard on the task at hand in Weston, not in distant places such as Ohio.
- Benjamin's hours of work increased in March when the lumbermen drove their timber downstream to market.
- Benjamin recorded the receipt of logs used to settle personal accounts while Uncle Samuel worked to sell them for a profit.
- Each lumberman employed personal log marks composed of a combination of letters of the alphabet, numbers and symbols.
- This precaution prevented others from claiming logs as they moved downstream.
- Benjamin had to use a separate account book based upon the various log marks and their owners, and then reconcile the differences within the account books.
- It was an arduous task.
- A break from these duties arrived one day when Uncle Samuel was working late with a customer, Charles McCollum.
- With evening arriving, Uncle Samuel asked Benjamin to take Mr. McCollum's 16-year-old daughter in the sleigh.
- A ride of three miles with a pretty girl was not to be lightly discarded by Benjamin, especially after a tedious day of bending over a desk and drawing off accounts.
- The ride proved to be eventful when the horse's ears pricked up within the journey's first mile.
- This sign of danger from the horse was noticed quickly by Benjamin and reinforced when two lank wolves emerged from a thicket.
- It was not Benjamin's fault that the horse's speed accelerated or Mr. McCollum's daughter grabbed his arm.
- The ride thrilled him.
- Upon dropping off the young lady and returning to B.F. Brown & Company, Benjamin thought about his recent hard work.
- He was earning more than he ever had in his life and wondered what his future held.
- After paying for rent, food and a few new clothes, he still had over 10 dollars in his possession.
- It troubled him that his parents expected him to send them the money for expenses in Bangor.

Life in the Community: Bangor, Maine
- Bangor, Maine, was known as the "Lumber Capital of the World" in the 1840s with its numerous sawmills along the Penobscot River.
- A large presence of wealth north of Bangor invited conflict between Maine and its northern neighbor, Canada.
- Since 1769, Massachusetts was responsible for the territory and controlled Maine as a province of the Commonwealth of Massachusetts.
- While under its control, disputes with Canada occurred often on the province's boundary to control the wealth in lumber.

Bangor, Maine.

- Because of the province's rapidly growing population and being geographically separated from Massachusetts, Maine became a state in 1820 under the Missouri Compromise.
- That agreement admitted both Maine and Missouri into the Union while keeping a balance between slave and free states.
- When Maine acquired its statehood, the population of Bangor was 1,800.
- Fourteen years later the city rapidly grew to a population of over 8,000.
- Lumber spurred the rapid growth, bringing with it numerous business investments; over 300 lumber mills were present along the Penobscot River by the 1830s.
- The lumber mills then attracted lumber companies, shingle mills, lumbermen and log drivers.
- The economic activity brought many Irish immigrants into Bangor from Canada in the 1830s.
- Foreign laborers competing for local jobs sparked a deadly riot in 1833 that lasted for days and required the state's militia to restore order.
- Demand for a police force to prevent future riots motivated the town to incorporate as the City of Bangor in 1834.
- The attraction and wealth associated with lumber caused an unofficial war between Britain's colony, Canada, and Maine commonly referred to as the Aroostook or Lumberjack's War in 1838-1839.
- The dispute was between the two countries' borders and access to the lumber.
- Local militia and government troops were required to control the conflict; under the Webster-Ashburton Treaty of 1842, the border between the United States and Canada was resolved.
- Timber demand continued to grow in the 1840s with lumber products primarily used in the nation's shipyards.
- Manufactured lumber products from Bangor were also sent to cities in Europe and the Caribbean.
- The city's first disaster struck in 1846 during the spring lumber drive: a four-mile ice buildup on the Penobscot River's falls north of the city.
- When it broke loose, it swept away a number of bridges, including the Penobscot River covered bridge, and flooded hundreds of shops and businesses in the city.

HISTORICAL SNAPSHOT
1848

- Britain suspended the Habeas Corpus Act in Ireland following the potato famine and protests
- The Treaty of Guadalupe Hidalgo ended the Mexican War with the United States
- Wisconsin entered the Union as the thirtieth state
- The first Woman's Rights Convention opened in Seneca Falls, New York, under the leadership of Elizabeth Cady Stanton
- German missionary-explorer Johannes Rebmann, became the first European to observe the snow-covered Mount Kilimanjaro, Africa's highest peak
- John Jacob Astor died, leaving a fortune of $20 million acquired in the fur trade and New York real estate
- The Pacific Mail Steamship Company contracted with engineers to build a rail link across the Isthmus of Panama to facilitate transportation between Atlantic Coast ports and San Francisco
- State of Maine Pure Spruce Gum was introduced, the world's first commercial chewing gum
- Britain took the Mosquito Coast from Nicaragua
- James Marshall found gold in Sutter's Mill in Coloma, California
- The ballet *Faust* premiered in Milan, Italy
- James K. Polk became the first U.S. president photographed in office
- French King Louis-Philippe abdicated the throne, resulting in the development of the Second French Republic
- Karl Marx and Frederick Engels published *The Communist Manifesto* in London, England
- Hungary became the constitutional monarchy under King Ferdinand of Austria
- The Territory of Oregon was organized by an act of Congress out of the U.S. portion of the Oregon Country below the forty-ninth parallel
- Waldo Hanchett patented the dental chair
- The first shipload of Chinese laborers arrived in San Francisco
- The Shaker song *Simple Gifts* was written by Joseph Brackett in Alfred, Maine
- American born Joseph Jenkins Roberts was sworn in as the first president of the independent African Republic of Liberia

Selected Prices

Coal Scuttle $25.00
Mare $230.00
Molasses, Gallon $13.34
Ox $600.00
Pillow Case $3.00
Saddle, Leather $95.00
Salt, Bushel $46.00
Spinning Wheel $14.38
Towels, Dozen $20.00
Washboard $1.43

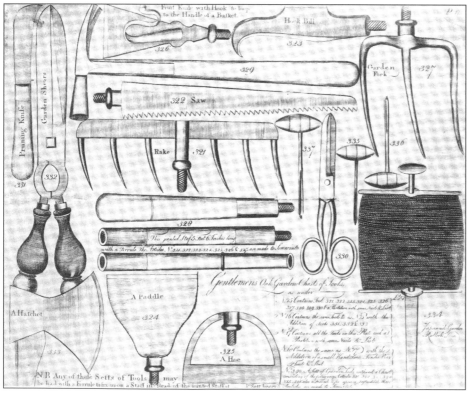

Gentlemens garden tools.

"Chorus of a Patriot Song During the Mexican War," *Down East Diary*, Edited by Charles Foster, 1975:

Palo Alto, Monterey
Bring out your Santa Anna
For every time we fire a gun
Fsht—Pop goes a Mexican-er

"Observations on Maine Land Speculation in Maine," *Niles Register*, June 27, 1835:

I have noticed among the speculators at the Bangor House, several gentlemen who have failed in Boston within two or three years. Their good luck this quarter has enabled them to discharge all their debts, and to have heavy purses left for future use. This is well. Enterprise combined with honesty deserves a rich reward.

Many speculators here are men of small means. But they have a kind of *dare devil* feeling which is decidedly better than money. A man who is not the owner of one hundred dollars, will buy a township and will sell it again within an hour, at a small advance and pocket the profit, merely transferring all the responsibilities from his own shoulders to those of some other person, or persons, better able to bear them. This is the grand secret of "trade and commerce" in this hot bed of speculation and enterprise.

The ten lots of land which were sold yesterday at 11 and 1200 dollars per lot, were purchased for the sum of $2,500 of a Boston gentleman, who took the land for a bad debt. Here is an increase for land! But this is an everyday story in Bangor.

"Life Among the Loggers," Charles Hallock, *Harper's New Monthly Magazine*, March 1860:

And now, with the men and teams on the ground, and a favorable depth of snow, the work begins in real earnest. The trees to be cut are selected with a practiced eye, and many huge and symmetrical trunks are disregarded, which to the uninitiated appear to be perfect in all respects, but exhibit to the lumberman the mark of the insidious "konkus," which is infallible. Skids are then laid to receive the falling giants, and the swampers busily cut their way to the selected points.

And now the reverberating strokes of the axes ring incessantly through the high arches; crash after crash thunders forth the knell of the doomed ones; and the wild shouting of the teamsters, the clank of the log-chains, and the unearthly shrieks of the bob-sleds as they groan beneath their ponderous burdens, combine to thrill the senses with an excitement as pleasurable as it is novel.

A Chinese executioner, who severs the necks of his victims with that peculiar "cheep, cheep" of the cleaver, which so plainly speaks the value of human life in that Celestial Elysium, could not perform his labor (or pastime) more nicely or expeditiously than the lumberman amputates the limbs and branches from the long trunks.

The barker dexterously strips off the bark, and the sled-tender is ready with team, tackle and fall, to raise the huge bodies of the fallen upon his sled, and transport them to the landing-places at the river, where they are cut into suitable lengths for driving to the booms in the spring.

These are the times that are trying to the oxen, and often the utmost exertions of four yokes are required to move the massive burdens. But by dint of volleys of encouragement and abuse, and a proper application of the mechanical forces and the whip, perseverance at length triumphs over gravity, and the huge load moves slowly and reluctantly forward to its destination.

This is the regular routine work through the long winter, yet diversified daily with that variety which is the spice of life and the nutmeg of existence. Sunday alone brings a cessation of labor; for the lumberman is always respectful of that clause of the Divine command which forbids all work on that sacred day.

To "fell, clear, and haul," continually for four or five long months, one might suppose would be monotonously irksome; but there is a pleasure in the ceaseless tramp from the swamp to the landing, and the landing to the swamp, in the companionship of the patient oxen, and the comfort of the never-absent pipe; a music in the jingling chains, the creaking sleds, and the echo of one's own song and whistle; a variety in the little vexations and difficulties of the way; and exciting episodes occasioned by sudden accidents, the unwelcome presence of wolves dodging among the brush along the route, or the chance encounters with bears or other noble game that unexpectedly cross the path.

"Editor's Note on a Country Store," *Harper's Weekly*, September 1853:

The proprietor generally kept himself at his town establishment, but sometimes he would visit his country-store, or "branch," staying now and then a week or more at a time, and always attending the little country church. As a matter of course, he was looked up to with emulation, if not astonishment, by the" go-to-meeting" young folk of the town. What *he* "wore to meeting" was of necessity the prevailing fashion until he introduced a new style at his next visit.

One day he asked his country-partner about the business and other matters in which they were interested, who said:

"Yes, goods go pretty quick, and at good prices."

"You keep those pig-skin caps, I see, yet? I am afraid I didn't make a great bargain in buying *them*. Can't you get rid of more of that big box-full?"

"No; haven't sold *one* yet; people don't like 'em; and I've had a great notion of throwing them out of the back-window, and getting rid of the trouble of 'em. I don't think they'll *go* here."

Our merchant looked at them a moment; and then quietly remarked:

"You have kept them out of sight, I see. So much the better. Now next Monday morning you get them out, brush them up, and I think we'll find some customers for them before the week is out."

The next Sunday this acute observer of the springs of human action appeared in church with one of those identical pig-skin caps, tipped jauntily on one side of his head, and a splendid gold watch-chain dangling from his vest-pocket.

As usual, he was the "observed of all observers;" and it is superfluous to add that in less than a fortnight after, at his metropolitan store, he received a large additional order for these suddenly popular pigskin caps.

1849 PROFILE

After getting into a serious jam with a girl in New Jersey, Alvin Grunn was reluctantly sent away to North Carolina by his uncle to become a postal worker.

Life at Home

- As soon as Alvin Grunn learned that his uncle was in town, he knew he was in real trouble.
- He had somehow gotten away with his escapade with Sally Keckley, even after they were caught sneaking back to her house at 4 am.
- Her brothers were pretty riled up, but Alvin, as usual, had talked the problem to death and they lost their will to kill him.
- Now that Sally had decided that she was with child, Alvin was concerned that his luck could be running out.
- Sally was only 16—six years younger than Alvin—and her widowed father's favorite.
- Sally was also convinced that she was in love with Alvin and he with her; Alvin was less convinced of these personal matters.
- Her brothers were very agitated.
- The situation could be deadly in a tight-knit community like Trenton, New Jersey, where men did not take advantage of girls and get away with it.
- His uncle, politically connected since the days of President Andrew Jackson, had a simple solution: send Alvin away, before he got himself killed, by getting him an appointment to help run a post office in rural North Carolina.
- Maybe he could stay out of trouble there and the girl's family would accept a sizeable gift of land to remain quiet.
- Alvin was devastated; his life revolved around the balls, taverns and gaiety of Trenton, not some God-forsaken place in North Carolina called Charlotte.

Alvin Grunn was sent to North Carolina after getting into trouble with a young lady.

Life was interesting for Alvin in Trenton, New Jersey.

- In 1840 the developing community of Charlotte had 12 stores, one bank agent, three taverns, one tannery, one printing office, one weekly newspaper, one common school, two ministers, six lawyers and six doctors.
- Personal property included 13 leisure carriages, 83 gold watches, 38 silver watches and 24 pianos.
- Most of the area residents were rural farmers widely scattered throughout the countryside.
- Gold mining was the principal business of the town.
- Discovered in 1799, gold had fueled the growth of the community and even attracted the U.S. Mint to assay ore and mint coins.
- Now its postal service was to be augmented by an additional unhappy federal employee, whose only thoughts were concerned with escaping the wilderness of North Carolina for the joys of New Jersey.
- Moving the mail was a big business in America in 1849.
- Postal employees accounted for 76 percent of the civilian federal workforce.
- Postmasters outnumbered soldiers 8,764 to 6,332 and were the most visible representatives of the burgeoning federal government across America.
- In the prior 20 years, 4,500 post offices, handling one million letters annually, had been expanded to embrace 13,600 locations handling 4.3 million pieces of mail.
- In influence, Alvin's uncle outranked entire towns thanks to his wealth, long ties to Washington politics and a willingness to bend the rules.
- Alvin's uncle had never married, but instead adopted the children of his brothers and sisters as if they were his own.
- Alvin's first alcoholic drink was served up by his uncle, along with explicit, confidential advice about pleasing girls.
- But now that Alvin's exploits had attracted unwanted attention, his uncle was now in charge; Alvin was going to become a postal employee.
- As his uncle commented later, "Who's going to notice one more rude postal clerk?"

Alvin found life in Charlotte, North Carolina quiet and boring.

Life at Work

- For eight years Alvin Grunn had clerked the post office in Charlotte, North Carolina, waiting impatiently for a letter announcing his next appointment.
- As if he had time to think about anything but work!
- Ever since the federal government cut the postage rates in 1845, everyone thought it their duty to write a letter whether they had anything to say or not.
- People who had never visited the post office before were writing two or three letters a month.
- Some people came every day—unaccompanied women included—to inquire after letters for them.
- It was madness; farmers even planned trips to town based on the expectation of mail.
- Alvin was thoroughly annoyed by the constant flow of customers.
- Farmers and merchants who banged on his home window during lunch or on Sundays were particularly irritating.
- When he moved to Charlotte, his duties were built around business letters and dozens and dozens of out-of-town newspapers that arrived on the 6:45 a.m. train.
- All the mail could be handled in an orderly, leisurely manner; most of all, everyone was polite and respectful of his position.
- For the first third of the century, most Americans, with the exception of merchants or the very rich, rarely exchanged letters.

Alvin was the postal clerk in Charlotte for eight years, always hoping to be transferred someplace else.

- The process was slow and expensive.
- At the turn of the century, a letter's journey between Portland, Maine, and Savannah, Georgia, required 40 days.
- Even the journey between New York City and upstate New York might consume 20 days.
- By 1811, better roads had cut a letter's travel time from New York City to upstate New York to 12 days.
- In 1828, there were 7,530 post offices and 29,956 postal employees, mail contractors and carriers, making the department the largest employer in the executive branch.
- Because the department awarded a large number of jobs and contracts, the Postmaster General's power grew as well.
- From 1816 to 1845, the postage on a single-sheet letter traveling more than 400 miles was $0.25.
- This expense led letter writers to economize by writing the second half of the letter at a 90 degree angle between the lines of the first in order to avoid paying postage for a second piece of paper.
- Newspapers, on the other hand, traveled for $0.01 each.
- Since its inception, the post was committed to the distribution of political news to ensure an informed public, even farmers who lived far from the major cities.
- As a result, 41 different types of newspapers passed through Alvin's postal office each month—many sent by relatives eager to share town news.
- Many wanted to share more—at less cost.
- One of Alvin's duties was to scan each newspaper for hidden notes or messages; Alvin even found one news story heavily edited with ink cross-throughs so that the remaining words formed a personal message.
- With that discovery, the $0.01 newspaper postage immediately rose to a quarter.
- Alvin also followed local custom and threw away flyers promoting the abolition of slavery or booklets that encouraged slaves to run away.
- Personal letters and merchant exchanges were expected to finance the main business of the post office and subsidize the low rates imposed on newspapers.
- Then, in 1845, Congress enacted substantial reductions in the cost of sending a letter.
- Letters could be mailed at $0.05 per half ounce for distances up to 300 miles and $0.10 per half ounce for greater distances.
- Within a few years, Americans became unwilling to live beyond the reach of a post office.
- As the country grew, people in new states and territories petitioned Congress for even more postal routes, regardless of their cost or profitability.

The burning of abolitionist flyers sent through the post.

- Thanks to all these changes, the workload had become overwhelming; Alvin didn't have a minute to read his favorite newspapers from New Jersey and New York each morning.
- Merchants began routinely sending paper money through the mail to settle accounts now that postage was calculated on weight and each bank note was no longer considered an additional page.
- Wives were penning long letters to husbands recently departed to the newly discovered gold fields of California.
- Families were mailing Daguerreotype portraits of themselves to relatives who had moved west to Tennessee and Kentucky.
- This was a fascination for all, rich and poor alike, and money was not a concern.
- Farmers were writing customers in New England as though they were personal friends and constantly exchanging seed packets as if one land was like another.
- And the new fad of sending letters to famous people to request an autograph was a waste of everyone's time and clearly not the intent of the improved postal rates, Alvin was convinced.
- Plus, the handwriting on some letters was simply atrocious.
- If the mark of a cultured, educated person was a beautiful, graceful penmanship, the nation was populated with dullards, Alvin had learned from his postal experience.

Letters to husbands who left for the California gold rush increased Alvin's workload.

Life in the Community: Charlotte, North Carolina

- America's first gold rush took place in North Carolina.
- The discovery of gold in 1799 and subsequent successes in the 1820s and 1830s made North Carolina the leading producer of gold in America until the California gold strike in 1849.
- Gold mining was a leading occupation, behind farming, in the 1830s, earning North Carolina the nickname of the "Golden State."
- Mining employed nearly 20,000 persons in the 1830s; most of the gold was exported to Paris, France.
- By the 1840s, the state had more than 14,000 people working at 3,400 manufacturing establishments across the state, including flour mills and saw mills.
- In 1849, the largest 11 cities in the South did not include a single one from North Carolina; the largest North Carolina city was the port town of Wilmington, which ranked ninety-ninth in the nation and sixteenth in the South.
- The largest Southern cities of that time were New Orleans, Louisiana, 116,000; Charleston, South Carolina, 43,000; Richmond, Virginia, 27,000; Mobile, Alabama, 21,000; and Savannah, Georgia.

Primitive sketch of Wilmington, North Carolina.

HISTORICAL SNAPSHOT
1849

- The photographic slide was invented

- French officer Claude-Etienne Minie invented a bullet known as the Minie ball

- Abraham Lincoln patented a lifting and buoying device for vessels; he was the only U.S. president to apply for a patent

- Elizabeth Blackwell became the first woman in the United States to receive a medical degree

- Colonel John W. Geary became the first postmaster of San Francisco

- Harriet Tubman escaped from slavery in Maryland

- M. Jolly-Bellin accidently discovered the process of dry cleaning when he upset a lamp containing turpentine and oil onto his clothing and observed the cleaning effect

- The safety pin was patented by Walter Hunt of New York City

- The U.S. Gold Coinage Act authorized the coining of the $20 Double Eagle gold coin

- The Pfizer drug company was founded in Brooklyn

- The U.S. Territory of Minnesota was organized

- A patent was granted for an envelope-making machine

- Joseph Couch patented a steam-powered percussion rock drill

- Zachary Taylor was sworn in as the twelfth American president

- California petitioned to be admitted into the Union as a free state

- The gas mask was patented by L.P. Haslett

Zachary Taylor.

Selected Prices

Bran, Bushel $1.84
Cabin, with Acre of Land $1,725.00
Cigars, Box $138.00
Dinner, Tavern $8.63
Dog House $1.38
Goose $10.12
Malt, Barrel $28.75
Medicine to Cure Drunkenness, Bottle $23.00
Thermometer $54.50
Yacht $690,000

America is a poem in our eyes; its ample geography dazzles the imagination.

—Ralph Waldo Emerson, 1843

"Black Walnut," *North American Review*, Boston, Massachusetts, October 1844:

The Black-walnut, the nut of which is so highly esteemed for the dessert, is a tree of most imposing appearance, and, when at its full size, scarcely inferior to the Oak and Chestnut in some of its effects in landscape. . . . The wood is very beautiful when used for cabinet-work, and seems to be rapidly superseding that of mahogany for a variety of purposes. For its rich color and high polish, we cannot hesitate to think it decidedly superior to that long established favorite; and we gladly take this opportunity to express the wish, that it may be much more generally introduced for the interior finishing of domestic apartments. Its effect, when thus employed, would be unrivaled even by the famous oak wainscoting of old England; and we have no doubt, that, when the graces and amenities of domestic architecture are a little more understood, it will come into common use among us.

"To One Beloved," by J.D. Prentiss, *The Bridal Wreath*, a wedding souvenir edited by Percy Bryant, Boston, 1845:

I think of thee when morning springs
  From sleep, with plumage bathed in dew,
And, like a young bird, lifts her wings
  Of gladness in the welkin blue.

And, when, at noon, the breath of love,
  O'er flower and stream is wandering free,
And sent in music from the grove,
  I think of thee, I think of thee.

I think of thee, when soft and wide
  The evening spreads her robes of light,
And, like a young and timid bride,
  Sits blushing in the arms of night.

And when the moon's sweet crescent springs,
  In light, o'er heaven's own deep, waveless sea
And stars are forth like blessed things
  I think of thee, I think of thee

I think of thee; that eye of flame,
  Those tresses falling bright and free,
That brow where 'Beauty writes her name,'
  On fancy rush; I think of thee.

Travels in the United States in 1847, by Domingo Sarmiento, 1847:

Since, as they say, "As the nest, so the bird," I will say a word or two about the villager. If he is a tavern keeper, a storekeeper, or belongs to some other sedentary profession, his daily costume will consist of the following articles: patent-leather boots, pants and coat of black cloth, a black satin waistcoat, a tie of twilled silk, a small cloth cap, and, hanging from a black cord, a gold charm in the shape of a pencil or a key. At the end of this cord, and deep in his pocket, is the most curious item of a Yankee's dress. If you want to study the transformations the watch has gone through from its invention down to our time, ask a Yankee you meet what time it is. You will see fossil watches, mastodon watches, haunted watches, watches which are the home of vermin, and inflated watches three stories high with drawbridges and the secret stairways which you descend with a lantern in order to wind up.

"New York in the Olden Time," *The Ladies Wreath,* New York, 1848:

Young women of all ranks, spun and wove most of their own apparel, and though they dressed gaily when going out to visit, or to attend church, never failed to change their dress for the home-made short- gown and petticoat on their return home. This was always done on Sunday evenings, when a visit from their beaux was a matter of course, as it was considered their best recommendation to be seen as frugal, and in readiness for any domestic avocation. The young men and boys did the same thing, and thus a Sunday dress lasted a whole lifetime, or de-scended as an heir-loom from generation to generation, for fashions never altered.

Journal of Sarah F. Davidson, Charlotte, North Carolina, February 7, 1837:

Has been a delightful spring-like day—walked in the garden—commenced gardening—and remained out nearly all day attending to the pruning of fruit trees and clearing away the decayed vegetation of the past year—derived pleasure from observing the varied hues of the smoke and flame arising from the burning masses for heterogeneous and decayed matter—also observed some traces of renewed vegetation and could not but indulge in place in pleasing anticipation of approaching spring. After tea attended to the instruction of our young servants—being much troubled and perplexed (relative to my duty) on this subject—and believing religious instruction cannot be well communicated without some knowledge of letters—about six weeks ago—I commenced learning them to read—and reading to them small portions of Scripture and requiring answers individually on reading each verse—It is a source of peculiar gratification to find my feeble efforts to instruct has already produced a good effect—and that the hours further spent by them in play and strolling the villages has been devoted to acquiring knowledge. By their faithful attendance and application—they can now—repeat the Lord's Prayer—His commandments—(and in the same degree understand) also can answer all the prominent questions which may be asked in the first and second chapters of Genesis—and the first and second chapters of Matthew and progressing as fast as I can recently expect in learning to read.

February 22, 1837:

I received a letter from my friend S. Williamson with a flattering promise that I should soon have the pleasure of enjoying her society—also my friend Ada and Harriet—Sarah—letter gives the cheering intelligence of newborn souls—among them my cousin M. M-Culloh. In praying for my kindred M. has been ever remembered though not in special manner—Never do I bow before a mercy seat without pleading for relatives friends and acquaintances. The work of grace has commenced oh may it continue until all and each shall be made anew Christ Jesus. She says several members are added to the Church and the people—particularly the young are much interested in the subject of religion. When will the people of Charlotte awake from their drowsy slumbers—and live and act for Eternity—this world this wicked world with its transient—fleeting enjoyments occupies too much of our time and thoughts. I am guilty and can say nothing to any one as reproof.

"Daguerreotypes," *Godey's Lady's Book*, Philadelphia, May 1849:

If our children and children's children to the third and fourth generation are not in possession of portraits of their ancestors, it will be no fault of Daguerreotypist of the present day; for, verily, they are limning faces at a rate that promises soon to make every man's house a Daguerrean Gallery. From little Bess, the baby, up to great-grandpa, all must now have their likenesses; and even the sober friend, who heretofore rejected all the vanities of portrait-taking, is tempted to sit in the operator's chair, and quick as thought, his features are caught and fixed by a sunbeam. In our great cities, a Daguerreotypist is to be found in almost every square; and there is scarcely a county in any state that has not one or more of these industrious individuals busy at work catching "the shadow" ere the "substance" fade. A few years ago it was not every man who could afford a likeness of himself, his wife or his children; these were luxuries known to those only who had money to spare; now it is hard to find the man who has not gone through the "operators" hands from once to a half-a-dozen times, or who has not the shadowy faces of his wife and children done up in purple morocco and velvet, together or singly, among his household treasures. Truly the sunbeam art is a most wonderful one, and the public feel it is a great benefit!

The Santa Fe Trail, by A Wislizenus, Memoir of a Tour of Northern Mexico in 1846 and 1847:

Traveling this morning quietly over the plain, we heard in the distance of several miles a singular, awful noise, like a combination of falling rocks, breaking of bones, screams of anguish and cries of children, but the impression which the mysterious concert had made upon my ears was but surpassed by the surprising effect, when with my eyes I descried the wonderful machine whose actions produced that unearthly music—a Mexican carreta. Imagine to yourself the cart, made without any nails or iron of any kind, with two solid wheels formed out of the trunk of a big tree, and in circumference rounded, or rather squared, and with a frame of ox-skins or sticks fastened together by rawhide, and this machine then put in motion by three yoke of oxen, and carrying a load, which on a better vehicle one animal could transport and much faster and easier, and you will have an idea of the primitive and only known vehicle used in northern Mexico.

"Mail," Alexis de Tocqueville, *Democracy in America,* 1831:

I traveled along a portion of the frontier of the United States in a sort of cart, which was termed the mail. Day and night we passed with great rapidity along the roads, which were scarcely marked out through immense forests. When the gloom of the woods became impenetrable, the driver lighted branches of pine, and we journeyed along by the light they cast. From time to time we came to a hut in the midst of the forest; this was a post-office. The mail dropped an enormous bundle of letters at the door of this isolated dwelling, and we pursued our way at full gallop, leaving the inhabitants of the neighboring log houses to send for their share of the treasure.

Two Years Before the Mast, by Richard Henry Dana, 1840:

No one has ever been on distant voyages and after a long absence received a newspaper from home, who cannot understand the delight that they give one. . . . Nothing carries you so entirely to a place, and makes you feel so perfectly at home, as a newspaper.

Letter from Theodore Tilton to His Wife:

Oh, how my heart abounds at the sight of your handwriting. . . . There is something in the exchange of letters that ranks next to the greeting of palm to palm. When I receive one of your letters the sheet seems to contain more than you were writing; it is something which has been touched by your hand, which has caught a pulse of your feeling, and which represents more than the words can possibly say.

1849 NEWS FEATURE

Letter, Denial of Justice to the Cherokees, *Newark Daily Advertiser*, March 14, 1849:

We are enabled, by a kindness of the reverend gentleman to whom it was addressed, to take the annexed extracts from a letter just received in the city from William P. Ross, Esq., a delegate of the Cherokee Nation, now about to leave Washington and return to his home, bearing to his long-suffering and much injured tribe another repetition of the old story of neglect and wrong, so often received by them, as the only answer from this great, rich, civilized and Christian people, for their humble and touching appeals for simple justice.

Washington, DC, March 11.

Your letter reached me on the fifth of March, when I felt depressed and disappointed at the failure of measures which I spent night and day to accomplish—measures founded on right, strengthened by long withholden justice, demanded by humanity, and favored, up to the last night of Congress, by the prospect of success. Yes, we have been again put off, disappointed, deprived of our rights for two long years more, and that by mere pretexts and excuses, which, if practiced between man and man, would lead to inevitable disgrace, between nations of equal strength, to something serious and destructive. But so it is. We are small and insignificant, unable to help ourselves, and must patiently, if not graciously, submit to the wrongs which we cannot avert.

At the unsolicited call of the authorities of my country, I left my home on the 20th December, and came on at a time when my associate became alarmed and left me, to return home, on account of the cholera, that was then raging in New Orleans, and prevailing along the great thoroughfare of travel—to settle up the Cherokee business with the Government, and secure payment for our country east of the Mississippi, which the U.S. have been in the full enjoyment of more than ten years, for which they promised prompt payment by the Treaty of 1846.

Shortly after my arrival here about the middle of January, the Senate put an amendment to the Indian Appropriations Bill to the House for our benefit, or more than

$1,200,000 in part payment for our demands. With this amendment, the bill was returned to the House, referred to the Committee on Ways and Means, where it was kept until within a day or two of the close of the session. It was then reported, so amended as would have kept us out of the money for several months, even if it had passed. The House itself added a still further amendment requiring us, before any money should be paid, to relinquish entirely a large and just claim against the government. In this form, and coupled with authority for the government to make a new loan of five million dollars to raise the means for our benefit, it passed the House, but was again returned to the Senate. The Senate refused to concur in the amendments; a committee of conference was appointed; that committee was equally divided, and could not agree; and so finally to save the bill, each House agreed to recede from its amendment, and the bill passed, leaving us entirely out, and putting us off to a "more convenient season," if one should ever arrive.

Under these circumstances, my long absence from my family and private business, and the longer withheld justice for my people, I feel the disappointment not a little. As soon as a result was known, it was my intention to have left immediately for home, but I determined, a day or two after his introduction to office, to address General Taylor a letter on our business. I did so and have since been waiting for a reply. So soon as that comes to hand, I will pack up my "duds" and make my way, as best as possible, toward "sun down."

I went to see the new president along with a countryman and a Choctaw. When introduced he received us very cordially and said we were the people among whom he had been. I expressed to him the gratification Cherokees felt that he was now President of United States. He thanked us repeatedly and seemed to feel deeply. I like the old man much, and heard him make a speech to the Redskins long before he ever dreamed of the Presidency. He was sometime in command of our frontier, and was the best officer we ever had there. He is well acquainted with the border, with many of our people, and I have great hope that he will make a good and just President. He cannot be worse toward us than some late presidents have been, and there is every reason to hope that he will be better. So may it be, is my hope and expectation.

William P. Ross, Esquire

1850–1859

At the mid-century mark, two distinct, dissimilar social structures had developed within the United States: one in the South and the other in the North. The agricultural South was focused on crops such as cotton, tobacco, sugar and rice, often grown with slave labor. The North, while still tied to farming, had diversified its economy with commerce and manufacturing, fueled by low-wage labor. Many came to believe that the two regions were so divergent that holding the Union together might prove impossible. The politics of fear invaded nearly every issue.

Fittingly, the period began with the Compromise of 1850, brokered by Henry Clay in a futile attempt to end sectional controversy and preserve the nation's unity. To the Southerners he offered the reenactment of a drastic fugitive slave law that mandated the return of runaways, plus the organization of the New Mexico and Utah territories. For the North, Clay called for admission of California as a free state and abolition of the slave trade in Washington, DC, the nation's capital. It proved to be a measure that merely delayed the actual outbreak of the Civil War for a decade.

At the same time the national economy was growing in a variety of ways. As a result of natural increase, immigration and the absorption of people living in acquired territories, 31.4 million people lived in the United States—six times more than in

1800. Similarly, labor productivity rose impressively. By the end of the decade, one person could produce twice as much wheat as in 1800, and more than four times as much cotton cloth. Between 1840 and 1860, the nation's agricultural output more than doubled in value, and its mining and manufacturing industries tripled.

In the North, the economy was aided by the wage earner class, often immigrants who flocked to industrial America. Thanks to this massive influx, foreign-born workers represented about 15 percent of employees in the 1850s. Industrial production increased 50 percent from 1850 to 1860, but this dependence on manufacturing had its downside. When the nation's economy dipped in 1857, cotton textile employment for the state of Rhode Island, for example, fell by 68 percent and iron works employment by 43 percent. Wages shrank by the same rate. Skilled workers accustomed to $1.25 a day saw their pay plummet to $0.60 per day. Yet, remittances by immigrants to relatives and friends in the Old World—often used to pay the cost of passage to discover America themselves—continued to grow during this period.

The decade before the Civil War also saw the expansion of slavery as Southern planters moved west to Louisiana, Tennessee, Arkansas and Texas. In the 1850s, the American South produced five million bales of cotton annually, or two thirds of the cotton grown in the world. Most was sold to the British, whose textile mills clothed Europe, America and East Asia. This made the South highly dependent on English manufacturing needs and thus made small, single crop cotton planters highly vulnerable to fluctuations in cotton prices. In 1850, 31 percent of the Southern white population owned slaves; 10 years later the percentage was down to 26 percent.

During this period, too, ambition and discovery were populating the frontier West, unleashing an army of eager fortune hunters willing to leave the past behind, often on a whim. The discovery of gold in California in 1849 had touched off a dramatic migration west by boat, by horse and by rail. In a similar fashion, earlier events had dispersed the national population when the discovery of salt mining deposits in Michigan drew workers from Cape Cod and copper mining drew unprecedented settlers to Colorado. This western expansion also accelerated the building of railroads nationwide. Ironically, the dramatic rise in rail construction, which drove the economy during this period, was largely funded by foreign investors, primarily the Germans and British.

In 1850, schools were also undergoing a revolutionary change. Based on a reform movement begun in the 1830s, most northern and western communities endorsed and supported free education, including compulsory attendance for students and training of teachers, along with a curriculum suitable for a changing workplace. At the outbreak of the Civil War in 1861, the United States could justifiably boast the most complete and highly developed public school system in the world.

1852 PROFILE

German immigrant Albert Hoffman began his career in 1839 as a 15-year-old apprentice to a wholesale liquor dealer.

Life at Home

- Albert Arnold Hoffman was born on July 14, 1824, in Borringhausen, a hamlet of Damme, in the Grand Duchy of Oldenburg, Germany.
- He was the fourth of six surviving children of Martha and Julius Hoffman; three additional children died in early childhood.
- As Albert grew, conditions in Germany became precarious; economic opportunities dissolved in the boggy region near the Netherlands as crop failures multiplied.
- Few job prospects and a lack of available land to farm drove many Germans to leave their homeland for America, a much advertised land of plenty.
- As the family was preparing to emigrate to America in February 1833, Albert's mother died.
- Albert knew her grave would be well tended by his oldest sister, and thus they could leave.
- His father sold the family farm to purchase passage and sail from Bremerhaven, Germany, with five of his children, aged nine to 16.
- The passage from Germany to Baltimore, Maryland, cost 35 talers per person, required six weeks, and was fraught with danger.
- They left behind both a rye field on the 12-acre family farm and their heritage; when they reached the United States, they anglicized their given names to be more American.
- Like many of their neighbors from Damme, the Hoffmans originally settled in Minster, Ohio, 100 miles north of Cincinnati.
- Albert's first job, at age 13, was as a waterboy on the Miami and Ohio Canal.

Albert Hoffman was a successful liquor merchant.

- In 1839, 15-year-old Albert moved to Cincinnati where he began as an apprentice with Edmund Dexter, wholesale liquor dealer and English immigrant.
- After several decades in the whiskey trade, Edmund Dexter had developed extensive contacts all the way to the East Coast; his mansion on the corner of 4th Street and Broadway was one of Cincinnati's premier showplaces and proof of his success.
- The business involved the buying, mixing and distribution of barrels of "white dog" liquor made by Ohio farmers from their surplus corn.
- For farmers, barrels of liquor were easier to store and ship than corn, which was bulky and subject to mold or mouse infestations.
- Since each individual farmer produced only a few barrels of the raw, colorless liquid, whose taste and alcohol content varied widely, it was the job of whiskey dealers to refine, combine and distribute a blended product.
- Albert was to learn the business from the ground up: where and when to buy; who could be trusted; how to calculate his profit margins in his head while still negotiating with the buyer or seller.
- Soon after Albert arrived in Cincinnati, he took a room at the Watkins Boardinghouse located two blocks from his new workplace.

Whiskey trade community in Cincinnati, Ohio.

- The boardinghouse was run by Mrs. Evelyn Watkins, a widow whose home was her principal means of support, and her two daughters; meals and lodging cost $3.00 per week per person.
- Cincinnati boasted 200 boardinghouses in 1840, more than a third of which were run by female proprietors.
- Albert shared both the room and a double bed with Michael Redd, a grocer; this was the customary arrangement at boardinghouses.
- While traveling, he had shared his sleeping quarters with up to five men and found it smelly and noisy.
- After work, residents met in each other's rooms or gathered in the large parlor where they entertained themselves in various amusements.
- Favorite pastimes included the card games euchre, casino and whist, a predecessor to bridge involving four players divided into two partnerships.
- Another popular game was "spin the trencher," which involved a player spinning a round wooden plate on its edge and calling the name of another player who was then required to catch the plate before it stopped spinning.
- Betting was often involved.
- During his first 10 years in Cincinnati, Albert also spent his time attempting to become a well-rounded gentleman; he took both French and music lessons.
- His music lessons were taught by a flutist who also performed with some of the leading talents of the day; the cost was $6.00 per three lessons.
- His French lessons were taught by Charles Moulinier, who was born in Italy in 1823 and emigrated to Cincinnati in 1840.
- Albert scheduled much of his day around his music and French lessons and proudly recorded his progress in his journal.
- But after 10 years of apprenticeship, 25-year-old Albert grew restless and was ready to strike out on his own in St. Louis, Missouri, which was one of the fastest-growing cities in the Midwest.
- Fully one-third of the population of St. Louis was German-speaking, which buoyed Albert's expectations for success.
- Albert chose as his partner John Edgar Drach, a tobacconist who had immigrated to Cincinnati in 1842.
- John's brother had already partnered with Albert's brother Heinz in a successful tobacco business in Cincinnati.
- But a move to an unknown city was intimidating and frightening.

Tobacco was the business of Albert's brother, Heinz.

Life at Work

- By 1849, after 10 years of work in the liquor trade, Albert Hoffman was experienced and savvy.
- While working for Edmund Dexter, he was often entrusted to work alone with thousands of dollars and highly complex business decisions.
- He loved and appreciated Edmund, but knew it was time to test his own skills.
- However, his decision was not without risk, starting with the trip itself.
- When Albert booked his fare to St. Louis via the steamboat *Thomas Jefferson*, he also composed a will that left $200, along with most of his favorite possessions, to various relatives.

Edmund Dexter.

- To his brother Henry he left his guitar; his flute and flute music was designated to brother Frank on the condition they would never be sold, and his piano was given to his sister.
- This trepidation was well founded, he believed; the average life of a steamboat was about four years.
- Collisions, boiler explosions and faulty construction made these vessels a dangerous mode of transportation; in 1849 alone, 88 steamboats were totally destroyed.
- During the trip, ice ran "very thick, sometimes covering the entire river, and of a solidity that made the boat shake like a leaf to go through it."
- Twice the boat became stuck in the ice.
- Eventually Albert's trip to St. Louis in February 1849 was successful, but his reception was not; his prospective landlord, himself an occasional whiskey merchant, refused to rent his building as promised, fearing competition.
- Unable to find a suitable building to lease, Albert and John decided to petition their friends and relatives for a $1,000 loan to build their own establishment on 3rd Street near the market—on the same day Zachary Taylor was inaugurated president of the United States, Albert duly recorded.
- Once the loan money started to flow in from Ohio, the partners contracted to build their store for $2,635 including labor and materials.
- But they were immediately slowed by the cholera epidemic that had arrived in St. Louis at almost the same time as Albert.
- Cholera was caused by contaminated food or water and killed its victims through severe dehydration, normally caused by diarrhea.
- On Sunday, May 20, 1849, Albert recorded, "The cholera at present is raging more or less throughout all the western cities. Here it continues with unabated force. This week 160 deaths from it alone."
- From May through July 1849, 7,000 people died and thousands more fled into the countryside, leaving the city of 45,000 largely deserted.

Steamboats were a dangerous form of transportation.

- Albert's high expectations for immediate success foundered with the fleeing residents of St. Louis.
- But the unmarried Albert was not entirely idle: "I came very near to making a fool of myself this week, in fact I did. I went with Herzer to an accommodation House. Fortunately every strumpet was engaged, and I had no opportunity of committing any folly."
- On another occasion, Albert got into such a heated argument while playing dominos at Bach's beer house that he recorded the entire incident in his journal and amended his will to "devote all my means to the prosecution of the person who shall murder me."
- Throughout the summer of 1849, Albert struggled with events beyond his control: "Yesterday was another great jubilee day for the cholera. Among the important deaths, important to us, was our builder D. Aufdenfelde. Poor fellow was suddenly taken about 12 and [by] 7 p.m. he was a corpse."
- By the time the residents of St. Louis returned, most were pleased by the opportunity to visit the newly opened whiskey and tobacco shop; Albert and his partner were $4,000 in debt and needed the business.
- Two years of struggle followed.
- In 1851 Albert recorded that his income was about the same as when he was a clerk in Cincinnati: $700 per year.
- Disregarding difficulties and considering marriage the full mark of a man, Albert became engaged to Elise Vollrath, a young woman who boarded at the house of his partner.
- On January 29, 1851, he recorded, "I am now worth 5,000 dollars. With my wife I receive nothing. Consequently all my property is honestly my own, I have not married for money or gain."
- On July 31, 1851, they were married at the Drach home.
- By the time Albert Hoffman Jr. was born in March 1852, his father could breathe again.

Considering marriage the full mark of a man, Albert married Elise Vollrath at age 27.

Life in the Community: Cincinnati, Ohio, and St. Louis, Missouri

- During the first decade Albert Hoffman lived in America, from 1833 to 1843, nearly 200,000 Germans entered the United States primarily through the ports of Baltimore, New York, Philadelphia and New Orleans.

St. Louis, Missouri.

Cincinnati, Ohio.

- Thousands traveled to Cincinnati, Ohio, where the northeast quadrant of the city became an ethnic enclave, 25 percent of Cincinnati's citizens having been born in German states.
- The German neighborhood was reached by crossing the Miami and Erie Canal; thus, locals began to refer to it as "the Rhine."
- The entire neighborhood then became known as the "over the Rhine" community.
- Encompassing nearly 100 city blocks, the neighborhood comprised churches, schools, markets and theaters.
- Gothic lettering on signs gave the streetscape a European look; four German-language newspapers united the community.
- Scores of vereine, or societies, were formed to cover every interest.
- The bachelor culture of the time was castigated by newspapers and periodicals which condemned the young unmarried men who moved in society "totally free of responsibility."
- German-born men like Albert Hoffman attended theater performances, frequented taverns and danced into the wee hours, earning themselves the name "rogue elephants."
- For nighttime entertainment, Albert had access to taverns such as Napoleon, the William Tell, Black Bear and the US Tavern.
- Popular theater productions included *King Lear* and *A Midsummer Night's Dream* at the National Gallery and musical recitals at the Athenaeum.
- The Mercantile Library provided the classics and new novels for those who wanted to read; the Turner Association was a German community organization dedicated to physical fitness through disciplined exercises.

Cincinnati and St. Louis were home to large, lively and robust German populations.

- The people of the "over the Rhine" community were considered extremely patriotic and eagerly celebrated all national holidays, including war victories.
- When presidential candidates visited the Queen City, as Cincinnati was known, Germans turned out in large numbers and conducted lively debates over drinks and cigars.
- St. Louis also claimed a robust German population.
- The Germans who fled the revolution in their homeland settled in such numbers that by the early 1850s, city ordinances had to be translated into German for their benefit.
- In 1850 the population of St. Louis was 77,860, nearly five times its size in 1840.

Historical Snapshot
1852

- Ohio made it illegal for women and children under 18 to work more than 10 hours a day
- Gun manufacturer Smith & Wesson was founded in Springfield, Massachusetts
- Louis Napoleon established the Second French Empire and called himself Emperor Napoleon III
- In Ireland, Edward Sabine showed a link between sunspot activity and changes in Earth's magnetic field
- The commercial value of Concord grapes in humid eastern states was discovered
- Dog tags were introduced
- James Joule and Lord Kelvin demonstrated that a rapidly expanding gas cools
- Emma Snodgrass was arrested in Boston for wearing pants
- The first Holstein cow was transported to North America on a Dutch ship on which sailors had requested milk
- Massachusetts ruled that all school-age children must attend school
- Harriet Beecher Stowe's *Uncle Tom's Cabin* was published in Boston
- Wells, Fargo & Company was established in San Francisco
- The first British public toilet was opened in London
- Miami Medical College in Cincinnati was founded
- Anti-Jewish riots broke out in Stockholm
- The first Chinese immigrants arrived in Hawaii
- The *Uncle Sam* cartoon figure made its debut in the *New York Lantern* weekly
- The first edition of Peter Mark Roget's Thesaurus was published
- Antonius Mathijsen developed plaster of Paris casts for setting fractures

Selected Prices

Boat Passage, Boston to Liverpool $1,680.00
Book, *Elements of Algebra* $13.86
Castor Oil, Bottle $3.00
Fiddle and Box $31.50
Land, 650 Acres $90,000
Lantern $16.80
Rail Fare, New York to Baltimore $126.00
Slave, Male, 14 Years Old $17,600
Spittoon $2.20
Steer $88.00

Diary of Joseph J. Mersman, Whiskey Merchant:

Saturday, April 1, 1848, Cincinnati, Ohio:

All fools day I fortunately escaped becoming the subject to it. Business kept me employed the whole day. After supper I had my French lesson. . . . I gave up my old guitar and kept my five dollars. From there went directly home. Expense $.15 c
Paid boarding and washing to April 2. $15.80

Monday, April 3, 1848, Cincinnati, Ohio:

Pleasant weather. Business also very pleasant, being able to do it all with ease, and have a little time left for my French study. I took my book home with me intending to study, but found it impossible to refuse Mr. Brown's invitation to accompany him to the Antheneaum to see Mrs. Wilkinson. She appeared in *The Wife*. I did not like her acting so well as I anticipated, having seen Mrs. Mowett in that beautiful piece. By the bye Mrs. W. is a very pretty little woman. This pretty fact made her find more favor with me, then her acting would have done. We did not stay to see the end of the evenings entertainment went home at 11. Smoked until half past. Expense 15c.

Wednesday, April 12, 1848, Cincinnati, Ohio:

Excellent weather. Business was very good to day. The evening I passed at home entirely, excepting only a walk to the alehouse immediately after my French lesson with Moulinier. Returned directly home. Smoked till 10 o'clock. then retired weary and sleepy. Expenses $.20

Sunday afternoon March 30, 1851, St. Louis, Missouri:

It is now two months since I married, and I can not but acknowledge that so far I prefer married to single life. It is true there are now and then little differences between self and wife. She has, unfortunately some of her good fathers quarrelsome and unpleasing disposition, but with kindness mixed with a delicate firmness which every true woman must admire in her husband, except where she wants to rule and dominate over him, and this my wife can, I dare say, already discover that she can never hope to do with me. That she loves me devotedly I have no reason to doubt, and every one to believe, and upon average I am happy as I expected. . . .

continued

Diary of Joseph J. Mersman, Whiskey Merchant . . . *(continued)*

Until lately I've entertained the idea of going to Cincinnati with my wife. Had already written my relations to this effect, but have now changed my mind. I would not burden my good brother-in-law Kattenhorn to this effect after his unbrotherly conduct, and Henry I fear has no accommodation for us. And the expenses are also serious hindrance, having to take much money out of the business. The best way to replace it is to save what we have and to use every exertion of making more. . . .

Jenny Lind concluded last week here her brilliant career. She gave five concerts. I was to none. Saved $10 at least. All our benevolent societies have enjoyed her bounty. The German Fräulein Verein of which by the bye my good mother-in-law is president, received $250. Her total donations amount to about 5,000 dollars.

Jenny Lind.

"Mutton Suet as a Household Remedy," *The General Scott Almanac,* Philadelphia, Pennsylvania, 1853:

It is very vexing and annoying, indeed, to have one's lips break out with cold sores, but like the measles, it is far better to strike out than to strike in. A drop of warm mutton suet applied to the sores at night, just before retiring will soon cause them to disappear. This is also an excellent remedy for parched lips and chapped hands. It should be applied at night in a liquid state, and be well rubbed and heated before a brisk fire, which often causes a smarting sensation, but the roughest of hands, by this treatment, will often be restored to their natural condition by one application. If everyone could but know the healing properties of so simple a thing as a little mutton suet, no housekeeper would ever be without it. Get a little from your butcher, fry it out yourself, run into little cakes, and put away ready for use. For cuts and bruises it is almost indispensable, and where there are children there always are plenty of cuts and bruises. Many a deep gash that would have frightened most women into sending for a physician at once, I have healed with no other remedy in a little mutton suet and plenty of good castile soap. A wound should always be kept clean, and the bandages changed every day or every other day. A drenching of warm soap suds from the purest soap that can be obtained is not only cleansing but healing; then cover the surface of the wound with a little bit of old white muslin dipped into melted mutton suet. Renew the drenching and the suet every time the bandages are changed, and you will be astonished to see how rapidly the ugliest wound will heal.

"Remedy for Poison Ivy," *The Farmers Calendar,* Baltimore, Maryland, 1854:

Dissolve sugar of lead a bit the size of a hazelnut in half a teacupful of sweet milk or warm water. Apply as warm as can be easily borne with a soft linty piece of linen rag. Three or four applications are stationed to effect a cure. It is a marvelous cure and by watching closely one can see the fever blisters turned from white to yellow during application. This remedy for ivy poison should prevent a great deal of suffering. It is well where a member of the family is easily poisoned to keep sugar of lead in the house at all time. Let it be labeled and kept where it can be found the moment it is wanted. Keep it well wrapped up that it may not lose its strength.

"Monthly Record of Current Events," *Harper's New Monthly Magazine,* September 1851:

Mr. William R. Ragland, Virginia, who died in 1849, by his last will and testament emancipated all his slaves, 90 in number, leaving to them also the plantation upon which he had resided or, in case it should be made illegal for them to remain upon it, the estate was to be sold, and the proceeds to be employed in settling the slaves elsewhere. The property thus bequeathed was stated to be worth $50,000. The will was contested by the relatives of the testator, but its validity has been established by the Supreme Court sitting in Richmond.

* *

A treaty has been concluded with the Sioux Indians, by which they cede to the United States a tract of land in Minnesota, estimated to contain 21,000,000 acres. They reserved themselves a tract in Upper Minnesota, 100 miles by 20 in extent. They are to receive $305,000 after the removal to the reservation; and an annual payment of $68,000 a year, for 50 years.

* *

During the month of July the number of Immigrants who arrived at the port of New York was 30,034; of whom about 20,000 were from Great Britain and Ireland, 4500 from Germany, and 4700 from France.

* *

In South Carolina a large meeting was held in Charleston, on the 29th of July, but those who are in favor of co-operation for the purpose of resistance, and opposed to separate state action, under present circumstances. John Rutledge, Esq., was chosen chairman. A letter was read from the Honorable Langdon Cheve, approving the object of the meeting, asserting the right of secession, but affirming it would not be "a moral or social one on thepart of one Southern state in reference to sister states of the South." He thought South Carolina to secede, but not alone; and that a union in favor of secession would take place. . . . A series of resolutions was passed, declaring that the measures of The Federal Government, taken in conjunction manifestation of feelings up north,

continued

"Monthly Record of Current Events," . . . *(continued)*

showed a subtle purpose to deprive the southern states of their rank as equals in the Confederacy; and tended to do the abolition of slavery and the establishment of a consolidated government; and the time it therefore come when the Union ought to be dissolved, and a Southern Confederacy formed; but they would still willingly give trial to any scheme proposed by the South, short of dissolution, for reinstating them in their rights. That, as the subject of controversy concerned all the Southern states as much as South Carolina, the true policy to be observed was concert of action; and that separate state action must be deprecated as tending to alienate the other states and thus "prevent the formation of the Southern Confederacy," delay would insure the co-operation of other states; while separate action would place South Carolina in the position of a foreign country; in which case the laws preventing the introduction of slaves in the United States would subject her "practically to the Wilmot Proviso in its worst form."

* *

A convention of free people of color has been held at Indianapolis, Indiana, to deliberate upon matters relating to their interest and prospects as a class. The convention while insisting upon their rights to remain in this country, passed resolutions affirming the expediency of emigrating, provided that the laws should become intolerably burdensome to them. Among the places mentioned as suitable for them to colonize were Canada, Mexico, Jamaica, and Central America. They expressed a strong disinclination to emigrate to Liberia.

* *

GREAT BRITAIN

The American Steamer Baltic arrived in New York August 16, having made the passage in nine days, 14 hours, 20 minutes apparent time; or, adding the difference of time between the ports, in nine days, 18 hours and 45 minutes, actual time. This is the shortest passage ever made.

* *

As the session of Parliament approaches its close, the proceedings begin to assume some features of interest. The bill to alter the form on the oath of agitation, so as to allow Jews to sit in Parliament passed the Commons with little opposition, its opponents contending themselves with expressing their abhorrence of the measure but leaving to the Peers the ungracious task of excluding from the other House members duly chosen, whom that House was anxious to receive. . . . In the Upper House, as was foreseen, the bill was lost.

"Literary Notices," *Harper's New Monthly Magazine*, September 1851:

The True Remedy for the Wrongs of Women, by Catharine E. Beecher, published by Philips, Sampson, and Co. This is not a controversial work. it is rather an eloquent plea for the education of woman. It contains little that is original, and nothing radical. The enterprise of the author of the promotion of education in the West is its main topic. Her narrative of the annoyances and perplexities to which she's been subjected in the prosecution of her plan slightly is graphic, and not without a tinge of bitterness. The volume displays throughout a masculine intellect, and sufficient energy of character for a field-marshal.

Episodes of Insect Life. A second volume of this fascinating chronicle of insect history is issued by J.S. Redfield, which will command the public favor no less than the former volume, by its sparkling delineations of rural life, and its beautiful illustrations of animal economy. The author has a decided genius for delicate observation; nothing escapes him, however minute, the study of insect idiosyncrasy; and with a rich vein of poetic sentiment, and a luxuriant bloom of all kindly and natural household feelings, he throws a delightful coloring imagination around his descriptions, though without impairing his evident fidelity to nature. The very titles in his chapters have a delicious quaintness that leads every one who opens the book to obtain a further taste of its quality.

1854 PROFILE

Isaac Sheppard, who was unsatisfied being a farmer like his father, decided to head to California to try his luck at gold mining.

Life at Home

- For two years Isaac Sheppard had been mining for gold with the hopes of finding extraordinary riches along the rivers and streams of California.
- Though he found some gold, the wealth he had anticipated when he left Plymouth, Vermont, after his twenty-first birthday hadn't arrived.
- The fourth oldest out of five children and the younger of two boys, he did not want to follow his father's life as a farmer.
- The routine of farm life bored him.
- Each year Isaac could anticipate when to plough the fields, plant the crop, shear the sheep and conduct the harvest—all without the strong sense of personal accomplishment that his father enjoyed.
- It was while washing the sheep in a brine to kill ticks that Isaac first discussed the idea of gold mining in California with his father.
- His father thought gold mining was a foolish thought and believed it unlikely that hundreds of men were earning $10 a day, as reported in the newspaper.
- One of Isaac's older friends, Clarence, had already left for California to find his wealth.
- Prior to Clarence's departure, Isaac agreed that he would write and share news of Vermont.
- It took seven months before he received a reply from Sacramento.
- Upon opening Clarence's letter, Isaac found a small, flattened golden nugget that weighed less than an eighth of an ounce.
- Although Isaac appraised it at roughly $2.00, it was proof, along with the Clarence's news, that gold was plentiful in California.
- Isaac shared the letter with his friend Daniel Myers, who also expressed excitement when he saw the gold.

Isaac Sheppard left Vermont at 21-years-old to make his fortune in the California gold rush.

Plymouth, Vermont.

- In that instant they both agreed that they would depart for California in the summer.
- To prepare for the expedition, Isaac would read Loomis's *Elements of Geology* out of his parents' sight late in the evening.
- He then could not wait to discuss the various geological indicators where gold resided with Daniel in his spare time.
- By midsummer Isaac informed his father of his plans; the same day the family sold over 1,300 pounds of wool to a Duttonsville factory for $523.60.
- The news upset his father, especially the timing: Isaac intended on leaving in the middle of the haying season.
- After a heated discussion over the journey's dangers and expense, Isaac agreed to assist his father haying for six weeks for $35.
- He later learned from his mother that his father hoped the delay would result in his changing his mind.
- Isaac wrote in his journal, "Owing to Father's peculiar manner of dealing with his children . . . he never would tell them anything about what he would do for them or what he thought best for them to do, until the very last minute . . . I should go anywhere and not be dependent upon anyone."
- Over the next several weeks, Isaac began acquiring his gear for the journey, which included two coats, four stockings, two pants, four shirts, one fur hat, two linen handkerchiefs, a spyglass, a pistol, one pound of bullets, half a pound of powder, a fine comb, a Bible and 80 sheets of letter paper.
- Because he lacked sufficient funds to complete the journey, he borrowed $200 from his older brother Timothy, $140 of it a certificate from the Bank of Rochester.
- He cashed the certificate and received bills from Black River Bank to add to the $172 for the journey.

- By late September, Isaac and Daniel left Plymouth and traveled 15 miles to Ludlow, Vermont.
- There Isaac paid $6.40 for his ticket on the railroad to New York City.
- When they arrived in New York they lodged a couple of nights at the Eagle Hotel at No. 18 Greenwich Street on the city's lower west side.
- Isaac was in awe at the city's size and the fact that over 500,000 people lived in this metropolis.
- On the first day they searched for passage to the Panamanian Isthmus and bought two steerage tickets for $155 each on the steamship *Philadelphia*.
- The day before the ship's departure, Isaac visited part of the Croton Water Reservoir which brought fresh water to New York.
- The distribution reservoir, built in the style of an Egyptian temple, held 20 million gallons of water.
- After touring the water reservoir, Isaac met Daniel at the dock and discovered that Daniel had purchased over $7 worth of the *New York News Daily*.
- Daniel planned to sell the roughly 700 copies in news-starved San Francisco for additional money.
- Life on board the *Philadelphia* was not without incident, especially in the crowded steerage where most of the passengers were located.
- The journey's challenges included the discomfort of the confined steerage space and rough seas, the combination of which created seasickness for many on board.
- Nausea struck Isaac hard and he stayed in bed for several days.
- One morning he awoke terribly sick and vomited a dozen times during the day; after a time, nothing but a yellowish green substance emerged from his stomach.
- Isaac wrote in his journal, "Top of Mizzen mast broke away. I was then on the deck awful sick and did not care much what became of us. Vomited most powerfully and ate nothing today."
- Near the end of the journey to Chagres, he overheard crew members discussing the ship's doctor's diagnosis of smallpox in a passenger and the need to place the passenger in quarantine on the ship's hurricane deck.
- Isaac's reaction was not like that of the other passengers aboard the *Philadelphia*.
- Many feared the chances of an epidemic and wanted to depart.
- To Isaac's benefit he had been inoculated with cow pox a year earlier when an epidemic occurred in Plymouth.
- Fortunately, the ship was only a two-day journey away from Chagres and the quarantine was in place prior to arriving in port.
- Upon their arrival at Chagres, Isaac found the village to be one of the filthiest places he ever saw.
- Situated on a low point of land, several thatched huts with cane sides occupied both sides of the Chagres River.
- Natives arrived with boats to pick up the passengers and deliver them ashore.
- For Isaac and his gear the charge was $2.00 for transport to Chagres.
- Daniel's materials, including the newspapers, cost $2.50 to transport.
- They stayed a couple of days in a bamboo hut for $0.25 each and made travel arrangements to reach Panama on a flat-bottom boat.
- After five days of traveling across the isthmus, Isaac and Daniel arrived in Panama.
- Isaac then booked passage with the Pacific Mail Steamship Company's steamer *California*.

- When he learned that the ship was continually delayed because the mail failed to arrive from other ships, he became frustrated.
- He was paying $2.00 a day for poor lodgings and had to wait an additional three days before leaving for San Francisco.
- En route to California, the ship stopped for coal and water in Acapulco.
- As it approached, the natives came around the ship in boats, some completely naked, with oranges, pineapples, coconuts and bananas to sell.
- Seasickness continued to haunt Isaac and prevented him from buying any of the fruit.
- In addition to Isaac's seasickness, Daniel became sick when the ship left Acapulco.
- He experienced severe fevers and vomiting for the next several days.
- Three days before arriving in San Francisco, Daniel died in the middle of the night.
- Isaac wrote in his journal, "My dear friend has left this earth after suffering a cruel disease and without finding our riches. . . . I am alone and without soul to confide my concerns."
- That morning before breakfast, Isaac attended Daniel Myers's burial at sea on the ship's starboard deck.
- Daniel's body was sewn inside a canvas bag and stretched upon a wooden board that foggy morning.
- The burial service was brief, with only a few words provided by a man who claimed to be a Baptist minister.
- Once done, Daniel's body was disposed into the sea.
- It was several hours later after the fog lifted, the steamer approached San Francisco.
- Upon debarking, Isaac attempted to sell some of Daniel's possessions, even the large stack of newspapers.
- By the end of the afternoon, all the newspapers were sold for $0.10 each and Isaac had over $70.
- Isaac had not changed his clothes in three weeks and decided to celebrate his new fortune that evening.
- After changing his attire, he ate a first-rate supper of wheat bread, butter, toast and tea before going to bed at the Maine Hotel.
- There, the fleas bit like tigers, but he slept well.

Isaac worked along the Sacramento River searching for gold.

Life at Work

- Finding work that paid well was initially a challenge when Isaac disembarked into Sacramento from the steamboat *Lea Bird*.
- Initially he agreed to work for $22 per week up river with a company but was not hired when he arrived late the first day.
- The only work he could find was with a black man who wanted to take on a couple of partners looking for gold.
- He and another fellow, Joseph Jordan from Virginia, agreed.
- Isaac would receive an equal share of the expense and gain from the claim.
- After working for three days, the entire amount of gold found was only worth $1.50.
- Frustrated with little prospects on this agreement, Isaac and Joseph agreed to find another opportunity.
- The pair decided to purchase a small claim along the Sacramento River and pan for gold.
- For the next three weeks, Isaac squatted along the edge of a stream flowing into the Sacramento River with a Mexican-made batea, or bowl.
- He submerged the batea with scooped dirt and gyrated it in an oscillating motion while constantly kneading the dirt with one hand.

Miners in Isaac's camp.

- Over a period of a few minutes, the dirt pile was gradually reduced, leaving behind a few specks of gold mixed with black sand.
- Because the sand could not be separated from the gold, it was left to dry on a cotton sheet next to a fire.
- Since the gold weighed more than the sand, Isaac only needed to blow the dry sand off and collect the gold.
- Each day Isaac collected about $5.00 in gold, but soon realized that was not enough; prices for everyday goods were extremely expensive in California, especially around the prospecting areas.
- The price of materials was mounting due to the high charges for transportation to the mines.
- Bacon cost $0.28 per pound, rice $0.10 per pound, beans $1.50 per bushel, flour $0.18 per pound, vinegar $1.00 per gallon and lumber at $100 per 1,000 feet.
- News became bleaker for miners in early November when Isaac was informed that Sacramento was burnt to the ground and the entire business district was consumed.
- A few days later a large fire consumed Marysville, and by November 10, a great fire consumed the city of San Francisco.
- Isaac was one of the many miners in the camps to hear the rumor that a gang of rascals were in the country and intended to burn every city they could.
- In San Francisco over $10 million in property was destroyed.
- With the destruction in so many cities, provisions in the region grew instantly scarce.
- Prices increased overnight with flour costing $0.27 per pound and lumber climbing to $300 per 1,000 feet.
- With the cost of living rising greatly, Isaac knew he needed to work harder and smarter to make his fortune.
- Both he and Joseph agreed to pool their resources for a larger claim.

Mining gold along Poor Man's Creek for one month, made Isaac $350.

- They inspected one claim that the owner, a Mr. Horan, wanted to sell along the Yuba River.
- All over the property were holes, along with five men digging around the site.
- Mr. Horan wanted to sell it for $500 to be used to return home to Philadelphia.
- He said that he had made his money back plus all expenses, and that the claim had an average yield of $35 to $60 if five men worked the site.
- The owner continued to explain it was currently generating roughly $10 a day, which was still doing well.
- Walking the grounds, Isaac inspected one hole that some men were working.
- He acquired a few buckets full of dirt from the spot and washed it out to discover the prospects of only $0.01 to $0.02 worth of gold.
- A week later they purchased half ownership of a 60-foot claim on Poor Man's Creek for $300, which gave Isaac a quarter of all the profits.
- A month later the property only took out $350 in gold, prompting Isaac and Joseph to sell their ownership for $250 in gold.
- Because they were unfamiliar with the area's attractive prospecting territory, they decided to work as laborers.
- Hopping from company to company, the men worked for $15 to $20 per week, saving their money in a "company purse" to be used for a future claim.
- One forenoon at a work site, Isaac visited a Chinamen's tent and looked over the curious things not commonly found in mining camps.
- The Chinamen showed him their opium pipe, gold scales and the razor which they used to shave themselves.
- The gold scales looked more like steelyards with a pan for gold instead of a hook, and the scale beam was made of ivory.
- The Chinese razor blade was about three inches long; it cut well even when they used it without lather, employing only water in their beards.

- Before Isaac departed, he traded three pieces of Chinese copper money for a cent which he planned to mail home to his family.
- He also thought of placing a small, flattened gold nugget he had discovered.
- In his letter he shared a number of stories, including the easiest discovery he had while in California.
- Isaac wrote that after dinner he was returning to his camp and discovered a small nugget along the road.
- Upon inspection it was worth over $5.00!
- He told his family about his health and activity with others prospecting for gold.
- Other news included the unusual weather conditions, especially the hurricane-like winds that occurred in December.
- When letters and packages arrived with supplies to the camps, a clamor often arose.
- Many hoped for news from friends from home, or even letters from women interested in marrying a man with good prospects.
- Joseph received a steady supply of letters from a number of women in Virginia.
- He had promised to send any lady who wrote him a piece of gold for each letter mailed to him.
- Isaac had not received any letters from home.
- Because much of the population in California was predominantly male, an informal code emerged that a miner would provide a visiting woman a piece of gold if she visited his claim.
- Neither Joseph nor Isaac had the opportunity to offer such a gift to a visitor.
- The only unexpected visitor was an Indian who arrived late one night and pounded on his cabin door.
- Isaac fired his pistol and told him to vamoose, but the Indian only laughed.
- So Isaac knocked him down and told him to leave by kicking him in the seat of his pants as fast as he could.
- The following day Isaac learned from another miner that a number of Indians were trading gold for food or cheap articles from a nearby merchant.
- Isaac visited the merchant and saw that he was selling whiskey, tobacco, raisins and other groceries in exchange for gold.
- The merchant shared a story about one bargain he acquired from an Indian.
- As the merchant was finishing weighing the gold on the scales and counterbalancing them with raisins, the hungry Indian seized the raisins and ran into the woods.
- In exchange for the $0.05 in raisins, he left more than $30 in gold.
- More extreme forms of theft typically occurred in the mining areas.

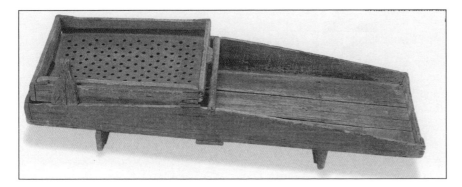

Used by miners to separate gold from the river's sand and dirt.

- In one case two men were almost whipped to death at the Red Banks for stealing $200.
- They confessed that they stole the money but would not honestly tell the place they hid the gold.
- Isaac was not in a whipping mood when someone stole his small money purse from his cabin.
- Fortunately, all that was missing was $4.30 and not his hidden bag with over $650 in gold to purchase a good claim.
- In his journal he wrote, "I may well congratulate myself on not losing any more, but after all I should have liked him better if he had left me a few quarters in change, for it is very scarce."
- Fearing a future theft, Isaac and Joseph decided to put their chances on a claim along Sheldon Canal.
- They purchased the claim for ownership for $500 and spent an additional $100 for materials for the site.
- Items included cradles, buckets, shovels and wood to construct sluicing boxes.
- For the next couple of weeks they dug trenches to bring water from the creek and fill in their manmade pond.
- When needed, they released the water to move down a second trench to their sluice boxes.
- As they filled the sluicing boxes with soil, water flowed over the iron tops dropping small pebbles into the holes.
- The sluicing boxes washed away the earth and captured small gold nuggets in the wooden cleats nailed along the bottom.
- Over the first two months, Isaac was pleased with his investment, for it was yielding $150 to $200 per week, but it was short lived.
- The availability of gold on their property was diminishing and starting to reduce the potential profit.
- Fortunately, water was becoming scarce by the late spring when the river waters diminished from the snow melt in the mountains, thus making the pond water the only item of value on the land.
- Isaac and Joseph agreed to sell their claim to Mr. Jennings for $400 so he could access the water to use for his nearby claims.
- After expenses, the two men calculated a profit of $1,491.85, half of which was owed to Isaac.
- After two years of mining in California and gaining little significant riches in gold, Isaac began to ponder if he should return home to Vermont while he had the money for such a voyage.

Life in the Community: San Francisco, California

- San Francisco was an exciting new city bursting with growth when it was chartered in 1850.
- Its population began to swell with American and international prospectors because of the Gold Rush.
- The population grew from 500 inhabitants to over 20,000 in less than a year.
- San Francisco was originally founded in 1776, not as a town but as a presidio, or fort, and a Catholic mission outpost to evangelize to the region's natives.
- In 1821, as more Spaniards were settling the area, formal streets were planned which created a new community named Yerba Buena.
- Immediately it became an attractive spot for American pioneer settlers.

San Francisco in 1847, before the gold rush.

San Francisco in 1850, bustling with new growth.

- In 1846, at the instigation of American settlers, Alta California was thrown into a state of revolt that was continued by the beginning of the Mexican-American war.
- As a result, Yerba Buena, along with the presidio and mission, were captured by the U.S. Navy.
- Within the year the town was renamed San Francisco.
- When gold was first discovered at Sutter's Mill in 1848, much of the town nearly disbanded in the search for gold.
- San Francisco rebounded and became an international gateway to gold seekers; the growth the city experienced created an uncontrollable rise in demand for goods and services.
- Staples, such as bread, cost upwards of 10 times the value one would pay in New York City.
- Rents and real estate skyrocketed almost overnight.
- One popular gambling house, the Elderado, charged by the month to rent a canvas tent.
- San Francisco's rapid growth also created a change in the city's social order.
- Reports of ex-doctors sweeping streets, ex-ministers becoming gamblers, and bankers waiting tables in cafés became common.
- Sailors, cooks, or day laborers frequently became heads of profitable establishments due to successful mining discoveries.
- For all the influx of peoples from the Pacific Rim and across the continent and Europe, San Francisco was a decidedly masculine town during the early 1850s.

Mining for gold in the hills of San Francisco.

- Tasks normally associated with women were done by men who usually charged a hefty price.
- It was cheaper to send one's clothes to China to be cleaned, or buy new ones than to send them to a local launderer.
- When a woman of class did arrive single in San Francisco, it wasn't long before she found a husband of her picking.
- San Francisco boasted over 100 different daily news publications written in languages such as Spanish, German and French.
- Those struggling for success founded other business ventures.
- Levi Strauss founded a clothing company by making pants from canvas tents, which were sold to prospectors.
- In 1852 Henry Wells and William Fargo began a small banking business buying gold for secure paper notes and an express business of transporting valuables.
- Their bank, being the city's first brick structure, was one of the most trusted in the region and later expanded operations to other mining communities and towns.
- The rapid construction of wooden structures and canvas tents made the city prone to fire; wood was also used to plank the street to prevent the thoroughfares from becoming muddy.
- The worst of the city's fires occurred in 1851 when roughly 16 city blocks were burned, destroying $12 million in real estate.
- But fire wasn't the only problem for San Francisco; another was crime.
- The police services in the city were overwhelmed.
- Gangs were present, composed of men who came in search of gold but resorted to crime; most were ethnically based, such as the Sydney Ducks, a gang whose members all hailed from Australia.
- In 1851 private citizens took matters into their own hands and formed a Committee on Vigilance; the committee arrested, tried and sentenced those elements of society deemed questionable and even helped guard the city against arson.

HISTORICAL SNAPSHOT
1854

- The Crimean War began with Britain and France declaring war on Russia
- The Republican Party was organized at Ripon, Wisconsin, by former Whigs and disaffected Democrats opposed to the extension of slavery
- Mexico's *La Reforma* period began with the issuance of the Plan de Ayutla, which called for the ouster of the dictator Antonio López de Santa Anna
- *New York Tribune* journalist James Redpath traveled through the slave states urging slaves to run away
- Arctic explorer Elisha Kent Kane passed 80 degrees north, the farthest point reached by any expedition
- The U.S. Mint opened a San Francisco branch and paid miners the official rate of $16 per ounce for gold
- The Kansas and Nebraska territories were created
- The Chicago & Rock Island Railroad reached Rock Island in the Mississippi, giving Chicago its first rail link to America's key waterway
- U.S. railroads used telegraph messages for the first time to send information ahead about the location of trains and thus alert engineers to possible safety problems
- A Vatican ruling made the Immaculate Conception of the Virgin an article of faith and established papal infallibility in all matters of faith and morals
- Abraham Lincoln made his first political speech at the Illinois State Fair
- English chemist Alexander William Williamson explained for the first time the function of a catalyst in a chemical reaction
- A cholera epidemic in Chicago killed 5 percent of the city's population

High society in San Francisco.

- The first Young Men's Hebrew Association was founded in Baltimore, Maryland
- U.S. Roman Catholics came under attack by the new American Party which opposed immigration and compared the Roman Catholic Church to Southern slave owners
- A paper mill at Roger's Ford in Chester County, Pennsylvania, produced paper from wood pulp at low cost
- *Walden, or Life in the Woods* by Henry David Thoreau was published
- The first street-cleaning machine in the U.S. was used in Philadelphia
- "The Charge of the Light Brigade" by Alfred Tennyson was written, glorifying Lord Cardigan's actions at the Battle of Balaclava
- "Jeanie with the Light Brown Hair" was a poplar song written by Stephen C. Foster
- The Otis safety elevator impressed visitors to the World's Fair in New York City

Selected Prices

Chamber Bucket $10.00
Cologne, Bottle $2.60
Daguerreotype $4.00
Heifer $100.00
Pie Dish $3.00
Sheep $40.00
Shoes, Child's $5.20
Smelling Salts, Vial $50.00
Umbrella $5.00
Washing Machine $60.00

Description of San Francisco in 1849, Letter from Dr. Charles F. Winslow to Samuel Fisher, June 19, 1849:

This place is growing very fast, houses going up in every direction, shanties and sheds and all other buildings of all manner of materials which can be obtained to make them of. Lumber is so scarce that it sells from 3 to 400 dollars per thousand. Land also is held at enormous prices, so much so that spots 12 feet by 12 feet on which many people have only tents are let for a hundred dollars a month. Prices of land which 2 years ago cost from 15 to 100 dollars are now sold at from 10,000 to 50,000 dollars. Men who 2 years ago were poor are now very rich. But their living here is very expensive.

Ship Advertisement for San Francisco, *New York Herald*, February 19, 1852:

NEW LINE FOR CALIFORNIA—DIRECT FOR SAN FRANCISCO, California—the splendid, 1,500 tons, copper fastened clipper ship GRECIAN will sail from her pier No. 4 East River on Saturday 28th February. For passengers only. This ship is entirely new and is fitted for passengers in the most commodious manner. . . . Stateroom, $2000, Bearth $160. Passengers going by this ship will, after the 21st day of February, be permitted to go on board, and will be free from expense until they arrive at San Francisco. The proprietor of this ship confidently expects to go from port to port in 90 days, as she will not take any freight, except small lots for passengers. . . . Another vessel will follow this immediately. For passage apply to ADAM SMITH, 25 Front Street.

"Chinese in California," *The New York Times,* September 29, 1854:

In California there are about 75,000 thousand Chinamen, generally in San Francisco and the mines. They are the best cooks, washers and servants in that country. They are capable of performing and enduring more labor and fatigue than any other people in that island, and have no spirit to retaliate for the many insults and injuries they receive. They, like the Jews, are a distinct people, and work in squads entirely by themselves in the mines, and save every farthing. Their living is brought from China by their own merchants; and all their trading is done among themselves, and they wear their own peculiar costume; few adopt the dress of this country.

In San Francisco whole streets are occupied by them. They have their own hotel-keepers, wholesale and retail merchants, grocers and physicians. In fact they do their own business independent of others. After obtaining sufficient income to make them independent at home, they usually return. They take little or no notice of strangers, only for their interest; are greatly addicted to gambling, and have gaming establishments and houses of prostitution publicly open day and night, like their neighbors.

Chinese shipping boxes.

"How We Get Gold in California," by a Miner of the Year '49
Harper's New Monthly Magazine, April 1860:

One of the richest *placeres* of California was an extensive sloping flat near the centre of Calaveras Country, at the foot of a range of quartz mountains, separating it from the valley of the Stanislaus, and known as "Carson's Flat." The gold deposits were first struck at this place in 1851. The discoverers sunk a small hole in the shallowest part of the flat where the bed-rock lay about ten feet below the surface. Here they panned out several thousand dollars during the first week; but though their labors were continued with great secrecy, they were speedily tracked and multitudes flocked to the place. A small town was built where Carson's Creek discharged into the Stanislaus, goods came pouring in, Jew clothiers, rum-dealers, and gamblers followed the crowds of working men, and in a month every foot of ground, supposed to be auriferous, was appropriated.

"The Gold Product of 1854," *The New York Times*, March 11, 1854:

The California returns, as indicated by the Mint report for the months of January and February, begin to excite remark, and fears are expressed that the product of 1854 will fall far short of that of the previous year. The Hartford *Times* of yesterday, makes a leader on the subject, drawn with considerable care in reference to the history and sudden decline in production in the Gold regions which preceded California, but not so well advised as to the causes of the apparent fall off from the country for the past few months.

The comparative deposits at the Mint in January and February of the present year, are scarcely a fair criterion of the probable result of the season. The amount was enhanced in January, 1853, by the accidental circumstance, that part of the gold by the second packet, due in December, 1852, was thrown over, and a like circumstance happened in March, 1853, which swelled the receipts to $7,534,000. The proper comparison would be for the eight months of the fiscal or Treasury year, which embrace both Summer and Winter production, viz:

July 1, 1852, to March 1, 1853 . . . . $34,670,000
July 1, 1853, to March 1, 1854 . . . . $30,270,000

An apparent loss of 12.79 percent $4,400,000

1858 Profile

Born to a wealthy family in Philadelphia in 1823, Emily Jameson chose to marry a plantation owner's son and move to low country South Carolina when she was 19 years old.

Life at Home

- Emily Jameson's father was a celebrated lawyer and her grandmother was a noted author of novels; Emily had been raised in an urban world of plenty.
- She was fluent in both French and Italian and fully capable of reading Goethe in German.
- The busy ports of Philadelphia regularly brought exquisite exotic imports from France, Italy and Britain, while local silversmiths, furniture makers and carriage shops turned out some of America's finest quality products.
- Between the 1820 and 1840 Philadelphia and its immediate suburbs had grown from 100,000 residents to well over 200,000; New York, America's major metropolis, went from 123,000 to over 312,000 in the same 20 years.
- In 1842 she married a naval officer from the low country plantations of South Carolina and moved 800 miles, where she lived with her new extended family for six years before building a home of her own.
- William's father owned four plantations on the Santee River, worked by 103 slaves.
- The primary crop was cotton, but they enjoyed homegrown corn, rice, flour, poultry, mutton and vegetables; sugar, coffee, salt, fruits, and candy were available only in Charleston.
- When Emily could obtain raisins from Philadelphia, they were saved for special occasions, along with the chocolate bon-bons created in the shape of fresh strawberries.

Emily Jameson married a plantation owner's son when she was 19 years old.

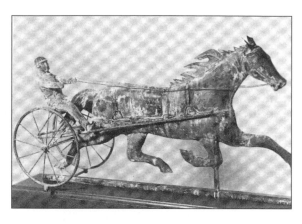

Horseracing was very popular on the plantation.

- Emily often missed the excitement of Philadelphia: "I have had quite enough green trees and roosters and am panting for brick walls and noise. I have been engaged in making preserves and jelly for next winter which I hope will turn out well. The strawberry seems so nice that I must bring on a jar with me."
- In South Carolina Emily quickly discovered that her new family was steeped with rabid hunters, expert farmers and devoted horsemen; a racetrack with regular races sponsored by the upper St. Johns Jockey Club had been constructed on the property.
- "It is ridiculous the care they take of them. The horses eat the most dainty things and have to be rubbed with whiskey and actually drink it too. Every day before they take exercise they eat twenty eggs," she wrote in letters home.
- Fascinated by botany, Emily maintained a regular correspondence concerning flower seeds, cuttings and root clippings.
- "I enclose 12 cents in this letter and wish you would buy me a paper of the best mignonette seed and also a paper of Heart's Ease seed of the large dark purple sort."
- Emily made regular trips away from the plantation, including an annual excursion to Philadelphia aboard a fast sailing regular packet schooner christened *Emma*.
- Trips overland to Virginia with friends included carriage rides across vanishing roads that reappeared as mud swamps and wet adventures aboard slow moving flat-bottom boats.
- "When we were about a quarter of a mile from the carriage a regular mountain storm came up and we were forced to get in again. . . . All four curtained in and the carriage would bump first one side and then the other and the horses would rear and slip and Miss Hannah shrieked and Miss Sally shuddered. Miss Hannah would insist on peeking through the curtains. I told her not to. She would call out, the horse fell then and now my side of the carriage is touching the ground. I could not help laughing but I was very glad to get home safe with only soreness from the jolt."
- Everyone's lives were dictated by the weather, making it a topic for discussion and humor.
- "The weather is quite warm enough to satisfy any reasonable person, planters and farmers not included of course. For those worthy individuals incorporate themselves so thoroughly in the feelings of their crops that instead of enjoying the cool nights and mornings and a blanket at night they're thinking of the shivering cotton which tho it warms others unfortunately cannot warm itself."

Life at Work

- Emily Jameson's home was a large frame four-bedroom house with big central rooms, a front hall, large piazzas and big double chimneys.
- Typical of plantation houses built near a river, it was constructed high off the ground on six substantial brick arches.

Emily Jameson's home.

- It was heated by fireplaces; the occasional Southern wintertime cold spell accompanied by snow could be miserable.
- "The ice was so thick in my room that we could not break it and even in Eliza Manning's room where she kept a fire burning all night, the water froze hard. I assure you it was entirely too cold to be pleasant."
- Meals were plentiful, leisurely and served three times daily.
- Even after a decade of living in the South, Emily continued her Philadelphia custom of eating wheat toast for breakfast and was always amazed at her husband's regular breakfast of hotcakes, waffles, biscuits and hominy.
- A typical dinner party might include vermicelli soup, boiled turkey, celery sauce, bouilli ham, wild duck, omelette soufflé, charlotte polonaise and plum pudding—much of which she helped prepare.
- Emily's passion was for desserts; she generally served three different kinds as a finale to her dinner parties.
- These included puddings made from blackberries and plums served with wine, or sugar-based sauce custards made from sugar, cream and eggs produced on the plantation.
- She was especially proud of her recipe for charlotte Russe, accented by napkins folded in a fan shape and finger glasses with a slice of lemon.
- To prepare these dishes, sugar was an essential ingredient and was kept—along with other staples—under lock and key.
- Therefore, Emily learned to use liberal amounts of molasses, boiled down from homegrown sorfhum.
- Life also centered around children, planting, housekeeping, reading and singing.

Plantation chickens produced eggs for Emily's fancy desserts.

Two of Emily's and William's five children.

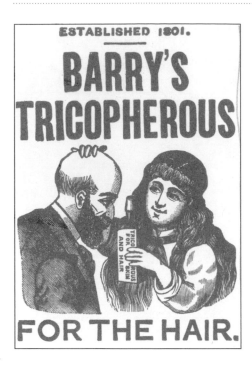

- Emily and William had five children, one of whom had died as a baby; Emily took an active role in teaching the children to read and play the piano.
- William taught them all how to ride at an early age.
- She also carefully recorded effective ways to fashion lard candles, window glass cleaner (pulverized indigo mixed with vinegar wine), and three types of soap: soap with concentrated lye, potash soap and cosmetic soap.
- Her formula for homemade hair wash included lac sulphur and sugar of lead with instructions to wash the whole head twice a week.
- To expel ants, Emily explained how a sugared sponge loaded with ants could be dropped in boiling water.
- During the summer months, when malaria was a constant threat, Emily and the children would rent a house on Sullivan's Island where the sea breezes brought relief from the heat.
- "Very nice fish can be bought at the Break water, nearly in front of our house. A remarkably nice fish called the Whiting and Sheep's-Heads are the most caught. Crabs and shrimps in any quantity tho I have refrained from getting any. Every inch of ground near Charleston is now taken up with English and Northern truck farmers. White potatoes are really splendid and I am provoked that there is no steamer running to Philadelphia for I want so much to send you a barrel."
- A particular pleasure during the summertime trips was reading serialized romance novels, for which Emily drew criticism from her highbrow sister.
- "I would have you to know that I am rather more cultivated and enlightened in my tastes than you think."
- Both William and Emily loved to read; their personal library numbered nearly 600 books including *Jane Eyre*, *The Poetical Works of Robert Southey*, and *Domby and Son* by Charles Dickens—which she found tiresome.
- Charleston had one of the first subscription libraries in the country, and Emily was one of its most loyal members.
- "I can get as many books out as I want," she wrote her parents.
- In addition, William subscribed to several periodicals, including *The Cultivator* at a cost of $10 a year to stay abreast of modern farming techniques.
- Newspapers and magazines such as the *London News* were also favorites and every copy was well circulated to all the other plantations by request.
- Emily especially enjoyed reading copies of the Saturday editions of the Philadelphia papers that described who was getting married and other social details concerning her friends.
- And to stay abreast of Northern fashion, she regularly read *Leslie's Fashion Monthly* which emphasized the Second Empire mode since Napoleon III had revived the French court.
- Long, leisurely days were spent with books and music; family singing, in German and Italian, was accompanied by a mother-of-pearl inlaid guitar from Spain and a Steinway piano imported from Hamburg Germany costing $500.
- To entertain guests, Emily and her sister-in-law would be asked to sing duets, often relying upon Jenny Lind's most popular songs such as "Coming Through the Rye," and "The Last Rose of Summer."

William Jameson taught his children how to ride at an early age.

- Christmas, too, was an important time of celebration for the entire family, attracting more than 40 relatives to her father-in-law's house.
- "This season of Christmas is here. In the first place, staying at Eutaw for nearly a week with a house there full of company involves a good deal of brushing up of the children's wardrobe, then there is to be the grandest Christmas tree ever known which is to be hung with wax lights and all manner of gilt things beside presents for the children. . . . And the servants' Christmas. Not only do I get them all rice, sugar and coffee and William kills a ox for them but there is no end to the business of exchanging. They come to me with eggs and chickens for which they wish me to give them sugar, coffee, wheat flour, tobacco etc. etc. Of course I never refuse, and the consequence is I am at a loss to know what to do with all I have. I have now upwards of 100 chickens straggling about and an immense box of salt filled eggs."

Life in the Community: Charleston, South Carolina

- Charleston, South Carolina, one of America's largest cities with a population of 40,000, was 40 miles away by railroad, plus a 10-mile carriage ride from the plantation.
- There Emily Jameson adored taking part in the gaiety of the teas, carriage rides, shopping on Kings Street and walking the Battery, where land met water, and going to dances.
- In February the entire family descended upon Charleston for the horse races, "by far the best time to see Charleston to advantage."
- The construction of a 120-mile railroad into the interior South Carolina 25 years before had dramatically altered plantation commerce.
- When Andrew Jackson was first elected to the presidency in 1828, only a few miles for a road track had been laid across the nation.

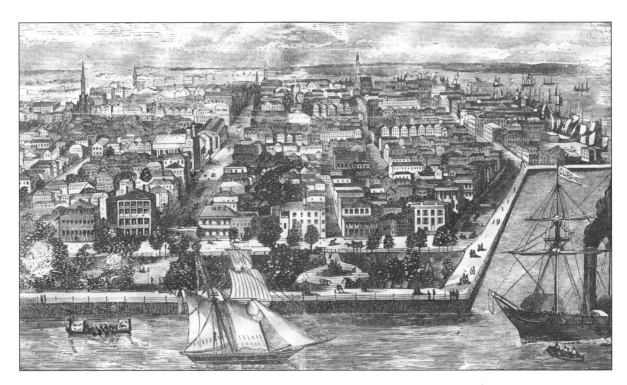

Charleston, South Carolina.

Creation of a railroad line attracted new businesses.

- By 1840 trains were running on more than 3,000 miles of track.
- Historically, cotton and rice had been hauled to the port of Charleston by flat-bottom boat through the Santee Canal, a sometimes risky mode for moving a year's worth of product to market.
- The creation of a railroad line attracted significant new business; the number of cotton bales arriving by train more than doubled from 187,000 bales in 1844 to 393,000 bales in 1859.
- The train also shipped large quantities of flour, grain, barrels of naval stores and livestock.
- By 1858 Charleston was also operating 11 schools with nearly 3,000 students as part of an effort to reduce illiteracy among white workers.
- It was a classless system in which children of the elite went to school with the working poor.
- At the same time, South Carolina maintained the country's strictest laws prohibiting the teaching of blacks, slave or free.
- Although well known as a city of commerce, Charleston was also in the center of the national debate over slavery.
- During the late 1850s, the debate was raging whether the northern Democratic Party could represent them or whether a southern party should be created to represent Southern issues.
- A third party faction known as the American party or "Know nothings" had placed its focus on nationalism, Protestantism, native Americanism, and was best known for its opposition to immigration, especially Catholic immigration.
- The United States Supreme Court's ruling in the Dred Scott decision in 1857 strengthened the hand of stay-the-course Southern conservatives and cut the legs of those eager to carry the South out of the Union immediately.
- But Southern plantation owners were eagerly searching for ways to protect their way of life.
- Newspapers, particular the *Charleston Standard*, were leading a campaign to reopen the African slave trade, a movement branded the "Congo Party" and rejected by the establishment.
- The discussion did popularize the concept that slavery would be best secured for all time by making practically every white man the owner of at least one slave.

HISTORICAL SNAPSHOT
1858

- RH Macy & Company opened its first store at 6th Avenue in New York City
- Italian chemist Stanislao Cannizzaro differentiated between atomic and molecular weights
- The Butterfield Overland Mail Company began delivering mail from St. Louis to San Francisco
- Charles R. Darwin and Alfred Wallace independently proposed natural selection theories of evolution
- The invention of the Mason jar stimulated use of large quantities of white sugar for preserves
- U.S. Senate candidate Abraham Lincoln first used the phrase "A house divided against itself cannot stand"
- Minnesota became the thirty-second state
- A pencil with an eraser attached to one end was patented by Hyman L. Lipman of Philadelphia
- An admission price of $0.50 was charged at the All Star baseball game between New York and Brooklyn
- Hamilton Smith patented a rotary washing machine
- The New York Symphony Orchestra held its first performance
- The first edition of Gray's *Anatomy of the Human Body* was published
- Mary Ann Evans published her first collection of tales, *Scenes of Clerical Life*, under the pseudonym George Eliot
- The first transatlantic cable was completed and then failed after less than one month in operation
- Mendelssohn's *Wedding March* was first played at the wedding of Queen Victoria's daughter Princess Victoria to the crown prince of Prussia

Selected Prices

Harness $84.00
Ladder $10.50
Pain Reliever $3.36
Pig $10.50
Pillowcases, Muslin, Pair $5.25
Pistol $367.50
Saddle Wallets $10.50
Saddle $126.00
Slave, 30-Year-Old Male $5,250.00
Tea Kettle $36.75

Letter from Emily Wharton Sinkler to her parents in Philadelphia, 1842:

Perhaps you would like to know how we spend our days. Breakfast is from half past eight to quarter to nine. I get up at seven. Mr. Sinkler five mornings out of seven gets up at four or five and mounts a horse and goes off to shoot English wild ducks or deer or foxes. All the family assemble at nine thirty for family prayers. There is a great variety of hot cakes, waffles, biscuits. I don't take to all these vanities, however, always eat toast for breakfast and supper. They make excellent wheat bread and toast it very nicely by the coals. Hominy is a very favorite dish. They eat it at all their meals. It is what is called grits in Philadelphia. We take breakfast in the hall and sit there all the morning. Soon after breakfast our little carriage comes to the door and we set off to take a drive. . . . The carriage is perfectly plain just holding two persons. The horses are very dark brown with plain black harness. When we set out the dogs come running up so we have a cortege of two greyhounds and two terriers generally. We are always preceded by Sampson on horseback to open gates. We are home at twelve or one and I then read and sew until dinner time. We dine between three and four. Eliza is an excellent housekeeper, and the ice cream here is really the best I ever tasted. We have supper at half past eight which is very much like breakfast except we have cold meat and after the cloth is removed wine and cordials. In the evening we have music, both piano and guitar.

Letter from Emily Sinkler to her parents in Philadelphia, February 11, 1843:

Housekeeping is very different at the South and the North though I think one thing is, people here give themselves to much trouble about it and have a great many servants about the house which of course causes great confusion. For instance there is but four bedrooms to be attended to in the house and there are five chambermaids to attend them so of course that makes five times as much confusion as necessary.

Journey through the Seaboard Slave States, Frederick Olmsted, 1856:

The plows at work, both with single and double mule teams, were generally held by women, and very well held, too. I watched with some interest for any indication that their sex unfitted them for the occupation. Twenty of them were plowing together, with double teams and heavy plows. They were superintended by a Negro man who carried a whip, which he frequently cracked at them, permitting no dawdling or delay at the turning; and they twitched their plows around on the head-land, jerking their reins, and yelling to their mules, with apparent ease, energy, and rapidity.

Throughout the Southwest the Negroes, as a rule, appeared to be worked much harder than in the Eastern and Northern Slave States. . . . They are constantly and steadily driven up to their work, and the stupid, plodding, machine-like manner in which they labor, is painful to witness. This was especially the case with the hoe-gangs. One of them numbered nearly two hundred hands (for the force of two plantations was working together), moving across the field in parallel lines, with a considerable degree of precision. I repeatedly rode through the lines at a canter, without producing the smallest change or interruption in the dogged action of the laborers, or causing one of them, so far as I could see, to lift an eye from the ground. . . . I think it told a more painful story than any I had ever heard, of the cruelty of slavery. It was emphasized by a tall and powerful Negro who walked to and fro in the rear of the line, frequently cracking his whip, and calling out in the surliest manner, to one and another, "Shove your hoe, there! Shove your hoe!" But I never saw him strike anyone with the whip.

Life on the Old Plantation in Ante-Bellum Days, or, A Story Based on Facts, by Irving E. Lowey, 1911:

That smoke-house was never without meat and lard, and that store-room contained barrels of flour, barrels of sugar, barrels of molasses and sacks of coffee from one year to another. And the corn, oh, there was no end to that. There were several barns, some big and some little, but when the corn was gathered and the "corn-shucking" was over and the crop was housed, the barns were full to overflowing. They would remind one of Pharaoh's barns in Egypt at the end of the seven years of plenty. There was very little cotton raised on that plantation in those days. Four or six bales were considered a good crop. But the corn, peas, potatoes, hogs, cattle, sheep and goats, there was no end to these. It was a rare thing to buy anything to eat on that plantation save sugar and coffee. Shoes were bought, but the clothing for the white folks and the slaves was made at home. It was the good old "home-spun." On rainy days, when it was too wet to do outdoor work, the men and boys got out corn, as they said in plantation language, for the mill, while the women and girls carded and spun cotton and wool. A task of so many hanks of yarn was given them for a day's work, which was a reasonable task, and when it was finished they carded and spun for themselves. They more or less completed their tasks before night, and by working after night they were enabled to do almost as much for themselves as they did for the white folks during the day. The weaving was almost invariably done by the young white ladies, or by some one of the servant girls who was taught especially to do it. Thus everybody on the place was kept well clothed, both the white folks and the slaves. That which the slave women carded and spun at night was their own, and they usually hired their young missus, or some other white woman of the neighborhood, to weave it into cloth for them, and thus they always had good, clean clothing for Sunday wear, so that they could go to "meetin'" without embarrassment.

On the east side of the white folks' house was the orchard. It occupied a space of about five or six acres and contained a large number of fruit trees of every description. There could be found the apple in variety, the peach, the pear, the apricot and the plum. On the west side was a large vegetable garden, which contained, in addition to the supply of vegetables for the table, several varieties of grapes. The arbors built for these grapes were large, strong and well cared for. And the slaves got their portion of all these delicious fruits. Of course, they were not allowed to steal them (but this does not signify that they never resorted to this method of obtaining fruit), but they could, and did, get fruit by asking for it.

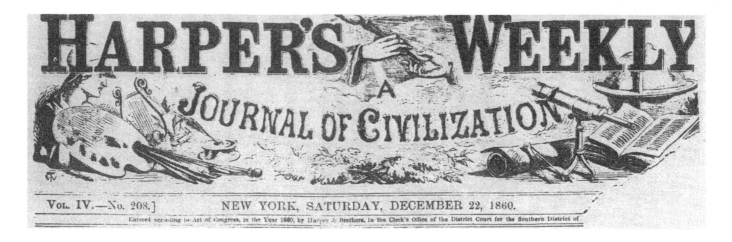

HARPER'S WEEKLY
A JOURNAL OF CIVILIZATION

VOL. IV.—No. 208.]   NEW YORK, SATURDAY, DECEMBER 22, 1860.

Entered according to Act of Congress, in the Year 1860, by Harper & Brothers, in the Clerk's Office of the District Court for the Southern District of

"Monthly Record of Current Events," *Harper's New Monthly Magazine*, September 1851:

In South Carolina a large meeting was held in Charleston, on the 29th of July, for those who are in favor of co-operation for the purpose of resistance, and opposed to separate state action, under present circumstances. John Rutledge, Esq., was chosen chairman. A letter was read from the Honorable Langdon Cheve, approving the object of the meeting, asserting the right of secession, but affirming it would not be "a moral or social one on the part of one Southern state in reference to sister states of the South." He thought South Carolina to secede, but not alone; and that a union in favor of secession would take place. . . . A series of resolutions was passed, declaring that the measures of The Federal Government, taken in conjunction manifestation of feelings up north, showed a subtle purpose to deprive the southern states of their rank as equals in the Confederacy; and tended to do the abolition of slavery and the establishment of a consolidated government; and the time it therefore come when the Union ought to be dissolved, and a Southern Confederacy formed; but they would still willingly give trial to any scheme proposed by the South, short of dissolution, for reinstating them in their rights. That, as the subject of controversy concerned all the Southern states as much as South Carolina, the true policy to be observed was concert of action; and that separate state action must be depre-cated as tending to alienate the other states and thus "prevent the formation of the Southern Confederacy," delay would insure the co-operation of other states; while separate action would place South Carolina in the position of a foreign country; in which case the laws preventing the introduction of slaves in the United States would subject her "practically to the Wilmot Proviso in its worst form."

CHARLESTON

MERCURY

EXTRA:

Passed unanimously at 1.15 o'clock, P. M., December 20th, 1860.

AN ORDINANCE

To dissolve the Union between the State of South Carolina and other States united with her under the compact entitled "The Constitution of the United States of America."

We, the People of the State of South Carolina, in Convention assembled, do declare and ordain, and it is hereby declared and ordained,

That the Ordinance adopted by us in Convention, on the twenty-third day of May, in the year of our Lord one thousand seven hundred and eighty-eight, whereby the Constitution of the United States of America was ratified, and also, all Acts and parts of Acts of the General Assembly of this State, ratifying amendments of the said Constitution, are hereby repealed; and that the union now subsisting between South Carolina and other States, under the name of "The United States of America," is hereby dissolved.

THE

UNION

IS

DISSOLVED!

1851 News Feature

"Joys And Perils of Lumbering," *Harper's New Monthly Magazine,* September 1851:

Lumbermen not only cut and haul from clumps and communities, but reconnoitre forest, hill, vale, and mountain side for scattering trees; and when they are deemed worth an effort, no location in which they may be found, however wild or daring, can oppose the skill and enterprise of our men.

For taking logs down mountain sides, we adopt various methods, according to the circumstances. Sometimes we construct what are termed a dry sluice-ways, which reach from the upper edge of a precipice down to the base of the hill. This is made by laying large poles or trunks from straight trees together the whole distance, which is so constructed as to keep the log from rolling off at the sides. Logs are rolled into the upper end, the descent or dip often being very steep; the log passes on with lightning-like velocity, quite burying itself in the snow and leaves below. From the roughness of the surfaces, the friction is very great, causing the bark and smoke to fly plentifully.

At other times, when the descent is more gradual, and not too steep, and when there is not a sufficient quantity to pay the expenses of a sluice-way, we fell a large tree, sometimes the Hemlock, trim out the top, and cut the largest limbs off a foot, more or less, from the trunk. This is attached to the end of the log by strong chains, and as the oxen draw the load, this drag thrusts its stumpy limbs in the snow and frozen earth, and best prevents the load from forcing the team forward too rapidly. Should the chain give way which attaches the hold-back to the load, nothing could save the team from sudden destruction.

There is a mountain on the "west branch" of the Penobscot where Pine-trees of excellent quality stand far up its sides, whose tops appear to sweep the very clouds. The side which furnishes timber rises in terraces of gigantic proportions, forming a succession of abrupt precipices and shelving table-land. There are three of these giant mountain steps, each of which produces lumber which challenges the admiration and enterprise of the logmen. The assent of these Alpine groves is too abrupt to allow the team to ascend in harness; we therefore unyoke and drive the oxen up winding pathways. The yokes and chains are carried up by the workman, and also the bob-sled in pieces, after taking it apart.

Ascending into the uppermost terrace, the oxen are re-yoked and the sled adjusted. The logs, being cut and prepared as usual, are loaded and hauled to the edge of the first precipice, unloaded, and rolled off the table of the second terrace, where they are again loaded, hauled, and tumbled off as before, to the top of the first rise, which they again pitch down to the base of the mountain where for the last time they are loaded and hauled to the landing.

To obtain logs in such romantic locations was really as hazardous as it was laborious, varying sufficiently from the usual routine of labor to invest the occasion with no ordinary interest. It was, indeed, an exhibition well calculated to awaken thrilling emotions to witness the descent of those massive logs, breaking and shivering whatever might obstruct their giddy plunge down the steep mountain side, making the valleys reverberate and ring merrily with the concussion.

In other instances loads are eased down hill sides by the use of "tackle and fall" or by a strong "warp" taking a "bight" round a tree and hitching-to one yoke of the oxen. In this manner the load is "tailed down" steeps where it would be impossible for the "tongue oxen" to resist the pressure of a load. Sometimes the warp parts under test to which it is thus subjected, when the whole load plunges onward like an avalanche, subjecting the poor oxen to a shocking death.

But the circumstance which calls forth the most interest and most exertion is the "rival load." When teams are located with sufficient proximity to admit of convenient intercourse, a spirit of rivalry is often rife between the different crews on various points. The "largest tree," the "smartest chopper," the "best cook" the "greatest day's work" and a score of other superlatives, all are invested with attractions for greater than the isolated circumstances of swamp life. . . .

But while the greater part of the swamp life is more or less merry, there are occasional interruptions to the joyousness that abounds. Logging roads are generally laid out with due regard to the conveniences of level or gently descending ground. But in some instances the unevenness of the country admits only of unfavorable alternatives. Sometimes there are moderate rises to ascend or descend on the way to the landing; the former are hard, the latter are dangerous to the team. I knew a teamster to lose his life in the following shocking manner: on one section of the main road there was quite a "smart pitch" of considerable length, on which the load invariably "drove" the man along at a forced trot. Down this slope our teamster had often passed without sustaining any injury to himself or oxen. One day, having, as usual, taken his load from the stump, he proceeded toward the landing, soon passing out of sight and hearing. Not making his appearance at the expiration of the usual time, it was suspected that something more than usual detained him. Obeying the impulses of proper solicitude on his behalf, some of the hands started to render service if it were needed. Coming to the head of the hill down which the road ran, they saw the team at the foot of it, standing with the forward oxen faced about up the road, but no teamster. In reaching the spot, a most distressing spectacle presented itself; there lay the teamster on the hard road, with one of the sled runners directly across his bowels, which, under the weight of several tons of timber, pressed down to the thickness of a man's hand. He was still alive and when they called out to him, just before reaching the sled, he spoke up as promptly as usual, "Here am I," as if nothing had been the matter. These were the only and last words he ever uttered. The "pry" was immediately set, which raised the deadfall from his crushed body, enabling them to extricate it from its dreadful position. Shortly afterwards, his consciousness left him, and never more returned. He could give no explanation; but we inferred, from the position of the forward oxen, that the load had forced the team into a run, by which the tongue cattle, pressed by the leaders, turning them around, which probably threw the teamster under the runner, and a whole load stopped when about to poise over his body.

He was taken to the camp, where all was done that could be done on the circumstances to save him, but to no purpose. His work was finished. He still lingered, in an apparently unconscious state, and at midnight, with his spirit forsaking its bruised and crushed tenement, ascended above the sighing pines, and entered the eternal state. The only words he uttered with those in reply to the calling of his name. As near as we can judge, he had lain two hours in the position in which he was found. It was astonishing to see how he had gnawed the rave of the sled. It was between three and four inches through. In his agony he had bitten it nearly half off. To do this, he must've pulled himself up with his hands, gnawed for awhile, then fallen back through near exhaustion and despair. He was taken out to the nearest settlement, and then buried. . . .

1860–1869

The decade of the 1860s proved to be a watershed period that reshaped the United States into a new nation. Prior to the 1860 presidential election, it was evident to most Americans that slavery would become the only campaign issue. Upon the election of Abraham Lincoln, the Southern states seceded from the United States and formed the Confederate States of America. The four-year Civil War between the American states enrolled over three million soldiers into military service. To finance the battle of state against state and brother against brother, the North substantially increased the taxes on tobacco and alcohol, while imposing the first income tax in the nation's history. Customs receipts also proved to be an important revenue source. The Treasury issued paper money called greenbacks, the value of which fluctuated wildly during the war years. The South used printing presses to keep the war financed, issuing nearly $1 billion in inadequately backed treasury notes. The resulting inflation rendered Confederate money virtually worthless. The physical devastation of the war, primarily in the South, was enormous: burned or plundered homes, pillaged farms, destroyed rail lines, ruined buildings, bridges and dams, devastated college campuses, and neglected roads all left the South in economic ruin. The direct monetary costs of the conflict were recorded at $15 billion, a figure that does not include the lost potential of the more than one million men and women who died on the battlefield or from disease. The approximately 10,455 Civil War military engagements, accidents, suicides, sicknesses, murders and executions resulted in total casualties of 1,094,453. Estimates of wounded Union Army personnel topped 275,000; Confederate records indicate 194,000 were wounded. At the war's conclusion, the United States experienced its first assassination of a U.S. president and was challenged to reincorporate the former Confederate states back into the Union. After freeing the existing slave population and providing African-American males the right to vote, the nation struggled with a wide range of issues concerning postwar reconstruction. Congress demanded severe measures to punish the Southern states. And when President Andrew Johnson's plans were not severe enough, they impeached him.

Communications advances that crossed the continent initially started with the development of the Pony Express in 1860 which carried letters from St. Joseph, Missouri, to Sacramento, California, within 10 days. The enterprise lasted only 18 months until the first transcontinental telegraph began service in 1861 and made communication faster and cheaper. Five years later in 1866, the Atlantic cable between Great Britain and the U.S. provided improved communications across the ocean with the European community.

The emergence of new writers who would influence the nation emerged in the decade. Mark Twain became nationally popular in 1865 when his tall tale "Jim Smiley and His Jumping Frog" was printed in the New York *Saturday Press*. Horatio Alger's first book that formed the Ragged Dick series appeared and taught the principles of hard work and avoiding life's temptations. One of the most published authors of the decade, Englishman Charles Dickens, visited New York City for a reading of his works in 1867. People stood in two lines a mile long for tickets, and scalpers demanded $20 for a ticket for the event.

The United States, which produced 90 percent of the nation's manufactured items prior to the war, easily resumed its manufacturing dominance following the war. As industry grew, the Civil War accelerated the organization of labor unions. Many workers raised social and economic questions concerning both free and slave labor. Over 10 national unions were formed between 1863 and 1866 addressing the issues of prosperity through higher wages and fewer work hours. By 1867, the eight-hour day was enacted in Illinois, New York and Missouri, but not enforced. Thoughts of prosperity also continued for those in the Western United States. Silver discovered in Virginia City, Nevada, created a rush to populate the region with hopes of discovering riches through the decade. At the same time, many questioned the prudence of America acquiring 586,400 square miles of Alaska by paying Russia $7.2 million. Although rich in furs and fish, it would be years before its natural resources were appreciated.

Railroad transportation dominated the decade as an effective method for commercial transport. Safety improvements with Westinghouse's air brake and the development of refrigerator railcars would improve commerce with the railroad industry. By the end of the decade, the United States' manufacturing strength and the completion of the transcontinental railroad in 1869 foreshadowed the emergence of the United States in the world.

1862 PROFILE

Jane Altman from Iowa endured the hardships of a journey across the country with her husband and his family to eventually settle in California.

Life at Home

- Jane Altman was happily tending to her home in Milton, Iowa, in 1862, when her husband Albert announced he had decided they should move west to California.
- Jane was not consulted.
- Albert had already discussed the move with his father and brother and persuaded both of them to make the journey together with him and his family.
- Jane had been taught to be respectful of the wisdom and authority of her husband; when Albert decided to move west, she did not argue.
- In all, about 30 other families from Iowa were interested in leaving; Jane was given two months to get ready for the move.
- In preparation, Albert sold some livestock to purchase a prairie schooner, a wagon especially designed for travel over the plains.
- Lighter than the Conestoga wagons used back East, the prairie schooner could be easily pulled by a team of four horses or mules.
- Romantics said the wagons looked like boats sailing across the prairie.
- For Jane the trip meant leaving her parents, brothers and sisters, and aunts and uncles behind—perhaps never to see them again.
- In her heart she did not wish to leave their farm, neighbors, and her comfortable home.
- She was especially sad to leave her new stove behind—a gift from her husband two years earlier.
- She took a great deal of pride in her baking, especially yeast bread, a dish difficult to make without an oven.
- She wondered in her journal who would pick the apples and flowers at the farm after she was gone.

Jane Altman reluctantly traveled to California with her family.

Albert decided, with his father and brother, to take his family to California.

- At least they wouldn't be leaving the horses, mules and chickens behind, but she wondered how the animals would fare, walking so many miles through the wilderness.
- For Jane it was hard to imagine where they might live, and what they might be doing once they reached California.
- She had seen and heard so many conflicting reports from travelers and newspaper accounts.
- She especially dreaded having to bid farewell to her parents, who were getting old now and might need her help.
- To cope, Jane made up her mind that she would, for the next five or six months, make the wagon her new home.
- The Altman family, consisting of Jane and Albert, their two sons, Albert's brother Charlie and his wife, Lou, plus Albert's father and a hired hand, left Iowa on April 27, 1862.
- They and the 30 other families traveled together in a wagon train that included cows and chickens, and large quantities of flour, sugar and coffee; they hoped they would find other provisions along the way.

Life at Work

- The first day the group rode through a prairie all morning, "nooned" at an old haystack, and camped for the night in a grove near a farmhouse, where the lady of the house offered them fresh milk to drink.
- They had come 16 miles; hundreds of miles lay ahead.
- Jane Altman cooked the evening meal over an open fire and missed her stove and other conveniences of her kitchen; from that day forward her journal became her closest confidante.

Thirty families traveled together in a wagon train.

- Jane paid particularly close attention to the weather on the trail; the morning frost made it difficult to prepare breakfast, she noted.
- On May 1, the fourth day, Jane was still having trouble fixing breakfast, and complained of the wet ground and the cold wind blowing from the northwest.
- In mid-May the wagons halted for several days and the women had a chance to catch up on their washing and baking.
- Jane was pleased to be able to make some yeast bread, for the first time in three weeks, and to serve something other than biscuits.
- The next day it rained hard, so the women did not even venture out.
- The men fixed breakfast outside, brought it into the wagon, and served the meal using a trunk for a table.
- By that afternoon, Jane wrote, "It had grown very cold through the day, and most of the men were wet through."
- By the next morning, a Sunday, the weather improved, and Jane took the children out for a walk to pick flowers.
- They found hazel bushes, picked up a few of the hazelnuts from the ground, and cracked them.
- The nuts were quite good, so they picked two quarts, "a luxury for this time of year."
- Sundays were traditionally a day of rest, but many of the women did their washing anyway.
- Two couples enjoyed a break from the routine chores and went out horseback-riding for their health.
- One afternoon toward the end of May, Jane and Lou, her sister-in-law, practiced shooting a revolver, and were pleased to hear the men say they had done "first rate for new beginners."
- That evening, the men amused themselves playing the fiddle, and other families came over to listen and do a little dancing.
- On June 28, Jane explained in her diary that they "stayed over" to let the cattle have a chance to rest.
- While the cattle rested, Albert was busy setting the tires of his wagon wheels and setting shoes on the horses, "which made a pretty hard day's work for him."

Some evenings, families got together for fiddle music and dancing.

- There was a blacksmith in the area, and Jane was pleased to report that he only charged "ten dollars for the shoeing of a yoke."
- The wagon train soon reached the Platte River, and they began traveling along the road known variously as the Oregon Trail or California Trail, depending on one's destination.
- The Platte River was wide, slow moving, and very shallow, and Jane described how "the boys waded across to an island."
- Later she described the river as being filled with small islands, and that "the boys have gone bathing."
- The hired man, Gus, helped her carry the clothes to the river to rinse them.
- They tried to wade over to a little island, hoping to hang the clothes there, but the water was too deep and they "were obliged to hang them on some low bushes close to the river."
- Toward the end of June, the men began building a raft, and Jane wrote, "Worked hard all day . . . half the men in the water, too."
- The next day proved even more strenuous as they started ferrying the wagons over the river; she wrote, "We had to take them apart and float the box and cover behind. The two boxes were fastened together by the rods, one before to tow in and the other to load . . . worked till dark."
- "We were the last but one to cross tonight. Got some of our groceries wet, some coffee sugar dissolved."
- But the loss of sugar was minor compared to the dangers that lurked along the way.
- "Annie McMillen had lagged behind, walking, when we stopped. The whole train had crossed the creek before they thought of her. The creek was so deep that it ran into the wagon boxes, so she could not wade."
- "A man on horseback went over for her, and another man on a mule went to help her on."

Jane's wagon train crossed the Platte River.

- "The mules refused to go clear across . . . went where the water was very deep, threw the man off and almost trampled him, but he got out safe, only well wet and with the loss of a good hat, which is no trifling loss here."
- Jane made note of the fact that Albert was "feeling rather indisposed," and later she wrote "his appetite was rather capricious, he not being well."
- A trace of homesickness can be detected in her next entry, as they passed "a lonely nameless grave on the prairie."
- It made her sad to think of being buried and left alone in "so wild a country with no one to plant a flower or shed a tear o'er one's grave."
- As the trip stretched into the fourth month, Jane began to carefully note all instances of accidents and illness, saying that she went calling on "a neighbor who has a sick child," or commenting that "a lady . . . was thrown from her horse and injured quite severely."
- A few days later she wrote, "In the night I heard Mrs. Wilson's baby crying very hard indeed . . . it had fallen from the wagon. It cried for nearly an hour . . . he struck his head."
- On the July 4, Jane wrote, "Here we are away off in the wilderness and can't even stay over a day to do any extra cooking. The men fired their guns. We wonder what the folks at home are doing and oh, how we wish we were there."
- One day she noticed a mail station and several other buildings on the opposite shore, and later "a little log hut which is used for a store."
- She added, rather sadly, that "It was really a welcome sight after going four hundred miles without seeing a house of any kind."
- The stress and anxiety became increasingly evident in her journal, as she noted: "We hear many stories of Indian depredations, but do not feel frightened yet," or "There was a little child run over by a wagon in Walker's train . . . just ahead of us. The child was injured quite seriously. . . ."
- "We came past a camp of thirty six wagons [that] have been camped for some time here in the mountains. They have had their cattle stampeded four or five times."
- "There was a woman died in this train yesterday. She left six children, one of them only two days old. Poor little thing, it had better have died with its mother."

Accidents were not uncommon on the trail.

The first Indians they encountered on the trail were dressed in grand style.

- Then she learned of another tragedy.
- A woman was run over by the cattle and wagons that had stampeded the day before. "She lived twenty-four hours . . . she gave birth to a child a short time before she died. The child was buried with her. She leaves a little two year old girl and a husband. They say he is nearly crazy with sorrow."
- As their wagon train approached Indian territory, the community drew closely together, knowing how much they needed one another for protection and moral support.
- The first Indians they encountered appeared to be friendly.
- One of the travelers, a Mr. Bullwinkle, bought antelope meat from some Indians, and gave big shares of it to Jane to cook up as a delicious breakfast for the family.
- As the wagon train passed through a small Indian village one morning, Jane observed that the Indians had about 100 ponies and 16 wigwams.
- That day at lunchtime, an Indian chief "rode up on a nice mule, his bridle . . . covered with silver plates, [with] Masonic emblems on it, and . . . dressed in grand style."
- Jane may have wondered how the chief acquired his fancy decorations—through trade or violence—but she didn't say.
- "He had a looking glass and comb suspended by a string, and a fan and silver ornaments made of half dollars made into fancy shapes; I cannot describe half the ornaments that he wore. He was real good looking for an Indian. He wore earrings as much as eight inches long. . . ."
- Once they reached the Snake River they began to hear of recent Indian attacks.
- She wrote, "We learned that a train of eleven wagons had been plundered of all that was in them and the teams taken and the men killed."

They were always on the look out for Indian attacks.

- "One was Mr. Bullwinkle who left us the 25th of last month at the crossing of Green River . . . . He was hit eight times. His dog was shot four times before he would let them get to the wagon. They took all that he had in his wagon, except his trunk and papers. It is supposed that they took six thousand dollars from him."

- The next day she continued, "The two men we brought up were buried early this morning with the other three, so they had five men side by side in this vast wilderness, killed by guns and arrows of the red demons. The chief appeared yesterday in a suit of Mr. Bullwinkle's on the battlefield."

- Captain Adams, who had been their leader, lost his son and daughter; "Poor father and mother lost one son and one daughter, all of his teams, clothing and four thousand dollars . . . . Is dependent on the bounty of strangers. . . ."

- One of the ladies of the plundered train, a Mrs. Ellen Ives, came to ride in the wagon with Jane.

- Her husband was taken into the wagon ahead.

- The two were newlyweds, as Jane explained: "She was married the morning she started for California. Not a very pleasant wedding tour."

- When the wagon train was attacked in the middle of the night, Jane dressed the children and hid them behind the wagon, beneath some mattresses and quilts.

- The attackers did not do much harm, perhaps because there were so many wagons traveling together—approximately 111—and they figured they had over 200 well-armed men.

- This attack and subsequent alarms left Jane feeling frightened and shaken.

- As she described it, "It is not an enviable situation to be placed in, not to know at night when you go to bed, whether you will all be alive in the morning or not."

- To relieve the tension, some of the adults went a short way from the road one day and "got our arms full of currant bushes laden with fruit, both red and white. We ate what we wished and had nearly two quarts to eat with sugar for supper. They were real refreshing."

- Jane expressed her feelings even more candidly, saying, "Oh dear, I do so want to get there. It is now almost four months since we have slept in a house. If I could only be set down at home with all the folks I think there would be some talking as well as resting."

Indian attacks left behind death and destruction.

- Her worries about her husband's health had continued to grow. "Albert is so very miserable too, that I don't enjoy myself as well as I would if he was well."
- And the feelings she expressed about the Indians grew more negative: "There have been Indians around today begging. We are glad to see them do so now, for we are disgusted with the wretched creatures."
- When a friend and neighbor died unexpectedly one night, she was angry his family and friends had to bury him with no proper boards for a coffin.
- "He was in his clothes with a sheet around him. It seems hard to have to bury one's friends in such a way. I do feel sorry for the poor wife and daughter, strangers in a strange land. All her relatives are in Ohio. . . ."
- By early September they learned that their wagon train was to be divided, with one group going on the Honey Lake route, and the other on the Carson River route.
- Their captain was assigned to the first group and Jane's family to the other.
- They hated to see him go.
- "We seem like a family of children without a father. We think he is the best Captain on the road. Some could hardly refrain from shedding tears at parting. Tears came into the Captain's eyes as he bade them goodbye. . . ."
- By September 9, the wagons had reached Humboldt City, and several women took a long walk up a steep hill to see the town.
- It had about 25 buildings, some of rough stone and some of adobe.
- They called on an emigrant woman whose husband was sick with typhoid fever and learned that the prices for flour, coffee, sugar and bacon were exorbitant indeed.
- One of the women decided to stay in Humboldt, despite the opposition raised by all her friends.
- Jane wrote later, "I was sorry to leave Mrs. McMillan . . . it does not seem like a good place for a woman to stay . . . there are only four families here . . . the rest are single men."
- Later, when they stopped for lunch, and no grass was growing anywhere, she admitted to herself, "I am just as homesick as I can be."
- By September 21, the train had reached an outpost of civilization, Empire City. She told how the streets were "full of freight wagons . . . and there is a quartz mill there, too, with buildings going up fast. . . ."

The wagon train reached civilization after six months on the trail.

- In her last entry, on October 8, Jane told of pitching their tent in a town, when a lady came by and told them about a house available for rent.
- "Charlie went with her to the house, made a bargain, provided it pleased all around, which it did, we picked up and went right over. . . . Slept in a house the first time for over five months."
- At the very end she wrote, "The house is very convenient. We pay ten dollars per month rent. The house is over half a mile from the business part of town."

Life in the Community: California

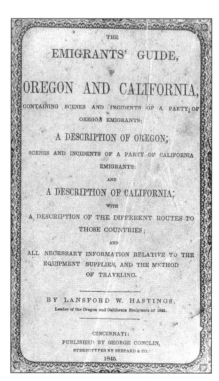

- An estimated 250,000 men, women and children traveled west during the 1850s and 1860s; about one-tenth of them died along the trail from illness, accidents, warfare, childbirth and starvation.
- In 1848, as word spread about the discovery of gold in California, people began streaming across the American continent, risking everything in hopes of becoming fabulously wealthy by panning for gold.
- Even though most of the "forty-niners" were disappointed and never found the riches they had hoped for.
- People back East kept hearing stories about the lucky few, and about other veins of gold being found in Colorado, Alaska, and other sites throughout the West.
- During the early years of the gold rush, it was predominantly men who attempted the risky journey; most of them planned to strike it rich quick and return home to their wives and children with a small fortune.
- These men left their wives to shoulder all the responsibilities of child care, managing the farm or family business, and of providing food and shelter without the help of their husbands.
- Many of the husbands never returned, and many wives did not know for certain if they were dead or alive.
- During the 1850s, several wagon trails were developed, and thousands of wagons began rolling westward, carrying entire families with all their earthly possessions, including livestock, household goods, cash, clothing and furniture.

- These optimistic people came from all walks of life, including farmers, clerks, hired hands, lawyers, doctors, ministers and opportunists of every sort and description, and instead of traveling alone, this time they were bringing their families along.
- Although Conestoga wagons were still in use back East, the families heading west learned that the large wagons, pulled by oxen, were not suited to the long journey across the prairies.
- Oxen did not have the stamina necessary for making such a long journey, and families were often stranded in the wilderness when one or more of their oxen died.
- The "prairie schooner" design became popular because it was so much lighter, about half the size of a Conestoga, and could be pulled by horses or mules.
- A typical wagon hauled huge quantities of flour, cornmeal, bacon, sugar, coffee, dried fruit, salt, baking soda, tea, rice and beans.
- According to some estimates, families packed about 300 pounds of dry goods per person for a journey lasting four or five months.
- Prairie schooners continued to bring thousands of families over the Oregon Trail through the 1860s but were less popular after the opening of the transcontinental railroad in 1869.
- In October 1858, as miners rushed to stake their claims in the mountains near Pike's Peak, many enterprising men organized companies to form towns, building cabins that could protect them from the hard winter conditions.
- Most of these towns lasted only a season or two, as miners left again to try their luck at a better location.
- Among the towns that were established, at least on paper, were Montana, Auraria, St. Charles Santa Fe, Nonpareil City, and Pike's Peak City.
- Speculators tried to sell lots in towns that never existed, and in some cases labor shortages and a lack of building materials slowed the construction of substantial cabins.
- Despite the surveys, the town charters, and the efforts of so many to promote towns and sell lots in them, these towns either never materialized or were quickly abandoned.
- By June of 1859, a newcomer described Auraria as "an inconsiderable village . . . a dull hole. . . . This town had its origin in rascality, and therefore deserves to prove a failure. There is no doubt that all the flaming reports of rich gold discoveries that blazed so dazzlingly through the newspapers, were concocted in this very spot, and sent forward by men who had never washed a pan of dirt, but who were largely interested in attracting hither a population, so that the value of their 'city lots' might be enhanced."

HISTORICAL SNAPSHOT
1862

- Paper money was introduced into the United States

- Richard J Gatling patented and manufactured the machine gun, which was used against Native Americans

- Victor Hugo's novel *Les Miserables* dramatically highlighted social problems in France

- Charles Darwin published the first thorough study of orchid pollination

- The U.S. Department of Agriculture was created

- Louis Pasteur convincingly disproved the theory concerning spontaneous generation of cellular life

- General Robert E. Lee took command of the Confederate armies of Virginia and North Carolina

- Jean Joseph Etienne Lenoir built the first gasoline-engine automobile

- The Homestead Act was passed, providing cheap land for settlement of the Nebraska Territory

- Congress established a Commissioner of Internal Revenue to deal with Civil War debt and collect tax on whiskey

- Slavery was abolished in Washington, DC

- The Sioux uprising erupted in Minnesota

- Union forces were defeated by Confederates at the second battle of Bull Run in Manassas, Virginia

- "The Battle Hymn of the Republic" by Julia Ward Howe was published in *The Atlantic Monthly* as an anonymous poem

- The Battle of Shiloh in Tennessee resulted in the deaths of 9,000 soldiers

- The United States population—north and south—was 31 million

Selected Prices

Buckwheat, Bushel $13.00

Commode $21.00

Home, Wood, Brooklyn, New York $27,500

Lumber, 100 Feet of Cherry $30.03

Map of the United States $42.00

Microscope $42.00

Pitcher $10.00

Sausage Grinder $42.00

Tallow, Pound $2.00

Whiskey, Glass $10.50

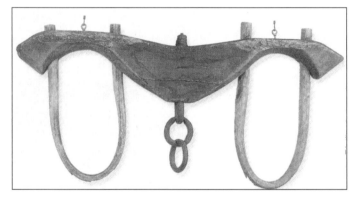

Diary of Mary Louisa Black, *The Oregon and Overland Trail*, 1865:

June 24

We passed the ferry this morning, they were crossing two wagons at a time and charging $7 for a four horse team and besides having to work the ropes themselves. Numbers were going above to ford, nooned on the Cachel la Poudre River in a nice shady place near a ranch. The crows mowed the grass for them. John Browned coffee. Corralled separate, no stampede. Plenty of prairie dogs along the road.

June 26

The Arapahoos, about 20, came into camp yesterday evening, exhibiting all the characteristics of natives excepting they had long hair filled with ornaments, that is three of their number. I suppose two to be chiefs & one of their squaws. Nooned 26 at the foot of Black Hills. . . .

June 27

Morning I rested well last night. They were in a rush to get started. No alarms during the night. We nooned near the top of the hills. Some of the teams belonging to the Coopers train stampeded, running against the hindmost wagon of our train, smashing one wheel. They took back a wheel and brought up the wagon and divided the load. Mr. Day fell on a large rock three times.

June 28

About 10 o'clock. Every one is busy. John is having his horses shod, while a great many are helping to repair the broken wagon. I was quite sick this morning with diarrhea. I took a full dose of laudanum this morning and some quinine about 8 and I feel some better and have just finished cutting out a pair of drawers for myself. The women have finished their washing. Horsemen came forward just now to halt the train, another stampede. Some of the mule teamsters would not lock coming down a long hill and ran by some ox teams causing them to stampede, that's the first report. Wat mounted the black mule and has accompanied the man to the rear. A cold mountain wind is facing us. . . .

June 29

We camped in the mountains again. I'm still sick this morning. Had a rundown just at daylight. Some mint, resembling Peppermint and tasted like penoroyl, John gathered the first evening we encamped in the mountains was a great relief to my stomach. The hills on the side were grey colored rocks with pines scattered over them. The stage passed this morning. Nooned on the roadside. Made a fire under a large pine to boil some tea. Soon after we halted, a soldier came running up to the doctor of our train to go back to the next station to take a arrow out of a man's back. The man lives at the station and has been hunting for them for a number of years. It was done right in the rear of our train by some Arappahoos who shook hands with him pretending friendly and when he turned to leave they shot him. The arrow passed through his lung the doctor says. The same Indians that visited our camp Sunday eve were the authors of the mischief, near as we can learn. The hunter knew them.

Original journal entry.

Letter from Mrs. W. W. Buck from Oregon to her family:

Of course we were all anxious to hear about the country we were bound for, and our captain said Dr. White could told us about the Oregon. He jumped upon the wagon tongue and all our eyes and ears were open to catch every word. He said: "Friends you are traveling to the Garden of Eden, a land flowing with milk and honey. And just let me tell you, the clover grows wild all over Oregon, and when you wade through it, it reaches your chin." We believed every word, and for days, I thought that not only our men, but our poor tired oxen, stepped lighter for having met Dr. White.

Diary of Cecelia McMullan Adams traveling from Illinois to Oregon, 1852:

June 25 Passed 7 graves . . . made 14 miles
June 26 Passed 8 graves
June 29 Passed 10 graves
June 30 Passed 10 graves . . . made 22 miles
July 1 Passed 8 graves . . . made 21 miles
July 2 One man in our company died. Passed 8 graves made 16 miles
July 4 Passed 2 graves . . . made 16 miles
July 5 Passed 9 graves . . . made 18 miles
July 6 Passed 6 graves . . . made 9 miles
July 11 Passed 15 graves . . . made 13 miles
July 12 Passed 5 graves . . . made 15 miles
July 18 Passed 4 grave . . . made 16 miles

Predicting the Weather, *The Old Farmer's Almanac,* 1867:

- Sheep run to and fro, jump from the ground, and fight in their gambols before a change in weather
- When cattle lie out, or pigs lie down for the night without covering themselves with litter, fine weather will continue
- Asses hanging their ears forward or rubbing themselves against walls or trees prognosticate rain
- Cats remaining indoors, devoid of vivacity, forecast wet or windy weather
- Frogs croaking more than usual, moles throwing up more soil than usual, toads in great numbers, and oxen licking their forefeet all mean rain
- Owls hooting and screeching during bad weather foretell fine weather near at hand
- Swallows flying near the ground, robins coming near the house, and sparrows chirping a great deal all mean rain or wind

BETWEEN SACRAMENTO, AND THE MINES

1863 PROFILE

At the outbreak of the Civil War, George Upton sold his gold mine and enlisted in the Union Army as a member of the California Volunteers.

Life at Home

- Thirty-three-year-old George Upton was familiar with life's challenges in California long before he joined the Union Army to fight Confederates.
- He quickly learned that drunks, Indians and boredom were more dangerous to his future than the Confederate army.
- George grew up in Whitestown, New York, where his father taught him his trade and gave him a valuable set of drafting instruments to secure his future.
- But gold fever struck him deep when at age 19 he heard tales of the immense potential for wealth in California.
- With his father's consent, George traveled to the Gold State and started working in the mines.
- As a resident in the territory, he even voted to admit California into the Union as a Free State on November 13, 1849.
- In 1861, after years of prospecting in the region, he obtained a valuable piece of land in Nevada with good mineral prospects.
- A few weeks later he heard news of the War of the Rebellion between the Union and the Southern states.
- When the call for volunteers developed in late July, he thought it was his duty to serve.
- He sold his land for a trifle and went to San Francisco to enlist.
- In San Francisco, George learned that Texans had invaded part of New Mexico and proclaimed the region as "the Confederate Territory of Arizona."
- At one of the city's saloons, he overheard several conversations proposing that the state of California secede from the Union and form the "Pacific Republic."
- One even proposed dividing the state into two parts with the northern half free and the southern half slave-holding.

George Upton was 33 when he enlisted in the Union Army.

- Regardless, George Upton registered as a solider at the Presidio along with hundreds of others vowing to smash the "secesh," the secessionist.
- A few days later, George's compatriots elected him a sergeant, even though he had no formal military training.
- Assigned to the infantry, Sgt. George Upton was issued his uniform and materials, which consisted of roughly 60 pounds of gear.
- His equipment included a blanket, a forage cap, a woolen shirt, a pair of stockings, a towel, two handkerchiefs, a sewing kit, a piece of soap and one toothbrush.
- George was also issued a Model 1855 Springfield rifle musket.
- It was the best rifle he had ever owned and he proved himself to be the best shot during target practice.
- On one afternoon he fired a Minié ball one-eighth from center, three balls one-fourth from center and two at half of center from a distance of 110 yards.
- A few days later George made a center shot from 150 yards away.
- But being a strong shot was not enough; skirmishes were necessary to prepare the company for combat.
- George's company conducted skirmishes with blank cartridges with fiber wads but without a Minié ball.
- But general discontent was rampant in the military of the west.
- Prior to departing for Yuma, a group of men refused to move when their company was ordered to pack their knapsacks.
- Other volunteers then decided to disobey the command.
- George, along with the rest of the soldiers, was then questioned on his willingness to obey orders.
- Thirty men refused and were then ordered to ground arms and were marched to the guardhouse.
- It was an inauspicious beginning to military life.
- Shortly thereafter, Sgt. Upton's company marched east towards Yuma, traveling in the evening due to the unbearable March heat.
- The company dropped from fatigue by nine o'clock in the morning.

The Army marched toward Fort Yuma in unbearable heat.

- After each man received a one-pint ration from a water keg, George wrote in his journal, "The boys lie around panting like polar bears in a warm climate."
- Seeing the bluff with Fort Yuma brought relief to George as he and his men arrived at the first leg of their destination.
- Upon arrival, they pitched camp outside Fort Yuma and rested.
- Due to the uncommonly high waters of the Colorado River, his company was unable to cross and had to wait for the waters to recede before heading off for Tucson.
- They waited almost three months.
- As they passed the time in Yuma, George was able to explore the area around the fort, including the Indian village.
- To his surprise, many of the Indians were more enterprising than Indians he knew in California.
- They grew their own vegetables and cooked for some of the soldiers.
- A few cut wood for the steamships arriving at the port for three dollars per cord.
- During his stay the First Calvary of the California Volunteers captured 24 men from the Showater Party who intended to join the Confederate army.
- After being paraded into Fort Yuma, each was asked to take an oath of allegiance to the federal government and denounce aid or comfort to any of its enemies.
- After the event, George commented in his journal, "It was a strong oath and if there was a secesher in the party, it must have been a bitter pill."
- In preparation for the long journey to Tucson, George's company was vaccinated against small pox.

Soldiers waited for the waters of the Colorado River to recede before crossing.

Westward migration resulted in conflicting lifestyles.

- The day after the inoculations, the Brigade Surgeon Robert Christian discovered that Upton had had typhoid and bilious fevers for the past three weeks.
- Sickness alone could not stop the festivities for July 4th, and George was pleased to have a distraction in Yuma, even though the town and the fort had little to offer.
- Aside from singing the "Star-Spangled Banner" and other patriotic airs, George expected a traditional reading of the Declaration of Independence.
- He later learned that a copy could not be found, which was unusual for a military post.
- As part of the celebration, each man was offered one gill, or half a cup, of "patriotism" and half the command procured passes for the day.
- Many of the men returned to camp drunk that evening, while five returned in chains for fighting.

- When it was time to depart Yuma for Tucson, George was thrilled to leave this boredom of Yuma, even to endure 250 miles of desert marching.
- Once again the extreme heat required them to hike only in the evening hours.
- The company followed the Butterfield Overland Mail Company's route along the Gila River for 140 miles.
- George was impressed with the saguaros cactus plants, some 20 feet high and 18 inches in diameter.
- During the nighttime marches, the largest concern was not the threat of attack by Confederate troops, but an ambush by the Apache Indians.
- George thought the troop size discouraged direct attacks and wrote, "We have not seen a Tonto yet."
- The last 50 miles of the desert march was the worst because of the lack of water.
- George guarded the water wagon and discovered many men drank their canteens dry out of fear of not getting their fair share of water.
- It was a struggle for George to refuse a thirsty man water, especially from his own canteen.
- Food provisions also ran low due to the lack of wild game, and someone had neglected to pack the jerked beef prior to departing Yuma.
- One morning George had to eat grasshoppers and pork rind for breakfast.
- No one died from the lack of food or water but a few men did perish at the hands of the Apache near the march's end.
- One was a good friend of George Upton, Private Charley O'Brien.
- Charley apparently fell behind the command; the Indians shot him, stripped and literally cut him in pieces before he was discovered missing. In his writings, George commented, "They have attacked every command so far and we expect to get some of it when we go. Who will be the victims time alone will tell."
- Just prior to arriving in Tucson, the company commander ordered all men to put on clean clothes.
- Major Fergusson declared that they were the cleanest looking company to arrive into Tucson from Yuma.

Indian attacks were not uncommon.

Life at Work

- As Sgt. George Upton's service in the Union army continued, military engagements became more common within the Arizona Territory.
- These skirmishes were not with Confederate soldiers but with the Indians in the area.
- Word of an Apache attack was common and nearly always caused a panic; frequently George's company was called quickly to arms and put into pursuit.
- Though the Apache were not favored by many, a few tame Apaches were in Tucson.
- George attended one of their powwows and observed the great noise 40 men dancing around a fire can make at midnight.
- Entertaining as the powwow was to George, the customs of the region were more interesting.
- His journal reflected his fascination with adobe rooftops covered in corn and pumpkins to be dried in the October air.
- One night, unable to get off that day, George and some friends sneaked out to attend a fandango on Plaza Segundo.
- George stayed until the musk and cigarita smoke drove him out.
- When his friends returned, he learned that General Carleton's black servant was out with an attractive señorita.
- When the servant took her out on the dance floor, the soldiers threw bricks and broke up the event.
- A few weeks later, George's company received orders to move to the town of Mesilla near Fort Fillmore along the Rio Grande, on the Texas border.
- Over the next three weeks, the winter elements had more of an influence than the fear of the Apache.
- Fatigue was common, and George had trouble sleeping in wet blankets and coats which typically froze stiff at night.

Native tribes had been organized on the land for centuries.

- Wood was scarce and limited the number of fires for warmth.
- One night George Upton's blanket froze stiff with half an inch of frost on top.
- Later he wrote in his journal, "Hard work to turn the boys out—snow, cold and everything froze. . . . Very bad traveling—snow, wind very plenty."
- Just before Christmas the company arrived at Mesilla, and George was pleased to find some civilization.
- The town had one tenpin alley, two billiard tables, a church and plenty of adobe houses.
- During the next couple of weeks, there were no drills or parades due to the Christmas season.
- For Christmas dinner, George and his men received a meal of beef stew.
- At night a minstrel show was performed through the New Year.
- During his time off, George received several letters from family and friends.
- One interesting piece of news from Mrs. Hill of California was a copy of Lincoln's Emancipation Proclamation.
- The document assisted George when he was accused of stealing someone's property one afternoon.
- George noticed a young ragged woman chopping wood with a dull axe.
- In conversation, he learned that she was in peonage, in voluntary servitude to pay a debt, and she wanted to leave her master.
- With his help, she fled to a nearby home, and George provided his horse blanket so she could be kept warm during the evening.
- Once he was confident she was safe, George returned to camp.
- The following morning, Lieutenant Fountain learned of Sgt. Upton's activity and demanded that he return the peon to her master.
- George was told his actions constituted the robbery of a man's property, for which George could be jailed.
- Sgt. George Upton explained to Lt. Fountain that the woman was a slave, and, in accordance with the president's Proclamation, he had confiscated her.
- The officer dismissed George and said nothing else about the matter.
- Most of the California Volunteers, including George, thought little of their officers.
- One time, a soldier was caught stealing company food and his offences were read out during dress parade.
- To George's frustration, the major acquitted the man, even with the evidence and witnesses.
- George enjoyed the sentencing of Captain Tuttle for open drunkenness while in charge of the parade at a fort.
- He was so inebriated, he fell flat on his face and had to be carried off by his men.
- Tuttle's punishment was six months' hard labor and the loss of his $5.00 pay for each month of his confinement.
- As the spring season approached, Indian activity became bolder, from harassing an expressman delivering mail on horseback to raiding the army's livestock.

George's army home.

Dealing with his men was sometimes troublesome for George.

- Though mail was having difficulty being delivered at times, military pay was still coming to the troops in the form of U.S. Greenbacks.
- Many of the local merchants had trouble understanding the concept of paper currency and why it had value equal to gold and silver coins.
- George, along with the rest of the California Volunteers, was pleased when the California legislature offered them an additional $5.00 per month from the state's treasury—in gold!
- The arrival of pay encouraged many of the soldiers to spend their wages on whiskey; to avoid the temptation, George attempted staying in on nights following disbursement of pay.
- Dealing with his men proved troublesome at times, but when needed, George could count on them.
- When they were converted from infantry to calvary, the extra duties of taking care of their horses and mules went with little complaint.
- George was pleased to see them adapt to the new situation and blacken their polished rifles.
- This prevented the sun from reflecting off the metal and betraying their position to the Apache.

Life in the Community: The New Mexico Territory
- The New Mexico Territory was a sparsely populated area of the American Southwest with a tenuous identity and a strong history.
- When Mexico gained its independence from Spain in 1821, Santa Fe became the capital of the province of New Mexico.

New Mexico Territory was inhabited by trappers and traders.

- No longer influenced by Spain, the region became inhabited by American trappers and traders.
- Most of the early migration to the region was to the southern part of the territory to the area around the Mesilla Valley, but Santa Fe in the north remained a burgeoning population center.
- Many of the initial traders anticipated finding Santa Fe as an exotic destination for trade only to discover why traders referred to it as the "Siberia of the Mexican Republic."
- Santa Fe encountered an occupation in 1846 when American army general, Stephen Watts Kearny, took the city and raised the American flag over the Plaza during the early stages of the Mexican War.
- Peace later came to the New Mexico Territory when it was obtained by the United States under the 1848 Treaty of Guadalupe Hidalgo.
- Because of the city's language diversity, Santa Fe had a bilingual newspaper in 1849 entitled *The New Mexican.*
- The four-page paper consisted of two pages in English and two in poorly translated Spanish.
- Much of the paper comprised local news because mail outside the territory arrived only once per month.
- National politics strongly influenced the future of the region in the Compromise of 1850.
- The New Mexico Territory was recognized as a slave-holding territory, even though geography and economics made it impractical.
- When the American Civil War started, Confederate troops from Texas invaded and captured a number of the region's towns, including Santa Fe.
- While under the occupation by Confederate forces, the territory was referred to as the Arizona Territory.
- Because of the territory's importance as a land link between California and the eastern United States, Union forces were quickly organized and pushed the Confederate occupiers back into Texas.
- The Union army's mission changed to focus on a pre-existing concern—the settlers' fears of attacks by the Apache and the Navaho.
- This resulted in the United States establishing many military forts and outposts within the region.

HISTORICAL SNAPSHOT
1863

- The Emancipation Proclamation, issued by President Lincoln, took effect January 1, technically freeing nearly four million U.S. slaves

- The first homestead under the Homestead Act was claimed near Beatrice, Nebraska

- Union forces suffered defeat at Chancellorsville, Virginia, with casualties totaling over 16,700

- West Virginia entered the Union as the thirty-fifth state

- Union forces defeated Robert E. Lee's forces in Gettysburg, Pennsylvania

- The National Banking Act was signed into law by President Lincoln to raise money to finance the Union war effort, establish a uniform national currency and provide a dependable market for government bonds

- The first black regiment, the 54th Massachusetts, left Boston to fight in the Civil War

- The International Machinists and Blacksmiths Union adopted a resolution at Boston demanding an eight-hour day instead of a 12-hour one

- The Central Pacific Railroad construction began with ground-breaking ceremonies at Sacramento, California

- Former Mississippi riverboat pilot Samuel Langhorne Clemens adopted the pen name "Mark Twain" in a published letter printed in Carson City's Territorial Enterprise

- *Tales of a Wayside Inn* by Henry Wadsworth Longfellow was published which included the poem "Paul Revere's Ride"

- Edouard Manet's painting, *Le déjeuner sur l'herbe*, was exhibited at the Salon des Refuses in Paris, depicting a nude woman picnicking with two clothed men

- A new Football Association established in England drew up definitive rules for "soccer"

- The first major U.S. racetrack for flat racing opened at Saratoga Springs, New York

- The first four-wheeled roller skates were patented by New York inventor James L. Plimpton

- The Capitol dome at Washington, DC, was capped to complete the structure's construction

- Disruption of sugar plantations in the South sent U.S. sugar prices soaring and brought an increase in sugar planting in the Hawaiian Islands

- President Lincoln proclaimed a national Thanksgiving Day to commemorate the feast given by the Pilgrims in 1621

THE RAIL CANDIDATE.

Selected Prices

Bull Calf $105.00
Bureau, Cedar $5.25
Forks, Silver, Dozen $396.00
Harper's Magazine, Annual Subscription $44.00
Morphine, Spoonful $3.30
Parlor Screen $21.00
Rifle, Colt Revolving $550.00
Rug, Sheepskin $15.75
Sleigh $42.00
Window Blind $52.50

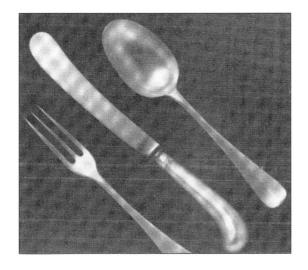

"Encounter with an Apache," *San Francisco Daily Alta,* June 11, 1862:

A soldier named Carver, a member of Company B, 2d Cavalry, California Volunteers, and attached to the body escort of Gen. Carleton, was ordered by him to ride off toward the river, and report the distance from the road to water; and was also instructed not to fire upon any Apache unless first attacked. Carver proceeded for some miles in a northerly direction, and at last arrived at the river, taking the precaution to carry his six-shooter cocked in his right hand. Just as he reached the river, an Apache sprang from the bushes, gun in hand, and the muzzle directed full upon Carver, who, fortunately, saw him at the same moment, and brought his colt to bear upon the savage. The latter stood ready for a few seconds, Carver likewise, both with weapons leveled, and both, doubtless, anxious to fire; but the Indian seemed to think the odds too great, at the short distance between them, some twelve feet, and Carver had positive orders not to fire first. The savage, who was in full panoply of war paint, then dropped his muzzle and said, "How de do?" "How do you do?" replied Carver. "You Captain?" asked the Indian. "No," answered Carver; "Are you a Chief?" "No," growled the ring-streaked and spotted Apache, and without further parley he plunged into the river and swam across, bearing his gun up out of the water as he went. The temptation to shoot was a sore one for Carver, but he would not disobey his orders.

Marching Song of the First California Calvary, *Santa Fe Gazette,* December 17, 1864:

We'll whip the Apache
We'll exterminate the race
Of thieves and assassins
Who the human form disgrace
We'll travel over mountain
And through the valley deep,
We'll travel without eating,
We'll travel without sleep.

"Report on the Navajos," *The New Mexican*, November 14, 1863:

The Navajoes

Are on the walks for plunder. Look out, rancheros, for your herds and flocks. On Thursday of last week, about nine miles below Santa Fe, by the road over the mesa, to Pena Blanca, a deep trail was made, by Indians crossing eastwardly, towards the Pecos. They were on foot, and from the deep, permanent trail they made upon the earth, are supposed to have been some two or three hundred. Such a movement bodeth no good. A detachment of soldiers were sent from here to scout for the Navajoes, but returned "without tidings." The Navajo is for plunder and escape again, and may succeed. "Can such things be, and overcome us like" a winter cloud, pestilence and tempest, "without our special wonder?"

"Life in Tucson, A Tour of Arizona," *Harper's New Monthly Magazine*, December 1864:

If the world were searched over I suppose there could not be found so degraded a set of villains as then formed the principal society of Tucson. Every man went armed to the teeth, and street-fights and bloody affrays were of daily occurrence. Since the coming of the California Volunteers, two years ago, the state of things in this delightful metropolis has materially changed. The citizens who are permitted to live here at all still live very much in the Greaser style—the tenantable houses having been taken away from them for the use of the officers and soldiers who are protecting their property from the Apaches. But then, they have claims for rent, which they can probably sell for something when any body comes along disposed to deal in that sort of paper. Formerly they were troubled a good deal about the care of their cattle and sheep: now they have no trouble at all; the cattle and sheep have fallen into the hands of Apaches, who have become unusually bold in their depredations; and the pigs which formerly roamed unmolested about the streets during the day, and were deemed secure in the back-yards of nights, have become a military necessity. Eggs are scarce, because the hens that used to lay them cackle no more in the hen farm. Drunkenness has been effectually prohibited by a written order limiting the sale of spirituous liquors to three specific establishments, the owners of which pay a license for hospital purposes, the fund whereof goes to the benefit of the sick and disabled, who have fallen a sacrifice to their zeal in the pursuit of hostile Indians. Gambling is also much discountenanced; and nobody gambles when he is out of money, or can't borrow any from other sources. The public regulations are excellent. Volunteer soldiers are stationed all over the town—at the mescal-shops, the monte-tables, and houses of ill-fame—for the preservation of public order, or go there of their own accord for that purpose, which amounts to the same thing. Public property is eminently secure. The Commissary's store-house is secured by a padlock on the door and a guard in front with a musket on his shoulder; so that nobody can go in at any time of the day or night and steal one hundred pounds of coffee and one hundred pounds of sugar, deposited there by private parties for safe-keeping, without killing the guard and breaking open the padlock, or cutting a hole through the adobe wall. If such a thing did occur it would be considered a reflection upon the entire post, and the loss would at once be reimbursed either from public or private sources. Otherwise people would naturally think very strange of such an occurrence.

Abraham Lincoln's Emancipation Proclamation, issued January 1, 1863, technically freed the slaves.

"Battle with the Indians, The California Volunteers and the Navajos in New Mexico—Rifle Balls vs. Arrows," *The New York Times,* March 29, 1864:

The fight commenced simultaneously on right, and left and centre; the Navajos made a stand for one volley from our carbines and they made the air black with arrows for about two minutes, and then they saw so many of their men falling, and none of us, they took to their heels and run for dear life. But it was no go, for we kept close to them, and kept giving the benefit of our breech-loading carbines. Their bows and arrows were like so many straws, for after the first volley, we found that we had the long range on them, and we made use of it. Their arrows are harmless over thirty yards, and they had no rocks to get behind, the battle being on the open plain, so that we chose our own distance and gave them fits. . . .

Just as the sun was going behind the hill we were ordered to cease fire and return home. We went over the battle-ground and found by the simple rule of addition, that out of 120 Indians we had killed 62.

1864 PROFILE

Alan Marsh was 24-years-old when the political itch compelled him to campaign "day and night" for Republican candidate Abraham Lincoln in 1860.

Life at Home

- Although already married with a child, Alan Marsh proudly organized a company of young men "just young enough and strong enough to do some tall yelling" for Republican candidate Abraham Lincoln.
- His wife, Martha, found his political enthusiasm juvenile, unproductive and distracting—especially when fall electioneering got in the way of the harvest.
- Four years Alan's junior, Martha had been tending to children and fields since she was 11, when cholera swept through eastern Iowa and killed both her parents and two older brothers within a week.
- All that was left behind was a partially planted wheat crop, two younger sisters, a newly established family cemetery and a promise that one day each grave would be graced with a headstone.
- Life was hard work and Martha didn't have time for Alan's foolishness.
- Winter was always coming, when God selected the heartiest of his children to live for one more year.
- Abraham Lincoln would do just fine without Alan's help; his riding from town to town with his fellow Republicans "whooping up the electorate" would not improve the harvest one whit.
- Then came the call for volunteers to put down the insurrection of the Southern states.

Alan Marsh avidly campaigned for Abraham Lincoln.

Abraham Lincoln was first elected President in 1860.

- Martha was insistent that Alan was not going.
- Alan listened—for awhile.
- When newly elected President Lincoln called for volunteers to put down the insurrection that threatened the unity of America, the first wave of volunteers was composed of excitable 18 year olds determined to prove their manhood.
- Within a year, they were more balanced—65 percent of the men who enlisted were over 21 years of age.
- By 1862, when Alan finally joined, the median age of a Union soldier was 24.
- Alan firmly believed it was his obligation to fight; if the country created by his father and grandfathers was to survive, it rested with their children to finish the work already begun.
- The general belief within his community was that any man who hired a substitute for $300 "isn't worthy of the name man and should be put in petticoats immediately."
- Martha, too, had come to understand that the entire family would be humiliated if Alan didn't go to war.
- Tavern talk said that "craven cowards and skulkers" who avoided the war would not be allowed to enjoy the peace.
- Alan joined up with four other community men; Martha even brought a flag to wave at his triumphant departure.
- As he boarded the train, he realized he was bidding farewell to baker's bread, cow's milk and other such comforts.
- Later he would write, "more men die of homesickness than all other diseases and when a man gives up and lies down he is a goner."
- His solution was simple: "keep the mind occupied with something new and keep going all the time except when asleep."

Life at Work

- Alan Marsh's introduction to bloodshed and the reality of war came quickly—within two weeks of leaving home.
- The Fifteenth Iowa Infantry were aboard a steamer at Pittsburg Landing having breakfast when the order came to go ashore.
- The Battle of Shiloh, Tennessee, was underway.
- Dressed in new uniforms, hardly soiled by sweat, Alan and his unit ran three miles toward the raging battle.
- Along the way, they met "thousands of men on the retreat who had thrown away their arms and were rushing toward the landing—most of these were hatless and had nothing on them except their clothes."
- Some had been shot, some simply ran, some were being carried on stretchers, a few were covered with blood from head to foot.
- As the Iowa Infantry crossed the ravine and deployed into the line of battle, the Confederates opened fire.
- A man near Alan took a bullet: "He sprang up in the air and gave one groan and fell dead."
- Alan felt compelled to minister to the corpse, but the officers ordered a charge; "no time for the gone."
- The company moved forward and was then pushed back over the same ground; Alan had to fight hard to restrain his instinct to flee the battlefield.
- By day's end the Fifteenth Iowa Infantry had retreated to the bluffs where they had disembarked from their boats at breakfast.
- The next day was more horrible than the first.
- First came the rain, which partially dampened the sounds of wounded, delirious men calling for their mothers or wives.
- Then came the opportunity in the light of day to walk among the bodies of dead and wounded soldiers, Union and Confederate, scattered over the ground.

Alan became a Union soldier at 26 and quickly experienced the bloodshed of war.

- Some of the wounded were so near death from exposure they were "mostly insane."
- He saw that the weapons beside the dead Confederates were antiques of various types: shotguns, older model smooth-bore muskets, and even some primitive pikes.
- A fellow soldier commented, "I hated to hear the rebels cheer when they make the charge, they put me in mind of small schoolchildren about the time school was out."
- On the battlefield, Alan came across a dead rebel who died in great agony; in one motion he pulled a button off the Confederate's coat as a memento of battle.
- In a letter home, Alan confessed, "War is hell broke loose and benumbs all the tender feelings of men and makes them all brutes."

The Battle of Shiloh.

- Twenty five thousand soldiers—Union and Confederate—died in the Battle of Shiloh.
- As the war progressed, Alan found it easier to pick food from Southern civilians, including chickens and roasted ears of corn.
- As a member of a group of armed soldiers invading homes, he came to understand that the civilians' food was their due because the soldiers were loyal and self-sacrificing.
- By the end of his fighting days, just before a bullet shattered his hand, Alan realized that in war burning down houses of civilians was simply "another way to defeat the enemy."
- He also loved to tell his fellow soldiers that Lincoln was a great president—a father figure for the nation—who would be praised by history.
- Slowly he also came to appreciate that if war was a man's rite of passage, then fighting would always be with us as each generation attempted to measure up to those who came before.

Shiloh, Tennessee.

Life in the Community: Shiloh, Tennessee

- Alan Marsh, like most Union soldiers, fought with men recruited from a single community or region.
- They had known each other from childhood and, if they survived the war, would know each other as old men.
- Everyone knew that a show of cowardice would be a brand to carry the rest of their lives.
- Thanks to a steady exchange of letters, information and gossip were passed back and forth between the men of the army and the people back home on a weekly basis.
- Soldiers learned from neighbors that their wives were "destitute of everything for her comfort and without food or wood."
- A private's monthly pay of $13 rarely covered the needs of both home and soldier.
- When one soldier's wife learned that her husband had been unfaithful, she wrote him immediately in a letter incorporating details only his fellow soldiers could have known.
- Another volunteer was shocked that his parents had learned that he had been found guilty of unworthy conduct.
- For some, the hunger for respect and admiration back home was best described in songs such as "Just Before the Battle, Mother," or "The Drummer Boy of Shiloh."

Letters from home kept the soldiers informed.

- Abraham Lincoln was re-elected president with Andrew Johnson as his vice president

- Both the Union and Confederate armies suffered significant losses in the Battle of Spotsylvania, Virginia

- Union Major General William T. Sherman's troops set fires that destroyed much of Atlanta during their march through the South

- Congress first authorized the use of the phrase "In God We Trust" on a coin

- Secretary of War Edwin Stanton signed an order establishing a military burial ground at Confederate General Robert E. Lee's home estate in Arlington, Virginia

- Maryland voters adopted a new constitution that included the abolition of slavery

- Nevada became the thirty-sixth state

- The first salmon cannery in the United States was established at Washington, California

- Inflation devalued Confederate currency to $4.60 per $100 note

- Both the University of Kansas and the University of Denver were formed

- The Geneva Convention established the neutrality of battlefield facilities

- The Knights of Pythias was founded in Washington, DC

- George Pullman and Ben Feld patented the railroad sleeping car

- U.S. wheat prices reached $4.00 per bushel

- Confederate agents set Barnum Museum on fire in an attempt to burn New York City

- European immigrants poured into America to take advantage of the Homestead Act free land

- Louis Pasteur invented pasteurization for wine

Selected Prices

Chicken Coop	$42.00
Clover Seed, Bushel	$65.52
Gunpowder, Pound, Smuggled by Confederacy	$63.00
Gunpowder, Pound	$3.78
Lard Can	$11.00
Milk Pan	$0.55
Piano	$550.00
Quinine, Ounce	$110.00
Window Shade	$1.32
Wood, Cord	$192.50

A Soldier's Letter Home from A. S. Bright, 1863:

Dear Uncle,

Sam Caldwell came in just as I finished writing last night. He left Washington yesterday morning. He brought us a chicken, a can of tomatoes, and some tobacco. I tell you that it was a great treat to us at present. He says to get anything we want sent to him and he will forward it to us, so John and I concluded to write and get you to send eatables. If you see any of the rest of the friends and they feel inclined to send us anything tell them we will not waste it. If convenient send me a little butter and a can of apple butter. If you have any apples put in two or three, for I have not seen an apple for a year. Send me some canned fruit and anything that is good to eat and send me a plug of tobacco and a hundreds tobys.

A. B.
Camp near Belle Plain, Virginia
December 27, 1863

"Editor's Easy Chair," *Harper's New Monthly Magazine*, October 1866:

A great historical event has occurred since our last talk, and it has been received almost as a matter of course. The distance between Europe and America has been practically annihilated; the Atlantic Ocean has been abolished; steam as an agent of communications has been antiquated; we read every morning the previous day's news from London or Paris, and there is no excitement whatever. Scarcely a bell has rung or a cannon roared. Not even a dinner has been eaten in honor of the great event, except by the gentleman immediately concerned; and the salvo of speeches which usually resounds upon much inferior occasions from end to end of the country has been omitted. Indeed, the first thing was caviling and sneering, and an insinuation that the ocean telegraph was no "great shakes" after all. Persons of a cynical turn, however, observed that the declamatory strain proceeded from the newspapers, upon which the success imposed a heavy outlay. The insatiable public must have all the news at the old expense; and experience has demonstrated that, to the public, no new news is worth more than three or five cents.

continued

"Editor's Easy Chair," *Harper's New Monthly Magazine,* . . . (continued)

Indeed, the possible results of the union of the two continents are so incalculable that all the commentators have avoided speculation. They will be so rapidly developed that we can well wait. The first and inevitable consequences has been the sweeping away of the old and intense general interest in the heading of "Three days (more or less) later from Europe" which has so long heralded the arrival of the ocean steamers. The steamers bring the cream no longer. That is shot electronically under the sea, and the ships suddenly convey only skim milk. They are yet young men who remember the arrival of the *Sirius* and the *Liverpool* and the *Great Western.* Their coming was the occasion of a thousand fold greater excitement than the laying of the cable. Yet if some visionary enthusiast had said to his friend as they watched with awe the steaming in or out of those huge ships, "Before we are bald and gray we shall look upon these vessels as we look from the express train upon the slow old stage-coaches," he would have been tolerated only as a harmless maniac. But this kind of maniac is very apt to prove the only wise man. The sole folly is in setting limits on the scope and results of invention.

That the cholera has not stricken the country with panic is mainly due to the thorough discussion of the subject ample preparation that was every where made. Yet the resistance of various kinds offered to the operations in the New York Board of Health has been a mortifying illustration of the want of a truly generous public spirit. Instead of aiding in every way the strenuous and essential efforts of the Board, they have been opposed by protests, injunctions, and slanders, as if they were a despotism aiming at oppression and injustice. "The public is an ass, my son," said a sententious old philosopher; "but don't treat it as such, or it will kick you."

The government tried to control disease within the community.

Diary of Asa Smith, 25-Year-Old Union Soldier from Massachusetts:

June 29, 1862
Near the James River, Virginia

About the time we got into position, we heard the rebel yell as they came upon our abandoned works, and knew they would soon be upon us. Soon artillery and musketry fire began up the line of the railroad, nearer to Richmond, and very quickly came toward us; and shell began to come in our direction. We remained here under this fire for about one hour and a half, and did not see a rebel soldier, as the infantry in the neighborhood were trying to advance down the cut, that's been entirely out of our sight.

The infantry fire became quite heavy, and remained so for at least an hour. Quite a number of unexploded shell and shrapnel came over, and only one did any damage. I saw this one coming right for us, but it was a little high and struck in the lines of the Pennsylvania 26th, killing a man. As he was lying on the ground it tore off one arm, one leg, and the foot of the remaining leg. The victim gave one shriek and died in a few minutes.

After a time firing ceased, and we were marched to the rear at a lively pace.

The roads were crowded with troops of all arms, making it hard work to move; but we were pushed unmercifully. After some time we reached Savage Station on the railroad, and found troops marching through the village toward the James River. Every road was full, and all were hustling lively.

Great quantities of supplies were being destroyed here, one large warehouse being filled with clothing. All were burned.

On we went toward White Oaks Swamp, through the narrow roads, through a growth of tall pine which shut out the breeze, while the sun's rays beat upon us fiercely. The air was full of dust, so it was impossible to tell the color of anyone's hair or of his uniform. The pace was hurried, we found ourselves getting short of water and becoming exhausted.

I staggered in the ranks, but did not fall out as did many. At last when it seemed as if I could go but a little farther, I was refreshed by a swallow of vinegar kindly given me by a comrade, and struggled along until we reached the swamp, where in the company with hundreds of others I go down upon my hands and knees and drank from the rut in the road, where men, horses, mules, guns, etc., had been passing all day. . . .

In the course of an hour or two, skirmishing commenced in front of McCall, followed very quickly by heavy firing of both artillery and infantry. In a little while it appeared to be nearer, and we were called to arms. We were formed behind a worm fence of a side hill, and in a few minutes a battery came galloping up and took the position previously noted by General Hooker.

Before long the Pennsylvanians began to approach us at a run, and attempted to break to the rear. We gathered in all that we could and reformed them (or part of them) in our rear. Very soon the enemy's artillery opened and quickly got the range, shells bursting in the air just in front so as to send the thesis directly among us. This continued for some time while the advance forces were being driven. Without any warning there came a sudden, sharp crack followed closely by others, the screeching of shell from the battery in the rear. The guns were so near that it seemed as though our eardrums would burst; but in a few minutes we became somewhat accustomed to the sounds, and minded them very little.

The enemy's shells flew thick and fast, and there were some close calls. One piece came down and grazed the side of my left shoe, partially burying itself in the ground. As I stooped and got hold of it, the Captain saw it, and said, "A miss is as good as a mile, Corporal," and I felt the same way about it.

"Monthly Records of Current Events,"
Harper's New Monthly Magazine,
October 1866:

Admission of Southern Representation to Congress

I do not wish them to come back into the Union a degraded and despised people. If they come back so, they
would not be fit to be a portion of the great American
people. I want them to come back with all their rights and
privileges.

—President Andrew Johnson, 1866

We see by the tone of the papers that these people are not ready for reconstruction. There is a mass of overwhelming evidence upon the subject. . . . The Southern man, whether arrived at the common age of man or not, knows he can go to any part of the north and speak his sentiments freely, and I did not want any part of this country represented in Congress until you and I can go and argue the principles of free government without fear of the knife or pistol, or of being murdered by a mob. And when men ask me how long I would keep these men out, I say, Keep them out until the heavens melt with fervent heat, until they will allow free speech and free press throughout their land. And if it should not come in this generation, we will swear her sons to keep them out until they become fit for a republican form of government.

—General B. F. Butler, 1866

In the struggle tomorrow we shall be fighting men of our own blood, Western men, who understand the use of firearms. The struggle will be a desperate one.

—P. G. T. Beauregard on the Battle of Shiloh, April 1862

1866 NEWS FEATURE

"The Freedman's Story," *Harper's New Monthly Magazine*, October 1866:

My name is Oby, they say it is because my father was an Obeah man when he lived down south in Florida and drove a stage. I have heard him say, to the contrary, that he belonged, at the time I was born, to a man by the name of Overton, and that is my true name. So when I went down to town the other day, and the Provost-Marshal asked me if I could sign my own name, I boldly wrote down "Mr. Overton Paragon."

I was raised at this place, by people who were ever so kind to me as long as I can remember them; but that was not very long, for they were poor white folks and could not keep me, or my mother, or my father either. So we were hired out to a very good master, who took good care of father especially, because he hired him for more than 20 years, and I was living with them in his house, though I could not do much work, being rather weakly and, I am afraid, lazy too. One fine day master comes downstairs and says to my father: Uncle James you have served me faithfully these ten years, and you know I only bought you because I did not want your master to set you in your old days to hard work. But I do not like to own you, and you are free. You can go whenever and wherever you choose. I can not give you your freedom in any other way, because the laws of the state do not permit me to do so, and we all have to obey the law; but you must understand that you can stay or go as you choose."

Father could not say much, for he was not handy with his tongue, but he told master did he did not want to leave him as long as he cared to keep him. But when master had gone up again, he comes in and tells mother, and Uncle Henry, who was there tells him he had better go across the line and live at the North. Father had been there when master sent him all the way to Boston with a fine horse—his name was Topaz—and they tried very hard then to make father stay. But he did not like their ways; he said they were not genteel at all like our old family servants, he came back and was mighty glad to be again in Old Virginia. So father staid, and mother staid, and I was taken up to the dining room, and mistress taught me to wait, to wash the china and the glass.

I was nearly grown—I may have been about nineteen or twenty years old—and the Yankees came down upon us. We had been expecting them often before, and many is the time Uncle Henry came running in where mother was and cried out, "God be thanked, they are coming, they are coming!" And mother asked him, "Who are you talking about?" He would say, "Our deliverers, the Yankees, whom God sends to make us all free!" But Mother did not like his ways at all, and when he was gone she would take me and brother Henry by her little stool close to the fire and say: "Now boys, don't think you'll be much better off when you're free. Folks have to work everywhere, free or slave, black or white; and it's much better for you to be with genteel folks, go to church, and nothing to do with poor niggers, than to be way off, where you have not anybody who cares for you."

Mother was mighty good to us, and I know she meant it all for the best, but to save my life, I could not help thinking of what Uncle Henry said, and what a fine thing it would be to be free, to have twelve dollars a month and nothing to do. So I went over to Colonel Wood's Aleck and we talked it over behind the wood-pile, where nobody could hear us, and he told me how he knew a great plenty more who would go away as soon as the Yankees came. He said they were fighting for us, and if we wanted to go you need not run away by night, like a poor three-hundred-dollar nigger, but we might ride off on a fine horse, in the middle of the day, and our masters would not say a word against it for fear of the Yankees. So I promised I would join him, and when we heard that General Sheridan was coming this way, with a hundred thousand men, we knew that the Confederates could not stand before him, and we agreed we would go off all together.

I remember it well; it was a dark night, but the stars were all out and the mud awfully deep, when all of a sudden Uncle Henry comes rushing in by the side gate, quite out of breath, and tells us that General Early has been beaten all to pieces, and that the Yankees are coming across the mountains. They did not know any thing of it in town, and I had heard Master say at supper-table that we need not be afraid; the Yankees would again go up the Valley of Lexington and pass us by. But we knew better, and mother would have told mistress, whom she was mighty fond of, but Uncle Henry would not let her, and mother was terribly worried about it. He told us that we must all put on our Sunday clothes, and be very polite to the soldiers, because they were coming to make us all free, and we were just as good now as they. Father was very uneasy about us, for he did not believe half of what the others said, and he shook his head and groaned as he sat before the fire and smoked his pipe; but he said nothing, only now and then he would look up, and when mother looked at him at the same time, he would shake his head and sigh, until it made me feel quite badly, and I did not know what to do.

At night, when the white folks had all gone to bed, we, Aleck and I, took an ash cake and a piece of middling, and we ran up the turnpike, miles and miles, until we came to the top of the long hill, where Doctor White's house stood before it was burned, and there we sat the livelong night, and watched the camp-fires against the dark mountain side, thinking what the Yankees were doing up there, and why they did not come to help us all. It was very hard to trot back again in the morning early, and go to work splitting wood for the cook before breakfast, but Aleck and I thought if we could but once see the blue coats coming down the hill, and see their horses standing by the side of the lake, we would be perfectly happy.

And so I did come about one time, clear morning. On Monday a man in gray had come racing up the turnpike, turning right and left under his broad-brimmed hat, and gone into town. Uncle Henry had met him as he came up, and shook his head and said: Now I should not wonder if that was a real Yankee." They all laughed at him, and asked him if he did not see the Confederate gray and the ragged hat the man wore. But he shook his head and said: Now, I'll tell you, boys it may be so, and it may not be so; but that man there did not ride like one of our folks, and he had eyes too busy in his head and hand too near his revolver to be one of our soldiers." That morning early there came two, and three, and at last the whole number of these graycoats, and someone said in a whisper, as we were standing at the stile close to the turnpike, "Those are the Jesse Scout, you believe me!" But we looked at the old man who said so, and as nobody knew him, and we do not believe him. It was all the same true; it turned out afterwards they were Jesse Scouts, as they called them from General Fremont's wife; and there had been a dozen of them in town all day long, and nobody had known them. We knew how little our soldiers cared about spies and that sort of men, so it was not very difficult to come in and find out every thing.

But on Tuesday, early in the morning, as soon as master had had his breakfast, we all slipped down and went down to the road, where we found a great many people standing about and talking of what the Yankees were going to do with the house, and the servants, and the town itself. Down by the lake, where the road from the house comes into the turnpike, and not far from the little lodge, stood a heap of gentleman, who had come up from town to beg pardon of the General, and ask him not to burn them all out. They were mightily scared, and Mr. Fowler, the tailor, who is a great goose, as I've heard it said often and often, looked white and shock in all his limbs. It could not be from the cold, for although the rain had stopped overnight, it was quite mild in the morning. Alongside of them, but a little apart, stood master and some of his friends; I don't know if they too had come to ask the Yankees to spare the house. Soon one man came flying down the hill, and then another, and then three or four together, galloping right past without ever stopping, and just crying one after another, "They are coming, they are coming!" I slipped up close to where master stood, and I could hear them say it was a mighty hard thing to stand there and not know whether they would have a house over their head next night or not; and what would become of the ladies and of the little ones. One I heard say distinctly, "Oh gentleman, we will all go before tonight, sure enough!" William Gibbons, who preaches down in the big bath-house every Sunday, said the gentleman was being very wicked, for if God would take us up we must all be ready at any time; and he, for one, was quite willing to go to heaven.

Every now and then someone would cry out, "There they are!" and we all looked up to the top the hill, behind which the road was hid, and when a man slowly rose over the brow it turned out that he was on horseback, and we thought sure enough there were the Yankees. So we stood hours and hours, and just when we thought they would not be coming that day, two men rode up the hill and down again slowly, then three more, then a dozen or more in a body, with flags in their hands; and at last the whole turnpike was blue, and we knew for a certainty they were come. We just looked at one another, and I felt mighty queer; but Uncle Henry and all the others, who stood way down by the stile, looked exactly as if they were going to shout to the sky and jump out of their skin. Aleck looked at me too, and winked, and shut his eyes, and shook all over, till I could not help myself, and I laughed, and they all laughed, and it set the others down at the stile a-laughing, and we held our sides and did not mind master and his friends looking at us as if they did not like it at all.

When the first officer came up to where Mr. Fowler stood, he rushed forward and came near falling between the horses' feet, and they all cried out together, I don't know what; but the tailor had the biggest mouth, and he talked loudest. So I suppose I heard him, one of the officers said something about private property been spared, but public property must be given up.

Just then master walked up himself, like a real gentleman that he is, and although he was on foot and had not even a spur on his boot, he looked as good a man as the big officers on their fine horses. One of them told him he was not the General, but they would send up a guard as soon as they got into town. Then they moved on, and such a sight! They looked very different from our poor Confederate soldiers, with their sleek horses and bright swords, and there was not a ragged jacket or a bare foot among them all. They had, everyone of them, a pile of good thing strapped on both behind and before their saddles, and a good many had a fine horse on the other side with all sorts of packages and parcels strapped upon their back, ever so high, but nobody in the saddle. But I thought, what wouldn't I give if I could but ride one of those fine horses and be a soldier and as good as any white man! I looked at Aleck, and I saw he thought so too; and what is best about it, he did not last long, it all came true, sure enough. We stood there and looked and looked until we were tired, for there was no end to the horses, and the big guns, and the wagons, and oh, they had every thing so nice and so whole, though they were bespattered from head to foot; I did not think soldiers could look so well. At last they were nearly all gone, and I and Aleck went back.

When we came to the other side of the lake we saw Miss Mary and some of the other young ladies standing by the window upstairs, and some of them were crying; but Miss Mary waved a little flag such as our soldiers have, right in the face the Yankees. But master looked up and gave her such a look! Miss Mary went away from the window and when they sent for her to come down to dinner, she told Flora to tell master she had a bad headache and did not want any dinner. Soon after the bell rang, and when I went to the front-door there stood a big Yankee soldier, with his sword by his side and the mud all over him, and he asked in a very soft voice if master was at home. I did not much like his talking to my master and he a Yankee, but I knew I must be polite to strangers, and I asked him to please walk in. He said he wanted to see master, would I request him to come to the front-door for a moment. I didn't tell exactly what it was that was there, but there was something in the officer's voice, and in the way he spoke to me, made me feel a big man, and as if nobody ought to call me Oby any more. Master is mighty good to me, but he always talks to me as if I was a little baby and had not any sense at all. Now the officer spoke right sternly, though his voice was so soft, but somehow did not hurt me in the least, and I felt all the better for it. I ran in and told master, who came out at once, not at all flurried like a grand old gentleman, and he begged the officer very politely to walk in. But he would not come in, and merely told master he was on General Sheridan's staff, and that he wished to know where he should place the guard. I wanted badly to hear what they were going to say to each other, but master sent me downstairs to tell Aunt Hannah to cook a big dinner for the soldiers. We've done that often enough when our poor Confederates came by, and there was not much left in the smokehouse; but when the folks in the kitchen heard it was for the Yankees they were going to cook they set to work with a will. Aunt Hannah said she would sit up all night to work for them blessed Yankees, and Flora laughed and cried out she hoped it was a handsome captain coming to take her to Boston. . . .

INDEX

Page numbers in italics indicate images. Bold entries indicate profile subjects.

Page numbers in italics indicate images. Bold entries indicate profile subjects.

Page numbers in italics indicate images. Bold entries indicate profile subjects.

Page numbers in italics indicate images. Bold entries indicate profile subjects.

Page numbers in italics indicate images. Bold entries indicate profile subjects.

Page numbers in italics indicate images. Bold entries indicate profile subjects.

Page numbers in italics indicate images. Bold entries indicate profile subjects.

Business Information ◆ Ratings Guides ◆ General Reference ◆ Education ◆
Statistics ◆ Demographics ◆ Health Information ◆ Canadian Information

Grey House Publishing

The Directory of Business Information Resources, 2009

With 100% verification, over 1,000 new listings and more than 12,000 updates, *The Directory of Business Information Resources* is the most up-to-date source for contacts in over 98 business areas – from advertising and agriculture to utilities and wholesalers. This carefully researched volume details: the Associations representing each industry; the Newsletters that keep members current; the Magazines and Journals - with their "Special Issues" - that are important to the trade, the Conventions that are "must attends," Databases, Directories and Industry Web Sites that provide access to must-have marketing resources. Includes contact names, phone & fax numbers, web sites and e-mail addresses. This one-volume resource is a gold mine of information and would be a welcome addition to any reference collection.

"This is a most useful and easy-to-use addition to any researcher's library." –The Information Professionals Institute

Softcover ISBN 978-1-59237-399-4, 2,500 pages, $195.00 | Online Database: http://gold.greyhouse.com Call (800) 562-2139 for quote

Hudson's Washington News Media Contacts Directory, 2009

With 100% verification of data, *Hudson's Washington News Media Contacts Directory* is the most accurate, most up-to-date source for media contacts in our nation's capital. With the largest concentration of news media in the world, having access to Washington's news media will get your message heard by these key media outlets. Published for over 40 years, Hudson's Washington News Media Contacts Directory brings you immediate access to: News Services & Newspapers, News Service Syndicates, DC Newspapers, Foreign Newspapers, Radio & TV, Magazines & Newsletters, and Freelance Writers & Photographers. The easy-to-read entries include contact names, phone & fax numbers, web sites and e-mail and more. For easy navigation, Hudson's Washington News Media Contacts Directory contains two indexes: Entry Index and Executive Index. This kind of comprehensive and up-to-date information would cost thousands of dollars to replicate or countless hours of searching to find. Don't miss this opportunity to have this important resource in your collection, and start saving time and money today. Hudson's Washington News Media Contacts Directory is the perfect research tool for Public Relations, Marketing, Networking and so much more. This resource is a gold mine of information and would be a welcome addition to any reference collection.

Softcover ISBN 978-1-59237-407-6, 800 pages, $289.00 | Online Database: http://gold.greyhouse.com Call (800) 562-2139 for quote

Nations of the World, 2009 A Political, Economic and Business Handbook

This completely revised edition covers all the nations of the world in an easy-to-use, single volume. Each nation is profiled in a single chapter that includes Key Facts, Political & Economic Issues, a Country Profile and Business Information. In this fast-changing world, it is extremely important to make sure that the most up-to-date information is included in your reference collection. This edition is just the answer. Each of the 200+ country chapters have been carefully reviewed by a political expert to make sure that the text reflects the most current information on Politics, Travel Advisories, Economics and more. You'll find such vital information as a Country Map, Population Characteristics, Inflation, Agricultural Production, Foreign Debt, Political History, Foreign Policy, Regional Insecurity, Economics, Trade & Tourism, Historical Profile, Political Systems, Ethnicity, Languages, Media, Climate, Hotels, Chambers of Commerce, Banking, Travel Information and more. Five Regional Chapters follow the main text and include a Regional Map, an Introductory Article, Key Indicators and Currencies for the Region. As an added bonus, an all-inclusive CD-ROM is available as a companion to the printed text. Noted for its sophisticated, up-to-date and reliable compilation of political, economic and business information, this brand new edition will be an important acquisition to any public, academic or special library reference collection.

"A useful addition to both general reference collections and business collections." –RUSQ

Softcover ISBN 978-1-59237-273-7, 1,700 pages, $175.00

The Directory of Venture Capital & Private Equity Firms, 2009

This edition has been extensively updated and broadly expanded to offer direct access to over 2,800 Domestic and International Venture Capital Firms, including address, phone & fax numbers, e-mail addresses and web sites for both primary and branch locations. Entries include details on the firm's Mission Statement, Industry Group Preferences, Geographic Preferences, Average and Minimum Investments and Investment Criteria. You'll also find details that are available nowhere else, including the Firm's Portfolio Companies and extensive information on each of the firm's Managing Partners, such as Education, Professional Background and Directorships held, along with the Partner's E-mail Address. *The Directory of Venture Capital & Private Equity Firms* offers five important indexes: Geographic Index, Executive Name Index, Portfolio Company Index, Industry Preference Index and College & University Index. With its comprehensive coverage and detailed, extensive information on each company, The Directory of Venture Capital & Private Equity Firms is an important addition to any finance collection.

"The sheer number of listings, the descriptive information and the outstanding indexing make this directory a better value than ...Pratt's Guide to Venture Capital Sources. Recommended for business collections in large public, academic and business libraries." –Choice

Softcover ISBN 978-1-59237-398-7, 1,300 pages, $565/$450 Lib | Online DB: http://gold.greyhouse.com Call (800) 562-2139 for quote

Business Information ✦ Ratings Guides ✦ General Reference ✦ Education ✦
Statistics ✦ Demographics ✦ Health Information ✦ Canadian Information

Grey House Publishing

The Encyclopedia of Emerging Industries
*Published under an exclusive license from the Gale Group, Inc.

The fifth edition of the *Encyclopedia of Emerging Industries* details the inception, emergence, and current status of nearly 120 flourishing U.S. industries and industry segments. These focused essays unearth for users a wealth of relevant, current, factual data previously accessible only through a diverse variety of sources. This volume provides broad-based, highly-readable, industry information under such headings as Industry Snapshot, Organization & Structure, Background & Development, Industry Leaders, Current Conditions, America and the World, Pioneers, and Research & Technology. Essays in this new edition, arranged alphabetically for easy use, have been completely revised, with updated statistics and the most current information on industry trends and developments. In addition, there are new essays on some of the most interesting and influential new business fields, including Application Service Providers, Concierge Services, Entrepreneurial Training, Fuel Cells, Logistics Outsourcing Services, Pharmacogenomics, and Tissue Engineering. Two indexes, General and Industry, provide immediate access to this wealth of information. Plus, two conversion tables for SIC and NAICS codes, along with Suggested Further Readings, are provided to aid the user. *The Encyclopedia of Emerging Industries* pinpoints emerging industries while they are still in the spotlight. This important resource will be an important acquisition to any business reference collection.

"This well-designed source…should become another standard business source, nicely complementing Standard & Poor's Industry Surveys. It contains more information on each industry than Hoover's Handbook of Emerging Companies, is broader in scope than The Almanac of American Employers 1998-1999, but is less expansive than the Encyclopedia of Careers & Vocational Guidance. Highly recommended for all academic libraries and specialized business collections." –Library Journal

Hardcover ISBN 978-1-59237-242-3, 1,400 pages, $325.00

Encyclopedia of American Industries
*Published under an exclusive license from the Gale Group, Inc.

The Encyclopedia of American Industries is a major business reference tool that provides detailed, comprehensive information on a wide range of industries in every realm of American business. A two volume set, Volume I provides separate coverage of nearly 500 manufacturing industries, while Volume II presents nearly 600 essays covering the vast array of services and other non-manufacturing industries in the United States. Combined, these two volumes provide individual essays on every industry recognized by the U.S. Standard Industrial Classification (SIC) system. Both volumes are arranged numerically by SIC code, for easy use. Additionally, each entry includes the corresponding NAICS code(s). The *Encyclopedia's* business coverage includes information on historical events of consequence, as well as current trends and statistics. Essays include an Industry Snapshot, Organization & Structure, Background & Development, Current Conditions, Industry Leaders, Workforce, America and the World, Research & Technology along with Suggested Further Readings. Both SIC and NAICS code conversion tables and an all-encompassing Subject Index, with cross-references, complete the text. With its detailed, comprehensive information on a wide range of industries, this resource will be an important tool for both the industry newcomer and the seasoned professional.

"Encyclopedia of American Industries contains detailed, signed essays on virtually every industry in contemporary society. ... Highly recommended for all but the smallest libraries." -American Reference Books Annual

Two Volumes, Hardcover ISBN 978-1-59237-244-7, 3,000 pages, $650.00

Encyclopedia of Global Industries
*Published under an exclusive license from the Gale Group, Inc.

This fourth edition of the acclaimed *Encyclopedia of Global Industries* presents a thoroughly revised and expanded look at more than 125 business sectors of global significance. Detailed, insightful articles discuss the origins, development, trends, key statistics and current international character of the world's most lucrative, dynamic and widely researched industries – including hundreds of profiles of leading international corporations. Beginning researchers will gain from this book a solid understanding of how each industry operates and which countries and companies are significant participants, while experienced researchers will glean current and historical figures for comparison and analysis. The industries profiled in previous editions have been updated, and in some cases, expanded to reflect recent industry trends. Additionally, this edition provides both SIC and NAICS codes for all industries profiled. As in the original volumes, *The Encyclopedia of Global Industries* offers thorough studies of some of the biggest and most frequently researched industry sectors, including Aircraft, Biotechnology, Computers, Internet Services, Motor Vehicles, Pharmaceuticals, Semiconductors, Software and Telecommunications. An SIC and NAICS conversion table and an all-encompassing Subject Index, with cross-references, are provided to ensure easy access to this wealth of information. These and many others make the *Encyclopedia of Global Industries* the authoritative reference for studies of international industries.

"Provides detailed coverage of the history, development, and current status of 115 of "the world's most lucrative and high-profile industries." It far surpasses the Department of Commerce's U.S. Global Trade Outlook 1995-2000 (GPO, 1995) in scope and coverage. Recommended for comprehensive public and academic library business collections." -Booklist

Hardcover ISBN 978-1-59237-243-0, 1,400 pages, $495.00

Business Information ✦ **Ratings Guides** ✦ **General Reference** ✦ **Education** ✦
Statistics ✦ **Demographics** ✦ **Health Information** ✦ **Canadian Information**

The Directory of Mail Order Catalogs, 2009

Published since 1981, *The Directory of Mail Order Catalogs* is the premier source of information on the mail order catalog industry. It is the source that business professionals and librarians have come to rely on for the thousands of catalog companies in the US. Since the 2007 edition, *The Directory of Mail Order Catalogs* has been combined with its companion volume, *The Directory of Business to Business Catalogs*, to offer all 13,000 catalog companies in one easy-to-use volume. Section I: Consumer Catalogs, covers over 9,000 consumer catalog companies in 44 different product chapters from Animals to Toys & Games. Section II: Business to Business Catalogs, details 5,000 business catalogs, everything from computers to laboratory supplies, building construction and much more. Listings contain detailed contact information including mailing address, phone & fax numbers, web sites, e-mail addresses and key contacts along with important business details such as product descriptions, employee size, years in business, sales volume, catalog size, number of catalogs mailed and more. *The Directory of Mail Order Catalogs*, now with its expanded business to business catalogs, is the largest and most comprehensive resource covering this billion-dollar industry. It is the standard in its field. This important resource is a useful tool for entrepreneurs searching for catalogs to pick up their product, vendors looking to expand their customer base in the catalog industry, market researchers, small businesses investigating new supply vendors, along with the library patron who is exploring the available catalogs in their areas of interest.

"This is a godsend for those looking for information." –Reference Book Review

Softcover ISBN 978-1-59237-396-3, 1,700 pages, $350/$250 Lib | Online DB: http://gold.greyhouse.com Call (800) 562-2139 for quote

Sports Market Place Directory, 2008

For over 20 years, this comprehensive, up-to-date directory has offered direct access to the Who, What, When & Where of the Sports Industry. With over 20,000 updates and enhancements, the *Sports Market Place Directory* is the most detailed, comprehensive and current sports business reference source available. In 1,800 information-packed pages, *Sports Market Place Directory* profiles contact information and key executives for: Single Sport Organizations, Professional Leagues, Multi-Sport Organizations, Disabled Sports, High School & Youth Sports, Military Sports, Olympic Organizations, Media, Sponsors, Sponsorship & Marketing Event Agencies, Event & Meeting Calendars, Professional Services, College Sports, Manufacturers & Retailers, Facilities and much more. The Sports Market Place Directory provides organization's contact information with detailed descriptions including: Key Contacts, physical, mailing, email and web addresses plus phone and fax numbers. *Sports Market Place Directory* provides a one-stop resources for this billion-dollar industry. This will be an important resource for large public libraries, university libraries, university athletic programs, career services or job placement organizations, and is a must for anyone doing research on or marketing to the US and Canadian sports industry.

"Grey House is the new publisher and has produced an excellent edition...highly recommended for public libraries and academic libraries with sports management programs or strong interest in athletics." -Booklist

Softcover ISBN 978-1-59237-348-2, 1,800 pages, $225.00 | Online Database: http://gold.greyhouse.com Call (800) 562-2139 for quote

Food and Beverage Market Place, 2009

Food and Beverage Market Place is bigger and better than ever with thousands of new companies, thousands of updates to existing companies and two revised and enhanced product category indexes. This comprehensive directory profiles over 18,000 Food & Beverage Manufacturers, 12,000 Equipment & Supply Companies, 2,200 Transportation & Warehouse Companies, 2,000 Brokers & Wholesalers, 8,000 Importers & Exporters, 900 Industry Resources and hundreds of Mail Order Catalogs. Listings include detailed Contact Information, Sales Volumes, Key Contacts, Brand & Product Information, Packaging Details and much more. *Food and Beverage Market Place* is available as a three-volume printed set, a subscription-based Online Database via the Internet, on CD-ROM, as well as mailing lists and a licensable database.

"An essential purchase for those in the food industry but will also be useful in public libraries where needed. Much of the information will be difficult and time consuming to locate without this handy three-volume ready-reference source." –ARBA

3 Vol Set, Softcover ISBN 978-1-59237-361-1, 8,500 pages, $595 | Online DB: http://gold.greyhouse.com Call (800) 562-2139 for quote

The Grey House Performing Arts Directory, 2009

The Grey House Performing Arts Directory is the most comprehensive resource covering the Performing Arts. This important directory provides current information on over 8,500 Dance Companies, Instrumental Music Programs, Opera Companies, Choral Groups, Theater Companies, Performing Arts Series and Performing Arts Facilities. Plus, this edition now contains a brand new section on Artist Management Groups. In addition to mailing address, phone & fax numbers, e-mail addresses and web sites, dozens of other fields of available information include mission statement, key contacts, facilities, seating capacity, season, attendance and more. This directory also provides an important Information Resources section that covers hundreds of Performing Arts Associations, Magazines, Newsletters, Trade Shows, Directories, Databases and Industry Web Sites. Five indexes provide immediate access to this wealth of information: Entry Name, Executive Name, Performance Facilities, Geographic and Information Resources. *The Grey House Performing Arts Directory* pulls together thousands of Performing Arts Organizations, Facilities and Information Resources into an easy-to-use source – this kind of comprehensiveness and extensive detail is not available in any resource on the market place today.

"Immensely useful and user-friendly … recommended for public, academic and certain special library reference collections." –Booklist

Softcover ISBN 978-1-59237-376-5, 1,500 pages, $185.00 | Online Database: http://gold.greyhouse.com Call (800) 562-2139 for quote

Business Information ✦ **Ratings Guides** ✦ **General Reference** ✦ **Education** ✦
Statistics ✦ **Demographics** ✦ **Health Information** ✦ **Canadian Information**

The Environmental Resource Handbook, 2008/09

The Environmental Resource Handbook is the most up-to-date and comprehensive source for Environmental Resources and Statistics. Section I: Resources provides detailed contact information for thousands of information sources, including Associations & Organizations, Awards & Honors, Conferences, Foundations & Grants, Environmental Health, Government Agencies, National Parks & Wildlife Refuges, Publications, Research Centers, Educational Programs, Green Product Catalogs, Consultants and much more. Section II: Statistics, provides statistics and rankings on hundreds of important topics, including Children's Environmental Index, Municipal Finances, Toxic Chemicals, Recycling, Climate, Air & Water Quality and more. This kind of up-to-date environmental data, all in one place, is not available anywhere else on the market place today. This vast compilation of resources and statistics is a must-have for all public and academic libraries as well as any organization with a primary focus on the environment.

> *"...the intrinsic value of the information make it worth consideration by libraries with environmental collections and environmentally concerned users." –Booklist*

Softcover ISBN 978-1-59237-195-2, 1,000 pages, $155.00 | Online Database: http://gold.greyhouse.com Call (800) 562-2139 for quote

New York State Directory, 2008/09

The New York State Directory, published annually since 1983, is a comprehensive and easy-to-use guide to accessing public officials and private sector organizations and individuals who influence public policy in the state of New York. *The New York State Directory* includes important information on all New York state legislators and congressional representatives, including biographies and key committee assignments. It also includes staff rosters for all branches of New York state government and for federal agencies and departments that impact the state policy process. Following the state government section are 25 chapters covering policy areas from agriculture through veterans' affairs. Each chapter identifies the state, local and federal agencies and officials that formulate or implement policy. In addition, each chapter contains a roster of private sector experts and advocates who influence the policy process. The directory also offers appendices that include statewide party officials; chambers of commerce; lobbying organizations; public and private universities and colleges; television, radio and print media; and local government agencies and officials.

> *"This comprehensive directory covers not only New York State government offices and key personnel but pertinent U.S. government agencies and non-governmental entities. This directory is all encompassing... recommended." -Choice*

New York State Directory - Softcover ISBN 978-1-59237-358-1, 800 pages, $145.00
Online Database: http://gold.greyhouse.com Call (800) 562-2139 for quote
New York State Directory with *Profiles of New York* – 2 Volumes, Softcover ISBN 978-1-59237-359-8, 1,600 pages, $225.00

The Grey House Homeland Security Directory, 2008

This updated edition features the latest contact information for government and private organizations involved with Homeland Security along with the latest product information and provides detailed profiles of nearly 1,000 Federal & State Organizations & Agencies and over 3,000 Officials and Key Executives involved with Homeland Security. These listings are incredibly detailed and include Mailing Address, Phone & Fax Numbers, Email Addresses & Web Sites, a complete Description of the Agency and a complete list of the Officials and Key Executives associated with the Agency. Next, *The Grey House Homeland Security Directory* provides the go-to source for Homeland Security Products & Services. This section features over 2,000 Companies that provide Consulting, Products or Services. With this Buyer's Guide at their fingertips, users can locate suppliers of everything from Training Materials to Access Controls, from Perimeter Security to BioTerrorism Countermeasures and everything in between – complete with contact information and product descriptions. A handy Product Locator Index is provided to quickly and easily locate suppliers of a particular product. This comprehensive, information-packed resource will be a welcome tool for any company or agency that is in need of Homeland Security information and will be a necessary acquisition for the reference collection of all public libraries and large school districts.

> *"Compiles this information in one place and is discerning in content. A useful purchase for public and academic libraries." –Booklist*

Softcover ISBN 978-1-59237-196-6, 800 pages, $195.00 | Online Database: http://gold.greyhouse.com Call (800) 562-2139 for quote

Business Information ♦ Ratings Guides ♦ General Reference ♦ Education ♦ Statistics ♦ Demographics ♦ Health Information ♦ Canadian Information

The Grey House Safety & Security Directory, 2009

The Grey House Safety & Security Directory is the most comprehensive reference tool and buyer's guide for the safety and security industry. Arranged by safety topic, each chapter begins with OSHA regulations for the topic, followed by Training Articles written by top professionals in the field and Self-Inspection Checklists. Next, each topic contains Buyer's Guide sections that feature related products and services. Topics include Administration, Insurance, Loss Control & Consulting, Protective Equipment & Apparel, Noise & Vibration, Facilities Monitoring & Maintenance, Employee Health Maintenance & Ergonomics, Retail Food Services, Machine Guards, Process Guidelines & Tool Handling, Ordinary Materials Handling, Hazardous Materials Handling, Workplace Preparation & Maintenance, Electrical Lighting & Safety, Fire & Rescue and Security. Six important indexes make finding information and product manufacturers quick and easy: Geographical Index of Manufacturers and Distributors, Company Profile Index, Brand Name Index, Product Index, Index of Web Sites and Index of Advertisers. This comprehensive, up-to-date reference will provide every tool necessary to make sure a business is in compliance with OSHA regulations and locate the products and services needed to meet those regulations.

"Presents industrial safety information for engineers, plant managers, risk managers, and construction site supervisors…" –Choice

Softcover ISBN 978-1-59237-375-8, 1,500 pages, $165.00

The Grey House Transportation Security Directory & Handbook

This is the only reference of its kind that brings together current data on Transportation Security. With information on everything from Regulatory Authorities to Security Equipment, this top-flight database brings together the relevant information necessary for creating and maintaining a security plan for a wide range of transportation facilities. With this current, comprehensive directory at the ready you'll have immediate access to: Regulatory Authorities & Legislation; Information Resources; Sample Security Plans & Checklists; Contact Data for Major Airports, Seaports, Railroads, Trucking Companies and Oil Pipelines; Security Service Providers; Recommended Equipment & Product Information and more. Using the *Grey House Transportation Security Directory & Handbook*, managers will be able to quickly and easily assess their current security plans; develop contacts to create and maintain new security procedures; and source the products and services necessary to adequately maintain a secure environment. This valuable resource is a must for all Security Managers at Airports, Seaports, Railroads, Trucking Companies and Oil Pipelines.

"Highly recommended. Library collections that support all levels of readers, including professionals/practitioners; and schools/organizations offering education and training in transportation security." -Choice

Softcover ISBN 978-1-59237-075-7, 800 pages, $195.00

The Grey House Biometric Information Directory

This edition offers a complete, current overview of biometric companies and products – one of the fastest growing industries in today's economy. Detailed profiles of manufacturers of the latest biometric technology, including Finger, Voice, Face, Hand, Signature, Iris, Vein and Palm Identification systems. Data on the companies include key executives, company size and a detailed, indexed description of their product line. Information in the directory includes: Editorial on Advancements in Biometrics; Profiles of 700+ companies listed with contact information; Organizations, Trade & Educational Associations, Publications, Conferences, Trade Shows and Expositions Worldwide; Web Site Index; Biometric & Vendors Services Index by Types of Biometrics; and a Glossary of Biometric Terms. This resource will be an important source for anyone who is considering the use of a biometric product, investing in the development of biometric technology, support existing marketing and sales efforts and will be an important acquisition for the business reference collection for large public and business libraries.

"This book should prove useful to agencies or businesses seeking companies that deal with biometric technology. Summing Up: Recommended. Specialized collections serving researchers/faculty and professionals/practitioners." -Choice

Softcover ISBN 978-1-59237-121-1, 800 pages, $225.00

Business Information ♦ Ratings Guides ♦ General Reference ♦ Education ♦
Statistics ♦ Demographics ♦ Health Information ♦ Canadian Information

Grey House Publishing

The Rauch Guide to the US Adhesives & Sealants, Cosmetics & Toiletries, Ink, Paint, Plastics, Pulp & Paper and Rubber Industries

The Rauch Guides save time and money by organizing widely scattered information and providing estimates for important business decisions, some of which are available nowhere else. Within each Guide, after a brief introduction, the ECONOMICS section provides data on industry shipments; long-term growth and forecasts; prices; company performance; employment, expenditures, and productivity; transportation and geographical patterns; packaging; foreign trade; and government regulations. Next, TECHNOLOGY & RAW MATERIALS provide market, technical, and raw material information for chemicals, equipment and related materials, including market size and leading suppliers, prices, end uses, and trends. PRODUCTS & MARKETS provide information for each major industry product, including market size and historical trends, leading suppliers, five-year forecasts, industry structure, and major end uses. Next, the COMPANY DIRECTORY profiles major industry companies, both public and private. Information includes complete contact information, web address, estimated total and domestic sales, product description, and recent mergers and acquisitions. *The Rauch Guides* will prove to be an invaluable source of market information, company data, trends and forecasts that anyone in these fast-paced industries.

"An invaluable and affordable publication. The comprehensive nature of the data and text offers considerable insights into the industry, market sizes, company activities, and applications of the products of the industry. The additions that have been made have certainly enhanced the value of the Guide." –Adhesives & Sealants Newsletter of the Rauch Guide to the US Adhesives & Sealants Industry

Paint Industry: Softcover ISBN 978-1-59237-127-3 $595 | Plastics Industry: Softcover ISBN 978-1-59237-128-0 $595 | Adhesives and Sealants Industry: Softcover ISBN 978-1-59237-129-7 $595 | Ink Industry: Softcover ISBN 978-1-59237-126-6 $595 | Rubber Industry: Softcover ISBN 978-1-59237-130-3 $595 | Pulp and Paper Industry: Softcover ISBN 978-1-59237-131-0 $595 | Cosmetic & Toiletries Industry: Softcover ISBN 978-1-59237-132-7 $895

Research Services Directory: Commercial & Corporate Research Centers

This ninth edition provides access to well over 8,000 independent Commercial Research Firms, Corporate Research Centers and Laboratories offering contract services for hands-on, basic or applied research. Research Services Directory covers the thousands of types of research companies, including Biotechnology & Pharmaceutical Developers, Consumer Product Research, Defense Contractors, Electronics & Software Engineers, Think Tanks, Forensic Investigators, Independent Commercial Laboratories, Information Brokers, Market & Survey Research Companies, Medical Diagnostic Facilities, Product Research & Development Firms and more. Each entry provides the company's name, mailing address, phone & fax numbers, key contacts, web site, e-mail address, as well as a company description and research and technical fields served. Four indexes provide immediate access to this wealth of information: Research Firms Index, Geographic Index, Personnel Name Index and Subject Index.

"An important source for organizations in need of information about laboratories, individuals and other facilities." –ARBA

Softcover ISBN 978-1-59237-003-0, 1,400 pages, $465.00

International Business and Trade Directories

Completely updated, the Third Edition of *International Business and Trade Directories* now contains more than 10,000 entries, over 2,000 more than the last edition, making this directory the most comprehensive resource of the worlds business and trade directories. Entries include content descriptions, price, publisher's name and address, web site and e-mail addresses, phone and fax numbers and editorial staff. Organized by industry group, and then by region, this resource puts over 10,000 industry-specific business and trade directories at the reader's fingertips. Three indexes are included for quick access to information: Geographic Index, Publisher Index and Title Index. Public, college and corporate libraries, as well as individuals and corporations seeking critical market information will want to add this directory to their marketing collection.

"Reasonably priced for a work of this type, this directory should appeal to larger academic, public and corporate libraries with an international focus." –Library Journal

Softcover ISBN 978-1-930956-63-6, 1,800 pages, $225.00

Business Information ✦ **Ratings Guides** ✦ General Reference ✦ Education ✦
Statistics ✦ Demographics ✦ Health Information ✦ Canadian Information

TheStreet.com Ratings Guide to Health Insurers

TheStreet.com Ratings Guide to Health Insurers is the first and only source to cover the financial stability of the nation's health care system, rating the financial safety of more than 6,000 health insurance providers, health maintenance organizations (HMOs) and all of the Blue Cross Blue Shield plans – updated quarterly to ensure the most accurate information. The Guide also provides a complete listing of all the major health insurers, including all Long-Term Care and Medigap insurers. Our *Guide to Health Insurers* includes comprehensive, timely coverage on the financial stability of HMOs and health insurers; the most accurate insurance company ratings available–the same quality ratings heralded by the U.S. General Accounting Office; separate listings for those companies offering Medigap and long-term care policies; the number of serious consumer complaints filed against most HMOs so you can see who is actually providing the best (or worst) service and more. The easy-to-use layout gives you a one-line summary analysis for each company that we track, followed by an in-depth, detailed analysis of all HMOs and the largest health insurers. The guide also includes a list of TheStreet.com Ratings Recommended Companies with information on how to contact them, and the reasoning behind any rating upgrades or downgrades.

> *"With 20 years behind its insurance-advocacy research [the rating guide] continues to offer a wealth of information that helps consumers weigh their healthcare options now and in the future." -Today's Librarian*

Issues published quarterly, Softcover, 550 pages, $499.00 for four quarterly issues, $249.00 for a single issue

TheStreet.com Ratings Guide to Life & Annuity Insurers

TheStreet.com Safety Ratings are the most reliable source for evaluating an insurer's financial solvency risk. Consequently, policyholders have come to rely on TheStreet.com's flagship publication, *TheStreet.com Ratings Guide to Life & Annuity Insurers*, to help them identify the safest companies to do business with. Each easy-to-use edition delivers TheStreet.com's independent ratings and analyses on more than 1,100 insurers, updated every quarter. Plus, your patrons will find a complete list of TheStreet.com Recommended Companies, including contact information, and the reasoning behind any rating upgrades or downgrades. This guide is perfect for those who are considering the purchase of a life insurance policy, placing money in an annuity, or advising clients about insurance and annuities. A life or health insurance policy or annuity is only as secure as the insurance company issuing it. Therefore, make sure your patrons have what they need to periodically monitor the financial condition of the companies with whom they have an investment. The TheStreet.com Ratings product line is designed to help them in their evaluations.

> *"Weiss has an excellent reputation and this title is held by hundreds of libraries. This guide is recommended for public and academic libraries." -ARBA*

Issues published quarterly, Softcover, 360 pages, $499.00 for four quarterly issues, $249.00 for a single issue

TheStreet.com Ratings Guide to Property & Casualty Insurers

TheStreet.com Ratings Guide to Property and Casualty Insurers provides the most extensive coverage of insurers writing policies, helping consumers and businesses avoid financial headaches. Updated quarterly, this easy-to-use publication delivers the independent, unbiased TheStreet.com Safety Ratings and supporting analyses on more than 2,800 U.S. insurance companies, offering auto & homeowners insurance, business insurance, worker's compensation insurance, product liability insurance, medical malpractice and other professional liability insurance. Each edition includes a list of TheStreet.com Recommended Companies by type of insurance, including a contact number, plus helpful information about the coverage provided by the State Guarantee Associations.

> *"In contrast to the other major insurance rating agencies...Weiss does not have a financial relationship worth the companies it rates. A GAO study found that Weiss identified financial vulnerability earlier than the other rating agencies." -ARBA*

Issues published quarterly, Softcover, 455 pages, $499.00 for four quarterly issues, $249.00 for a single issue

TheStreet.com Ratings Consumer Box Set

Deliver the critical information your patrons need to safeguard their personal finances with *TheStreet.com Ratings' Consumer Guide Box Set*. Each of the eight guides is packed with accurate, unbiased information and recommendations to help your patrons make sound financial decisions. TheStreet.com Ratings Consumer Guide Box Set provides your patrons with easy to understand guidance on important personal finance topics, including: *Consumer Guide to Variable Annuities, Consumer Guide to Medicare Supplement Insurance, Consumer Guide to Elder Care Choices, Consumer Guide to Automobile Insurance, Consumer Guide to Long-Term Care Insurance, Consumer Guide to Homeowners Insurance, Consumer Guide to Term Life Insurance, and Consumer Guide to Medicare Prescription Drug Coverage*. Each guide provides an easy-to-read overview of the topic, what to look out for when selecting a company or insurance plan to do business with, who are the recommended companies to work with and how to navigate through these often-times difficult decisions. Custom worksheets and step-by-step directions make these resources accessible to all types of users. Packaged in a handy custom display box, these helpful guides will prove to be a much-used addition to any reference collection.

Issues published twice per year, Softcover, 600 pages, $499.00 for two biennial issues

TheStreet.com Ratings Guide to Stock Mutual Funds

TheStreet.com Ratings Guide to Stock Mutual Funds offers ratings and analyses on more than 8,800 equity mutual funds – more than any other publication. The exclusive TheStreet.com Investment Ratings combine an objective evaluation of each fund's performance and risk to provide a single, user-friendly, composite rating, giving your patrons a better handle on a mutual fund's risk-adjusted performance. Each edition identifies the top-performing mutual funds based on risk category, type of fund, and overall risk-adjusted performance. TheStreet.com's unique investment rating system makes it easy to see exactly which stocks are on the rise and which ones should be avoided. For those investors looking to tailor their mutual fund selections based on age, income, and tolerance for risk, we've also assigned two component ratings to each fund: a performance rating and a risk rating. With these, you can identify those funds that are best suited to meet your - or your client's – individual needs and goals. Plus, we include a handy Risk Profile Quiz to help you assess your personal tolerance for risk. So whether you're an investing novice or professional, the *Guide to Stock Mutual Funds* gives you everything you need to find a mutual fund that is right for you.

"There is tremendous need for information such as that provided by this Weiss publication. This reasonably priced guide is recommended for public and academic libraries serving investors." -ARBA

Issues published quarterly, Softcover, 655 pages, $499 for four quarterly issues, $249 for a single issue

TheStreet.com Ratings Guide to Exchange-Traded Funds

TheStreet.com Ratings editors analyze hundreds of mutual funds each quarter, condensing all of the available data into a single composite opinion of each fund's risk-adjusted performance. The intuitive, consumer-friendly ratings allow investors to instantly identify those funds that have historically done well and those that have under-performed the market. Each quarterly edition identifies the top-performing exchange-traded funds based on risk category, type of fund, and overall risk-adjusted performance. The rating scale, A through F, gives you a better handle on an exchange-traded fund's risk-adjusted performance. Other features include Top & Bottom 200 Exchange-Traded Funds; Performance and Risk: 100 Best and Worst Exchange- Traded Funds; Investor Profile Quiz; Performance Benchmarks and Fund Type Descriptions. With the growing popularity of mutual fund investing, consumers need a reliable source to help them track and evaluate the performance of their mutual fund holdings. Plus, they need a way of identifying and monitoring other funds as potential new investments. Unfortunately, the hundreds of performance and risk measures available, multiplied by the vast number of mutual fund investments on the market today, can make this a daunting task for even the most sophisticated investor. This Guide will serve as a useful tool for both the first-time and seasoned investor.

Editions published quarterly, Softcover, 440 pages, $499.00 for four quarterly issues, $249.00 for a single issue

TheStreet.com Ratings Guide to Bond & Money Market Mutual Funds

TheStreet.com Ratings Guide to Bond & Money Market Mutual Funds has everything your patrons need to easily identify the top-performing fixed income funds on the market today. Each quarterly edition contains TheStreet.com's independent ratings and analyses on more than 4,600 fixed income funds – more than any other publication, including corporate bond funds, high-yield bond funds, municipal bond funds, mortgage security funds, money market funds, global bond funds and government bond funds. In addition, the fund's risk rating is combined with its three-year performance rating to get an overall picture of the fund's risk-adjusted performance. The resulting TheStreet.com Investment Rating gives a single, user-friendly, objective evaluation that makes it easy to compare one fund to another and select the right fund based on the level of risk tolerance. Most investors think of fixed income mutual funds as "safe" investments. That's not always the case, however, depending on the credit risk, interest rate risk, and prepayment risk of the securities owned by the fund. TheStreet.com Ratings assesses each of these risks and assigns each fund a risk rating to help investors quickly evaluate the fund's risk component. Plus, we include a handy Risk Profile Quiz to help you assess your personal tolerance for risk. So whether you're an investing novice or professional, the *Guide to Bond and Money Market Mutual Funds* gives you everything you need to find a mutual fund that is right for you.

"Comprehensive... It is easy to use and consumer-oriented, and can be recommended for larger public and academic libraries." -ARBA

Issues published quarterly, Softcover, 470 pages, $499.00 for four quarterly issues, $249.00 for a single issue

TheStreet.com Ratings Guide to Banks & Thrifts

Updated quarterly, for the most up-to-date information, *TheStreet.com Ratings Guide to Banks and Thrifts* offers accurate, intuitive safety ratings your patrons can trust; supporting ratios and analyses that show an institution's strong & weak points; identification of the TheStreet.com Recommended Companies with branches in your area; a complete list of institutions receiving upgrades/downgrades; and comprehensive coverage of every bank and thrift in the nation – more than 9,000. TheStreet.com Safety Ratings are then based on the analysts' review of publicly available information collected by the federal banking regulators. The easy-to-use layout gives you: the institution's TheStreet.com Safety Rating for the last 3 years; the five key indexes used to evaluate each institution; along with the primary ratios and statistics used in determining the company's rating. *TheStreet.com Ratings Guide to Banks & Thrifts* will be a must for individuals who are concerned about the safety of their CD or savings account; need to be sure that an existing line of credit will be there when they need it; or simply want to avoid the hassles of dealing with a failing or troubled institution.

"Large public and academic libraries most definitely need to acquire the work. Likewise, special libraries in large corporations will find this title indispensable." -ARBA

Issues published quarterly, Softcover, 370 pages, $499.00 for four quarterly issues, $249.00 for a single issue

Business Information ✦ **Ratings Guides** ✦ General Reference ✦ Education ✦
Statistics ✦ Demographics ✦ Health Information ✦ Canadian Information

TheStreet.com Ratings Guide to Common Stocks

TheStreet.com Ratings Guide to Common Stocks gives your patrons reliable insight into the risk-adjusted performance of common stocks listed on the NYSE, AMEX, and Nasdaq – over 5,800 stocks in all – more than any other publication. TheStreet.com's unique investment rating system makes it easy to see exactly which stocks are on the rise and which ones should be avoided. In addition, your patrons also get supporting analysis showing growth trends, profitability, debt levels, valuation levels, the top-rated stocks within each industry, and more. Plus, each stock is ranked with the easy-to-use buy-hold-sell equivalents commonly used by Wall Street. Whether they're selecting their own investments or checking up on a broker's recommendation, TheStreet.com Ratings can help them in their evaluations.

"Users... will find the information succinct and the explanations readable, easy to understand, and helpful to a novice." -Library Journal

Issues published quarterly, Softcover, 440 pages, $499.00 for four quarterly issues, $249.00 for a single issue

TheStreet.com Ratings Ultimate Guided Tour of Stock Investing

This important reference guide from TheStreet.com Ratings is just what librarians around the country have asked for: a step-by-step introduction to stock investing for the beginning to intermediate investor. This easy-to-navigate guide explores the basics of stock investing and includes the intuitive TheStreet.com Investment Rating on more than 5,800 stocks, complete with real-world investing information that can be put to use immediately with stocks that fit the concepts discussed in the guide; informative charts, graphs and worksheets; easy-to-understand explanations on topics like P/E, compound interest, marked indices, diversifications, brokers, and much more; along with financial safety ratings for every stock on the NYSE, American Stock Exchange and the Nasdaq. This consumer-friendly guide offers complete how-to information on stock investing that can be put to use right away; a friendly format complete with our "Wise Guide" who leads the reader on a safari to learn about the investing jungle; helpful charts, graphs and simple worksheets; the intuitive TheStreet.com Investment rating on over 6,000 stocks — every stock found on the NYSE, American Stock Exchange and the NASDAQ; and much more.

"Provides investors with an alternative to stock broker recommendations, which recently have been tarnished by conflicts of interest. In summary, the guide serves as a welcome addition for all public library collections." -ARBA

Issues published quarterly, Softcover, 370 pages, $499.00 for four quarterly issues, $249.00 for a single issue

TheStreet.com Ratings' Reports & Services

- Ratings Online — An on-line summary covering an individual company's TheStreet.com Financial Strength Rating or an investment's unique TheStreet.com Investment Rating with the factors contributing to that rating; available 24 hours a day by visiting www.thestreet.com/tscratings or calling (800) 289-9222.
- Unlimited Ratings Research — The ultimate research tool providing fast, easy online access to the very latest TheStreet.com Financial Strength Ratings and Investment Ratings. Price: $559 per industry.

Contact TheStreet.com for more information about Reports & Services at www.thestreet.com/tscratings or call (800) 289-9222

TheStreet.com Ratings' Custom Reports

TheStreet.com Ratings is pleased to offer two customized options for receiving ratings data. Each taps into TheStreet.com's vast data repositories and is designed to provide exactly the data you need. Choose from a variety of industries, companies, data variables, and delivery formats including print, Excel, SQL, Text or Access.

- Customized Reports - get right to the heart of your company's research and data needs with a report customized to your specifications.
- Complete Database Download – TheStreet.com will design and deliver the database; from there you can sort it, recalculate it, and format your results to suit your specific needs.

Contact TheStreet.com for more information about Custom Reports at www.thestreet.com/tscratings or call (800) 289-9222

Business Information ✦ Ratings Guides ✦ General Reference ✦ **Education** ✦
Statistics ✦ Demographics ✦ Health Information ✦ Canadian Information

Grey House
Publishing

The Value of a Dollar 1600-1859, The Colonial Era to The Civil War

Following the format of the widely acclaimed, *The Value of a Dollar, 1860-2004*, *The Value of a Dollar 1600-1859, The Colonial Era to The Civil War* records the actual prices of thousands of items that consumers purchased from the Colonial Era to the Civil War. Our editorial department had been flooded with requests from users of our *Value of a Dollar* for the same type of information, just from an earlier time period. This new volume is just the answer – with pricing data from 1600 to 1859. Arranged into five-year chapters, each 5-year chapter includes a Historical Snapshot, Consumer Expenditures, Investments, Selected Income, Income/Standard Jobs, Food Basket, Standard Prices and Miscellany. There is also a section on Trends. This informative section charts the change in price over time and provides added detail on the reasons prices changed within the time period, including industry developments, changes in consumer attitudes and important historical facts. This fascinating survey will serve a wide range of research needs and will be useful in all high school, public and academic library reference collections.

"The Value of a Dollar: Colonial Era to the Civil War, 1600-1865 will find a happy audience among students, researchers, and general browsers. It offers a fascinating and detailed look at early American history from the viewpoint of everyday people trying to make ends meet. This title and the earlier publication, The Value of a Dollar, 1860-2004, complement each other very well, and readers will appreciate finding them side-by-side on the shelf." -Booklist

Hardcover ISBN 978-1-59237-094-8, 600 pages, $145.00 | Ebook ISBN 978-1-59237-169-3 www.greyhouse.com/ebooks.htm

The Value of a Dollar 1860-2009, Fourth Edition

A guide to practical economy, *The Value of a Dollar* records the actual prices of thousands of items that consumers purchased from the Civil War to the present, along with facts about investment options and income opportunities. This brand new Third Edition boasts a brand new addition to each five-year chapter, a section on Trends. This informative section charts the change in price over time and provides added detail on the reasons prices changed within the time period, including industry developments, changes in consumer attitudes and important historical facts. Plus, a brand new chapter for 2005-2009 has been added. Each 5-year chapter includes a Historical Snapshot, Consumer Expenditures, Investments, Selected Income, Income/Standard Jobs, Food Basket, Standard Prices and Miscellany. This interesting and useful publication will be widely used in any reference collection.

"Business historians, reporters, writers and students will find this source... very helpful for historical research. Libraries will want to purchase it." –ARBA

Hardcover ISBN 978-1-59237-403-8, 600 pages, $145.00 | Ebook ISBN 978-1-59237-173-0 www.greyhouse.com/ebooks.htm

Working Americans 1880-1999
Volume I: The Working Class, Volume II: The Middle Class, Volume III: The Upper Class

Each of the volumes in the *Working Americans* series focuses on a particular class of Americans, The Working Class, The Middle Class and The Upper Class over the last 120 years. Chapters in each volume focus on one decade and profile three to five families. Family Profiles include real data on Income & Job Descriptions, Selected Prices of the Times, Annual Income, Annual Budgets, Family Finances, Life at Work, Life at Home, Life in the Community, Working Conditions, Cost of Living, Amusements and much more. Each chapter also contains an Economic Profile with Average Wages of other Professions, a selection of Typical Pricing, Key Events & Inventions, News Profiles, Articles from Local Media and Illustrations. The *Working Americans* series captures the lifestyles of each of the classes from the last twelve decades, covers a vast array of occupations and ethnic backgrounds and travels the entire nation. These interesting and useful compilations of portraits of the American Working, Middle and Upper Classes during the last 120 years will be an important addition to any high school, public or academic library reference collection.

"These interesting, unique compilations of economic and social facts, figures and graphs will support multiple research needs. They will engage and enlighten patrons in high school, public and academic library collections." –Booklist

Volume I: The Working Class Hardcover ISBN 978-1-891482-81-6, 558 pages, $145.00 | Volume II: The Middle Class Hardcover ISBN 978-1-891482-72-4, 591 pages, $145.00 | Volume III: The Upper Class Hardcover ISBN 978-1-930956-38-4, 567 pages, $145.00 | www.greyhouse.com/ebooks.htm

Working Americans 1880-1999 Volume IV: Their Children

This Fourth Volume in the highly successful *Working Americans* series focuses on American children, decade by decade from 1880 to 1999. This interesting and useful volume introduces the reader to three children in each decade, one from each of the Working, Middle and Upper classes. Like the first three volumes in the series, the individual profiles are created from interviews, diaries, statistical studies, biographies and news reports. Profiles cover a broad range of ethnic backgrounds, geographic area and lifestyles – everything from an orphan in Memphis in 1882, following the Yellow Fever epidemic of 1878 to an eleven-year-old nephew of a beer baron and owner of the New York Yankees in New York City in 1921. Chapters also contain important supplementary materials including News Features as well as information on everything from Schools to Parks, Infectious Diseases to Childhood Fears along with Entertainment, Family Life and much more to provide an informative overview of the lifestyles of children from each decade. This interesting account of what life was like for Children in the Working, Middle and Upper Classes will be a welcome addition to the reference collection of any high school, public or academic library.

Hardcover ISBN 978-1-930956-35-3, 600 pages, $145.00 | Ebook ISBN 978-1-59237-166-2 www.greyhouse.com/ebooks.htm

Business Information ✦ Ratings Guides ✦ General Reference ✦ **Education** ✦
Statistics ✦ Demographics ✦ Health Information ✦ Canadian Information

Working Americans 1880-2003 Volume V: Americans At War

Working Americans 1880-2003 Volume V: Americans At War is divided into 11 chapters, each covering a decade from 1880-2003 and examines the lives of Americans during the time of war, including declared conflicts, one-time military actions, protests, and preparations for war. Each decade includes several personal profiles, whether on the battlefield or on the homefront, that tell the stories of civilians, soldiers, and officers during the decade. The profiles examine: Life at Home; Life at Work; and Life in the Community. Each decade also includes an Economic Profile with statistical comparisons, a Historical Snapshot, News Profiles, local News Articles, and Illustrations that provide a solid historical background to the decade being examined. Profiles range widely not only geographically, but also emotionally, from that of a girl whose leg was torn off in a blast during WWI, to the boredom of being stationed in the Dakotas as the Indian Wars were drawing to a close. As in previous volumes of the *Working Americans* series, information is presented in narrative form, but hard facts and real-life situations back up each story. The basis of the profiles come from diaries, private print books, personal interviews, family histories, estate documents and magazine articles. For easy reference, *Working Americans 1880-2003 Volume V: Americans At War* includes an in-depth Subject Index. The Working Americans series has become an important reference for public libraries, academic libraries and high school libraries. This fifth volume will be a welcome addition to all of these types of reference collections.

Hardcover ISBN 978-1-59237-024-5, 600 pages, $145.00 | Ebook ISBN 978-1-59237-167-9 www.greyhouse.com/ebooks.htm

Working Americans 1880-2005 Volume VI: Women at Work

Unlike any other volume in the *Working Americans* series, this Sixth Volume, is the first to focus on a particular gender of Americans. *Volume VI: Women at Work*, traces what life was like for working women from the 1860's to the present time. Beginning with the life of a maid in 1890 and a store clerk in 1900 and ending with the life and times of the modern working women, this text captures the struggle, strengths and changing perception of the American woman at work. Each chapter focuses on one decade and profiles three to five women with real data on Income & Job Descriptions, Selected Prices of the Times, Annual Income, Annual Budgets, Family Finances, Life at Work, Life at Home, Life in the Community, Working Conditions, Cost of Living, Amusements and much more. For even broader access to the events, economics and attitude towards women throughout the past 130 years, each chapter is supplemented with News Profiles, Articles from Local Media, Illustrations, Economic Profiles, Typical Pricing, Key Events, Inventions and more. This important volume illustrates what life was like for working women over time and allows the reader to develop an understanding of the changing role of women at work. These interesting and useful compilations of portraits of women at work will be an important addition to any high school, public or academic library reference collection.

Hardcover ISBN 978-1-59237-063-4, 600 pages, $145.00 | Ebook ISBN 978-1-59237-168-6 www.greyhouse.com/ebooks.htm

Working Americans 1880-2005 Volume VII: Social Movements

Working Americans series, Volume VII: Social Movements explores how Americans sought and fought for change from the 1880s to the present time. Following the format of previous volumes in the Working Americans series, the text examines the lives of 34 individuals who have worked -- often behind the scenes --- to bring about change. Issues include topics as diverse as the Anti-smoking movement of 1901 to efforts by Native Americans to reassert their long lost rights. Along the way, the book will profile individuals brave enough to demand suffrage for Kansas women in 1912 or demand an end to lynching during a March on Washington in 1923. Each profile is enriched with real data on Income & Job Descriptions, Selected Prices of the Times, Annual Incomes & Budgets, Life at Work, Life at Home, Life in the Community, along with News Features, Key Events, and Illustrations. The depth of information contained in each profile allow the user to explore the private, financial and public lives of these subjects, deepening our understanding of how calls for change took place in our society. A must-purchase for the reference collections of high school libraries, public libraries and academic libraries.

Hardcover ISBN 978-1-59237-101-3, 600 pages, $145.00 | Ebook ISBN 978-1-59237-174-7 www.gale.com/gvrl/partners/grey.htm

Working Americans 1880-2005 Volume VIII: Immigrants

Working Americans 1880-2007 Volume VIII: Immigrants illustrates what life was like for families leaving their homeland and creating a new life in the United States. Each chapter covers one decade and introduces the reader to three immigrant families. Family profiles cover what life was like in their homeland, in their community in the United States, their home life, working conditions and so much more. As the reader moves through these pages, the families and individuals come to life, painting a picture of why they left their homeland, their experiences in setting roots in a new country, their struggles and triumphs, stretching from the 1800s to the present time. Profiles include a seven-year-old Swedish girl who meets her father for the first time at Ellis Island; a Chinese photographer's assistant; an Armenian who flees the genocide of his country to build Ford automobiles in Detroit; a 38-year-old German bachelor cigar maker who settles in Newark NJ, but contemplates tobacco farming in Virginia; a 19-year-old Irish domestic servant who is amazed at the easy life of American dogs; a 19-year-old Filipino who came to Hawaii against his parent's wishes to farm sugar cane; a French-Canadian who finds success as a boxer in Maine and many more. As in previous volumes, information is presented in narrative form, but hard facts and real-life situations back up each story. With the topic of immigration being so hotly debated in this country, this timely resource will prove to be a useful source for students, researchers, historians and library patrons to discover the issues facing immigrants in the United States. This title will be a useful addition to reference collections of public libraries, university libraries and high schools.

Hardcover ISBN 978-1-59237-197-6, 600 pages, $145.00 | Ebook ISBN 978-1-59237-232-4 www.greyhouse.com/ebooks.htm

Business Information ✦ Ratings Guides ✦ General Reference ✦ **Education** ✦
Statistics ✦ Demographics ✦ Health Information ✦ Canadian Information

Grey House
Publishing

Working Americans 1770-1896 Volume IX: From the Revolutionary War to the Civil War

Working Americans 1770-1869: From the Revolutionary War to the Civil War examines what life was like for the earliest of Americans. Like previous volumes in the successful Working Americans series, each chapter introduces the reader to three individuals or families. These profiles illustrate what life was like for that individual, at home, in the community and at work. The profiles are supplemented with information on current events, community issues, pricing of the times and news articles to give the reader a broader understanding of what was happening in that individual's world and how it shaped their life. Profiles extend through all walks of life, from farmers to merchants, the rich and poor, men, women and children. In these information-packed, fun-to-explore pages, the reader will be introduced to Ezra Stiles, a preacher and college president from 1776; Colonel Israel Angell, a continental officer from 1778; Thomas Vernon, a loyalist in 1776, Anna Green Winslow, a school girl in 1771; Sarah Pierce, a school teacher in 1792; Edward Hooker, an attorney in 1805; Jeremiah Greenman, a common soldier in 1775 and many others. Using these information-filled profiles, the reader can develop an understanding of what life was like for all types of Americans in these interesting and changing times. This new edition will be an important acquisition for high school, public and academic libraries as well as history reference collections.

Hardcover ISBN 978-1-59237-371-0, 660 pages, $145.00

The Encyclopedia of Warrior Peoples & Fighting Groups

Many military groups throughout the world have excelled in their craft either by fortuitous circumstances, outstanding leadership, or intense training. This new second edition of *The Encyclopedia of Warrior Peoples and Fighting Groups* explores the origins and leadership of these outstanding combat forces, chronicles their conquests and accomplishments, examines the circumstances surrounding their decline or disbanding, and assesses their influence on the groups and methods of warfare that followed. Readers will encounter ferocious tribes, charismatic leaders, and daring militias, from ancient times to the present, including Amazons, Buffalo Soldiers, Green Berets, Iron Brigade, Kamikazes, Peoples of the Sea, Polish Winged Hussars, Teutonic Knights, and Texas Rangers. With over 100 alphabetical entries, numerous cross-references and illustrations, a comprehensive bibliography, and index, the *Encyclopedia of Warrior Peoples and Fighting Groups* is a valuable resource for readers seeking insight into the bold history of distinguished fighting forces.

"Especially useful for high school students, undergraduates, and general readers with an interest in military history." –Library Journal

Hardcover ISBN 978-1-59237-116-7, 660 pages, $135.00 | Ebook ISBN 978-1-59237-172-3 www.greyhouse.com/ebooks.htm

The Encyclopedia of Invasions & Conquests, From the Ancient Times to the Present

This second edition of the popular *Encyclopedia of Invasions & Conquests*, a comprehensive guide to over 150 invasions, conquests, battles and occupations from ancient times to the present, takes readers on a journey that includes the Roman conquest of Britain, the Portuguese colonization of Brazil, and the Iraqi invasion of Kuwait, to name a few. New articles will explore the late 20th and 21st centuries, with a specific focus on recent conflicts in Afghanistan, Kuwait, Iraq, Yugoslavia, Grenada and Chechnya. In addition to covering the military aspects of invasions and conquests, entries cover some of the political, economic, and cultural aspects, for example, the effects of a conquest on the invade country's political and monetary system and in its language and religion. The entries on leaders – among them Sargon, Alexander the Great, William the Conqueror, and Adolf Hitler – deal with the people who sought to gain control, expand power, or exert religious or political influence over others through military means. Revised and updated for this second edition, entries are arranged alphabetically within historical periods. Each chapter provides a map to help readers locate key areas and geographical features, and bibliographical references appear at the end of each entry. Other useful features include cross-references, a cumulative bibliography and a comprehensive subject index. This authoritative, well-organized, lucidly written volume will prove invaluable for a variety of readers, including high school students, military historians, members of the armed forces, history buffs and hobbyists.

"Engaging writing, sensible organization, nice illustrations, interesting and obscure facts, and useful maps make this book a pleasure to read." –ARBA

Hardcover ISBN 978-1-59237-114-3, 598 pages, $135.00 | Ebook ISBN 978-1-59237-171-6 www.gale.com/gvrl/partners/grey.htm

Encyclopedia of Prisoners of War & Internment

This authoritative second edition provides a valuable overview of the history of prisoners of war and interned civilians, from earliest times to the present. Written by an international team of experts in the field of POW studies, this fascinating and thought-provoking volume includes entries on a wide range of subjects including the Crusades, Plains Indian Warfare, concentration camps, the two world wars, and famous POWs throughout history, as well as atrocities, escapes, and much more. Written in a clear and easily understandable style, this informative reference details over 350 entries, 30% larger than the first edition, that survey the history of prisoners of war and interned civilians from the earliest times to the present, with emphasis on the 19th and 20th centuries. Medical conditions, international law, exchanges of prisoners, organizations working on behalf of POWs, and trials associated with the treatment of captives are just some of the themes explored. Entries are arranged alphabetically, plus illustrations and maps are provided for easy reference. The text also includes an introduction, bibliography, appendix of selected documents, and end-of-entry reading suggestions. This one-of-a-kind reference will be a helpful addition to the reference collections of all public libraries, high schools, and university libraries and will prove invaluable to historians and military enthusiasts.

*"Thorough and detailed yet accessible to the lay reader.
Of special interest to subject specialists and historians; recommended for public and academic libraries." - Library Journal*

Hardcover ISBN 978-1-59237-120-4, 676 pages, $135.00 | Ebook ISBN 978-1-59237-170-9 www.greyhouse.com/ebooks.htm

Business Information ✦ Ratings Guides ✦ General Reference ✦ **Education** ✦
Statistics ✦ Demographics ✦ Health Information ✦ Canadian Information

The Encyclopedia of Rural America: the Land & People

History, sociology, anthropology, and public policy are combined to deliver the encyclopedia destined to become the standard reference work in American rural studies. From irrigation and marriage to games and mental health, this encyclopedia is the first to explore the contemporary landscape of rural America, placed in historical perspective. With over 300 articles prepared by leading experts from across the nation, this timely encyclopedia documents and explains the major themes, concepts, industries, concerns, and everyday life of the people and land who make up rural America. Entries range from the industrial sector and government policy to arts and humanities and social and family concerns. Articles explore every aspect of life in rural America. *Encyclopedia of Rural America*, with its broad range of coverage, will appeal to high school and college students as well as graduate students, faculty, scholars, and people whose work pertains to rural areas.

"This exemplary encyclopedia is guaranteed to educate our
highly urban society about the uniqueness of rural America. Recommended for public and academic libraries." -Library Journal

Two Volumes, Hardcover, ISBN 978-1-59237-115-0, 800 pages, $250.00

The Religious Right, A Reference Handbook

Timely and unbiased, this third edition updates and expands its examination of the religious right and its influence on our government, citizens, society, and politics.   From the fight to outlaw the teaching of Darwin's theory of evolution to the struggle to outlaw abortion, the religious right is continually exerting an influence on public policy.   This text explores the influence of religion on legislation and society, while examining the alignment of the religious right with the political right.   A historical survey of the movement highlights the shift to "hands-on" approach to politics and the struggle to present a unified front.   The coverage offers a critical historical survey of the religious right movement, focusing on its increased involvement in the political arena, attempts to forge coalitions, and notable successes and failures. The text offers complete coverage of biographies of the men and women who have advanced the cause and an up to date chronology illuminate the movement's goals, including their accomplishments and failures. This edition offers an extensive update to all sections along with several brand new entries. Two new sections complement this third edition, a chapter on legal issues and court decisions and a chapter on demographic statistics and electoral patterns.   To aid in further research, *The Religious Right*, offers an entire section of annotated listings of print and non-print resources, as well as of organizations affiliated with the religious right, and those opposing it.   Comprehensive in its scope, this work offers easy-to-read, pertinent information for those seeking to understand the religious right and its evolving role in American society. A must for libraries of all sizes, university religion departments, activists, high schools and for those interested in the evolving role of the religious right.

" Recommended for all public and academic libraries." - Library Journal

Hardcover ISBN 978-1-59237-113-6, 600 pages, $135.00 | Ebook ISBN 978-1-59237-226 3 www.greyhouse.com/ebooks.htm

From Suffrage to the Senate, America's Political Women

From Suffrage to the Senate is a comprehensive and valuable compendium of biographies of leading women in U.S. politics, past and present, and an examination of the wide range of women's movements.   Up to date through 2006, this dynamically illustrated reference work explores American women's path to political power and social equality from the struggle for the right to vote and the abolition of slavery to the first African American woman in the U.S. Senate and beyond. This new edition includes over 150 new entries and a brand new section on trends and demographics of women in politics. The in-depth coverage also traces the political heritage of the abolition, labor, suffrage, temperance, and reproductive rights movements.   The alphabetically arranged entries include biographies of every woman from across the political spectrum who has served in the U.S. House and Senate, along with women in the Judiciary and the U.S. Cabinet and, new to this edition, biographies of activists and political consultants. Bibliographical references follow each entry. For easy reference, a handy chronology is provided detailing 150 years of women's history. This up-to-date reference will be a must-purchase for women's studies departments, high schools and public libraries and will be a handy resource for those researching the key players in women's politics, past and present.

"An engaging tool that would be useful in high school, public, and academic libraries
looking for an overview of the political history of women in the US." –Booklist

Two Volumes, Hardcover ISBN 978-1-59237-117-4, 1,160 pages, $195.00 | Ebook ISBN 978-1-59237-227-0
www.gale.com/gvrl/partners/grey.htm

Business Information ✦ Ratings Guides ✦ General Reference ✦ **Education** ✦
Statistics ✦ Demographics ✦ Health Information ✦ Canadian Information

An African Biographical Dictionary

This landmark second edition is the only biographical dictionary to bring together, in one volume, cultural, social and political leaders – both historical and contemporary – of the sub-Saharan region. Over 800 biographical sketches of prominent Africans, as well as foreigners who have affected the continent's history, are featured, 150 more than the previous edition. The wide spectrum of leaders includes religious figures, writers, politicians, scientists, entertainers, sports personalities and more. Access to these fascinating individuals is provided in a user-friendly format. The biographies are arranged alphabetically, cross-referenced and indexed. Entries include the country or countries in which the person was significant and the commonly accepted dates of birth and death. Each biographical sketch is chronologically written; entries for cultural personalities add an evaluation of their work. This information is followed by a selection of references often found in university and public libraries, including autobiographies and principal biographical works. Appendixes list each individual by country and by field of accomplishment – rulers, musicians, explorers, missionaries, businessmen, physicists – nearly thirty categories in all. Another convenient appendix lists heads of state since independence by country. Up-to-date and representative of African societies as a whole, An African Biographical Dictionary provides a wealth of vital information for students of African culture and is an indispensable reference guide for anyone interested in African affairs.

> *"An unquestionable convenience to have these concise, informative biographies gathered into one source, indexed, and analyzed by appendixes listing entrants by nation and occupational field." –Wilson Library Bulletin*

Hardcover ISBN 978-1-59237-112-9, 667 pages, $135.00 | Ebook ISBN 978-1-59237-229-4 www.greyhouse.com/ebooks.htm

American Environmental Leaders, From Colonial Times to the Present

A comprehensive and diverse award winning collection of biographies of the most important figures in American environmentalism. Few subjects arouse the passions the way the environment does. How will we feed an ever-increasing population and how can that food be made safe for consumption? Who decides how land is developed? How can environmental policies be made fair for everyone, including multiethnic groups, women, children, and the poor? *American Environmental Leaders* presents more than 350 biographies of men and women who have devoted their lives to studying, debating, and organizing these and other controversial issues over the last 200 years. In addition to the scientists who have analyzed how human actions affect nature, we are introduced to poets, landscape architects, presidents, painters, activists, even sanitation engineers, and others who have forever altered how we think about the environment. The easy to use A–Z format provides instant access to these fascinating individuals, and frequent cross references indicate others with whom individuals worked (and sometimes clashed). End of entry references provide users with a starting point for further research.

> *"Highly recommended for high school, academic, and public libraries needing environmental biographical information." –Library Journal/Starred Review*

Two Volumes, Hardcover ISBN 978-1-59237-119-8, 900 pages $195.00 | Ebook ISBN 978-1-59237-230-0 www.greyhouse.com/ebooks.htm

World Cultural Leaders of the Twentieth & Twenty-First Centuries

World Cultural Leaders of the Twentieth & Twenty-First Centuries is a window into the arts, performances, movements, and music that shaped the world's cultural development since 1900. A remarkable around-the-world look at one-hundred-plus years of cultural development through the eyes of those that set the stage and stayed to play. This second edition offers over 120 new biographies along with a complete update of existing biographies. To further aid the reader, a handy fold-out timeline traces important events in all six cultural categories from 1900 through the present time. Plus, a new section of detailed material and resources for 100 selected individuals is also new to this edition, with further data on museums, homesteads, websites, artwork and more. This remarkable compilation will answer a wide range of questions. Who was the originator of the term "documentary"? Which poet married the daughter of the famed novelist Thomas Mann in order to help her escape Nazi Germany? Which British writer served as an agent in Russia against the Bolsheviks before the 1917 revolution? A handy two-volume set that makes it easy to look up 450 worldwide cultural icons: novelists, poets, playwrights, painters, sculptors, architects, dancers, choreographers, actors, directors, filmmakers, singers, composers, and musicians. *World Cultural Leaders of the Twentieth & Twenty-First Centuries* provides entries (many of them illustrated) covering the person's works, achievements, and professional career in a thorough essay and offers interesting facts and statistics. Entries are fully cross-referenced so that readers can learn how various individuals influenced others. An index of leaders by occupation, a useful glossary and a thorough general index complete the coverage. This remarkable resource will be an important acquisition for the reference collections of public libraries, university libraries and high schools.

> *"Fills a need for handy, concise information on a wide array of international cultural figures."-ARBA*

Two Volumes, Hardcover ISBN 978-1-59237-118-1, 900 pages, $195.00 | Ebook ISBN 978-1-59237-231-7 www.greyhouse.com/ebooks.htm

---

Business Information ✦ Ratings Guides ✦ General Reference ✦ **Education** ✦
Statistics ✦ Demographics ✦ Health Information ✦ Canadian Information

Political Corruption in America: An Encyclopedia of Scandals, Power, and Greed

The complete scandal-filled history of American political corruption, focusing on the infamous people and cases, as well as society's electoral and judicial reactions. Since colonial times, there has been no shortage of politicians willing to take a bribe, skirt campaign finance laws, or act in their own interests. Corruption like the Whiskey Ring, Watergate, and Whitewater cases dominate American life, making political scandal a leading U.S. industry. From judges to senators, presidents to mayors, *Political Corruption in America* discusses the infamous people throughout history who have been accused of and implicated in crooked behavior. In this new second edition, more than 250 A–Z entries explore the people, crimes, investigations, and court cases behind 200 years of American political scandals. This unbiased volume also delves into the issues surrounding Koreagate, the Chinese campaign scandal, and other ethical lapses. Relevant statutes and terms, including the Independent Counsel Statute and impeachment as a tool of political punishment, are examined as well. Students, scholars, and other readers interested in American history, political science, and ethics will appreciate this survey of a wide range of corrupting influences. This title focuses on how politicians from all parties have fallen because of their greed and hubris, and how society has used electoral and judicial means against those who tested the accepted standards of political conduct. A full range of illustrations including political cartoons, photos of key figures such as Abe Fortas and Archibald Cox, graphs of presidential pardons, and tables showing the number of expulsions and censures in both the House and Senate round out the text. In addition, a comprehensive chronology of major political scandals in U.S. history from colonial times until the present. For further reading, an extensive bibliography lists sources including archival letters, newspapers, and private manuscript collections from the United States and Great Britain. With its comprehensive coverage of this interesting topic, *Political Corruption in America: An Encyclopedia of Scandals, Power, and Greed* will prove to be a useful addition to the reference collections of all public libraries, university libraries, history collections, political science collections and high schools.

"...this encyclopedia is a useful contribution to the field. Highly recommended." - CHOICE
"Political Corruption should be useful in most academic, high school, and public libraries." Booklist

Two Volumes, Hardcover ISBN 978-1-59237-297-3, 500 pages, $195.00 | Ebook ISBN 978-1-59237-308-6
www.greyhouse.com/ebooks.htm

Religion and Law: A Dictionary

This informative, easy-to-use reference work covers a wide range of legal issues that affect the roles of religion and law in American society. Extensive A–Z entries provide coverage of key court decisions, case studies, concepts, individuals, religious groups, organizations, and agencies shaping religion and law in today's society. This *Dictionary* focuses on topics involved with the constitutional theory and interpretation of religion and the law; terms providing a historical explanation of the ways in which America's ever increasing ethnic and religious diversity contributed to our current understanding of the mandates of the First and Fourteenth Amendments; terms and concepts describing the development of religion clause jurisprudence; an analytical examination of the distinct vocabulary used in this area of the law; the means by which American courts have attempted to balance religious liberty against other important individual and social interests in a wide variety of physical and regulatory environments, including the classroom, the workplace, the courtroom, religious group organization and structure, taxation, the clash of "secular" and "religious" values, and the relationship of the generalized idea of individual autonomy of the specific concept of religious liberty. Important legislation and legal cases affecting religion and society are thoroughly covered in this timely volume, including a detailed Table of Cases and Table of Statutes for more detailed research. A guide to further reading and an index are also included. This useful resource will be an important acquisition for the reference collections of all public libraries, university libraries, religion reference collections and high schools.

Two Volumes, Hardcover ISBN 978-1-59237-298-0, 500 pages, $195.00 | Ebook ISBN 978-1-59237-309-3
www.greyhouse.com/ebooks.htm

Human Rights in the United States: A Dictionary and Documents

This two volume set offers easy to grasp explanations of the basic concepts, laws, and case law in the field, with emphasis on human rights in the historical, political, and legal experience of the United States. Human rights is a term not fully understood by many Americans. Addressing this gap, the new second edition of *Human Rights in the United States: A Dictionary and Documents* offers a comprehensive introduction that places the history of human rights in the United States in an international context. It surveys the legal protection of human dignity in the United States, examines the sources of human rights norms, cites key legal cases, explains the role of international governmental and non-governmental organizations, and charts global, regional, and U.N. human rights measures. Over 240 dictionary entries of human rights terms are detailed—ranging from asylum and cultural relativism to hate crimes and torture. Each entry discusses the significance of the term, gives examples, and cites appropriate documents and court decisions. In addition, a Documents section is provided that contains 59 conventions, treaties, and protocols related to the most up to date international action on ethnic cleansing; freedom of expression and religion; violence against women; and much more. A bibliography, extensive glossary, and comprehensive index round out this indispensable volume. This comprehensive, timely volume is a must for large public libraries, university libraries and social science departments, along with high school libraries.

"...invaluable for anyone interested in human rights issues ... highly recommended for all reference collections."
- American Reference Books Annual

Two Volumes, Hardcover ISBN 978-1-59237-290-4, 750 pages, $225.00 | Ebook ISBN 978-1-59237-301-7
www.greyhouse.com/ebooks.htm

Business Information ♦ Ratings Guides ♦ General Reference ♦ **Education** ♦
Statistics ♦ Demographics ♦ Health Information ♦ Canadian Information

Grey House
Publishing

The Comparative Guide to American Elementary & Secondary Schools, 2008

The only guide of its kind, this award winning compilation offers a snapshot profile of every public school district in the United States serving 1,500 or more students – more than 5,900 districts are covered. Organized alphabetically by district within state, each chapter begins with a Statistical Overview of the state. Each district listing includes contact information (name, address, phone number and web site) plus Grades Served, the Numbers of Students and Teachers and the Number of Regular, Special Education, Alternative and Vocational Schools in the district along with statistics on Student/Classroom Teacher Ratios, Drop Out Rates, Ethnicity, the Numbers of Librarians and Guidance Counselors and District Expenditures per student. As an added bonus, *The Comparative Guide to American Elementary and Secondary Schools* provides important ranking tables, both by state and nationally, for each data element. For easy navigation through this wealth of information, this handbook contains a useful City Index that lists all districts that operate schools within a city. These important comparative statistics are necessary for anyone considering relocation or doing comparative research on their own district and would be a perfect acquisition for any public library or school district library.

> *"This straightforward guide is an easy way to find general information.*
> *Valuable for academic and large public library collections." –ARBA*

Softcover ISBN 978-1-59237-223-2, 2,400 pages, $125.00 | Ebook ISBN 978-1-59237-238-6 www.greyhouse.com/ebooks.htm

The Complete Learning Disabilities Directory, 2009

The Complete Learning Disabilities Directory is the most comprehensive database of Programs, Services, Curriculum Materials, Professional Meetings & Resources, Camps, Newsletters and Support Groups for teachers, students and families concerned with learning disabilities. This information-packed directory includes information about Associations & Organizations, Schools, Colleges & Testing Materials, Government Agencies, Legal Resources and much more. For quick, easy access to information, this directory contains four indexes: Entry Name Index, Subject Index and Geographic Index. With every passing year, the field of learning disabilities attracts more attention and the network of caring, committed and knowledgeable professionals grows every day. This directory is an invaluable research tool for these parents, students and professionals.

> *"Due to its wealth and depth of coverage, parents, teachers and others… should find this an invaluable resource." -Booklist*

Softcover ISBN 978-1-59237-368-0, 900 pages, $145.00 | Online Database $195.00 | Online Database & Directory Combo $280.00

Educators Resource Directory, 2007/08

Educators Resource Directory is a comprehensive resource that provides the educational professional with thousands of resources and statistical data for professional development. This directory saves hours of research time by providing immediate access to Associations & Organizations, Conferences & Trade Shows, Educational Research Centers, Employment Opportunities & Teaching Abroad, School Library Services, Scholarships, Financial Resources, Professional Consultants, Computer Software & Testing Resources and much more. Plus, this comprehensive directory also includes a section on Statistics and Rankings with over 100 tables, including statistics on Average Teacher Salaries, SAT/ACT scores, Revenues & Expenditures and more. These important statistics will allow the user to see how their school rates among others, make relocation decisions and so much more. For quick access to information, this directory contains four indexes: Entry & Publisher Index, Geographic Index, a Subject & Grade Index and Web Sites Index. *Educators Resource Directory* will be a well-used addition to the reference collection of any school district, education department or public library.

> *"Recommended for all collections that serve elementary and secondary school professionals." –Choice*

Softcover ISBN 978-1-59237-179-2, 800 pages, $145.00 | Online Database $195.00 | Online Database & Directory Combo $280.00

Business Information ◆ Ratings Guides ◆ General Reference ◆ Education ◆
Statistics ◆ **Demographics** ◆ Health Information ◆ Canadian Information

Grey House Publishing

Profiles of New York | Profiles of Florida | Profiles of Texas | Profiles of Illinois | Profiles of Michigan | Profiles of Ohio | Profiles of New Jersey | Profiles of Massachusetts | Profiles of Pennsylvania | Profiles of Wisconsin | Profiles of Connecticut & Rhode Island | Profiles of Indiana | Profiles of North Carolina & South Carolina | Profiles of Virginia | Profiles of California

The careful layout gives the user an easy-to-read snapshot of every single place and county in the state, from the biggest metropolis to the smallest unincorporated hamlet. The richness of each place or county profile is astounding in its depth, from history to weather, all packed in an easy-to-navigate, compact format. Each profile contains data on History, Geography, Climate, Population, Vital Statistics, Economy, Income, Taxes, Education, Housing, Health & Environment, Public Safety, Newspapers, Transportation, Presidential Election Results, Information Contacts and Chambers of Commerce. As an added bonus, there is a section on Selected Statistics, where data from the 100 largest towns and cities is arranged into easy-to-use charts. Each of 22 different data points has its own two-page spread with the cities listed in alpha order so researchers can easily compare and rank cities. A remarkable compilation that offers overviews and insights into each corner of the state, each volume goes beyond Census statistics, beyond metro area coverage, beyond the 100 best places to live. Drawn from official census information, other government statistics and original research, you will have at your fingertips data that's available nowhere else in one single source.

"The publisher claims that this is the 'most comprehensive portrait of the state of Florida ever published,' and this reviewer is inclined to believe it...Recommended. All levels." –Choice on Profiles of Florida

Each Profiles of... title ranges from 400-800 pages, priced at $149.00 each

America's Top-Rated Cities, 2008

America's Top-Rated Cities provides current, comprehensive statistical information and other essential data in one easy-to-use source on the 100 "top" cities that have been cited as the best for business and living in the U.S. This handbook allows readers to see, at a glance, a concise social, business, economic, demographic and environmental profile of each city, including brief evaluative comments. In addition to detailed data on Cost of Living, Finances, Real Estate, Education, Major Employers, Media, Crime and Climate, city reports now include Housing Vacancies, Tax Audits, Bankruptcy, Presidential Election Results and more. This outstanding source of information will be widely used in any reference collection.

"The only source of its kind that brings together all of this information into one easy-to-use source. It will be beneficial to many business and public libraries." –ARBA

Four Volumes, Softcover ISBN 978-1-59237-349-9, 2,500 pages, $195.00 | Ebook ISBN 978-1-59237-233-1
www.greyhouse.com/ebooks.htm

America's Top-Rated Smaller Cities, 2008/09

A perfect companion to *America's Top-Rated Cities*, *America's Top-Rated Smaller Cities* provides current, comprehensive business and living profiles of smaller cities (population 25,000-99,999) that have been cited as the best for business and living in the United States. Sixty cities make up this 2004 edition of America's Top-Rated Smaller Cities, all are top-ranked by Population Growth, Median Income, Unemployment Rate and Crime Rate. City reports reflect the most current data available on a wide-range of statistics, including Employment & Earnings, Household Income, Unemployment Rate, Population Characteristics, Taxes, Cost of Living, Education, Health Care, Public Safety, Recreation, Media, Air & Water Quality and much more. Plus, each city report contains a Background of the City, and an Overview of the State Finances. *America's Top-Rated Smaller Cities* offers a reliable, one-stop source for statistical data that, before now, could only be found scattered in hundreds of sources. This volume is designed for a wide range of readers: individuals considering relocating a residence or business; professionals considering expanding their business or changing careers; general and market researchers; real estate consultants; human resource personnel; urban planners and investors.

"Provides current, comprehensive statistical information in one easy-to-use source... Recommended for public and academic libraries and specialized collections." –Library Journal

Two Volumes, Softcover ISBN 978-1-59237-284-3, 1,100 pages, $195.00 | Ebook ISBN 978-1-59237-234-8
www.greyhouse.com/ebooks.htm

Profiles of America: Facts, Figures & Statistics for Every Populated Place in the United States

Profiles of America is the only source that pulls together, in one place, statistical, historical and descriptive information about every place in the United States in an easy-to-use format. This award winning reference set, now in its second edition, compiles statistics and data from over 20 different sources – the latest census information has been included along with more than nine brand new statistical topics. This Four-Volume Set details over 40,000 places, from the biggest metropolis to the smallest unincorporated hamlet, and provides statistical details and information on over 50 different topics including Geography, Climate, Population, Vital Statistics, Economy, Income, Taxes, Education, Housing, Health & Environment, Public Safety, Newspapers, Transportation, Presidential Election Results and Information Contacts or Chambers of Commerce. Profiles are arranged, for ease-of-use, by state and then by county. Each county begins with a County-Wide Overview and is followed by information for each Community in that particular county. The Community Profiles within the county are arranged alphabetically. *Profiles of America* is a virtual snapshot of America at your fingertips and a unique compilation of information that will be widely used in any reference collection.

A Library Journal Best Reference Book "An outstanding compilation." –Library Journal

Four Volumes, Softcover ISBN 978-1-891482-80-9, 10,000 pages, $595.00

To preview any of our Directories Risk-Free for 30 days, call (800) 562-2139 or fax (518) 789-0556
www.greyhouse.com books@greyhouse.com

Business Information ♦ Ratings Guides ♦ General Reference ♦ Education ♦
Statistics ♦ Demographics ♦ Health Information ♦ Canadian Information

The Comparative Guide to American Suburbs, 2007/08

The Comparative Guide to American Suburbs is a one-stop source for Statistics on the 2,000+ suburban communities surrounding the 50 largest metropolitan areas – their population characteristics, income levels, economy, school system and important data on how they compare to one another. Organized into 50 Metropolitan Area chapters, each chapter contains an overview of the Metropolitan Area, a detailed Map followed by a comprehensive Statistical Profile of each Suburban Community, including Contact Information, Physical Characteristics, Population Characteristics, Income, Economy, Unemployment Rate, Cost of Living, Education, Chambers of Commerce and more. Next, statistical data is sorted into Ranking Tables that rank the suburbs by twenty different criteria, including Population, Per Capita Income, Unemployment Rate, Crime Rate, Cost of Living and more. *The Comparative Guide to American Suburbs* is the best source for locating data on suburbs. Those looking to relocate, as well as those doing preliminary market research, will find this an invaluable timesaving resource.

"Public and academic libraries will find this compilation useful…The work draws together figures from many sources and will be especially helpful for job relocation decisions." – Booklist

Softcover ISBN 978-1-59237-180-8, 1,700 pages, $130.00 | Ebook ISBN 978-1-59237-235-5 www.greyhouse.com/ebooks.htm

The American Tally: Statistics & Comparative Rankings for U.S. Cities with Populations over 10,000

This important statistical handbook compiles, all in one place, comparative statistics on all U.S. cities and towns with a 10,000+ population. *The American Tally* provides statistical details on over 4,000 cities and towns and profiles how they compare with one another in Population Characteristics, Education, Language & Immigration, Income & Employment and Housing. Each section begins with an alphabetical listing of cities by state, allowing for quick access to both the statistics and relative rankings of any city. Next, the highest and lowest cities are listed in each statistic. These important, informative lists provide quick reference to which cities are at both extremes of the spectrum for each statistic. Unlike any other reference, *The American Tally* provides quick, easy access to comparative statistics – a must-have for any reference collection.

"A solid library reference." -Bookwatch

Softcover ISBN 978-1-930956-29-2, 500 pages, $125.00 | Ebook ISBN 978-1-59237-241-6 www.greyhouse.com/ebooks.htm

The Asian Databook: Statistics for all US Counties & Cities with Over 10,000 Population

This is the first-ever resource that compiles statistics and rankings on the US Asian population. *The Asian Databook* presents over 20 statistical data points for each city and county, arranged alphabetically by state, then alphabetically by place name. Data reported for each place includes Population, Languages Spoken at Home, Foreign-Born, Educational Attainment, Income Figures, Poverty Status, Homeownership, Home Values & Rent, and more. Next, in the Rankings Section, the top 75 places are listed for each data element. These easy-to-access ranking tables allow the user to quickly determine trends and population characteristics. This kind of comparative data can not be found elsewhere, in print or on the web, in a format that's as easy-to-use or more concise. A useful resource for those searching for demographics data, career search and relocation information and also for market research. With data ranging from Ancestry to Education, *The Asian Databook* presents a useful compilation of information that will be a much-needed resource in the reference collection of any public or academic library along with the marketing collection of any company whose primary focus in on the Asian population.

"This useful resource will help those searching for demographics data, and market research or relocation information… Accurate and clearly laid out, the publication is recommended for large public library and research collections." -Booklist

Softcover ISBN 978-1-59237-044-3, 1,000 pages, $150.00

The Hispanic Databook: Statistics for all US Counties & Cities with Over 10,000 Population

Previously published by Toucan Valley Publications, this second edition has been completely updated with figures from the latest census and has been broadly expanded to include dozens of new data elements and a brand new Rankings section. The Hispanic population in the United States has increased over 42% in the last 10 years and accounts for 12.5% of the total US population. For ease-of-use, *The Hispanic Databook* presents over 20 statistical data points for each city and county, arranged alphabetically by state, then alphabetically by place name. Data reported for each place includes Population, Languages Spoken at Home, Foreign-Born, Educational Attainment, Income Figures, Poverty Status, Homeownership, Home Values & Rent, and more. Next, in the Rankings Section, the top 75 places are listed for each data element. These easy-to-access ranking tables allow the user to quickly determine trends and population characteristics. This kind of comparative data can not be found elsewhere, in print or on the web, in a format that's as easy-to-use or more concise. A useful resource for those searching for demographics data, career search and relocation information and also for market research. With data ranging from Ancestry to Education, *The Hispanic Databook* presents a useful compilation of information that will be a much-needed resource in the reference collection of any public or academic library along with the marketing collection of any company whose primary focus in on the Hispanic population.

"This accurate, clearly presented volume of selected Hispanic demographics is recommended for large public libraries and research collections."-Library Journal

Softcover ISBN 978-1-59237-008-5, 1,000 pages, $150.00

Business Information ✦ Ratings Guides ✦ General Reference ✦ Education ✦
Statistics ✦ **Demographics** ✦ Health Information ✦ Canadian Information

Ancestry in America: A Comparative Guide to Over 200 Ethnic Backgrounds

This brand new reference work pulls together thousands of comparative statistics on the Ethnic Backgrounds of all populated places in the United States with populations over 10,000. Never before has this kind of information been reported in a single volume. Section One, Statistics by Place, is made up of a list of over 200 ancestry and race categories arranged alphabetically by each of the 5,000 different places with populations over 10,000. The population number of the ancestry group in that city or town is provided along with the percent that group represents of the total population. This informative city-by-city section allows the user to quickly and easily explore the ethnic makeup of all major population bases in the United States. Section Two, Comparative Rankings, contains three tables for each ethnicity and race. In the first table, the top 150 populated places are ranked by population number for that particular ancestry group, regardless of population. In the second table, the top 150 populated places are ranked by the percent of the total population for that ancestry group. In the third table, those top 150 populated places with 10,000 population are ranked by population number for each ancestry group. These easy-to-navigate tables allow users to see ancestry population patterns and make city-by-city comparisons as well. This brand new, information-packed resource will serve a wide-range or research requests for demographics, population characteristics, relocation information and much more. *Ancestry in America: A Comparative Guide to Over 200 Ethnic Backgrounds* will be an important acquisition to all reference collections.

*"This compilation will serve a wide range of research requests for population characteristics
… it offers much more detail than other sources." –Booklist*

Softcover ISBN 978-1-59237-029-0, 1,500 pages, $225.00

Weather America, A Thirty-Year Summary of Statistical Weather Data and Rankings

This valuable resource provides extensive climatological data for over 4,000 National and Cooperative Weather Stations throughout the United States. Weather America begins with a new Major Storms section that details major storm events of the nation and a National Rankings section that details rankings for several data elements, such as Maximum Temperature and Precipitation. The main body of Weather America is organized into 50 state sections. Each section provides a Data Table on each Weather Station, organized alphabetically, that provides statistics on Maximum and Minimum Temperatures, Precipitation, Snowfall, Extreme Temperatures, Foggy Days, Humidity and more. State sections contain two brand new features in this edition – a City Index and a narrative Description of the climatic conditions of the state. Each section also includes a revised Map of the State that Includes not only weather stations, but cities and towns.

"Best Reference Book of the Year." –Library Journal

Softcover ISBN 978-1-891482-29-8, 2,013 pages, $175.00 | Ebook ISBN 978-1-59237-237-9 www.greyhouse.com/ebooks.htm

Crime in America's Top-Rated Cities

This volume includes over 20 years of crime statistics in all major crime categories: violent crimes, property crimes and total crime. *Crime in America's Top-Rated Cities* is conveniently arranged by city and covers 76 top-rated cities. Crime in America's Top-Rated Cities offers details that compare the number of crimes and crime rates for the city, suburbs and metro area along with national crime trends for violent, property and total crimes. Also, this handbook contains important information and statistics on Anti-Crime Programs, Crime Risk, Hate Crimes, Illegal Drugs, Law Enforcement, Correctional Facilities, Death Penalty Laws and much more. A much-needed resource for people who are relocating, business professionals, general researchers, the press, law enforcement officials and students of criminal justice.

"Data is easy to access and will save hours of searching." –Global Enforcement Review

Softcover ISBN 978-1-891482-84-7, 832 pages, $155.00

**Business Information ✦ Ratings Guides ✦ General Reference ✦ Education ✦
Statistics ✦ Demographics ✦ Health Information ✦ Canadian Information**

Grey House
Publishing

The Complete Directory for People with Disabilities, 2009

A wealth of information, now in one comprehensive sourcebook. Completely updated, this edition contains more information than ever before, including thousands of new entries and enhancements to existing entries and thousands of additional web sites and e-mail addresses. This up-to-date directory is the most comprehensive resource available for people with disabilities, detailing Independent Living Centers, Rehabilitation Facilities, State & Federal Agencies, Associations, Support Groups, Periodicals & Books, Assistive Devices, Employment & Education Programs, Camps and Travel Groups. Each year, more libraries, schools, colleges, hospitals, rehabilitation centers and individuals add *The Complete Directory for People with Disabilities* to their collections, making sure that this information is readily available to the families, individuals and professionals who can benefit most from the amazing wealth of resources cataloged here.

"No other reference tool exists to meet the special needs of the disabled in one convenient resource for information." –Library Journal

Softcover ISBN 978-1-59237-367-3, 1,200 pages, $165.00 | Online Database: http://gold.greyhouse.com Call (800) 562-2139 for quote

The Complete Learning Disabilities Directory, 2009

The Complete Learning Disabilities Directory is the most comprehensive database of Programs, Services, Curriculum Materials, Professional Meetings & Resources, Camps, Newsletters and Support Groups for teachers, students and families concerned with learning disabilities. This information-packed directory includes information about Associations & Organizations, Schools, Colleges & Testing Materials, Government Agencies, Legal Resources and much more. For quick, easy access to information, this directory contains four indexes: Entry Name Index, Subject Index and Geographic Index. With every passing year, the field of learning disabilities attracts more attention and the network of caring, committed and knowledgeable professionals grows every day. This directory is an invaluable research tool for these parents, students and professionals.

"Due to its wealth and depth of coverage, parents, teachers and others… should find this an invaluable resource." -Booklist

Softcover ISBN 978-1-59237-368-0, 900 pages, $145.00 | Online Database: http://gold.greyhouse.com Call (800) 562-2139 for quote

The Complete Directory for People with Chronic Illness, 2007/08

Thousands of hours of research have gone into this completely updated edition – several new chapters have been added along with thousands of new entries and enhancements to existing entries. Plus, each chronic illness chapter has been reviewed by a medical expert in the field. This widely-hailed directory is structured around the 90 most prevalent chronic illnesses – from Asthma to Cancer to Wilson's Disease – and provides a comprehensive overview of the support services and information resources available for people diagnosed with a chronic illness. Each chronic illness has its own chapter and contains a brief description in layman's language, followed by important resources for National & Local Organizations, State Agencies, Newsletters, Books & Periodicals, Libraries & Research Centers, Support Groups & Hotlines, Web Sites and much more. This directory is an important resource for health care professionals, the collections of hospital and health care libraries, as well as an invaluable tool for people with a chronic illness and their support network.

"A must purchase for all hospital and health care libraries and is strongly recommended for all public library reference departments." –ARBA

Softcover ISBN 978-1-59237-183-9, 1,200 pages, $165.00 | Online Database: http://gold.greyhouse.com Call (800) 562-2139 for quote

The Complete Mental Health Directory, 2008/09

This is the most comprehensive resource covering the field of behavioral health, with critical information for both the layman and the mental health professional. For the layman, this directory offers understandable descriptions of 25 Mental Health Disorders as well as detailed information on Associations, Media, Support Groups and Mental Health Facilities. For the professional, The Complete Mental Health Directory offers critical and comprehensive information on Managed Care Organizations, Information Systems, Government Agencies and Provider Organizations. This comprehensive volume of needed information will be widely used in any reference collection.

"… the strength of this directory is that it consolidates widely dispersed information into a single volume." –Booklist

Softcover ISBN 978-1-59237-285-0, 800 pages, $165.00 | Online Database: http://gold.greyhouse.com Call (800) 562-2139 for quote

Business Information ◆ Ratings Guides ◆ General Reference ◆ Education ◆
Statistics ◆ Demographics ◆ **Health Information** ◆ Canadian Information

Grey House
Publishing

The Comparative Guide to American Hospitals, Second Edition

This new second edition compares all of the nation's hospitals by 24 measures of quality in the treatment of heart attack, heart failure, pneumonia, and, new to this edition, surgical procedures and pregnancy care. Plus, this second edition is now available in regional volumes, to make locating information about hospitals in your area quicker and easier than ever before. The Comparative Guide to American Hospitals provides a snapshot profile of each of the nations 4,200+ hospitals. These informative profiles illustrate how the hospital rates when providing 24 different treatments within four broad categories: Heart Attack Care, Heart Failure Care, Surgical Infection Prevention (NEW), and Pregnancy Care measures (NEW). Each profile includes the raw percentage for that hospital, the state average, the US average and data on the top hospital. For easy access to contact information, each profile includes the hospital's address, phone and fax numbers, email and web addresses, type and accreditation along with 5 top key administrations. These profiles will allow the user to quickly identify the quality of the hospital and have the necessary information at their fingertips to make contact with that hospital. Most importantly, *The Comparative Guide to American Hospitals* provides easy-to-use Regional State by State Statistical Summary Tables for each of the data elements to allow the user to quickly locate hospitals with the best level of service. Plus, a new 30-Day Mortality Chart, Glossary of Terms and Regional Hospital Profile Index make this a must-have source. This new, expanded edition will be a must for the reference collection at all public, medical and academic libraries.

"These data will help those with heart conditions and pneumonia make informed decisions about their healthcare and encourage hospitals to improve the quality of care they provide. Large medical, hospital, and public libraries are most likely to benefit from this weighty resource."-Library Journal

Four Volumes Softcover ISBN 978-1-59237-182-2, 3,500 pages, $325.00 | Regional Volumes $135.00 |
Ebook ISBN 978-1-59237-239-3 www.greyhouse.com/ebooks.htm

Older Americans Information Directory, 2008

Completely updated for 2008, this sixth edition has been completely revised and now contains 1,000 new listings, over 8,000 updates to existing listings and over 3,000 brand new e-mail addresses and web sites. You'll find important resources for Older Americans including National, Regional, State & Local Organizations, Government Agencies, Research Centers, Libraries & Information Centers, Legal Resources, Discount Travel Information, Continuing Education Programs, Disability Aids & Assistive Devices, Health, Print Media and Electronic Media. Three indexes: Entry Index, Subject Index and Geographic Index make it easy to find just the right source of information. This comprehensive guide to resources for Older Americans will be a welcome addition to any reference collection.

"Highly recommended for academic, public, health science and consumer libraries..." –Choice

1,200 pages; Softcover ISBN 978-1-59237-357-4, $165.00 | Online Database: http://gold.greyhouse.com Call (800) 562-2139 for quote

The Complete Directory for Pediatric Disorders, 2008

This important directory provides parents and caregivers with information about Pediatric Conditions, Disorders, Diseases and Disabilities, including Blood Disorders, Bone & Spinal Disorders, Brain Defects & Abnormalities, Chromosomal Disorders, Congenital Heart Defects, Movement Disorders, Neuromuscular Disorders and Pediatric Tumors & Cancers. This carefully written directory offers: understandable Descriptions of 15 major bodily systems; Descriptions of more than 200 Disorders and a Resources Section, detailing National Agencies & Associations, State Associations, Online Services, Libraries & Resource Centers, Research Centers, Support Groups & Hotlines, Camps, Books and Periodicals. This resource will provide immediate access to information crucial to families and caregivers when coping with children's illnesses.

"Recommended for public and consumer health libraries." –Library Journal

Softcover ISBN 978-1-59237-150-1, 1,200 pages, $165.00 | Online Database: http://gold.greyhouse.com Call (800) 562-2139 for quote

The Directory of Drug & Alcohol Residential Rehabilitation Facilities

This brand new directory is the first-ever resource to bring together, all in one place, data on the thousands of drug and alcohol residential rehabilitation facilities in the United States. The Directory of Drug & Alcohol Residential Rehabilitation Facilities covers over 1,000 facilities, with detailed contact information for each one, including mailing address, phone and fax numbers, email addresses and web sites, mission statement, type of treatment programs, cost, average length of stay, numbers of residents and counselors, accreditation, insurance plans accepted, type of environment, religious affiliation, education components and much more. It also contains a helpful chapter on General Resources that provides contact information for Associations, Print & Electronic Media, Support Groups and Conferences. Multiple indexes allow the user to pinpoint the facilities that meet very specific criteria. This time-saving tool is what so many counselors, parents and medical professionals have been asking for. *The Directory of Drug & Alcohol Residential Rehabilitation Facilities* will be a helpful tool in locating the right source for treatment for a wide range of individuals. This comprehensive directory will be an important acquisition for all reference collections: public and academic libraries, case managers, social workers, state agencies and many more.

"This is an excellent, much needed directory that fills an important gap..." –Booklist

Softcover ISBN 978-1-59237-031-3, 300 pages, $135.00

Business Information ♦ Ratings Guides ♦ General Reference ♦ Education ♦
Statistics ♦ Demographics ♦ **Health Information** ♦ Canadian Information

Grey House
Publishing

The Directory of Hospital Personnel, 2009

The Directory of Hospital Personnel is the best resource you can have at your fingertips when researching or marketing a product or service to the hospital market. A "Who's Who" of the hospital universe, this directory puts you in touch with over 150,000 key decision-makers. With 100% verification of data you can rest assured that you will reach the right person with just one call. Every hospital in the U.S. is profiled, listed alphabetically by city within state. Plus, three easy-to-use, cross-referenced indexes put the facts at your fingertips faster and more easily than any other directory: Hospital Name Index, Bed Size Index and Personnel Index. *The Directory of Hospital Personnel* is the only complete source for key hospital decision-makers by name. Whether you want to define or restructure sales territories… locate hospitals with the purchasing power to accept your proposals… keep track of important contacts or colleagues… or find information on which insurance plans are accepted, *The Directory of Hospital Personnel* gives you the information you need – easily, efficiently, effectively and accurately.

"Recommended for college, university and medical libraries." -ARBA

Softcover ISBN 978-1-59237-402-1, 2,500 pages, $325.00 | Online Database: http://gold.greyhouse.com Call (800) 562-2139 for quote

The HMO/PPO Directory, 2009

The HMO/PPO Directory is a comprehensive source that provides detailed information about Health Maintenance Organizations and Preferred Provider Organizations nationwide. This comprehensive directory details more information about more managed health care organizations than ever before. Over 1,100 HMOs, PPOs, Medicare Advantage Plans and affiliated companies are listed, arranged alphabetically by state. Detailed listings include Key Contact Information, Prescription Drug Benefits, Enrollment, Geographical Areas served, Affiliated Physicians & Hospitals, Federal Qualifications, Status, Year Founded, Managed Care Partners, Employer References, Fees & Payment Information and more. Plus, five years of historical information is included related to Revenues, Net Income, Medical Loss Ratios, Membership Enrollment and Number of Patient Complaints. Five easy-to-use, cross-referenced indexes will put this vast array of information at your fingertips immediately: HMO Index, PPO Index, Other Providers Index, Personnel Index and Enrollment Index. *The HMO/PPO Directory* provides the most comprehensive data on the most companies available on the market place today.

"Helpful to individuals requesting certain HMO/PPO issues such as co-payment costs, subscription costs and patient complaints. Individuals concerned (or those with questions) about their insurance may find this text to be of use to them." -ARBA

Softcover ISBN 978-1-59237-369-7, 600 pages, $325.00 | Online Database: http://gold.greyhouse.com Call (800) 562-2139 for quote

Medical Device Register, 2009

The only one-stop resource of every medical supplier licensed to sell products in the US. This award-winning directory offers immediate access to over 13,000 companies - and more than 65,000 products – in two information-packed volumes. This comprehensive resource saves hours of time and trouble when searching for medical equipment and supplies and the manufacturers who provide them. Volume I: The Product Directory, provides essential information for purchasing or specifying medical supplies for every medical device, supply, and diagnostic available in the US. Listings provide FDA codes & Federal Procurement Eligibility, Contact information for every manufacturer of the product along with Prices and Product Specifications. Volume 2 - Supplier Profiles, offers the most complete and important data about Suppliers, Manufacturers and Distributors. Company Profiles detail the number of employees, ownership, method of distribution, sales volume, net income, key executives detailed contact information medical products the company supplies, plus the medical specialties they cover. Four indexes provide immediate access to this wealth of information: Keyword Index, Trade Name Index, Supplier Geographical Index and OEM (Original Equipment Manufacturer) Index. *Medical Device Register* is the only one-stop source for locating suppliers and products; looking for new manufacturers or hard-to-find medical devices; comparing products and companies; know who's selling what and who to buy from cost effectively. This directory has become the standard in its field and will be a welcome addition to the reference collection of any medical library, large public library, university library along with the collections that serve the medical community.

"A wealth of information on medical devices, medical device companies… and key personnel in the industry is provide in this comprehensive reference work... A valuable reference work, one of the best hardcopy compilations available." -Doody Publishing

Two Volumes, Hardcover ISBN 978-1-59237-373-4, 3,000 pages, $325.00

The Directory of Health Care Group Purchasing Organizations, 2008

This comprehensive directory provides the important data you need to get in touch with over 800 Group Purchasing Organizations. By providing in-depth information on this growing market and its members, *The Directory of Health Care Group Purchasing Organizations* fills a major need for the most accurate and comprehensive information on over 800 GPOs – Mailing Address, Phone & Fax Numbers, E-mail Addresses, Key Contacts, Purchasing Agents, Group Descriptions, Membership Categorization, Standard Vendor Proposal Requirements, Membership Fees & Terms, Expanded Services, Total Member Beds & Outpatient Visits represented and more. Five Indexes provide a number of ways to locate the right GPO: Alphabetical Index, Expanded Services Index, Organization Type Index, Geographic Index and Member Institution Index. With its comprehensive and detailed information on each purchasing organization, *The Directory of Health Care Group Purchasing Organizations* is the go-to source for anyone looking to target this market.

"The information is clearly arranged and easy to access…recommended for those needing this very specialized information." –ARBA

1,000 pages; Softcover ISBN 978-1-59237-287-4, $325.00 | Online Database: http://gold.greyhouse.com Call (800) 562-2139 for quote

Business Information ◆ Ratings Guides ◆ General Reference ◆ Education ◆
Statistics ◆ Demographics ◆ Health Information ◆ **Canadian Information**

Grey House
Publishing

Canadian Almanac & Directory, 2009

The Canadian Almanac & Directory contains sixteen directories in one – giving you all the facts and figures you will ever need about Canada. No other single source provides users with the quality and depth of up-to-date information for all types of research. This national directory and guide gives you access to statistics, images and over 100,000 names and addresses for everything from Airlines to Zoos - updated every year. It's Ten Directories in One! Each section is a directory in itself, providing robust information on business and finance, communications, government, associations, arts and culture (museums, zoos, libraries, etc.), health, transportation, law, education, and more. Government information includes federal, provincial and territorial - and includes an easy-to-use quick index to find key information. A separate municipal government section includes every municipality in Canada, with full profiles of Canada's largest urban centers. A complete legal directory lists judges and judicial officials, court locations and law firms across the country. A wealth of general information, the *Canadian Almanac & Directory* also includes national statistics on population, employment, imports and exports, and more. National awards and honors are presented, along with forms of address, Commonwealth information and full color photos of Canadian symbols. Postal information, weights, measures, distances and other useful charts are also incorporated. Complete almanac information includes perpetual calendars, five-year holiday planners and astronomical information. Published continuously for 160 years, *The Canadian Almanac & Directory* is the best single reference source for business executives, managers and assistants; government and public affairs executives; lawyers; marketing, sales and advertising executives; researchers, editors and journalists.

Hardcover ISBN 978-1-59237-370-3, 1,600 pages, $325.00

Associations Canada, 2009

The Most Powerful Fact-Finder to Business, Trade, Professional and Consumer Organizations
Associations Canada covers Canadian organizations and international groups including industry, commercial and professional associations, registered charities, special interest and common interest organizations. This annually revised compendium provides detailed listings and abstracts for nearly 20,000 regional, national and international organizations. This popular volume provides the most comprehensive picture of Canada's non-profit sector. Detailed listings enable users to identify an organization's budget, founding date, scope of activity, licensing body, sources of funding, executive information, full address and complete contact information, just to name a few. Powerful indexes help researchers find information quickly and easily. The following indexes are included: subject, acronym, geographic, budget, executive name, conferences & conventions, mailing list, defunct and unreachable associations and registered charitable organizations. In addition to annual spending of over $1 billion on transportation and conventions alone, Canadian associations account for many millions more in pursuit of membership interests. *Associations Canada* provides complete access to this highly lucrative market. *Associations Canada* is a strong source of prospects for sales and marketing executives, tourism and convention officials, researchers, government officials - anyone who wants to locate non-profit interest groups and trade associations.

Hardcover ISBN 978-1-59237-401-4, 1,600 pages, $325.00

Financial Services Canada, 2008/09

Financial Services Canada is the only master file of current contacts and information that serves the needs of the entire financial services industry in Canada. With over 18,000 organizations and hard-to-find business information, Financial Services Canada is the most up-to-date source for names and contact numbers of industry professionals, senior executives, portfolio managers, financial advisors, agency bureaucrats and elected representatives. Financial Services Canada incorporates the latest changes in the industry to provide you with the most current details on each company, including: name, title, organization, telephone and fax numbers, e-mail and web addresses. *Financial Services Canada* also includes private company listings never before compiled, government agencies, association and consultant services - to ensure that you'll never miss a client or a contact. Current listings include: banks and branches, non-depository institutions, stock exchanges and brokers, investment management firms, insurance companies, major accounting and law firms, government agencies and financial associations. Powerful indexes assist researchers with locating the vital financial information they need. The following indexes are included: alphabetic, geographic, executive name, corporate web site/e-mail, government quick reference and subject. *Financial Services Canada* is a valuable resource for financial executives, bankers, financial planners, sales and marketing professionals, lawyers and chartered accountants, government officials, investment dealers, journalists, librarians and reference specialists.

Hardcover ISBN 978-1-59237-278-2, 900 pages, $315.00

Directory of Libraries in Canada, 2008/09

The Directory of Libraries in Canada brings together almost 7,000 listings including libraries and their branches, information resource centers, archives and library associations and learning centers. The directory offers complete and comprehensive information on Canadian libraries, resource centers, business information centers, professional associations, regional library systems, archives, library schools and library technical programs. *The Directory of Libraries in Canada* includes important features of each library and service, including library information; personnel details, including contact names and e-mail addresses; collection information; services available to users; acquisitions budgets; and computers and automated systems. Useful information on each library's electronic access is also included, such as Internet browser, connectivity and public Internet/CD-ROM/subscription database access. The directory also provides powerful indexes for subject, location, personal name and Web site/e-mail to assist researchers with locating the crucial information they need. *The Directory of Libraries in Canada* is a vital reference tool for publishers, advocacy groups, students, research institutions, computer hardware suppliers, and other diverse groups that provide products and services to this unique market.

Hardcover ISBN 978-1-59237-279-9, 850 pages, $315.00

Business Information ✦ Ratings Guides ✦ General Reference ✦ Education ✦
Statistics ✦ Demographics ✦ Health Information ✦ **Canadian Information**

Canadian Environmental Directory, 2009

The Canadian Environmental Directory is Canada's most complete and only national listing of environmental associations and organizations, government regulators and purchasing groups, product and service companies, special libraries, and more! The extensive Products and Services section provides detailed listings enabling users to identify the company name, address, phone, fax, e-mail, Web address, firm type, contact names (and titles), product and service information, affiliations, trade information, branch and affiliate data. The Government section gives you all the contact information you need at every government level – federal, provincial and municipal. We also include descriptions of current environmental initiatives, programs and agreements, names of environment-related acts administered by each ministry or department PLUS information and tips on who to contact and how to sell to governments in Canada. The Associations section provides complete contact information and a brief description of activities. Included are Canadian environmental organizations and international groups including industry, commercial and professional associations, registered charities, special interest and common interest organizations. All the Information you need about the Canadian environmental industry: directory of products and services, special libraries and resource, conferences, seminars and tradeshows, chronology of environmental events, law firms and major Canadian companies, *The Canadian Environmental Directory* is ideal for business, government, engineers and anyone conducting research on the environment.

Softcover ISBN 978-1-59237-374-1, 900 pages, $325.00

Canadian Parliamentary Guide, 2008

An indispensable guide to government in Canada, the annual *Canadian Parliamentary Guide* provides information on both federal and provincial governments, courts, and their elected and appointed members. The Guide is completely bilingual, with each record appearing both in English and then in French. The Guide contains biographical sketches of members of the Governor General's Household, the Privy Council, members of Canadian legislatures (federal, including both the House of Commons and the Senate, provincial and territorial), members of the federal superior courts (Supreme, Federal, Federal Appeal, Court Martial Appeal and Tax Courts) and the senior staff for these institutions. Biographies cover personal data, political career, private career and contact information. In addition, the Guide provides descriptions of each of the institutions, including brief historical information in text and chart format and significant facts (i.e. number of members and their salaries). The Guide covers the results of all federal general elections and by-elections from Confederations to the present and the results of the most recent provincial elections. A complete name index rounds out the text, making information easy to find. No other resources presents a more up-to-date, more complete picture of Canadian government and her political leaders. A must-have resource for all Canadian reference collections.

Hardcover ISBN 978-1-59237-310-9, 800 pages, $184.00